lonely planet

San Francisco

"All you've got to do is decide to go
and the hardest part is over.

So go!"

Ashley Harrell, Alison Bing,
Greg Benchwick, Celeste Brash, Adam Karlin

Contents

Plan Your Trip   4

Explore San Francisco   48

Understand San Francisco   237

Survival Guide   263

San Francisco Maps   287

(left) **Columbus Tower p112**

(above) **Lombard Street p129** One of SF's most iconic streets.

(right) **Rainbow Honor Walk p167** The Castro pays tribute to LGBTIQ+ heroes.

Welcome to San Francisco

Grab your coat and a handful of glitter, and enter a wonderland of fog and fabulousness. So long, inhibitions; hello, San Francisco!

Outlandish Notions

Consider permission permanently granted to be outlandish: other towns may surprise you, but in San Francisco you will surprise yourself. Good times and social revolutions tend to start here, from manic gold rushes to blissful hippie 'be-ins'. If there's a skateboard move yet to be busted, a technology still unimagined, a poem left unspoken or a green scheme untested, chances are it's about to happen here. Yes, right now. This town has lost almost everything in earthquakes and dot-com gambles, but never its nerve.

Food & Drink

Every available Bay Area–invented technology is needed to make dinner decisions in this city, with the most restaurants and farmers markets per capita in North America – all supplied by pioneering local organic farms. San Francisco set the gold standard for Wild West saloons, until drinking was driven underground in the 1920s with Prohibition. Today San Francisco celebrates its historic saloons and speakeasies – and with Wine Country and local distillers providing a steady supply of America's finest hooch, the West still gets wild nightly.

Natural Highs

San Francisco is a 7-by-7-mile peninsula that looks like California's thumb, pointed optimistically upwards. Take this as a hint to look up: you'll notice San Francisco's crooked Victorian rooflines, wind-sculpted treetops, and fog tumbling over the Golden Gate Bridge.

Heads are perpetually in the clouds atop San Francisco's 48 hills. Cable cars provide easy access to Russian and Nob Hills, and splendid panoramas reward the slog up to Coit Tower. Earn exhilarating highs on Telegraph Hill's garden-lined stairway walks, and windswept hikes around Lands End. If there's another kind of high you're seeking, that can also be arranged: marijuana is legal here for adults 18 and over with ID, and dispensaries and delivery are at your service.

Neighborhood Microclimates

Microclimates add magic realism to San Francisco days: when it's drizzling in the outer reaches of Golden Gate Park, it might be sunny in the Mission. A difference of a few degrees between neighborhoods grants permission for salted-caramel ice cream in Dolores Park, or a hasty retreat to tropical heat inside the California Academy of Sciences' rainforest dome. This town will give you goose bumps one minute, and warm you to the core the next.

LUCIANO MORTULA - LGM / SHUTTERSTOCK ©

Why I Love San Francisco

By Alison Bing, Writer

On my way from Hong Kong to New York, I stopped in San Francisco for a day. I walked up Grant Ave to Waverly Pl, just as temple services were starting – the fog was scented with incense and roast duck. I felt the magnetic pull to City Lights, and in the nonfiction cellar, I noticed a sign painted by a 1920s cult: 'I am the door'. It's true. San Francisco is the threshold between East and West, body and soul, fact and fiction.

That was more than 20 years ago. I'm still here. Now it's your turn to open that door, and find yourself in San Francisco.

For more about our writers, see p320

Top: The Painted Ladies alongside Alamo Square Park (p179)

San Francisco's
Top 10

1

Golden Gate Bridge *(p58)*

1 Other suspension bridges are impressive feats of engineering, but the Golden Gate Bridge tops them all for razzle-dazzle showmanship. On sunny days, it transfixes crowds with its radiant glow – thanks to 28 daredevil painters who reapply around 1000 gallons of International Orange paint each week. When afternoon fog rolls in, the bridge performs its disappearing act: now you see it, now you don't and, abracadabra, it's sawn in half. Return tomorrow for its dramatic unveiling, just in time for the morning commute.

◉ *The Marina, Fisherman's Wharf & the Piers*

Alcatraz *(p54)*

2 From its 19th-century founding to detain Civil War deserters and Native American dissidents until its closure by Bobby Kennedy in 1963, Alcatraz was America's most notorious jail. No prisoner is known to have escaped alive – but once you enter D-Block solitary and hear carefree city life humming across the bay, the 1.25-mile swim through riptides seems worth a shot. For maximum chill factor, book the spooky twilight jailhouse tour. Freedom never felt so good as it does on the return ferry to San Francisco.

◉ *The Marina, Fisherman's Wharf & the Piers*

PHITHA TANPAIROJ / SHUTTERSTOCK ©

BLAZG / SHUTTERSTOCK ©

Golden Gate Park (p191)

3 You may have heard that SF has a wild streak a mile wide, but that streak also happens to be 4.5 miles long. Golden Gate Park lets locals do what comes naturally: roller-discoing, drum-circling, starfish-petting, orchid-sniffing and stampeding toward the Pacific with a herd of bison. It's hard to believe these lush 1017 acres were once scrubby sand dunes, and that San Franciscans have preserved this stretch of green since 1866, blocking development of casinos and resorts. Today everything SF needs is here: inspiration, nature and murals with microbrewed beer at the Beach Chalet. TOP LEFT: JAPANESE TEA GARDEN (P192)

⊙ *Golden Gate Park & the Avenues*

Mission Murals (p145)

4 Love changed the course of art history in the 1930s, when modern-art power couple Diego Rivera and Frida Kahlo honeymooned in San Francisco. Kahlo completed her first portrait commissions during her time in the city, and Rivera created mural masterpieces that inspired generations of San Francisco muralists. Today San Francisco's Mission district is an urban-art show-stopper, featuring more than 400 murals. Balmy Alley has some of the oldest, while 24th St and the landmark San Francisco Women's Building are covered with glorious portrayals of community pride and political dissent. LEFT: PRECITA EYES (P147) RUNS MURAL TOURS

⊙ *The Mission, Dogpatch & Potrero Hill*

The Castro (p165)

5 Somewhere over the rainbow crosswalk, you'll realize you've officially arrived in the Castro district – the most out-and-proud neighborhood on the planet for more than 50 years. Walk in the footsteps of trans trailblazers along Castro St's LGBTIQ+ walk of fame, get to know civil rights champions at America's first GLBT History Museum and join history perpetually in progress at San Francisco's month-long, million-strong Pride celebrations in June.

⊙ *The Castro*

Coit Tower *(p110)*

6 Wild parrots might mock your progress up Telegraph Hill, but they can't expect to keep scenery like this to themselves. Filbert St Steps pass cliffside cottage gardens to reach SF's monument to independent thinking: Coit Tower. Firefighting millionaire Lillie Hitchcock Coit commissioned this deco monument honoring firefighters, and muralists captured 1930s San Francisco in its lobby frescoes. Coit Tower's paintings and panoramic viewing platform show San Francisco at its best: a city of broad perspectives, outlandish and inspiring.

👁 *North Beach & Chinatown*

Cable Cars *(p127)*

7 Carnival rides can't compare to the time-traveling thrills of cable cars, San Francisco's steampunk public transit. Novices slide into strangers' laps – cable cars were invented in 1873, long before seat belts – but regulars just grip the leather hand straps, lean back and ride the downhill plunges like pro surfers. Follow their lead, and you'll soon master the San Francisco stance and find yourself conquering the city's hills without even breaking a sweat.

🏃 *Downtown, Civic Center & SoMa*

6

Ferry Building (p78)

8 Global food trends start in San Francisco. To sample tomorrow's menu today, head to the Ferry Building, the city's monument to trailblazing local, sustainable food. Don't miss the Saturday farmers market, where top chefs jostle for first pick of rare heirloom varietals and foodie babies blissfully teethe on organic California peaches. Picnic on Pier 14 with food-truck finds overlooking the sparkling bay and let lunch and life exceed expectations.

🍴 *Downtown, Civic Center & SoMa*

Barbary Coast Nights (p120)

9 In the mid-19th century you could start a San Francisco bar crawl with smiles and 10¢ whiskey – and end up two days later involuntarily working on a ship bound for Patagonia. Now that double-crossing barkeep Shanghai Kelly is no longer a danger to drinkers, revelers can relax at North Beach's once-notorious Barbary Coast saloons. These days you can pick your own poison: historically correct cocktails at Comstock Saloon, cult California wines in the back-room speakeasy at Pawn Shop and pitchers at the knickknack-adorned Specs, and enough potions at Devil's Acre to keep you snoring to Patagonia and back. RIGHT: SPECS (P120)

🍷 *North Beach & Chinatown*

SFMOMA (p81)

10 San Francisco Museum of Modern Art has always been ahead of its time. The institution sprung onto the San Francisco art scene in 1935 and immediately invested in art forms that were innovative for the time: photography, murals, film and installation. Since then SFMOMA has grown nearly three-fold, dedicating entire wings to new media projects, giant paintings and futuristic design. It's worthwhile to spend an afternoon covering all seven floors, and to grab a table at the museum's delightful restaurant In Situ. Corey Lee's Michelin-starred operation basically serves up edible art.

👁 *Downtown, Civic Center & SoMa*

What's New

Pot Central

Now that marijuana is legal in California for medical and recreational use by adults aged 18 and up, you'll probably get a whiff of California-grown 'kind bud' while you're in San Francisco – even though use is supposedly restricted to private, indoor use. Be mindful of neighbors, and for your own safety, buy marijuana only from licensed dispensaries – such as Apothecarium (p174), Sparc (p188) or Mission Cannabis Club (p163) – or legit delivery services like HelloMD (www.hello md.com) and Eaze (www.eaze.com).

New LGBTIQ+ Cultural Districts

The nation's first Transgender Cultural District (p87) is in the Tenderloin neighborhood, where transgender patrons of Compton's Cafeteria protested police harassment back in 1966 – kicking off a nationwide movement for transgender civil rights. Meanwhile, on the other side of Market St, SoMa's LGBTIQ+ Leather District has served as a refuge and community hub since the 1960s.

Super-sized SFMOMA

The half-billion-dollar expansion at the San Francisco Museum of Modern Art (p81) is open, tripling the museum in size and scope. Around 11,000 new acquisitions are still being unveiled. Don't miss far-out new media art on the top floor, the world-class 3rd-floor photography collection or groundbreaking ground-floor food gallery In Situ (p90).

Tiki Time

Tropical cocktail enthusiasts will not suffer for a place to drink in San Francisco, where a new zombie-, rum- or tiki-themed bar seems to open every week. The latest favorites include Zombie Village (p97), from the same people behind yet another outrageous tiki bar, Pagan Idol (p93), and Obispo (p155), a decidedly anti-tiki rum bar.

Public Art on High

It's a bird! It's a plane! It's all kinds of stuff displayed on a circular screen attached to the top nine stories of the Salesforce Tower. The installation is called Day for Night (p254), and it involves 11,000 LED lights that broadcast images captured by cameras around the city.

Tune Up

Put your ear to the ground SF and you may just stumble on a new sound venue. There's the 15,000 sq ft concert space August Hall (p99; and its basement speakeasy/bowling alley) and a music-inspired art gallery, Family Affair (p180), with synesthesia-inducing shows that include things like video art of sonic collages.

Dogpatch Creative Corridor

Hop on the T streetcar to 22nd St to discover creativity flourishing in the Dogpatch (p148): Minnesota St art gallery openings, local designer studios, hot brunch spots and buzzy new wine bars (p154).

Lucky Ladies

For as long as anybody can remember, there was only Wild Side West. But shiny new lesbian bar Jolene's (p154) has opened in the Mission, and it puts on femme-focused parties like UHaul, along with live music, performances and theme nights (queer prom, anybody?).

For more recommendations and reviews, see **lonelyplanet. com/san-francisco**

Need to Know

For more information, see Survival Guide (p263)

Currency
US dollar ($)

Language
English

Visas
USA Visa Waiver Program (VWP) allows nationals from 38 countries to enter the US without a visa. See the **US Customs & Border Protection** (https://www.cbp.gov/travel/international-visitors) website and register with the **US Department of Homeland Security** (https://esta.cbp.dhs.gov/esta).

Money
ATMs widely available; credit cards accepted at most hotels, stores and restaurants. Many farmers-market stalls and food trucks and some bars are cash only. Keep small bills for cafes, bars and hotel service, where cash tips are appreciated.

Cell Phones
Most US cell (mobile) phones besides the iPhone operate on CDMA – check with your provider.

Time
Pacific Standard Time (GMT/UTC minus eight hours)

Tourist Information
SF Visitor Information Center (www.sanfrancisco.travel/visitor-information-center) Muni Passports, activities deals, culture and event calendars.

Daily Costs

Budget:
Less than $150
⇒ Dorm bed: $33–60
⇒ Burrito: $6–9
⇒ Food-truck fare: $5–15
⇒ Mission murals: free
⇒ Live North Beach music, comedy or musical comedy: free–$15
⇒ Castro Theatre show: $12

Midrange:
$150–350
⇒ Downtown hotel/home-share: $130–195
⇒ Ferry Building meal: $20–45
⇒ Mission share-plates meal: $25–50
⇒ Symphony rush tickets: $25
⇒ Muni Passport: $29

Top End:
More than $350
⇒ Boutique hotel: $195–390
⇒ Chef's tasting menu: $90–260
⇒ City Pass (Muni, cable cars plus four attractions): $94
⇒ Alcatraz night tour: $45.50
⇒ Opera orchestra seats: $90–150

Advance Planning
Two months before Make reservations at Benu, Chez Panisse or French Laundry; start walking to build stamina for Coit Tower climbs and Mission bar crawls.

Three weeks before Book Alcatraz tour, Chinatown History Tour or Precita Eyes Mission Mural Tour.

One week before Search for tickets to American Conservatory Theater, SF Symphony, SF Opera and Oasis drag shows – and find out what else is on the following weekend.

Useful Websites
SFGate (www.sfgate.com) *San Francisco Chronicle* news and event listings.

48 Hills (https://48hills.org) Independent SF news and culture coverage.

7x7 (www.7x7.com) Trend-spotting SF restaurants, bars and style.

Craigslist (http://sfbay.craigslist.org) SF-based source for jobs, dates and free junk.

Lonely Planet (www.lonelyplanet.com/san-francisco) Destination information, hotel bookings, traveler forum and more.

WHEN TO GO

June and July bring fog and chilly 55°F (13°C) weather to SF; August, September and October are best for warm weather, street fairs and harvest cuisine.

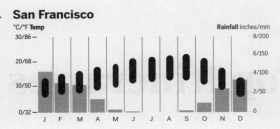

San Francisco

Arriving in San Francisco

San Francisco International Airport (SFO) Fast rides to downtown SF on BART cost $9.65; ride-share $35 to $60, plus tip; door-to-door shuttle vans $19 to $25, plus tip; SamTrans express bus 398 to Temporary Transbay Terminal $2.50; or taxi $50 to $65, plus tip.

Oakland International Airport (OAK) Catch BART from the airport to downtown SF ($10.95); take a shared shuttle van to downtown SF for $25 to $47; or pay $40 to $80, plus tip, for a ride-share or taxi to SF destinations.

Temporary Transbay Terminal Greyhound buses arrive/depart downtown SF's transit center.

Emeryville Amtrak station (EMY) Located outside Oakland, this depot serves West Coast and nationwide train routes; Amtrak runs free shuttles to/ from San Francisco's Ferry Building, Caltrain, Civic Center and Fisherman's Wharf.

For much more on **arrival** see p264

Getting Around

San Franciscans mostly walk, bike, ride Muni or ride-share instead of taking a car or cab. Traffic is notoriously bad and parking is next to impossible. Avoid driving until it's time to leave town. For Bay Area transit options, departures and arrivals, call 511 or check www.511.org. A *Muni Street & Transit Map* is available online.

Cable cars Frequent, slow and scenic, from 6am to 12:30am daily. Single rides cost $7; for frequent use, get a Muni Passport ($23 per day).

Muni streetcar and bus Reasonably fast, but schedules vary by line; infrequent after 9pm. Fares are $2.75 cash, or $2.50 with a reloadable Clipper card.

BART High-speed transit to East Bay, Mission St, SF airport and Millbrae, where it connects with Caltrain.

Taxi Fares are about $3 per mile; meters start at $3.50.

For much more on **getting around** see p266

Sleeping

San Francisco hotel rates are among the world's highest. Plan ahead to find a bargain

Accommodations Websites

BedandBreakfast.com (www. bedandbreakfast.com) Listings include local B&Bs and neighborhood inns.

HotelTonight (www.hotel tonight.com) SF-based hotel-search app offering last-minute discounted bookings.

Lonely Planet (www.lonely planet.com/usa/san-francisco/ hotels) Recommendations and bookings.

For much more on **sleeping** see p226

Top Itineraries

Day One

North Beach & Chinatown (p108)

 Grab a leather strap on the Powell-Mason cable car and hold on: you're in for hills and thrills. Hop off at **Washington Square Park**, where parrots squawk encouragement for your hike up to **Coit Tower** for 1930s murals celebrating SF workers and 360-degree panoramas. Take scenic **Filbert Street Steps** to the **Embarcadero** to wander across Fog Bridge and explore the freaky Tactile Dome at the **Exploratorium**.

> **Lunch** Savor local oysters and Dungeness crab at the Ferry Building (p78).

The Marina, Fisherman's Wharf & the Piers (p52)

Catch your prebooked ferry to **Alcatraz**, where D-Block solitary raises goose bumps. Make your island-prison break, taking in **Golden Gate Bridge** views on the ferry ride back. Hop the Powell-Mason cable car to North Beach, to take in free-speech landmark **City Lights Books** and mingle with SF's freest spirits at the **Beat Museum**.

> **Dinner** Pasta at Cotogna (p88) or modern Chinese at Mister Jiu's (p119).

North Beach & Chinatown (p108)

 Since you just escaped prison, you're tough enough to handle too-close-for-comfort comics at **Cobb's Comedy Club** or razor-sharp satire at **Beach Blanket Babylon**. Toast the wildest night in the west with potent Pisco sours at **Comstock Saloon** or Chinese mai tais at **Li Po**.

Day Two

Golden Gate Park & the Avenues (p189)

 Hop the N Judah to Golden Gate Park to see carnivorous plants enjoying insect breakfasts at the **Conservatory of Flowers** and spiky dahlias wet with dew in the **Dahlia Garden**. Follow Andy Goldsworthy's artful sidewalk fault lines to find flawless Oceanic masks and tower-top views inside the **de Young Museum**, then take a walk on the wild side inside the rainforest dome of the **California Academy of Sciences**. Enjoy a moment of Zen with green tea at the **Japanese Tea Garden** and bliss out in the secret redwood grove at the **San Francisco Botanical Garden**.

> **Lunch** Join surfers at Outerlands (p197) for grilled cheese and soup.

Golden Gate Park & the Avenues (p189)

 Beachcomb **Ocean Beach** up to the **Beach Chalet** to glimpse 1930s frescoes celebrating Golden Gate Park. Follow the **Coastal Trail** past **Sutro Baths** and Lands End for **Golden Gate Bridge** vistas and priceless paper artworks at the **Legion of Honor**.

> **Dinner** Marvel at the elegance of each dish at Japanese Wako (p196).

Nob Hill & Russian Hill (p124)

Psychedelic posters and top acts make for rock-legendary nights at the **Fillmore**.

Legion of Honor (p194)

Day Three

North Beach & Chinatown (p108)

 Take the **California cable car** to pagoda-topped Grant St for an eye-opening **Red Blossom** tea tasting and then a jaw-dropping history of Chinatown at the **Chinese Historical Society of America**. Wander temple-lined **Waverly Place** and artistically inclined **Ross Alley** to find your fortune at the **Golden Gate Fortune Cookie Company**.

> ✖️ **Lunch** Hail dim-sum carts for dumplings at City View (p119).

The Marina, Fisherman's Wharf & the Piers (p52)

☀️ To cover the waterfront, take the **Powell-Hyde cable car** past zigzagging **Lombard Street** to the **San Francisco Maritime National Historical Park**, where you can see what it was like to stow away on a schooner. Save the world from Space Invaders at **Musée Mécanique** or enter underwater stealth mode inside a real WWII submarine: the **USS Pampanito**. Watch sea lions cavort as the sun fades over **Pier 39**, then hop onto the vintage F-line streetcar.

> ✖️ **Dinner** Inspired NorCal fare at Rich Table (p183) satisfies and surprises.

The Haight & Hayes Valley (p176)

 Browse Hayes Valley boutiques before your concert at the **SF Symphony** or **SFJAZZ Center**, and toast your good fortune at **Smuggler's Cove**.

Day Four

The Mission, Dogpatch & Potrero Hill (p143)

 Wander 24th St past mural-covered bodegas to **Balmy Alley**, where the Mission *muralista* movement began in the 1970s. Stop for a 'secret breakfast' (bourbon and cornflakes) ice-cream sundae at **Humphry Slocombe**, then head up Valencia to **Ritual Coffee Roasters**. Pause for pirate supplies and Fish Theater at **826 Valencia** and duck into **Clarion Alley**, the Mission's outdoor graffiti-art gallery. See San Francisco's first building, Spanish adobe **Mission Dolores**, and visit the memorial to the Native Ohlone who built it.

> ✖️ **Lunch** Dine on just-baked wonders at Tartine Manufactory (p152).

The Haight & Hayes Valley (p176)

☀️ Spot Victorian 'Painted Ladies' around **Alamo Square** and browse **NoPa boutiques**. Stroll tree-lined Panhandle park to Stanyan, then window-shop your way down hippie-historic **Haight Street** past record stores, vintage emporiums, drag designers and **Bound Together Anarchist Book Collective**.

> ✖️ **Dinner** Early walk-ins may score sensational small plates at Frances (p171).

The Castro (p165)

 Sing along to tunes pounded out on the Mighty Wurlitzer organ before shows at the deco-fabulous **Castro Theatre**. Club kids cruise over to **440 Castro**, while straight-friendly crowds clink tiki drinks amid airplane wreckage at **Last Rites**.

If You Like...

Vista Points

Coit Tower Up Greenwich St stairs, atop Telegraph Hill, inside the 1930s tower, upon the viewing platform: 360-degree panoramas. (p110)

Lands End Shipwrecks, Golden Gate views and Monterey pines line the hike from Sutro Baths to the Legion of Honor. (p200)

Corona Heights Park Rocky outcropping with views over the Haight, the Castro and the Mission to the silvery bay beyond. (p167)

Dolores Park On the southwestern corner, overlook sunbathers, picnickers and kids swarming the Aztec play pyramid all the way to the bay. (p146)

Alamo Square Park Peek over the shoulders of 'Painted Lady' Victorian mansions to glimpse City Hall and the Transamerica Pyramid. (p179)

Local Hangouts

Dolores Park Athletes, radical politicos, gay sunbathers, happy doggies and delighted toddlers: on sunny days, they all converge on this grassy hillside. (p146)

Japantown The unofficial living room of film-festival freaks, Lolita goths, anime aficionados and grandmas who fought for civil rights. (p51)

Coffee to the People The quadruple-shot Freak Out with hemp milk could wake the Grateful Dead at this radical Haight coffeehouse. (p186)

Washington Square Mellow out with poets and tai-chi masters while wild parrots eye your focaccia from the trees. (p111)

City Lights Books (p111)

Cafe Flore Glassed-in Castro corner venue serving coffee with a side of local eye candy since the '70s. (p173)

Historic Sites

Mission Dolores The first building in SF was this Spanish adobe mission, built by conscripted Ohlone and Miwok tribespeople. (p147)

Alcatraz 'The Rock' was a Civil War jail, an A-list gangster penitentiary and disputed territory claimed by Native American activists and the FBI. (p54)

City Lights Books Publishing poetry got City Lights cofounder Lawrence Ferlinghetti arrested – and won a landmark case for free speech. (p111)

Chinese Historical Society of America California's first licensed woman architect, Julia Morgan, built the elegant, tiled-roofed Chinese YWCA with clinker bricks. (p112)

City Hall Home to the first 1960s sit-in, America's first publicly gay elected official and the first citywide composting law. (p87)

Hidden Alleyways

Balmy Alley Hot topics and artistic talents have surfaced since the 1970s in this backstreet decorated by SF *muralistas*. (p145)

Spofford Alley Revolutions were plotted and bootlegger gun battles waged here – but peace has brought Chinese orchestras and marathon mah-jongg games. (p115)

Jack Kerouac Alley This byway named after the Beat author is

inscribed with his words, right on the road. (p111)

Ross Alley Ladies who entered this alley once risked their reputations, but now its most colorful characters are in the murals. (p115)

Macondray Lane This cottage-lined lane was the perfect setting for a mysterious landlady in Armistead Maupin's *Tales of the City*. (p129)

Movie Locations

Nob Hill Steve McQueen's muscle car goes flying over the summit in *Bullitt* – and somehow lands in SoMa. (p51)

Human Rights Campaign Action Center Harvey Milk's camera shop in *Milk* was this real-life Castro location, now home to the LGBTIQ+ civil-rights organization. (p167)

Transamerica Pyramid Godzilla stomps through the Golden Gate Bridge in the 2014 sci-fi remake, but mysteriously spares downtown's signature landmark. (p82)

Alcatraz Even America's highest-security prison can't contain Clint Eastwood in *Escape from Alcatraz*. (p54)

Fort Point Hitchcock was right: swirling noir-movie fog and giddy Golden Gate views make for a thrilling case of *Vertigo*. (p60)

Alamo Square Park SF's picturesque Painted Ladies have stolen scenes in sci-fi classics (*Invasion of the Body Snatchers*), rom-coms (*So I Married an Axe Murderer*) and TV shows (*Full House*). (p179)

For more top San Francisco spots, see the following:
➡ Eating (p25)
➡ Drinking & Nightlife (p31)
➡ Entertainment (p35)
➡ Shopping (p42)
➡ Sports & Activities (p45)

PLAN YOUR TRIP IF YOU LIKE...

Free Stuff

Stern Grove Festival Free concerts at Golden Gate Park's natural amphitheater, from Afrobeat jazz to SF Opera. (p35)

Hardly Strictly Bluegrass Headliners like Elvis Costello, Gillian Welch and banjo legend Béla Fleck plus 100 other acts in Golden Gate Park. (p35)

Cable Car Museum Glimpse the inner workings of San Francisco's transportation icon, which remains largely unchanged since its 1873 invention. (p126)

Amoeba Music concerts Rockers, DJs and hip-hop heroes give free shows in-store. (p186)

Giants baseball Catch a glimpse of the action and join the party at the Embarcadero waterfront promenade behind left field. (p99)

Golden Gate Bridge Yeah, you've probably heard of this. Walk across, hop a bus or rent a bike. (p58)

de Young Museum Many SF museums are free the first Tuesday of the month, including the de Young; sculpture garden access is always free. (p191)

Month By Month

February

Lion dancing, freakishly warm days and alt-rock shows provide brilliant breaks in the February drizzle.

✹ Noise Pop

Winter blues, be gone: discover your new favorite indie band and catch rockumentary premieres and rockin' pop-up events during the Noise Pop festival. Held the last week of February.

✹ Lunar New Year Parade

Chase the 200ft dragon, legions of lion dancers and frozen-smile runners-up for the Miss Chinatown title during Lunar New Year celebrations.

April

Reasonable room rates and weekends crammed with cultural events will put some spring in your step in San Francisco.

✹ Cherry Blossom Festival

Japantown blooms and booms in April when the Cherry Blossom Festival (p43) arrives with *taiko* drums and homegrown hip-hop, yakitori stalls and eye-popping anime cosplay.

☆ San Francisco International Film Festival

The nation's oldest film festival (p36) is still looking stellar, with hundreds of films and directors and plenty of star-studded premieres. Plan ahead for two weeks of screenings at Castro Theatre, Alamo Drafthouse Cinema and Roxie Cinema.

🔒 Art Market SF

Gallerists converge on Fort Mason to showcase contemporary art at this fair (p43), and satellite art fairs pop up in motels and parking lots in the Marina.

May

As inland California warms up, fog settles over the Bay Area – but goose bumps haven't stopped the naked joggers and conga lines yet.

🏃 Bay to Breakers

Run costumed or naked from Embarcadero to Ocean Beach for Bay to Breakers (p46), while joggers dressed as salmon run upstream. SF's outlandish race is held on the third Sunday in May.

✹ Carnaval

Brazilian, or just faking it with a wax and a tan? Shake your tail feathers in the Mission and conga through the inevitable fog during Carnaval; last weekend of May.

June

Since 1970 SF Pride has grown into a month-long extravaganza, with movie premieres and street parties culminating in the million-strong Pride Parade.

🎪 Haight Ashbury Street Fair

Free music, tie-dye galore, and wafting pot smoke – the Summer of Love stages a comeback in the Haight every mid-June since 1977, when Harvey Milk helped make the first Haight Ashbury Street Fair (p43) happen.

☆ Frameline Film Festival

Here, queer and ready for a premiere since 1976, San Francisco's Frameline LG-BTQ+ Film Festival (p36) is the oldest, biggest lesbian, gay, bisexual, transgender and queer film fest anywhere. Binge-watch up to 150 films from 40 countries over two weeks in late June.

🎪 Pride Parade

Come out wherever you are: SF goes wild for LGBTIQ+ pride on the last Sunday of June, with 1.2-plus million people, seven stages, tons of glitter and oodles of thongs at the Pride Parade. Join crowds cheering for civil-rights pioneers, gays in uniform, proud families and rainbow-flag drag.

🎪 SF Jazz Festival

Minds are blown by jazz greats and upstarts play career-defining sets during the SF Jazz Festival (www. sfjazz.org), featuring Grammy winners and crossover global talents; held at the SFJAZZ Center (p186) and other venues.

July

Wintry summer days make bundling up advisable, but don't miss July barbecues and outdoor events, including charity hikes, free concerts and fireworks.

🏃 AIDS Walk

Until AIDS takes a hike, you can: the 10km fundraising AIDS Walk through Golden Gate Park benefits various AIDS organizations and has raised $90 million over the three decades it's been running. Held the third Sunday in July.

🎪 Stern Grove Festival

Music for free among the redwood and eucalyptus trees, every summer since 1938. Free concerts during the Stern Grove Festival (p35) include hip-hop, world music and jazz, but the biggest events are performances by SF Ballet, SF Symphony and SF Opera. Held 2pm Sundays July and August.

August

Finally the San Francisco fog rolls back and permits sunset views from Ocean Beach, just in time for one last glorious summer fling in Golden Gate Park and a harvest feast at Fort Mason.

☆ Outside Lands

Golden Gate Park hosts major marquee acts and gleeful debauchery at Wine Lands, Beer Lands and star-chef food trucks during Outside Lands (p35). It's one of America's top music and comedy festivals; tickets sell out months in advance.

🍴 Eat Drink SF

Loosen your belt to make room for three days of culinary events (p29) celebrating California's bounty, starting with a taco-off and culminating in a Grand Tasting at Fort Mason.

September

Warm weather arrives at last and SF celebrates with more outrageous antics than usual, including public spankings and Shakespearean declarations of love.

🎪 Folsom Street Fair

Bondage enthusiasts emerge from dungeons worldwide for San Francisco's wildest street party on Folsom St, between 7th and 11th Sts. Enjoy leather, beer and public spankings for local charities the last Sunday of the month.

🎪 SF Shakespeare Festival

The play's the thing in the Presidio, outdoors and free of charge on sunny September weekends during the Shakespeare Festival (p36). Kids' summer workshops are also held for budding Bards, culminating in performances throughout the Bay Area.

October

Expect golden sunshine – this is San Francisco's true summer – and free events for fans of music and literature.

🎪 Litquake

Stranger-than-fiction literary events take place the second week of October during SF's literary festival (p36), with authors leading lunchtime story sessions and spilling trade secrets

over drinks at the legendary Lit Crawl.

☆ Hardly Strictly Bluegrass

The West goes wild for free
bluegrass (p35) and roots
music at Golden Gate Park,
with three days of concerts
and seven stages of head-
liners. Held early October.

November

**Party to wake the dead
and save the planet as
San Francisco celebrates
its Mexican history and
perennial craftiness.**

🎎 Día de los Muertos

Zombie brides and Aztec
dancers in feather regalia
party like there's no tomorrow on Día de los Muertos,
paying their respects to
altars to the dead along the
Mission processional route
on November 2.

🔒 West Coast Craft

Get hip, handmade style
without lifting a finger at
West Coast Craft (p43),
featuring 100-plus indie
makers just in time for the
holidays.

December

**December days may
be overcast, but nights
sparkle with holiday lights
and events citywide.**

☆ Kung Pao Kosher

A San Francisco holiday
tradition to rival the San
Francisco Ballet's *The
Nutcracker,* Kung Pao
Kosher is a Jewish comedy
marathon held in a Chinese
restaurant at Christmas.

Top: Street parade celebrating Carnaval (p20)

Bottom: Hardly Strictly Bluegrass

THETAHOEGUY / SHUTTERSTOCK ©

EDDIEHERNANDEZPHOTOGRAPHY / SHUTTERSTOCK ©

With Kids

San Francisco has the fewest kids per capita of any US city and, according to SPCA data, 5000 to 35,000 more dogs than children live here. Yet many locals make a living entertaining kids – from Pixar animators to video-game designers – and this town is full of attractions for young people.

rousel at the Children's Creativity Museum (p84)

Alcatraz & the Piers

Prison tours of Alcatraz (p54) fascinate children, while older kids enjoy the spooky evening tours. Hit the award-winning, hands-on exhibits at the Exploratorium (p64) to investigate the science of skateboarding and glow-in-the-dark animals, then free the world from Space Invaders at Musée Mécanique (p62). Don't be shy: bark back at the sea lions at Pier 39 (p61), and ride a unicorn on the pier's vintage San Francisco carousel.

Freebies

See SF history in motion at the free Cable Car Museum (p126), and take free mechanical pony rides and peek inside vintage stagecoaches at the Wells Fargo History Museum (p82). Cool kids head to 24th St to see Balmy Alley murals and hang with skaters at Potrero del Sol/La Raza Skatepark (p46). The free Randall Junior Museum (p167) introduces kids to urban wildlife, earth science and the fascinating Golden Gate model railroad. Daredevils can conquer the concrete Seward Street slides (p174) in the Castro, hillside concrete slides at the Golden Gate Park (p191) kids playground, and the Winfield Street slides in Bernal Heights. Lunchtime concerts are free at Old St Mary's (p112) and, in summer, at Yerba Buena Gardens (p84) and **Justin Herman Plaza** (Map p301, C2; www. sfrecpark.org; cnr Market St & the Embarcadero; ▣2, 6, 7, 9, 14, 21, 31, 32, Ⓑ Embarcadero, Ⓜ Embarcadero). Kids can graze on free samples at the Ferry Building (p78), and score free toys in exchange for a bartered song, drawing or poem at 826 Valencia (p146).

Nature Lovers

Penguins, buffalo and an albino alligator call Golden Gate Park (p191) home. Chase butterflies through the rainforest dome, pet starfish in the petting zoo and squeal in the Eel Forest at the California Academy of Sciences (p192). Get a whiff of insect breath from carnivorous flowers at the Conservatory of Flowers (p193) – pee-eeww! – and brave the shark tunnel at Aquarium of the Bay (p62). San Francisco

SABRINA DALBESIO / LONELY PLANET ©

NEED TO KNOW

Change facilities Best public facilities are at **Westfield San Francisco Centre** (Map p294, C5; www.westfield.com/sanfrancisco; 865 Market St; ⊙10am-8:30pm Mon-Sat, 11am-7pm Sun; 🚻; 🚋Powell-Mason, Powell-Hyde, Ⓜ Powell, 🅑Powell) and San Francisco Main Library (p86). Availability and cleanliness vary elsewhere.

Emergency care San Francisco General Hospital (p272).

Strollers and car seats Bring your own or hire from a rental agency like **Cloud of Goods** (☑415 634 9141; www.cloudofgoods.com; 100 Produce Ave).

Kiddie menus Mostly in cafes and downtown diners; call ahead about dietary restrictions. Most San Francisco kids eat from the same menu as their parents.

Zoo (p195) is out of the way but worth the trip for monkeys, lemurs and giraffes.

Cable Cars & Boats

When junior gearheads demand to know how cable cars work, the Cable Car Museum (p126) lets them glimpse the inner workings for themselves. Take a joyride on the Powell-Hyde cable car to Fisherman's Wharf, where you can enter submarine stealth mode aboard the USS Pampanito (p63) and climb aboard schooners and steamships at the Maritime National Historical Park (p62). Future sea captains will enjoy model-boat weekend regattas at Spreckels Lake in Golden Gate Park (p191).

Warm Days

On sunny Sundays when Golden Gate Park is mostly closed to traffic, rent paddleboats at Stow Lake (p193) or strap on some rentals at Golden Gate Park Bike & Skate (p201). Crissy Field (p59) and the southern end of Baker Beach (p60) are better bets for kid-friendly beaches than Ocean Beach, where fog and strong currents swiftly end sandcastle-building sessions; drownings happen at Ocean, and swimming and even wading is considered a risk; heed the signs and watch your children carefully. Hit Chinatown for teen-led Chinatown Alleyway Tours (p121), and cookies at Golden Gate Fortune Cookie Company (p123).

Museums & Interactive Activities

The Children's Creativity Museum (p84) allows future tech moguls to design their own video games and animations, while the Exploratorium (p64) has interactive displays that let kids send fog signals and figure out optical illusions for themselves. At the Walt Disney Family Museum (p65), kids can get to know their favorite characters better – and find out about the animators who brought them to life. Kids are strongly encouraged to explore art in San Francisco, with free admission for those aged 12 and under at the Asian Art Museum (p80), SFMOMA (p81), Legion of Honor (p194), de Young Museum (p191), Museum of the African Diaspora (p83) and Contemporary Jewish Museum (p83). To make your own hands-on fun, hit Paxton Gate (p163) kids' store for shadow puppets and organic play dough.

Playgrounds

Golden Gate Park (p191) Swings, monkey bars, play castles with slides, hillside slides and a vintage carousel.

Dolores Park (p146) Jungle gym, Mayan pyramid and picnic tables.

Yerba Buena Gardens (p84) Grassy downtown playground surrounded by museums, cinemas and kid-friendly dining.

Huntington Park (p129) Top-end playground in ritzy hilltop park.

Portsmouth Square (p113) Chinatown's outdoor playroom.

Old St Mary's Square (p112) Skateboarders and play equipment.

Peppers at the Ferry Plaza Farmers Market (p79)

 # Eating

Other US cities boast bigger monuments, but San Francisco packs more flavor. Chef Alice Waters set the Bay Area standard for organic, sustainable, seasonal food back in 1971 at Chez Panisse, and today you'll find California's pasture-raised meats and organic produce proudly featured on the Bay Area's trend-setting, cross-cultural menus. Congratulations: you couldn't have chosen a better time or place for dinner.

NEED TO KNOW

Price Ranges

The following price ranges refer to a main course, not including drinks, tax and tip:

$ less than $15

$$ $15–25

$$$ more than $25

Tipping

Together, tax and tip add 25% to 35% to the bill. SF follows the US tipping standard: 20% to 25% is generous; 15% is the bare minimum, unless something went horribly wrong with the service you received.

Surcharges

Some restaurants tack on a 4% to 5% surcharge to cover the cost of providing health care to restaurant employees – health-care coverage is required by SF law. If you don't appreciate restaurants passing on their business costs to customers, say so in an online restaurant review. Just don't blame your server, who may not directly benefit from the surcharge.

Opening Hours

Many restaurants are open seven days a week, though some close Sunday and/or Monday night. Breakfast is served 8am to 10am; lunch is usually 11:30am to 2:30pm; dinner starts around 5:30pm, with last service between 9pm and 9:30pm on weekdays and 10pm at weekends. Weekend brunch is from 10am to 2pm.

Berkeley's Chez Panisse (p207)

food to the inner city, including California-grown produce and mom-and-pop food trucks.

Alemany Farmers Market (http://sfgsa.org; 100 Alemany Blvd; ☺dawn-dusk Sat) Operating since 1943, California's first farmers market offers bargain California-grown produce and ready-to-eat artisan food.

Castro Farmers Market (p175) Local produce and artisan foods at moderate prices, plus charmingly offbeat folk-music groups.

DIY DINING

For California-fresh ingredients, you can't beat SF farmers markets, Rainbow Grocery (p163) and Bi-Rite. (p161) Downtown are several handy Whole Foods (www.whole foodsmarket.com) and Trader Joes (www. traderjoes.com) stores.

Farmers Markets

NorCal idealists who headed back to the land in the 1970s started the nation's organic-farming movement. Today the local bounty can be sampled across SF, the US city with the most farmers markets per capita.

Ferry Plaza Farmers Market (p79) Star chefs, heirloom ingredients, and food trucks at weekends.

Mission Community Market (p149) Nonprofit, neighborhood-run market with 30 local vendors offering farm-fresh ingredients and artisan-food meals.

Heart of the City Farmers Market (p92) Low-cost, farmer-run market bringing healthy, fresh

Fine Dining

Reservations are a must at popular San Francisco restaurants – the sooner you make them, the better the options you'll have. Most restaurants have online reservations through their websites or OpenTable (www.opentable.com), but if the system shows no availability, call the restaurant directly – some seats may be held for phone reservations and early-evening walk-ins, and there may be last-minute cancellations or room at the bar. Landmark restaurants like Chez Panisse (p207) and small, celebrated SF bistros like Benu (p91), Rich Table (p183), State Bird Provisions (p138) and Frances (p171) offer limited seating, so call a month ahead and take what's available.

If you don't have a reservation, your best bets for a walk-in table are restaurant-dense

Top: Mission Cheese (p150)

Bottom: Ferry Plaza Farmers Market (p79)

areas like 24th or Valencia Sts (in the Mission), Japantown, Polk St (in Russian Hill), the Avenues (especially around 9th Ave), Hayes Valley, Chinatown or North Beach. Go early (5pm-ish) or eat late (after 9pm).

Service is well informed and friendly, never snooty. If you don't see sourcing footnotes or mentions of sustainable, organic ingredients on the menu, ask – it's an SF server's job to know where and how your food was sourced. Mention any dietary limitations when reserving, and you should be cheerfully accommodated. Nice jeans are acceptable and personable interactions appreciated.

Food Trucks & Carts

Feeling hungry and adventurous? You're in the right place. Just be street-food smart: look for prominently displayed permits as a guarantee of proper food preparation, refrigeration and regulated working conditions.

SF's largest gathering of gourmet trucks is Off the Grid (p67), which hosts several events weekly. Sunday brings OTG picnics to the Presidio and Friday sees 30-plus food trucks circle their wagons in Fort Mason. Trucks and carts are mostly cash-only businesses, and lines for popular trucks can take 10 to 20 minutes.

For the best selection of gourmet food on the go, don't miss the Ferry Building (p78) kiosks and Saturday farmers market. To pre-party before hitting SoMa clubs, hit **SoMa StrEat Food Park** (Map p298; http://somastreatfoodpark.com; 428 11th St; dishes $5-12; ⏰11am-3pm & 5-9pm Mon-Fri, 11am-9pm Sat, to

5pm Sun; 📶; 🚌9, 27, 47), a permanent food-truck parking lot with over a dozen trucks, picnic tables, beer and DJs.

For the best gourmet to go, try empanadas from **El Sur** (📞415-530-2803; www.elsursf.com; empanadas $3.50-5), clamshell buns stuffed with duck and mango from the **Chairman** (www.hailthechairman.com; buns $3.75-6, bowls $7-9), free-range herbed roast chicken from **Roli Roti** (www.roliroti.com; mains $8-11), and dessert from **Kara's Cupcakes** (Map p292; 📞415-563-2253; www.karascupcakes.com; 3249 Scott St; cupcakes $2.50-3.75; ⏰10am-8pm Sun-Thu, to 9pm Fri & Sat; 🚌28, 30, 43) 🌿.

You can track food trucks at Roaming Hunger (www.roaminghunger.com/sf/vendors) or on Twitter (@MobileCravings/sf-food-trucks, @streetfoodsf). Start getting hungry now for October's SF Street Food Festival (www.sfstreetfoodfest.com), featuring hundreds of mom-and-pop food vendors – proceeds provide training and kitchens for low-income culinary entrepreneurs.

Pop-Up Restaurants

To test out possible restaurant ventures or trial new culinary concepts, guest chefs occasionally commandeer SF bars, cafes and restaurants with creative pop-up menus. Educational community food nonprofit 18 Reasons (p163) hosts pop-ups where chefs share cooking tips with diners. For a three-day pop-up feast, plan your visit to coincide with **Eat Drink SF** (www.eatdrink-sf.com; ⏰last weekend Aug) in August.

Look for announcements on EaterSF (http://sf.eater.com), Grub Street San Fran-

---

SF CRAVING: DIM SUM

Since one in three San Franciscans has Asian roots, SF's go-to comfort foods aren't just burgers and pizza – though you'll find plenty of those – but also kimchi, tandoori and, above all, dim sum. Dim sum is Cantonese for what's known in Mandarin as *xiao che* ('small eats'); some also call it *yum cha* ('drink tea'). At traditional dim-sum places like Yank Sing (p90) and City View (p119), waitstaff roll carts past your table with steaming baskets of dumplings, platters of garlicky greens and, finally, crispy sweet sesame balls.

If you prefer to cut to the chase, step up to the counter at Chinatown's Good Mong Kok (p119) and get dumplings to go, straight from the steamer. Expect a queue for traditional dim-sum hot spots in Chinatown and along Geary St and Clement St, and for gourmet bao (buns) at the Chairman food truck.

But at SF's genre-defying dim-sum innovators like China Live (p117), Dragon Beaux (p195) and Hakkasan (p89), you'll find inventive, succulent dumplings that would be right at home on fine-dining tasting menus. For James Beard–acclaimed California twists on dim-sum dining, reserve at fusion sensations State Bird Provisions (p138) or Mister Jiu's (p119).

Dim sum

cisco (http://sanfrancisco.grubstreet.com) and Inside Scoop (http://insidescoopsf.sfgate.com) for upcoming pop-ups. Bring cash and arrive early: most pop-ups don't accept credit cards, and popular dishes run out fast.

Top Chefs

San Francisco is a magnet for award-winning chefs – many of whom just so happen to be women, including Iron Chef Traci Des Jardins of Mijita (p87); James Beard Award winner Nancy Oakes at Boulevard (p91); Michelin-starred Dominique Crenn from Petit Crenn (p184); and Melissa Perello of Frances (p171) – and you may recognize their names from TV.

Eating by Neighborhood

Downtown, Civic Center & SoMa (p87) Vietnamese and bargain eats in the Tenderloin; bar bites, tasting menus and sandwiches in SoMa; business lunches and date-night dinners downtown.

North Beach & Chinatown (p113) Dim sum, spicy Sichuan and proper banquets in Chinatown; pizza, pasta and brunches in North Beach.

The Mission, Dogpatch & Potrero Hill (p149) Tacos, innovative Californian food, vegetarian and Asian soul food.

The Marina, Fisherman's Wharf & the Piers (p66) Fusion fare in the Marina; seafood and fast food on Fisherman's Wharf; food trucks and vegetarian fare in Fort Mason.

The Castro (p170) Boisterous bistros, Scandinavian brunches and tasty Thai food in the Castro.

The Haight & Hayes Valley (p181) Market-inspired menus, sunny brunches and dessert in Hayes Valley; brunch and trendy bistros in NoPa.

Japantown, Fillmore & Pacific Heights (p136) Cross-cultural soul food in the Fillmore and Pacific Heights; sushi, ramen and *izakaya* in Japantown.

Golden Gate Park & the Avenues (p195) Dim sum, surfer cuisine and pastry galore in the Avenues.

Nob Hill & Russian Hill (p129) Hilltop treats and adventurous date-night dining in Russian Hill.

Lonely Planet's Top Choices

Benu (p91) Fine dining meets DJ styling in ingenious remixes of Pacific Rim classics and the best ingredients in the West.

Rich Table (p183) Tasty, inventive California fare with French fine-dining finesse makes you feel clever by association.

1760 (p130) Korean flavors, Italian accents and French technique bring California dreaming to the plate.

Californios (p153) Roots cuisine celebrating California's sunny coastal flavors and the Mission's deep Latin American heritage.

In Situ (p90) SFMOMA's gallery of contemporary cuisine serves the signature dishes of top international chefs.

Tartine Manufactory (p152) The seasons's finest fixings piled atop slabs of hearty, just-baked bread.

NorCal Cuisine

Rich Table (p183) Mind-bending, seasonal dishes abound at this local restaurant.

Al's Place (p150) California dreams are shared here, with imaginative plates of pristine seafood and seasonal specialties.

Chez Panisse (p207) Alice Waters' Berkeley bistro has championed local, sustainable, fabulous food since 1971.

Mister Jiu's (p119) Bringing pristine ingredients and wild creativity to the table inside a historic Chinatown banquet hall.

Al Fresco Dining

Boulette's Larder (p88) Sunny, market-inspired lunches at the Ferry Building waterfront.

Greens (p68) Sit on the dock of the bay with black-bean chili that will distract you from the Golden Gate Bridge.

Beach Chalet (p198) Toast the bison with bubbly over brunch at Golden Gate Park's heated backyard.

La Palma Mexicatessen (p149) Peak Mission: fresh tamales with sidewalk seating, surrounded by murals.

Mission Cheese (p150) Gloat over your California goat's-cheese selections and trend-spot Mission street fashion.

Off the Grid (p67) First course: empanadas; next course: pork-belly bun; dessert: cupcakes.

Local Organic Fusion

1760 (p130) Global cuisines combine in exquisitely presented dishes.

Cala (p184) Alta California seafood meets Baja California flavors.

Mr. Pollo (p149) Travel-inspired tasting menus feature local seafood and Colombian arepas with sake.

Kaiyo (p68) Meet your new favorite cuisine: Japanese Peruvian Californian.

Noosh (p136) Middle Eastern mezze with wild western flair and ultra-fresh ingredients.

NICK OTTO / ALAMY STOCK PHOTO / GETTY IMAGES ©

Smuggler's Cove (p184)

Drinking & Nightlife

No matter what you're having, SF bars, cafes and clubs are here to oblige, with anything from California wines and Bay spirits to local roasts. Adventurous drinking is abetted by local bartenders, who've been making good on gold rush saloon history with potent drinks in deceptively delicate vintage glasses. SF baristas take their micro-roasts seriously and local DJs invent their own software.

Cocktails

Tonight you're gonna party like it's 1899: you'll recognize SF drink historians by their Old Tom gin selections and vintage tiki barware displays. All that authenticity-tripping over cocktails may sound self-conscious, but after enjoying strong pours at vintage saloons, tiki bars and speakeasies, consciousness is hardly an issue.

Pacific trade winds blow strong through SF happy hours at SF's trendsetting tiki hot spots Pagan Idol (p93), Louie's Gen-Gen Room at Liholiho Yacht Club (p89), Last Rites (p172), Smuggler's Cove (p184) and Zombie Village (p97) – but the Tonga Room (p132) and Trad'r Sam (p198) still set the standard for old-school tiki.

Top-shelf SF Bay liquor includes St George gin, 1512 Barbershop white rye, Anchor Old Tom gin, Sutherland Distilling rum, Hangar One vodka, Workhorse rye, Spirit Works sloe gin, Old Potrero whiskey and Emperor Norton absinthe.

Happy-hour specials or well drinks run $7 to $10 and gourmet choices with premium hooch run $10 to $15. With a $1 to $2 tip per drink, bartenders return the favor with heavy pours next round – that's why it's called getting tip-sy.

NEED TO KNOW

Opening Hours

Downtown and SoMa bars draw happy-hour crowds from 4pm to 7pm; otherwise, bars are hopping by 9pm, with last call 10:30pm to 11:30pm weekdays and 1:30am weekends. Clubs kick in around 10pm and many close at 2am – check before you invest in cover.

Smoking

Not legal indoors. Some bars have smoking patios – including Rye (p97), Bar Agricole (p94), Irish Bank (p94), many Castro bars – or backyards – such as El Rio (p155), Wild Side West (p158) and Zeitgeist (p153). Otherwise, you'll be puffing on the sidewalk. Pot's legal in SF, but secondhand smoke is still unwelcome. Vaping is subject to mockery.

Websites

To find out what's up where this weekend, check SF Weekly (www.sfweekly.com) and Funcheap SF (http://sf.funcheap.com), and skim calendars at SF Station (www.sfstation.com), UrbanDaddy (www.urbandaddy.com/home/sfo) and Thrillist (www.thrillist.com).

Wine

To get the good stuff, you don't need to commit to a bottle or escape to Wine Country. San Francisco restaurants, wine bars and urban wineries are increasingly offering top-notch, small-production California wines by the glass or *alla spina* (on tap). Organically grown, sustainable and even biodynamic wines are showcased on most SF restaurant lists.

Toast city living at **Bluxome Street Winery** (Map p298; ☑415-543-5353; www.bluxomewinery.com; 53 Bluxome St; tastings $16-20; ◎1-8pm; Ⓜ N, T) and in Dogpatch, where San Francisco's best vintages are blended and served in industrial warehouses. Cult wine retailers sell hard-to-find wines at reasonable prices; try Bi-Rite (p161), Ferry Plaza Wine Merchant (p93), Dig (p148) and California Wine Merchant (p70).

To pair your wine with SF's finest street food, consult the Twitter feed or Facebook page of your chosen wine bar. Indian Paradox (p181) pairs South Asian street food with Italian and Californian vintages, and many SF wine bars list upcoming food truck visits and pop-ups.

If heading to Napa or Sonoma, plan your trip for late fall, when you can taste new releases and score harvest specials.

Beer

SF's first brewery (1849) was built before the city was, and beer has been a staple ever since. Drink in the great outdoors at Biergarten (p181), Zeitgeist (p153), Beach Chalet (p198) and Wild Side West (p158). For house brews, it doesn't get more local than beer brewed on-site at Anchor Brewing Company (p164), 21st Amendment Brewery (p90), Magnolia Brewpub (p148) and **Social** (Map p318; ☑415-681-0330; www.socialkitchenandbrewery.com; 1326 9th Ave; ◎5pm-midnight Mon-Thu, to 1am Fri, 11:30am-1am Sat, 11:30am-11pm Sun; Ⓠ6, 7, 43, 44, Ⓜ N). Budget $4 to $7 a pint for draft microbrews, $2 to $3 for Pabst Blue Ribbon (PBR) – plus $1 tip.

Still not satiated? Attend meet-ups with local brewers at the SF Brewers' Guild (www.sfbrewersguild.org); pick up trade secrets at City Beer Store & Tasting Room (p96); or take a brewing class at **Workshop** (Map p314; ☑415-874-9186; www.workshopsf.org; 1798 McAllister St; workshops $42-125; Ⓠ5, 7, 21, 24, 43).

Cafes

When San Francisco couples break up, the thorniest issue is: who gets the cafe? San Franciscans are fiercely loyal to specific roasts and baristas – especially in the Mission, Hayes Valley and North Beach – and the majority of first internet dates meet on neutral coffee grounds. When using free cafe wi-fi, remember: order something every hour, deal with interruptions graciously and don't leave laptops unattended. Phone calls are many baristas' pet peeve but texting is fine.

An American coffee costs $2.50 to $4 and espresso drinks $3.50 to $5. Leave a buck in the tip jar for espresso drinks, especially when staying a while.

Clubs

DJs set the tone at clubs in SF, where the right groove gets everyone on the dance floor – blending gay and straight in a giddy motion blur.

Most clubs charge $10 to $25 at the door. For discounted admission, show up before

Beach Chalet (p198)

10pm or sign up to the club's online guest list (look for a VIP or RSVP link). Seating may be reserved for bottle service at high-end clubs. You'll usually only wait 15 minutes to get in anywhere, unless you're stumbling drunk.

SF is pretty casual, though club bouncers do turn away people wearing flip-flops, shorts or T-shirts (unless they're spiffy), especially at retro nights and salsa clubs.

Last call at many clubs is around 11:30pm on weekdays and 1:30am at weekends. Many clubs close around 2am, though some stay open until 4am. After-hours clubs like EndUp (p94) rage until the sun rises.

Drinking & Nightlife by Neighborhood

The Marina, Fisherman's Wharf & the Piers (p70) Straight bars with frat vibes in the Marina.

Downtown, Civic Center & SoMa (p93) Dives, chichi lounges and old-school gay bars in Civic Center and the Tenderloin; clubs, drag showcases and leather bars in SoMa.

North Beach & Chinatown (p120) Barbary Coast saloons, historic dives, cafes and deco lounges.

The Mission, Dogpatch & Potrero Hill (p153) Coffee roasters, hipster saloons, friendly wine bars, salsa clubs, and straight-friendly LGBTIQ+ clubs in the Mission.

The Castro (p171) Gay bars and clubs in the Castro.

The Haight & Hayes Valley (p184) Beer and boho lounges in the Haight; wine bars and coffee kiosks in Hayes Valley.

Golden Gate Park & the Avenues (p197) Irish and tiki bars in the Richmond District; coffee and beer in the Sunset District.

Lonely Planet's Top Choices

Stookey's Club Moderne (p131) Toast the end of Prohibition at this 1930s deco bar, with drinks, entertainment, and noir-movie-extra regulars to match.

Specs (p120) Swill Anchor Steam by the pitcher with salty characters in SF's definitive Merchant Marine dive.

Comstock Saloon (p120) Vintage Wild West saloon with potent, period-perfect concoctions and dainty bar bites.

Bar Agricole (p94) Drink your way to a history degree with well-researched cocktails – anything with hellfire bitters earns honors.

Pagan Idol (p93) Tiki to a T, with Hemingway-esque rum drinks served in skulls and volcano eruptions.

Trick Dog (p153) The ultimate theme bar switches up drinks and decor every few months to match SF obsessions: murals, horoscopes, conspiracy theories...

Best Retro Cocktails

Stookey's Club Moderne (p131) Art deco bar with bartenders shaking the stiffest Corpse Reviver cocktails in town.

Comstock Saloon (p120) Enjoy authentic cocktails, such as a Martinez, at this 1907 saloon.

Bourbon & Branch (p97) Not since Prohibition have secret passwords and gin knowledge proved so handy.

Bon Voyage (p154) If 1950s world travelers suddenly woke up in this San Francisco bar, they could pick up partying exactly where they left off.

Aub Zam Zam (p184) Bohemian den of iniquity since 1960 – the Haight's original Persian jazz martini bar.

Best for Beer

Specs (p120) Order a pitcher of Anchor Steam at this bar filled with seafaring mementos.

Zeitgeist (p153) Surly women bartenders tap 40 microbrews to guzzle in the beer garden.

City Beer Store & Tasting Room (p96) Beer sommeliers earn the title here, with expert-led tastings, brewing and pairing tips.

Wild Side West (p158) The bathroom fixtures that were thrown into this beer garden in 1977 to dissuade lesbian partiers today make fine planters.

Best for Wine

Ungrafted (p154) Go with the flow like a pro – everyone's a sommelier here.

Riddler (p185) Women-run bar with bubbles for days, from Sonoma brut to proper French Champagne.

20 Spot (p155) Expect the unexpected: unusual wines and double-deviled eggs in a former punk-record storefront.

Atalena Vinoteca (p70) Drink your way around the Mediterranean from your portside perch at Fisherman's Wharf.

Best Cafes

Sightglass Coffee (p94) This SoMa roastery looks industrial but serves small-batch roasts from family farms.

Blue Bottle Coffee Kiosk (p185) The back-alley garage

that kicked off the Third Wave coffee-roastery craze.

Trouble Coffee Co (p198) Driftwood seating, espresso in stoneware and surfers hunched over coconuts.

Andytown Coffee (p198) Ocean Beach days demand Snowy Plover gelato and espresso combos.

Best Dance Clubs

EndUp (p94) Epic 24-hour dance sessions in an urban-legendary SoMa gay club since 1973.

El Rio (p155) Get down in the Mission and flirt internationally in the backyard.

Rickshaw Stop (p97) Beats won't quit at this all-ages, all-orientations, all-fabulous shoebox club.

Madrone Art Bar (p184) Nudge aside the art installations and clear the floor: it's a Prince/Michael dance-off.

Best Tiki Bars

Pagan Idol (p93) Full-on tiki with rum drinks served in the make-believe belly of a wooden sailing ship.

Tonga Room (p132) Typhoons have struck SF every 20 minutes nightly since 1945 in this classic tiki bar.

Smuggler's Cove (p184) Roll with the rum punches at this Barbary Coast shipwreck bar.

Last Rites (p172) Toast narrow escapes from grim fates with rum concoctions amid airplane wreckage.

Zombie Village (p97) Drink from skulls inside huts until the apocalypse or last call – whichever comes first.

Entertainment

SF is one of the top five US cities for the number of creative types per square mile – and when they all take to the stage, look out. Though there's a world-famous orchestra, opera, jazz center, film festival, theater and ballet, the scene isn't all about marquee names or sit-down shows: you can see cutting-edge dance, comedy and music here for the price of an IMAX movie.

Opera & Classical Music

Between San Francisco Opera (p98) seasons, hear opera by the Grammy-winning, 12-man chorus **Chanticleer** (www.chanticleer.org) and the **Pocket Opera Company** (www.pocketopera. org; ☺Feb-Jun).

In 2018 Esa Pekka-Salonen was announced as the new music director of the Grammy Award–winning San Francisco Symphony (p97), as of the 2020–2021 season; he will take over from Michael Tilson Thomas. **San Francisco Performances** (www.performances. org) hosts world-class classical performances at the Herbst Theater while Revolution Cafe (p159) hosts chamber music at Classical Revolution in the Mission.

The symphony and opera season typically runs September through June; check SF Classical Voice (www.sfcv.org) for dates.

SF Opera offers America's least expensive opera tickets (starting from $10); SF Symphony offers rush tickets and Sound-Box rehearsal-stage shows ($20 to $35). SF Opera and SF Symphony perform gratis at the **Stern Grove Festival** (www.sterngrove.org; Stern Grove; ☺Jun-Aug). Stop by Old St Mary's (p112) for regular Tuesday noon concerts, and check http://noontimeconcerts.org for other donation-requested concerts.

Live Music

Eclectic SF clubs host funk, reggae, bluegrass and punk; check online calendars.

Hear bluegrass, the original music of SF's gold rush, at the **Hardly Strictly Bluegrass** (www.hardlystrictlybluegrass.com; ☺Oct) festival and at Berkeley's Freight & Salvage Coffeehouse (p209). Host Peter Thompson brings encyclopedic knowledge of American roots music to KALW's breakthrough bluegrass national public radio program, Bluegrass Signal (www.kalw.org; 91.7FM).

For funk and hip-hop Oakland has tougher rap and faster beats, but SF plays it loose and funky at Mezzanine (p101) and the Independent (p186). Psychedelic rock legends play at the Fillmore Auditorium (p139), but alt-rock storms the stage at the **Outside Lands** (www. sfoutsidelands.com; 3-day pass standard/VIP $375/795; ☺Aug) festival, Warfield (p99) and the Great American Music Hall (p98). Meanwhile, punk's not dead at Bottom of the Hill (p159), Edinburgh Castle (p97) and **Slim's** (Map p298; ☑415-255-0333; www.slimspresents. com; 333 11th St; tickets $15-30; ☺box office 5pm-close on show nights; ☐9, 12, 27, 47).

Major jazz talents are in residence year-round at the SFJAZZ Center (p186), and jazz ensembles regularly play the Revolution Cafe (p159), Chapel (p159), the Royale (p99), Club Deluxe (p186) and Stookey's Club Moderne (p131).

Theater

Before winning Tonys and a Pulitzer Prize, *Angels in America* got its wings at the American Conservatory Theater (p98). You can see the next theatrical breakthrough in progress at the ACT's Strand Theater (p99). In summer the **San Francisco Mime Troupe** (www. sfmt.org) performs free political-comedy satire in Dolores Park, while the **SF Shakespeare**

PLAN YOUR TRIP ENTERTAINMENT

NEED TO KNOW

Arts Calendar

Check **KQED's The Do List** (www.kqed.org/arts/program/the-do-list) for an excellent selection of upcoming performing-arts events.

Discounts

Sign up at **Gold Star Events** (www.goldstarevents.com) for discounts on comedy, theater, concerts and opera, or stop by the **TIX Bay Area** (Map p294; ☑415-433-7827; http://tixbayarea.org; 350 Powell St; ☐Powell-Mason, Powell-Hyde, ⒷPowell, ⓂPowell) Union Sq ticket booth for cheap tickets for same-day or next-day shows.

Festival (www.sfshakes.org; ⊘Sep) is held gratis in the Presidio.

Theatre Bay Area (www.theatrebayarea.org) is a comprehensive calendar of 100 Bay Area theater companies. Find SF Broadway show listings at SHN (www.shnsf.com).

Marquee shows run $35 to $150, but same-day, half-price tickets are often available. Indie theater runs $10 to $35.

Comedy & Spoken Word

For laughs, go for drag comedy at Oasis (p99), Marsh (p159) monologues, campy Beach Blanket Babylon (p122), HBO headliners at Cobb's Comedy Club (p122) and the Punch Line (p99), or get onstage with BATS Improv (p72) comedy workshops.

This town has tales like you wouldn't believe – hear every eyebrow-raising detail at SF's annual **Litquake** (www.litquake.org; ⊘mid-Oct), the San Francisco Main Library (p86) and Booksmith (p186) author events. For raucous readings, check out Writers with Drinks at the Make-Out Room (p160), storytelling slams at Public Works (p100), Pint-Sized Plays at PianoFight (p98), and Mortified's teen-diary excerpts at DNA Lounge (p100).

Dance

SF supports the longest-running US ballet company, the San Francisco Ballet (p98),

and multiple independent troupes at the Yerba Buena Center for the Arts (p100). Experimental styles are championed at the Oberlin Dance Collective (p158) and **Joe Goode Performance Group** (Map p302; ☑415-561-6565; www.joegoode.org; 401 Alabama St; tickets $18-38; ⊘shows 7pm or 8pm; ☐22, 33), and you can invent your own style at Dance Mission (p164). Dancers' Group (www.dancersgroup.org) has a comprehensive dance calendar.

Cinema

Cinemaniacs adore SF's vintage movie palaces, including the Roxie (p159), Castro (p173) and Balboa (p199) cinemas. For major releases and resurrected cult movies with drinks and dinner, head to Alamo Drafthouse (p158). Foreign films and award contenders show at the **Embarcadero Center Cinema** (Map p301; ☑415-352-0835; www.landmarktheatres.com; 1 Embarcadero Center, Promenade Level; tickets $11-14; ⓂEmbarcadero, ⒷEmbarcadero), while New People Cinema (p140) hosts anime and Asian American Film Festival premieres, and IMAX blockbusters screen at AMC Metreon 16 (p100). Most tickets run $10 to $16, with weekday matinees around $8.

Beyond the **SF International Film Festival** (www.sffs.org; ⊘Apr), the city hosts **LGBTQ+** (www.frameline.org; tickets $10-35; ⊘Jun), **Green** (www.greenfilmfest.org; ⊘Sep), Asian American (https://caamedia.org), Jewish (https://jfi.org/film-festival) and Arab (https://arabfilminstitute.org) film festivals.

Entertainment by Neighborhood

Downtown, Civic Center & SoMa (p97) Symphony, opera, theater, punk, jazz, rock and comedy.

North Beach & Chinatown (p122) Comedy, jazz, folk, blues and spoken word.

The Mission, Dogpatch & Potrero Hill (p158) Dance, alt-bands, punk, bluegrass, experimental theater and spoken word.

Golden Gate Park & the Avenues (p199) Festivals and free concerts.

Lonely Planet's Top Choices

San Francisco Symphony (p97) Sets the tempo for modern classical, with innovative musical director Esa Pekka-Salonen and guest artists like Metallica.

SFJAZZ Center (p186) Top talents reinvent standards and create new works inspired by mariachis, skateboarders, poets, Joni Mitchell and Angela Davis.

San Francisco Opera (p98) Divas like Renée Fleming bring down the house with classics and original contemporary works such as *The (R)evolution of Steve Jobs*.

American Conservatory Theater (p98) Daring theater, from operas by Tom Waits and William Kentridge to breakthrough Lauren Yee plays – plus experimental works at the Strand Theater.

Castro Theatre (p173) Organ overtures and cult classics with enthusiastic audience participation raise the roof at this art-deco movie palace.

Best for Laughs

Oasis (p99) Drag comedy variety acts so funny you'll cough up glitter.

Cobb's Comedy Club (p122) Comics from the streets to Comedy Central test risky new material.

Beach Blanket Babylon (p122) Laugh your wig off with San Francisco's over-the-top Disney-drag cabaret.

Punch Line (p99) Breakthrough comedians like Ellen Degeneres, Chris Rock and Margaret Cho started here.

Best Theater & Dance

American Conservatory Theater (p98) Landmark theater that hosts premiere work from major playwrights and launches breakthrough shows.

San Francisco Ballet (p98) Elegant lines and gorgeous original staging from America's oldest ballet company.

Oberlin Dance Collective (p158) Style and substance in balance, with muscular, meaningful original choreography.

Yerba Buena Center for the Arts (p100) Modern dance troupes throw down and represent SF's cutting edge.

Magic Theatre (p70) Original works by major playwrights, performed in a converted army base.

Best Live Music Venues

San Francisco Symphony (p97) The Grammy-winning symphony constantly wows audiences with their performances.

SFJAZZ Center (p186) Jazz legends from across the globe perform at this center.

San Francisco Opera (p98) Rivalling New York's Met Opera, SF Opera shows world premieres and features incredible costumes and sets.

Fillmore Auditorium (p139) Rock-legendary since the '60s, with the psychedelic posters to prove it.

Great American Music Hall (p98) Marquee acts in a historic, intimate venue that was once a bordello.

Best for Movies

Castro Theatre (p173) Featuring both new films and classics,with showtime heralded by the Wurlitzer organ, plus wildly popular drag reenactments of cult flicks and singalong musicals.

Alamo Drafthouse Cinema (p158) Come for premieres with beer and pizza, stay for D-movie nights with themed cocktails.

Roxie Cinema (p159) Vintage cinema screening cult classics, documentary premieres and indie films not yet distributed.

Balboa Theatre (p199) Art-deco cinema features first-run and art-house films, plus family matinees.

Best Free Entertainment

Hardly Strictly Bluegrass (p35) See bluegrass greats like Alison Krauss jam alongside Elvis Costello, Patti Smith and Dwight Yoakam – for free.

Stern Grove Festival (p35) SFJAZZ legends and symphony soloists perform in the great outdoors.

San Francisco Mime Troupe (p35) Social satire, Kabuki and musical comedy make scenes in Dolores Park.

SF Shakespeare Festival (p35) Audiences warm to *The Winter's Tale* at foggy Presidio performances.

Amoeba Music (p186) Free in-store concerts by rock and alt-pop radio favorites, plus oddballs and cult bands.

PLAN YOUR TRIP ENTERTAINMENT

Participants in San Francisco's Pride Parade

LGBTIQ+

It doesn't matter where you're from or who you love: if you're here and queer, welcome home. San Francisco is America's pinkest city, and though New York Marys may call it the retirement home of the young — the sidewalks roll up early here — there's nowhere easier to be out and proud.

Brava Theater (p158) is run by and for women

LGBTIQ+ Scene

In San Francisco, you don't need to trawl the urban underworld for a gay scene. The intersection of 18th and Castro is the historic center of the gay world, but dancing queens and trans club kids head to SoMa to mix it up at thump-thump clubs. Drag shows have been a nightlife staple here since the 1800s, though you'll never need a professional reason to blur gender lines here – next to baseball, gender-bending is SF's favorite sport.

Where are all the women into women? They're busy sunning on the patio at Wild Side West (p158) or El Rio (p155), screening documentaries at the Roxie Cinema (p159), hitting happy hour at Jolene's (p154), inventing new technologies at SF women's/nonbinary hackerspaces, working it out on the dance floor at Rickshaw Stop (p97) or The Cafe (p173), and raising kids in Noe Valley and Bernal Heights.

The Mission remains the preferred 'hood of womxn, femmes, bois, dykes on bikes, transpeople and nonbinary folx right across the rainbow spectrum. Gender need not apply in SF, where the Department of Motor Vehicles (DMV) officially acknowledges trans-queer identities.

Party Planning

On Sundays in the 1950s, SF bars held gay old times euphemistically called 'tea dances' – and Sunday afternoons remain a happening time to go out, most notably at the Eagle Tavern (p95) – but most parties happen Thursday through Sunday nights.

NEED TO KNOW

News & Events

San Francisco has two gay newspapers, plus a glossy nightlife rag.

The Bay Area Reporter (www.ebar.com) Released every Wednesday since 1971; news and events.

San Francisco Bay Times (http://sfbay times.com) News and calendar listings.

Gloss Magazine (www.glossmagazine. net) Nightlife and parties.

Support & Activism

LYRIC (https://lyric.org) For queer youth.

Human Rights Campaign Action Center (p167) For political organizing.

GLBT History Museum (p167) For context.

Transgender Law Center (www. transgenderlawcenter.org) For civil-rights activism and support.

Homobiles (p270) Nonprofit LGBTIQ+ taxi service.

Strut (www.sfaf.org) Before you play, get PrEP.

Women's Community Venues

Women's Building (p146) Mural-graced landmark housing nine women's organizations.

Lyon-Martin Women's Health Services (http://lyon-martin.org) For health and support.

Brava Theater (p158) For arts.

Comfort & Joy (http://playajoy.org), the queer Burning Man collective, lists happening dance parties and creative community events.

Marriage Equality in SF

San Francisco was the first city to authorize same-sex marriages, back in 2004 – but some 4036 honeymoons ended abruptly when their marriages were legally invalidated by the state. Court battles ensued, and California voters narrowly passed a measure to legally define marriage as between a man and a woman.

PLAN YOUR TRIP LGBTIQ+

GETTING MARRIED IN SF

If you decide you want to get hitched in San Francisco, first of all: congratulations! The city is duly honored. The process is simple. Make an appointment to get your marriage license at City Hall, bring federal ID or a birth certificate, and be prepared to spend around $200 in fees. You do not have to be a California resident or US citizen, and you and your spouse can be any gender. Once you have your license, you can get married the same day. Yes, really!

San Francisco City Hall is a marriage equality landmark, and also a romantic, highly photogenic place for a wedding – the Rotunda is filled with light and has double staircases for bonus drama. You can choose a civil ceremony performed by a city official, or officiated by any person who's a registered justice of the peace. In California, anyone can get ordained online at www.themonastery.org/ordination.

For the complete requirements and details on getting married in San Francisco, check out the city's official wedding website: https://sfgov.org/countyclerk/marriage. May you live a long and happy life together, and return often to San Francisco.

But for star-crossed San Francisco couples, there was a happy ending. Countersuits were initiated and, in 2013, the US Supreme Court upheld California courts' ruling in favor of state civil rights protections, setting a nationwide precedent. Upon further appeal, the Supreme Court declared laws prohibiting same-sex marriage unconstitutional nationwide in 2015. The day of the decision, many longtime partners got hitched at City Hall – some for the second or third time, to the same person.

LGBTIQ+ by Neighborhood

Downtown, Civic Center & SoMa Raging dance clubs, leather bars, drag shows and men's sex clubs in SoMa; bars, trans venues and queer cabaret in the Tenderloin.

The Mission, Dogpatch & Potrero Hill Women's and trans-queer bars, arts venues and community spaces in the Mission.

The Castro Gay history, activism, men's cruising bars, drag nights and queer clubbing.

Lonely Planet's Top Choices

Pride (p246) The most extravagant celebration on the planet culminates in the Dyke March, Pink Party and an exhilarating 1.2-million-strong Pride Parade.

Castro Theatre (p173) A 1929 movie palace with cult classics, drag nights and LGBTQ+ film festival premieres.

Rainbow Honor Walk (p167) Get to know LGBTIQ+ icons as you walk through the Castro.

Oasis (p99) Original, fearless and funny drag theater and comedy showcases.

GLBT History Museum (p167) Historical context and insight into the gay community.

Best Dance Floors

Aunt Charlie's Lounge (p97) Knock-down, drag-out winner for gender-bending shows and dance-floor freakiness in a tiny space.

El Rio (p155) Mix it up with world music, salsa, house, live bands and SF's flirtiest patio.

Stud (p95) Shows and DJs nightly, plus the tantalizing aroma of bourbon, cologne and testosterone.

Powerhouse (p95) DJs most nights, gogo dancers and strong drinks at the classic SoMa cruise bar.

EndUp (p94) Hit your groove Saturday night and work it until Monday.

Best for Women

Jolene's (p154) Women on the dance floor, at the bar, all over the wallpaper, right at home.

Wild Side West (p158) Cheers to queers and beers in the herstory-making sculpture garden.

Rickshaw Stop (p97) All-ages parties and extra estrogen at semi-monthly Cockblock.

Women's Building (p146) Glorious murals crown this community institution.

Brava Theater (p159) Original shows by, for and about women, queer and trans folx.

Best Daytime Scene

Dolores Park (p146) Sun and cityscapes on hillside 'Gay Beach,' plus political protests.

Baker Beach (p60) Only Baker Beach regulars know you can get goose bumps *there*.

Cafe Flore (p173) Fab gay scene-watching: blind dates, LGBTIQ+ parents with kids, occasional dogs in drag.

El Rio (p155) Sunday's Daytime Realness brings back-patio drag fabulousness.

Eagle Tavern (p95) At Sunday-afternoon beer busts, leather daddies drink alongside gay scenesters.

Best Places to Stay

Parker Guest House (p236) Top choice for comfort and style.

Inn on Castro (p236) Vintage Victorian styled with disco-era furnishings.

Beck's Motor Lodge (p235) Upgraded motel rooms in the heart of the Castro.

Inn San Francisco (p235) Swanky B&B in the heart of the Mission.

Best for Trans & Nonbinary Points of Interest

Compton's Transgender Cultural District (p87) In the world's first landmarked transgender district, see the exact spot where the US movement for trans civil rights began in 1966.

Tenderloin Museum Walking Tours (p104) Walk in the footsteps of trans trailblazers on docent-led tours.

AsiaSF (p100) Waitresses serve drinks and sass with a not-so-secret secret: they're transgender.

Homobiles (p270) Safe rides are just a text message away.

Transgender Law Center (p39) Because knowing your rights is SF's finest souvenir.

LGBTIQ+ Trailblazers

Human Rights Campaign Action Center (p167) Been there, signed the petition, bought the T-shirt supporting civil rights at Harvey Milk's camera storefront.

Castro Theatre (p173) Frameline LGBTQ+ Film Festival premieres, singalong movie nights and drag recreations of cult classics.

Rainbow Honor Walk (p167) Plaques honoring LGBTIQ+ heroes line Market and Castro Sts.

GLBT History Museum (p167) Proud moments and historic challenges, captured for posterity.

Oasis (p99) SF's dedicated drag venue, hostessed by SF drag icons Heklina and D'Arcy Drollinger.

Rare Device (p187)

Shopping

All those tricked-out dens, well-stocked spice racks and fabulous ensembles don't just pull themselves together – San Franciscans scour their city for them. Eclectic originality is SF's signature style, and that's not one-stop shopping. But consider the thrill of the hunt: while shopping, you can watch fish theater, sample chocolate and trade fashion tips with professional drag queens.

Adventures in Retail

Indie designers and vintage shops supply original style on SF's most boutique-studded streets: Haight, Divisadero, Valencia, Hayes, upper Grant, Fillmore, Union and Polk. For further adventures in alt-retail, don't miss West Coast Craft and Art Market San Francisco.

STYLE SECRETS

Polk Street Vintage looks, local art, indie designers and smart gifts.

Valencia Street Made-in-SF gifts, West Coast style and scents, pirate supplies.

Haight Street Vintage, drag glam, steampunk gear and hats galore, plus anarchist comics, vinyl LPs and skateboards for total SF makeovers.

Hayes Valley Local designers, gourmet treats, home decor.

Fillmore St Makeup bars, upscale designers, resale boutiques.

Powell Street Lined with flagship stores and cheap glamour: Gap, Uniqlo, H&M and Urban Outfitters.

Union Square Ringed by department stores and megabrands, including Neiman Marcus, Macy's, Saks and Apple.

Retail Events

Want to take your shopping spree up a notch? San Franciscans are a festive bunch with widely diverse interests – no matter what you're looking for, there's an event in San Francisco to celebrate it.

Art Market San Francisco (http://artmarket sf.com; Fort Mason Center; ☺last weekend Apr) At Fort Mason, San Francisco's signature art fair attracts curators with major museum pieces but also sells affordable original works for as little as $80. For further art action, look for renegade satellite fairs in Fort Mason's parking lot and nearby motels.

West Coast Craft (http://westcoastcraft. com; Fort Mason Center; ☺mid-Jun & mid-Nov) That laid-back, homespun California look takes handiwork – or you can leave it to the pros at West Coast Craft where you'll find 100-plus indie makers.

Litquake (p36) Stranger-than-fiction literary events take place during SF's outlandish literary festival, with the first ever Lit Crawl Book Fair taking place in 2019.

Haight Ashbury Street Fair (www.haightash burystreetfair.org; ☺mid-Jun) Free music on two stages, plus macramé, tie-dye galore and wafting pot smoke all along Haight St to Masonic St – the Summer of Love stages a comeback in the Haight every year since 1977, when Harvey Milk helped make the first Haight Street Fair happen.

Cherry Blossom Festival (www.nccbf.org; ☺Apr) Japantown blooms when the Cherry Blossom Festival arrives with *taiko* drums, art and craft exhibits, food stalls and anime cosplay. The biggest West Coast celebration of Japanese culture since 1968, the festival draws 220,000 people over a week of events, culminating in a raucous Grand Parade on the final Sunday.

Shopping by Neighborhood

The Marina, Fisherman's Wharf & the Piers (p72) Date outfits, accessories, wine and design in the Marina.

Downtown, Civic Center & SoMa (p101) Department stores, global megabrands, discount retail and Apple's flagship store.

NEED TO KNOW

Opening Hours

Most stores are open daily from 10am to 6pm or 7pm, though hours often run 11am to 8pm Saturday and 11am to 6pm Sunday. Stores in the Mission and the Haight tend to open later and keep erratic hours; many Downtown stores stay open until 8pm.

Sales Tax

Combined SF city and California state sales taxes tack 8.75% onto the price of your purchase. This tax is not refundable.

Returns

Try before you buy and ask about return policies. Many stores offer returns for store credit only. When in doubt, consider a gift certificate; in California, they never expire – and you can often use them online.

Online Resources

Check **Urban Daddy** (www.urbandaddy. com) for store openings and pop-ups, **Thrillist** (www.thrillist.com) for gear and gadgets, and **Refinery 29** (www.refinery 29.com) for sales and trends.

Japantown, Fillmore & Pacific Heights (p140) Home design, stationery, toys, accessories and anime in Japantown; haute resale, designers and decor in Pacific Heights.

Nob Hill & Russian Hill (p133) Indie designers, vintage and local art in Russian Hill.

The Mission, Dogpatch & Potrero Hill (p160) Local makers, community-supported bookstores, indie art galleries, artisan foods, dandy style and vintage whatever.

The Haight & Hayes Valley (p186) Design boutiques, decor, food and coffee in Hayes Valley; quirky gifts and accessories in NoPa; head shops, music, vintage and skate gear in the Haight.

The Castro (p174) Local designer decor, men's fashion and gifts for coming-out parties.

Lonely Planet's Top Choices

City Lights Books (p111) If you can't find nirvana in the Poetry Chair upstairs, try Lost Continents in the basement.

826 Valencia (p146) Your friendly neighborhood pirate-supply store and publishing house; proceeds support on-site youth writing programs.

Gravel & Gold (p161) Get good Californian vibrations from G&G's SF-made, feel-good clothing and beach-shack housewares.

Bi-Rite (p161) SF's best-curated selection of local artisan chocolates, cured meats and small-production wines.

Park Life (p199) Art, books, Aesthetics team T-shirts and design objects make SF seem exceptionally gifted.

Apothecarium (p174) Wonderland of cannabis edibles to whet your California appetite.

Best Gourmet Gifts

Bi-Rite (p161) Foodie heaven with a wall of chocolates, a selection of local wine and cheese and an altar-like deli counter.

Rainbow Grocery (p163) Vast selection of NorCal's finest coffees, cheeses and organic airplane snacks.

Recchiuti Chocolates (p101) Idyllic gourmet s'mores, sea-salted caramels and whiskey-pairing truffles.

Apothecarium (p174) America's best-designed marijuana dispensary with a broad selection of cannabis.

Heath Ceramics (p161) The tableware of choice of top SF chefs, handmade on-site at the Mission studio.

Omnivore (p174) Rare vintage cookbooks and author events with star chefs.

Best SF Fashion Designers

Gravel & Gold (p161) California's hippie homesteader movement celebrated in clothing and housewares.

Paloma (p187) Retro-motorcycle-gang scarves, billiard-ball cocktail rings and handmade leather bags banged out on-site.

Nooworks (p162) Eighties new-wave designs reinvented with edgy art-schooled graphics.

Amour Vert (p187) Feel-good fashion: flattering silhouettes cut from earth-friendly materials.

Paul's Hat Works (p199) Tip of the hat to the hatmaker capping off SF looks since the 1930s.

Best for the Person Who Has Everything

826 Valencia (p146) Eccentric pirate-supply store selling eye patches, spyglasses and McSweeney's literary magazines.

Good Vibrations (p133) Adult toys, informed staff and zero judgment.

New People (p141) Ninja shoes, Lolita Goth petticoats and graphic-art smocks at this Japantown showcase.

Bound Together Anarchist Book Collective (p186) One-stop shopping for DIY organic farming manuals, radical comics and prison literature.

Foggy Notion (p200) Presidio hiking-trail scents, un-washing powder for Ocean Beachy hair and other SF beauty secrets.

Best Eclectic Decor

Rare Device (p187) Handcrafted ceramics, toys and other indie decor beyond standard design magazines.

Adobe Books & Backroom Gallery (p162) Art freshly made on-site by the artist in residence, plus out-of-print books and zines galore.

San Francisco Rock Posters (p122) Original psychedelic Fillmore posters bring instant SF street cred to any pad.

Cliff's Variety (p175) Disco balls, jars of rubber nuns and other essential decor for SF theme parties.

Workshop Residence (p161) Local artists work with local fabricators to produce limited-edition housewares, decor and more.

Kitesurfing in San Francisco Bay

Sports & Activities

San Franciscans love the outdoors, and their historic conservation efforts have protected acres of parks, beaches and woodlands for all to enjoy. This city lives for sunny days spent biking, skating, surfing and drifting on the Bay. Foggy days are spent making art projects, but nights are for dancing and Giants games.

Spectator Sports

See the Giants play baseball on their home turf at the Giants Stadium (p99). You might also be able to catch some Giants action for free at the Embarcadero waterfront boardwalk. The Golden State Warriors play NBA basketball to win, and they're moving back to SF to play in a new stadium in 2019. To see the 49ers (p46) in action, you'll need to drive an hour south of SF to Santa Clara, where they now play in Levi's Stadium.

Tickets can be booked through team websites or Ticketmaster (www.ticketmaster. com). If games are sold out, search the 'Tickets' category on www.craigslist.org. The *San Francisco Chronicle* (www.sfgate.com) offers complete sports coverage, but *The Examiner* (www.sfexaminer.com) also has sports stats and predictions.

Outdoor Activities

On sunny weekends, SF is out kite-flying, surfing or biking. Even on foggy days, don't neglect sunscreen: UV rays penetrate SF's thin cloud cover.

BICYCLING

Every weekend, thousands of cyclists cross Golden Gate Bridge to explore the Marin

Headlands and Mt Tamalpais. Since the 1970s, 'Mt Tam' has been the Bay Area's ultimate mountain-biking challenge.

Many SF streets have bicycle lanes and major parks have bike paths. The safest places to cycle in SF are Golden Gate Park (car-free on Sunday), the Embarcadero and the wooded Presidio. SF bikers' favorite street-biking route is the green-painted, flat bike lane connecting Market St and Golden Gate Park called the Wiggle (www.sfbike. org/our-work/street-campaigns/the-wiggle).

The San Francisco Bicycle Coalition (p266) produces the *San Francisco Bike Map & Walking Guide,* which outlines the Wiggle route and shows how to avoid traffic and hills. For further planning put your smartphone to work finding the perfect route using the San Francisco Bike Route Planner (http://amarpai.com/bikemap).

RUNNING
Crissy Field (p59) has a 2.5-mile jogging track, and trails run 3 miles through Golden Gate Park (p191) from the Panhandle to Ocean Beach. The Presidio (p65) offers ocean breezes through eucalyptus trees. SF's major races are more festive than competitive, including **Bay to Breakers** (www. baytobreakers.com; race registration from $65; ☷3rd Sun May) – bring a costume, or at least a feather boa.

SKATING & SKATEBOARDING
SF is the home of roller disco and the skateboard magazine *Thrasher.* Inline skaters skate the Embarcadero Friday nights and disco-skate in Golden Gate Park on Sunday. Golden Gate Park Bike & Skate (p201) rents inline and four-wheeled roller skates in good weather.

Potrero del Sol/La Raza Skatepark (Map p302; cnr 25th & Utah Sts; ☷8am-9pm; ☐9, 10, 27, 33, 48, ⓑ24th St Mission) has ramps for kids and bowls for pros; **SoMa West Skatepark** (Map p302; ☑415-551-3000; https://sfrecpark.org/ destination/soma-west-skate-park; 1369 Stevenson St; ☷9am-9pm; ⓜF) is a newer, grittier urban park under the freeway. Haight St is urban skating at its obstacle-course best, especially the downhill slide from Baker to Pierce.

For signature SF skateboards and skate gear, hit Mission Skateboards (p162) and **FTC Skateboarding** (Map p314; ☑415-626-0663; www.ftcsf.com; 1632 Haight St; ☷11am-7pm; ☐6, 7, 33, 37, 43, ⓜN); for skate fashion and street graphics, check out **Upper Playground** (Map p314; ☑415-861-1960; www.upper playground.com; 220 Fillmore St; ☷11am-7pm; ☐6, 7, 22, ⓜN).

GOLF & MINIGOLF
Tee up and enjoy mild weather, clipped greens and gorgeous views on SF's top public courses: Lincoln Park Golf Course (p194) and Golden Gate Municipal Golf Course (p201). If minigolf is more your speed, book a tee time at Urban Putt (p163) or Stagecoach Greens (p105).

Water Sports & Activities
SAILING
Sailing is best April through August, and classes and rentals are available from

---

SAN FRANCISCO 49ERS

The **49ers** (☑415-656-4900; www.sf49ers.com; Levi's Stadium, Santa Clara; tickets $48-570; ⓡCaltrain Santa Clara Station) were the National Football League's dream team from 1981 to 1994, claiming five Super Bowl championships. But after decades of chilly, fumbled games at foggy Candlestick Park, the 49ers moved to Santa Clara's **Levi's Stadium** in 2014. Some fans argue the team should be renamed, since Santa Clara is 38 miles from San Francisco. Locals hoped the move would lift the jinx, but the 49ers weren't on the field when Levi's Stadium hosted Super Bowl 50 in 2016. In that same year, the team drew attention when quarterback Colin Kaepernick began a long-standing practice of kneeling during the national anthem to protest the treatment of minorities in the USA. In 2017 the controversial gesture resulted in Vice President Mike Pence walking out of a 49ers game.

To reach the stadium, take Caltrain one hour south to Santa Clara station, then catch the game-day shuttle. Since Levi's Stadium is in Silicon Valley, it's tricked out with technology, from the power-generating solar roof to wi-fi–enabled concessions. Maybe there's hope yet: in a superstitious effort to align the team with the San Francisco Giants' impressive winning streak (largely attributed to thick-bearded pitcher Brian Wilson), the team's bread-loving mining mascot Sourdough Sam now sports a beard.

Spinnaker Sailing (p105) or City Kayak (p105). Newbies may feel more comfortable on a catamaran with Adventure Cat (p75) or a booze cruise with Red & White Fleet (p74).

Whale-watching season peaks mid-October through December, when the mighty mammals are easy to spot from Point Reyes. Book whale-watching tours through Oceanic Society Expeditions (p75).

SURFING & WINDSURFING

About a 90-minute drive south of SF, Santa Cruz is NorCal's top surf destination for kooks (newbies) and pros alike. SF's Ocean Beach (p195) is surfed by locals at daybreak in winter, but these Pacific swells are not for beginners. Mavericks (http://titansof mavericks.com/) big-wave surfing competition is held each February in Half Moon Bay (30 minutes south of SF); it's strictly invitation-only for pros willing to risk it all.

A safer bet is Bay windsurfing and body-surfing off the beach at Crissy Field (p59). Hit up Mollusk (p200) for specialty boards and Aqua Surf Shop (p200) for rental gear. Check the surf report (📞415-273-1618) before you suit up.

SWIMMING

Ocean Beach (p195) is best for walking – the Pacific undertow is dangerous, with drownings occurring every year. Don't turn your back on the Pacific: Northern California occasionally gets 'sneaker waves' that whisk unsuspecting strollers and casual waders out to sea. Hardy swimmers brave chilly Bay waters at Aquatic Park (p63) or Baker Beach (p60), which is nude around the northern end.

Local pools The Embarcadero YMCA, which is attached to the Harbor Court Hotel (p233) has a well-kept pool; city pool schedules are listed at http://sfrecpark.org.

Alcatraz Sharkfest Swim Swim 1.5 miles from Alcatraz to Aquatic Park. Entry is $275; check Envirosports (www.envirosports.com) for info.

Sports & Activities by Neighborhood

The Marina, Fisherman's Wharf & the Piers (p74) Running, biking, windsurfing, kayaking, skating and yoga in the Marina.

The Mission, Dogpatch & Potrero Hill (p163) Arts, dance, skateboarding and yoga in the Mission.

The Haight & Hayes Valley Skateboarding and bicycling in the Haight and Hayes Valley.

Downtown, Civic Center & SoMa (p104) Swimming, kayaking and sailing in SoMa.

Golden Gate Park & the Avenues (p200) Surfing, biking, archery, golf, disc golf, and lawn bowling in the Avenues.

Lonely Planet's Top Choices

Golden Gate Park (p191) Lawn-bowling, skating and cycling – especially on car-free Sundays.

Potrero del Sol/La Raza Skatepark Skate the bowl if you've got the skills.

Stow Lake (p201) Glide across the lake by paddleboat.

Urban Putt (p163) Minigolf through SF landmarks.

Spinnaker Sailing (p105) Sail across the bay.

Crissy Field (p59) Kitesurfing with a Golden Gate Bridge backdrop.

Explore San Francisco

SAN FRANCISCO'S
TOP SIGHTS

Neighborhoods at a Glance

❶ The Marina, Fisherman's Wharf & the Piers p52

Since the gold rush, this waterfront has been the point of entry for new arrivals – and it remains a major attraction for sea lion antics and getaways to Alcatraz. The Marina has chic boutiques built over a former cow pasture and organic dining along the waterfront. The Presidio's got Shakespeare on the loose and public nudity on a former army base.

❷ Downtown, Civic Center & SoMa p76

Downtown has it all: art galleries, swanky hotels, first-run theaters, malls and entertainment megaplexes. Civic Center is a zoning conundrum, with great performance venues and Asian art treasures on one side of City Hall and dive bars and soup kitchens on the other. Head to South of Market (SoMa) for high-tech deals, high art and dirty dance floors.

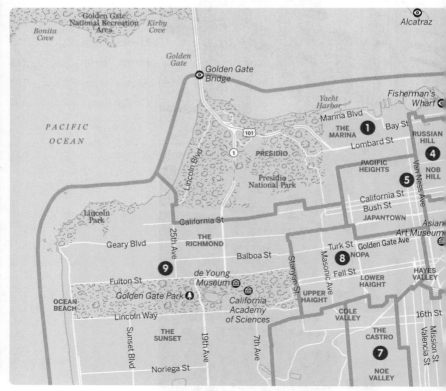

❸ North Beach & Chinatown p108

Dumplings and rare teas are served under pagoda roofs on Chinatown's main streets – but its historic back alleys are filled with temple incense, mah-jongg tile clatter and distant echoes of revolution. Wild parrots circle over the Italian cafes and bohemian bars of North Beach, serving enough espresso to fuel your own Beat poetry revival.

❹ Nob Hill & Russian Hill p124

Summit San Francisco's twin downtown hills and you'll discover everyone's heads are in the clouds up here – billionaires and penniless poets, rock stars and rock-star chefs, urban hikers and spiritual seekers. Just follow your own bliss – head to a tiki bar happy hour, attend a cathedral organ recital, or watch the Bay Bridge lights twinkle.

❺ Japantown, Fillmore & Pacific Heights p134

Don't let the quaint Victorians and upscale boutiques fool you: this neighborhood rocks. Japanese Americans have called it home for over a century and today Japantown is where cosplay kids come to rock Lolita goth fashion at anime premieres. The Fillmore has been a nightlife hub since its 1940s jazz heyday and hilltop Pacific Heights is all about the mansions.

❻ The Mission, Dogpatch & Potrero Hill p143

The best way to enjoy the Mission is with a book in one hand and a burrito in the other, amid murals, sunshine and the usual crowd of creatives, techies, and skaters. Potrero Hill is a bedroom community for Silicon Valley refugees. In the Dogpatch, you can brunch like a champion, mingle with wine barflies or chat up innovators and artists in revamped waterfront warehouses.

❼ The Castro p165

Rainbow flags wave their welcome to all in the world's premier LGBTIQ+ culture destination – club kids, career activists, leather daddies and sequined drag queens. Check the plaques on Castro sidewalks and notice whose footsteps you're walking in.

❽ The Haight & Hayes Valley p176

Hippie idealism lives in the Haight, with street musicians, anarchist comic books and psychedelic murals galore. Browse local designs and go gourmet in Hayes Valley, where Zen monks and jazz legends drift down the sidewalks.

❾ Golden Gate Park & the Avenues p189

Hardcore surfers and gourmet adventurers meet in the foggy Avenues around Golden Gate Park. This is one totally chill global village, featuring bluegrass and Korean BBQ, disc golf and tiki cocktails, French pastries and cult-movie matinees.

The Marina, Fisherman's Wharf & the Piers

THE MARINA & COW HOLLOW | FISHERMAN'S WHARF & THE PIERS | PRESIDIO

Neighborhood Top Five

1 Golden Gate Bridge (p58) Strolling it after the fog clears, revealing magnificent views of downtown with sailboats plying the waves below.

2 Alcatraz (p54) Feeling cold winds blow as you imagine the misery of prison life – not to mention the ingenuity required for an escape.

3 Pier 39 (p61) Giggling at the shenanigans of braying and barking sea lions, then retreating to the carnival-like attractions, novelty shops and tacky restaurants nearby.

4 Exploratorium (p64) Letting your curiosity run amok in this hands-on museum of science, art and human perception. Don't miss the Tactile Dome.

5 Musée Mécanique (p62) Marveling at a collection of vintage mechanical amusements and 19th-century arcade games.

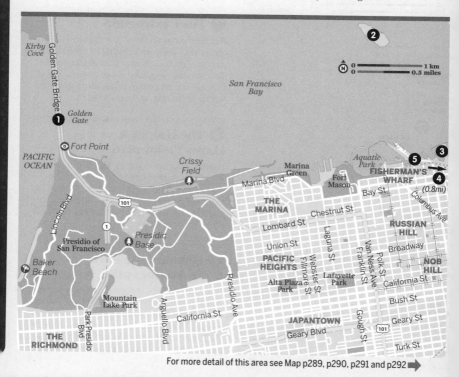

For more detail of this area see Map p289, p290, p291 and p292 ➡

Explore the Marina, Fisherman's Wharf & the Piers

Fisherman's Wharf is the epicenter of tourism in San Francisco; the few remaining fishermen moor their boats around Pier 47. Locals don't usually visit the Wharf because it's entirely geared to tourists. Budget two hours to a half-day maximum. Weekends are packed by early afternoon: come first thing in the morning to avoid crowds. Summertime fog usually clears by midday (if it clears at all), so visit the Golden Gate Bridge during the early afternoon – but be warned that the fog blows in around 4pm. Carry a jacket and definitely wear pants, unless you're here during a rare heat wave (locals spot the tourists by their shorts). Most people walk farther than they anticipate: wear comfortable shoes and sunscreen. Cow Hollow and the Marina have good boutique-shopping strips, bars and restaurants. Explore them later in the day, after working hours but while the shops are still open, when the busy sidewalks provide a glimpse of the fancy-pants Marina crowd.

Local Life

Nature walks San Franciscans love the outdoors – joggers and dog walkers flock to the waterfront trails at Crissy Field and to the hills of the Presidio for wooded trails and site-specific art installations.

Bar-hopping The Marina District bars on Fillmore St, from Union St to Chestnut St, are ground zero for party-girl sorority sisters and the varsity jocks who love them. Not all locals approve.

City views For dramatic views of Fisherman's Wharf and the San Francisco skyline – and a break from the crowds – hop on a ferry at Pier 41.

Getting There & Away

Streetcar Historic F Market streetcars run along Market St, then up the Embarcadero to Fisherman's Wharf. On the E line, the same cars follow the Embarcadero to the Wharf along the waterfront.

Cable car The Powell-Hyde and Powell-Mason lines run up Powell St to the Wharf; the Mason line is quicker, but the hills are better on the Hyde line.

Bus Major routes to the Wharf and/or the Marina from downtown include the 19, 30, 47 and 49. The free PresidiGo (p60) shuttle is based at the Presidio Transit Center (p60) and loops the Presidio.

Ferry Ferries (p74) run from Pier 41 and the Ferry Building to Sausalito, Tiburon, Larkspur, Angel Island, Oakland, Alameda and Vallejo. There's an ongoing expansion of the terminal.

Lonely Planet's Top Tip

To escape the crowds, head west of Ghirardelli Sq. First, make your way on foot or by bike to Aquatic Park, then cut west along the waterfront path, through Fort Mason to Marina Green. Aim for the bobbing masts of the yacht club along Marina Blvd, stopping to explore the piers but keeping your eye on the prize: the Golden Gate Bridge.

 ### Best Waterfront Vistas

➡ Golden Gate Bridge (p58)
➡ Warming Hut (p59)
➡ Crissy Field (p59)
➡ Aquatic Park (p63)
➡ Pier 39 (p61)

 ### Best Places to Eat

➡ Gary Danko (p69)
➡ Atelier Crenn (p69)
➡ Kaiyo (p68)
➡ Off the Grid (p67)
➡ Greens (p68)

For reviews, see p66.➡

 ### Best Places to Drink

➡ Interval Bar & Cafe (p70)
➡ Buena Vista Cafe (p70)
➡ Gold Dust Lounge (p70)
➡ Pier 23 (p72)
➡ Atalena Vinoteca (p70)

For reviews, see p69.➡

TOP SIGHT
ALCATRAZ

Alcatraz: for over 150 years, the name has given the innocent chills and the guilty cold sweats. Over the decades it's been a military prison, a forbidding maximum-security penitentiary and disputed territory between Native American activists and the FBI. So it's no surprise that the first step you take onto 'the Rock' seems to cue ominous music: dunh-dunh-dunnnnh!

Early History

It all started innocently enough back in 1775, when Spanish lieutenant Juan Manuel de Ayala sailed the *San Carlos* past the 22-acre island that he called Isla de los Alcatraces (Isle of the Pelicans). In 1859 a new post on Alcatraz became the first US West Coast fort and it soon proved handy as a holding pen for Civil War deserters, insubordinates and the court-martialed. Among the prisoners were Native American scouts and 'unfriendlies,' including 19 Hopis who refused to send their children to government boarding schools, where speaking Hopi and practicing their religion were punishable by beatings. By 1902 the four cell blocks of wooden cages were rotting, unsanitary and ill-equipped for the influx of US soldiers convicted of war crimes in the Philippines. The army began building a new concrete military prison in 1909, but upkeep was expensive and the US soon had other things to worry about: WWI, financial ruin and flappers.

Prison Life

In 1922, when the 18th Amendment to the Constitution declared selling liquor a crime, rebellious Jazz Ag-

DON'T MISS

➡ Introductory films and self-guided audio tour

➡ D-Block solitary-confinement cells

➡ Any site-specific temporary art installations

➡ Waterfront vistas along the (seasonal) Agave Trail

PRACTICALITIES

➡ Map p214, H4

➡ Alcatraz Cruises 415-981-7625

➡ www.alcatrazcruises.com

➡ tours adult/child 5-11 day $38.35/23.50, night $45.50/27.05

➡ call center 8am-7pm, ferries depart Pier 33 half-hourly 8:45am-3:50pm, night tours 5:55pm & 6:30pm

ers weren't prepared to give up their tipple – and gangsters kept the booze coming. Authorities were determined to make a public example of criminal ringleaders and in 1934 the Federal Bureau of Prisons took over Alcatraz as a prominent showcase for its crime-fighting efforts. The Rock averaged only 264 inmates, but its roster read like a list of America's Most Wanted. A-list criminals doing time on Alcatraz included Chicago crime boss Al 'Scarface' Capone, dapper kidnapper George 'Machine Gun' Kelly, hot-headed Harlem mafioso and sometime poet 'Bumpy' Johnson, and Morton Sobell, the military contractor found guilty of Soviet espionage along with Julius and Ethel Rosenberg.

Today, first-person accounts of daily life in the Alcatraz lockup are included on the excellent self-guided audio tour. But take your headphones off for just a moment and you'll notice the sound of carefree city life traveling from across the water: this is the torment that made perilous escapes into riptides worth the risk. Although Alcatraz was considered escape-proof, in 1962 the Anglin brothers and Frank Morris stuffed their beds with dummies, floated away on a makeshift raft and were never seen again. Security and upkeep proved prohibitively expensive and finally the island prison was abandoned to the birds in 1963.

Native American Occupation

Native Americans claimed sovereignty over the island in the '60s, noting that Alcatraz had long been used by the Ohlone people as a spiritual retreat. But federal authorities refused their proposal to turn Alcatraz into a Native American study center. Then, on the eve of Thanksgiving 1969, 79 Native American activists boated to the island and took it over. During the next 19 months, several thousand Native Americans would visit the occupied island. Public support eventually pressured President Richard Nixon in 1970 to restore Native territory and strengthen self-rule for Native nations. Each Thanksgiving Day since 1975, an 'Un-Thanksgiving' ceremony has been held at dawn on Alcatraz, with Native leaders and supporters showing their determination to reverse the course of colonial history. After the government regained control of the island, it became a national park and by 1973 it had already become a major tourist draw. Today the cell blocks' 'free Indian land' water-tower graffiti and rare wildlife are all part of the attraction.

WALKING

Visiting Alcatraz means walking – a lot. The ferry drops you off at the bottom of a 130ft-high hill, which you'll have to ascend to reach the cell block. The quarter-mile path is paved, but if you're not fully fit you'll be panting by the top. For people with mobility impairment, there's a twice-hourly tram from dock to cell house. Wear sturdy shoes, as you may want to explore some of the unpaved bird-watching trails.

Most people spend three to four hours; bring lunch to linger longer. Note: eating is allowed only at the ferry dock. There's limited food on the island, only bottled water, coffee and nuts.

GETTING THERE

A ferry with **Alcatraz Cruises** (Map p290; ☏415-981-7625; www.alcatrazcruises.com; Pier 33; tours day adult/child/family $38.35/23.50/115.70, night adult/child $45.50/27.05; Ⓜ E, F) is the only way to reach the island. You must reserve a specific departure time – book at least a week ahead for the best choice.

Alcatraz

A HALF-DAY TOUR

Book a ferry from Pier 33 and ride 1.5 miles across the bay to explore America's most notorious former prison. The trip itself is worth the money, providing stunning views of the city skyline. Once you've landed at the ❶ **Ferry Dock & Pier**, you begin the 580yd walk to the top of the island and prison; if you need assistance to reach the top, there's a twice-hourly tram.

As you climb toward the ❷ **Guardhouse**, notice the island's steep slope; before it was a prison, Alcatraz was a fort. In the 1850s, the military quarried the rocky shores into near-vertical cliffs. Ships could then only dock at a single port, separated from the main buildings by a sally port (a drawbridge and moat in what became the guardhouse). Inside, peer through floor grates to see Alcatraz's original prison.

Volunteers tend the brilliant ❸ **Officers' Row Gardens**, an orderly counterpoint to the overgrown rose bushes surrounding the burned-out shell of the ❹ **Warden's House**. At the top of the hill, by the front door of the ❺ **Main Cellhouse**, beautiful shots unfurl all around, including a view of the ❻ **Golden Gate Bridge**. Above the main door of the administration building, notice the ❼ **historic signs & graffiti**, before you step inside the dank, cold prison to find the ❽ **Frank Morris cell**, former home to Alcatraz's most notorious jail-breaker.

TOP TIPS

➡ Book at least one month prior for self-guided daytime visits, longer for ranger-led night tours. For info on garden tours, see www.alcatraz gardens.org.

➡ Be prepared to hike; a steep path ascends from the ferry landing to the cell block. Most people spend two to three hours on the island. You need only reserve for the outbound ferry; take any ferry back.

➡ There's no food (just water) but you can bring your own; picnicking is allowed at the ferry dock only. Dress in layers as weather changes fast and it's usually windy.

ADRIEN.G/SHUTTERSTOCK ©

Historic Signs & Graffiti
During their 1969–71 occupation, Native Americans graffitied the water tower: 'Home of the Free Indian Land.' Above the cellhouse door, examine the eagle-and-flag crest to see how the red-and-white stripes were changed to spell 'Free.'

DOPTIS/SHUTTERSTOCK ©

Warden's House
Fires destroyed the warden's house and other structures during the Indian Occupation. The government blamed the Native Americans; the Native Americans blamed agents provocateurs acting on behalf of the Nixon administration to undermine public sympathy.

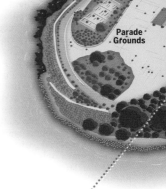

Parade Grounds

Officers' Row Gardens
In the 19th century soldiers imported topsoil to beautify the island with gardens. Well-trusted prisoners later gardened – Elliott Michener said it kept him sane. Historians, ornithologists and archaeologists choose today's plants.

Main Cellhouse
During the mid-20th century, the maximum-security prison housed the day's most notorious troublemakers, including Al Capone and Robert Stroud, the 'Birdman of Alcatraz' (who actually conducted his ornithology studies at Leavenworth).

View of the Golden Gate Bridge
The Golden Gate Bridge stretches wide on the horizon. Best views are from atop the island at Eagle Plaza, near the cellhouse entrance, and at water level along the Agave Trail (September to January only).

Power House

Recreation Yard

Water Tower

Officers' Club

6

5

8

Lighthouse

7

3

2

4

Guard Tower

Guardhouse
Alcatraz's oldest building dates to 1857 and retains remnants of the original drawbridge and moat. During the Civil War the basement was transformed into a military dungeon – the genesis of Alcatraz as a prison.

Frank Morris Cell
Peer into cell 138 on B-Block to see a recreation of the dummy's head that Frank Morris left in his bed as a decoy to aid his notorious – and successful – 1962 escape from Alcatraz.

1

Ferry Dock & Pier
A giant wall map helps you get your bearings. Inside nearby Building 64, short films and exhibits provide historical perspective on the prison and details about the Native American Occupation.

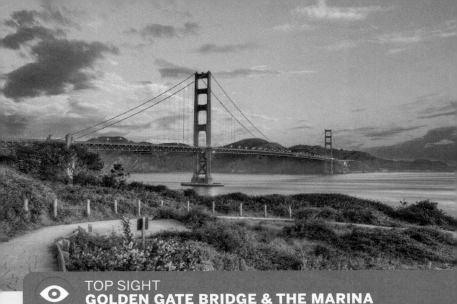

MICHAEL LAWENKO DELA PAZ / GETTY IMAGES ©

TOP SIGHT

GOLDEN GATE BRIDGE & THE MARINA

The city's most spectacular icon towers 80 stories above the roiling waters of the Golden Gate, the narrow entrance to San Francisco Bay. It's hard to believe that SF's northern gateway lands not into a tangle of city streets but into the Presidio, an army base turned national park where forested paths and grassy promenades look largely as they have since the 19th century.

SF's Iconic Bridge

San Francisco's famous suspension bridge, painted a signature shade called International Orange, was almost nixed by the Navy in favor of concrete pylons and yellow stripes. Joseph B Strauss rightly receives praise as the engineering mastermind behind this iconic marvel, but without the aesthetic intervention of architects Gertrude and Irving Murrow and incredibly quick work by daredevil laborers, this 1937 landmark might have been just another traffic bottleneck.

How It Came to Be

Nobody thought it could happen. Not until the early 1920s did the City of San Francisco seriously investigate building a bridge over the treacherous, windblown strait. The War Department owned the land on both sides and didn't want to take chances with ships: safety and solidity were its goals. But the green light was given to the counter-proposal by Strauss and the Murrows for a subtler suspension span, economic in form, that harmonized with the natural environment. Before the War Department could insist on an eyesore, laborers dove into the treacherous riptides of the bay and got the bridge

DON'T MISS

- ➡ Fort Point
- ➡ Cross-section of suspension cable, behind Bridge Pavilion visitors center
- ➡ Bridge towers emerging as fog clears
- ➡ Municipal pier behind Warming Hut

PRACTICALITIES

- ➡ Map p214, F5
- ➡ ☏toll information 877-229-8655
- ➡ www.goldengate bridge.org/visitors
- ➡ Hwy 101
- ➡ northbound free, southbound $7-8
- ➡ 🚌28, all Golden Gate Transit buses

under way in 1933. Just four years later workers balancing atop swaying cables completed what was then the world's longest suspension bridge – nearly 2 miles long, with 746ft suspension towers, higher than any construction west of New York.

Crossing the Bridge

For on-site information, stop into the **Bridge Pavilion Visitor Center** (Map p291; 415-426-5220; www.ggnpc.org; Golden Gate Bridge toll plaza; 9am-6pm).

Pedestrians take the eastern sidewalk. Dress warmly! From the parking area and bus stop (off Lincoln Blvd), a pathway leads past the toll plaza, then it's 1.7 miles across. If 3.4 miles round-trip seems too much, take a bus to the north side via Golden Gate Transit, then walk back (for exact instructions, see www.goldengatebridge.org/visitors). Note: pedestrian access is open 5am to 9pm summer, to 6:30pm winter.

By bicycle, from the toll-plaza parking area ride toward the Roundhouse, then follow signs to the western sidewalk, reserved for bikes only. (Caution: locals pedal fast; avoid collisions.) Bicycles can cross 24 hours but travel the eastern sidewalk certain hours; see www.goldengatebridge.org.

From the toll plaza, it's 4.5 miles to Sausalito; ferry back to SF via Golden Gate Ferry (p74; to downtown) or Blue & Gold Fleet (p74; to Fisherman's Wharf). Bikes are allowed on ferries.

Muni bus 28 runs west from Fort Mason (corner Marina Blvd and Laguna St) to the bridge parking lot, then cuts south down 19th Ave, intersecting with the N-Judah metro line at Judah St. Marin County–bound Golden Gate Transit buses (10, 70/71 and 101; $4.25 one way) are the fastest, most comfortable way from downtown; alert the driver and disembark at the toll plaza *just before* the bridge. On Sunday only, Muni bus 76 travels from downtown, crosses the bridge and loops through the spectacular Marin Headlands.

Parking at the toll plaza is extremely limited. Find additional parking west along Lincoln Blvd.

Crissy Field

War is for the birds at **Crissy Field** (Map p291; 415-561-4700; www.nps.gov; 1199 East Beach; 30, PresidiGo Shuttle), a military airstrip turned waterfront nature preserve with knockout Golden Gate views. Where military aircraft once zoomed in for landings, bird-watchers now huddle in the silent rushes of a reclaimed tidal marsh. Joggers pound beachside trails and the only security alerts are raised by puppies suspiciously sniffing surfers. On foggy days, stop by the certified-green **Warming Hut** (Map

WALKING TOURS

City Guides (415-557-4266; www.sfcityguides.org) FREE offers free tours of the bridge, departing Sunday and Thursday at 11am, from the statue of Joseph Strauss by the visitor center on the bridge's SF side; plan to tip $5 per person.

On the foggiest days, up to one million gallons of water, in the form of fog, blow through the Golden Gate hourly.

TOP TIPS

➔ Hitchcock had it right: seen from below at Fort Point, the bridge induces a thrilling case of *Vertigo*.

➔ For wider vistas, explore the headlands just southwest of the toll plaza, atop high bluffs dotted with wildflowers.

➔ Fog aficionados prefer the lookout at Vista Point, in Marin, on the bridge's sunnier northern side, to watch gusting clouds rush through the bridge cables. Better still, find your way up the Marin Headlands to look down upon the span.

➔ Crissy Field reveals the span's entirety, with windsurfers and kite-fliers adding action to snapshots.

p291; ☑415-561-3042; www.parksconservancy.org/visit/eat/warming-hut.html; 983 Marine Dr; items $4-9; ⊙9am-5pm; P 🚻; ☐PresidiGo shuttle) 🛍 to browse regional-nature books and warm up with fair-trade coffee. Offshore, the area is very popular with windsurfers and kitesurfers.

Fort Point

A triple-decker, brick-walled US military fortress, **Fort Point** (Map p291; ☑415-504-2334; www.nps.gov/fopo; Marine Dr; ⊙10am-5pm Fri-Sun; P; ☐28) FREE was completed in 1861, with 126 cannons, just in time to protect the bay against certain invasion during the Civil War...or not, as it turned out. Without a single shot having been fired, Fort Point was abandoned in 1900. When the bridge was built overhead, engineers added an extra span to preserve it. Alfred Hitchcock saw deadly potential in Fort Point, and shot the trademark scene from *Vertigo* of Kim Novak leaping from the lookout to certain death into the bay...or not, as it turned out. Fort Point has since given up all pretense of deadliness and now showcases Civil War displays and knockout panoramic viewing decks.

On Saturdays once monthly from March through October, staff demonstrate crabbing from the pier, available by lottery only (see website); November to February, inquire about spooky Saturday-night candlelight tours (reservations required).

Baker Beach

Picnic amid wind-sculpted pines, fish from craggy rocks or frolic nude at mile-long **Baker Beach** (Map p291; ☑10am-5pm 415-561-4323; www.nps.gov/prsf; ⊙sunrise-sunset; P; ☐29, PresidiGo Shuttle), with spectacular views of the bridge. Crowds come weekends, especially on fog-free days, so arrive early. For nude sunbathing (mostly straight girls and gay boys), head to the northern end. Families in clothing stick to the southern end, nearer the parking lot. Mind the currents and the c-c-cold water.

Presidio Base

What began in 1776 as a Spanish fort, built by conscripted Ohlone people, is now a treasure trove of surprises, set in an urban national park, the Presidio of San Francisco (p65).

Begin at the Main Post parade grounds to gather maps and shuttle schedules at the visitor center (p65), then explore the free Officers' Club (p66) to learn the Presidio's checkered history, and warm up on fireside sofas, cozy on foggy days. Mickey Mouse fans head to the Walt Disney Family Museum (p65); fans of the macabre hike to the **Pet Cemetery**, off Crissy Field Ave, where handmade tombstones mark the final resting places of hamsters and kitties. East of the parade grounds, toward the Palace of Fine Arts, lies the **Letterman Campus**, home to nonprofits and *Star Wars* creator George Lucas' Lucas Arts (now owned by Disney) – offices are closed to visitors, but you can pay your respects to the Yoda statue outside. Sunday afternoons April to October, Off the Grid (p67) sets up food trucks on the parade grounds.

There's excellent hiking, too. To find exciting site-specific sculptures by environmental artist Andy Goldsworthy, **Presidio Trust** (Map p291; ☑415-561-5300; www.presidio.gov; Montgomery St, Bldg 103; ⊙8am-5pm Mon-Fri; ☐PresidiGo Shuttle) publishes good maps to scenic overlooks; they're available free at the visitor center.

Free **PresidiGo** (☑415-561-2739; www.presidio.gov/shuttle) buses loop the park, via two routes, from the **Presidio Transit Center** (Map p291; www.presidio.gov/places/presidio-transit-center; 215 Lincoln Blvd). Service runs every 30 minutes from 5:45am to 8pm weekdays, and 9am to 6:30pm weekends. There's service to downtown, free to the public on weekends and during certain weekday hours. Download maps, pass information and schedules from the PresidiGo website.

◉ TOP SIGHT
FISHERMAN'S WHARF

You won't find many fishermen at Fisherman's Wharf – though some still moor here, they're difficult to spot beyond the blinking neon and side-by-side souvenir shops. The Wharf may not be the 'real San Francisco,' but it's lively and holds a few surprises. Stick near the waterfront, where sea lions bray, street performers alarm unsuspecting passersby, and an aquarium and carousel entice kids.

Pier 39

The focal point of Fisherman's Wharf isn't the waning fishing fleet but the carousel, carnival-like attractions, shops and restaurants of **Pier 39** (pictured; Map p289; ☎415-705-5500; www.pier39.com; cnr Beach St & the Embarcadero; P 🚻; 🚌47, 🚋Powell-Mason, Ⓜ E, F). Developed in the 1970s to revitalize tourism, the pier draws thousands of tourists daily, but it's really just a big outdoor shopping mall. On the plus side, its visitor center rents strollers, stores luggage and has free phone-charging stations.

By far the best reason to walk the pier is to spot the famous **sea lions** (Map p289; ☎415-623-4734), who took over this coveted waterfront real estate in 1989. These unkempt squatters have been making a public display ever since and now they're San Francisco's favorite mascots. The valuable boat slips accommodate as many as 1000 sea lions that 'haul out' onto the docks between January and July. Follow signs along the pier's western edge – you can't miss 'em.

San Francisco Carousel

A chariot awaits to whisk you and the kids past the Golden Gate Bridge, Alcatraz and other SF landmarks hand-painted onto this Italian **carousel** (Map p289; 1 ride $5, 3 rides $10;

DON'T MISS

→ Sea lions at Pier 39
→ Musée Mécanique
→ San Francisco Maritime National Historical Park
→ Aquatic Park

PRACTICALITIES

→ Map p289, C2
→ www.fishermans wharf.org
→ admission free
→ 🚻
→ 🚌19, 30, 47, 49, 🚋Powell-Mason, Powell-Hyde, Ⓜ F

WATERFRONT RESTAURANTS

It's hard to resist waterfront restaurants and their breathtaking views, but you really should, unless you go only for drinks and appetizers. Wharf restaurants are generally way overpriced and the food can't compare to what's available in nearby neighborhoods. Go simple – maybe a cup of chowder or some crab Louis from the fish stands at the foot of Taylor St.

A few third- and fourth-generation fishermen remain in the bay, but to withstand the drop in salmon and other local stocks some now use their boats for tours, surviving off the city's new lifeblood: tourism. Find the remaining fleet around Pier 47.

◷10am-9pm Sun-Thu, to 10pm Fri & Sat; ⊞), twinkling with 1800 lights, at the bayside end of Pier 39.

Aquarium of the Bay

Sharks circle overhead, manta rays sweep by and seaweed sways all around at the **Aquarium of the Bay** (Map p289; ☑415-623-5300; www.aquariumofthe bay.org; adult/child/family $27.95/17.95/75; ◷10am-8pm late May-early Sep, shorter hrs rest of yr; ⊞), where you wander through glass tubes surrounded by sea life from San Francisco Bay. Not for the claustrophobic, perhaps, but the thrilling fish-eye view leaves kids and parents amazed. Kids love the critters and touch pools upstairs, and the new virtual reality theater.

Musée Mécanique

A flashback to penny arcades, the **Musée Mécanique** (Map p289; ☑415-346-2000; www.museemecan ique.com; Pier 45, Shed A; ◷10am-8pm; ⊞; ⊟47, ⊠Powell-Mason, Powell-Hyde, ⊠E, F) houses a mind-blowing collection of vintage mechanical amusements. Sinister, freckle-faced Laughing Sal has freaked out kids for over a century, but don't let this manic mannequin deter you from the best arcade west of Coney Island. A quarter lets you start brawls in Wild West saloons, peep at belly dancers through a vintage Mutoscope and even learn a cautionary tale about smoking opium.

San Francisco Maritime National Historical Park

Five historic ships are floating museums at this **maritime national park** (Map p289; ☑415-447-5000; www.nps.gov/safr; 499 Jefferson St, Hyde St Pier; 7-day ticket adult/child under 16 $15/free; ◷9:30am-5pm Oct-May, to 5:30pm Jun-Sep; ⊞; ⊟19, 30, 47, ⊠Powell-Hyde, ⊠F), Fisherman's Wharf's most authentic attraction. Moored along Hyde St Pier, the three most interesting are the 1891 schooner *Alma*, which hosts guided sailing trips in summer; 1890 steamboat *Eureka*; and iron-hulled *Balclutha*, which brought coal to San Francisco. It's free to walk the pier; pay only to board ships.

National Park Visitors Center

San Francisco grew from its docks. This 10,000-sq-ft **visitor center** (Map p289; ☑415-447-5000; www.nps.gov/safr; 499 Jefferson St; ◷9:30am-5pm Oct-May, to 5:30pm Jun-Sep; ⊞; ⊟19, 30, 47, ⊠Powell-Hyde, ⊠E, F) FREE for the nearby maritime national historical park details how it happened, in a permanent exhibit that re-creates the 19th-century waterfront. Also on display is a rich collection of maritime artifacts, from a giant 1850s first-order lighthouse lens to scale models of 19th-century schooners. Kids love running around the vast space. Rangers provide maps and information about the surrounding area's trails and walks, as well as all national parks and monuments of the American West.

USS Pampanito

The **USS Pampanito** (Map p289; ☑415-775-1943; www.maritime.org/pamphome.htm; Pier 45; adult/child/family $20/10/45; ◷9am-8pm, can vary seasonally; 🖘; 🚌19, 30, 47, 🚋Powell-Hyde, ⓜE, F), a WWII-era US Navy submarine, completed six wartime patrols, sank six Japanese ships, battled three others and lived to tell the tale. Submariners' stories of tense moments in underwater stealth mode will have you holding your breath, and all those cool brass knobs and mysterious hydraulic valves will make 21st-century technology seem overrated.

SS Jeremiah O'Brien

It's hard to believe that the historic 10,000-ton **SS Jeremiah O'Brien** (Map p289; ☑415-554-0100; www.ssjeremiahobrien.org; Pier 45; adult/child/family $20/10/45; ◷10am-4pm; 🖘; 🚌19, 30, 47, 🚋Powell-Hyde, ⓜE, F) was turned out by San Francisco's shipbuilders in under eight weeks. Harder still to imagine how she dodged U-boats on a mission delivering supplies to Allied forces on D-Day. Of the 2710 Liberty ships launched during WWII, only this one is still fully operational. Check the website for upcoming four-hour cruises.

Aquatic Park

Fisherman's Wharf's eccentricity is mostly staged, but at **Aquatic Park** (Map p289; ☑415-561-7000; www.nps.gov/safr; 🖘; 🚌19, 30, 47, 🚋Powell-Hyde) FREE it's the real deal: extreme swimmers dive into the bone-chilling waters of the bay in winter, while oblivious old men cast fishing lines and listen to AM-radio sports. Aside from being the city's principal swimming beach (with bathrooms, but no life-guard), the park is ideal for people-watching and sandcastle building. For perspective on the Wharf, wander out along the enormous Municipal Pier at the foot of Van Ness Ave.

Maritime Museum

The **Maritime Museum** (Aquatic Park Bathhouse; Map p289; www.maritime.org; 900 Beach St; ◷10am-4pm; 🖘; 🚌19, 30, 47, 🚋Powell-Hyde) FREE was built as a casino and public bathhouse in 1939 by the Depression-era Works Progress Administration (WPA). Beautifully restored murals depict the mythical lands of Atlantis and Mu and the handful of exhibits include maritime ephemera and dioramas. Note the entryway slate carvings by celebrated African American artist Sargent Johnson and the back veranda's sculptures by Beniamino Bufano.

Ghirardelli Square

Willy Wonka would tip his hat to Domingo Ghirardelli, whose business became the West's largest chocolate factory in 1893. After the company moved to the East Bay, developers reinvented the factory as a mall and ice-cream parlor in 1964. Today, **Ghirardelli Square** (Map p289; ☑415-775-5500; www.ghirardellisq.com; 900 North Point St; ◷10am-9pm; 🚋Powell-Hyde) has entered its third incarnation as a boutique time-share/spa complex with wine-tasting rooms. The square looks quite spiffy, with local boutiques and, of course, **Ghirardelli Ice Cream** (Map p289; ☑415-474-3938; www.ghirardelli.com; 900 North Point St, Ghirardelli Sq; ice creams $11-16; ◷8:30am-11pm Sun-Thu, to midnight Fri & Sat; 🖘; 🚌19, 30, 47, 🚋Powell-Hyde).

◉ TOP SIGHT
EXPLORATORIUM

Is there a science to skateboarding? Do toilets really flush counterclockwise in Australia? Combining science with art, San Francisco's dazzling hands-on Exploratorium nudges you to question how you know what you know. As thrilling as the exhibits is the setting: a 9-acre, glass-walled pier jutting over San Francisco Bay, with vast outdoor portions you can explore for free.

Covering 330,000 sq ft of indoor-outdoor space, the 600-plus exhibits have buttons to push, cranks to ratchet and dials to adjust, all made by artists and scientists at the in-house building shop. Try a punk hairdo, courtesy of the static-electricity station. Turn your body into the gnomon of a sundial. Slide, climb and feel your way – in total darkness – through the labyrinth of the **Tactile Dome** (Map p290; ☑415-528-4444; www.exploratorium.edu; Pier 15; admission day/after dark $15/10; ⊙10am-5pm Tue-Sun, extended hrs Fri & Sat summer, over 18yr only 6-10pm Thu; ⊞; Ⓜ E, F).

In 2013 the Exploratorium moved to its purpose-built solar-powered space, constructed in concert with scientific agencies, including the National Oceanic and Atmospheric Administration (NOAA), which hardwired the pier with sensors delivering real-time data on weather, wind, tides and the bay.

Frank Oppenheimer founded the Exploratorium in 1969. He'd been a physicist on the atom bomb, was blackballed during the McCarthy era, then reemerged as a high-school teacher, eschewing secret scientific study in favor of public education. The Exploratorium is his lasting legacy.

DON'T MISS

➡ Tactile Dome (reservations required)
➡ 'Visualizing the Bay' exhibit
➡ Tinkering Studio
➡ Plankton exhibit
➡ Everyone Is You and Me (mirror)

PRACTICALITIES

➡ Map p290, A5
➡ ☑415-528-4444
➡ www.exploratorium.edu
➡ Pier 15/17
➡ adult/child $29.95/19.95, 6-10pm Thu $19.95
➡ ⊙10am-5pm Tue-Sun, over 18yr only 6-10pm Thu
➡ Ⓟ ⊞
➡ Ⓜ E, F

◉ SIGHTS

Sights along Fisherman's Wharf are geared entirely to tourists, particularly to families, and it's easy to get stuck with so much vying for your attention. Stick to the waterside and keep moving. Once you're west of Van Ness Ave, locals supplant tourists and you get a better sense of how people actually live along the waterfront. Though everything looks close together on the map, on the ground you'll do a lot of walking.

◉ The Marina & Cow Hollow

FORT MASON CENTER AREA

Map p292 (☑415-345-7500; www.fortmason.org; cnr Marina Blvd & Laguna St; ℙ; ☐22, 28, 30, 43, 47, 49) San Francisco takes subversive glee in turning military installations into venues for nature, fine dining and out-there experimental art. Evidence: Fort Mason, once a shipyard and embarkation point for WWII troops, now a vast cultural center and gathering place for events, drinking and eating. Wander the waterfront, keeping your eyes peeled for fascinating outdoor art-and-science installations designed by the Exploratorium.

The mess halls are replaced by vegan-friendly Greens, a Zen-community-run restaurant, and also the Long Now Foundation, whose compelling exhibits reconsider extinction and the future of time. Warehouses contain cutting-edge theater at the Magic (p70) and improvised comedy workshops at BATS Improv (p72). The Herbst Pavilion counts major arts events and fashion shows among its arsenal – see the website for upcoming events. Hidden art exhibits include the 'Tasting the Tides' water fountain, which lets you taste, with the touch of a button, the varying salinity of the bay – it's next to the firehouse, with glorious water views.

CARTOON ART MUSEUM MUSEUM

Map p289 (☑415-227-8666; http://cartoonart. org; 781 Beach St; adult/child $10/4; ⊙11am-5pm Thu-Tue; ☐19, 30, 47, ⓖPowell-Hyde) Founded on a grant from Bay Area cartoon legend Charles M Schultz of *Peanuts* fame, this bold museum isn't afraid of the dark, political or racy – cases in point: R Crumb drawings from the '70s and a retrospective of political cartoons from the *Economist* by Kevin 'Kal' Kallaugher. Lectures and openings are rare opportunities to mingle with comic legends, Pixar Studios heads and obsessive collectors.

WAVE ORGAN PUBLIC ART

Map p292 (www.exploratorium.edu/visit/wave-organ; Marina Small Craft Harbor jetty; ⊙daylight hrs; ♿; ☐22, 30) **FREE** A project of the Exploratorium, the Wave Organ is a sound sculpture of PVC tubes and concrete pipes capped with found marble from San Francisco's old cemetery, built into the tip of the yacht-harbor jetty. Depending on the waves, winds and tide, the installation emits sound like nervous humming from a dinnertime line cook or spooky heavy breathing over the phone in a slasher film.

◉ Fisherman's Wharf & the Piers

FISHERMAN'S WHARF PIER
See p61.

EXPLORATORIUM MUSEUM
See p64.

◉ Presidio

GOLDEN GATE BRIDGE BRIDGE
See p58.

ALCATRAZ HISTORIC SITE
See p54.

PRESIDIO OF SAN FRANCISCO PARK

Map p291 (☑415-561-4323; www.nps.gov/prsf; ⊙dawn-dusk; ℙ; ☐28, 43) Explore that splotch of green on the map between Baker Beach and Crissy Field and you'll find parade grounds, Yoda, a centuries-old adobe wall and some fascinating art projects. What started as a Spanish fort built by Ohlone conscripts in 1776 is now a treasure hunt of surprises. Begin your adventures at the Main Post to get trail maps at the **visitor center** (Map p291; ☑415-561-4323; www.presidio.gov; 210 Lincoln Blvd; ⊙10am-5pm; ☐PresidiGo Shuttle) and inquire about site-specific art installations by Andy Goldsworthy.

WALT DISNEY FAMILY MUSEUM MUSEUM

Map p291 (☑415-345-6800; www.waltdisney. org; 104 Montgomery St; adult/student/child $25/20/15; ⊙10am-6pm Wed-Mon, last entry

WORTH A DETOUR

SCENIC STAIRWAYS

Appreciating San Francisco's brilliant vistas means hiking up some serious hills. Sure, you could ride a cable car, but you'd miss all those hidden staircases, backyard gardens and cascades of fragrant flowers. Better wear your walking shoes.

Here's a short list of staircases worth the climb. Add some to your itinerary, and you'll be rewarded with knockout views – and strong thighs. Mind your step on damp days, when wet leaves make some routes slippery. Be sure to stop and look around, and you might glimpse San Francisco's wild parrots zipping between hilltops – you'll hear them before you see them.

Filbert Street Steps (p110)

Francisco Street Steps (Map p308; 📵30, 📵Powell-Mason)

Lyon Street Steps (Map p291; Lyon St)

Baker Street Steps (Map p292; Baker St; 📵3)

Vallejo Street Steps (p128)

16th Avenue Tiled Steps (Map p318; www.16thavenuetiledsteps.com; 1700 16th Ave, cnr Moraga St; ☉sunrise-sunset; 📵66)

5pm; 🅿 🚻; 📵43, PresidiGo shuttle) An 1890s military barracks in the Presidio houses 10 galleries that chronologically tell the exhaustively long story of Walt Disney's life. Opened in 2009, the museum gets high marks for design, integrating 20,000 sq ft of contemporary glass-and-steel exhibition space with the original 19th-century brick building, but it's definitely geared toward grown-ups and will bore kids after an hour (too much reading).

PRESIDIO OFFICERS' CLUB   HISTORIC BUILDING
Map p291 (📞415-561-4400; www.presidio.gov/officers-club; 50 Moraga Ave; ☉10am-5pm Tue-Sun; 📵PresidiGo shuttle) FREE The Presidio's oldest building dates to the late 1700s, and was fully renovated in 2014, revealing gorgeous Spanish-Moorish adobe architecture. The free **Heritage Gallery** shows the history of the Presidio, from Native American days to the present, along with temporary exhibitions (in 2019, this was an exploration of the Presidio's role in the unjust incarceration of 120,000 Japanese Americans during WWII).

PALACE OF FINE ARTS   MONUMENT
Map p291 (📞510-599-4651; www.lovethepalace.org; Palace Dr; ☉24hr; 📵28, 30, 43) FREE Like a fossilized party favor, this romantic, ersatz Greco-Roman ruin is the city's memento from the 1915 Panama-Pacific International Exposition. The original, designed by celebrated Berkeley architect Bernard Maybeck, was of wood, burlap and plaster, then later reinforced. By the 1960s it was crumbling. The structure was recast in concrete so that future generations could gaze at the rotunda relief to glimpse 'Art under attack by materialists, with idealists leaping to her rescue.' A glorious spot to wander day or night.

SWEDENBORGIAN CHURCH   CHURCH
Map p291 (📞415-346-6466; www.sfswedenborgian.org; 2107 Lyon St; ☉10am-6pm Mon-Fri, services 11am-noon Sun; 📵3, 43) Radical ideals in the form of distinctive buildings make beloved SF landmarks; this standout 1894 example is the collaborative effort of 19th-century Bay Area progressive thinkers, such as naturalist John Muir, California Arts and Crafts leader Bernard Maybeck and architect Arthur Page Brown. Inside, nature is everywhere – in hewn-maple chairs, in mighty madrone trees supporting the roof and in scenes of northern California that took muralist William Keith 40 years to complete.

🍴 EATING

Mid-November to June, the specialty is Dungeness crab. If you're a foodie, explore the Wharf before lunch, west to east (if you're arriving by cable car, ride the Powell-Hyde line), then go to the Ferry Building to sample some sweet crab, on foot (1-mile/20-minute walk) or via the F-Market streetcar, which goes directly there. In the Marina, good restaurants line Chestnut St, from Fillmore to Divisadero Sts, and Union St, between Fillmore St and Van Ness Ave. There's also good-priced ethnic fare on Lombard St, if you're willing to hunt. Greens (p68) gives reason to trek to Fort Mason.

★ GIO GELATI GELATO

Map p292 (☑415-867-1306; https://giogelati. com; 1998 Union St; gelato from $4.50; ☺10am-10pm Sun-Thu, to 11pm Fri & Sat; ☐22, 41, 45) Gelato chef Patrizia Pasqualetti was well-known in Italy for her family's gelato shop, and here in SF she's re-creating those tried-and-true flavors, only with local fruit, dairy and nuts. The results are pure creamy deliciousness, and favorites among the 30 flavors include sour cherry crunch and the Portuguese milk with caramelized figs.

VEGAN PICNIC VEGAN $

Map p292 (☑415-323-3043; www.veganpicnic. com; 1977a Union St; mains $7-14; ☺8am-6:30pm Mon-Fri, from 9am Sat & Sun; ☑; ☐22, 41, 45) If all vegan meatballs, faux crispy chicken sandwiches and imitation salami subs tasted this good, every cow, chicken and pig could run free. Okay maybe not, but this places really nails its meat flavors. Staff members couldn't be nicer and you'll especially think so when they present you with free, lip-smackin' samples.

LUCCA DELICATESSEN DELI $

Map p292 (☑415-921-7873; www.luccadeli.com; 2120 Chestnut St; sandwiches $8-15; ☺9am-6:30pm Mon-Fri, to 6pm Sat & Sun; ☐28, 30, 43) Open since 1929, this classic Italian deli is an ideal spot to assemble picnics for Marina Green. Besides perfect prosciutto and salami, nutty cheeses and fruity Chiantis, expect made-to-order sandwiches on fresh-baked Acme bread, including yummy meatball subs. There's hot homemade soup from 11am to 3pm.

OFF THE GRID FOOD TRUCK $

Map p292 (☑415-339-5888; www.offthegridsf. com; 2 Marina Blvd, Fort Mason Center; items $6-15; ☺5-10pm Fri Mar-Oct; ☑; ☐22, 28) Spring through fall, some 30 food trucks and pop-up cubes circle their wagons at SF's largest mobile-gourmet hootenannies on Friday night at Fort Mason Center, and 11am to 4pm Sunday for **Picnic at the Presidio** on the Main Post lawn. Arrive early for the best selection and to minimize waits.

ITALIAN HOMEMADE ITALIAN $

Map p292 (☑415-655-9325; www.italianhome madecompany.com; 1919 Union St; mains $13-16; ☺11am-10pm Sun-Wed, to 11pm Thu-Sat; ☑; ☐22, 41, 45) You'd be hard-pressed to find pasta fresher than this – cooks roll out sheets of dough right in the window. The formula is simple: pick your pasta, add a sauce. The Bolognese is most popular and, because the proprietor is from Bologna, you can bet on its quality. Kids love seeing how their dinner is made, and fusilli and penne are available gluten free.

ROOSTER & RICE THAI $

Map p292 (☑415-776-3647; www.roosterandrice. com; 2211 Filbert St; mains $11-14; ☺11:30am-8pm Mon-Sat; ☐22, 41, 45) ☑ This quick-eats hole-in-the-wall place makes one dish (with a vegetarian variation) – *khao mun gai* (Thai-style chicken and rice), made with organic poached chicken, white or brown rice, and flavor-packed chili sauce on the side. Add $2 for veggies. The only drawback is limited seating; consider getting it to go.

PLUTO'S FRESH FOOD AMERICAN $

Map p292 (☑415-775-8867; www.plutosfresh food.com; 3258 Scott St; mains $7-13; ☺11am-10pm; ☑☑; ☐28, 30, 43) When you're hungry for a wholesome meal but don't want to fuss, Pluto's serves good food fast, with build-your-own salads, burgers, stick-to-your-ribs mac 'n' cheese and carved-to-order roast beef and turkey with all the fixings. Order at the counter, then snag a seat. Kids' meals cost just $5.25.

FISHERMAN'S WHARF CRAB STANDS SEAFOOD $

Map p289 (Taylor St; mains $5-22; ᴍF) Men and women in rolled-up sleeves stir steaming cauldrons of Dungeness crab at several side-by-side takeout crab stands at the foot of Taylor St, the epicenter of Fisherman's Wharf. Crab season typically runs winter through spring, but you'll find shrimp and other seafood year-round.

BLUE BARN GOURMET SANDWICHES $

Map p292 (☑415-896-4866; www.bluebarngour met.com; 3344 Steiner St; salads & sandwiches $12-17; ☺11am-8:30pm Mon-Thu, to 8pm Fri-Sun; ☑☑☑; ☐22, 28, 30, 43) ☑ Toss aside ordinary salads. For $13.95, build a mighty mound of organic produce, topped with six fixings, including artisan cheeses, caramelized onions, heirloom tomatoes, candied

LOCAL KNOWLEDGE

FISHERMAN'S WHARF FOOD TRUCKS

Three side-by-side food trucks near the corner of Jones and Jefferson Sts provide perfect alternatives to the Wharf's overpriced restaurants:

Carmel Pizza (Map p289; 415-676-1185; www.carmelpizzaco.com; 2826 Jones St; pizzas $13-21; 11:30am-8pm Mon-Fri, from noon Sat & Sun; 47, Powell-Mason, F) bakes gooey-delicious single-serving pizza in a wood-fired oven.

Codmother (Map p289; 415-606-9349; www.codmother.com; 496 Beach St; mains $7-13; 11am-5pm Mon & Wed-Fri, to 11:30am-6pm Sat & Sun; 47, Powell-Mason, F) serves note-perfect fish and chips, plus Baja-style fish tacos.

Tanguito (Map p289; 415-577-4223; 2850 Jones St; dishes $4-13; 11:30am-6:30pm Tue-Fri, noon-7:30pm Sat, to 6pm Sun; 47, Powell-Mason, F) makes its own Argentinian-style empanadas with chicken or steak, stellar saffron rice and even paella (if you can wait 45 minutes). Note early closing times and outdoor-only seating.

pecans and pomegranate seeds; add extra for grilled organic meats and seafood. For something hot, try the grilled cheese with *soppressata* salami, *manchego* cheese and Mission-fig jam. On balmy days, sit on the back patio.

IN-N-OUT BURGER   BURGERS $

Map p289 (800-786-1000; www.in-n-out.com; 333 Jefferson St; meals under $10; 10:30am-1am Sun-Thu, to 1:30am Fri & Sat; ; 30, 47, Powell-Hyde) Gourmet burgers have taken SF by storm, but In-N-Out has had a good thing going for more than 60 years: prime chuck beef processed on-site, plus fries and shakes made with ingredients you can pronounce, all served by employees paid a living wage. Consider ordering yours off the menu 'Animal style,' cooked in mustard with grilled onions.

★KAIYO   FUSION $$

Map p292 (415-525-4804; https://kaiyosf.com; 1838 Union St; small plates $12-28, share plates $19-28; 5-10pm Tue, Wed & Sun, to 11pm Thu & Sat, 10:30am-3pm Sat & Sun; 41, 45) For a deliciously deep dive into the cuisine of the Japanese-Peruvian diaspora, head to Cow Hollow's most playful and inventive new restaurant, where the Pisco and whiskey cocktails are named for anime characters and a neon-green moss wall runs the length of the *izakaya*-style dining room. But the real adventure is the food.

★GREENS   VEGETARIAN, CALIFORNIAN $$

Map p292 (415-771-6222; www.greensrestaurant.com; Fort Mason Center, 2 Marina Blvd, Bldg A; mains $18-28; 5:30-9pm Mon, 11:30am-2:30pm & 5:30-9pm Tue-Thu, 11:30am-2:30pm & 5-9pm Fri, 10:30am-2:30pm & 5-9pm Sat & Sun; ; 22, 28, 30, 43, 47, 49) Career carnivores won't realize there's zero meat in the hearty black-bean chili, or in Greens' other flavor-packed vegetarian dishes, made using ingredients from a Zen farm in Marin. And, oh, what views! The Golden Gate rises just outside the window-lined dining room. The on-site cafe serves to-go lunches, but for sit-down meals, including Saturday and Sunday brunch, reservations are recommended.

BALBOA CAFE   GASTROPUB $$

Map p292 (415-921-3944; www.balboacafe.com/san-francisco; 3199 Fillmore St; mains lunch $14-25, dinner $14-33; kitchen 11:30am-10pm Sun-Wed, to 11pm Thu-Sat, bar to 2am; 22, 28, 30, 43) Equal parts bar and grill, Balboa is a mainstay for classic cooking in a pub operational since 1913. The decor retains an old-world look, with massive oak bar, wood-paneled walls and brass trim – a fitting backdrop for well-wrought cocktails and dishes including Caesar salad, steaks and burgers. Local luminaries frequent the bar. Good brunch. Make reservations.

ARGUELLO   MEXICAN $$

Map p291 (415-561-3650; www.arguellosf.com; 50 Moraga Ave; mains $18-25; 11am-4pm Tue, to 9pm Wed-Fri, 11am-3pm & 5-9pm Sat, 11am-4pm Sun; ; 43, PresidiGo shuttle) Located within the Presidio Officers' Club, this lively Mexican restaurant by James Beard Award–winner Traci Des Jardins features cooking techniques and dishes from a different Mexican state each month, including small plates good for sharing and several mains (look for the standout marinated pork shoulder).

BELGA
BELGIAN $$

Map p292 ([📞]415-872-7350; http://belgasf.com; 2000 Union St; mains $12-26; ⏰11am-9:30pm Mon-Fri, 10am-10pm Sat & Sun; 🚌22, 41, 45) Happening and swank, Belga resembles a European brasserie, with side-by-side tables flanking red-leather banquettes – fitting for northern French and Belgian specialties like mussels and fries, wood-fired roasts and sausages, *spaetzle* (boiled dumplings) and cabbage, gratins and *carbonnade* (beef stew in beer), all made with a lighter Californian sensibility. Reservations recommended.

BRAZEN HEAD
PUB FOOD $$

Map p292 ([📞]415-921-7600; http://brazenheadsf. com; 3166 Buchanan St; mains $16-30; ⏰4pm-2am; 🚌22, 28, 30) You have to know where you're going to find the Brazen Head, a tiny pub with low lighting and cozy nooks, and reliably good onion soup and steaks. The kitchen stays open till 1am – rare in early-to-bed SF.

ROSE'S CAFÉ
ITALIAN, CALIFORNIAN $$

Map p292 ([📞]415-775-2200; www.rosescafesf. com; 2298 Union St; mains lunch $10-17, dinner $17-30; ⏰8am-4:30pm Mon-Fri, to 4pm Sat & Sun; [📶]; 🚌22, 41, 45) 🍴 The ideal refueling spot while you're browsing Union St boutiques. Follow your salads and house-made soups with rich organic polenta with gorgonzola and thyme, or a simple grass-fed beef burger, then linger over espresso or tea. Shop if you must, but return to this sunny corner cafe from 4pm to 6pm for half-price wine by the glass and tap beer on weekdays.

⭐ATELIER CRENN
FRENCH $$$

Map p292 ([📞]415-440-0460; www.ateliercrenn. com; 3127 Fillmore St; tasting menu $335; ⏰5-9pm Tue-Sat; 🚌22, 28, 30, 43) The menu arrives in the form of a poem and then come the signature white chocolate spheres filled with a burst of apple cider. If this seems an unlikely start to a meal, just wait for the geoduck rice tart in a glass dome frosted by liquid nitrogen, and about a dozen more plates inspired by the childhood of chef Dominique Crenn in Brittany, France.

GARY DANKO
CALIFORNIAN $$$

Map p289 ([📞]415-749-2060; www.garydanko.com; 800 North Point St; 3-/5-course menu $92/134; ⏰5:30-10pm; 🚌19, 30, 47, 🚋Powell-Hyde) Gary Danko wins James Beard Awards for his impeccable Californian *haute cuisine*. Smoked-glass windows prevent passersby from tripping over their tongues at the exquisite presentations – glazed oysters with Osetra caviar, horseradish-crusted salmon medallions, lavish cheeses and chestnut *crémeux* with spiced honey cake. Reservations a must.

A16
ITALIAN $$$

Map p292 ([📞]415-771-2216; www.a16sf.com; 2355 Chestnut St; pizzas $18-22, mains $18-38; ⏰lunch 11:30am-2:30pm Fri-Sun, dinner 5:30-10pm Mon-Thu, 5:30-11pm Fri & Sat, 5-10pm Sun; 🚌28, 30, 43) Even before A16 won a James Beard Award, it was hard to book, but persevere: the house-made mozzarella *burrata*, blister-crusted pizzas from the wood-burning oven and 15-page Italian wine list make it worth your while. Skip the spotty desserts and instead double up on adventurous appetizers, including house-cured *salumi*.

IZZY'S STEAKS & CHOPS
STEAK $$$

Map p292 ([📞]415-644-5330; www.izzyssteaks. com; 3345 Steiner St; mains $20-35; ⏰5-9:30pm Mon-Fri, from 4pm Sat & Sun; 🚌22, 28, 30, 43) Izzy's casual dining room is a throwback to Barbary Coast saloons, with old-time memorabilia and trophy heads lining the walls. Of all the steak houses in SF, this one's the most relaxed, with no dress code. It has all the usual classics, like rib-eye steak and creamed spinach. Reservations essential.

SCOMA'S
SEAFOOD $$$

Map p289 ([📞]415-771-4383; www.scomas.com; Pier 47; mains $28-40; ⏰11:30am-10pm Fri & Sat, to 9:30pm Sun, noon-9:30pm Mon-Thu; [🅿]; 🚋Powell-Hyde, Ⓜ️F) Enjoy a flashback to the 1960s, with waiters in white dinner jackets, pine-paneled walls decorated with signed photographs of forgotten celebrities, and plate-glass windows overlooking the docks – Scoma's is the Wharf's long-standing staple for seafood. Little changes, except the prices. Expect classics like *cioppino* (seafood stew) and crab thermidor – never groundbreaking, always good – that taste better when someone else buys.

🍷 DRINKING & NIGHTLIFE

Fisherman's Wharf bars cater almost entirely to tourists but can be good fun, if pricey. If you're at a Wharf hotel but prefer a local nightlife scene, head

a mile up Polk St from the waterfront. Clustered around Fillmore and Greenwich Sts, Marina watering holes – which author Armistead Maupin called 'breeder bars' – cater to a frat-boy crowd.

★ INTERVAL BAR & CAFE   BAR
Map p292 (www.theinterval.org; 2 Marina Blvd, Fort Mason Center, Bldg A; ◷10am-midnight; ☐10, 22, 28, 30, 47, 49) Designed to stimulate discussion of philosophy and art, the Interval is a favorite spot in the Marina for cocktails and conversation. It's inside the Long Now Foundation, with floor-to-ceiling bookshelves, which contain the canon of Western lit, rising above the prototype of a 10,000-year clock – a fitting backdrop for a daiquiri, gimlet or aged Tom Collins, or single-origin coffee, tea and snacks.

★ BUENA VISTA CAFE   BAR
Map p289 (☑415-474-5044; www.thebuenavista. com; 2765 Hyde St; ◷9am-2am Mon-Fri, 8am-2am Sat & Sun; ☎; ☐30, 45, 47, ☐Powell-Hyde) Warm your cockles with a prim little goblet of bitter-creamy Irish coffee, introduced to America at this destination bar that once served sailors and cannery workers. That old Victorian floor manages to hold up carousers and families alike, served community-style at round tables overlooking the cable-car turnaround at Victoria Park.

ATALENA VINOTECA   WINE BAR
Map p289 (☑415-350-5778; https://altalena vinoteca.com; 448 Beach St; glass of wine $10-18; ◷11am-9pm Sun-Thu, to 9:30pm Fri & Sat; ☐47, ☐Powell-Mason, ⓜF) There aren't many places around Fisherman's Wharf that can be described 'elegant.' Okay so there's only one...and it's this new wine bar. There's a lovely selection of wines from France, Italy, Spain, Portugal and California, and some salads, charcuterie and paninis that make for fantastic pairings.

GOLD DUST LOUNGE   BAR
Map p289 (☑415-397-1695; www.golddustsf.com; 165 Jefferson St; ◷1pm-2am; ☐47, ☐Powell-Mason, ⓜE, F) The Gold Dust is so beloved by San Franciscans that when it lost its lease on the Union Sq building it had occupied since the 1930s, then reopened in 2013 at the Wharf – with the same precarious Victorian brass chandeliers and twangy rockabilly band – the mayor declared it 'Gold Dust Lounge Day.'

RADHAUS   BEER HALL
Map p292 (☑415-445-4556; http://radhaussf. com; 2 Marina Blvd, Fort Mason Center, Bldg A; ◷11am-10pm; ☐10, 22, 28, 30, 47, 49) It always feels like Octoberfest at this gleaming, Bavarian-style beer hall, installed in Fort Mason in 2018. Offerings include nine taps of German beer, along with wine, kombucha and cider, to be paired with all the brats, currywurst, weisswurst and chicken schnitzel you can stomach.

WEST COAST WINE & CHEESE   WINE BAR
Map p292 (☑415-376-9720; www.westcoastsf. com; 2165 Union St; ◷5-10pm Mon & Tue, 5pm-midnight Wed, 4pm-midnight Thu & Fri, 2pm-midnight Sat, 2-10pm Sun; ☐22, 41, 45) A rack of more than 700 bottles frames the wall at this austerely elegant storefront wine bar, which pours wines exclusively from California, Oregon and Washington. All pair with delectable small bites (dishes $8 to $16), including house-made charcuterie and cheese plates.

CALIFORNIA WINE MERCHANT   WINE BAR
Map p292 (☑415-567-0646; www.californiawine merchant.com; 2113 Chestnut St; ◷11am-midnight Sun-Wed, to 1am Thu-Sat; ☐22, 30, 43) Part wine store, part wine bar, this small shop and wine club on busy Chestnut St caters to neighborhood wine aficionados, with a frequently changing list of 50 wines by the glass, available in half pours. Arrive early to score a seat, or stand and gab with the locals. Weekday happy hours run from noon to 6pm.

☆ ENTERTAINMENT

MAGIC THEATRE   THEATER
Map p292 (☑415-441-8822; www.magictheatre. org; Fort Mason Center, Bldg D, 3rd fl, cnr Marina Blvd & Laguna St; tickets $30-85; ☐22, 28, 30, 43, 47, 49) The Magic is known for taking risks and staging provocative plays by both up-and-coming and seasoned playwrights. If you're interested in seeing new theatrical works and getting under the skin of the Bay Area theater scene, the Magic is an excellent starting point. Check the calendar online.

PIER 23   LIVE MUSIC
Map p290 (☑415-362-5125; www.pier23cafe. com; Pier 23; ◷shows 6-9pm Wed, 4-9pm Thu, 7-10pm Fri & Sat 5-8pm Sun-Tue; ⓜE, F) FREE It resembles a surf shack, but this old waterfront restaurant regularly features R&B,

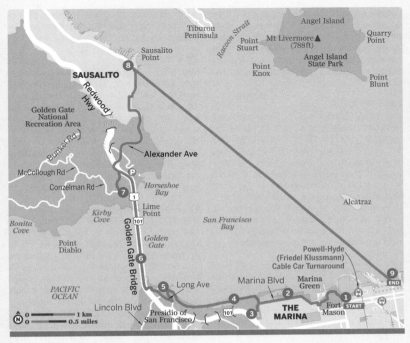

Neighborhood Ride
Cycling Tour: Freewheeling Over the Bridge

START MARITIME MUSEUM
FINISH PIER 41
LENGTH 8 MILES; TWO TO FOUR HOURS

Built in Streamline Moderne style, the 1939 ❶ **Maritime Museum** (p63) resembles an art-deco ocean liner. Head behind the building to the sandy shore along Aquatic Park and dip your toes into the icy bay.

Joggers, Frisbee throwers and kite fliers congregate at ❷ **Marina Green**. A right turn bisects two boat marinas; at the end is the curious Wave Organ. Flash back to the 1915 Panama–Pacific International Expo at the ❸ **Palace of Fine Arts** (p66). Hear how your voice echoes inside. Watch kids chase swans, while you pose for photos beside gorgeous Greco-Roman arches.

Head to ❹ **Crissy Field** (p59) to watch windsurfers and kiteboarders attempt one of SF's windiest beaches. Take the Golden Gate Promenade, a foot-and-bike path skirting the field, toward Fort Point. Fuel up on organic sandwiches and coffee at

❺ **Warming Hut** (p59). Afterwards, back-track to Long Ave and hang a sharp right up super-steep Lincoln Blvd toward the bridge. This is the hardest part of the route because of the hill. If all else fails, you can walk and push your bike.

With everyone craning their necks, it's no surprise bicycles sometimes collide on the ❻ **Golden Gate Bridge** (p58); keep your eyes peeled. Before crossing, stop at the visitor center and see the exhibits. You'll be grateful you brought a tight-fitting hat and windbreaker if the fog suddenly blows in.

Just across the bridge, turn left onto Conzelman Rd and ascend the ❼ **Marin Headlands** to look down on the bridge from a former WWII bunker, Battery Spencer – you can either pedal up the giant hill or walk your bike. Or just enjoy the views and pedal past. Swanky ❽ **Sausalito**, with bayside vistas and galleries aplenty, is ideal for a stroll, but first get the ferry schedule at the dock to coordinate your timing.

Take the ferry from Sausalito back to ❾ **Pier 41** at Fisherman's Wharf.

reggae, Latin bands, DJs, mellow rock, the occasional jazz pianist and even 'silent disco,' where everybody listens to wireless headphones (and dances). Wander out to the bayside patio to soak in the views. The dinner menu features pier-worthy options like batter-fried oysters and whole roasted crab.

BATS IMPROV
THEATER

Map p292 (☎415-474-6776; www.improv.org; Fort Mason Center, Bldg B, 3rd fl, cnr Marina Blvd & Laguna St; tickets $17-20; ⊗shows 8pm Fri & Sat; 🚌22, 28, 30, 43) Bay Area Theater Sports explores all things improv, from audience-inspired themes to whacked-out musicals at completely extemporaneous weekend shows. Or take center stage yourself at a three-hour improv-comedy workshop (held once a week over six-week sessions). Think fast: classes fill quickly. Admission prices vary depending on the show/workshop.

LOU'S FISH SHACK
LIVE MUSIC

Map p289 (☎415-771-5687; http://lousfishshacksf.com; 300 Jefferson St; ⊗shows 7-11pm Fri & Sat, 4-8pm Sun; 🚇; 🚌30, 47, 🚋Powell-Mason, Ⓜ F) FREE Lou's presents live blues on Friday and Saturday nights and Sunday afternoons. Primarily a restaurant, it also has a few bar tables near the bandstand and a tiny dance floor upstairs, making it a good backup when you're staying nearby and want to hear live music but don't want to travel. And, unlike bona fide blues bars, Lou's welcomes kids.

🛍 SHOPPING

Wharf shopping yields T-shirts, fridge magnets and miniature cable cars – the latter are perfect souvenirs; best are wood or metal. There's (far) better shopping on Polk St (Russian Hill) and the Marina. First choice is Cow Hollow – Union St between Gough and Fillmore Sts – where indie boutiques flank upmarket chains.

⭐ SUI GENERIS ILLA
CLOTHING

Map p292 (☎415-800-7584; www.suigenerisconsignment.com; 2147 Union St; ⊗11am-7pm Mon-Sat, to 5pm Sun; 🚌22, 41, 45) *Sui generis* is Latin for 'one of a kind' – which is what you'll find at this high-end designer consignment shop that features recent seasons' looks, one-of-a-kind gowns and a few archival pieces by key couturiers from decades

past. No jeans, no pants – unless they're leather or superglam. Yes, it's pricey, but far cheaper than you'd pay shopping retail.

⭐ ATYS
HOMEWARES

Map p292 (☎415-441-9220; www.atysdesign.com; 2149b Union St; ⊗11am-6:30pm Mon-Sat, noon-6pm Sun; 🚌22, 41, 45) Tucked in a courtyard, this design showcase is like a museum store for exceptional, artistic household items – to wit, a mirrored coat rack, a rechargeable flashlight that turns a wineglass into a lamp, and a zero-emissions, solar-powered toy airplane. Expect sleek, modern designs of superior quality that you won't find anywhere else.

EPICUREAN TRADER
FOOD & DRINKS

Map p292 (☎415-780-1628; www.theepicureantrader.com; 1909 Union St; ⊗7:30am-9pm Sun-Wed, to 10pm Thu-Sat; 🚌22, 41, 45, 47, 49) 🍴 A must-visit for discerning bartenders and fans of the artisanal foods movement, this grocery, liquor store and deli carries only small-batch products, many locally made, with an emphasis on bar supplies – grass-flavored gin with elderflower tonic, anyone? The deli makes perfect paninis on bread from Tartine; for dessert, there's Humphry Slocombe ice cream by the scoop.

ANOMIE
FASHION & ACCESSORIES

Map p292 (☎415-872-9943; www.shopanomie.com; 2149 Union St; ⊗11am-7pm; 🚌22, 41, 45) An essential stop on a Union St shopping raid, Anomie carries multiple small-production, independent designers of casual women's clothing, all subtly fashion forward, plus a changing lineup of accessories, jewelry, candles and bath supplies. Many pieces are in the online shop, so you can get a sense of the featured designers before you trek to the Marina.

FLAX ART & DESIGN
DESIGN

Map p292 (☎415-530-3510; http://flaxart.com; 2 Marina Blvd, Bldg D; ⊗10am-6:30pm Mon-Sat, to 6pm Sun; 🚌22, 28, 30, 43) The city's finest art-supply store carries a dizzying array of ink, paints, pigment, brushes, frames, pens, pencils, markers and glues, plus paper in myriad varieties, from stationery and wrapping to drawing pads and sketch tablets. If you're a serious designer or artist, Flax is a must-visit.

AMBIANCE
FASHION & ACCESSORIES

Map p292 (☎415-923-9796; www.ambiancesf.com; 1858 Union St; ⊗11am-7pm Sun-Fri, from

10am Sat; 🚊41, 45) The Union St outpost of this four-store SF-based chain showcases midrange designers, with a good mix of trendy and classic cuts in jeans, dresses, shirts, shoes and locally made jewelry. Half the store is devoted to sale items with prices at least 20% below retail, sometimes yielding great bargains.

ELIZABETHW
PERFUME

Map p289 (✆415-441-8354; www.elizabethw.com; 900 North Point St; ☉10am-7pm Mon-Thu, to 9pm Fri & Sat, to 8pm Sun; 🚊19, 30, 47, 🚋Powell-Hyde) Local scent maker elizabethW supplies the tantalizing aromas of changing seasons without the sweaty brows or frozen toes. 'Te' smells like a Georgia porch in summertime, 'Vetiver' like autumn in Maine. For a true SF fragrance, 'Leaves' is as audaciously green as Golden Gate Park in January. Also carries locally made bath and body products.

SPORTS BASEMENT
SPORTS & OUTDOORS

Map p291 (✆415-934-2900; www.sportsbase ment.com; 610 Old Mason St; ☉9am-9pm Mon-Fri, 8am-8pm Sat & Sun; 🚊30, 43, PresidiGo Shuttle) Specializing in odd lots of sporting goods at closeout prices, this 80,000-sq-ft sports-and-camping emporium is also the best place to rent wet suits for swims at Aquatic Park, gear for last-minute trips to Yosemite, or bikes to cross the nearby Golden Gate Bridge – and free parking makes it easy to trade your rental car for a bike.

PLUMPJACK WINES
WINE

Map p292 (✆415-346-9870; www.plumpjack wines.com; 3201 Fillmore St; ☉11am-8pm Mon-Sat, to 6pm Sun; 🚊22, 28, 30, 43) Discover new favorite Californian vintages for under $25 at the distinctive wine boutique that won founder and Governor Gavin Newsom respect even from Green Party gourmets. A more knowledgeable staff is hard to find anywhere in SF, and they'll set you up with the right bottles to cross party lines. Plump-Jack Wines also has a store in Noe Valley.

MY ROOMMATE'S CLOSET
CLOTHING

Map p292 (✆415-447-7703; www.shopmrc.com; 3044 Fillmore St; ☉11am-7pm Mon-Sat, 11am-6pm Sun; 🚊22, 41, 45) All the half-off bargains and none of the clawing dangers of a sample sale. Stocks constantly change but have included cloud-like Catherine Malandrino chiffon party dresses, executive Diane von Furstenberg wrap dresses and designer denim at prices approaching reality.

FOG CITY LEATHER
CLOTHING

Map p292 (✆415-567-1996; http://fogcityleath er.com; 2060 Union St; ☉11:30am-6pm Wed-Sun; 🚊22, 41, 45) Nothing screams San Francisco quite as much as a new leather outfit – it's what Hillary Clinton wore in SF the first time she spoke publicly after losing the election – and Fog City's clothes are made to be statement pieces. Though it carries practical motorcycle jackets, too, what's great here are the fashion styles – buttery soft and in a rainbow of colors.

SF SALT CO
HOMEWARES

Map p289 (✆800-480-4540; www.sfsalt.com; Pier 39; ☉10am-9pm Oct-Apr; 🚊47, 🚋Powell-Mason, Ⓜ️E, F) Here's an unusual gift: bring back the bay to those who couldn't join you. SF Salt mines salt from San Francisco Bay to make bath salts, adding only essential oils and/or fragrances. The 'detox soak,' made with lavender oil, rosemary oil and sea kelp, is especially appealing. After being surrounded by dense crowds at the Wharf, you're gonna need it.

HOUDINI'S MAGIC SHOP
TOYS

Map p289 (✆415-433-1422; www.houdini.com; Pier 39; ☉10am-9pm; 🚲; 🚊47, 🚋Powell-Mason, Ⓜ️E, F) For the prankster in your life, Houdini's stocks all the classic gags – rubber chickens, exploding caps, marked cards, escapable handcuffs – plus a surprisingly good collection of vintage and modern books on magic. A staff of well-suited magicians will teach you, in the privacy of a 'magic-teaching booth,' how to deploy your new tricks.

BOOKS INC
BOOKS

Map p292 (✆415-931-3633; www.booksinc.net; 2251 Chestnut St; ☉10am-10pm Mon-Sat, to 9pm Sun; 🚊22, 28, 30, 43) One of the city's best remaining independent bookstores, Books Inc carries new-release hardcovers, good fiction, extensive magazines and travel books. Check the bulletin boards for readings and literary events.

Y & I BOUTIQUE
FASHION & ACCESSORIES

Map p292 (✆415-202-0775; www.shopyandi.com; 2101 Chestnut St; ☉10:30am-7pm Mon-Wed & Fri, to 8pm Thu, 10am-7pm Sat, to 6pm Sun; 🚊22, 30, 43) When Marina girls need an outfit that won't break the bank, they shop Y & I for their cute dresses, priced at $50 to $200, by brands including Everly and Yumi Kim, plus fun sandals and shoes under $100 and

THE BAY BY BOAT

Some of the best views of San Francisco are from the water – if the weather's fair, be sure to take a boat ride. Oh, and a fun fact: by 2020, every ferry and tour boat in the bay will be running on renewable diesel fuel made of fat, vegetable oils and grease. Following is a list of operators that will get you (sustainably) out on the bay and provide some stellar photo ops, too. Be warned: it's always at least 10 degrees cooler on the bay's chilly waters. Bring a jacket.

Bay cruises The quickest way to familiarize yourself with the view from the bay is aboard a narrated one-hour cruise that loops beneath the Golden Gate Bridge. **Red & White Fleet** (Map p289; ☑415-673-2900; www.redandwhite.com; Pier 43½; adult/child $33/23; 🚻; 🚋47, ⓂE, F) operates multiple trips; **Blue & Gold Fleet** (Map p289; ☑415-705-8200; www.blueandgoldfleet.com; Pier 41; adult/child 60min ferry tour $33/22, 30min high-speed boat ride $30/21; ⊙9am-6:30pm, varies seasonally; 🚻; 🚋47, ⓂE, F) offers 30-minute trips aboard its high-speed *Rocketboat*. (Note: Blue & Gold's Alcatraz-themed cruise only sails *around* the island, not to it.)

Sailboat tours If you prefer sailboats to ferries, hit the bay aboard the Adventure Cat – a catamaran with a trampoline between its hulls – for a 90-minute bay cruise or sunset sail. Or charter a private sailboat, with or without skipper, from Spinnaker Sailing (p105).

Paddle tours Explore the bay's calm eastern shoreline in a canoe or kayak from City Kayak (p105), which guides tours, including full-moon paddles, and rents boats to experienced paddlers.

Whale-watching tours To go beyond the Golden Gate and on to the open ocean, take one of the excellent trips operated by the Oceanic Society.

Alcatraz trips Only Alcatraz Cruises (p55) is licensed to sail to the notorious island and you'll need advance reservations, but other ferries sail nearby, providing a fleeting glimpse.

Sausalito and Tiburon trips It's a quick, inexpensive ferry ride to these neighboring waterside villages across the bay from SF. **Golden Gate Ferry** (☑511, 415-455-2000; www.goldengateferry.org) and Blue & Gold Fleet operate services.

Angel Island trips Spend the day hiking and picnicking at this state park in the middle of the bay. From San Francisco, take Blue & Gold Fleet.

Oakland trips Ferries land at Jack London Sq, where you can eat bayside and have a beer at historic Heinold's First & Last Chance Saloon, whose sloping bar has been operating since 1883. Take San Francisco Bay Ferry (p267).

Alameda trips Ferry to Oakland's small-town neighbor (via San Francisco Bay Ferry) and go wine and spirits tasting. Rosenblum Cellars is adjacent to the ferry landing. Or bring a bike and pedal to wineries and distilleries that lie a little farther afield.

a big selection of all-handmade jewelry starting at just $20. Home goods are also available here.

TOPDRAWER GIFTS & SOUVENIRS
Map p292 (☑415-771-1108; www.topdrawershop.com; 1840 Union St; ⊙11am-7pm; 🚋41, 45) The first boutique outside Japan of Japanese brand Itoya showcases ingenious gadgets for travel you never knew you needed, including reversible house slippers, collapsible bottles, travel alarms and portable bento boxes, plus pouches and totes to carry them home. Three additional stores

have opened in the Bay Area, including one in the Mission.

🏃 SPORTS & ACTIVITIES

★**OCEANIC SOCIETY EXPEDITIONS** CRUISE
Map p292 (☑415-256-9604; www.oceanicsociety.org; 3950 Scott St; whale-watching trips per person $135; ⊙office 9am-5pm Mon-Fri; 🚋30) The Oceanic Society runs top-notch, natural-

ist-led, ocean-going weekend boat trips – sometimes to the Farallon Islands – during both whale-migration seasons. Cruises depart from the yacht harbor and last all day. Kids must be 10 years or older. Reservations required; group pricing and private charters are also available.

ADVENTURE CAT   CRUISE

Map p289 (☎415-777-1630; www.adventurecat. com; Pier 39, Dock J; adult/child $45/25, sunset cruise $60; ⚓; ☐47, Ⓜ E, F) There's no better view of San Francisco than from the water, especially at twilight on a fogless evening aboard a sunset cruise. Adventure Cat uses catamarans, with a windless indoor cabin for grandparents and a trampoline between hulls for bouncy kids. Three daily cruises depart March through October; weekends only in November.

FLYER   SCENIC FLIGHTS

Map p289 (www.theflyer-sanfrancisco.com; Pier 39; adult/child 12 & under $25/16; ⊙10am-8pm; ⚓; ☐49, ☐Powell-Mason, Ⓜ E, F) Pier 39's latest gimmick allows visitors to virtually lift off over the Golden Gate Bridge and soar around the city, cruising by its iconic, 3D attractions and coasting through Redwood National Forest. The ride is just a few short minutes, but the footage – shot with drones and helicopters and blended with CGI – will definitely impress the kiddies. Okay, and you.

CHEESE SCHOOL
OF SAN FRANCISCO   COOKING

Map p289 (☎415-346-7530; www.thecheese school.com; 900 North Point St; ⊙11am-8pm; ☐19, 30, 47, ☐Powell-Hyde) This elegant, two-story space does quadruple duty as a school, cafe, event space and cheese shop. Visitors experiment with making homemade mozzarella and pairing artisan cheeses with the perfect glass of wine or beer. Check the website for information on classes and tasting events.

FIRE ENGINE TOURS   TOURS

Map p289 (☎415-333-7077; http://sanfrancisco fireenginetours.com; 650 Beach St; adult/child $59/39; ⊙tours 11am, 1pm & 3pm) Hot stuff: a 90-minute ride in an open-air vintage fire engine over Golden Gate Bridge. Dress warmly! Tours depart from the Cannery at Beach St.

PLANET GRANITE   CLIMBING

Map p291 (☎415-692-3434; https://planetgran ite.com/sf/; 924 Mason St; day use adult $20-25,

child $16; ⊙6am-11pm Mon-Fri, 8am-8pm Sat, to 6pm Sun; ☐28) Take in spectacular bay views as you ascend false-rock structures inside this kick-ass 25,000-sq-ft glass-walled climbing center at Crissy Field – ideal for training before climbs at Yosemite. Master top ropes of 45ft or test your strength ascending giant boulders and vertical-crack climbing walls; finish in the full gym or stretch in a yoga session. Check the website for schedules.

BLAZING SADDLES   CYCLING

Map p289 (☎415-202-8888; www.blazingsad dles.com/san-francisco; 2715 Hyde St; bicycle rental per hr $8-15, per day $32-88, electric bikes per day $48-88; ⊙8am-8pm, shortened hrs in winter; ⚓; ☐Powell-Hyde) Blazing Saddles is tailored to visitors, with a main shop on Hyde St and six rental stands around Fisherman's Wharf, convenient for biking the Embarcadero or to the Golden Gate Bridge. It also rents tandem and electric bikes and offers a 24-hour return service – a big plus. Reserve online for a 20% discount; rental includes all extras (bungee cords, packs etc).

PRESIDIO GOLF COURSE   GOLF

Map p291 (☎415-561-4661; www.presidiogolf. com; cnr Arguello Blvd & Finley Rd; 18 holes non-resident $125-145, SF resident $69-80, NorCal resident $88-97; ⊙sunrise-sunset; ☐33) Whack balls with military-style precision on the course once reserved for US forces. The Presidio course, now operated by Touchstone Golf, overlooks the bay and is considered one of the country's best. Book up to seven days in advance on the website; look for specials on the Presidio Golf Course app. Rates include cart.

HOUSE OF AIR   TRAMPOLINING

Map p291 (☎415-965-2470; https://houseofair. com; 926 Old Mason St; 1hr $15-19; ⊙10am-8pm Sun & Mon, 2-9pm Tue-Thu, 10am-9pm Fri & Sat; ⚓; ☐28) If you resented your gym teacher for not letting you jump like you wanted on the trampoline, you can finally have your way at this incredible Crissy Field trampoline park, with multiple jumping areas where you can literally bounce off the walls on 42 attached trampolines. Kids get dedicated areas. Reservations strongly recommended – book three days ahead, especially at weekends.

Downtown, Civic Center & SoMa

FINANCIAL DISTRICT & JACKSON SQUARE | UNION SQUARE | SOMA | CIVIC CENTER & THE TENDERLOIN

Neighborhood Top Five

1 Ferry Building (p78) Grazing the Northern California food scene with incredible bay views at this showcase for the Bay Area's food purveyors and organic farmers.

2 San Francisco Museum of Modern Art (p81) Getting lost in mesmerizing installation art at the new triple-sized SFMOMA – and discussing it over museum-quality meals at In Situ.

3 San Francisco Symphony (p97) Watching impresario Michael Tilson Thomas conduct Beethoven from the tips of his toes at the Grammy-winning symphony.

4 Asian Art Museum (p80) Seeing all the way across the Pacific via the museum's priceless treasures.

5 Embarcadero (p99) Wandering south for daytime people-watching, sneaking peeks at Giants games, and getting dazzling nighttime views of the Bay Lights.

For more detail of this area see Map p294, p296, p298, and p301 ➡

Explore Downtown, Civic Center & SoMa

The cluster of monumental stone buildings and plazas around City Hall is called Civic Center. Start your day at the Asian Art Museum (p80), then take your pick of dozens of local food stalls at Heart of the City Farmers Market (p92) or the Twitter building marketplace (p86). North and east of Civic Center is the less-than-savory Tenderloin, which most first-time visitors are advised to skip – though adventurous gallery-goers brave Market St between 8th and 6th for groundbreaking arts nonprofits. Hop the F line to Powell St for shopping around Union Sq, or head onward to Montgomery to discover splendid architecture among the Financial District's mighty temples of money. Come nightfall, SoMa bars, nightclubs and drag cabarets encourage outrageousness. If you scored tickets to the SF Symphony or Opera, catch the California cable car to Van Ness and stroll downhill to your show.

Local Life

Markets Ferry Building and Civic Center farmers-market days are foodie magnets, with heirloom produce, local artisan foods and free samples galore.

Arts revival The blighted blocks of SoMa and Market St west of Powell aren't much to look at from the outside, but inside they're full of ideas: arts nonprofits stage provocative shows in formerly derelict dives.

Happy hours Whether your preferred tipple is wine, beer or a craft cocktail, you're spoiled for choice downtown – and weekday drink specials beckon.

Getting There & Away

Streetcar Historic F-Market streetcars run above Market St, between the Castro and Fisherman's Wharf.

Cable car Powell-Hyde and Powell-Mason lines link downtown with the Wharf; the California St line runs perpendicular, over Nob Hill.

Bus Buses 2, 5, 6, 7, 14, 19, 21, 27, 30, 31, 38, 41, 45 and 47 serve Downtown and/or SoMa.

Ferry Ferries run from the Ferry Building to Larkspur, Sausalito, Tiburon, Oakland, Alameda and Vallejo.

Metro J, K/T, L, M and N metro lines run under Market St. The N continues to the Caltrain station, connecting SoMa to the Haight and Golden Gate Park. The T runs from downtown, via SoMa, stopping along 3rd St.

BART Downtown stations are Embarcadero, Montgomery, Powell and Civic Center.

Lonely Planet's Top Tip

Most tourists begin cable-car trips at Powell St but often get stuck waiting in the long lines at the cable-car turnaround at Powell and Market Sts – and subjected to panhandlers and clamorous street performers. Either queue up for the Powell St cable car before noon, or hop the lesser-traveled, more historic California St line near the Embarcadero.

DOWNTOWN, CIVIC CENTER & SOMA

Best Places to Eat

➡ In Situ (p90)
➡ Ferry Building (p78)
➡ Benu (p91)
➡ Cotogna (p88)
➡ Liholiho Yacht Club (p89)
➡ Yank Sing (p90)

For reviews, see p87.➡

Best Places to Drink

➡ Bar Agricole (p94)
➡ Bourbon & Branch (p97)
➡ Aunt Charlie's Lounge (p97)
➡ Stud (p95)
➡ Zombie Village (p97)

For reviews, see p93.➡

Best Entertainment

➡ San Francisco Symphony (p97)
➡ American Conservatory Theater (p98)
➡ Giants Stadium (p99)
➡ Oasis (p99)

For reviews, see p97.➡

TOP SIGHT
FERRY BUILDING

Other towns have gourmet ghettos, but San Francisco puts its love of food front and center at the Ferry Building. The once-grand port was overshadowed by a 1950s elevated freeway – until the overpass collapsed in 1989's Loma Prieta earthquake. The Ferry Building survived and became a symbol of San Francisco's reinvention, marking your arrival onto America's forward-thinking food frontier.

Ferry Building

Like a grand salute, the Ferry Building's trademark 240ft tower greeted dozens of ferries daily after its 1898 inauguration. But with the opening of the Bay and Golden Gate Bridges, ferry traffic subsided in the 1930s. An overhead freeway was built, obscuring the building's stately facade and turning it black with exhaust fumes. Only after the 1989 earthquake did city planners realize what they'd been missing: with its grand halls and bay views, this was the perfect place for a new public commons.

Today the grand arrivals hall tempts commuters to miss the boat and get on board with SF's latest culinary trends instead. Indoor kiosks sell locally roasted espresso, artisan cheese and cured meats, plus organic ice-cream flavors to match – that's right, Vietnamese coffee, cheese and prosciutto. People-watching wine bars and award-winning restaurants are further enticements to stick around and raise a toast to San Francisco.

DON'T MISS

➜ Ferry Plaza Farmers Market picnics by the bay

➜ Food kiosks in the Ferry Building's grand arrivals hall

➜ Bay Bridge views along the Embarcadero waterfront promenade

PRACTICALITIES

➜ Map p301, D2

➜ ☏415-983-8000

➜ www.ferrybuildingmarketplace.com

➜ cnr Market St & the Embarcadero

➜ ⊙10am-7pm Mon-Fri, 8am-6pm Sat, 11am-5pm Sun

➜ ♿

➜ ☐2, 6, 9, 14, 21, 31, Ⓜ Embarcadero, Ⓑ Embarcadero

Farmers Market

Even before Ferry Building renovations were completed in 2003, the Ferry Plaza Farmers Market began operating out front on the sidewalk. Soon the foodie action spread to the bayfront plaza, with 50 to 100 local food purveyors catering to hometown crowds three times a week. While locals sometimes grumble that the prices are higher here than at other markets, there's no denying that the Ferry Plaza market offers seasonal, sustainable, handmade gourmet treats and specialty produce not found elsewhere.

Join SF's legions of professional chefs and semi-professional eaters, and taste-test the artisan goat cheese, fresh-pressed California olive oil, wild boar and organic pluots for yourself. The Saturday morning **farmers market** (Map p301; ☑415-291-3276; www. cuesa.org; street food $3-12; ◷10am-2pm Tue & Thu, from 8am Sat; ☑️👶) ✈ offers the best people-watching – it's not uncommon to spot celebrities – but arrive early if you're shopping, before those pesky *Top Chef* contestants snap up the best finds.

Bay Bridge Lights

The Bay Bridge looms large on the horizon south of the Ferry Building, and even larger in the minds of San Franciscans. Fear of crossing the bridge is invoked by city residents as a legitimate excuse for skipping social engagements in Berkeley and Oakland – and when you watch Friday-night bridge traffic crawl as you stroll the Embarcadero, you'll concede the point (word to the wise: take BART). Some San Franciscans are still shaken by memories of the 1989 Loma Prieta earthquake, which collapsed the bridge's eastern span – the damage cost taxpayers $6.4 billion and took 12 years to fix.

But the Bay Bridge is finally winning the admiration of San Franciscans, thanks to one local artist's bright idea. In 2013 lighting artist Leo Villareal strung 25,000 LED lights onto the vertical suspension cable of the Bay Bridge's western span, transforming it into a 1.8-mile-long nightly light show. The **Bay Lights** blink in never-repeating patterns – one second the bridge looks like bubbly champagne, then a lava-lamp forest, then Vegas-style fountains spraying 50 stories high. You could stare at it for hours...hopefully not while driving. The installation was meant to be temporary, but thanks to hypnotized local donors, it was permanently installed in 2016.

TOP TIPS

➡ You can still catch ferries at the Ferry Building and, on sunny days, crossing the sparkling bay is a great escape. Hop Golden Gate Transit Ferries (p267) to Larkspur, Tiburon and Sausalito, explore Oakland and Alameda via **San Francisco Bay Ferry** (☑415-705-8200; https://sanfranciscobay ferry.com), or head to Napa car-free on the Vallejo Ferry (p267).

➡ Otherwise, follow the Embarcadero waterfront promenade south from the Ferry Building to Giants Stadium (p99) for San Francisco's favorite leisurely stroll.

The Ferry Building is foodie central, with options ranging from food trucks and Ferry Plaza Farmers Market finds on the south side to oysters and bubbly at Hog Island Oyster Company (p88).

GETTING THERE

➡ The vintage F-line streetcar stops at the Ferry Building.

➡ Catch the BART or Muni to Embarcadero station.

➡ Hop off the California St cable car at its downtown terminus and walk two blocks.

TOP SIGHT
ASIAN ART MUSEUM

The most comprehensive collection of Asian art outside Asia covers 6000 years and thousands of miles of terrain. A trip through the galleries is a treasure-hunting expedition, from cutting-edge Japanese minimalism and seductive Hindu temple carvings to the jewel-box gallery of lustrous Chinese jade – just don't bump into those priceless Ming vases.

Suggested Itinerary

The Asian Museum's curatorial concept is to follow the evolution of Asian art from West to East toward San Francisco, along Buddhist pilgrimage trails and trade routes. In a couple of hours you should be able to hit the highlights, but if you're tight on time, you might head directly to ground-floor special exhibitions or follow the mapped trail of masterworks. Parents can pick up Explorer Cards for kids to find favorite animals and characters in the galleries.

Start your wander through the wonders of Asia on the 3rd floor, where you'll find a treasure trove of Hindu temple carvings and Indian jewels (pictured). Detour through dizzying Iranian geometric tiles and Javanese shadow puppets, and turn a corner to find Tibetan prayer wheels. Ahead are Chinese jades and snuff bottles, and downstairs on the 2nd floor are Chinese calligraphy, Korean celadon bowls and an entire Japanese tea-ceremony room. Look for artworks by contemporary artists responding to pieces in the collection, and don't miss artists' demonstrations in Samsung Hall before you return to the ground-floor special exhibits.

DON'T MISS

➡ South Asian and Persian miniatures

➡ Japanese tea-house artifacts

➡ 3000-year-old Chinese bronze rhinoceros wine vessel with a twinkle in its eye

➡ Breakthrough contemporary Asian art

➡ Thursday-night live artist-led events

PRACTICALITIES

➡ Map p296, B5

➡ ☎415-581-3500

➡ www.asianart.org

➡ 200 Larkin St

➡ adult/student/child $15/10/free, 1st Sun of month free

➡ ⊙10am-5pm Tue, Wed & Fri-Sun, to 9pm Thu

➡ Ⓜ Civic Center, Ⓑ Civic Center

TOP SIGHT
SAN FRANCISCO MUSEUM OF MODERN ART

The expanded San Francisco Museum of Modern Art is a mind-boggling feat, nearly tripling in size to accommodate a sprawling collection of modern and contemporary masterworks over seven floors – but then, SFMOMA has defied limits ever since its 1935 founding. The museum was a visionary early investor in then-emerging art forms including photography, installations, video, digital art and industrial design.

Suggested Itinerary

There are free gallery tours, but exploring on your own inspires the thrill of discovery, which is what SFMOMA is all about. Following this itinerary, you should be able to cover collection highlights in two to four hours. Start on the 3rd floor with SFMOMA's standout photography collection and special exhibitions. Meditate amid serene paintings in the Agnes Martin room surrounded by 4th-floor abstract art, then get an eyeful of Warhol's Pop Art on the 5th floor.

Head to the 6th floor for an exhibition of German art after 1960, and then hit the 7th floor for a showcase of cutting-edge contemporary works and intriguing media arts installations. Head downstairs via the atrium to see how SFMOMA began, with colorful local characters admiring equally colorful characters by Diego Rivera, Frida Kahlo and Henri Matisse on the 2nd floor.

Sunny days are ideal for restorative coffee and impromptu panini in the rooftop cafe and sculpture garden. And after SFMOMA's 10-floor feast for the eyes, you'll be properly hungry for contemporary culinary masterpieces painstakingly re-created by In Situ (p90) chef Corey Lee.

DON'T MISS

➡ Photography collection
➡ Video and new-media installations
➡ Julie Mehretu mural
➡ 7th-floor contemporary art
➡ In Situ restaurant

PRACTICALITIES

➡ SFMOMA
➡ Map p298, E3
➡ ☎415-357-4000
➡ www.sfmoma.org
➡ 151 3rd St
➡ adult/ages 19-24/under 18yr $25/19/free
➡ ⏱10am-5pm Fri-Tue, to 9pm Thu, atrium 8am Mon-Fri
➡ 🌢
➡ 🚌5, 6, 7, 14, 19, 21, 31, 38, Ⓜ Montgomery, Ⓑ Montgomery

⦿ SIGHTS

The Financial District centers on Montgomery St – the 'Wall St of the West' – and stretches to Jackson Square, the city's oldest neighborhood, with low-slung brick buildings and high-end antiquarians. Union Square refers to the square *and* the surrounding retail-shopping and hotel district. Tech and biotech are converting South of Market (SoMa) into a second downtown. Museums and galleries cluster around 3rd and Mission, but otherwise SoMa's long, industrial blocks are gritty and tedious. Civic Center is the area around City Hall bordered north and east by the seedy Tenderloin district – best avoided without a mapped route to a specific destination.

⦿ Financial District & Jackson Square

FERRY BUILDING   LANDMARK
See p78.

**DIEGO RIVERA'S ALLEGORY
OF CALIFORNIA FRESCO**   PUBLIC ART
Map p301 (www.sfcityguides.org; 155 Sansome St; tours free; ⊙tours by reservation with SF City Guides 3pm 1st & 3rd Mon of month; BMontgomery, MMontgomery) FREE Hidden inside San Francisco's Stock Exchange tower is a priceless treasure: Diego Rivera's 1930–31 *Allegory of California* fresco. Spanning a two-story stairwell between the 10th and 11th floors, the fresco shows California as a giant golden goddess offering farm-fresh produce, while gold miners toil beneath her and oil refineries loom on the horizon. *Allegory* is glorious, but cautionary – while Californian workers, inventors and dreamers go about their business, the pressure gauge in the left-hand corner is entering the red zone.

**TRANSAMERICA PYRAMID
& REDWOOD PARK**   NOTABLE BUILDING
Map p301 (www.thepyramidcenter.com; 600 Montgomery St; ⊙10am-3pm Mon-Fri; MEmbarcadero, BEmbarcadero) The defining feature of San Francisco's skyline is this 1972 pyramid, built atop a whaling ship abandoned in the gold rush. A half-acre redwood grove sprouted out front, on the site of Mark Twain's favorite saloon and the newspaper office where Sun Yat-sen drafted his Procla-

mation of the Republic of China. Although these transplanted redwoods have shallow roots, their intertwined structure helps them reach dizzying heights – Twain himself couldn't have penned a more perfect metaphor for San Francisco.

WELLS FARGO HISTORY MUSEUM   MUSEUM
Map p301 (☑415-396-2619; www.wellsfargohistory.com/museums; 420 Montgomery St; ⊙9am-5pm Mon-Fri; ♿; MMontgomery, BMontgomery) FREE Gold miners needed somewhere to stash and send cash, so Wells Fargo opened in this location in 1852. Today this storefront museum covers gold rush–era innovations, including the Pony Express, transcontinental telegrams and statewide stagecoaches. Wells Fargo was the world's largest stagecoach operator c 1866, and you can climb aboard a preserved stagecoach to hear pioneer-trail stories while kids ride a free mechanical pony. Notwithstanding the blatant PR for Wells Fargo, the exhibits are well researched, fascinating and free.

⦿ Union Square

PALACE HOTEL   HISTORIC BUILDING
Map p294 (☑415-512-1111; www.sfpalace.com; 2 New Montgomery St; BMontgomery, MMontgomery) A true SF survivor, the Palace opened in 1875 but was gutted during the 1906 earthquake. Opera star Enrico Caruso was jolted from his Palace bed by the quake and fled San Francisco, never to return. The Palace reopened by 1909 and it was here that Woodrow Wilson gave his League of Nations speech 10 years later. Visit by day to see the Garden Court stained-glass ceiling, then peek into the **Pied Piper Bar** to see Maxfield Parrish's *Pied Piper* mural.

49 GEARY   GALLERY
Map p294 (www.sfada.com; 49 Geary St; ⊙11am-6pm Tue-Sat; ☒5, 6, 7, 9, 21, 31, 38, MPowell, BPowell) FREE Pity the collectors silently nibbling endive in austere Chelsea galleries – at 49 Geary, First Thursday art openings mean unexpected art, popcorn and outspoken crowds. Four floors of two dozen galleries feature standout international and local works, including photography at Fraenkel Gallery and Scott Nichols Gallery, Ai Weiwei installations at Haines Gallery, and Christian Maychack's architectural excess at Gregory Lind. For quieter contemplation, visit on a weekday.

JAMES FLOOD BUILDING HISTORIC BUILDING
Map p294 (cnr Market & Powell Sts; MPowell, BPowell) This 1904 stone building survived the 1906 earthquake and retains its original character, notwithstanding the Gap flagship downstairs. Upstairs, labyrinthine marble hallways are lined with frosted-glass doors, just like a noir movie set. No coincidence: in 1921 the SF office of infamous Pinkerton Detective Agency hired a young investigator named Dashiell Hammett, author of the 1930 noir classic *The Maltese Falcon*.

☉ SoMa

SAN FRANCISCO MUSEUM OF MODERN ART MUSEUM
See p81.

CONTEMPORARY JEWISH MUSEUM MUSEUM
Map p298 (☑415-655-7856; www.thecjm.org; 736 Mission St; adult/student/child $14/12/free, after 5pm Thu $8; ⏰11am-5pm Mon, Tue & Fri-Sun, to 8pm Thu; ♿; ☐14, 30, 45, BMontgomery, MMontgomery) That upended blue-steel box miraculously balancing on one corner atop the Contemporary Jewish Museum is appropriate for an institution that upends conventional ideas about art and religion. Architect Daniel Libeskind designed this museum to be rational, mystical and powerful. But it's the contemporary art commissions that truly bring the building to life.

MUSEUM OF THE AFRICAN DIASPORA MUSEUM
Map p298 (MoAD; ☑415-358-7200; www.moadsf.org; 685 Mission St; adult/child/student $10/free/$5; ⏰11am-6pm Wed-Sat, noon-5pm Sun;

DOWNTOWN, CIVIC CENTER & SOMA SIGHTS

TIMOTHY PFLUEGER'S JAWDROPPING SKYSCRAPERS

When a downtown skyscraper makes you stop, stare and crane your neck, it's probably Timothy Pflueger's fault. San Francisco's prolifically fanciful architect was responsible for downtown's most jaw-dropping buildings from 1925 to 1948, in styles ranging from opulent art deco to monumental minimalism. Movie buffs and architecture aficionados will want to hop the F line to catch a movie in Pflueger's 1922 palatial Mexican-baroque Castro Theatre, then take BART to Oakland to see how his 1931 glittering mosaic deco Paramount Theatre inspired *Wizard of Oz* Emerald City sets. But first, stop and stare at these Pflueger masterpieces downtown.

Pacific Telephone & Telegraph Company Building (Map p298; 140 New Montgomery St; ☐14, BMontgomery, MMontgomery) Recently renovated and gilt to the hilt indoors, this 1925 building made Pflueger's reputation with its black-marble deco lobby and soaring, streamlined shape. Winston Churchill made his first transatlantic telephone call here in 1929, but ironically the tower now seems to interfere with cell-phone coverage. Notice the cable-like lines running right up the building, past stylized telegraph insulators to fierce stone eagles. Today it's the headquarters for review site Yelp, as well as Morocco-moderne Mourad (p91) restaurant.

450 Sutter St (Map p294; 450 Sutter St; ☐38, ☐Powell-Mason, Powell-Hyde) A 26-story deco dental building fit for the gods, this 1929 Mayan-revival stone skyscraper has a lobby covered floor to ceiling with cast-bronze snakes representing healing, grimacing figures apparently in need of dentistry, and panels covered with mystifying glyphs – early insurance forms, perhaps? With glowing inverted-pyramid lights, this landmark makes getting a cavity filled seem like a spiritual experience.

I Magnin Building (Map p294; cnr Stockton & Geary Sts; ☐38, ☐Powell-Mason, Powell-Hyde) When Timothy Pflueger's radical design was revealed on Union Sq in 1948, SF society was shocked: San Francisco's flagship clothing store appeared completely naked. Stripped of deco adornment, Pflueger's avant-garde white-marble plinth caused consternation – until Christian Dior himself pronounced it 'magnifique.' Today it's a collection of luxury boutiques with new interiors. Pflueger's daring building remains Union Sq's most timeless fashion statement, and was his final work before his untimely death of a heart attack at 54. His legacy includes a dozen other Bay Area landmarks, including the Bay Bridge, plus the arts institution he co-founded: the San Francisco Museum of Modern Art (p81).

P ⬛; 🖥14, 30, 45, Ⓜ Montgomery, Ⓑ Montgomery) MoAD assembles an international cast of characters to tell the epic story of diaspora, including a moving video of slave narratives told by Maya Angelou. Standouts among quarterly changing exhibits have included homages to '80s New Wave icon Grace Jones, architect David Adjaye's photographs of contemporary African landmarks and Alison Saar's sculptures of figures marked by history. Public events include poetry slams, Yoruba spiritual music celebrations and lectures examining the legacy of the Black Panthers' free-school-breakfast program.

SPUR URBAN CENTER GALLERY   CULTURAL CENTER

Map p298 (📞415-781-8726; www.spur.org; 654 Mission St; ◷9am-5pm; 🖥12, 14, Ⓑ Montgomery, Ⓜ Montgomery) FREE Cities are what you make of them, and urban-planning nonprofit SPUR invites you to reimagine San Francisco (and your own hometown) with gallery shows that explore urban living, from soundscapes to elder-housing design. Exhibitions are free, thought-provoking and visually appealing, featuring local and international artists. For the ultimate SF treasure hunt, check out SPUR's map and guide to POPOs (privately owned public open spaces), which are actually open to all. Search 'POPO San Francisco' on the website or download the app.

CHILDREN'S CREATIVITY MUSEUM   MUSEUM

Map p298 (📞415-820-3320; http://creativity. org/; 221 4th St; $12.95; ◷10am-4pm Tue-Sun summer, Wed-Sun rest of yr; ⬛; 🖥14, Ⓜ Powell, Ⓑ Powell) No velvet ropes or hands-off signs here: kids rule, with high-tech displays double-daring them to make music videos, film claymation movies and construct play castles. Jump into live-action video games and sign up for workshops with Bay Area superstar animators, techno whizzes and robot builders. For low-tech fun, take a spin on the vintage-1906 **Looff Carousel** outside, operating 10am to 5pm daily; one $4 ticket covers two rides ($1 discount with museum admission).

CALIFORNIA HISTORICAL SOCIETY   MUSEUM

Map p298 (📞415-357-1848; www.californiahis toricalsociety.org; 678 Mission St; adult/child $10/free; ◷gallery & store 11am-5pm Tue-

Sun, library 1-5pm Wed-Fri; ⬛; Ⓜ Montgomery, Ⓑ Montgomery) Enter a Golden State of enlightenment at this Californiana treasure trove, featuring themed exhibitions drawn from the museum's million-plus California photographs, paintings and ephemera. Past exhibits have unearthed Prohibition-era wine labels, protest posters from the Summer of Love and 1971 instructions for interpretive-dancing your way through San Francisco by dance pioneer Anna Halprin. Events are rare opportunities to discuss 1970s underground comix, 1940s SF gay bars and gold rush–era saloon menu staples (whiskey, opium and tamales).

YERBA BUENA GARDENS   PARK

Map p298 (📞415-820-3550; www.yerbabuena gardens.com; cnr 3rd & Mission Sts; ◷6am-10pm; ⬛; Ⓜ Montgomery, Ⓑ Montgomery) Breathe a sigh of relief: you've found the lush green getaway in the concrete heart of SoMa, between Yerba Buena Center for the Arts and Metreon entertainment complex. This is a prime spot to picnic, hear free noontime summer concerts (see website) or duck behind the fountain for a smooch. Martin Luther King Jr Memorial Fountain is a wall of water that runs over the Reverend's immortal words: '...until justice rolls down like water and righteousness like a mighty stream.'

CROWN POINT PRESS   GALLERY

Map p298 (📞415-974-6273; www.crownpoint. com; 20 Hawthorne St; ◷10am-5pm Mon, to 6pm Tue-Sat; 🖥14, Ⓑ Montgomery, Ⓜ Montgomery) FREE Bet you didn't think anyone could capture Chuck Close's giant portraits, Robert Bechtle's hyper-realistic street scenes or Kiki Smith's painstaking wall paintings on paper – yet here they are. Crown Point Press printmakers work with international artists to turn singular visions into large-scale, limited-edition woodblocks and etchings. When master printmakers are at work, you're often invited to watch – and if you're inspired to make your own, you can pick up how-to books and tools here.

SF ARTS COMMISSION GALLERY   GALLERY

Map p296 (📞415-252-2255; www.sfartscommis sion.org; 401 Van Ness Ave, Suite 126, War Memorial Veterans Bldg; ◷11am-6pm Tue-Sat; Ⓜ Van Ness) 🖉 Get in on the ground floor of the next SF art movement at this public showcase for local talent, with past exhibits ranging from Susan O'Malley's silk-screened words of advice from San Franciscans to rock photogra-

DOWNTOWN ROOFTOP GARDENS

Above the busy sidewalks, there's a serene world of unmarked public rooftop gardens that grant perspective on downtown's skyscraper canyons. They're called POPOs (privately owned public open spaces). Local public-advocacy urbanist group SPUR publishes a downloadable app that lists them all.

Local favorites:

One Montgomery Terrace (Map p294; 1 Montgomery St; ⏱10am-6pm Mon-Sat; Ⓜ Montgomery, ⒷMontgomery) has great Market St views of old and new SF. Enter through Crocker Galleria, take the elevator to the top, then ascend the stairs; or enter Wells Fargo at One Montgomery and take the elevator to 'R.'

Sun Terrace (Map p301; 343 Sansome St; ⏱10am-5pm Mon-Fri; Ⓜ Embarcadero, ⒷEmbarcadero) has knockout vistas of the Financial District and Transamerica Pyramid from atop a slender art-deco skyscraper. Take the elevator to the 15th floor.

pher Jim Marshall's iconic shots of Jimi and Janis. Beyond gallery exhibitions, the commission also shows art in City Hall and in an empty storefront at 155 Grove St.

◉ Civic Center & the Tenderloin

ASIAN ART MUSEUM MUSEUM
See p80.

LUGGAGE STORE GALLERY GALLERY
Map p296 (☑415-255-5971; www.luggagestore gallery.org; 1007 Market St; ⏱noon-5pm Wed-Sat; ☐6, 7, 9, 21, ⓂCivic Center, ⒷCivic Center) Like a dandelion pushing through sidewalk cracks, this plucky nonprofit gallery has brought signs of life to one of the Tenderloin's toughest blocks for two decades. By giving SF street artists a gallery platform, the Luggage Store helped launch graffiti-art star Barry McGee, muralist Rigo and street photographer Cheryl Dunn. Find the graffitied door and climb to the 2nd-floor gallery, which rises above the street without losing sight of it.

GLIDE MEMORIAL UNITED METHODIST CHURCH CHURCH
Map p296 (☑415-674-6090; www.glide.org; 330 Ellis St; ⏱celebrations 9am & 11am Sun; ♿; ☐38, ⓂPowell, ⒷPowell) When the rainbow-robed Glide gospel choir enters singing their hearts out, the 2000-plus congregation erupts in cheers, hugs and dance moves. Raucous Sunday Glide celebrations capture San Francisco at its most welcoming and uplifting, embracing the rainbow spectrum of culture, gender, orientation, ability and

socioeconomics. After the celebration ends, the congregation keeps the inspiration coming, serving 2000 meals a day and connecting homeless individuals and families with shelter and emotional support. Yes, Glide welcomes volunteers.

SF CAMERAWORK GALLERY
Map p296 (☑415-487-1011; www.sfcamerawork. org; 1011 Market St, 2nd fl; ⏱noon-6pm Tue-Fri, to 5pm Sat; ☐6, 7, 9, 21, ⒷCivic Center, ⓂCivic Center) FREE Since 1974, this nonprofit art organization has championed experimental photo-based imagery beyond classic B&W prints and casual digital snapshots. Since moving into a spacious Market St gallery, Camerawork's far-reaching exhibitions have examined memories of love and war in Southeast Asia, taken imaginary holidays with slide shows of vacation snapshots scavenged from the San Francisco Dump and showcased SF-based artist Sanaz Mazinani's mesmerizing Islamic-inspired photo montages made of tiny Trumps.

TENDERLOIN NATIONAL FOREST PARK
Map p296 (☑831-318-0253; www.luggagestore gallery.org/tnf; Ellis St, btwn Leavenworth & Hyde Sts; ⏱noon-5pm; ☐27, 31, 38, ⒷPowell, ⓂPowell) FREE Urban blight is interrupted by bucolic splendor on one of the Tenderloin's grittiest blocks. Once littered with hypodermic needles and garbage, dead-end Cohen Alley has been transformed by a nonprofit artists' collective. A grove of trees is taking root, concrete walls are covered with murals by local artists, and asphalt has been replaced with mosaic pathways and koi ponds. If you feel so inspired – and, really, who wouldn't? – garden tools are available to help maintain SF's scrappiest natural wonder.

LOCAL KNOWLEDGE

SOMA'S SPIRIT OF INVENTION

Few San Francisco visitors realize that most of the personal technology they use every day was invented within 50 miles of where they're standing – all those handy search engines, websites and apps, plus the smart phones, glasses and watches they run on. But even fewer people realize how many of the most widely used apps were invented within the half-sq-mile area of SoMa District – including Instagram, Twitter, Pinterest and Airbnb.

Is there something in the water in SoMa? No, but there may be something in the beer. By joining techies for downtime in SoMa start-up hubs, you can get a sneak preview of the next big technology. Several of Silicon Valley's most important start-up incubator spaces are in SoMa, including RocketSpace (http://rocketspace.com), PARISOMA (www.parisoma.com) and Impact Hub (https://bayarea.impacthub.net). Check their websites for happy hours, meet-ups and pitch nights, where you can hear technology ideas and beta-test the next big tech launch and/or flop.

When you are seized with your own technology breakthrough – yep, it happens to everyone in SF eventually – you're in the right place to make it happen. San Francisco has several hackerspaces where you can socialize over circuitry with people who could probably break into your bank account but who instead graciously share pointers. Two hackerspaces that host events open to nonmembers are the Mission's non-profit women's maker/hackerspace, Double Union (https://www.doubleunion.org; check online for open-house hack sessions and workshops), and anarchically creative nonprofit Mission hackerspace Noisebridge (https://www.noisebridge.net; donations welcome).

Don't be discouraged if your invention doesn't turn out as planned. As the Silicon Valley saying goes: if at first you don't succeed, fail better. Most technologies become obsolete eventually – some just do it faster than others. On Friday afternoons you can pay your respects to bygone blogs and glimpse the inner workings of the Wayback Machine at the Internet Archive (p194), housed in a converted 1927 neoclassical temple in the Richmond District.

So what else is left to invent in San Francisco? Time machines, for starters. Drink to the future at the Interval Bar & Cafe (p70), and check out their Tuesday night lectures on art, design, history, nature, technology and time.

TWITTER HEADQUARTERS   LANDMARK
Map p296 (Western Furniture Exchange & Merchandise Mart; https://about.twitter.com/com pany; 1355 Market St; 🚊6, 7, 21, Ⓜ Civic Center, Ⓑ Civic Center) 🚶 Market St's traffic-stopping 1937 Mayan deco landmark was built to accommodate 300 wholesale furniture-design showrooms – but, a decade ago, fewer than 30 remained. The city offered tax breaks to Twitter to move here from its **South Park** (Map p298; S Park St; Ⓜ N, T) headquarters and, after a $1.2-million LEED-certified green makeover including a rooftop farm, Twitter nested here. Only employees can access Twitter's free video arcade and Birdfeeder cafeteria, but the ground-floor public space, **The Market**, offers 22,000 sq ft of local gourmet fare.

ROOT DIVISION   GALLERY
Map p298 (📞415-863-7668; www.rootdivision. org; 1131 Mission St; donations welcome; ⊙gallery 2-6pm Wed-Sat, also by appointment; 🚼; 🚊6, 9, 71, Ⓑ F, Ⓑ Civic Center, Ⓜ Civic Center) **FREE** Get back to your creative roots at this arts nonprofit, which hosts curated shows on themes ranging from garden art to calligraphy made with human-hair brushes. Root Division keeps the inspiration coming, offering artists subsidized studio space in exchange for providing community art classes ranging from felt sculpture to electronic art – see the schedule for upcoming workshops for youth and adults. Don't miss events like the annual Misfit Maker Factory, where artists create works for sale.

SAN FRANCISCO
MAIN LIBRARY   CULTURAL CENTER
Map p296 (📞415-557-4400; www.sfpl.org; 100 Larkin St; ⊙10am-6pm Mon & Sat, 9am-8pm Tue-Thu, noon-6pm Fri, noon-5pm Sun; 🚼; 🚊5, 6, 7, 19, 21, 31, Ⓑ Civic Center, Ⓜ Civic Center) **FREE** A grand light well illuminates SF's favorite

subjects: poetry in the Robert Frost Collection, civil rights in the Hormel LGBTQIA Center, SF music zines in the Little Maga/Zine Center and comic relief in the Schmulowitz Collection of Wit and Humor. Check out the wallpaper made from the old card catalog on the 3rd to 5th floors – artists Ann Chamberlain and Ann Hamilton invited 200 San Franciscans to add multilingual commentary to 50,000 cards.

CITY HALL
HISTORIC BUILDING

Map p296 (📞tour info 415-554-6139; http://sfgov.org/cityhall/city-hall; 400 Van Ness Ave; ☺8am-8pm Mon-Fri, tours 10am, noon & 2pm; ♿; Ⓜ Civic Center, Ⓑ Civic Center) 𝐅𝐑𝐄𝐄 Rising from the ashes of the 1906 earthquake, this beaux arts landmark echoes with history. Demonstrators protesting red-scare McCarthy hearings on City Hall steps in 1960 were blasted with fire hoses – yet America's first sit-in worked. America's first openly gay official supervisor, Harvey Milk, was assassinated here in 1978, along with Mayor George Moscone – but, in 2004, 4037 same-sex couples were legally wed here. Recently, City Hall has made headlines for approving pioneering environmental initiatives and citywide sanctuary status.

COMPTON'S TRANSGENDER CULTURAL DISTRICT
AREA

(www.facebook.com/pages/category/community-organization/comptons-transgender-cultural-district-1601956093204763) The world's first legally recognized transgender district was created to commemorate historical sites and preserve existing non-profits, businesses and nightlife venues to help the community remain vibrant. Boundaries include Market St between Taylor St and Jones St, to the south side of Ellis St between Mason St and Taylor St, and the north side of Ellis St between Taylor St and Jones St, as well as the 6th St corridor between Market St and Howard St.

✖ EATING

Downtown and South of Market (SoMa) are best known for high-end restaurants (for which you'll need reservations), but lunchtime eateries in the neighborhood cater to office workers, with meals around $12 to $25. The Financial District is dead at night, when only midrange and top-end joints stay open. The Tenderloin (west of Powell St, south of Geary St, north of Market St) feels sketchy and rough but, as always in San Francisco, bargain eats reward the adventurous. Some cheap eateries in the 'Loin close earlier than their posted hours.

✖ Financial District & Jackson Square

MIJITA
MEXICAN $

Map p301 (📞415-399-0814; www.mijitasf.com; 1 Ferry Bldg, cnr Market St & the Embarcadero; dishes $4-10; ☺10am-7pm Mon-Thu, to 8pm Fri, 9am-8pm Sat, 9am-3pm Sun; ✒♿; 🚌2, 6, 9, 14, 21, 31, Ⓜ Embarcadero, Ⓑ Embarcadero) 🍽 Jealous seagulls circle above your outdoor bayside table, eyeing your sustainable fish tacos and tangy jicama and grapefruit salad. James Beard Award–winning chef Traci Des Jardins honors her Mexican grandmother's cooking at this sunny taqueria – the Mexico City–style quesadilla is laced with *epazote* (Mayan herbs) and the *aguas fresca* (fruit punch) is made from just-squeezed juice.

COWGIRL CREAMERY
CHEESE $

Map p301 (Sidekick Cafe & Milk Bar; 📞415-392-4000; www.cowgirlcreamery.com/sidekick-cafe-milk-bar; 1 Ferry Bldg, cnr Market St & the Embarcadero; cheese plate $13, sandwiches $6-13; ☺7am-7pm Mon-Sat, 9am-5pm Sun; Ⓑ Embarcadero, Ⓜ Embarcadero) To do in San Francisco: see Golden Gate Bridge; ride cablecar; develop opinion on Red Hawk, the distinctively stinky, washed-rind cheese that put Cowgirl Creamery on the map. The robust, complex flavor profile isn't for everybody, but if it's for you, it's *really* for you. Or maybe you'll prefer the milder Mt Tam, or some other gourmet selection, possibly melted on a sandwich?

GOLDEN WEST
SANDWICHES $

Map p294 (📞415-216-6443; http://theauwest.com; 8 Trinity Alley; lunch $9-12; ☺8am-2pm Mon-Fri; 🚌3, 8, 30, 45, Ⓑ Montgomery, Ⓜ Montgomery) Eureka! Wedged between brokerage firms under the glowing sign that says Au (the periodic-table symbol for gold) is an elusive FiDi find: a memorable lunch with top-notch California-grown ingredients that won't break the bank. Menu items are seasonal, but look for short-rib sandwiches with caramelized onions and house-made mayo or spicy chicken salads with mango, organic greens and pumpkin seeds.

EL PORTEÑO EMPANADAS ARGENTINE $

Map p301 (☑415-513-4529; www.elportenosf.
com; 1 Ferry Bldg, cnr Market St & the Embarcadero; empanadas $6.50; ⏱7:30am-8:15pm Mon-Sat, 8am-7:15pm Sun; ☑🖉; ⒷEmbarcadero, ⓂEmbarcadero) 🖉 Pocket change left over from farmers-market shopping scores Argentine pocket pastries packed with local flavor at El Porteño. Vegetarian versions like *acelga* (organic Swiss chard and Gruyère) and *humita* (Brentwood sweet corn and caramelized onions) are just as mouthwatering as classic *jamon y queso* (prosciutto and fontina). Save room for *dulce de leche alfajores* (cookies with gooey caramel centers).

COTOGNA ITALIAN $$

Map p301 (☑415-775-8508; www.cotognasf.
com; 490 Pacific Ave; mains $19-38; ⏱11:30am-10:30pm Mon-Thu, to 11pm Fri & Sat, 5-9:30pm Sun; ☑; ☐10, 12) Chef-owner Michael Tusk racks up James Beard Awards for a quintessentially Italian culinary balancing act: he strikes ideal proportions among a few pristine flavors in rustic pastas, wood-fired pizzas and salt-crusted branzino. Reserve, especially for bargain $69 multi-course Sunday suppers with $35 wine pairings – or plan a walk-in late lunch/early dinner. Top-value Italian wine list (bottles from $50).

BOULETTE'S LARDER
& BOULIBAR MEDITERRANEAN, CALIFORNIAN $$

Map p301 (☑415-399-1155; www.bouletteslarder.com; 1 Ferry Bldg, cnr Market St & the Embarcadero; mains $18-24; ⏱Larder 8-10:30am & 11:30am-3pm Tue-Sat, 10am-2:30pm Sun, Boulibar 11:30am-3pm & 6-9:30pm Tue-Fri, 11:30am-3pm & 4:30-8pm Sat; ⓂEmbarcadero, ⒷEmbarcadero) Dinner theater can't beat brunch at Boulette's communal table, strategically placed inside a working kitchen amid a swirl of chefs with views of the Bay Bridge. At adjoining Boulibar, get tangy Middle Eastern mezze platters, beautifully blistered wood-fired pizzas and flatbreads at indoor picnic-style tables – perfect for people-watching, despite sometimes rushed service. Get inspiration to go with Larder spice mixes.

SLANTED DOOR VIETNAMESE $$

Map p301 (☑415-861-8032; www.slanteddoor.
com; 1 Ferry Bldg, cnr Market St & the Embarcadero; mains $18-42; ⏱11am-2:30pm & 5:30-10pm Mon-Sat, 11:30am-3pm & 5:30-10pm Sun; ☐2, 6, 9, 14, 21, 31, ⓂEmbarcadero, ⒷEmbarcadero) 🖉 Live the dream at this bayfront bistro, where California-fresh, Vietnamese-inspired dishes are served with sparkling waterfront views. Chinatown-raised chef-owner Charles Phan is a James Beard Award winner and a local hero for championing California-grown ingredients in signature dishes like garlicky grass-fed 'shaking beef' and Dungeness crab heaped atop cellophane noodles. Book weeks ahead, or settle for Out the Door takeout.

HOG ISLAND
OYSTER COMPANY SEAFOOD $$

Map p301 (☑415-391-7117; www.hogislandoysters.com; 1 Ferry Bldg, cnr Market St & the Embarcadero; 6 oysters $19-21; ⏱11am-9pm; ☐2, 6, 9, 14, 21, 31, ⓂEmbarcadero, ⒷEmbarcadero) 🖉 Slurp the bounty of the North Bay with East Bay views at this local, sustainable oyster bar. Get them raw, grilled with chipotle-bourbon butter, or Rockefeller (cooked with spinach, Pernod and cream). Not the cheapest oysters in town, but consistently the best – with excellent wines. Stop by Hog Island's farmers-market stall, 8am to 2pm Saturday.

KUSAKABE SUSHI, JAPANESE $$$

Map p301 (☑415-757-0155; http://kusakabe-sf.
com; 584 Washington St; 8-course tasting menu $98, 11-course tasting menu $168; ⏱5-10:45pm, last seating 8:45pm; ☐8, 10, 12, 41) Trust chef Mitsunori Kusakabe's *omakase* (tasting menu). Sit at the counter while the chef adds a herbal hint to fatty tuna with the inside of a *shiso* leaf. After you devour the menu – mostly with your hands 'to release flavors' – you can special-order Hokkaido sea urchin, which the chef perfumes with the outside of the *shiso* leaf. Soy sauce isn't provided – or missed. Wine ($130) and sake ($160) pairings are also available.

QUINCE CALIFORNIAN $$$

Map p301 (☑415-775-8500; www.quincerestaurant.com; 470 Pacific Ave; 10-course tasting menu $295, wine pairing $275, abbreviated menu $180, wine pairing $150; ⏱5:30-9pm Mon-Thu, 5-9:30pm Fri & Sat; ☐3, 10) 🖉 Chef Michael Tusk's tasting menu of Northern California bounty is an adventure and an investment – if you're not entirely sold on this season's menu (see online), go à la carte in the salon instead. It's slightly more affordable and no less swanky, with seasonal plates that involve caviar. A standout Acquerello risotto dish comes with white sturgeon caviar, meyer lemon and crème fraîche.

KOKKARI GREEK $$$

Map p301 (☑415-981-0983; www.kokkari.com; 200 Jackson St; mains $25-56; ⏱11:30am-2:30pm & 5:30-10pm Mon-Thu, 11:30am-2:30pm & 5:30-11pm Fri, 5-11pm Sat; ☑; ☐8, 10, 12, 41) This is one Greek restaurant where you'll want to lick your plate instead of break it, with starters like chargrilled octopus with a zing of lemon and oregano, and a signature lamb, eggplant and yogurt moussaka as rich as the Pacific Stock Exchange. Reserve to avoid waits, or make a meal of hearty Mediterranean appetizers at the happening bar.

✖ Union Square

SUSHIRRITO JAPANESE, FUSION $

Map p294 (☑415-544-9868; www.sushirrito.com; 226 Kearny St; dishes $10-14; ⏱10am-8pm Mon-Fri, from 11am Sat, noon-4pm Sun; ☑; ☐30, 45, ☐Montgomery, ⓂMontgomery) 🍴 Ever get a sushi craving, but you're hungry enough for a burrito? Join the crowd at Sushirrito, where fresh Latin and Asian ingredients are rolled in rice and nori seaweed, then conveniently wrapped in foil. Pan–Pacific Rim flavors shine in Geisha's Kiss, with line-caught yellowfin tuna and *piquillo* peppers, and vegetarian Buddha Belly, with spicy Japanese eggplant, kale and avocado.

EMPORIO RULLI CAFE $

Map p294 (www.rulli.com; Union Sq; pastries $4-8; ⏱8am-7pm; 🚸; ⓂPowell, ⒷPowell) Food is secondary to people-watching at this glass-pavilion cafe perched atop Union Sq – stake out a prime outdoor table and order snacks at the counter. On sunny days, this is a welcome midday stop for gelato, Italian pastries or ham or prosciutto croissants – plus powerful espresso drinks or wine. In the winter, there's ice skating just beside the cafe.

★LIHOLIHO YACHT CLUB HAWAIIAN, CALIFORNIAN $$

Map p296 (☑415-440-5446; http://lycsf.com; 871 Sutter St; dishes $11-37; ⏱5-10:30pm Mon-Thu, to 11pm Fri & Sat; ☐2, 3, 27, 38, ⒸCalifornia) Who needs yachts to be happy? Aloha abounds over Liholiho's pucker-up-tart cocktails and gleefully creative Calwaiian/Hawafornian dishes – surefire mood enhancers include spicy beef-tongue *bao,* duck-liver mousse with pickled pineapple on brioche, and Vietnamese slaw with tender squid and crispy tripe. Reservations are tough; arrive early/late for bar dining, or head downstairs to

---

LOCAL KNOWLEDGE

ALFRESCO DINING DOWNTOWN

During the odd heat wave in SF, when it's too hot to stay indoors without air-con (which nobody in SF has) and warm enough to eat outside, two downtown streets become go-to destinations for dining alfresco: Belden Pl (www.belden-place.com) and Claude Lane. Both are pedestrian alleyways lined with European-style restaurants and convivial sidewalk seating. The food is marginally better on Claude Lane, notably at Cafe Claude. Belden is sunnier and more colorful – the restaurants here make up for average fare with big smiles and generous wine pours.

Louie's Gen-Gen Room speakeasy for shamelessly tasty bone-marrow-butter waffles.

CAFE CLAUDE FRENCH $$

Map p294 (☑415-392-3505; www.cafeclaude.com; 7 Claude Lane; mains $15-26; ⏱11:30am-10pm; ☐30, 45, ⓂMontgomery, ⒷMontgomery) Escape down an SF alleyway to a sleek French cafe, with zinc bar, umbrella tables outside and staff chattering *en français*. Lunch is served all day and jazz combos play Thursday to Sunday during dinner. Expect classics like *coq au vin* and gently garlicky *escargots,* always good, if not great – but wine and romance make it memorable.

HAKKASAN DIM SUM $$$

Map p294 (☑415-829-8148; http://hakkasan.com; 1 Kearny St; mains $20-38; ⏱11:30am-2pm & 5-10pm Tue-Fri, 11:30am-3pm & 5-10pm Sat; ⓂMontgomery, ⒷMontgomery) Bootstrapping start-ups and venture capitalists alike hit Hakkasan for three-course lunch specials ($39) or elegant dim sum (get XO brandy scallop dumplings and prawn and chive dumplings). Celebrate birthdays and IPOs in style with generous bartender pours and decadent mains like Peking duck with sustainable caviar. For dinner, count on two to three dishes per person; $15 parking available.

✖ SoMa

SENTINEL SANDWICHES $

Map p298 (☑415-769-8109; www.thesentinelsf.com; 37 New Montgomery St; sandwiches $9-12;

DOWNTOWN, CIVIC CENTER & SOMA EATING

⊙7am-2:30pm Mon-Fri; 🚇12, 14, Ⓜ️Montgomery, Ⓑ️Montgomery) Rebel SF chef Dennis Leary revolutionizes the humble sandwich with top-notch seasonal ingredients: lamb gyros get radical with pesto and eggplant, and corned beef crosses borders with Swiss cheese and house-made Russian dressing. Check the website for daily menus and call in your order, or expect a 10-minute wait – sandwiches are made to order. Enjoy in nearby Yerba Buena Gardens.

YANK SING
DIM SUM $

Map p298 (☎415-781-1111; www.yanksing.com; 101 Spear St; dim sum plates $6-14; ⊙11am-3pm Mon-Fri, 10am-4pm Sat & Sun; 🚇6, 9, 14, 21, 31, Ⓑ️Embarcadero, Ⓜ️Embarcadero) San Francisco's most iconic dim sum experience has earned its accolades, and remains the go-to choice for its pork and broth-filled Shanghai dumplings and unparalleled Peking duck by the slice. The cart service is efficient and impeccable, and the kind staff members speak fluent English, Cantonese and Mandarin. Reservations are a must.

TONY BALONEY'S
SANDWICHES $

Map p298 (☎415-863-1514; 1098 Howard St; sandwiches $3-7; ⊙6am-6pm Mon-Fri, 6:15am-4pm Sat; 🚇12, 14, 19) Long-standing mom-and-pop deli where the service couldn't be sweeter and the sandwiches still cost under $7. It's perfect for picnic supplies, and the chicken pesto sandwich is a legend. Definitely go Dutch crunch.

VIVE LA TARTE
CAFE $

Map p298 (☎415-643-5444; https://vivelatarte.com; 1160 Howard St; mains $9-18; ⊙8am-5pm; 🚇12, 14, 19) What began as a catering business out of a VW Westfalia graduated into this beloved cafe and Belgian-Californian bakery, now set in a bright, industrial-chic space with high ceilings and a wide-open kitchen. Menu standouts include rotating focaccia, pastries, quiches and heaping breakfast plates, but the best reason to stop in is the cheesecake, made with a gingery Belgian biscuit crust.

DOTTIE'S TRUE BLUE CAFÉ
AMERICAN, BREAKFAST $

Map p296 (☎415-885-2767; 28 6th St; mains $9-17; ⊙7:30am-3pm Thu, Fri, Mon & Tue, to 4pm Sat & Sun; Ⓑ️Powell, Ⓜ️Powell) Consider yourself lucky if you wait outside less than half an hour and get hit up for change only once – but fresh-baked goods come to those who wait at Dottie's. Cinnamon-ginger pancakes, grilled chili-cheddar cornbread, scrambles with whiskey-fennel sausage and other breakfast staples hot off Dottie's griddle are tried and true blue.

★IN SITU
CALIFORNIAN, INTERNATIONAL $$

Map p298 (http://insitu.sfmoma.org; 151 3rd St, SFMOMA; mains $20-50; ⊙11am-3:30pm Thu-Mon, 5-9pm Thu-Sat, 11am-3:30pm & 5-8pm Sun; 🚇5, 6, 7, 14, 19, 21, 31, 38, Ⓑ️Montgomery, Ⓜ️Montgomery) The landmark gallery of modern cuisine attached to SFMOMA also showcases avant-garde masterpieces – but these ones you'll lick clean. Chef Corey Lee collaborates with more than 100 star chefs worldwide, scrupulously recreating their signature dishes with California-grown ingredients so that you can enjoy Nathan Myhrvold's caramelized carrot soup, Tim Raue's wasabi lobster and Albert Adrià's Jasper Hill Farm cheesecake in one unforgettable sitting.

CATHEAD'S BBQ
BARBECUE $$

Map p298 (☎415-861-4242; http://catheadsbbq.com; 1665 Folsom St; mains $12-19; ⊙11am-8pm Wed-Sun; 🚇9, 12, 14, 47, Ⓜ️Van Ness) She was from Michigan; he was from Tennessee. But this BBQ-loving couple brought their respective meat traditions with them to SF and absolutely nailed it. Carnivores line up for the irresistible plates of Coca-Cola smoked brisket, pulled pork and sweet tea BBQ chicken. For the (unfortunate) vegetarians there's Maker's Mark portobello mushrooms.

COCKSCOMB
CALIFORNIAN $$

Map p298 (☎415-974-0700; http://cockscombsf.com; 564 4th St; mains $14-26; ⊙11:30am-1:45pm & 5-10:30pm Mon-Fri, 5-10:30pm Sat; ☎; 🚇30, 45, 47, Ⓜ️N, T) 🌱 Rules need not apply in San Francisco: concrete warehouses can become cozy bistros, duck-fat cauliflower and oysters are daily dietary requirements, and veggie burgers are served rare and 'bleeding' plant-based heme juice. Cockscomb's rebel chef-owner Chris Cosentino is a *Top Chef* regular and a champion of nose-to-tail dining – even the faint of heart will be converted by his beef-heart tartare.

21ST AMENDMENT BREWERY
AMERICAN $$

Map p298 (☎415-369-0900; http://21st-amendment.com; 563 2nd St; mains $10-20; ⊙kitchen 11:30am-10pm Mon-Sat, 10am-10pm Sun, bar to midnight; 🖉 🚻; 🚍10, MN,T) Perfectly placed before Giants games, 21st Amendment brews stellar IPA and Hell or High Watermelon wheat beer. The vegetarian-friendly bar-and-grill menu – pizza, beef and veggie burgers, and signature tot-chos (tater-tot nachos) – checks your buzz, but the cavernous space is so loud, nobody'll notice you're shouting. Kids get ice-cream floats made with homemade root beer. Ground zero for techies who lunch.

ZERO ZERO
PIZZA $$

Map p298 (📞415-348-8800; www.zerozerosf.com; 826 Folsom St; pizzas $13-20; ⏱11:30am-10pm Sun-Thu, to 11pm Fri & Sat; MPowell, BPowell) The name is a throw-down of pizza credentials – '00' flour is the secret to puffy-edged Neapolitan crust – and these pies deliver on that promise, with inspired SF-themed toppings. The Geary is a cross-cultural adventure involving Manila clams, bacon and Calabrian chilies, but the real crowd-pleaser is the Castro, which is fittingly loaded with house-made sausage.

★BENU
CALIFORNIAN, FUSION $$$

Map p298 (📞415-685-4860; www.benusf.com; 22 Hawthorne St; tasting menu $310; ⏱5:30-8:30pm Tue-Thu, to 9pm Fri & Sat; 🚍10, 12, 14, 30, 45) SF has pioneered Asian fusion cuisine for 150 years, but the pan-Pacific innovation chef-owner Corey Lee brings to the plate is gasp-inducing: foie-gras soup dumplings – what?! Dungeness crab and truffle custard pack such outsize flavor into Lee's faux-shark's fin soup, you'll swear Jaws is in there. A Benu dinner is an investment, but don't miss star sommelier Yoon Ha's ingenious pairings ($210).

BOULEVARD
CALIFORNIAN $$$

Map p298 (📞415-543-6084; www.boulevardrestaurant.com; 1 Mission St; mains lunch $16-30, dinner $29-54; ⏱11:30am-2pm & 5:30-9:30pm Mon-Thu, to 10pm Fri, 5:30-10pm Sat, 5:30-9:30pm Sun; MEmbarcadero, BEmbarcadero) The 1889 belle epoque Audiffred Building once housed the Coast Seamen's Union, but for 20-plus years James Beard Award–winning chef Nancy Oakes has made culinary history here. Reliably tasty, effortlessly elegant dishes include juicy wood-oven-roasted Berkshire pork prime rib chops, crisp California quail, and wild halibut with scallop prawn dumplings, plus decadent, nostalgia-inducing cakes and ice cream, and SF's best service.

1601 BAR & KITCHEN
CALIFORNIAN, FUSION $$$

Map p298 (📞415-552-1601; http://1601sf.com; 1601 Howard St; mains $23-29; ⏱5:30-10pm Tue-Thu, to 11pm Fri & Sat; 🚍9, 12, 47, MVan Ness) 🍴 Rising star chef alert: Brian Fernando is turning Sri Lankan inspirations into Californian cravings. Velvety halibut ceviche in coconut milk is an instant obsession, Marin Sun Farms goat stew with red basmati rice for two is date worthy, and you'll want the house-smoked turmeric salmon and fenugreek-chili-vinegar home fries again for breakfast. Ingenuity without pretension, and fabulous tasting menu ($110). Offerings change daily.

MOURAD
MOROCCAN, MEDITERRANEAN $$$

Map p298 (📞415-660-2500; http://mouradsf.com; 140 New Montgomery St; mains $19-40, family-style platters $75-165, tasting menu $155; ⏱11:30am-2pm & 5:30-10pm Mon-Fri, 5-10pm Sat & Sun; 🚍12, 14, BMontgomery, MMontgomery) 🍴 In the historic Pacific Telephone & Telegraph building (check out the splendid black-marble deco lobby), *Iron Chef* star Mourad Lahlou creates such conversation-starting dishes as couscous, parsnip, saffron and maitake mushroom. Moroccan family-style platters, accompanied by abundant sides, serve two to six – a taste/texture sensation, if you can agree on a protein (go lamb shoulder).

🍴 Civic Center & the Tenderloin

ARIA KOREAN TAPAS
KOREAN $

Map p296 (📞415-292-6914; https://ariasf.com; 932 Larkin St; 10 pieces of chicken $9, mains $9-11; ⏱11:30am-3pm & 4:30-9pm; 🚍19, 38, 47, 49) The space is cramped, dingy and covered in street art, including several graffiti chickens. But the Korean 'tapas' are sublime, and Aria is famous for its lip-smacking organic Korean fried chicken thighs, glazed with a garlic soy or a sweet and spicy sauce. Other favorites include the *kimbap* (Korean sushi rolls with marinated rib eye or veggies) and the *tteokbokki* (spicy rice cakes).

SAIGON SANDWICH SHOP
VIETNAMESE $

Map p296 (📞415-474-5698; 560 Larkin St; sandwiches $4-5; ⏱7am-5:30pm; 🚍19, 31) Don't get distracted by Tenderloin street scenes while you wait – be ready to order your *banh mi* (Vietnamese sandwiches) when the Saigon boss ladies call 'Next!' or you'll get skipped.

HEART OF THE CITY FARMERS MARKET

Bringing farm freshness to the city's concrete-paved center since 1981, this nonprofit, farmer-operated **market** (Map p296; www.hotcfarmersmarket. org; United Nations Plaza; ⊗7am-5:30pm Wed, to 5pm Sun; 🖭; 🚍6, 7, 9, 21, MCivic Center, BCivic Center) is on a mission to provide local, affordable, healthy food to low-income inner-city communities. Seasonal scores include organic berries from Yerena Farms, Buddha's-hand citrus from De Santis Farms and dry-farmed (water-saving) tomatoes and fruit from Miramonte Farms Organics. Bargain prices.

Act fast and be rewarded with a baguette piled high with your choice of roast pork, chicken, pâté, meatballs or tofu, plus pickled carrots, cilantro, jalapeño and thinly sliced onion.

GOLDEN ERA   VEGAN $

Map p296 (☎415-487-8687; https://goldenera vegan.com; 395 Golden Gate Ave; mains $10-13; ⊗10:30am-8:30pm; 🖋; MCivic Center, BCivic Center) You may need to step over a sleeping homeless person to enter this bright and cheerful vegan eatery, but what could possibly be more San Francisco than that? And truly, the affordable Pan-Asian soups, salads, noodle dishes, curries and stir-fried vegetables are worth it. The meatless substitute dishes are especially beloved, and pair well with teas and fresh juices.

Z ZOUL   SUDANESE $

Map p296 (☎415-757-0187; http://zzoulcafe ca.com; 295 Eddy St; mains $7-17; ⊗10:30am-9:30pm Mon-Fri, to 8:30pm Sat; 🖋; 🚍5, 6, 7, 21, 31, 🚋Powell-Mason, Powell-Hyde, BPowell, MPowell) Would you like a side of humanitarianism with that lamb shank? Brave the Tenderloin and check out San Francisco's only Sudanese restaurant, owned and operated by refugee Aref Elgaali. The gifted chef and storyteller enjoys sharing his history and his traditional foods, the most interesting of which include *kisra* (thin fermented bread) with pepper relish, *theeli* (a pureed spinach stew) and *jabana* coffee.

The coffee beans are grown near an Ethiopian camp for Sudanese refugees that Aref is proud to support, and he spices it up with cardamom and dried ginger.

RED CHILLI   NEPALI $

Map p296 (☎415-931-3529; www.redchillisf.com; 522 Jones St; mains $8-11; ⊗11:30am-10:30pm; 🚍2, 3, 27, 38) Mt Everest is for amateurs – gourmet adventurers brave the Tenderloin's mean streets for Red Chilli's bargain butter chicken, Kathmandu rolls (naan wraps) and pickle-spice lamb *achar*. Can't decide? Get rice-plate combos, but don't skip the *momos* (Nepalese dumplings). This family-run storefront diner is welcoming, charmingly kitschy and convenient before/after Bourbon & Branch (p97) cocktails – otherwise, get delivery.

ESAN CLASSIC   NORTHERN THAI $$

Map p296 (☎415-800-7646; https://esanclassic. com; 739 Larkin St; mains $10-36; ⊗11am-4pm & 5pm-midnight; 🖋; 🚍19, 31, 38, 47, 49) Do not attempt to order *pad thai* at this fashionable younger sibling of nearby **Lers Ros** (Map p296; ☎415-931-6917; www.lersros.com/ larkin; 730 Larkin St; mains $10-22; ⊗11am-midnight; 🚍19, 31, 38, 47, 49), where the 120-dish menu is inspired by the cuisine of the lesser-explored Isan region of northeastern Thailand. No. Admire the vintage motorcycle parked by the host stand, look deeply into the eyes of the oversized anime girls painted on the walls, and order the chicken innards with basil.

HOOKER'S SWEET TREATS   DESSERTS $$

Map p296 (☎415-936-5137; www.hookerssweet treats.com; 442 Hyde St; 10-piece caramel box $24; ⊗8am-2pm Tue-Fri, 10am-2pm Sat; 🚍2, 3, 19, 27, 38, 47, 49) 🖋 Bring your sweet tooth to Hookers, named in honor of generations of sweet and salty Tenderloin sex workers. Get lemon blueberry bread pudding and an espresso to have here and award-winning caramels to go - try 3rd Nut with fair-trade chocolate, pistachios and sea salt.

BRENDA'S FRENCH SOUL FOOD   CREOLE $$

Map p296 (☎415-345-8100; www.frenchsoul food.com; 652 Polk St; mains $13-19; ⊗8am-3pm Mon & Tue, to 10pm Wed-Sat, to 8pm Sun; 🚍19, 31, 38, 47, 49) Chef-owner Brenda Buenviaje blends New Orleans–style Creole cooking with French technique to invent 'French soul food.' Expect updated classics like cayenne-spiked crawfish beignets, fluffy cream biscuits, impeccable Hangtown Fry (eggs, bacon and cornmeal-crusted oysters) and fried chicken with collard greens and hot-pepper jelly. Long waits on sketchy sidewalks are unavoidable – but you can order takeout.

 DRINKING & NIGHTLIFE

Most nightclubs are in SoMa, but they're spread across a large area – don't walk in heels. The highest concentration of bars and clubs is around 11th and Folsom Sts. The SoMa scene pops on weekends and shrivels on weekdays. Financial District bars are packed from 5pm to 8pm Wednesday through Friday, empty suddenly and close by midnight. Braggadocious bro-grammers and after-hours office drama spoil the scene, and things get sloppy on Fridays. For cheaper drinks, brave the Tenderloin to swill with hipsters, free spirits and career drinkers. Prices rise as you move toward the Financial District, exceeding $12 east of Powell St.

🍷 Financial District & Jackson Square

IMPERIAL TEA COURT   TEAHOUSE
Map p301 (📱415-544-9830; www.imperialtea.com; 1 Ferry Bldg, cnr Market St & the Embarcadero; tea $6-12; ⏲10am-7pm Mon-Fri, 8am-6:30pm Sat, 10am-5pm Sun; Ⓜ Embarcadero, Ⓑ Embarcadero) Enter through the traditional moon gate, wander beneath the Chinese lanterns and have a seat at one of the rosewood tables, where you can choose from more than 100 loose-leaf teas to perfectly complement a bowl of hand-pulled noodles. The oolong selection is particularly impressive, and each is presented in a porcelain saucer as part of a Gaiwan ceremony, calling to mind the Ming Dynasty.

BIX   BAR
Map p301 (📱415-433-6300; www.bixrestaurant.com; 56 Gold St; ⏲bar 4:30-10pm Mon-Thu, 11:30am-midnight Fri, 5:30pm-midnight Sat, 5:30-10pm Sun; 🚌1, 8,10, 12, 41) Head down a Jackson Square alleyway and back in time at Bix, a speakeasy-style supper club with white-jacketed staff shaking martinis at the mahogany bar. The restaurant is open for lunch between 11:30am and 2:30pm and

again at 5:30pm for dinner. The bar is the real draw, though, with nightly live piano and jazz combos.

FERRY PLAZA WINE MERCHANT   WINE BAR
Map p301 (📱415-391-9400; www.fpwm.com; 1 Ferry Bldg, cnr Market St & the Embarcadero; ⏲11am-7pm Mon, 10am-8pm Tue, 10am-9pm Wed-Fri, 8am-8pm Sat, 10am-7pm Sun; Ⓜ Embarcadero, Ⓑ Embarcadero) Are you feeling flinty or flirty? With at least 25 wines available to try by 2oz taste or 5oz pour, as well as flights in the club series, you're bound to find a flavor profile to match your mood with ready assistance from well-informed staff. The bar is jammed Saturdays, but otherwise staff take time to introduce exciting new California releases.

🍸 Union Square

PAGAN IDOL   LOUNGE
Map p294 (📱415-985-6375; www.paganidol.com; 375 Bush St; ⏲4pm-2am Mon-Fri, from 6pm Sat; Ⓑ Montgomery, Ⓜ F, J, K, L, M) Volcanoes erupt inside Pagan Idol every half hour. Order your island cocktail and brace for impact – these tiki drinks are no joke. Flirt with disaster over a Hemingway is Dead: rum, bitters and grapefruit served in a skull. Book online to nab a hut for groups of four to six.

LOCAL EDITION   BAR
Map p294 (📱415-795-1375; www.localeditionsf.com; 691 Market St; ⏲5pm-2am Mon-Thu, from 4:30pm Fri, from 7pm Sat; Ⓜ Montgomery, Ⓑ Montgomery) Get the scoop on the SF cocktail scene at this speakeasy in the basement of the historic Hearst newspaper building. The lighting is so dim you might bump into typewriters, but that's no excuse to dodge a Good Question: a cocktail of hibiscus-infused sherry, jenever, thyme, salt, pepper and mystery. Book tables ahead for swinging live-music nights.

PACIFIC COCKTAIL HAVEN   COCKTAIL BAR
Map p294 (PCH; www.pacificcocktailsf.com; 580 Sutter St; ⏲5pm-midnight Mon, 5pm-2am Tue-Thu, 4pm-2am Fri & Sat; 🚌1, 🚋Powell-Mason, Powell-Hyde, California) Sip your way around the Pacific Rim from the comfort of your downtown San Francisco barstool. Expand your hooch horizons to the South Pacific with Lime in da Coconut (vodka, coconut, salted pistachio, lime and crushed ice) and sail off into the

sunset with the off-menu Eastern Promises (Bombay Sapphire East gin, pink pepper and lemongrass bitters).

GASPAR BRASSERIE & COGNAC ROOM
BAR

Map p294 (☑415-576-8800; http://gaspar brasserie.com; 185 Sutter St; ☺upstairs bar 5:30-10pm Mon-Fri, restaurant 11:30am-2pm & 5:30-10pm Mon-Fri; Ⓑ Montgomery, Ⓜ Montgomery) When gold-rush prospectors struck it rich, they upgraded from rotgut rye to fine French cognac – and history repeats itself nightly at Gaspar's. SF's biggest, best selection of cognac cocktails features the drop-dead-delicious (off-menu) Corpse Reviver #1 (cognac, calvados, vermouth, orange). Come boom or bust, don't miss 4:30pm to 6:30pm happy hours for $1.50 oysters and $8 wine and cocktails.

RICKHOUSE
BAR

Map p294 (☑415-398-2827; www.rickhousebar. com; 246 Kearny St; ☺5pm-2am Mon, 3pm-2am Tue-Fri, 6pm-2am Sat; Ⓜ Montgomery, Ⓑ Montgomery) Like a shotgun shack plunked downtown, Rickhouse is lined from floor to ceiling with repurposed whiskey casks imported from Kentucky and back-bar shelving from an Ozarks nunnery that once secretly brewed hooch. Cocktails are strong on whiskey and bourbon – but the Californio with gold-dust bitters does rye proud. Round up a posse to help finish that vast bowl of Admiral's Whiskey Punch.

IRISH BANK
PUB

Map p294 (☑415-788-7152; www.theirishbank. com; 10 Mark Lane; ☺11:30am-2am; Ⓜ 2, 3, 30, 45, Ⓜ Montgomery, Ⓑ Montgomery) Perfectly pulled pints and thick-cut fries with malt vinegar are staples at this cozy Irish pub, hidden inside an alleyway near the Chinatown gate. Settle into your snug for juicy burgers, brats and anything else you could want with lashings of mustard. Sociable tables beneath the alley awning are ideal for easy banter and stigma-free smoking – rare in California.

🍴 SoMa

COIN-OP
BAR

Map p298 (☑628-444-3277; http://coinopsf. com; 508 4th St; ☺4pm-2am Mon-Fri, from 2pm Sat & Sun; Ⓜ 30, 45, 47, Ⓜ N, T) Finally, someplace where introverts and extroverts can drink, flirt shyly over shuffleboard and fight off nefarious ninjas together. Pinball wizards compete for high scores, while retro video-gamers take on Street Fighter and Super Mario Brothers at throwback 1980s prices. Prepare to be wowed by the bar made of vintage TVs and the California craft beer selection during happy hour (the first two hours of operation daily).

SIGHTGLASS COFFEE
CAFE

Map p298 (☑415-861-1313; www.sightglass coffee.com; 270 7th St; ☺7am-7pm; Ⓜ 12, 14, 19, Ⓑ Civic Center, Ⓜ Civic Center) Follow cult coffee aromas into this sunny SoMa warehouse, where family-grown, high-end coffee is roasted daily. Aficionados sip signature Owl's Howl Espresso downstairs or head directly to the mezzanine Affogato Bar to get ice cream with that espresso. Daredevils should try the sparkling coffee cascara shrub – soda made with the cherry fruit of coffee plants.

BAR AGRICOLE
BAR

Map p298 (☑415-355-9400; www.baragricole. com; 355 11th St; ☺5-11pm Mon-Thu, 5pm-midnight Fri & Sat; Ⓜ 9, 12, 27, 47) 🍸 Drink your way to a history degree with well-researched cocktails: Whiz Bang with house bitters, whiskey, vermouth and absinthe scores high, but El Presidente with white rum, farmhouse curaçao and California-pomegranate grenadine takes top honors.

BLOODHOUND
BAR

Map p298 (☑415-863-2840; www.bloodhoundsf. com; 1145 Folsom St; ☺4pm-2am; Ⓜ 12, 14, 19, 27, 47) The murder of crows painted on the ceiling is an omen: nights at Bloodhound often assume mythic proportions. Vikings would feel at home amid these antler chandeliers, while bootleggers would appreciate barn-wood walls and top-shelf hooch served in mason jars. Shoot pool or chill on leather couches until your jam comes on the jukebox.

ENDUP
GAY, CLUB

Map p298 (☑415-646-0999; www.facebook. com/theendup; 401 6th St; cover $10-60; ☺11pm Fri-8am Sat, 10pm Sat-4am Mon; Ⓜ 12, 19, 27, 47) Forget Golden Gate Bridge – once you End-Up watching the sunrise over the 101 freeway ramp from this rollicking dance club's backyard oasis (complete with leafy waterfall), you've officially arrived in SF. Dance sessions are marathons fueled by EndUp's

SOMA'S LEGENDARY LGBTIQ+ SCENE

Sailors have cruised Polk St and Tenderloin gay/trans joints since the 1940s, Castro bars boomed in the 1970s and women into women have been hitting Mission dives since the '60s – but SoMa warehouses have been the biggest weekend gay scene for decades now. From leather bars and drag cabarets to full-time LGBTIQ+ clubs, SoMa has it all. True, internet cruising has thinned the herd, many women still prefer the Mission and some nights are slow starters – but the following fixtures on the gay drinking scene pack at weekends.

Eagle Tavern (Map p298; www.sf-eagle.com; 398 12th St; cover $5-10; ☺5pm-2am Mon-Thu, from 2pm Fri, from noon Sat & Sun; ▣9, 12, 27, 47) Sunday afternoons, all roads in the gay underground lead to the historic Eagle for all-you-can-drink beer busts ($15) from 3pm to 6pm. Wear leather – or flirt shamelessly – and blend right in; arrive before 3pm to beat long lines and score free BBQ. Thursdays bring mixed crowds for rockin' bands; Fridays and Saturdays range from bondage to drag. Check online.

Lone Star Saloon (Map p298; ☑415-863-9999; http://lonestarsf.com; 1354 Harrison St; ☺4pm-2am Mon-Thu, from 2pm Fri, from noon Sat & Sun; ▣9, 12, 27, 47) Like California grizzlies to a honeycomb, big guys with bushy beards pack the legendary Lone Star. There's a huge back patio and a competitive pool table, perpetually thronged by manly men and their admirers since 1989 – this is SF's original all-male bear bar. Owner-bartenders Charlie and Bruce sling $3 beers during weekday 2pm to 8pm happy hours; Sundays are jammed.

Stud (Map p298; ☑415-863-6623; www.studsf.com; 399 9th St; cover $5-8; ☺5pm-2am Tue-Thu, 5pm-4am Fri, 7pm-4am Sat, 7pm-2am Sun; ▣12, 19, 27, 47) Rocking the gay scene since 1966, the Stud makes history nightly as America's first worker-owned co-op club. Theme nights run amok, with free karaoke dance party Tuesdays and QTease burlesque shows that make Saturdays blush. Regular DJs and visual artists amp up the freak factor, and monthly Monsters on Acid parties mean lasers in the air and skid marks on the dance floor.

Powerhouse (Map p298; ☑415-522-8689; www.powerhouse-sf.com; 1347 Folsom St; cover free-$10; ☺4pm-2am Sun-Thu, from 3pm Fri & Sat; ▣9, 12, 27, 47) Thursdays through Sundays are best at Powerhouse, a sweaty SoMa bar for leathermen, shirtless gym queens and the occasional porn star. Draft beer is cheap, specials keep the crowd loose and dance erupts around the pool table at weekends. Smokers grope on the smoky back patio, while oddballs lurk in corners. Powerhouse is a gay men's scene – no gawkers.

Hole in the Wall (Map p298; ☑415-431-4695; www.holeinthewallsaloon.com; 1369 Folsom St; ☺2pm-2am Mon-Fri, from noon Sat & Sun; ▣9, 12, 47) Filthy bikers and loudmouth punks proudly call this Hole their home. The tangle of neon and bike parts hanging over the bar sets the mood amid walls plastered with vintage party handbills and erotica. Tattooed regulars give the pool table a workout. Check online for beer busts and drink specials for men who arrive on two wheels.

Club OMG (Map p298; ☑415-896-6473; www.clubomgsf.com; 43 6th St; cover free-$10; ☺5-10pm Tue, to 2am Thu & Fri, 7pm-2am Sat; Ⓜ Powell, Ⓑ Powell) Minuscule but magnetic OMG lures 20s to 40ish gays to San Francisco's skid row to get down, drink up and strip to skivvies. Latin-diva DJs make Fridays and Scandalous Sundays *muy caliente*, and the undress code is strict on Underwear Party Wednesdays. Drag shows and comedy get the party started weeknights; come early to claim two-for-one drinks at the glowing bar.

24-hour license, so Saturday nights have a way of turning into Monday mornings. Laughable bathrooms; serious weapon/drug checks.

CAT CLUB CLUB
Map p298 (☑415-703-8965; www.sfcatclub.com; 1190 Folsom St; cover free-$12; ☺9pm-3am Tue-Sat, to midnight Sun; ▣12, 19, 27, 47, Ⓜ Civic

Center, **B**Civic Center) You never really know your friends till you've seen them belt out A-ha's 'Take on Me' at Class of '84, Cat Club's Thursday-night retro dance party, where the euphoric bi/straight/gay/undefinable scene seems like an outtake from some John Hughes art-school flick. Tuesdays it's free karaoke, Wednesdays Bondage-a-Go-Go, Fridays Goth and Saturdays '80s and '90s power pop – dress the part and rock out.

CITY BEER STORE & TASTING ROOM BAR

Map p298 (⌨415-503-1033; www.citybeerstore. com; 1148 Mission St; ⊙noon-midnight; 🚍12, 14, 19) Sample exceptional local and Belgian microbrews in 6oz to 20oz pours at SF's top beer store. Mix and match a six-pack of stouts or ales to go, or join the crowd enjoying featured craft brews of the day on draft. Learn to discern sours and IPAs at brewery-hosted sipping sessions – and pace yourself with smoked trout carpaccio or a slow-roasted lamb sandwich.

111 MINNA BAR, CLUB

Map p298 (⌨415-974-1719; www.111minnagallery. com; 111 Minna St; cover free-$20; ⊙7:30-9pm Mon-Thu, to 2am Fri, 10pm-2am Sat; **M**Montgomery, **B**Montgomery) Minna St is named after a gold rush–era madam, and today 111 Minna works three jobs on this street corner: art gallery–cafe (7am to 5pm weekdays), happy-hour (3:30pm to as late as 9pm weekdays) and weekend club. Don't miss '90s hip-hop nights or Trap x Art, when artpartiers make their mark on blank canvas and the dance floor.

HOUSE OF SHIELDS BAR

Map p298 (www.thehouseofshields.com; 39 New Montgomery St; ⊙2pm-2am Mon-Fri, from 3pm Sat & Sun; **M**Montgomery, **B**Montgomery) Flash back 100 years at this gloriously restored mahogany bar with original 1908 chandeliers and old-fashioned cocktails without the frippery. You won't find any TVs or clocks, so it's easy to lose all track of time. This is one bar Nob Hill socialites and downtown bike messengers can agree on – especially over potent Sazeracs in dimly lit corners.

PAWN SHOP WINE BAR

Map p298 (⌨415-874-8041; https://thepawn shopsf.com; 993 Mission St; ⊙4-11pm Mon, to midnight Tue-Thu, to 1am Fri, 10am-midnight Sat, 10am-11pm Sun; 🚍6, 7, 9, 14, **B**Powell, **M**Powell) Pick up the golden phone and ask for 'the pawn master.' He might mess with you, but stick

to your guns and you'll be invited into a fake store filled with vintage televisions, dust-covered instruments and obscure DVDs. Then you'll duck past a display case that doubles as a secret door, and into a tapas and wine bar with a decidedly tropical vibe.

MONARCH BAR, CLUB

Map p298 (⌨415-284-9774; www.monarchsf. com; 101 6th St; ⊙5:30pm-2am Tue-Thu, to 3am Fri & Sat, 9pm-2am Sun; 🚍6, 7, 9, 14, **B**Powell, **M**Powell) A boom-town club on a skid-row block, Monarch has a plush parlor bar and a cozy library bar on the main floor, plus a downstairs dance club with killer sound system and party-ready DJs (entry $5 to $20; cash only). Upgrade from merely happy to 'amazing hours' from 5:30pm to 8:30pm weekdays, when contortionists and circus burlesque acts perform over the bar.

WATERBAR BAR

Map p298 (⌨415-284-9922; www.waterbarsf. com; 399 the Embarcadero; ⊙11:30am-9:30pm Sun & Mon, to 10pm Tue-Sat; **B**Embarcadero, **M**N, T) Waterbar's glass-column aquariums and Bay Bridge vistas are SF's surest way to impress a date over drinks. Leave the dining room to Silicon Valley start-up founders trying to impress investors and head for the oval oyster bar, where wine is $7 from 2pm to 5:30pm and a daily featured oyster is just $1.05 – including 5¢ donated to various causes.

83 PROOF BAR

Map p298 (⌨415-296-8383; www.83proof.com; 83 1st St; ⊙2pm-midnight Mon & Tue, to 2am Wed & Thu, noon-2am Fri, 8pm-2am Sat; 🚍14, **M**Montgomery, **B**Montgomery) On average weeknights when the rest of downtown is dead, you may have to shout to be heard over 83's flirtatious, buzzing crowd. High ceilings make room for five shelves of top-notch spirits behind the bar – including 300-plus whiskeys – so trust your bartender to make an old-fashioned that won't hurt at work tomorrow. Arrive early for loft seating.

1015 FOLSOM CLUB

Map p298 (⌨415-991-1015; www.1015.com; 1015 Folsom St; cover $10-30; ⊙10pm-2am Thu, to 3am Fri & Sat; 🚍12, 27) Among the city's biggest clubs, Ten Fifteen packs for marquee EDM DJs and hip-hop acts, and has seen performances from the likes of LCD Soundsystem, Virgil Abloh and Maceo Plex. Five dance floors and bars mean you'll lose your posse if you're distracted. Prepare for entry pat-downs; there's a serious no-drugs (or weapons) policy.

⚲ Civic Center & the Tenderloin

★ BOURBON & BRANCH — BAR
Map p296 (☎415-346-1735; www.bourbonand branch.com; 501 Jones St; ☺6pm-2am; 🚊27, 38) 'Don't even think of asking for a cosmo' reads the House Rules at this Prohibition-era speakeasy, recognizable by its deliciously misleading Anti-Saloon League sign. For award-winning cocktails in the liquored-up library, whisper the password ('books') at the O'Farrell entrance. Reservations required for front-room booths and Wilson & Wilson Detective Agency, the noir-themed speakeasy-within-a-speakeasy (password supplied with reservations).

★ ZOMBIE VILLAGE — COCKTAIL BAR
Map p296 (☎415-474-2284; www.thezombie village.com; 441 Jones St; ☺5pm-2am Mon-Fri, from 6pm Sat; 🚊27, 38) San Francisco probably didn't need anymore tiki bars, but we're certainly not going to complain about Zombie Village, the latest from Future Bars Group, also behind Bourbon & Branch, Rickhouse (p94) and Local Edition (p93). Guests step off the gritty Tenderloin streets and into a dark and mystical tiki wonderland, where the rum flows like wine and skulls are everywhere.

★ AUNT CHARLIE'S LOUNGE — GAY, CLUB
Map p296 (☎415-441-2922; www.auntcharlies lounge.com; 133 Turk St; cover free-$5; ☺noon-midnight Mon & Wed, to 2am Tue & Thu, to 12:30am Fri, 10am-12:30am Sat, 10am-midnight Sun; 🚊27, 31, Ⓜ Powell, Ⓑ Powell) Vintage pulp-fiction covers come to life when the Hot Boxxx Girls storm the battered stage at Aunt Charlie's on Friday and Saturday nights at 10:15pm ($5; call for reservations). Thursday is Tubesteak Connection ($5, free before 10pm), when bathhouse anthems and '80s disco draw throngs of art-school gays. Other nights bring guaranteed minor mayhem, seedy glamour and Tenderloin dive-bar shenanigans. Cash only.

RICKSHAW STOP — CLUB
Map p296 (☎415-861-2011; www.rickshawstop. com; 155 Fell St; cover $5-35; 🚊21, 47, 49, Ⓜ Van

Ness) Welcome to the high-school prom you always wanted: indie bands, DIY decor, glitter drag and '90s getups in a former TV studio. Regular events include Popscene indie bands, Brazilian breakbeat nights, Nerd Nite lecture mixers and monthly gay Asian house party GAMeBoi. Some nights welcome ages 18-plus, others 21-plus; doors open around 8pm and main acts kick off around 10pm.

RYE — LOUNGE
Map p296 (☎415-474-4448; www.ryesf.com; 688 Geary St; ☺5:30pm-2am Mon-Fri, from 6pm Sat, from 7pm Sun; 🚊2, 3, 27, 38) Swagger into this sleek sunken lounge for cocktails that look sharp and pack more heat than Steve McQueen in *Bullitt*. The soundtrack is '80s and the drinks strictly old school – bartenders mix their own rye Pimm's No 5 Cup with ginger and proper English cucumber. Come early to sip at your leisure on leather couches and leave before the smokers' cage overflows.

EDINBURGH CASTLE — PUB
Map p296 (☎415-885-4074; 950 Geary St; ☺5pm-2am; 🚊19, 38, 47, 49) Bagpiper murals on the walls, the *Trainspotting* soundtrack blaring, ale on tap, Tuesday pub quiz and vinegary fish and chips until 9pm provide all the Scottish authenticity you could ask for, short of haggis. This flag-waving bastion of drink comes fully equipped with dartboard, pool tables, DJs on Saturday and occasional comedy shows.

☆ ENTERTAINMENT

The heart of San Francisco is also its epicenter of the arts. Those passionate about symphony, opera, jazz, film, theater or ballet are served by frequent world-class performances in and around downtown, and there are also a number of venues hosting edgy comedy, dance and live music.

☆ Financial District, Union Square & Civic Center

★ SAN FRANCISCO SYMPHONY — CLASSICAL MUSIC
Map p296 (☎box office 415-864-6000, rush-ticket hotline 415-503-5577; www.sfsymphony.org;

Grove St, btwn Franklin St & Van Ness Ave; tickets $20-150; 📱21, 45, 47, Ⓜ️Van Ness, ⒷCivic Center) From the moment conductor Michael Tilson Thomas bounces up on his toes and raises his baton, the audience is on the edge of their seats for another thunderous performance by the Grammy-winning SF Symphony. Don't miss signature concerts of Beethoven and Mahler, live symphony performances with such films as *Star Trek,* and creative collaborations with artists from Elvis Costello to Metallica.

SAN FRANCISCO OPERA   OPERA

Map p296 (📞415-864-3330; www.sfopera. com; 301 Van Ness Ave, War Memorial Opera House; tickets from $10; 📱21, 45, 47, 49, ⒷCivic Center, Ⓜ️Van Ness) Opera was SF's gold-rush soundtrack – and SF Opera rivals the Met, with world premieres of original works ranging from Stephen King's *Dolores Claiborne* to *Girls of the Golden West,* filmmaker Peter Sellars' collaboration with composer John Adams. Expect haute-couture costumes and radical sets by painter David Hockney. Score $10 same-day standing-room tickets at 10am; check website for Opera Lab pop-ups.

GREAT AMERICAN MUSIC HALL   LIVE MUSIC

Map p296 (📞415-885-0750; www.gamh.com; 859 O'Farrell St; shows $20-45; ⏰box office noon-6pm Mon-Fri, 5pm-close on show nights; 🐾; 📱19, 38, 47, 49) Everyone busts out their best sets at this opulent 1907 bordello turned all-ages venue – indie rockers like the Band Perry throw down, international legends such as Salif Keita grace the stage, and John Waters hosts Christmas extravaganzas. Pay $25 extra for dinner with prime balcony seating to watch shows comfortably, or rock out with the standing-room scrum downstairs.

SAN FRANCISCO BALLET   DANCE

Map p296 (📞tickets 415-865-2000; www.sfballet. org; 301 Van Ness Ave, War Memorial Opera House; tickets $22-150; ⏰ticket sales over the phone 10am-4pm Mon-Fri; 📱5, 21, 47, 49, Ⓜ️Van Ness, ⒷCivic Center) The USA's oldest ballet company is looking sharp in more than 100 shows annually, from *The Nutcracker* (the US premiere was here) to modern originals. Performances are at the War Memorial Opera House from January to May, and you can score $15 to $20 same-day standing-room tickets at the box office (open four hours before curtain on performance days only).

AMERICAN CONSERVATORY THEATER   THEATER

Map p294 (ACT; 📞415-749-2228; www.act-sf.org; 405 Geary St; ⏰box office 10am-6pm Mon, to curtain Tue-Sun; 📱8, 30, 38, 45, 🚋Powell-Mason, Powell-Hyde, ⒷPowell, Ⓜ️Powell) Breakthrough shows launch at this turn-of-the-century landmark, which has hosted ACT's productions of Tony Kushner's *Angels in America* and Robert Wilson's *Black Rider,* with William S Burroughs' libretto and music by Tom Waits. Major playwrights like Tom Stoppard, Dustin Lance Black and Eve Ensler premiere work here, while the ACT's newer Strand Theater stages more experimental works.

PIANOFIGHT   THEATER, CABARET

Map p296 (📞415-816-3691; www.pianofight. com; 144 Taylor St; cover free-$30; ⏰5-10pm Mon & Tue, to midnight Wed & Thu, to 1am Fri & Sat; 📱5, 6, 7, 21, 31, 🚋Powell-Mason, Powell-Hyde, Ⓜ️Powell St, ⒷPowell St) Watch SF make merciless fun of itself at PianoFight supper club, featuring comedy showcases, ukulele-for-your-life Variety Show Death Matches, and Pint-Sized Plays timed to last as long as your beer. All ages welcome, and performers and audience members often mingle in the bar after the shows.

SOUNDBOX   CLASSICAL MUSIC

Map p296 (📞415-503-5299; http://sfsoundbox. com; 300 Franklin St; cover $45; ⏰9pm-midnight Fri & Sat, doors open 8pm; 📱5, 7, 21, Ⓜ️Van Ness) Once only musicians were allowed backstage at the Symphony's cavernous rehearsal space, because the acoustics weren't fit for audiences – but with digital upgrades supplying sublime sound, club-style multimedia projections, and craft cocktails, one-off performances here threaten to upstage polished Symphony Hall performances. Arrive at least 30 minutes early to nab a cocktail table; latecomers mingle on leather benches.

BAR FLUXUS   LIVE PERFORMANCE

Map p294 (📞415-421-1894; www.barfluxus.com; 18 Harlan Pl; ⏰4pm-2am Mon-Thu & Sat, from 3pm Fri, 6pm-1am Sun; ⒷMontgomery, Ⓜ️Montgomery) Hidden in an alley behind Hotel des Arts (p232), and brought to you by the folks from Madrone (p184), comes this wacky downtown art bar. The interior is color-filled and deeply saturated in quirk, with an intimate little stage that's perfect for literary events, performance art, comedy nights and even puppet shows.

AUGUST HALL
LIVE PERFORMANCE

Map p294 (Fifth Arrow; ☑415-872-5745; www.
augusthallsf.com; 420 Mason St; ☑8, 30, 38, 45,
☑Powell-Mason, Powell-Hyde, ☐Powell) In 2018
the city's newest music venue slid into the
former home of douchey nightclub Ruby
Skye, and lots of San Franciscans are happy
about it. The 15,000-sq-ft concert hall has a
revamped stage, as well as a new sound and
lighting booth, and the main floor lends itself to sweaty dancing.

BLACK CAT
JAZZ

Map p296 (☑415-358-1999; www.blackcatsf.
com; 400 Eddy St; cover $10-30; ⊙5:30pm-2am
Tue-Sun, shows 6:30pm, 8pm & 10pm; ☑27, 31)
Jazz cats have stalked the Tenderloin ever
since Miles Davis, Billie Holiday, Charlie
Parker and Dave Brubeck played underground clubs here – and Black Cat is out to
restore the laid-back, lowdown glory of the
capital of West Coast cool. Upstairs is a bar-
restaurant, but downstairs is where the action is nightly, from gypsy-klezmer be-bop
to brass-band rebellion.

STRAND THEATER
THEATER

Map p296 (☑415-749-2228; www.act-sf.org/
home/box_office/strand.html; 1127 Market St;
☑F, ☐Civic Center, ☑Civic Center) What a
comeback: this 1917 theater has shed its
1970s porn-palace notoriety and reclaimed
the limelight as the American Conservatory
Theater venue for commissioned pieces by
cutting-edge playwrights – though the scar-
let decor winks knowingly at its red-light
past. Upstairs is a prime performance space
for jazz and cabaret, with vast windows letting in moonlight and the Strand's neon
marquee glow.

WARFIELD
LIVE MUSIC

Map p296 (☑888-929-7849; www.thewarfield
theatre.com; 982 Market St; ⊙box office 10am-
4pm Sun & 90min before shows; ☑Powell, ☐Pow-
ell) Big acts with international followings
play this former vaudeville theater. Marquee
names like Wu-Tang Clan, Iggy Pop, Kanye
West and Sarah Silverman explain the line
down this seedy Tenderloin block and the
packed, pot-smoky balconies. Beer costs $9
to $10 and water $4, so you might as well get
cocktails. Street parking isn't advisable – try
the garage at 5th and Mission.

ROYALE
LOUNGE, JAZZ

Map p296 (☑415-441-4099; www.theroyalesf.com;
800 Post St; ⊙4pm-midnight Sun-Wed, to 2am Thu-

Sat; ☑2, 3, 27, 38) The pool table and TV are
mostly ignored at this artsy Parisian-style
cafe-bar, where the local crowd roars for free
live jazz, DJs, vintage soul and reggae, plus
art openings. Royale's bartender-owners
pour mean craft cocktails and local beer, and
conversationalists get served first – so switch
off your phone and make a night of it.

PUNCH LINE
COMEDY

Map p301 (☑415-397-7573; www.punchlinecom
edyclub.com; 444 Battery St; cover $15-25, plus
2-drink minimum; ⊙shows 8pm Tue-Thu & Sun,
7:30pm & 9:45pm Fri & Sat; ☑Embarcadero,
☐Embarcadero) Known for launching big talent (including Robin Williams, Chris Rock,
Ellen DeGeneres and David Cross), this
historic stand-up venue is small enough for
you to hear sighs of relief backstage when
jokes kill and teeth grind when they bomb.
Strong drinks loosen up the crowd, but you
might not be laughing tomorrow.

☆ SoMa

★ GIANTS STADIUM
BASEBALL

Map p298 (AT&T Park; ☑415-972-2000, tours 415-
972-2400; http://sanfrancisco.giants.mlb.com;
24 Willie Mays Plaza; tickets $14-349, stadium
tour adult/child/senior $22/12/17; ⊙tour times
vary; ☑; ☑N, T) Baseball fans roar April to
October at the Giants' 81 home games. As
any orange-blooded San Franciscan will
remind you, the Giants have won three
World Series since 2010 – and you'll know
the Giants are on another winning streak
when superstitious locals wear team colors
(orange and black) and bushy beards (the
Giants' rallying cry is 'Fear the Beard!').

★ OASIS
CABARET

Map p298 (☑415-795-3180; www.sfoasis.com;
298 11th St; tickets $15-35; ☑9, 12, 14, 47, ☑Van
Ness) Forget what you've learned about
drag on TV – at this dedicated dragstrav-
aganza venue, the shows are so fearless,
freaky-deaky and funny you'll laugh until
it stops hurting. In a former gay bathhouse,
drag-legendary owners Heklina and D'Arcy
Drollinger mount original shows (sometimes literally), host drag-star DJs like Sharon Needles, and perform *Star Trek, Three's
Company* and *Sex and the City* in drag.

ALONZO KING LINES BALLET
DANCE

Map p296 (☑415-863-3040; www.linesballet.
org; 26 7th St; ☑F, ☐Civic Center, ☑Civic Center)

ⓘ CATCHING A GIANTS GAME

The downside of the Giants' winning streak is that Giants (p99) games often sell out, even though the stadium is among America's most expensive ballparks – the average cost for a family of four, including hot dogs and beer, is upwards of $200. Don't despair: season-ticket holders sell unwanted tickets through the team's Double Play Ticket Window (see http://sanfrancisco.giants.mlb.com).

If you can't find tickets, consider renting a kayak (p104) to paddle around McCovey Cove and wait for a 'splash hit.' Or head to the park's eastern side along the waterfront, where you may be able to stand at the archways and watch innings for free. You'll need to show up hours early with die-hard local fans for a decent view – or be prepared to just glimpse the game and enjoy the party instead. Go Giants!

Long, lean dancers perform complicated, angular movements that showcase impeccable technical skills. Original works have included dance set to songs in endangered languages, and collaborations with poet Bob Holman and Grateful Dead drummer Mickey Hart. King also offers classes and workshops.

YERBA BUENA CENTER FOR THE ARTS
PERFORMING ARTS

Map p298 (YBCA; ☎415-978-2700; www.ybca.org; 700 Howard St; tickets free-$25; ⊙box office 11am-6pm Tue, Wed, Fri-Sun, to 8pm Thu, galleries closed Mon; ☛; ☐14, ℳPowell, ℬPowell) Rock stars would be jealous of art stars at YBCA openings, which draw overflowing crowds of art-school groupies with shows ranging from cyberpunk video art to hip-hop showdowns and Indian kathak–American tap-dance fusion freestyle. Most touring dance and jazz companies perform at YBCA's main theater (across the sidewalk from the gallery).

PUBLIC WORKS
LIVE MUSIC

Map p298 (☎415-496-6738; http://publicsf.com; 161 Erie St; ☐14, 49, ℬ16th St Mission) Go Public for story-slam nights with NPR's the Moth, appearances by Questlove, European electronica fascinators like Jan Blomqvist, SF Opera pop-up nights, and DJ sets ranging from euphoric bhangra to Honey Soundsystem queer dance parties. On-site Roll Up Gallery art shows celebrate such enduring SF obsessions as hydroponics, science fiction, Burning Man and sourdough bacteria. Cash only, despite sketchy alleyway entry.

ASIASF
CABARET

Map p298 (☎415-255-2742; www.asiasf.com; 201 9th St; from $44; ⊙7:15-11pm Wed, Thu & Sun, to 2am Fri, 5pm-2am Sat; ☐12, 14, 19, ℳCivic Center, ℬCivic Center) First ladies of the world, look out: these dazzling Asian divas can out-hostess you in half the time and half the clothes. Cocktails and Asian-inspired dishes are served with sass by AsiaSF's transgender stars. Hostesses rock the bar/runway hourly, and at weekends everyone hits the downstairs dance floor. Three-course dinners run $44 to $69 – and, honey, those tips are well earned.

DNA LOUNGE
LIVE PERFORMANCE

Map p298 (☎415-626-1409; www.dnalounge.com; 375 11th St; cover $9-35; ⊙9pm-5am; ☐9, 12, 27, 47) SF's reigning megaclub hosts bands, literary slams and big-name DJs, with two floors of late-night dance action just seedy enough to be interesting. Occasional Saturday mash-up party Bootie brings Justin/Justin (Bieber/Timberlake) jams; Fridays are Hubba-Hubba Burlesque revues and writers reading teenage diaries at Mortified; Mondays are usually Goth/industrial bands at 18-plus Death Guild. Check the calendar; early arrivals may hear crickets.

AMC METREON 16
CINEMA

Map p298 (☎415-369-6201; www.amctheatres.com; 135 4th St; adult/child $15.99/12.99; ☐14, ℳPowell, ℬPowell) Sprawling across the top floor of the Metreon mall complex, the 16-screen Metreon cinema has comfortable stadium seats with clear views of digital-projection screens, plus 3D screenings ($4 extra per ticket) and a 3D IMAX theater ($7 extra for 3D screenings). For dinner before showtime, there's a passable ground-floor food court and a Super Duper Burger out front at 783 Mission St.

HOTEL UTAH SALOON
LIVE MUSIC

Map p298 (☎415-546-6300; www.hotelutah.com; 500 4th St; cover free-$10; ⊙11:30am-2am; ☐30, 47, ℳN, T) This Victorian saloon ruled SF's '70s underground scene, when upstarts

Whoopi Goldberg and Robin Williams took to the stage – and fresh talents surface here during Monday open-mic nights, indie-label debuts and twangy weekend showcases. In the '50s the bartender graciously served Beats and drifters but snipped off suits' ties; now you can wear whatever.

MEZZANINE
LIVE MUSIC

Map p298 (☑415-625-8880; www.mezzaninesf.com; 444 Jessie St; cover $20-60; Ⓜ Powell, Ⓑ Powell) Big nights come with bragging rights at Mezzanine, with one of the city's best sound systems and crowds hyped for breakthrough shows by hip-hop greats like Wyclef and Mystikal, pop powerhouses like Lupe Fiasco, and Saturday Controvrsy dance-offs (spoiler alert for Rihanna-versus-Beyonce nights: B wins, every time). No in/out privileges.

SHOPPING

Union Square is the city's principal shopping district, with flagship stores and department stores, including international chains. Downtown shopping district borders are (roughly) Powell St (west), Sutter St (north), Kearny St (east) and Market St (south), where the Westfield mall (p24) sprawls. The epicenter of the Union Square shopping area is around Post St, near Grant Ave. Stockton St crosses Market St and becomes 4th St, flanked by flagship stores and AMC Metreon cinema and mall. For boutique offerings, head toward Jackson Sq and along Commercial St.

Financial District

★ WILLIAM STOUT ARCHITECTURAL BOOKS
BOOKS

Map p301 (☑415-391-6757; www.stoutbooks.com; 804 Montgomery St; ☺10am-6:30pm Mon-Fri, to 5:30pm Sat; 🚌1, 10, 12, 41, 🚋California) You can't fit SFMOMA into your pocket, but you can put it on your coffee table – California architectural obsessions begin at William Stout, with 1st-edition catalogs for SFMOMA designers Snøhetta and retro classics like *Cabins, Love Shacks and Other Hide-outs*. This is SF's best-kept design secret, where Apple designers and skateboard makers alike find inspiration at reasonable prices.

★ HEATH CERAMICS
HOMEWARES

Map p301 (☑415-399-9284; www.heathceramics.com; 1 Ferry Bldg, cnr Market St & the Embarcadero; ☺10am-7pm Mon-Fri, 8am-6pm Sat, 10am-5pm Sun; Ⓜ Embarcadero, Ⓑ Embarcadero) Odds are your favorite SF meal was served on Heath Ceramics, Bay Area chefs' tableware of choice ever since Alice Waters started using Heath's modern, hand-thrown dishes at Chez Panisse. Heath's muted colors and streamlined, mid-century designs stay true to Edith Heath's originals c 1948. Pieces are priced for fine dining, while studio seconds are sold at the Sausalito store.

★ RECCHIUTI CONFECTIONS
CHOCOLATE

Map p301 (☑415-834-9494; www.recchiuticonfections.com; 1 Ferry Bldg, cnr Market St & the Embarcadero; ☺10am-7pm Mon-Fri, 8am-6pm Sat, 10am-5pm Sun; Ⓜ Embarcadero, Ⓑ Embarcadero) No San Franciscan can resist award-winning Recchiuti: Pacific Heights parts with old money for its *fleur de sel* caramels; Noe Valley's foodie kids prefer S'more Bites to the campground variety; North Beach toasts to the red-wine-pairing chocolate box; and the Mission approves SF-landmark chocolates designed by Creativity Explored – proceeds benefit the Mission arts-education nonprofit for artists with developmental disabilities.

FOG CITY NEWS
BOOKS, CHOCOLATE

Map p298 (☑415-543-7400; www.fogcitynews.com; 455 Market St; ☺10am-7pm Mon-Fri, 11am-6pm Sat; Ⓜ Embarcadero, Ⓑ Embarcadero) The perfect stop before a long flight, Fog City stocks a vast variety of domestic magazines and newspapers, plus 700 international titles from 25 countries – plus a chocolate selection so big it has its own database, featuring 200-plus candy bars. Historic photos of SF line the walls between the wooden magazine racks and fridges stocked with old-fashioned bottled soda pop.

MCEVOY RANCH
FOOD

Map p301 (☑415-291-7224; www.mcevoyranch.com; 1 Ferry Bldg, cnr Market St & the Embarcadero; ☺9am-7pm Mon-Fri, 8am-6pm Sat, 10am-5pm Sun; Ⓜ Embarcadero, Ⓑ Embarcadero) In addition to its famous olive oils, this locally based marketplace inside the Ferry Building sells organic treats and all-natural body products.

GALLERY JAPONESQUE — HOMEWARES

Map p301 (📞415-391-8860; http://japonesque
gallery.com; 824 Montgomery St; ⏰10:30am-
5:30pm Tue-Fri, 11am-5pm Sat; 🚋10, 12, 41)
Wabi-sabi is the fine appreciation for im-
perfect, organic forms and materials, and
the stock in trade of Gallery Japonesque.
Owner Koichi Hara arranges antique
Japanese bamboo baskets and contemporary ceramics alongside Kaname Higa's
post-apocalyptic ballpoint-pen landscapes
and Hiromichi Iwashita's graphite-coated,
chiseled-wood panels that look like bonfire
embers.

🏠 Union Square

BRITEX FABRICS — ARTS & CRAFTS

Map p294 (📞415-392-2910; www.britexfabrics.
com; 117 Post St; ⏰10am-6pm Mon-Sat; 🚋38,
🚋Powell-Mason, Powell-Hyde, Ⓜ️Powell, Ⓑ️Pow-
ell) Since 1952, runways can't compete with
Britex' fashion drama. Designers bicker
over dibs on caution-orange chiffon, glam
rockers dig through velvet goldmines and
Hollywood costumers make vampire-movie
magic with jet buttons and hand-dyed ribbon. Fake fur flies and remnants roll as
costumers prepare for Burning Man, Hal-
loween and your average SF weekend.

WINGTIP — FASHION & ACCESSORIES

Map p301 (📞415-765-0993; http://wingtip.com;
550 Montgomery St; ⏰10am-6pm Mon-Sat;
Ⓑ️Montgomery, Ⓜ️Montgomery) Get the look of
an outdoorsy professor who invested early
in Apple at this old-school men's store in
the handsome 1908 Bank of Italy building.
Visiting power brokers will find FiDi wardrobe basics and accessories from cigars to
fly-fishing lures, and score perks: commit
to spend $1200 in-store or online and gain
access to a swanky top-floor clubhouse,
which includes a wine cave, a barber shop,
a tailor shop and a cocktail bar.

MACY'S — DEPARTMENT STORE

Map p294 (www.macys.com; 170 O'Farrell St;
⏰10am-9pm Mon-Sat, 11am-7pm Sun; 🚋Powell-
Mason, Powell-Hyde, Ⓜ️Powell, Ⓑ️Powell) Seven
floors of name brands spanning a city block
and the historic marble I Magnin building
(p83) offer charming old-school amenities – including actual powder rooms. The
strong-willed brave perfume police and
slightly insulting free-makeover offers to
reach shoe sales (totally worth it), but those

SPCA holiday windows will totally convince
anyone to adopt a kitten.

LEVI'S FLAGSHIP STORE — CLOTHING

Map p294 (📞415-501-0100; www.us.levi.com;
815 Market St; ⏰9am-9pm Mon-Sat, 10am-8pm
Sun; 🚋Powell-Mason, Powell-Hyde, Ⓜ️Powell,
Ⓑ️Powell) The flagship store in Levi Strauss'
hometown sells classic jeans that fit without fail, plus limited-edition Japanese sel-
vage pairs and remakes of Levi's original
copper-riveted miner's dungarees. Scour
discount racks for limited-edition Levi's
Made & Crafted items, as well as men's
and women's clearance sections. Hemming
costs $20.

ISAIA — CLOTHING

Map p294 (📞415-500-4930; www.isaia.it; 140
Maiden Lane; ⏰10am-6pm Mon-Sat, noon-5pm
Sun; 🚋38, Ⓑ️Powell, Ⓜ️Powell) In 2017 this upscale Italian menswear boutique slid into
San Francisco's only Frank Lloyd Wright
Building. Originally designed as a VC Morris gift shop in 1948, the store now brims
with mostly handmade cashmere blazers,
fine sweaters, smart ties and even a $10,000
wool suit.

MARGARET O'LEARY — FASHION & ACCESSORIES

Map p294 (📞415-391-1010; www.margareto
leary.com; 1 Claude Lane; ⏰10am-5pm Tue-Sat;
🚋8, 30, 45, Ⓜ️Montgomery, Ⓑ️Montgomery)
Ignorance of the fog is no excuse in San
Francisco – but should you confuse SF
for LA (the horror!) and neglect to pack
the obligatory sweater, Margaret O'Leary
will sheathe you in knitwear, no questions
asked. The SF designer's warm yet whisper-
light signatures include Scottish-cashmere
cardigans, nubby linen ponchos, studded
handbags and Ocean Beachy tie-dyed cotton pullovers.

BARNEYS — DEPARTMENT STORE

Map p294 (📞415-268-3500; www.barneys.com;
77 O'Farrell St; ⏰10am-7pm Mon-Wed & Fri, to
8pm Thu, noon-7pm Sun; 🚋Powell-Mason, Powell-Hyde, Ⓜ️Powell, Ⓑ️Powell) The West Coast
outpost of the high-end New York fashion
landmark has similar signatures, including
inspired window displays and up-to-70%-
off sales. But Barneys SF feels more boutique than department store, showcasing
emerging designers upstairs, cult fragrances downstairs and a sprawling double-floor
men's shop with shoes, jackets and man-
bags galore.

LOCAL KNOWLEDGE

SAN FRANCISCO'S HOMELESS

It's inevitable: panhandlers will ask you for spare change during your visit to San Francisco, especially around Union Sq and downtown tourist attractions. This is nothing new. Sadly, San Francisco been plagued by homelessness for as long as most residents can remember, and there are reasons for that.

Some historians date San Francisco's challenges with homelessness to the 1940s, when shell-shocked WWII Pacific Theater veterans were discharged here without sufficient support. Local homeless advocates say the real crisis in California started in the 1960s, when then-governor Ronald Reagan slashed funding to mental hospitals, drug-rehab programs and low-income-housing programs – policies he continued as president in the 1980s. Wherever the problem started, police crackdowns and a lack of appropriate social services in other cities nationwide have created a 'weed and seed' effect: homeless populations forced out of other cities come to San Francisco for its milder climate, history of tolerance and safety-net services.

Over the years, many of San Francisco City Hall's schemes to address homelessness saw minimal success. Former mayor Willie Brown proposed seizing homeless people's shopping carts – a notorious failure. Ex-mayor Gavin Newsom's controversial 2002 'Care Not Cash' policy replaced cash payments with social services, which left some San Franciscans unable to pay rent. The equally controversial 2010 'Sit/Lie Ordinance' made daytime sidewalk loitering punishable by fines, which has been disproportionately enforced with vulnerable homeless teens in the Haight.

The better news is that since 2004, the city has doubled what it spends on the homelessness problem (to a cool $300 million a year), and the homeless population fell to 7499 in 2017. A new counseling program has shown promise, and hundreds of shelter beds and supportive housing units have been added. On the streets, though, the problem feels worse than ever: the opioid epidemic has spilled addicts onto the streets, while gentrification has triggered homeless migrations within the city. Given San Francisco's growing income inequality, the problem may get worse before it gets better.

So you may well sympathize with homeless San Franciscans who ask you to share food or spare change. Whether you choose to or not, know that there are also other ways you can make an immediate difference. You can volunteer with or make a donation to an SF homeless-services organization like Glide (p85), or you could offer your services to an organization back home. Homelessness isn't a uniquely San Franciscan problem – it's a global human tragedy.

🔒 SoMa

BARBARY COAST DISPENSARY   CANNABIS
Map p298 (📞415-243-4400; https://barbary coastsf.com; 952 Mission St; ⊘8am-9:45pm; 🚌6, 7, 9, 14, Ⓑ Powell; Ⓜ Powell) At a time when most SF dispensaries still feel like clinics and give off a buzz-killing, prescription-only vibe, this place feels decidedly recreational. The red tufted booths and antique chandeliers will have you feeling like you stepped into a steampunk Victorian apothecary, and the budtenders are friendly people who know their weed.

MR S LEATHER   ADULT
Map p298 (📞415-863-7764; www.mr-s-leather. com; 385 8th St; ⊘11am-8pm; 🚌12, 19, 27, 47) Only in San Francisco would you find an S&M superstore, with such musts as suspension stirrups, latex hoods and, for that special someone, a chrome-plated codpiece. If you've been a very bad puppy, there's an entire doghouse department catering to you, and gluttons for punishment will find home-decor inspiration in dungeon furniture.

SAN FRANCISCO RAILWAY MUSEUM GIFT SHOP   GIFTS & SOUVENIRS
Map p298 (📞415-974-1948; www.streetcar.org/ museum; 77 Steuart St; ⊘10am-5pm Tue-Sun; 🚇Embarcadero, Ⓑ Embarcadero) The next best thing to taking an SF cable car home with you is getting a toy streetcar from this tiny, free Municipal Railway museum showcasing SF public transit. Earn instant SF street cred with baseball caps and T-shirts emblazoned with Muni slogans, including everyone's favorite: 'Information gladly given,

but safety requires avoiding unnecessary conversation.'

🔒 Civic Center & the Tenderloin

HERO SHOP FASHION & ACCESSORIES
Map p296 (☎415-829-3129; http://heroshopsf.com; 982 Post St; ☉11am-7pm Mon-Sat; ☐2, 3, 19, 27, 38, 47, 49) On the cutting edge of the Tenderloin, Hero transforms casual browsers into SF fashionistas with statement pieces by rising-star local designers: Stevie Howell's boho silk tunics, Future Glory's handmade marbled-leather handbags, Culk's souvenir sweatshirts. It's no accident Hero's selection seems unusually well edited – owner Emily Holt left her job as *Vogue*'s fashion-trend editor to open this boutique.

GENERAL BEAD JEWELRY, GIFTS
Map p298 (☎415-621-8187; www.etsy.com/shop/generalbead; 637 Minna St; ☉noon-6pm; ☐14, 19, Ⓜ Civic Center, Ⓑ Civic Center) Wild beading ambitions strike suddenly within these walls lined with bulk beads, inducing visions of DIY drag and handmade holiday gifts like sparkling mirages: multi-tiered necklaces, sequined samba costumes, mosaic frames, fringed lampshades that double as hats...To practice restraint, order smaller quantities downstairs from beadbedecked staff behind the counter, who will ring up your sale on bejeweled calculators.

THE MAGAZINE BOOKS
Map p296 (☎415-441-7737; www.themagazinesf.com; 920 Larkin St; ☉noon-7pm Tue-Sat; ☐19, 38, 47, 49) The mother lode of magazines since 1973. The Magazine's old wooden shelves barely contain all the 1940s pinup mags, 1950s *Vogue,* trippy 1960s underground hippie newspapers, 1970s Italian boxing fanzines and '80s new-wave music 'zines – plus a back room packed with early issues of *Playboy* and vintage gay erotica. Many titles cost under a buck, and few are over $15.

🏃 SPORTS & ACTIVITIES

Walking and cycling tours dominate the scene downtown, but you'll also find plenty of outdoor adventure, including kayaking and sailing in SoMa, a plethora of activity at the Yerba Buena Center and a fantastic Tenderloin bathhouse.

★ DANDYHORSE SF BIKE TOURS CYCLING
Map p298 (☎415-890-2453; www.dandysftours.com; 33 Gordon St; tours from $69; ☉8am-7pm; ☐12, 19, 27, 47) The ultimate embodiment of San Francisco's DIY spirit, local resident Nick Normuth custom-built a bunch of bikes, studied up on the city and started a cycling tour. The adventure begins in an adorable headquarters in SoMa, and branches out to the Mission, the Castro, Golden Gate Park and beyond, depending on which tour you've signed up for.

EMPEROR NORTON'S FANTASTIC TIME MACHINE WALKING
Map p294 (☎415-548-1710; www.sftimemachine.com; $30; ☉11am Thu & Sat, waterfront tour 11am Sun; ☐30, 38, Ⓑ Powell St, Ⓜ Powell St, 🚋 Powell-Mason, Powell-Hyde) Huzzah, San Francisco invented time-travel contraptions! They're called shoes, and you wear them to follow the self-appointed Emperor Norton (aka historian Joseph Amster) across 2 miles of the most dastardly, scheming, uplifting and urban-legendary terrain on Earth... or at least west of Berkeley. Sunday waterfront tours depart from the Ferry Building; all others depart from Union Sq's Dewey Monument.

TENDERLOIN MUSEUM WALKING TOURS WALKING
Map p296 (☎415-351-1912; www.tenderloinmuseum.org/tours; 398 Eddy St; adult/with museum admission/night tour $10/15/20; ☉2pm Tue-Sun, 21+ night tour 6pm 1st & 3rd Wed; Ⓑ Powell, Ⓜ Powell, 🚋 Powell-Mason, Powell-Hyde) The Tenderloin's notoriety as a red-light district keeps tourists from witnessing historic sites where Muhammad Ali boxed, Miles Davis recorded, and LGBTIQ+ activists fought for their right to be served in cafeterias – and established America's first Transgender Historic District. Resident Tenderloin Museum historians lead intrepid visitors past these and other groundbreaking Tenderloin locales; walking shoes and city smarts essential.

CITY KAYAK KAYAKING
Map p298 (☎888-966-0953, 415-294-1050; www.citykayak.com; Pier 40, South Beach Harbor; kayak rentals per hr $35-125, lesson & rental $54, tours $54-89; ☉rentals noon-3pm, return by 5pm Thu-Mon; ☐30, 45, Ⓜ N, T) You haven't seen

San Francisco until you've seen it from the water. Newbies to kayaking can take lessons and paddle calm waters near the Bay Bridge; experienced paddlers can rent kayaks to brave currents near the Golden Gate (conditions permitting; get advice first). Sporty romantics: twilight tours past the Bay Bridge lights are ideal for proposals. Check website for details.

STAGECOACH GREENS   MINIGOLF

Map p298 (ParkLab Greens, Spark Social SF; ☑415-310-3246; www.parklab.com/spark-social-sf; 1379 4th St; golf admission adult/child under 12 $16/10; ☺11am-9pm Tue-Sun; 🚼; 🚌55, Ⓜ T) An outdoor mini-golf course might sound ill-advised in chilly, foggy San Francisco, but what if you added a beer garden? And brought in two dozen food trucks? And nearby there were fire pits surrounded by swings, and you could request s'mores service? Enter ParkLab Greens and Spark Social FL, a couple of partnering, neighboring community spaces filled with fun stuff that happens to include this 18-hole, boom-and-bust-of-the-West–inspired course.

ONSEN BATH   BATHHOUSE

Map p296 (☑415-441-4987; www.onsensf.com; 466 Eddy St; 1¾hr bath $35; ☺3:30-10pm Mon & Wed, from 11am-10pm Thu & Fri, 10am-10pm Sat & Sun; 🚌19, 31, 38, Ⓑ Civic Center, Ⓜ Civic Center) Hot-tubbing is a California custom that predates the swinging '70s and hippie '60s, with Victorian-era Sutro Baths and *onsen* (spa baths) founded by SF's Japanese American pioneers. Cultivate your own authentic California glow in Onsen's redwood and cedar saunas, a communal tub, cold plunge shower and cozy teahouse and Japanese restaurant.

YERBA BUENA ICE SKATING
& BOWLING CENTER   SKATING, BOWLING

Map p298 (☑415-820-3541; www.skatebowl. com; 750 Folsom St; skating adult/child under 6 $12.50/8, skate rental $5.50, bowling per lane per hr $22-48, shoe rental $5.75; ☺noon-9pm Sun & Mon, to 10pm Tue-Thu, to midnight Fri & Sat; 🚼; 🚌14, Ⓜ Powell, Ⓑ Powell) While the suits are working the floor at Moscone Convention Center, upstairs you can skate carefree figure eights or throw strikes at this rooftop family-fun center. Book bowling lanes ahead – especially for glow-in-the-dark Ultra Bowling. Check website or call for availability and deals, including a $23 per lane happy hour bowl, with free shoe rentals (4pm to 6pm on Tuesday and Wednesday).

SPINNAKER SAILING   BOATING

Map p298 (☑415-543-7333; www.spinnaker-sailing.com; Pier 40, South Beach Harbor; skippered charters from $445, lessons from $338; ☺10am-5pm; 🚌30, 45, Ⓜ N, T) Do 'luff', 'cringle' and 'helms-a-lee' mean anything to you? If yes, captain a boat from Spinnaker and sail into the sunset. If not, charter a skippered vessel or take classes and learn to talk like a sailor – in a good way.

Powell-Hyde (Friedel Klussmann) Cable Car Turnaround ⑤ ⑥

Powell-Mason Cable Car Turnaround ④

Beach St

North Point St

The Embarcadero (Herb Caen Way)

San Francisco Bay

0 — 1 km
0 — 0.5 miles

Bay St

NORTH BEACH

Filbert St ⑦

Grant Ave ⑧

Columbus Ave

Stockton St

Battery St

Sansome St

Broadway

Lombard St

Van Ness Ave

Powell-Hyde St Cable Car Line ③

Powell-Mason St Cable Car Line

Jones St

California St Cable Car Turnaround END ⑩

Broadway

Jackson St
Washington St

NOB HILL

California St Cable Car Line

⑨ **CHINATOWN**

Ⓜ Ⓑ Embarcadero

California St
Pine St
Bush St

California St Cable Car Turnaround

② Powell-Mason & Powell-Hyde St Cable Car Lines

Bush St

Market St

Folsom St Ⓜ

Ⓜ Ⓑ Montgomery St

Geary St

Powell St
Mason St

Hyde St

Geary Blvd

① Ⓜ Ⓑ Powell St
START

Brannan St Ⓜ

JOSEPH M. ARSENEAU / SHUTTERSTOCK ©

San Francisco by Cable Car

The ultimate SF joyride is in a cable car, San Francisco's steampunk public transit. These wood-trimmed trollies may look like throwbacks to the Victorian era, and in fact they're relatively unchanged since their invention in 1873. But the cable car remains the peak technology to conquer San Francisco's steep hills.

At the ❶ **Powell St Cable Car Turnaround** (p127), you'll see operators turn the car atop a revolving wooden platform and a vintage kiosk where you can buy an all-day Muni Passport for $23, instead of paying $7 per ride. Board the red-signed Powell-Hyde cable car and begin your 338ft ascent of Nob Hill.

As your cable car lurches uphill, you can imagine horses struggling up this slippery crag. Nineteenth-century city planners were skeptical of inventor Andrew Hallidie's 'wire-rope railway' – but after more than a century of near-continuous operation, his wire-and-hemp cables have seldom broken. Hallidie's cable cars even survived the 1906 earthquake and fire that destroyed 'Snob Hill; mansions, returning the faithful to the rebuilt ❷ **Grace Cathedral** (p128) – hop off to say hello to SF's gentle patron St Francis, carved by sculptor Beniamino Bufano.

Back on the Powell-Hyde car, enjoy Bay views as you careen past crooked, flower-lined ❸ **Lombard Street** (p129) toward ❹ **Fisherman's Wharf** (p61). Hop off to explore the ❺ **USS Pampanito** (p63) and witness Western saloon brawls in vintage arcade games at the ❻ **Musée Mécanique** (p62) before hitching the Powell-Mason cable car to North Beach.

Check out Diego Rivera's 1934 cityscape at the ❼ **San Francisco Art Institute** (p129), or follow your rumbling stomach directly to ❽ **Liguria Bakery** (p116). Stroll through North Beach and Chinatown alleyways, or take the Powell-Mason line to time-travel through the ❾ **Chinese Historical Society of America** (p112). Nearby, catch a ride on the city's oldest line: the California St cable car to the terminus near the ❿ **Ferry Building** (p78).

BENNYMARTY / GETTY IMAGES ©

Top: Powell-Hyde cable car turnaround
Bottom: Passing Bush St, traveling along Powell

North Beach & Chinatown

Neighborhood Top Five

1 **Chinatown Alleyways** (p115) Hearing mah-jongg tiles, temple gongs and Chinese orchestras as you wander story-filled SF backstreets.

2 **Coit Tower** (p110) Climbing Filbert Street Steps past heckling parrots and fragrant gardens to this panoramic, mural-lined tower.

3 **City Lights Books** (p111) Reflecting in the Poet's Chair and celebrating free speech.

4 **Chinese Historical Society of America** (p112) Time-traveling through old Chinatown at this museum, housed in the historic Julia Morgan–designed Chinatown YWCA.

5 **Li Po** (p121) Picking up where Jack Kerouac and Allen Ginsberg left off at a historic Beat hangout.

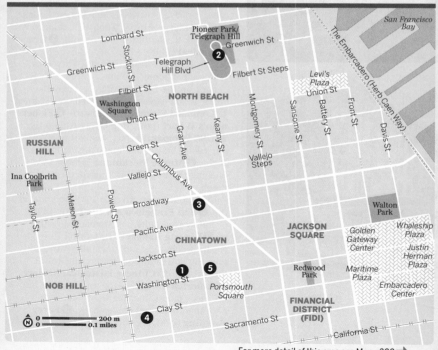

For more detail of this area see Map p308 ➡

Explore North Beach & Chinatown

From downtown, enter Dragon's Gate (p113) onto Chinatown's main tourist drag, Grant Ave. Hard to believe this pagoda-topped, souvenir-shopping strip was once the wildest spot in the West – at least until you see the fascinating displays at the Chinese Historical Society of America (p112). Duck into Chinatown's historic alleyways to glimpse a neighborhood that's survived against daunting odds, then detour for dim sum at City View (p119). Cross into North Beach via Jack Kerouac Alley (p111) and City Lights (p111), birthplace of Beat literature. Fuel up with espresso at Caffe Trieste (p120) for your North Beach Beat walking tour, and hike the garden-lined Filbert Street Steps (p110) to giddy panoramas and daring murals at Coit Tower (p110). Descend for a bar crawl and a hot slice at Golden Boy (p116) or a proper feast at Mister Jiu's (p119).

Local Life

Hangouts Join regular crowds of poets at Caffe Trieste (p120), martial-arts masters at Washington Square (p111) and skaters at Old St Mary's Square (p112).

Foodie discoveries Even been-there, ate-that San Franciscans find new taste sensations at Z & Y (p119), Mister Jiu's (p119) and China Live (p117).

Local celebrity sightings Keep an eye out for Sean Penn at Tosca Cafe (p117), Sofia Coppola at Columbus Tower (p112), Tom Waits and Carlos Santana at 101 Music (p123) and Countess Lola Montez reincarnated at Drag Me Along Tours (p121).

Five-buck bargains Fly a butterfly kite from Chinatown Kite Shop (p123), carbo-load at Liguria Bakery (p116) and drink beer with atmosphere at Specs (p120).

Getting There & Away

Muni The newly extended T line streetcar service links Chinatown and North Beach to Downtown and Dogpatch.

Bus Key routes passing through Chinatown and North Beach are 1, 10, 12, 30, 39, 41 and 45.

Cable car From downtown or Fisherman's Wharf, take the Powell-Mason or the Powell-Hyde line through Chinatown and North Beach. The California St cable car passes through the southern end of Chinatown.

Lonely Planet's Top Tip

Wild hawks and parrots circle above North Beach, as if they too were looking for a parking spot. The weekend parking situation is so dire that locals avoid North Beach and Chinatown – forgetting there's public parking underneath Portsmouth Sq and at **Good Luck Parking Garage**, where spots are stenciled with fortune-cookie wisdom: 'You have found the love of your life. Stop looking.'

 Best for Art

→ City Lights Books (p111)
→ Coit Tower (p110)
→ Jack Kerouac Alley (p111)
→ Li Po (p121)

 Best Places to Eat

→ Golden Boy (p116)
→ Good Mong Kok (p119)
→ Liguria Bakery (p116)
→ Mister Jiu's (p119)
→ Z & Y (p119)
→ Molinari (p116)

For reviews, see p113.

 Best Places to Drink

→ Specs (p120)
→ Comstock Saloon (p120)
→ Li Po (p121)
→ Vesuvio (p120)
→ Devil's Acre (p120)
→ Caffe Trieste (p120)

For reviews, see p119. →

NORTH BEACH & CHINATOWN

TOP SIGHT
COIT TOWER

The exclamation point on San Francisco's skyline is Coit Tower, the stark white deco building that firefighting millionaire Lillie Hitchcock Coit left her fortune to build as a monument to SF firefighters.

The tower's lobby murals depict city life during the Depression: people lining up at soup kitchens, organizing dockworkers' unions, partying despite Prohibition and reading books – including Marxist manifestos – in Chinese, Italian and English.

When they were completed in 1934, these federally funded artworks were controversial. Authorities denounced the 26 artists that painted them as communists, and demanded that radical elements be removed. The artists refused, and in a last-minute compromise, park employees painted over one hammer-and-sickle symbol.

The censors were overruled: San Franciscans embraced the murals as symbols of the city's openness. In 2012 voters passed a measure to preserve them as historic landmarks, and today the murals are freshly restored – and as bold as ever.

In the 19th century, a ruthless entrepreneur began quarrying and blasting away roads on the side of Telegraph Hill. City Hall eventually stopped the quarrying, but the view of the bay from the **Filbert Street Steps** (Map p308; 🚌39) is still (wait for it) dynamite. The steep climb leads past hidden cottages along Napier Lane, sweeping Bay Bridge vistas and colorful wild-parrot flocks.

DON'T MISS

➡ Uncensored, bold murals that show SF as it was – parties, protests and all
➡ 360-degree viewing-platform panorama
➡ Bay views and sculpture gardens along Filbert St Steps
➡ Secret murals revealed on stairway mural tours

PRACTICALITIES

➡ Map p308, D2
➡ ☎415-249-0995
➡ www.sfrecpark.org
➡ Telegraph Hill Blvd
➡ nonresident elevator fee adult/child $8/5, mural tour full/2nd fl only $8/5
➡ ⏱10am-6pm Apr-Oct, to 5pm Nov-Mar
➡ 🚌39

◉ SIGHTS

Standing atop the Filbert St Steps, you can understand what Italian fishermen, Beat poets and wild parrots saw in North Beach: there's more sky than ground here, and it's sociable but never entirely tamed. Coit Tower punctuates the scenery, lifting North Beach out of the fog of everyday life.

Across Columbus Ave is Chinatown, survivor of gold booms and busts, anti-Chinese riots, bootlegging wars and trials by fire and earthquake. Yet Chinatown repeatedly made history, providing labor for America's first cross-country railroad, rebuilding San Francisco and leading the charge for China's revolution and US civil rights.

◉ North Beach

COIT TOWER   PUBLIC ART
See p110.

★CITY LIGHTS BOOKS   CULTURAL CENTER
Map p308 (☑415-362-8193; www.citylights.com; 261 Columbus Ave; ☺10am-midnight; ♿; ☒8, 10, 12, 30, 41, 45, ☐Powell-Mason, Powell-Hyde, Ⓜ︎T)
Free speech and free spirits have rejoiced here since 1957, when City Lights founder and poet Lawrence Ferlinghetti and manager Shigeyoshi Murao won a landmark ruling defending their right to publish Allen Ginsberg's magnificent epic poem *Howl*. Celebrate your freedom to read freely in the designated Poet's Chair upstairs overlooking Jack Kerouac Alley, load up on zines on the mezzanine and entertain radical ideas downstairs in the new Pedagogies of Resistance section.

MULE GALLERY   GALLERY
Map p308 (☑415-543-2789; http://mulegallery. com; 80 Fresno St; ☺1-6pm Wed-Fri; ☒8, 10, 12, 41, ☐Powell-Mason, Ⓜ︎T) **FREE** Upstart San Francisco artists buck art-world trends and kick out brave new work at the backstreet Mule Gallery. Recent shows have featured artworks by Bay Area letterpress printers, and 'craftivism' workshops with textile artist Diana Weymar to embroider presidential tweets onto vintage children's book illustrations. Check the website for upcoming salon conversations with SF artists and activists.

BEAT MUSEUM   MUSEUM
Map p308 (☑800-537-6822; www.kerouac.com; 540 Broadway; adult/student $8/5, walking tours $30; ☺museum 10am-7pm, walking tours 2-4pm Sat; ☒8, 10, 12, 30, 41, 45, ☐Powell-Mason, Ⓜ︎T)
The closest you can get to the complete Beat experience without breaking a law. The 1000-plus artifacts in this museum's literary-ephemera collection include the sublime (the banned edition of Ginsberg's *Howl*, with the author's own annotations) and the ridiculous (those Kerouac bobblehead dolls are definite head-shakers). Downstairs, watch Beat-era films in ramshackle theater seats redolent with the odors of literary giants, pets and pot. Upstairs, pay your respects at shrines to individual Beat writers. A seismic retrofit may mean closures; call ahead.

JACK KEROUAC ALLEY   STREET
Map p308 (btwn Grant & Columbus Aves; ☒8, 10, 12, 30, 41, 45, ☐Powell-Mason) 'The air was soft, the stars so fine, the promise of every cobbled alley so great...' This ode by the *On the Road* and *Dharma Bums* author is embedded in his namesake alley, a fittingly poetic, streetwise shortcut between Chinatown and North Beach via his favorite haunts City Lights, Vesuvio (p120) and a stool near the golden Buddha statue at Li Po (p121) – Kerouac was a true believer in literature, Buddhism, and beer.

BOB KAUFMAN ALLEY   STREET
Map p308 (🚻; ☒8, 10, 12, 30, 41, 45, ☐Powell-Mason, Ⓜ︎T) What's that – your hometown *doesn't* have a street named after an African American Catholic-Jewish-voodoo anarchist street poet? Revered in France as the American Rimbaud, Bob Kaufman co-founded legendary *Beatitudes* magazine in 1959 and was a prolific spoken-word jazz artist. Yet he took a Buddhist vow of silence after John F Kennedy's assassination that he kept until the Vietnam War ended – 12 years later. This hidden alleyway (off Grant Ave near Filbert St) duly honors him: it's offbeat, streetwise and often profoundly silent.

WASHINGTON SQUARE   PARK
Map p308 (http://sfrecpark.org/destination/ washington-square; cnr Columbus Ave & Union St; ☒8, 30, 39, 41, 45, ☐Powell-Mason, Ⓜ︎T) Wild parrots, tai chi masters, and nonagenarian churchgoing *nonnas* (grandmothers) are the local company you'll keep on this lively patch of lawn. This was the city's earliest

official park, built in 1850 on the ranch-land of pioneering entrepreneur and San Francisco founder Juana Briones – there's a bench dedicated to her. Parrots keep their distance in the treetops, but like anyone else in North Beach, they can probably be bribed into friendship with a focaccia from Liguria Bakery (p116), on the square's northeastern corner.

COLUMBUS TOWER   HISTORIC BUILDING

Map p308 (Sentinel Building; 916 Kearny St; 🚌8, 10, 12, 30, 41, 45, 🚃California, Ⓜ T) If these copper-clad walls could talk, they'd name-drop shamelessly. The tower's original oc-cupant was political boss Abe Ruef, ousted in 1907 and sent to San Quentin for brib-ing city supervisors. Grammy-winning folk group the Kingston Trio bought the tower in the 1960s, and the Grateful Dead recorded in the basement. Since 1972 it's been owned by *Godfather* director Francis Ford Coppola, who shares offices with *Joy Luck Club* director Wayne Wang and Oscar-winning actor-director Sean Penn. Coppola runs ground-floor Cafe Zoetrope (p121).

◉ Chinatown

CHINATOWN ALLEYWAYS   AREA
See p115.

★CHINESE HISTORICAL SOCIETY OF AMERICA   MUSEUM

Map p308 (CHSA; ☎415-391-1188; www.chsa.org; 965 Clay St; ⊙noon-5pm Tue-Fri, 11am-4pm Sat & Sun; ♿; 🚌1, 8, 30, 45, 🚃California, Powell-Mason, Powell-Hyde, Ⓜ T) FREE Picture what it was like to be Chinese in America during the gold rush, transcontinental railroad construc-tion, and Beat heyday in this 1932 landmark, built as Chinatown's YWCA. CHSA histori-ans unearth fascinating artifacts: 1920s silk *qipao* dresses, WWII Chinatown nightclub posters, and Frank Wong's Chinatown min-iatures. Exhibits share personal insights and historical perspectives on Chinese American historical milestones – including the Civil Rights movement, Cold War, and Chinese Exclusion Act, which officially excluded Chi-nese immigrants from US citizenship and civil rights from 1882 to 1943.

CHINESE CULTURE CENTER   GALLERY

Map p308 (☎415-986-1822; www.cccsf.us; Hilton Hotel, 3rd fl, 750 Kearny St; suggested donation $5; ⊙during exhibitions 10am-4pm Tue-Sat; ♿; 🚌1,

8, 10, 12, 30, 41, 45, 🚃California, Powell-Mason, Powell-Hyde, Ⓜ T) You can see all the way to China from the Hilton's 3rd floor inside this cultural center, which hosts exhibits rang-ing from showcases of contemporary Chi-nese ink-brush painters to installations of kung-fu punching bags studded with fight-ing words. In odd-numbered years, don't miss Present Tense Biennial, where 30-plus Bay Area artists present personal takes on Chinese culture. Visit the Center's satellite gallery at 41 Ross Alley for contemporary collaborations; for local historical perspec-tives, book the Center's Chinatown Heritage Walking Tours (p121).

TIN HOW TEMPLE   TEMPLE

Map p308 (Tien Hau Temple; 125 Waverly Pl; do-nation customary; ⊙10am-4pm, except holidays; 🚌1, 8, 30, 45, 🚃California, Powell-Mason, Powell-Hyde) There was no place to go but up in Chinatown in the 19th century, when laws restricted where Chinese San Franciscans could live and work. Atop barber shops, laundries and diners lining Waverly Pl (p115), you'll spot lantern-festooned balco-nies of temples – including Tin How Tem-ple, built in 1852. Its altar miraculously survived the 1906 earthquake. To pay your respects, follow sandalwood-incense aro-mas up three flights of stairs. Entry is free, but offerings are customary for temple up-keep. No photography inside, please.

CHINESE TELEPHONE EXCHANGE   HISTORIC BUILDING

Map p308 (743 Washington St; 🚌1, 30, 45, 🚃Cali-fornia, Powell-Hyde, Powell-Mason, Ⓜ T) Califor-nia's earliest high-tech adopters weren't 1970s Silicon Valley programmers – they were Chinatown switchboard operators c 1894. To connect callers, operators spoke six languages fluently and memorized 1500-plus Chinatown residents by name, residence and occupation. Managers lived at the pagoda-topped exchange, operating the switchboard 365 days a year until 1949. Since people born in China were prohibited from entering the US during the 1882–1943 Chinese Exclusion era, the exchange pro-vided Chinatown residents with their only family contact for 60 years.

OLD ST MARY'S CATHEDRAL & SQUARE   CHURCH

Map p308 (☎415-288-3800; www.oldsaintmarys. org; 660 California St; ⊙11am-6pm Mon & Tue, to 7pm Wed-Fri, 9am-6:30pm Sat, to 4:30pm

CHINATOWN'S CLINKER-BRICK ARCHITECTURE

As you walk through Chinatown, take a close look at the brick buildings around you. Some of the bricks are blackened, twisted and bubbled. You might notice bricks jutting out from the wall at odd angles, because they're not flat enough to be laid flush. You've spotted clinker bricks, warped and discolored by fire over a century ago.

Clinker bricks are part of Chinatown's extraordinary survival story. Chinatown was originally largely built by non-Chinese landlords in cheap, unreinforced brick – and when the great 1906 earthquake hit, those buildings toppled. Fire swept Chinatown at such high temperatures that the bricks began to melt and turn glassy, becoming clinker bricks. Many residents returned to find they had lost everything – their homes, workplaces, social centers, churches and temples were reduced to rubble. The streets were choked with clinker bricks.

Bricklayers typically toss out over-fired clinker bricks as defective, because they're hard to lay straight and don't insulate well – but Chinatown couldn't wait for better materials to start rebuilding. With the backing of City Hall, ruthless developers like Abe Ruef – of Columbus Tower fame – were conspiring to relocate Chinatown outside San Francisco. When Chinatown residents caught wind of the plan, they marched back into their still-smoking neighborhood, cleared the streets, and started rebuilding Chinatown, brick by brick. They made ingenious use of warped bricks others would consider useless, turning them on their ends to create decorative patterns.

Chinatown not only stood its ground – it made an architectural statement. Architect Julia Morgan incorporated clinker bricks as a poignant decorative motif for Chinatown's 1908 Donaldina Cameron House (920 Sacramento St), a refuge for women and children who escaped indentured servitude. Chinatown's architecture of survival soon became a signature of California's 1920s Arts and Crafts movement, and today clinker bricks can be seen on religious buildings and family homes across the state.

Sun; 🚌1, 30, 45, 🚋California) California's first cathedral was started in 1853 by an Irish entrepreneur determined to give wayward San Francisco some religion - despite the cathedral's location on brothel-lined Dupont St. The 1906 earthquake miraculously spared the church's brick walls but destroyed a bordello across the street, making room for St Mary's Sq. Today, skateboarders do tricks of a different sort in the park, under the watchful eye of Beniamino Bufano's 1929 pink-granite-and-steel statue of Chinese revolutionary Sun Yat-sen.

PORTSMOUTH SQUARE
PARK

Map p308 (http://sfrecpark.org/destination/portsmouth-square; cnr Washington St & Walter Lum Pl; 🅿 ♿; 🚌1, 8, 10, 12, 30, 41, 45, 🚋California, Powell-Hyde, Powell-Mason, Ⓜ T) Chinatown's unofficial living room is named after John B Montgomery's sloop, which staked the US claim on San Francisco in 1846. SF's first city hall moved into Portsmouth Sq's burlesque Jenny Lind Theater in 1852, and today the square is graced by the Goddess of Democracy, a bronze replica of the statue that Tiananmen Sq protesters made in 1989. Tai chi practitioners greet the dawn,

toddlers rush the playground at noon and chess players plot moves well into the night.

DRAGON'S GATE
MONUMENT

Map p308 (cnr Grant Ave & Bush St; 🚌1, 8, 30, 45, 🚋California, Ⓜ T) Enter through the Dragon archway donated by Taiwan in 1970, and you'll find yourself on the street formerly known as Dupont in its notorious red-light heyday. The pagoda-topped 'Chinatown deco' architecture beyond this gate was innovated by Chinatown merchants led by Look Tin Ely in the 1920s – a pioneering initiative to lure tourists with a distinctive modern look. It worked: dragon streetlights chased away shady characters, and now light the way to bargain souvenirs and tea shops.

✖ EATING

Fair warning: in the picturesque, historic neighborhoods of Chinatown & North Beach, a crowd outside a restaurant may not be an indication of quality, but Instagrammability, familiarity and/or price. Chinatown restaurants pack on weekends for dim sum – go early or late.

MARINZOLICH / GETTY IMAGES ©

Asian

1. The Transamerica Pyramid (p82) from Chinatown
2. Spofford Alley 3. Ross Alley 4. Waverly Place

Chinatown Alleyways

The 41 historic alleyways packed into Chinatown's 22 blocks have seen it all since 1849: gold rushes and revolution, incense and opium, fire and icy receptions. These narrow backstreets are lined with towering buildings because there was nowhere to go but up in Chinatown after 1870, when laws limited Chinese immigration, employment and housing.

Waverly Place

The soul of Chinatown is **Waverly Place** (🚌1, 30, 🚋California, Powell-Mason, Ⓜ️T) and its historic clinker-brick buildings and flag-festooned temple balconies. Services have been held on the street's Tin How Temple (p112) since 1852 – even after San Francisco's 1906 earthquake and fire, when altars were still smoldering.

Ross Alley

Colorful murals hint at the colorful gold rush characters who once roamed SF's oldest alleyway. More recently **Ross Alley** (🚌1, 30, 45, 🚋Powell-Mason, Ⓜ️T) has been the picturesque backdrop for action movies like *The Karate Kid, Part II* and *Big Trouble in Little China*.

Spofford Alley

As sunset falls on sociable **Spofford Alley** (🚌1, 30, 45, 🚋Powell-Mason, Ⓜ️T), you'll hear clicking mah-jongg tiles and a Chinese orchestra warming up. But, generations ago, you might have overheard Sun Yat-sen and his conspirators at number 36 plotting the 1911 overthrow of China's last dynasty.

Guided Tours

Chinatown Alleyway Tours (p121) and Chinatown Heritage Walking Tours (p121) offer community-supporting, time-traveling strolls through defining moments in American history.

When choosing an Italian restaurant in North Beach, use this rule of thumb: if a host has to lure you inside with a 'Ciao, bella!' keep walking. Ditto for any restaurant with a gimmicky or too-obvious name – side-eye at you, Mona Lisa. Try smaller neighborhood restaurants on side streets off Grant Ave and Washington St, where staff gossip in Italian.

✖ North Beach

★ GOLDEN BOY PIZZA $

Map p308 (☎415-982-9738; www.goldenboy pizza.com; 542 Green St; slices $3.25-4.25; ☺11:30am-midnight Sun-Thu, to 2am Fri & Sat; ☐8, 30, 39, 41, 45, ☐Powell-Mason) 'If you don't see it don't ask 4 it' reads the menu – Golden Boy has kept punks in line since 1978, serving Genovese focaccia-crust pizza that's chewy, crunchy and hot from the oven. You'll have whatever second-generation Sodini family *pizzaioli* (pizza-makers) are making and like it – especially pesto and clam-and-garlic. Grab square slices and draft beer at the bomb-shelter counter and boom: you're golden.

★ LIGURIA BAKERY BAKERY $

Map p308 (☎415-421-3786; 1700 Stockton St; focaccia $4-6; ☺8am-2pm Tue-Fri, 7am-2pm Sat, 7am-noon Sun; 🖋 🚼; ☐8, 30, 39, 41, 45, ☐Powell-Mason, Ⓜ T) Bleary-eyed art students and Italian grandmothers line up by 8am for cinnamon-raisin focaccia hot out of the 100-year-old oven, leaving 9am dawdlers a choice of tomato or classic rosemary and garlic. Latecomers, beware: when they run out, they close. Take yours in waxed paper or boxed for picnics – just don't kid yourself that you're going to save some for later. Cash only.

★ MOLINARI DELI $

Map p308 (☎415-421-2337; www.molinarisalame. com; 373 Columbus Ave; sandwiches $11-14.50; ☺9am-6pm Mon-Fri, to 5:30pm Sat; ☐8, 10, 12, 30, 39, 41, 45, ☐Powell-Mason, Ⓜ T) Observe this quasi-religious North Beach noontime ritual: enter Molinari, and grab a number and a crusty roll. When your number's called, let wisecracking staff pile your roll with heavenly fixings: milky buffalo mozzarella, tangy sun-dried tomatoes, translucent sheets of prosciutto di Parma, slabs of legendary house-cured salami, drizzles of olive oil and balsamic. Enjoy hot from the panini press at sidewalk tables.

MARA'S ITALIAN PASTRY DESSERTS $

Map p308 (☎415-397-9435; 503 Columbus Ave; pastries $2-6; ☺7am-10:30pm Sun-Thu, to midnight Fri & Sat; ☐8, 30, 39, 41, 45, ☐Powell-Mason, Ⓜ T) Join early risers for double shots of espresso and *crostata* (jam tart), or wander in at night between bars and Beach Blanket Babylon (p122) for *torta di mandorla* (almond-meal tart with a layer of jam) and chocolate-chip-ricotta cannoli. Twice-baked, extra-crunchy biscotti are an acquired taste for non-Italians – try dunking them in *vin santo* – but pine-nut-studded chewy *pignoli* cookies are cross-cultural crowd-pleasers.

MAMA'S BRUNCH $

Map p308 (☎415-362-6421; www.mamas-sf.com; 1701 Stockton St; brunch mains $11-16; ☺8am-3pm Tue-Sun; 🖋 🚼; ☐8, 30, 39, 41, 45, ☐Powell-Mason, Ⓜ T) Generations of North Beachers have entrusted the most important meal of the day to Mama and Papa Sanchez, whose sunny Victorian storefront diner has soothed barbaric Barbary Coast hangovers for 50 years. Local farm-egg omelets and *kugelhopf* (house-baked brioche) French toast are cure-alls, but weekend specials like Dungeness-crab eggs Benedict make waits down the block worthwhile. Cash or debit card only.

TONY'S COAL-FIRED PIZZA & SLICE HOUSE PIZZA $

Map p308 (☎415-835-9888; http://tonys-coalfired.com; 1556 Stockton St; slices $5-6.50; ☺11:30-11pm Wed-Sun, to 10pm Mon, to 8pm Tue; ☐8, 30, 39, 41, 45, ☐Powell-Mason, Ⓜ T) Fuggedaboudit, New York pizza loyalists: in San Francisco, you can grab a cheesy, thin-crust slice from nine-time world-champion pizza-slinger Tony Gemignani. What, you were expecting kosher-salt shakers and bottled Coke from a vintage machine? Done. Difference is, here you can take that slice to sunny Washington Sq and watch tai chi practice and wild parrots year-round. Sorry, Manhattan – whaddayagonnado?

MARIO'S BOHEMIAN CIGAR STORE CAFE CAFE $

Map p308 (☎415-362-0536; 566 Columbus Ave; sandwiches $7-15; ☺10am-11pm; ☐8, 30, 39, 41, 45, ☐Powell-Mason, Ⓜ T) A boho North Beach landmark on Washington Sq, Mario's gave up smoking in the 1970s and turned to piping-hot panini. Generations of artistic movements have been fueled by Mario's oven-baked onion-focaccia sandwiches with meatballs, eggplant, or grilled chicken. This is a prime corner for people-watching over carafes of Chianti or pints of Anchor Steam.

CHINA LIVE
CHINESE $$

Map p308 (☑415-788-8188; http://chinalivesf. com; 644 Broadway; small plates $11-22; ⏰11:30am-10pm Mon-Thu, to 11pm Fri, 10:30am-11pm Sat, 10:30am-10pm Sun; ☑10, 12, ☒Powell-Hyde, ⓜT) San Francisco has steadily craved Chinese food since 1848, and this fancy food hall delivers regional Chinese taste sensations with Californian flair – it's San Francisco chef George Chen's Asian version of New York's Eataly emporium. Menus change seasonally, but recurring favorites at the main-floor restaurant include slurp-worthy Shanghai *xiao long bao* (soup dumplings), zesty chrysanthemum salad and crispy, kumquat-glazed Peking duck.

E' TUTTO QUA
ITALIAN $$

Map p308 (☑415-989-1002; www.etuttoqua. com; 270 Columbus Ave; mains $18-32; ⏰5-11pm Sun-Thu, to midnight Sat & Sun; ☑8, 10, 12, 30, 41, 45, ☒Powell-Mason, ⓜT) The Colosseum is 6000 miles from the corner of Columbus and Broadway, but you'll eat like a gladiator at E' Tutto Qua (translation: It's All Here). Boisterous Roman service and over-the-top decor create a party atmosphere – but they're serious about homemade pasta, grilled meats and top-flight Italian wines. Order the lamb chops and truffled *paccheri* (tube pasta) and emerge victorious.

RISTORANTE IDEALE
ITALIAN $$

Map p308 (☑415-391-4129; www.idealerestaurant.com; 1309 Grant Ave; pasta $16-20; ⏰5:30-10:30pm Mon-Thu, to 11pm Fri & Sat, 5-10pm Sun; ☑8, 10, 12, 30, 41, 45, ☒Powell-Mason, ⓜ5) Other North Beach restaurants fake Italian accents, but this trattoria has Italians in the kitchen, on the floor and at the table. Roman chef-owner Maurizio Bruschi serves authentic, al dente *bucatini amatriciana* (tube pasta with tomato-pecorino sauce and house-cured pancetta) and ravioli and gnocchi handmade in-house ('of course!'). North Beach's best-value Italian wine list ensures everyone goes home with Italian accents.

NAKED LUNCH
SANDWICHES $$

Map p308 (☑415-577-4951; www.nakedlunchsf. com; 504 Broadway; sandwiches $11-19; ⏰4:30-11pm Mon, 11:30am-2pm & 4:30-11pm Wed-Thu, 11:30am-2pm & 4:30-2am Fri, 11am-2am Sat; ☒; ☑8, 10, 12, 30, 41, ☒Powell-Mason, ⓜT) Decadent cravings worthy of a William S Burroughs novel are satisfied by this patio pub tucked between XXX entertainment venues. For brunch, the free-range, fried-chicken sandwich and full bar are plenty indulgent – but the truffled egg-and-bacon breakfast pizza is the stuff of legend. Browse Burroughs at the Beat Museum (p111) until happy hour (4:30-7pm).

TOSCA CAFE
ITALIAN $$

Map p308 (☑415-986-9651; www.toscacafesf. com; 242 Columbus Ave; mains $15-22; ⏰5pm-2am; ☑8, 10, 12, 30, 41, 45, ☒Powell-Mason, ⓜT) After this historic North Beach speakeasy was nearly evicted, devotees like Robert De-Niro and Johnny Depp rallied – now chef-owner April Bloomfield's in charge. The 1930s murals and red-leather banquettes are restored, and the kitchen serves rustic Italian classics (get the meatballs). Jukebox opera and spiked house cappuccino here deserve SF-landmark status. Reservations essential, especially for Sunday prix-fixe ($45, optional $10 wine pairing).

CAFE JACQUELINE
FRENCH $$$

Map p308 (☑415-981-5565; 1454 Grant Ave; soufflés per person $15-30; ⏰5:30-11pm Wed-Sun; ☑; ☑8, 30, 39, 41, 45, ☒Powell-Mason, ⓜT) The terror of top chefs is the classic French soufflé – but since 1979, Chef Jacqueline has been turning out perfectly puffy creations that float across the tongue like fog over the Golden Gate Bridge. With the right person to share that seafood soufflé, dinner could hardly get more romantic...until you order the chocolate version for dessert.

PARK TAVERN
CALIFORNIAN $$$

Map p308 (☑415-989-7300; www.parktavernsf. com; 1652 Stockton St; mains dinner $18-37, brunch $13-19; ⏰5-9pm Mon, to 10pm Tue-Thu, to 11pm Fri, 10am-11pm Sat, 10am-9pm Sun; ☑8, 30, 39, 41, 45, ☒Powell-Mason, ⓜT) Once an old boys' club, this modern, women-owned bistro makes cheeky California updates to continental classics: Kobe beef tartare with duck liver pâté on sourdough, truffled fries dipped in soft-cooked egg and caviar, lardo-wrapped shrimp dubbed 'demons on horseback.' Brunch brings blueberry fritters, oatmeal-raisin pancakes, and Bellinis. Never mind the noise; have a Paloma and join the happy din.

Neighborhood Walk
North Beach Beat

START CITY LIGHTS BOOKS
END LI PO
LENGTH 1.5 MILES; TWO HOURS

At ❶**City Lights Books** (p111), home of
Beat poetry and free speech, pick up something to inspire your journey into literary
North Beach – Ferlinghetti's *San Francisco
Poems* and Ginsberg's *Howl* make excellent
company.

Head to ❷**Caffe Trieste** (p120) for opera on the jukebox and potent espresso in
the back booth, where Francis Ford Coppola
drafted *The Godfather* screenplay.

At ❸**Washington Square** (p111),
you'll spot parrots in the treetops and octogenarians in tai chi tiger stances on the
lawn – pure poetry in motion. At the corner,
❹**Liguria Bakery** (p116) will give you
something to write home about: focaccia
hot from a century-old oven.

Peaceful ❺**Bob Kaufman Alley** (p111)
was named for the legendary street-corner
poet who kept a 12-year vow of silence that
lasted until the Vietnam War ended – when
he finally walked into a North Beach cafe
and recited his poem 'All Those Ships That
Never Sailed.'

Dylan jam sessions erupt in the bookshop, Allen Ginsberg spouts poetry nude
in backroom documentary screenings,
and stoned visitors grin beatifically at it all.
Welcome to the ❻**Beat Museum** (p111),
spiritual home to all 'angelheaded hipsters
burning for the ancient heavenly connection' (to quote Ginsberg's *Howl*).

The obligatory literary bar crawl begins
at ❼**Specs** (p120) amid merchant-marine
memorabilia, tall tales from old-timers,
and pitchers of Anchor Steam. *On the Road*
author Jack Kerouac once blew off Henry
Miller to go on a bender across the street at
❽**Vesuvio** (p120), until bartenders ejected him into the street now named for him:
❾**Jack Kerouac Alley** (p111). Note the
words of Chinese poet Li Po embedded in
the alley: 'In the company of friends, there is
never enough wine.'

Follow the lead of Kerouac and Ginsberg
and end your night under the laughing Buddha at ❿**Li Po** (p121) – there may not be
enough wine, but there's plenty of beer.

✕ Chinatown

★GOOD MONG KOK
DIM SUM $

Map p308 (📞415-397-2688; 1039 Stockton St; dumpling orders $2-5; ⏱7am-6pm; 🚌30, 45, 🚋Powell-Mason, California, Ⓜ️T) Ask Chinatown neighbors about their go-to dim sum and the answer is either grandma's or Good Mong Kok. Lines snake out the door of this counter bakery for dumplings whisked from vast steamers into takeout containers to enjoy in Portsmouth Sq. The menu changes by the minute/hour, but expect classic pork *siu mai,* shrimp *har gow* and BBQ pork buns; BYO chili sauce and black vinegar.

HOUSE OF NANKING
CHINESE $

Map p308 (📞415-421-1429; http://houseofnanking.net; 919 Kearny St; mains $10-16; ⏱11am-10pm Mon-Fri, noon-10pm Sat, noon-9:30pm Sun; 🚌8X, 10, 12, 30, 45, 🚋Powell-Mason, Ⓜ️T) 🍃 Meekly suggest an interest in seafood, nothing deep-fried, maybe some greens? – and your server will nod brusquely, grab the menu and return laden with Shanghai specialties: gingery greens with poached scallops, garlicky noodles and black-bean-glazed eggplant. Expect bossy service and a wait for a shared table – but also bold flavors at reasonable prices.

CITY VIEW
DIM SUM $

Map p308 (📞415-398-2838; http://cityviewdimsum.com; 662 Commercial St; dishes $3-8; ⏱11am-2:30pm Mon-Fri, from 10am Sat & Sun; ♿; 🚌1, 8, 10, 12, 30, 45, 🚋California) Take a seat in the sunny dining room and make way for carts loaded with delicate shrimp and leek dumplings, garlicky Chinese broccoli, tangy spareribs, coconut-dusted custard tarts and other tantalizing traditional dim sum. Arrive before the midday lunch rush to nab prime seating near the kitchen for first dibs on passing carts.

★MISTER JIU'S
CHINESE, CALIFORNIAN $$

Map p308 (📞415-857-9688; http://misterjius.com; 28 Waverly Pl; mains $14-45; ⏱5:30-10:30pm Tue-Sat; 🚌30, 🚋California, Ⓜ️T) Success has been celebrated in this historic Chinatown banquet hall since the 1880s – but today, scoring a table at Mister Jiu's is reason enough for celebration. Build memorable banquets from chef Brandon Jew's ingenious Chinese/Californian signatures: quail and Mission-fig sticky rice, hot and sour Dungeness crab soup, Wagyu sirloin and tuna heart fried rice. Don't skip dessert – pastry chef Melissa Chou's salted plum sesame balls are flavor bombs.

★Z & Y
SICHUAN $$

Map p308 (📞415-981-8888; www.zandyrestaurant.com; 655 Jackson St; mains $9-20; ⏱11am-9:30pm Sun-Thu, to 10:30pm Fri & Sat; 🚌8, 10, 12, 30, 45, 🚋Powell-Mason, Powell-Hyde, Ⓜ️T) Graduate from ho-hum sweet-and-sour to sensational Sichuan dishes that go down in a blaze of glory. Warm up with spicy pork dumplings and heat-blistered string beans, take on the housemade *tantan* noodles with peanut-chili sauce, and leave lips buzzing with fish poached in flaming chili oil and buried under red Szechuan chili peppers. Go early; worth the inevitable wait.

LAI HONG LOUNGE
DIM SUM $$

Map p308 (📞415-397-2290; www.lhklounge.com; 1416 Powell St; dim sum $5-17; ⏱10am-2:30pm & 5:30-8:30pm Mon-Fri, from 9am Sat & Sun; 🚌8, 10, 12, 30, 41, 45, 🚋Powell-Hyde, Ⓜ️T) Like a greatest-hits album, Lai Hong's menu features remastered dim-sum classics: properly plump shrimp dumplings, crisp Peking duck, baked barbecue-pork buns with the right ratio of savory-sweet pork to caramelized bun. Mark your order on the menu – no carts – to hand to a server, then bide your time while the food is cooked to order. Expect a wait outdoors.

TRESTLE
CALIFORNIAN $$

Map p308 (📞415-772-0922; http://trestlesf.com; 531 Jackson St; 3-course meals $38; ⏱5:30-10pm Mon-Thu, to 10:30pm Fri & Sat, to 9:30pm Sun; 🚌8, 10, 12, 30, 45, Ⓜ️T) If you've got a start-up budget but venture capitalist tastes, you're in luck here: $38 brings three courses of tasty, rustic comfort food. You get two options per course – typically soup or salad, meat or seafood, fruity or chocolatey dessert – so you and your date can taste the entire menu. Get the bonus handmade-pasta course ($10). Seating is tight, but the mood's friendly.

DRINKING & NIGHTLIFE

Pick your poison: stiff drinks in actual Wild West saloons, rare oolong in Chinatown tea boutiques, espresso in boho cafes where poems and blockbusters are

written, or cocktails at historic comedy clubs that can make or break comedians.

🍷 North Beach

★COMSTOCK SALOON
BAR

Map p308 (📞415-617-0071; www.comstocksaloon.com; 155 Columbus Ave; ⏰4pm-midnight Mon, to 2am Tue-Thu, noon-2am Fri, 11:30am-2am Sat, 11:30-4pm Sun; 🚌8, 10, 12, 30, 45, 🚋Powell-Mason, Ⓜ️T) During this 1907 saloon's heyday, patrons relieved themselves in the marble trough below the bar – now you'll have to tear yourself away from Comstock's authentic pisco punch and martini-precursor Martinez (gin, vermouth, bitters, maraschino liqueur). Arrive to toast Emperor Norton's statue at happy hour (4pm to 6pm) and stay for the family meal (whatever kitchen staff's eating).

★SPECS
BAR

Map p308 (Specs Twelve Adler Museum Cafe; 📞415-421-4112; 12 William Saroyan Pl; ⏰5pm-2am Mon-Fri; 🚌8, 10, 12, 30, 41, 45, 🚋Powell-Mason, Ⓜ️T) The walls here are plastered with merchant-marine memorabilia, and you'll be plastered too if you try to keep up with the salty characters holding court in back. Surrounded by seafaring mementos – including a massive walrus organ over the bar – your order seems obvious: pitcher of Anchor Steam, coming right up. Cash only.

★DEVIL'S ACRE
BAR

Map p308 (📞415-766-4363; www.thedevilsacre.com; 256 Columbus Ave; ⏰5pm-2am Tue, from 3pm Wed-Sat, 2pm-midnight Sun, 5pm-midnight Mon; 🚌8, 10, 12, 30, 41, 45, 🚋Powell-Mason, Ⓜ️T) Potent potions and lipsmacking quack cures are proudly served at this apothecary-style Barbary Coast saloon. Tartly quaffable Lachlan's Antiscorbutic (lime, sea salt, two kinds of gin) is a surefire cure for scurvy and/or sobriety; when in doubt, go Call a 'Treuse (Chartreuse, lemon, vanilla, egg white). There's happy hour until 7pm, but no food; switch to nonalcoholic 'remedies'.

★VESUVIO
BAR

Map p308 (📞415-362-3370; www.vesuvio.com; 255 Columbus Ave; ⏰8am-2am; 🚌8, 10, 12, 30, 41, 45, 🚋Powell-Mason) Guy walks into a bar, roars and leaves. Without missing a beat, the bartender says to the next customer, 'Welcome to Vesuvio, honey – what can I get you?'

Jack Kerouac blew off Henry Miller to go on a bender here and, after you've joined neighborhood characters on the stained-glass mezzanine for 8pm microbrews or 8am Kerouacs (rum, tequila and OJ), you'll see why.

★CAFFE TRIESTE
CAFE

Map p308 (📞415-392-6739; www.caffetrieste.com; 601 Vallejo St; ⏰6:30am-10pm Sun-Thu, to 11pm Fri & Sat; 📶; 🚌8, 10, 12, 30, 41, 45, Ⓜ️T) Poetry on bathroom walls, opera on the jukebox, live accordion jams and Beat poetry on bathroom walls: Caffe Trieste remains North Beach at its best, since the 1950s. Linger over legendary espresso and scribble your screenplay under the Sardinian fishing mural just as young Francis Ford Coppola did. Perhaps you've heard of the movie: *The Godfather*. Cash only.

15 ROMOLO
BAR

Map p308 (📞415-398-1359; www.15romolo.com; 15 Romolo Pl; ⏰5pm-2am; 🚌8, 10, 12, 30, 41, 45, 🚋Powell-Mason, Ⓜ️T) Strap on your spurs: it's gonna be a wild Western night at this back-alley Basque saloon squeezed between burlesque joints. The strong slay the Jabberwocky (gin, sherry, bitters, fortified wine), but the brazen Baker Beach (mezcal, manzanilla sherry, apricot, vermouth, lemon) makes grown men blush. Bask in $9 Basque Pincon punch at 5pm to 7:30pm happy hours, and pace yourself with tasty *pintxos* (tapas).

SALOON
BAR

Map p308 (📞415-989-7666; www.sfblues.net/Saloon.html; 1232 Grant Ave; live music free-$5; ⏰noon-2am; 🚌8, 10, 12, 30, 41, 45, 🚋Powell-Mason) Blues in a red saloon that's been a dive since 1861 – this is North Beach at its most colorful. Legend has it that when the city caught fire in 1906, loyal patrons saved the Saloon by dousing it with buckets of hooch. Today it's SF's oldest bar, and blues and rock bands perform nightly plus weekend afternoons. Cash only.

TONY NIK'S
LOUNGE

Map p308 (📞415-693-0990; www.tonyniks.com; 1534 Stockton St; ⏰4pm-2am Mon-Fri, from 2pm Sat & Sun; 🚌8, 30, 39, 41, 45, 🚋Powell-Mason, Ⓜ️T) Vintage neon points the way to Tony Nik's, keeping North Beach nicely naughty since 1933. This tiny cocktail lounge is co-owned by the original Tony 'Nik' Nicco's grandson, who has preserved the glass-brick entry, deco woodwork and Rat Pack–worthy martini recipe. Arrive early to snag a vintage banquette in back, or hang with neighborhood characters at the mood-lit bar.

CAFE ZOETROPE
CAFE, BAR

Map p308 (☑415-291-1700; www.cafecoppola.com/cafezoetrope; Columbus Tower, 916 Kearny St; ⊗11:30am-10pm Mon-Fri, noon-9pm Sat, noon-9pm Sun; ☐8,10,12,30,41,45, Ⓜ️T) During Prohibition, historic Columbus Tower (p112) housed a speakeasy – but now you can drink here in plain sight, at filmmaker Francis Ford Coppola's ground-floor sidewalk bistro. Sip Coppola's signature Napa wines surrounded by *Godfather* movie memorabilia, and consider the Caesar salad – first served at Columbus Tower in 1924 – but whatever you do, take the cannoli.

🍷 Chinatown

★LI PO
BAR

Map p308 (☑415-982-0072; www.lipolounge.com; 916 Grant Ave; ⊗2pm-2am; ☐8, 30, 45, Powell-Mason, Powell-Hyde, Ⓜ️T) Beat a hasty retreat to red-vinyl booths where Allen Ginsberg and Jack Kerouac debated the meaning of life under a golden Buddha. Enter the 1937 faux-grotto doorway and dodge red lanterns to place your order: Tsingtao beer or a sweet, sneaky-strong Chinese mai tai made with *baijiu* (rice liquor). Brusque bartenders, basement bathrooms, cash only – a world-class dive bar.

RÉVEILLE
CAFE

Map p308 (☑415-789-6258; http://reveillecoffee.com; 200 Columbus Ave; ⊗7am-6pm Mon-Fri, 8am-5pm Sat & Sun; 🖪🐾; ☐8, 10, 12, 30, 41, 45, Powell-Mason, Ⓜ️T) If this sunny flat-iron storefront doesn't lighten your mood, cappuccino with a foam-art heart will. Réveille's coffee is like San Francisco on a good day: nutty and uplifting, without a trace of bitterness. Check the circular marble counter for just-baked chocolate-chip cookies and sticky buns. No wi-fi makes for easy conversation, and sidewalk-facing counters offer some of SF's best people-watching.

PLENTEA
TEAHOUSE

Map p308 (☑415-757-0223; www.plenteasf.com; 341 Kearny St; ⊗11am-11pm; 🖪; ☐1, 8, 30, 45, California, Ⓜ️T) 🍃 Chinatown's

---

CHINATOWN WALKING TOURS

Chinatown Alleyway Tours (Map p308; ☑415-984-1478; www.chinatownalleywaytours.org; Portsmouth Sq; adult/student $26/16; ⊗tours 11am Sat; 🖪; ☐1, 8, 10, 12, 30, 41, 45, California, Powell-Mason, Powell-Hyde) Teenage Chinatown residents guide you on two-hour tours through backstreets that have seen it all: Sun Yat-sen plotting China's revolution, '49ers squandering fortunes on opium, services held in temple ruins after the 1906 earthquake. Your presence here helps the community remember its history and shape its future – Chinatown Alleyway Tours are a nonprofit, youth-led program of the Chinatown Community Development Center. Credit cards are accepted for advance online reservations only; drop-ins should bring exact change, because guides don't carry cash.

Chinatown Heritage Walking Tours (Map p308; ☑415-986-1822; https://tour.cccsf.us; Chinese Culture Center, Hilton Hotel, 3rd fl, 750 Kearny St; adult $30-40, student $20-30; 🖪; ☐1, 8, 10, 12, 30, 41, 45, California, Powell-Mason, Powell-Hyde) These local-led, kid-friendly tours wind through backstreets to key historic sights, including the Golden Gate Fortune Cookie Factory, Tin How Temple and Portsmouth Sq. Tours follow one of two themes: Chinatown History and Food Walk, covering Chinatown's daily life and cultural influence, or Dynasty to Democracy, exploring Chinatown's efforts for rights, justice and opportunity for all. Proceeds support the nonprofit Chinese Culture Center (p112); make bookings online or by phone three days in advance.

Drag Me Along Tours (Map p308; ☑415-857-0865; www.dragmealongtours.com; Portsmouth Sq; $30; ⊗tours 11am Sun; ☐1, 8, 10, 12, 30, 41, 45, California, Powell-Mason, Powell-Hyde, Ⓜ️T) Explore San Francisco's bawdy Barbary Coast with a bona-fide legend: gold-rush burlesque star Countess Lola Montez, reincarnated in drag by SF historian Rick Shelton. In two action-packed hours, her Highness leads you through Chinatown alleyways where Victorian ladies made and lost reputations, past North Beach saloons where sailors were shanghaied. Barbary Coast characters gambled, loved and lived dangerously – expect adult content. Reservations required; cash only.

TEA TASTING

Several Grant Ave tea importers let you sample for free, but the hard sell may begin before you finish sipping. For a more relaxed, enlightening teatime experience, **Red Blossom Tea Company** (Map p308; ☑415-395-0868; www.red-blossomtea.com; 831 Grant Ave; ⏰10am-5pm Mon-Thu, to 6pm Fri & Sat, 11am-5pm Sun; ☐1, 10, 12, 30, 35, 41, ⓕPowell-Mason, Powell-Hyde, California, ⓜT) offers half-hour premium tea flights with tips on preparing tea for maximum flavor ($35 for up to four participants). Book ahead at weekends; seating is limited.

latest, greatest import is Taiwanese bubble tea: milky iced tea polka-dotted with *boba* (chewy, gently sweet tapioca pearls). PlenTea fills vintage milk bottles with just-brewed, cetified-organic bubble tea in your choice of flavors: green, black or oolong, plus fresh seasonal mango, peach or strawberry. For original SF flavor, get the bittersweet matcha latte, malted black Nutella, or decadent oolong with sea-salt cream.

BUDDHA LOUNGE   BAR

Map p308 (☑415-362-1792; 901 Grant Ave; ⏰1pm-2am; ☐8, 30, 45, ⓕPowell-Mason, Powell-Hyde, ⓜT) Vintage red neon promises evenings worthy of WWII sailors on shore leave. Drink in the atmosphere, but stick to basic well drinks and beer straight from a laughing-Buddha bottle. Cue selections on the eclectic jukebox (Queen, Outkast, the Clash), ask the bartender for dice, and you're in for the duration. Bathrooms are in the former-opium-den basement. Cash only.

ENTERTAINMENT

★**BEACH BLANKET BABYLON**   CABARET

Map p308 (BBB; ☑415-421-4222; www.beachblanketbabylon.com; 678 Green St, aka Beach Blanket Babylon Blvd; $30-155; ⏰shows 8pm Wed, Thu & Fri, 6pm & 9pm Sat, 2pm & 5pm Sun; ☐8, 30, 39, 41, 45, ⓕPowell-Mason, ⓜT) Snow White searches for Prince Charming in San Francisco: what could possibly go wrong? This Disney-spoof musical-comedy cabaret has been running since 1974, but topical jokes keep it outrageous – and wigs as big as parade floats are gasp-worthy. Spectators must be over 21 to

handle racy humor, except at cleverly sanitized Sunday matinees. Reservations essential; arrive one hour early for best seats.

BIMBO'S 365 CLUB   LIVE MUSIC

Map p308 (☑415-474-0365; www.bimbos365club.com; 1025 Columbus Ave; from $20; ⏰box office 10am-4pm; ☐8, 30, 39, 41, 45, ⓕPowell-Mason, ⓜT) Get your kicks at this 1931 speakeasy with stiff drinks, bawdy vintage bar murals, parquet dance floors for high-stepping like Rita Hayworth (she was in the chorus line here) and intimate live shows by the likes of Beck, Talib Kweli, Chris Isaak and Nouvelle Vague. Dress snazzy and bring bucks to tip the powder-room attendant – this is a classy joint. It's 21+; two-drink minimum; cash only.

COBB'S COMEDY CLUB   COMEDY

Map p308 (☑415-928-4320; www.cobbscomedyclub.com; 915 Columbus Ave; $17-46; ⏰box office 1-6pm Wed, 4-6pm Thu-Sun; ☐8, 30, 39, 41, 45, ⓕPowell-Mason, ⓜT) There's no room to be shy at Cobb's, where bumper-to-bumper shared tables make the audience cozy – and vulnerable. The venue is known for launching local talent and giving big-name acts (Ali Wong, John Oliver, Michelle Wolf) a place to try risky new material. Check the website for shows, drag brunches and showcases like Really Funny Comedians (Who Happen to Be Women). It's 21+; two-drink minimum.

SHOPPING

Crank up your quirk factor in North Beach and Chinatown, where a day's haul might include vintage posters, dragon kites, rare albums, hand-painted silk robes, piles of freshly published City Lights poetry and a new tattoo.

North Beach

★**SAN FRANCISCO ROCK POSTERS & COLLECTIBLES**   VINTAGE, ART

Map p308 (☑415-956-6749; www.rockposters.com; 1851 Powell St; ⏰10am-6pm Mon-Sat; ☐8, 30, 39, 41, 45, ⓕPowell-Mason, ⓜT) Are you ready to rock?! Enter this trippy temple to classic rock gods – but leave your lighters at home because these concert posters are valuable. Expect to pay hundreds for first-run psychedelic Fillmore concert posters featuring the Grateful Dead – but you can score bargain handbills for San Francisco acts like Santana, the Dead Kennedys and Sly and the Family Stone.

ARTIST & CRAFTSMAN SUPPLY
ARTS & CRAFTS

Map p308 (☑415-931-1900; www.artistcraftsman. com; 555 Pacific Ave; ☉8:30am-7:30pm Mon-Fri, 10am-7pm Sat, 11am-6pm Sun; 🚼; 🚌8, 10, 12, 41, Ⓜ️T) Ditch your day job and take up painting at this employee-owned art-supply store, housed in the former Hippodrome burlesque theater. This Barbary Coast hot spot later became the Gay Nineties club – check out the figures cavorting in the entry reliefs and peek into the original speakeasy tunnel downstairs. Two floors of supplies anticipate every SF inspiration and rainy-day kids' project.

EDEN & EDEN
GIFTS & SOUVENIRS

Map p308 (☑415-983-0490; www.edenandeden. com; 560 Jackson St; ☉10am-7pm Mon-Fri, to 6pm Sat; 🚌8, 10, 12, 41, Ⓜ️T) Detour from reality at Eden & Eden, a Dadaist design boutique where espresso cups give you side-eye, lightning strikes on dresses, shaggy tea cozies make teapots look bearded and those suede lips are coin purses that swallow loose change. Prices are surprisingly reasonable for far-out, limited-edition and repurposed-vintage finds from local and international designers.

REAL OLD PAPER
ART, VINTAGE

Map p308 (☑415-527-8333; https://realoldpaper. com; 801 Columbus Ave; ☉noon-6pm Tue-Sat; 🚌8, 30, 39, 41, 45, Ⓜ️T, 🚠Powell-Mason) See the world from the comfort of your living room with a wall of Real Old Paper finds: vintage travel posters, Dutch *Star Wars* promotions, Pacific WWII rationing propaganda and advertisements for Italian vermouth brands. But wait, there's more: collectors Jennifer and Andrew England are always excited to show you new acquisitions not yet on the walls.

AL'S ATTIRE
FASHION & ACCESSORIES

Map p308 (☑415-693-9900; www.alsattire.com; 1300 Grant Ave; ☉11am-7pm Mon-Sat, noon-6pm Sun; 🚌8, 10, 12, 30, 41, 45, 🚠Powell-Mason, Ⓜ️T) Hepcats and slick chicks get their handmade threads at Al's, where vintage styles are reinvented in noir-novel twill, dandy high-sheen cotton and mid-century flecked tweeds. Prices aren't exactly bohemian for these bespoke originals, but turquoise wing tips are custom-made to fit your feet and svelte hand-stitched jackets have silver-

screen star quality. Ask about custom orders for weddings, Grammys and other shindigs.

101 MUSIC
MUSIC

Map p308 (☑415-392-6368; 1414 Grant Ave; ☉10am-8pm Mon-Sat, from noon Sun; 🚌8, 30, 39, 41, 45, 🚠Powell-Mason, Ⓜ️T) You'll have to bend over those earthquake-defying bins to let DJs and hard-core collectors pass (hey, wasn't that Tom Waits?!), but among the $5–25 discs are obscure releases and original recordings by Nina Simone, Janis Joplin and San Francisco's own Dead Kennedys. Don't knock your head on vintage Les Pauls.

🔒 Chinatown

★GOLDEN GATE FORTUNE COOKIES
FOOD & DRINKS

Map p308 (☑415-781-3956; www.goldengatefortunecookies.com; 56 Ross Alley; ☉9am-6pm; 🚌8, 30, 45, 🚠Powell-Mason, Powell-Hyde, Ⓜ️T) Find your fortune at this bakery, where cookies are stamped from vintage presses – just as they were in 1909, when fortune cookies were invented for SF's Japanese Tea Garden (p192). Write your own fortunes for custom cookies (50¢ each), or get cookies with regular or risqué fortunes (pro tip: add 'in bed' to regular ones). Cash only; $1 tip for photos.

CHINATOWN KITE SHOP
TOYS

Map p308 (☑415-989-5182; www.chinatownkite. com; 717 Grant Ave; ☉10am-8pm; 🚼; 🚌1, 10, 12, 30, 35, 41, 🚠Powell-Hyde, Powell-Mason, California, Ⓜ️T) Be the star of Crissy Field and wow any kids in your life with a fierce 9ft-long flying dragon, a pirate-worthy wild parrot (SF's city bird), surreal floating legs or a flying panda that looks understandably stunned. Pick up a two-person, papier-mâché lion-dance costume and invite a date to bust ferocious moves with you next lunar new year.

KIM + ONO
FASHION & ACCESSORIES

Map p308 (☑415-989-8588; https://kimandono. com; 729 Grant Ave; ☉10am-6pm Mon-Thu, to 6:30pm Fri & Sun, 10am-8pm Sat; 🚌30, 45, 🚠California, Powell-Mason, Ⓜ️T) Hollywood pinups borrowed their slinky silk-robe style from Chinatown burlesque stars back in the '30s – and now you can rock that retro hottie look in boudoir-to-streetwear designs by Chinatown sister-duo designers Renee and Tiffany. Each kimono has something extra: hand-painted blossoms, branches and vines, with the occasional crane peeking over the shoulder.

Nob Hill & Russian Hill

Neighborhood Top Five

❶ Diego Rivera Gallery (p128) Seeing San Francisco as the Mexican muralist maestro did – a fascinating work in progress.

❷ Vallejo Street Steps (p128) Seeing North Beach unfurl below you like a magic carpet, hovering between the Bay Bridge and downtown skyscrapers.

❸ Lombard Street (p129) Leaping off the Powell-Hyde cable car to photograph the hill's famous switchbacks.

❹ Cable Car Museum (p126) Witnessing San Fran-cisco's original 1873 steam-punk technology in action.

❺ Stookey's Club Moderne (p131) Toasting the definitive end of Prohibition with live jazz and histori-cally inspired cocktails at this swell deco bar.

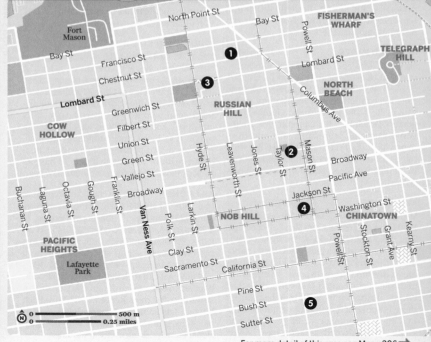

For more detail of this area see Map p306 ➡

Explore Nob Hill & Russian Hill

Russian and Nob Hills have the city's most stunning views – but first you have to get here. Be bold: hop a cable car or take a stairway hike. On the way, you'll discover panoramic views and hidden art treasures by an all-star cast, including muralist Diego Rivera, street artist Keith Haring, mosaic maestro Millard Sheets, poet Ina Coolbrith and novelist Armistead Maupin. Besides, there's no getting around these peaks if you really want to see the city – Nob Hill stands between downtown and Chinatown, and Russian Hill rises between North Beach and Fisherman's Wharf. After hilltop sunsets or happy-hour toasts, head downhill to Polk St for shopping, dinner and nightlife.

Local Life

Sunsets Find a bench at George Sterling Park (p128) to see the sunset and watch the fog hurdle over the Golden Gate Bridge – or climb Filbert St to Vallejo Street Steps (p128) to see the Oakland hills glitter with sunsets reflected in picture windows.

Hidden art treasures Veer off touristy Lombard St to see the Diego Rivera mural at the San Francisco Art Institute (p129), head downhill to glimpse Millard Sheets' Lombard Financial Center Mosaics (p128), and spot Keith Haring's angels and Beniamino Bufano's lovable statue of the city's patron saint inside Grace Cathedral (p128).

Hangouts See skateboarders attempt new tricks on the stairs at Huntington Park (p129) as you wander Grace Cathedral's outdoor labyrinth.

Literary secrets Find legendary locations that inspired Jack Kerouac's *On the Road,* George Sterlings' ode 'Cool Grey City of Love,' Ina Coolbrith's poem 'When the Grass Shall Cover Me' and Armistead Maupin's *Tales of the City.*

Getting There & Away

Bus Buses 10 and 12 link downtown with Russian and Nob Hills; the 10 continues to Pacific Heights. Bus 27 connects the Mission, SoMa and Downtown to Nob Hill. Buses 41 and 45 connect downtown to Russian Hill and Cow Hollow.

Cable car The Powell-Hyde cable car serves Russian and Nob Hills; the Powell-Mason line serves Nob Hill; and the California line runs from downtown through Chinatown and over Nob Hill to Van Ness Ave.

Car Don't drive if you can avoid it. With gradients from 24 to 31.5%, Nob Hill and Russian Hill are not good for your brakes or your blood pressure. Leave driving to pro taxi drivers who know the city.

Lonely Planet's Top Tip

Once you've tried to climb these hills with the help of a cable car, you'll realize that those vintage 1873 contraptions aren't just here for looks. Powell-Hyde and Powell Mason lines cover these hills, but fair warning: both lines start at Powell St terminus, where waits are notoriously long. If the cars are packed, they might not stop at all marked stops – but it's worth a shot if you're tired and quick to hop on board. Alternatively, take the California St line, which rarely has queues.

 Best Places to Eat

➡ Acquerello (p131)

➡ 1760 (p130)

➡ Hot Sauce & Panko (p129)

➡ Swan Oyster Depot (p130)

➡ Dim Sum Club (p130)

For reviews, see p129. ➡

 Best Places to Drink

➡ Stookey's Club Moderne (p131)

➡ Tonga Room (p132)

➡ Amélie (p132)

➡ Hi-Lo Club (p132)

For reviews, see p131. ➡

Best Shopping

➡ Good Vibrations (p133)

➡ Studio (p133)

➡ Relove (p133)

➡ Legion (p133)

➡ Molte Cose (p133)

For reviews, see p133. ➡

 NOB HILL & RUSSIAN HILL

TOP SIGHT
CABLE CAR MUSEUM

That clamor you hear riding cable cars is the sound of San Francisco's peak technology at work. Gears click and wire-hemp ropes whir as these vintage contraptions are hoisted up and over hills too steep for horses or buses – and you can inspect those cables close-up here, in the city's still-functioning cable-car barn.

Museum Memorabilia

Gearheads, rejoice: three original 1870s cable cars have survived miraculously intact and are still showcased at the Cable Car Museum. The mile-long Clay St cable-car line owned by cable-car inventor Andrew Hallidie is long gone, but the tiny wooden Clay St Railroad Car No 8 dating from 1873 remains the pride and joy of SF.

To demonstrate San Francisco's peak technology, this little car traveled cross-country from Chicago's World Fair to Baltimore railroad yards. Then disaster struck: San Francisco's great 1906 earthquake and fire destroyed most of the city's cable cars and lines. When the Clay St car came home at last for the 1939 Golden Gate Exposition, the city wasn't taking any risks it would be lost again – and kept it safe in deep storage through WWII.

DON'T MISS

➡ Original 1870s cable cars
➡ Cables in motion
➡ Riding the car

PRACTICALITIES

➡ Map p306, E5
➡ ☎415-474-1887
➡ www.cablecarmuseum.org
➡ 1201 Mason St
➡ donations appreciated
➡ ⊙10am-6pm Apr-Sep, to 5pm Oct-Mar
➡ ♿
➡ 🚋Powell-Mason, Powell-Hyde

But this cable barn museum isn't just a warehouse for antiques – it's the functioning cable powerhouse that keeps the Powell-Mason line running. Follow the cables running down the street, through an open channel and into the powerhouse, where they wind around massive bull wheels without losing momentum or tension. Head to the upstairs deck to see the powerhouse in action and watch cables whir over the wheels – as awesome a feat of physics now as when Andrew Hallidie invented the mechanism in 1873.

Slow Turns

Now that you've seen how cable cars work, it's time to experience one in action. Jump on a south-bound cable car one block over and hang on: the cable car tilts steeply as it climbs the 30-degree grade of Nob Hill and there are no seat belts on the cable car's slippery wooden benches. Grab a hand strap and take the ride standing like a pro surfer and you'll earn honorary San Franciscan status.

When you reach the end of the line at **Powell St Cable Car Turnaround** (Map p294; www.sfmta.com; cnr Powell & Market Sts; ⓖPowell-Mason, Mason-Hyde, ⓂPowell, ⒷPowell), you may breathe a sigh of relief – but for cable-car conductors, this is the toughest moment of the ride. Cable cars can't go in reverse, so they need to be turned around by hand at the terminus. After you step off the car, turn around to watch cable-car operators as they leap out of the car, grip the chassis of the trolley and slooowly turn the car atop a revolving wooden platform.

Judging the Queue

The best way to secure a spot on a cable car is to board at a turnaround, or cable-car terminus. Lines are shortest to get on the California cable car – the most historic line – but the ride isn't as long or scenic as on the Powell-Mason and Powell-Hyde lines. Powell-Mason cars are quickest to the Wharf, but Powell-Hyde cars traverse more terrain and hills.

Both lines start at the Powell St Turnaround, where riders line up midmorning to early evening, with raucous street performers, doomsday preachers and occasional protesters on the sidelines providing local color. The line at the Friedel Klussman Memorial Turnaround in Fisherman's Wharf is just as long as at Powell St Turnaround, but it thins out rapidly around sunset.

If you're not sure how long the wait will be, count heads and do math: cable cars hold 60 people (29 seated, 31 standing) but depart before they're full to leave room for passengers boarding en route. Cars depart every five to 10 minutes at peak times.

TAKE A BREAK

Hop the Powell-Mason or Powell-Hyde line or walk three steep blocks for a peak SF experience: tropical happy hour specials and pupu platters at tiki Tonga Room (p132).

Don't miss the Cable Car Museum shop for SF memorabilia that comes with local street cred. Your purchases of scale-model cable cars and actual cable-car bells help keep this nonprofit museum running and open to all for free.

NOB HILL & RUSSIAN HILL CABLE CAR MUSEUM

◉ SIGHTS

You'll need to limber up to reach the top of Nob and Russian Hills – but on a clear day, the payoff is an unparalleled panorama from the Bay Bridge all the way to Golden Gate Bridge. These side-by-side hilltops are the city's best vantage points for sunsets: see the sun sink into fog swirling around the Golden Gate Bridge from George Sterling Park, or watch East Bay hillsides glitter with golden rays reflected in bay windows as you walk the outdoor labyrinth at Grace Cathedral. In cloudy weather, head indoors to discover SF's peak art experiences.

CABLE CAR MUSEUM HISTORIC SITE
See p126.

★LOMBARD FINANCIAL CENTER MOSAICS PUBLIC ART
Map p306 (2750 Van Ness Ave; ⏍47, 49, ⏍Mason-Hyde) A couple years ago, blighted trees in front of this bank were cut down and a treasure hidden for almost half a century was revealed: mosaics by California modernist master Millard Sheets. He designed this bank branch as a clean canvas for mosaics highlighting San Francisco history, with the modern city silhouetted by the setting sun. During bank hours (9am to 5pm), head inside to admire floor-to-ceiling artwork by Sheets' studio: dazzling stained-glass windows and curving murals covering centuries of San Francisco history.

★DIEGO RIVERA GALLERY GALLERY
Map p306 (⏍415-771-7020; www.sfai.edu; 800 Chestnut St; ⏍9am-7pm; ⏍30, ⏍Powell-Mason) FREE Diego Rivera's 1931 *The Making of a Fresco Showing the Building of a City* is a *trompe l'oeil* fresco within a fresco, showing the artist himself pausing to admire his own work and the efforts of workers around him, as they build the modern city of San Francisco. The fresco covers an entire wall of the Diego Rivera Gallery in the San Francisco Art Institute. For sweeping views of the city Diego admired, head to the terrace cafe for espresso and panoramic bay vistas.

★GRACE CATHEDRAL CHURCH
Map p306 (⏍415-749-6300; www.gracecathedral.org; 1100 California St; suggested donation adult/child $3/2; ⏍8am-6pm Mon-Sat, to 7pm Sun, services 8:30am, 11am & 6pm Sun; ⏍1, ⏍California) San Francisco's Episcopal cathedral has been rebuilt three times since the gold rush and the current reinforced-concrete Gothic cathedral took 40 years to complete. Spectacular stained-glass windows include a 'Human Endeavor' series dedicated to science, depicting Albert Einstein uplifted in swirling nuclear particles. San Francisco history unfolds on murals covering the 1906 earthquake to the 1945 UN charter signing. People of all faiths wander indoor and outdoor inlaid-stone labyrinths, meant to guide restless souls through three spiritual stages: releasing, receiving and returning.

VALLEJO STREET STEPS ARCHITECTURE
Map p306 (Vallejo St, btwn Mason & Jones Sts; ⏍Powell-Mason, Powell-Hyde) Reach staggering heights with spectacular views along this staircase connecting North Beach with Russian Hill – ideal for working off a pasta dinner. Ascend Vallejo toward Mason St, where stairs rise toward Jones St, passing Ina Coolbrith Park. Sit at the top for nighttime views of the shimmering Bay Bridge lights, then continue west to Polk St for nightlife.

GEORGE STERLING PARK PARK
Map p306 (www.sfparksalliance.org; cnr Greenwich & Hyde Sts; ⏍; ⏍19, 41, 45, ⏍Powell-Hyde) 'Homeward into the sunset/Still unwearied we go/Till the northern hills are misty/With the amber of afterglow.' Poet George Sterling's poem 'City by the Sea' seems impossibly romantic – but when you watch the sunset over the Golden Gate Bridge from his namesake hilltop park, you'll see his point of view. This is the ideal vantage point to appreciate the town Sterling called 'the cool grey city of love.'

MASONIC AUDITORIUM & TEMPLE NOTABLE BUILDING
Map p306 (⏍415-292-9137; www.masonicheritage.org; 1111 California St; ⏍lobby 9am-5pm Mon-Fri, museum 10am-3pm Mon-Thu & by appointment; ⏍; ⏍1, ⏍California) FREE Rock stars and conspiracy theorists alike are mysteriously drawn to the Masonic – a major concert venue and the Masons' main temple for California. Freemasonry venerates architecture and this 1958 structure captures that sense of awe with sublime mid-century-modern style. The marble lobby is graced with a massive stained-glass window depicting Freemasonry symbols alongside scenes from early California. For

reasons known best to artist Emile Norman and California Masons, this 1958 modernist marvel contains fabric swatches and soil samples from across California.

LOMBARD STREET   STREET

Map p306 (🚋Powell-Hyde) You've seen the eight switchbacks of Lombard St's 900 block in a thousand photographs. The tourist board has dubbed it 'the world's crookedest street,' which is factually incorrect: Vermont St in Potrero Hill deserves that award, but Lombard is much more scenic, with its red-brick pavement and lovingly tended flowerbeds. It wasn't always so bent; before the arrival of the car it plunged straight down the hill.

INA COOLBRITH PARK   PARK

Map p306 (www.sfparksalliance.org/our-parks/parks/ina-coolbrith-park; cnr Vallejo & Taylor Sts; 🚌41, 45, 🚋Powell-Mason) On San Francisco's literary scene, all roads eventually lead to Ina Coolbrith. She was California's first poet laureate, editor of Mark Twain, colleague of Ansel Adams and mentor to Jack London, Isadora Duncan, George Sterling and Charlotte Perkins Gilman. But her friends didn't know her secret: her uncle was Mormon prophet Joseph Smith. This hidden, flowery hilltop park is a fitting honor: poetic, secretive, inspiring. Climb past gardens and balconies, and listen for the fog whooshing in the treetops.

FILBERT STREET HILL   HILL

Map p306 (🚌41, 45, 🚋Powell-Hyde) With a 31.5% grade, the honor of steepest street in San Francisco is shared by Filbert St and **22nd St** (Map p312; btwn Church & Vicksburg Sts; Ⓜ J) in the Castro. Filbert is shorter, but wins top marks for end-of-the-world views. From the tippy top near Hyde St, look over North Beach churches to see Coit Tower rising above the horizon, framed by the glittering lights of the Bay Bridge by night. The hill spans the 1100 block of Filbert St between Hyde and Leavenworth Sts – limber up.

HUNTINGTON PARK   PARK

Map p306 (http://sfrecpark.org; California St, btwn Mason & Taylor Sts; 👶; 🚌1, 🚋California) The crowning jewel of Nob Hill is this posh park – once the exclusive stomping ground of billionaires, now a park enjoyed by all, from gleeful toddlers at the playground to street skaters making YouTube videos on the steps. The centerpiece of the 1.3-acre park is the four-sided 'Fountain of the Tortoises,' a century-old recreation of a 400-year-old limestone fountain in Rome. Hop off the cable car for picnics, playground sessions and glimpses of golden East Bay hills around sunset.

SAN FRANCISCO ART INSTITUTE   GALLERY

Map p306 (SFAI; ☎415-771-7020; www.sfai.edu; 800 Chestnut St; ⏰Walter & McBean Galleries 11am-7pm Tue, to 6pm Wed-Sat, Diego Rivera Gallery 9am-7pm; 🚌30, 🚋Powell-Mason) FREE Since the 1870s, SFAI has been at the vanguard of Bay Area art movements – including 1960s Bay Area abstraction, 1970s conceptual art and 1990s new-media art. See Diego Rivera's 1931 *The Making of a Fresco Showing the Building of a City* alongside new student work in the Diego Rivera Gallery, see groundbreaking contemporary works showcased in the Walter and McBean Gallery since 1969 and find your own artistic inspiration in panoramic vistas from the terrace cafe.

MACONDRAY LANE   STREET

Map p306 (btwn Jones & Leavenworth Sts; 🚌41, 45, 🚋Powell-Mason, Powell-Hyde) The scenic route down from Ina Coolbrith Park – via steep stairs, past gravity-defying wooden cottages – is so charming, it looks like something from a novel. And so it is: Armistead Maupin used this shady, hidden byway as the model for Barbary Lane in his *Tales of the City* series.

✕ EATING

Some of the most memorable date-night spots in town await along Polk St – and the happy hour deals are sweet, too. Climb Russian Hill along Hyde St to reach prime picnic spots and neighborhood bistros. To cap off a romantic evening, hop a cable car.

★ HOT SAUCE AND PANKO   CHICKEN $

Map p306 (☎415-359-1908; http://hotsauceandpanko.com; 1468 Hyde St; wings $7-11; ⏰11:30am-7pm Wed-Sat, to 5pm Sun; 🚋Powell-Hyde) What's for lunch? Just wing it at Hot Sauce and Panko, an eccentric hilltop corner store stocking hundreds of versions of two namesake items, plus 30 (!) variations on chicken wings. House hot sauce gives a sensational slow burn and lime-chili fish sauce is a flavor bomb – but housemade *go-*

LOCAL KNOWLEDGE

DINING ON THE CABLE-CAR LINE

For a peak dining experience, hitch a ride on a cable car to hilltop hotspots. Let the weather be your guide: get cozy in a romantic hilltop wine bar on foggy days, or grab tasty takeout near George Sterling Park to make the most of sunny afternoons. Start your journey before you feel a rumble in your stomach – cable-car service can be erratic – and leave extra time if you've got reservations to make. Just make sure you board the correct line, going in the right direction.

➡ Seven Hills (p130)
➡ Hot Sauce and Panko (p129)
➡ Venticello (p131)
➡ Union Larder (p131)
➡ Za (p130)
➡ Swensen's (p130)

jujang (Korean fermented-chili sauce) will have you licking your lips for hours.

DIM SUM CLUB   DIM SUM $

Map p306 (📞415-529-2615; 2550 Van Ness Ave; dim sum $3-9; ⏰11am-3pm & 5-9pm; 🚃45, 49) Who knew such authentic *dim sum* was hiding in a Russian Hill motel? Chinese grandmas, of course. Families gather in this friendly dining room around lazy Susans piled with their pick of today's dishes: succulent shrimp and pork *siu mai,* juicy *xiao long bao* (soup dumplings), quite possibly the best *jian dui* (sesame balls) in town and wonton soup that's fragrant and restorative.

SWENSEN'S   ICE CREAM $

Map p306 (www.swensensicecream.com; 1999 Hyde St; cones from $3.75; ⏰noon-10pm; 🚃41, 45, 🚋Powell-Hyde) Bite into your ice-cream cone and get instant brain freeze, plus a hit of nostalgia – this is the original Swensen's ice-cream shop, opened in 1948. Oooh-ouch, that peppermint stick really takes you back, doesn't it? The 16oz root-beer floats are the 1950s version of Prozac, but the classic hot-fudge sundae is pure serotonin with sprinkles on top. Cash only.

CHEESE PLUS   DELI $

Map p306 (www.cheeseplus.com; 2001 Polk St; sandwiches $10-13; ⏰10am-7:30pm Mon-Fri,

from 9am Sat, 9am-7pm Sun; 🚃10, 12, 19, 27, 47, 49) Foodies, rejoice: here's one deli where they won't blink if you request aged, drunken chèvre instead of provolone on your sandwich. The specialty is classic grilled cheese, made with artisan *fromage du jour* – but for extra protein to fuel urban hikes, the Crissy Field comes loaded with oven-roasted Sonoma turkey and sustainable Niman Ranch bacon.

ZA   PIZZA $

Map p306 (📞415-771-3100; www.zapizzasf.com; 1919 Hyde St; slices $5-6; ⏰noon-10pm Sun-Wed, to 11pm Thu-Sat; 🚃41, 45, 🚋Powell-Hyde) Surfers and start-uppers cross town and climb hills for Za – because dude, you don't get gourmet, cornmeal-dusted, thin-crust slices like this every day. Get your pizza piled with fresh toppings, a pint of Anchor Steam and a cozy bar setting – all for under $10.

★1760   CALIFORNIAN $$

Map p306 (📞415-359-1212; www.1760sf.com; 1760 Polk St; dishes $15-22; ⏰5:30-9:30pm Mon-Thu, to 11pm Fri & Sat; 🍴; 🚃45, 49) 🍷 Every night is a culinary throw-down at 1760: chef Carl Foronda must find the right techniques and culinary inspirations to highlight today's star ingredients. No single cuisine dominates and unexpected strengths shine – shiitake add depth to Korean-style short rib, while tomato confit makes papardelle with ragu sing. This is what democracy in the kitchen looks like – all equally inspired and exquisitely presented. Trust your sommelier.

★SWAN OYSTER DEPOT   SEAFOOD $$

Map p306 (📞415-673-1101; 1517 Polk St; dishes $10-28; ⏰10:30am-5:30pm Mon-Sat; 🚃1, 19, 47, 49, 🚋California) Superior flavor without the superior attitude of typical seafood restaurants. Justifiably famous since 1912 for signature oysters and crab salads, there's almost always a wait for the few stools at its vintage lunch counter – but the upside of high turnover is incredibly fresh seafood. Arrive before noon to avoid hour-long waits, or order takeout to enjoy in George Sterling Park (p128).

SEVEN HILLS   ITALIAN, CALIFORNIAN $$

Map p306 (📞415-775-1550; www.sevenhillssf.com; 1550 Hyde St; mains $20-37; ⏰5:30-9:30pm Mon-Thu, 5-10pm Fri & Sat, to 9:30pm Sun; 🚃10, 12, 🚋Powell-Hyde) Romans and San Franciscans converge around the table at this tiny Russian Hill storefront trattoria, where market-fresh ingredients find peak expression. Anthony Florian's short market-driven menu is revised daily, featuring house-made pastas, quality California meats and fish caught hours earlier. Tables are close but service is stellar, and clever sound-canceling technology keeps the happy din to a dull roar.

UNION LARDER
CALIFORNIAN **$$**

Map p306 (☑415-323-4845; http://unionlarder. com; 1945 Hyde St; dishes $15-28; ⊙5-10pm Tue, to 10:30pm Wed, 4-10:30pm Thu, noon-10:30pm Fri & Sat, 5-9pm Sun; ☐Powell-Hyde) For wine with a side of food and people-watching, Union Larder sets the scene with backlit wine bottles rising to the ceiling and vaulted windows overlooking the cable-car line. The short, diverse menu features oysters, salumi (some house-made), succulent stinky cheeses, composed salads and knockout sandwiches, plus some 50 wines by the glass. Meet new friends at shared tables or the bar; no reservations.

VENTICELLO
ITALIAN **$$**

Map p306 (☑415-922-2545; http://venticello. com; 1257 Taylor St; mains $19-35; ⊙5:30-9:30pm Sun-Wed, to 10pm Thu-Sat; ☐1, ☐Powell-Hyde) Date night awaits up Nob Hill and down the stairs. To make your grand entrance to Venticello's two-story-high dining room, you descend via a staircase – which may be why so many of the Nob Hill regulars dress up for this otherwise casual neighborhood Italian bistro. Standout menu items include spaghetti carbonara, risotto and anything from the wood-fired oven – especially pizzas.

LEOPOLD'S
GERMAN **$$**

Map p306 (www.leopoldssf.com; 2400 Polk St; mains $20-29; ⊙dinner 5:30-9:30pm Sun-Mon, to 10pm Tue-Fri, noon-2:30pm & 5:30-10pm Sat, noon-2:30pm Sun; ☐19, 41, 45, 47, 49) Polk St was once better known as Polkstrasse by German immigrants and Leopold's pays homage to neighborhood heritage with lip-schmacking Austrian-German alpine cooking, served beer-hall style in pinewood booths. Hearty specialties include chicken soup with dumplings, goulash, schnitzel, flatbread and house-made salumi – *lecker*! The boisterous crowd gets loud, but after a boot full of beer you'll hardly notice.

★ACQUERELLO
CALIFORNIAN, ITALIAN **$$$**

Map p306 (☑415-567-5432; www.acquerello. com; 1722 Sacramento St; 3-/4-/5-course menu $105/130/150; ⊙5:30-9:30pm Tue-Thu, to 10pm Fri & Sat; ☐1, 19, 47, 49, ☐California) A converted chapel is a fitting location for feasts that turn Italian culinary purists into true believers in Cal-Italian cuisine. Chef Suzette Gresham's ingenious handmade pastas and seasonal signatures include heavenly abalone risotto, devilish lamb with sweetbreads, and truffled squab *canneloni* that deserve angelic choir accompaniment. An anteroom where brides once steadied their nerves is now lined with limited-production Italian vintages seldom seen outside Tuscan castles.

LA FOLIE
FRENCH **$$$**

Map p306 (☑415-776-5577; www.lafolie.com; 2316 Polk St; 4-course menu $150, 5-course veg menu $150, 6-course tasting menu $175; ⊙5:30-10pm Tue-Sat; ☐19, 41, 45, 47) Casually sophisticated La Folie has bravely upheld French standards in laid-back California since 1988. Courses are leisurely paced and chef-owner Roland Passot applies the same painstaking finesse to asparagus tips with quail egg as butter-poached lobster – vegetarians are welcome here. Next door, La Folie Lounge serves exquisite tiny soufflés, impeccable *gougères* (savoury choux pastries) and *tarte flambée* at happy hour (5pm–7pm Tuesday to Thursday).

DRINKING & NIGHTLIFE

Nob Hill rewards dedicated barflies with some of the best cocktails and giddiest views in town – but you'll have to brave the climb here. For bar crawls that require less staggering, head over to Polk St, Russian Hill's main drag. Back in the 1940s, sailors would come from the docks directly to Polk St, which was San Francisco's main gay-bar strip. Now you'll find full-time LGBTIQ+ bars all over town and only a couple on Polk. But on a good night, Polk St regulars are still as upbeat and outgoing as sailors on shore leave.

★STOOKEY'S CLUB MODERNE
LOUNGE

Map p306 (www.stookeysclubmoderne.com; 895 Bush St; ⊙4:30pm-2am Mon-Sat, to midnight Sun; ☐1, ☐Powell-Hyde, Powell-Mason, California) Dangerous dames lure unsuspecting sailors into late-night schemes over potent hooch at this art-deco bar straight out of a Dashiell Hammett thriller. Chrome-lined 1930s Streamline Moderne decor sets the scene for intrigue and wisecracking white-jacketed bartenders shake the stiffest Corpse Reviver cocktails in town. Arrive early to find room on the hat-rack for your fedora, especially on live jazz nights.

★TONGA ROOM   LOUNGE

Map p306 (reservations 415-772-5278; www. tongaroom.com; Fairmont San Francisco, 950 Mason St; cover $5-7; 5-11:30pm Sun, Wed & Thu, to 12:30am Fri & Sat; 1, California, Powell-Mason, Powell-Hyde) Tonight's San Francisco weather: partly foggy, with 100% chance of typhoons every 20 minutes inside the Tonga Room. No need to duck for cover – rain only falls on the indoor pool, where bands play on a boat. For a more powerful hurricane, order one in a plastic coconut. Score bargain Zombies and pupu platters at happy hour (5pm to 7pm Wednesday–Friday).

HI-LO CLUB   BAR

Map p306 (http://hilosf.com; 1423 Polk St; 4pm-2am; 1, 19, 47, 49, California) Trashy meets fancy at Hi-Lo, where discerning barflies sip clever cocktails from vintage glassware. This joint resembles a candlelit squat – tarnished-tin ceilings, well-worn floors, paint-peeling walls. If Van Gogh were in town, he'd come here for a Carthusian Sazerac (absinthe, rye, genapy). Great vintage soul, rock and punk soundtrack – come early, while you can still hear it.

HOPWATER DISTRIBUTION   BEER HALL

Map p306 (http://hopwaterdistribution.com; 850 Bush St; 5-11pm Sun-Wed, to 1am Thu-Sat; 30, 45, Powell-Hyde, Powell-Mason) A sanctuary for beer drinkers above the downtown fray, with 30+ ales, IPAs, pilsners and lagers on tap. The full kitchen offers choice pairings: buttermilk-fried-chicken sandwiches, bacon-studded deviled eggs and dastardly delicious Dungeness crab tater tots. Sit upstairs for bird's-eye views of the scene – during peak hours, it gets loud up here, but the crowd's friendly.

BIG 4   BAR

Map p306 (415-771-1140; www.big4restaurant. com; Huntington Hotel, 1075 California St; 11:30am-midnight; 1, California) Nob Hill society was once dominated by four ruthless railroad barons – but now it's your turn to give the orders in this swanky hill-top cocktail bar. Settle into a club chair to marinate in the oak-paneled old-boys'-club atmosphere and listen to piano players on weekends. Approach the grand mahogany bar for classic martinis and raise a toast to changing times.

HARPER & RYE   COCKTAIL BAR

Map p306 (415-562-7493; http://web.harper andrye.com; 1695 Polk St; 4pm-2am; 1, 19, 47, 49, California) Small-batch, craft and artisan aren't just buzzwords here – Harper & Rye bartenders name their cocktails after neighbors, family and friends, and treat each one accordingly. Floor-to-ceiling weathered wood and exposed steel give this joint honest, straightforward appeal – head to the mezzanine to overlook the upbeat local crowds. Seasonal punch is easy-drinking, but intended for four, not one (ahem).

AMÉLIE   BAR

Map p306 (415-292-6916; www.ameliewinebar. com; 1754 Polk St; 5pm-1am; 1, 10, 12, 19, 27, 47, 49, Powell-Hyde, California) With lipstick-red counters, well-priced pours and plates piled with cheese and charcuterie, this wine bar is a shameless charmer – especially at happy hour (5pm to 7pm), when flights of three cost just $12. Weekends pack (make reservations!); weekdays it's an ideal spot to dawdle over raviole du Dauphiné (cheesy pasta) lavished with black-truffle shavings.

CINCH   GAY

Map p306 (415-776-4162; http://cinchsf.com; 1723 Polk St; 9am-2am Mon-Fri, from 6am Sat & Sun; 1, 19, 27, 47, 49, California) The last of the old-guard Polk St gay bars still has an anything-goes saloon vibe, with pool, pinball, darts and an action-packed smokers patio. Friday drag cabarets are hosted by Anna Conda, mistress of chaos. Holidays are also a blast here and over-the-top decorations stay up for as long as management pleases.

TOP OF THE MARK   BAR

Map p306 (www.topofthemark.com; Mark Hopkins Hotel, 999 California St; cover free-$10; 4:30-11:30pm Sun-Thu, to 12:30am Fri & Sat; 1, California) Twirl above the clouds on the city's highest dancefloor. Friday and Saturday evenings, a full jazz band plays; Wednesdays and Thursdays have live piano music. Genteel mayhem ensues at Sunday Champagne brunches, but evenings are romantic – and it's often empty at sunset.

Cover is free for hotel guests and before 8pm weekdays. Martinis run $15+, but these views are priceless.

 SHOPPING

Upper Polk St (from California St to Broadway) is lined with indie boutiques, vintage shops and historic Polk St specialties: leathers and sex toys. Veer off the beaten path to find original art and local crafts.

★GOOD VIBRATIONS   ADULT

Map p306 (☑415-345-0400; www.goodvibes. com; 1620 Polk St; ☺shop 10am-9pm Sun-Thu, to 10pm Fri & Sat, museum 12:30-6:30pm Fri-Wed, to 8:30pm Thu; ☒1, 19, 47, 49, ☐California) 'Wait, I'm supposed to put that where?' The understanding salespeople in this worker-owned cooperative are used to giving rather explicit instructions, so don't hesitate to ask. Margaret Cho is on the board here, so you know they're not shy. Check out the display of antique vibrators, including one that looks like a floor waxer – thank goodness for modern technology.

★RELOVE   VINTAGE, FASHION & ACCESSORIES

Map p306 (☑415-800-8285; http://shoprelove. com; 1815 Polk St; ☺11am-8pm Tue-Sat, to 6pm Sun, noon-6pm Mon; ☒1, 10, 12, 19, 27, 47, 49, ☐California) ✐ 'More style, less waste' is the credo here, and this dream walk-in-closet of vintage and indie fashion delivers – recent scores include handwoven maxidresses, vintage varsity jackets, Issey Miyake pleated skirts and SF-made Anna Monet horsehair earrings. Relove creates distinctive head-to-toe looks for all genders, but sizes skew small.

LEGION   ARTS & CRAFTS

Map p296 (☑415-733-7900; www.legionsf.com; 808 Sutter St; ☺11am-6pm Tue-Sat; ☒2, 3, 27) This indie art and craft gallery may be off the beaten path, but its fans are legion. Curator-owners bring California's outlandish outlooks indoors with Chelsea Wong's storytelling SF streetscapes, BTW Ceramics' anarchic graffiti-splatter mugs, Bay Area artist Sami Cronk's smiling cherry cotton blanket and Goest's Way Out West candles. Check website for current shows and gallery openings.

MOLTE COSE   FASHION & ACCESSORIES, VINTAGE

Map p306 (☑415-921-5374; www.moltecose. com; 2044 Polk St; ☺11am-6:30pm Mon-Fri, to 6pm Sat, noon-5pm Sun; ☒10, 12, 19, 47, 49) Like a movie set in progress circa 1963, Molte Cose is an obsessively researched collection of one-off gifts and vintage finds artfully displayed on glove models, cake stands and deco vanities. The inspired choice includes vintage cufflinks, shaving kits, hip flasks and locally made kids' gear. Next-door Belle Cose focuses on charming vintage and new women's fashion and lingerie.

PICNIC   CLOTHING, HOMEWARES

Map p306 (☑415-346-6556; www.picnicsf.com; 1808 Polk St; ☺11am-6pm Tue-Sat, noon-6pm Sun; ☒19, 27, 47, 49, ☐Powell-Hyde) Modern gifts for modern women and the people they love – bold, unique, price-savvy. Gift yourself and others with picnic-ready multitools, versatile striped jumpsuits, porcelain hedgehogs that sprout wild strawberries, and scratch-off '99 Bottles of Craft Beer on the wall' posters. Most items are under $50, but no one back home would ever guess.

STUDIO   ART

Map p306 (☑415-931-3130; www.studiogallerysf. com; 1641 Pacific Ave; ☺11am-7pm Mon, Thu & Fri, to 6pm Sat & Sun, by appointment Tue & Wed; ☒1, 19, 47, 49, ☐California) Spiff up your pad with original Bay Area art at great prices. Featured works show a strong sense of place, including Michael Reardon's lightwashed watercolors of Golden Gate Park, Natalie Ciccoricco's embroidered snapshots and Nina Fabunmi's atmospheric oils of rainy SF nights. Some works are postcard-sized or smaller to brighten snug apartments. Check website for monthly openings with local artists.

JOHNSON LEATHERS   FASHION & ACCESSORIES

Map p306 (☑415-775-7393; www.johnsonleath er.com; 1833 Polk St; ☺10am-6pm Mon-Sat, from 11am Sun; ☒10, 12, 19, 27, 47, 49) Looking good in leather since 1979, Johnson Leathers custom-tailors classic cuts to suit all styles and genders. The motorcycle gear is made with quality leather that's all-weather and all-purpose – Johnson's outfits both the San Francisco Police Department's motorcycle patrol *and* the Hells Angels, plus people playing those roles on San Francisco weekends (you know who you are). These jackets last decades.

Japantown, Fillmore & Pacific Heights

Neighborhood Top Five

❶ Fillmore Auditorium (p139) Rocking out with music legends in San Francisco's shrine to psychedelic '60s counterculture.

❷ Kabuki Springs & Spa (p142) Unwinding in communal Japanese baths to take the edge off foggy SF days.

❸ Japan Center (p136) Slurping ramen, playing anime arcade games, cultivating bonsai gardens and browsing Japanese design mags – all inside a mid-century modern mall.

❹ Sasa (p136) Reaching the next level of Japanese dining with one magic

password: *omakase* (chef's choice).

❺ Japantown Cultural & Historical Walking Tour (p142) Getting a local, personal introduction to the peaceful neighborhood that was once a civil rights battleground.

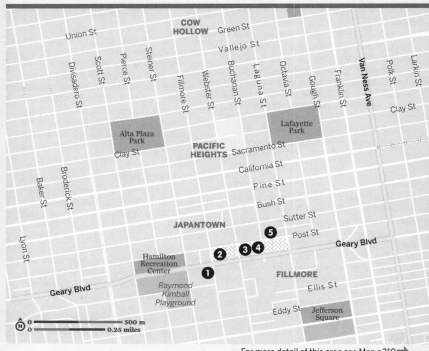

For more detail of this area see Map p310

Explore Japantown, Fillmore & Pacific Heights

The downhill slide of Fillmore St leads from the scenic hilltop parks and chic boutiques of Pacific Heights, through the Instagrammable cultural and culinary hotspots of Japantown, to the buzzworthy dinner and music venues of the Fillmore. To cover the neighborhood, start on Fillmore and Geary Sts, then head north and hang an east on Post St. Duck into Japan Center, head upstairs and browse your way easy across the mall to emerge in Peace Pagoda Place. Wander pedestrian Osaka Way to Sutter St, where you'll head west to Cottage Row for a moment of reflection in the Zen bonsai garden. Head north up to Bush Street, where a left leads you back to Fillmore St.

Window-shop your way uphill on Fillmore until the street becomes residential around Jackson St, then walk west to Alta Plaza Park for giddy hilltop city-view picnics. Here you'll find puppies in sweaters on parade and kids racing around the well-kept playground. For another peak moment, head east to terraced hilltop Lafayette Park – or return to Fillmore and cross Geary for adventurous dining options and epic shows at the Fillmore Auditorium.

Local Life

Music Several live-music venues lie near Geary and Fillmore Sts – the famous Fillmore Auditorium (p139), plus a couple of intimate jazz clubs.

Shopping Fillmore is lined with designer boutiques from local and international designers – but for more fun and adventurous browsing, head to Japantown to hit Japan Center (p136), New People (p141) and the shops along Osaka Way promenade.

Cinema For dinner and a movie, locals come to Japantown. AMC Kabuki (p140) Cinema hosts first-run features and San Francisco International Film Festival premieres; New People Cinema (p140) hosts indie film fests and anime.

Getting There & Away

Bus Lines 1, 2, 3 and 38 connect downtown with Japantown and Pacific Heights, heading west toward the Richmond District. Bus 10 links Pac Heights with downtown via Russian and Nob Hills. Bus 22 connects the Marina, Pac Heights, Japantown and the Fillmore to the Haight and Mission. Buses 41 and 45 connect downtown to Russian Hill and Cow Hollow.

Cable Car The California line's western terminus is at Van Ness, a few blocks east of Pacific Heights.

Lonely Planet's Top Tip

The 38 Geary bus will pick you up downtown and drop you right at Geary and Fillmore – but where's the adventure in that? Hop the California line west from the foot of Market St to Van Ness Ave, then walk to Pacific Heights or Japantown. Instead of taking busy California St west of Van Ness, walk along Victorian-lined Sacramento St (one block north of California), detouring through lovely Lafayette Park.

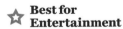

JAPANTOWN, FILLMORE & PACIFIC HEIGHTS

SIGHTS

Most neighborhood sights are in Japantown, but the uphill stretch of Fillmore Street above Geary is flanked with stately Victorian houses. Many have been whitewashed to suit modern minimalist tastes, which is a shame – San Franciscan Victorians were originally built by and for shameless exhibitionists, from their bombastic ornament to vivid color schemes. But when you spot a Victorian still showing its true colors, it's an irresistible photo-op – but since not all San Franciscans are exhibitionists, do respect privacy and public property.

★JAPAN CENTER   NOTABLE BUILDING

Map p310 (www.sfjapantown.org; 1737 Post St; ☉10am-midnight; P; 🚌2, 3, 22, 38, 38L) Time-travel to 1968 as you cross Japan Center's indoor wooden bridges, with *noren* (curtains) and *maneki-neko* (cat figurines) waving welcomes from restaurant entryways. Hard to believe, but this *kawaii*-cute mall started with a knock-down fight. While Japanese American residents were interned during World War II, the city planned to tear down Japantown. Postwar, 1500 recently returned Japantown residents were uprooted to build the mall. But Japantown residents and businesses rallied, stopping evictions and converting the mall into a community hub.

HAAS-LILIENTHAL HOUSE   HISTORIC BUILDING

Map p310 (☎415-441-3000; www.haas-lilienthalhouse.org; 2007 Franklin St; adult/child $10/8; neighborhood walking tours free; ☉noon-2:30pm Wed & Sat, 11am-3:30pm Sun; 👪; 🚌1, 10, 12, 19, 27, 47, 49) If these red-velvet parlor walls could talk this 1886 Queen Anne–style Victorian could tell you about earthquakes, booms, busts and untimely deaths. This turreted mansion looks like a Clue game setting – was the murderer Colonel Mustard with a rope in the ballroom, or Miss Scarlet with a candlestick in the pantry? Docents devoted to Victoriana lead one-hour house tours plus neighborhood walking tours and seasonal events, from fancy-dress Victorian Valentine balls to eerily accurate haunted house tours.

PEACE PAGODA   MONUMENT

Map p310 (Peace Plaza, Japan Center; P; 🚌22, 38) The spiritual center of Japantown's commercial district is minimalist master Yoshiro Taniguchi's Peace Pagoda. It was donated by San Francisco's sister city of Osaka, Japan in 1968. Presented with this five-tiered concrete stupa, San Francisco seemed stupa-fied about what to do with it. Over the years the city clustered shrubs around its stark nakedness, drained leaky reflecting pools and paved over surrounding gardens. Finally, with cherry trees and boulder benches restored to the plaza, the pagoda is in its element, *au naturel*.

COTTAGE ROW   STREET

Map p310 (🚌2, 3, 22, 38) Detour to days of yore, when this neighborhood was a sleepy seaside village – before lumber barons arrived with bombastic Victorian fanfare. Serene clapboard cottages that once housed Japanese fisherfolk line a brick-paved pedestrian promenade, where plum trees and bonsai take center stage. Homes are private, but the central Zen mini-park is perfect for sushi picnics. Cottage Row is off Sutter St, between Webster and Fillmore Sts.

✕ EATING

Japan Center is packed with Japanese restaurants of varying price and quality; noodle shops line the Osaka Way promenade north of Post St. Upper Fillmore St has a good selection of restaurants north of Sutter St.

★SASA   JAPANESE $

Map p310 (☎415-683-9674; www.sasasf.com; 22 Peace Plaza, Japan Center, East Wing, 2nd Floor; 6-10 small plates $25-60, individual plates $5-18; ☉noon-2:30pm & 5:30-9:30 Tue-Sun; 🚌22,38) Like an unexpected first-class upgrade, Sasa delights with exceptional attention to detail. Here katsu is made with kurobuta pork, silken organic *chawanmushi* (egg custard) comes studded with local Dungeness crab and nigiri sushi showcases thoughtfully sourced delicacies like Santa Barbara sea urchin and Hokkaido scallop. Trust the *omakase* (chef's tasting menu) – never has a second floor of a mall been this close to heaven.

★NOOSH   CALIFORNIAN, TURKISH $

Map p310 (☎415-231-5985; 2001 Fillmore St; small plates $5-15; ☑👪; 🚌1,22,38) Follow the spice route into the future with

A NEIGHBORHOOD DIVIDED

Walk around Japantown, Pacific Heights and the Fillmore and you'll notice these sub-neighborhood distinctions aren't just architectural and cultural – differences of race and class are obvious here. But the history of these three overlapping communities is inextricably linked and so too is their future.

In the 1880s, Japanese American fisherfolk and traders began to settle this quiet hillside, away from downtown tenements and conveniently sheltered from the stinky dairies of Cow Hollow. But when gold rush billionaires caught a glimpse of the views atop Pacific Heights, they staked out prime sites for grand hilltop mansions. Spotting an opportunity, real estate speculators copied Pac Heights billionaires' swanky style downhill, with Victorian flats rapidly constructed in sections – precursors to modern pre-fab architecture. These flats were affordable and accessible to many, including small-scale, middle-class Asian, Jewish and African American business owners.

World War II changed everything. Issued by President Roosevelt in 1942, Executive Order 9066 required that Japanese Americans vacate their homes and report for incarceration in internment camps as suspected 'enemy aliens.' Japantown community leaders immediately filed lawsuits against this violation of civil rights and due process – but the order stood. Government reparations would not be made for 45 years.

Meanwhile, the US needed battleships for war in the Pacific. Women and African Americans took up the shipbuilding effort in Bay Area shipyards – but there wasn't enough available housing near ports for the influx of workers. Many African Americans were settled in the Fillmore and lower Pacific Heights, where Japanese Americans had been evicted from their homes. By 1945 the Fillmore had become a community hub for the city's 30,000 African American workers.

After WWII, Japanese Americans returned from internment to await resettlement – only to discover that the city had other plans for the neighborhood. Redevelopment schemes were extending upmarket Pacific Heights developments downhill, displacing both Japantown and the African American Fillmore district. Over 15 years, more than 38 square blocks of small businesses and historic, affordable family homes were bulldozed. But the community stood its ground. African Americans and Japanese Americans worked together to demand fair housing and civil rights and together stopped the luxury-condo takeover of their neighborhood. Affordable housing was rebuilt and community institutions like the Japanese Cultural and Community Center of Northern California established.

Today as you walk around Japantown and the Fillmore, you'll spot many community triumphs: legacy small businesses, nonprofit community centers, historic Victorian flats saved from wrecking balls and mid modern apartment complexes that pioneered affordable housing developments. Look down on Fillmore St sidewalks around O'Farrell and you'll find brick markers noting where community institutions once stood and a Walk of Fame honoring neighborhood luminaries – including several leaders of the US Civil Rights movement. But the fight to keep this historic city neighborhood economically, culturally and ethnically diverse is still ongoing here – as it is across the Bay Area and throughout the US.

Istanbul-inspired, San Francisco-invented sensations: satiny lamb belly with smoked yoghurt, nutty confit sunchoke kebabs, fermented red pepper and California almond *muhammara* dip. Chef/co-owners Laura and Sayat Ozyilmaz satisfy cravings for something fresh and modern, yet soulful – their signature flatbread with aromatic preserved lemon baba ghanoush is so instantly and deeply satisfying, it'll vie for your pizza affections.

⭐ **MARUFUKU RAMEN** RAMEN $
Map p310 (☎415-872-9786; www.marufukuramen.com/; 1581 Webster St, Suite 235, Japan Center, West Wing, 2nd Floor; $13-17; 🚍22,38) No Silicon Valley technology excites as much local geekery as a bowl of Marufuku ramen. Its advantages are much discussed: tonkotsu broth cooked for 20 hours to achieve milky density, noodles handcut ultra-thin to avoid clumping, topped with egg that's soft-cooked, never hard-boiled. Here's all

you need to know: rich, tasty noodles. Value tip: save some broth and get extra noodles for $2.50.

★BENKYODO JAPANESE $

Map p310 (☑415-922-1244; www.benkyodocompany.com; 1747 Buchanan St; mochi $1.50; ⏰8am-5pm Tue-Fri, to 4pm Sat; 🚻; 🚌2, 3, 22, 38) Since 1906, family-owned Benkyodo has survived earthquakes, world wars, even Japanese American internment – and still the Okamura family keeps making life sweeter each day with handmade mochi and *manju* (rice-based confections). Every morning, rice is pounded into pillowy, chewy wrappers that envelop seasonal fillings – fragrant mango, crowd-pleasing peanut butter and best of all, velvety red bean. Cash only.

WISE SONS BAGEL & BAKERY BAKERY $

Map p310 (☑415-872-9046; http://wisesonsdeli.com; 1520 Fillmore St; dishes $3-11; ⏰7am-3pm Mon-Sat, 8am-3pm Sun; 🖋🚻; 🚌22, 38) "Thou shalt boil thy bagels before baking," proclaimed Jewish grandmas everywhere – and who are Wise Sons to disobey? Fillmore was once the hub of SF's Jewish community and this deli honors its roots with pastrami Ruebens on house-baked rye, crispy latkes (potato pancakes) with apple sauce and proper bagels. Since this is SF, load yours with pastrami-spiced salmon or harissa *schmear*.

B. PATISSERIE BAKERY $

Map p310 (☑415-440-1700; http://bpatisserie.com; 2821 California St; dishes $4-12; ⏰8am-6pm Tue-Sun; 🚌1, 24) 🖋 Once even Pacific Heights gourmands weren't sure how to pronounce kouign amann (it's 'queen-ah-man') – until James Beard–winning pastry chef Belinda Leong turned Brittany's buttery, caramelized pastry into a San Francisco sensation. Celebrate the seasons with limited-edition flavors – pumpkin for fall, black sesame for lunar new year – but leave room for meltaway ham-and-cheese croissants and mind-bending mochi donuts.

NIJIYA SUPERMARKET JAPANESE, SUPERMARKET $

Map p310 (☑415-563-1901; www.nijiya.com; 1737 Post St; bento boxes $6-14; ⏰10am-8pm; 🚌2, 3, 22, 38) Picnic under the Peace Pagoda (p136) with reliably fresh sushi or teriyaki bento boxes from Nijiya's deli counter, plus Berkeley-brewed Takara Sierra Cold sake or Hitachino white beer from the drinks aisle – and you'll still have change from $20 for a Japanese candy spree. Grab tropical gummies, *matcha* (green tea) KitKat and something called "cheese candy". You'll be a food Instagram hero.

★STATE BIRD PROVISIONS CALIFORNIAN $$

Map p310 (☑415-795-1272; http://statebirdsf.com; 1529 Fillmore St; dishes $8-30; ⏰5:30-10pm Sun-Thu, to 11pm Fri & Sat; 🚌22, 38) 🖋 Even before winning multiple James Beard Awards, State Bird attracted lines for 5:30pm seatings not seen since the Dead played neighboring Fillmore Auditorium. Carts arrive tableside laden with California-inspired, dim-sum-sized "provisions" like jerk octopus and pastrami pancakes. Progress to larger but equally esoteric seasonal signatures, from kimchi-spiced Dungeness crab with bottarga to parmesan-feathered California state bird (quail) atop slow-cooked onions. Book ahead.

OUT THE DOOR VIETNAMESE $$

Map p310 (OTD; ☑415-923 9575; www.outthedoors.com; 2232 Bush St; mains lunch $14-25, dinner $20-30; ⏰11am-2:30pm & 5:30-9:30pm Mon-Fri, 9am-2:30pm & 5:30-9:30pm Sat & Sun; 🚌2, 3, 22) 🖋 A casual offshoot of the famous Slanted Door (p88), home cooking gets an upgrade: brunch brings silken scrambled eggs with five-spice pork belly and cinnamony buttermilk pancakes while lunch means decadent Dungeness crab cellophane noodles and tangy grapefruit and jicama salad. Reserve online.

PIZZERIA DELFINA PIZZA $$

Map p310 (☑415-440-1189; www.pizzeriadelfina.com; 2406 California St; pizzas $14-21; ⏰11:30am-10pm Sun, Mon, Wed & Thu, 5-10pm Tue, 11:30am-11pm Fri & Sat; 🖋; 🚌1, 3, 22) 🖋 Wait: broccoli rabe on pizza with no sauce? Believe it – Pizzeria Delfina proves the Italian/Californian theory that a few farm-fresh ingredients, well-prepared and meticulously balanced, can become a proper feast. Toothsome thin-crust pizzas puff at the edges, barricading gooey buffalo mozzarella and San Marzano tomato sauce against shirt onslaughts. Brave tantalizing waits with help from Italian wines or local beer.

THE PROGRESS CALIFORNIAN $$$

Map p310 (☑415-673-1294; https://theprogress-sf.com; 1525 Fillmore St; small plates $16-36; ⏰5:30-10pm Sun-Thu, to 11pm Fri & Sat; 🖋;

📖22, 38) 🖊 The sister bistro of State Bird Provisions seems laid-back – the *wabi-sabi* wooden decor resembles a weatherbeaten boat and Stuart Brioza and Nicole Krasinski's Pacific coastal menu is quintessentially Californian. But surf-meets-turf fare reveals James Beard Award–winning flair – sustainable California sturgeon caviar drifts across potato clouds, while briny Manila clams and earthy roast maitake mushrooms bond over squash soup dumplings. Dessert is an afterthought; enjoy more vegetables.

🍷 DRINKING & NIGHTLIFE

Bars are missing the point here – why just get a drink when you could get one with an award-winning meal or world-class entertainment? Neighborhood hangouts range from Fillmore jazz joints to Japantown karaoke bars and Pacific Heights cafes.

SCOPO DIVINO
WINE BAR

Map p310 (📞415-928-3728; www.scopodivino. com; 2800 California St; ☺3-11pm Mon-Fri, 11am-11pm Sat-Sun) Wine, music and conversation blend brunch into happy hour at Scopo Divino. The wine selection does Sonoma proud with old-vine zins and fog-kissed whites and showcases intriguing Italian blends – take the Taste of Italy flight. Live jazz keeps Fillmore supperclub traditions alive and swinging Wednesdays, Thursdays and Sundays. For brunch, pair tart cherry bellinis with duck confit hash or chicken and waffles.

BOBA GUYS
TEAHOUSE

Map p310 (www.bobaguys.com; 1522 Fillmore St; ☺11am-9pm Mon-Thu, noon-11pm Fri & Sat, noon-6pm Sun; 📖22, 38) 🖊 Ping-pong buddies Andrew and Bin got thirsty and transformed superhero-style into Boba Guys. This is their dream milk tea made with premium small-batch teas and organic milk from Sonoma – plus your choice of tapioca balls or grass jelly made fresh daily. For hangovers, order yours with a side of kimchi fried rice from onsite Sunday Bird pop-up. Expect waits.

ELITE CAFE
COCKTAIL BAR

Map p310 (📞415-346-8400; http://theelitecafe. com; 2049 Fillmore St; ☺4-10pm Tue-Thu, 11-2:30 & 4-10pm Fri, 10am-3:30pm & 4-10pm Sat-Sun) You've been delightfully misled: this 1930s New Orleans-style cocktail joint isn't another hipster coffee shop and despite its upmarket address, it's not elitist. They cheerfully serve brunch mimosas by the liter at 10am Sunday – and you can score $2 oysters at 4-6pm happy hours, even on weekends. Relax and people-watch at sidewalk tables over legit Pimms Cup and restorative jambalaya.

SOCIAL STUDY
BAR

Map p310 (http://thesocialstudysf.com; 1795 Geary Blvd; ☺5-10:30pm Mon, noon-11pm Tue-Thu, to 1am Fri & Sat, noon-10:30pm Sun; 📶; 📖22, 38) Observe San Franciscans in their native habitat at Social Study, where days begin earnestly with powerful coffee, wi-fi and tasty study snacks, then relax into a rec-room groove over craft beer and wine by the glass, board games and movies projected onto brick walls. DJs amp up the house-party vibe Thursday-Saturday nights.

☆ ENTERTAINMENT

From the 1930s to the '60s, the Fillmore was home to the West Coast jazz scene – today clubs cluster around Geary Blvd. Local cinemas are ideal for foggy days and film festival nights.

★FILLMORE AUDITORIUM
LIVE MUSIC

Map p310 (📞415-346-6000; http://thefillmore. com; 1805 Geary Blvd; tickets from $20; ☺box office 10am-3pm Sun, plus 30min before doors open to 10pm show nights; 📖22, 38) Jimi Hendrix, Janis Joplin, the Grateful Dead – they all played the Fillmore and the upstairs bar is lined with vintage psychedelic posters to prove it. Bands that sell out stadiums keep rocking this historic, 1250-capacity dance hall, and for major shows, free posters are still handed out. To squeeze up to the stage, be polite and lead with the hip.

★AUDIUM
SOUNDSCAPE

Map p310 (📞415-771-1616; www.audium.org; 1616 Bush St; $20; ☺performances 8:15pm Thur, Fri & Sat; 📖2, 3, 19, 38, 47, 49, 📖California) Sit in total darkness as Stan Shaff plays his unique musical instrument: an auditorium constructed in 1962 as a living sound sculpture, lined floor to ceiling with 176 speakers. In extended, psychedelic "room compositions," meditative tones build to 1970s sci-fi sound effects before resolving into oddly endearing Moog-synthesizer wheezes. A truly San Franciscan experience that induces altered states – prepartying recommended.

BOOM BOOM ROOM
LIVE MUSIC

Map p310 (☎415-673-8000; www.boomboom room.com; 1601 Fillmore St; cover varies; ☺4pm-2am Tue-Sun; ☐22, 38) Jumping since the '30s, the Boom Boom remains a classic Fillmore venue for blues, soul and funk. Except for the outdoor murals and vintage photos indoors, there's nothing fancy about this joint – curtained stage, Formica tables, bar slinging potent well drinks, well-stomped checkered linoleum dance floor – but it rocks six nights a week with top touring talent. Shows start around 9pm.

SHEBA PIANO LOUNGE
JAZZ

Map p310 (☎415-440-7414; www.shebapiano lounge.com; 1419 Fillmore St; ☺5pm-1am; ☐22, 31, 38) Hot jazz comes extra spicy at Sheba's – a Fillmore supperclub where jazz combos play nightly, while sister co-owners Israel and Net Alamayehu dish out Ethiopian vegetarian combination platters that leave lips buzzing. Besides solid selections of Californian beers and wines, Ethiopian tej (honey wine) is a not-too-sweet treat. Arrive before 8pm showtime to score a coveted fireside table.

NEW PEOPLE CINEMA
CINEMA

Map p310 (☎415-525-8600; www.newpeople world.com; New People, 1746 Post St; tickets free-$15; ☐2, 3, 22, 38) Underground cinema draws small but dedicated crowds to this independent 143-seat basement theater. Local indie films, international documentaries, current-release Japanese films and anime get properly showcased here, with HD projection and booming surround sound. Check the website for special screenings for International Women's Day, Japanese American Internment Remembrance Day and SF and Asian American Film Festivals.

AMC KABUKI 8
CINEMA

Map p310 (☎415-346-3243; www.amctheatres. com; 1881 Post St; adult $8 matinee, $16 evening; ☐2, 3, 22, 38) 🖉 A go-to for rainy day matinees, featuring big-name flicks and film festival favorites. Pro tips: reserve a stadium seat online ($2 extra) and arrive early to beat the line to the bar for wine, beer and well drinks to pair with your movie snacks (hence the 21-plus designation for most shows).

🛍 SHOPPING

Japantown is packed with authentic Japanese wares, street fashion and kitschy-fun gift shops, especially in and immediately around Japan Center. Pacific Heights caters to an upmarket demographic – hence its nickname, Specific Whites. Along upper Fillmore St, there's designer window-shopping and beauty bars galore all the way up to Broadway. For more high-end indie boutiques, head to Presidio Heights – Sacramento St, west of Presidio Ave.

★ KINOKUNIYA BOOKS
BOOKS

Map p310 (☎415-567-7625; www.kinokuniya. com/us; 1581 Webster St, Japan Center; ☺10:30am-8pm; ☐22, 38) Like warriors in a showdown, the manga, bookstore and stationery divisions of Kinokuniya vie for your attention. You must choose where your loyalties lie: with vampire comics downstairs, stunning Daido Moriyama photography books and Harajuku street fashion mags upstairs, or across the hall to stationery where whiskey-barrel wood Pure Malt pens and journals featuring a pensive fried egg cartoon character vie for your 'eggsistential thoughts.'

★ SANKO KITCHEN ESSENTIALS
CERAMICS, HOMEWARES

Map p310 (https://sankosf.com; 1758 Buchanan St; ☺9am-5pm; ☐2, 3, 22, 38) Upgrade from ho-hum minimalism with Japanese goods bound to bring joy: bronzed Traveler's Company pen cases, square-handled charcoal Hasami porcelain mugs, Makoo recycled leather totes, old-school Casio calculator watches. Alongside must-have Japanese design objects are original pieces handmade by San Francisco artisans – including those stoneware ramen bowls and bunny chopstick holders.

★ SOKO HARDWARE
HOMEWARES

Map p310 (☎415-931-5510; 1698 Post St; ☺9am-5:30pm Mon-Sat; ☐2, 3, 22, 38) A Japantown go-to since 1925, Soko has an exceptional selection of hard-to-find housewares, from hot-water ladles for Japanese baths to properly tuned wind chimes. When (not if) Japantown inspires you to bring small graces to your own corner of the world, Soko is your source for essential ikebana, bonsai, tea-ceremony and Zen rock-garden supplies.

MARGARET O'LEARY   CLOTHING

Map p310 (☑415-771-9982; www.margareto leary.com; 2400 Fillmore St; ☺10am-7pm Mon-Sat, 11am-5:30pm Sun; ☐1, 3, 10, 22, 24) At her flagship store, San Francisco designer Margaret O'Leary showcases whisper-light cardigans of Scottish cashmere and organic cotton ideal for year-round wear in San Francisco. To keep the fog at Bay, layer nubby nautical striped sweaters under hand-knit jackets. For investment pieces, they're fairly priced – and the sale racks hold major scores.

NEW PEOPLE   CLOTHING, SHOES

Map p310 (☑415-345-1975; www.newpeople world.com; 1746 Post St; ☺noon-7pm Mon-Sat, to 6pm Sun; ☐2, 3, 22, 38) A three-story emporium devoted to Japanese pop culture, New People brings Tokyo style to SF. Get dolled up in Lolita petticoat dresses at 2nd-floor Baby the Stars Shine Bright, rock platforms with hoodies and other Harajuku street fashion at Maruq, or freestyle in Sou-Sou's modern graphic shifts inspired by *kantoui* (tunics) *w*orn circa 500BC.

KATSURA GARDEN   BONSAI

Map p310 (☑415-931-6209; 1825 Post St, Japan Center; ☺10am-6pm Mon-Sat, 11am-5:30pm Sun; ☐2, 3, 22, 38) Small wonders are the specialty of Katsura Garden, bonsai garden masters. Years of training go into each tiny tree gracing these shelves, from the miniature juniper that looks like it grew on a windswept molehill to the stunted maple that sheds five tiny, perfect red leaves each autumn. Pick up bonsai and ikebana supplies to keep inspiration flowing.

JONATHAN ADLER   HOMEWARES

Map p310 (☑415-563-9500; www.jonathanadler. com; 2133 Fillmore St; ☺10am-6pm Mon-Sat, 11am-5pm Sun; ☐1, 3, 22) Vases with handlebar mustaches and cookie jars labeled "LSD" may seem like holdovers from a Big Sur bachelor pad c 1974, but they're snappy interior inspirations from California pop-art potter Jonathan Adler. Don't worry whether that mirrored Lucite bar cart

matches your mid-century couch because as Adler says, 'Minimalism is a bummer.'

PAPER TREE   ARTS & CRAFTS

Map p310 (The Origami Store; ☑415-921-7100; 1743 Osaka Way; ☺10am-5pm Mon & Wed-Sat, 11am-4pm Sun; ☖; ☐22,38) Hang a left at Ruth Asawa's bronze Origami Fountains and discover worlds of possibility. Family-run since 1968, this paper-craft emporium is fueling a local origami revival. Beyond classic paper airplanes and cranes, origami is now used for art (notice the glass-encased paper cocoon-dress), work (Google's self-driving car prototype was origami) and play (fold your own Death Star with the Star Wars kit).

BITE LIP LAB   COSMETICS

Map p310 (☑415-872-9661; http://bitebeauty. com; 2132 Fillmore St; ☺11am-7pm; ☐1, 3, 22) San Francisco prides itself on innovation, but this one's Canadian: custom-blended lipstick, with food-grade essential oils and nontoxic, organic ingredients. Specialists find your color matches from over 200 shades – or like a true SF fashionista, you can design and name your own signature shade. Finishes come in matte, shimmer, gloss and creamy *amuse bouche*. Book appointments online; all genders welcome.

KOHSHI   GIFTS & SOUVENIRS

Map p310 (☑415-931-2002; www.kohshisf.com; 1737 Post St, Suite 355, West Mall, Japan Center; ☺11am-7pm Wed-Mon; ☐2, 3, 22, 38) Fragrant Japanese incense for every purpose, from long-burning sandalwood for Zen meditation to cinnamon-tinged Gentle Smile to atone for laundry left too long. For such a small shop, the gifting possibilities seem endless here – including ninja tea mugs, *kokedama* (ornamental plants growing from moss-covered balls) and red Daruma figurines for making wishes.

CROSSROADS TRADING   FASHION & ACCESSORIES

Map p310 (www.crossroadstrading.com; 1901 Fillmore St; ☺11am-7pm Sun-Thu, to 8pm Fri-Sat; ☐2, 3, 22, 38) Hey bargain hunters: see those upscale design boutiques lining Fillmore St? You can probably score their recent designs for less at Crossroads, thanks to Pacific Heights clotheshorses who ditch last season's wardrobe here – that's why this Crossroads beats other SF branches. For even sweeter deals, trade in your own

JAPANTOWN HISTORY WALK

In Peace Pagoda Plaza, on the outside wall of Japan Center's east wing, you'll notice an intriguing sign that asks: "What happened here?" This sign marks the beginning of the Japantown History Walk, a self-guided adventure that guides you around 10 blocks to 17 pivotal locations in Japantown. Take a picture of this sign as a map reference and handy timeline of key events in Japantown's history. Then follow your map to explore the origins of San Francisco sushi, Japanese baseball, WWII internment, civil rights and Japantown's enduring community.

stylish, gently worn clothes for credit. Men's selection is limited; women's is impressive.

ICHIBAN KAN   GIFTS & SOUVENIRS

Map p310 (☑415-409-0472; www.ichibankan usa.com; 22 Peace Plaza, Suite 540, Japan Center, East wing; ⊙10am-8pm; 🚇2, 3, 22, 38) It's a wonder you got this far in life without penguin soy-sauce dispensers, Pikachu socks, extra-spiky hair wax and the ultimate in gay gag gifts, the handy "Closet Case" – all here at bargain prices. The plush toy selection is exclamation-inducing – polar bears in sunglasses! Smiling tofu! Rainbow duckies! And untranslatable Japanese snacks add adventure to any road trip.

SPORTS & ACTIVITIES

★KABUKI SPRINGS & SPA   BATHHOUSE

Map p310 (☑415-922-6000; www.kabukisp rings.com; 1750 Geary Blvd; adult $30; ⊙10am-10pm, call-gender Tue, women-identified only Wed, Fri & Sun, men-identified only Mon, Thu & Sat; 🚇22, 38) Gooong! That's a subtle hint to chatty spa-goers to shush, restoring meditative silence to Japantown's communal, clothing-optional bathhouse. Salt-scrub in the steam room, soak in the hot pool, take a cold plunge, reheat in the sauna, rinse and repeat. Men/transmen and women/trans-

women alternate days except all-gender Tuesdays, when bathing suits are required. Bath access is $15 with spa treatments, including shiatsu massage.

JAPANESE ARTS & COOKING
WORKSHOPS AT JCCNC   COOKING, ARTS

Map p310 (☑415-567-5505; www.jcccnc.org; 1840 Sutter Street; workshops $15-65; ⊙workshop times vary; 🚼; 🚇22,38) Japantown has inspiration to spare – so nonprofit Japanese Cultural and Community Center of Northern California (JCCCNC) generously offers affordable workshops with acclaimed local artisans, chefs and artists. Get hands-on experience with Japanese traditions, such as ikebana, *washi ningyo* (paper dolls), *doburoku* (home brew sake), *kaiseki* (seasonal meal) cooking and *magawappa* bento box woodcraft. Check the calendar for upcoming events and workshops.

JAPANTOWN CULTURAL &
HISTORICAL WALKING TOUR   WALKING TOUR

Map p310 (☑415-921-5007; www.njahs.org/walk ing-tours/; NJAHS Japantown Peace Gallery, 1684 Post St; $10-15 per person; ⊙by prior booking Mon-Fri 10am-5pm; 🚼; 🚇22, 38) Get insider's perspectives on Japantown from local National Japanese Historical Society docents sharing cultural insights and personal stories. Tours depart NJAHS Japantown Peace Gallery. From Wednesday to Friday, NJAHS also offers fascinating tours of the Presidio's Fourth Army Intelligence School where Japanese American soldiers were trained for top-secret missions in WWII and for postwar US occupation of Japan.

PLAYLAND JAPAN   GAME ARCADE

Map p310 (☑510-501-6546; 1737 Post St, Unit 323; per game from 50¢; ⊙2:30-8:30pm Mon-Thu, 12:30-10pm Fri, 11am-10pm Sat, 11am-8pm Sun; 🚼; 🚇2, 3, 22, 38) Logically you realize adorable plush pink alpacas are near-impossible to grab with a clumsy remote-controlled claw, but that won't keep you from trying Takoyaki Catcher and other irresistible Japanese arcade games. Ask attendants for pointers on taiko drum games and anime adventures – instructions are in Japanese – and if at first you don't succeed, buy the alpaca up front.

The Mission, Dogpatch & Potrero Hill

Neighborhood Top Five

❶ Mission murals (p145) Seeing garage doors, storefronts and entire alleyways transformed into canvases, with more than 500 murals by local and international artists.

❷ Dolores Park (p146) Playing, picnicking and people-watching entire days away, while avoiding any form of adult responsibility.

❸ Valencia St (p163) Strolling the city's liveliest corridor, grabbing a bite or a cocktail at a trendy new restaurant, and popping into lifestyle and novelty stores.

❹ Mission Dolores (p147) Getting a handle on California history at San Francisco's oldest building, a whitewashed adobe church dating back to 1782.

❺ Dogpatch's Creative Corridor (p147) Appreciating local art, design, wine- and chocolate-making ensconced in waterfront warehouses.

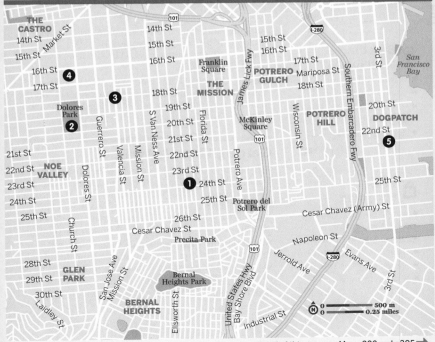

For more detail of this area see Map p302 and p305 ➡

Lonely Planet's Top Tip

The Mission is packed with restaurants, bars, boutiques, galleries and clubs; while you should be fine in the daytime, it's not always the safest area to walk alone in at night. Recruit a friend and be alert in the Mission east of Valencia, in Potrero Hill below 18th St and around deserted Dogpatch warehouses. Don't bring the bling – this isn't LA – and don't leave belongings unattended.

Best Places to Eat

➡ Tartine Manufactory (p152)

➡ La Palma Mexicatessen (p149)

➡ Al's Place (p150)

➡ Californios (p153)

➡ Mr Pollo (p149)

For reviews, see p149.➡

Best Places to Drink

➡ El Rio (p155)

➡ Trick Dog (p153)

➡ %ABV (p155)

➡ Ungrafted (p154)

➡ Zeitgeist (p153)

For reviews, see p153.➡

Best Shopping

➡ Adobe Books & Backroom Gallery (p162)

➡ Gravel & Gold (p161)

➡ Community Thrift (p160)

➡ Needles & Pens (p161)

➡ Mission Comics & Art (p160)

For reviews, see p160.➡

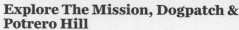

Explore The Mission, Dogpatch & Potrero Hill

Get to know San Francisco from the inside out, from pirate stores to painted alleyways, from salsa dives to art deco cinemas. Begin with almighty Valencia St, the city's most vibrant shopping corridor, to score new looks and old books, and then saunter through mural-covered Balmy Alley on your way south to the city's up-and-coming southern stretches. Pop into lesser-explored Potrero Hill galleries just south of 16th St and dip down to the Dogpatch's unnervingly hip Minnesota Street Project; you'll be fueled up for conversations through multiple tacos tastings and late into the night at the 'hood's hottest wine bars and cocktail lounges. After you've wandered hither and thither, get those hands dirty at a cooking class, craft workshop or the rock-climbing gym. Cap things off with an epic bar crawl and some Saturday night salsa dancing with suave strangers packed into Mission clubs.

Local Life

Learning something new Upcycle trash into art at SCRAP (Scroungers' Center for Re-Usable Art Parts; ☏415-647-1746; www.facebook.com/scrapsf; 801 Toland St; ◷10am-6pm Mon-Fri, to 5pm Sat; 🚼; 🚌9, 23, 24, 44) 🎗, hone knife skills at 18 Reasons (p163), vogue at Dance Mission (p164) and tell likely stories at 826 Valencia (p146).

Doing dessert After another lap of Mission murals, you're ready for boozy ice cream at Humphry Slocombe (p150) and salted-caramel eclairs from Craftsman & Wolves (p150).

Looking the part Define your own streetwise Mission style with local designers at Gravel & Gold (p161), Betabrand (p162), Nooworks (p162), Baggu (p160) and Aggregate Supply (p163).

Getting There & Away

Bus Bus 14 runs from downtown to the Mission District along Mission St. Bus 22 runs from Dogpatch and the Mission through the Haight to the Marina. Bus 49 follows Mission St and Van Ness Ave to Fisherman's Wharf, while bus 33 links Potrero and the Mission to the Castro, the Haight and Golden Gate Park.

Streetcar The J streetcar heads from downtown through the Mission. The T Muni line from downtown via SoMa stops along 3rd St between 16th and 22nd, in Potrero's Dogpatch district.

BART Stations at 16th and 24th Sts serve the Mission.

TOP SIGHT
MISSION MURALS

Diego Rivera has no idea what he started. Inspired by the Mexican maestro's 1930s works in San Francisco, generations of Mission muralists have covered alleys and community institutions with 500-plus murals in a splendid show of political dissent, community pride and graffiti-art bravado.

When 1970s Mission *muralistas* objected to US foreign policy in Latin America, they took to the streets with paintbrushes – beginning with **Balmy Alley**. Bodegas, taquerias and community centers lining 24th St are now covered with murals of mighty Mayan goddesses and Aztec warriors, honoring the district's combined native and Mexican origins. Aztec serpent-god Quetzalcoatl has kept watch over **24th & York Mini Park** (Map p302; www.sfparks alliance.org/our-parks/parks/24th-and-york-mini-park; cnr York & 24th Sts; ☉sunrise-sunset; 🚼; 🚌9, 12, 27, 48, Ⓑ24th St) since 1972 and former neighbor Galería de la Raza once repurposed billboards for Digital Mural Project proclamations such as 'Abolish borders!'

Before Barry McGee and Chris Johansen sold out shows at international art fairs, they could be found at Clarion Alley (p146), gripping spray-paint cans. In 1993–94 an all-star team of seven women *muralistas* and local volunteers covered the Women's Building (pictured; p146) with *Maestrapeace*, featuring icons of female strength. Atop literary nonprofit 826 Valencia (p146) is a gold-leafed mural celebrating human attempts to communicate, created by Pulitzer Prize–winning graphic novelist Chris Ware.

DON'T MISS

➡ Balmy Alley
➡ Clarion Alley
➡ *Maestrapeace* at the Women's Building
➡ 826 Valencia mural by Chris Ware

PRACTICALITIES

➡ Map p302, E7
➡ ☏415-285-2287
➡ www.precitaeyes.org
➡ btwn 24th & 25th Sts
➡ 🚌10, 12, 14, 27, 48, Ⓑ24th St Mission

◉ SIGHTS

The **Mission** is a crossroads of contradictions and at its heart is Mission St, SF's faded 'miracle mile' of art deco cinemas, now occupied by 99¢ stores and shady characters, surrounded by colorful murals and trend-setting restaurants. West of Mission St, Valencia St has quirky boutiques, reasonable restaurants and seven-figure condos. Calle 24 (24th St) is SF's designated Latino Cultural District, with community centers, churches, bodegas, *panaderias* (bakeries) and taquerias all swathed in murals. Further east, Potrero Hill has become a bedroom community for Silicon Valley tech execs – but, just downhill, culinary schools and art studios have creatively repurposed warehouses in Potrero Flats and waterfront Dogpatch.

BALMY ALLEY   PUBLIC ART
See p145.

★826 VALENCIA   CULTURAL CENTER
Map p302 (☑415-642-5905; www.826valencia. org; 826 Valencia St; ◷noon-6pm; ♿; 🚌14, 33, 49, Ⓑ16th St Mission, Ⓜ J) Avast, ye scurvy scallywags! If ye be shipwrecked without yer eye patch or McSweeney's literary anthology, lay down ye doubloons and claim yer booty at this here nonprofit pirate store. Below decks, kids be writing tall tales for dark nights a'sea, and ye can study writing movies, science fiction and suchlike, if that be yer dastardly inclination.

★WOMEN'S BUILDING   NOTABLE BUILDING
Map p302 (☑415-431-1180; www.womensbuilding. org; 3543 18th St; 🚌14, 22, 33, 49, Ⓑ16th St Mission, Ⓜ J) A renowned and beloved Mission landmark since 1979, the nation's first women-owned-and-operated community center is festooned with one of the neighborhood's most awe-inspiring murals. The *Maestrapeace* mural was painted in 1994 and depicts hugely influential women, including Nobel Prize–winner Rigoberta Menchú, poet Audre Lorde, artist Georgia O'Keeffe and former US Surgeon General Dr Joycelyn Elders.

★DOLORES PARK   PARK
Map p302 (http://sfrecpark.org/destination/ mission-dolores-park; Dolores St, btwn 18th & 20th Sts; ◷6am-10pm; ♿🐕; 🚌14, 33, 49, Ⓑ16th

St Mission, Ⓜ J) Welcome to San Francisco's sunny side, the land of street ball and Mayan-pyramid playgrounds, semiprofessional tanning and taco picnics. Although the grassy expanses are mostly populated by relaxing hipsters, political protests and other favorite local sports do happen from time to time, and there are free movie nights and mime troupe performances in summer. Climb to the upper southwestern corner for superb views of downtown, framed by palm trees.

★CLARION ALLEY   PUBLIC ART
Map p302 (https://clarionalleymuralproject.org; btwn 17th & 18th Sts; 🚌14, 22, 33, Ⓑ16th St Mission, Ⓜ16th St Mission) In this outstanding open-air street art showcase, you'll spot artists touching up pieces and making new ones, with the full consent of neighbors and Clarion Alley Collective's curators. Only a few pieces survive for years, such as Megan Wilson's daisy-covered *Tax the Rich* or Jet Martinez' glimpse of Clarion Alley inside a forest spirit. Incontinent art critics often take over the alley's eastern end – pee-eew! – so topical murals usually go up on the western end.

ANGLIM GILBERT GALLERY   GALLERY
Map p305 (☑415-433-2710; http://anglimgilbert gallery.com; 1275 Minnesota St, 2nd fl; ◷11am-6pm Tue-Sat; 🚌48, 🚃T) **FREE** The Bay Area hits the big time here, with gallery director Ed Gilbert continuing Anglim's 30-year legacy of launching art movements, from Beat assemblage to Bay Area conceptualists. Major artists range from political provocateur Enrique Chagoya to sublime sculptor Deborah Butterfield, yet shows here maintain a hair-raising edge, such as an upraised fist pushed through gallery walls in David Huffman's *Panther*.

CASEMORE KIRKEBY   GALLERY
Map p305 (☑415-851-9808; http://casemore kirkeby.com; 1275 Minnesota St, 1st fl; ◷11am-6pm Tue-Sat; 🚌48, 🚃T) **FREE** Ever since gold-rush miners captured their newfound wealth with ferrotype portraits, San Francisco has staked claims to artistic fame with photography – and Casemore Kirkeby continues to push the boundaries. Group shows explore techniques ranging from Aspen Mays' photograms to Sean McFarland's manufactured landscapes. Todd Hido retrospectives showcase his color photography mastery in eerie suburban nocturnes.

GENTRIFICATION IN THE MISSION

As you frolic around the Mission, popping into precious and pricey little boutiques and fueling up on $14 peanut-washed Bulleit Bourbon cocktails or $10 hand-whisked *matchas* (green tea), you may notice a strange placard high up in a window: 'No Locals on this Corner. We'll Miss You When We're Gone.' On a Saturday afternoon, you may encounter a group of Latinx residents and neighborhood activists chanting about stopping evictions. Or on a weekday morning, you could see a group of scooters blocking a shuttle route for tech-company employees, many of whom now call the Mission home.

Here's why: the arrival of these wealthy employees has jacked up housing costs in a neighborhood long populated by South and Central American immigrants living on minimum wage. The median household income in the Mission was $37,000 in 1990, and many of those households were filled with entire extended families. Now, lots of those homes are being bought up by big-name tech employees making four or five times that amount.

The neighborhood was already coveted for its flat streets, sunny weather, cultural cachet and proximity to the freeway and public transportation. And as new money comes into the Mission, along with fancy restaurants and shops, it's become even more desirable. Crime has become less of a problem. A new park, Chan Kaajal Park, replaced a former parking lot and features an interactive water plaza. And certainly there are new economic opportunities here for those in a position to capitalize.

Today, Valencia St offers some of the best food, shopping and people-watching in the city, and travelers flock to it for these reasons. But during your visit, do keep in mind that some of the Latinx residents, whose families have been here for five decades, are still trying to get by on meager incomes from their 99¢ stores, bodegas and taco shops.

You can learn more about the neighborhood by studying the gorgeous murals on Balmy (p145) and Clarion alleys or, better yet, jump on a mural tour with **Precita Eyes** (Map p302; ☑415-285-2287; www.precitaeyes.org; 2981 24th St; adult $20, child $3; ☐12, 14, 48, 49, ⓑ24th St Mission) for the full scoop on the neighborhood's artists. You can also show support for long-standing local businesses by grabbing an empanada at a place like **Chile Lindo** (Map p302; ☑415-621-6108; www.chilelindo.com; 2944 16th St; empanadas $5-6; ◷8am-4pm Mon-Fri, from 10am Sat; ☐14, 22, 33, ⓑ16th St Mission) 🍴, or a handmade tamale at La Palma Mexicatessen (p149).

Check in with **Calle 24 Latino Cultural District** (Map p302; www.calle24sf.org/; 3250 24th St) to find out about events that may be going on during your visit and other ways to get involved.

MUSEUM OF CRAFT & DESIGN MUSEUM
Map p305 (☑415-773-0303; www.sfmcd.org; 2569 3rd St; adult/student $8/6; ◷11am-6pm Tue-Sat, noon-5pm Sun; ☐22, 48, Ⓜ T) Elephants created from sewn-together maps, benches made from repurposed shovel handles, factory-floor scenes recreated entirely in duct tape: one-off original works not meant for mass production reignite wonder at the Museum of Craft & Design. Check the online schedule for hands-on workshops where accomplished artisans lead projects related to museum shows, from upcycled book furnishings to block-printed tea towels.

SOUTHERN EXPOSURE GALLERY
Map p302 (☑415-863-2141; www.soex.org; 3030 20th St; donations welcome; ◷noon-6pm Tue-

Sat; ☐12, 22, 27, 33, ⓑ16th St Mission) Art really ties the room together at nonprofit arts center Southern Exposure, where works are carefully crafted not just with paint and canvas, but a sense of community. Past projects featured science fiction visions of a near future imagined by artists of color, and 24 artists making artworks according to other artists' instructions. Don't miss So-Ex's annual auction, where major Bay Area artists create installations and the audience snaps up museum-worthy bargains.

MISSION DOLORES CHURCH
Map p302 (Misión San Francisco de Asís; ☑415-621-8203; www.missiondolores.org; 3321 16th St; adult/child $7/5; ◷9am-4:30pm May-Oct, to 4pm Nov-Apr; ☐22, 33, ⓑ16th St Mission, Ⓜ J)

WORTH A DETOUR

DOGPATCH DETOUR

Potrero Hill's convenient location off Hwy 101 has made it a Silicon Valley bedroom community – but, just downhill around 22nd and 3rd Sts, upstart creatives are taking over waterfront warehouses. After the shipping business moved to Oakland in the 1950s, this blue-collar longshoreman's neighborhood was left in dry dock for decades – even waterfront dive bars like Tom's Dry Dock closed (though the sign remains).

But sprawling brick shipping warehouses proved ideal for the **San Francisco Art Institute's** MFA graduate-student studios – and now that muni's T line has made the area accessible from downtown, the Museum of Craft & Design (p147) is attracting legions of crafty design thinkers to the neighborhood. Discover original designs galore in the museum's shop and explore Dogpatch studios for limited-edition finds. Cottage industries are booming with support from Workshop Residence (p161), where artists and designers collaborate to produce limited-edition, locally fabricated pieces. Freed from noise complaints from NIMBY neighbors, former factories converted into lofts also house inventors' workshops for TV's *Mythbusters* and all-women hacker/makerspace **Double Union** (https://doubleunion.org). Dogpatch's spirit of invention is captured in thoughtfully designed, multi-functional unisex gear by **Triple Aught Design** (Map p305; ☎415-520-3214; www.tripleaughtdesign.com; 660 22nd St; ⏰10am-7pm Tue-Fri, to 6pm Sat & Sun; 🚌22, 48, Ⓜ T), worthy of James Bond, with sleek Stealth hoodies perfect for parties or parkour.

In this starkly industrial landscape, savvy tech entrepreneurs and longtime Bay Area arts patrons Deborah and Andy Rappaport spotted a vital opening. Defunct factories could provide much-needed studio and display space for artists and nonprofits increasingly displaced by skyrocketing San Francisco rents. The Rappaports funded the conversion of a block of disused factory space into the **Minnesota Street Project** (www.minnesotastreetproject.com; 1295 Minnesota St), a groundbreaking arts complex filled with low-cost art studios, nonprofit art centers and rent-subsidized gallery space. The project has launched new galleries featuring SF talents like Casemore Kirkeby (p146) and been a lifeline for galleries in transition, including Anglim Gilbert (p146) and Eleanor Harwood.

But don't be deceived by the industrial waterfront: Dogpatch's dockworkers' district also has some of San Francisco's oldest Victorian and brick buildings, miraculously standing their ground through quakes and development schemes. One prime example is the 1859 **Yellow Building**, whose latest incarnation hosts a sister branch for Hayes Valley's MAC (p187) clothing store, with **Dig** (Map p305; ☎415-648-6133; http://digwinesf.com; 1005 Minnesota St; ⏰noon-7pm Tue-Fri, to 5pm Sat; 🚌22, 48, Ⓜ T) wine shop in its backyard.

When you work up a thirst walking along the sunny industrial waterfront and Victorian-lined backstreets, Dogpatch microbreweries and local wine bars come in handy. The Haight's **Magnolia Brewery** (Map p314; ☎415-864-7468; www.magnoliapub.com; 1398 Haight St; mains $14-26; ⏰11am-10pm Mon-Thu, to 11pm Fri, 10am-11pm Sat, to 10pm Sun; 🚌6, 7, 33, 43) 🌿 brews here, and Ungrafted (p154) wine bar specializes in champagne.

Hungry yet? **'āina** (Map p305; ☎415-814-3815; www.ainasf.com; 900 22nd St; mains $8-29, tasting menu $123; ⏰10am-2:30pm Wed-Fri, from 9am Sat & Sun, 5:30pm-10pm Wed-Sun; 🚌22, 48, Ⓜ T) has the city's best new brunch and for no-fuss brews and burgers on a sunny dock, head down to the **Ramp** (Map p305; ☎415-621-2378; www.rampsf.com; 855 Terry Francois St; mains $10-15; ⏰11am-6pm Mon-Fri, 10:30am-3:30pm Sat & Sun, bar 11am-8:30pm; 🚌22, Ⓜ T).

Dogpatch is always ready for dessert – this stretch of waterfront has become San Francisco's sweet spot. The **Mr & Mrs Miscellaneous** (Map p305; ☎415-970-0750; 699 22nd St; ice cream $4-8; ⏰11:30am-6pm Wed-Sat, to 5pm Sun; 🚌22, 48, Ⓜ T) factory-outlet ice-cream parlor does a brisk business in bourbon-caramel ice cream, while chocolatier Michael Recchiuti (p160) concocts experimental candy in Dogpatch before launching it at the Ferry Building (p101). Even people who swear they're not into dessert go wild for Poco Dolce (p161), San Francisco's savory, sustainably sourced chocolate confections with a touch of gray sea salt.

The city's oldest building and its namesake, whitewashed adobe Misión San Francisco de Asís was founded in 1776 and rebuilt from 1782. Today the modest adobe structure is overshadowed by the ornate adjoining 1913 **basilica**, built after the 1876 brick Gothic cathedral collapsed in the 1906 earthquake. It now features stained-glass windows depicting California's 21 missions and, true to Mission Dolores' name, seven panels depict the Seven Sorrows of Mary.

CREATIVITY EXPLORED   GALLERY
Map p302 (☑415-863-2108; www.creativity explored.org; 3245 16th St; donations welcome; ⊙10am-5pm Mon-Wed & Fri, to 7pm Thu, noon-5pm Sat; ☐14, 22, 33, 49, Ⓑ16th St Mission, ⓂJ) Brave new worlds are captured in celebrated artworks destined for museum retrospectives, international shows and even Marc Jacobs handbags and CB2 pillowcases – all by local artists with developmental disabilities who create at this nonprofit center. Intriguing themes range from monsters to Morse code, and openings are joyous celebrations with the artists, their families and rock-star fan base.

ELEANOR HARWOOD GALLERY   GALLERY
Map p305 (☑415-867-7770; www.eleanorharwood. com; 1275 Minnesota St, 2nd fl; ⊙1-5pm Tue, 11am-5pm Wed-Sat & by appointment; ☐10, 27, 33, 48, Ⓑ24th St Mission) FREE A curiosity cupboard of major Bay Area talents. Works showcased here are entrancing and meticulous – past shows have featured Dana Hemenway's dazzling extension-cord macramé wall lamps and Francesca Pastine's plaster planets sculpted out of intricately folded and carved issues of *Artforum* magazine.

✖ EATING

Mission eateries inspire culinary movements, while gourmet start-ups fill Dogpatch warehouses.

★MR POLLO   INTERNATIONAL $
Map p302 (2823 Mission St; four-course tasting menu $30; ⊙6-10pm Mon-Sat; ☐12, 14, 48, 49, Ⓑ24th St Mission) This hole-in-the-wall restaurant contains just six tables and serves one of the most delicious, but least expensive, tasting menus in all of San Francisco. Vegetarians or anyone fussy should skip it, as the four always-changing courses are often heavy on meat. But adventurous omnivores will fully appreciate the artful cuisine, prepared with seasonal ingredients and inspired by the chef's travels.

★MISSION COMMUNITY MARKET   MARKET $
Map p302 (http://missioncommunitymarket.org; Bartlett St, btwn 21st & 22nd Sts; ⊙4-8pm Thu mid-Feb–mid-Nov; ☑🚲; ☐14, 48, 49, Ⓑ24th St Mission) 🍴 Back-alley bounty brings ravenous crowds on Thursdays to this nonprofit, neighborhood-run market, come rain or shine. More than 30 local farmers and food artisans offer California produce and inspired SF street food – look for Coastside Farms' smoked albacore, Far West Fungi's mushrooms, Flour Chylde pastries and Izalco Catering's *pupusas* (tortilla pockets). Enjoy shade, seating and mariachis at mural-lined La Placita.

★MITCHELL'S ICE CREAM   ICE CREAM $
(☑415-648-2300; www.mitchellsicecream.com; 688 San Jose Ave; ice creams $4-9; ⊙11am-11pm; ☐14, 49, Ⓑ24th St Mission, ⓂJ) When you see happy dances break out on Mission sidewalks, you must be getting close to Mitchell's. One glance at the menu induces gleeful gluttony: classic Kahlua mocha cream, exotic tropical *macapuno* (young coconut)... or *both*?! Avocado and *ube* (purple yam) are acquired tastes, but they've been local favorites for generations – Mitchell's has kept fans coming back for seconds since 1953.

★LA PALMA MEXICATESSEN   MEXICAN $
Map p302 (☑415-647-1500; www.lapalmasf.com; 2884 24th St; tamales, tacos & huaraches $3-10; ⊙8am-6pm Mon-Sat, to 5pm Sun; ☑; ☐12, 14, 27, 48, Ⓑ24th St Mission) 🍴 Follow the applause: that's the sound of organic tortilla-making in progress. You've found the Mission mother lode of handmade tamales, and *pupusas* (tortilla pockets) with potato and *chicharones* (pork crackling), *carnitas* (slow-roasted pork), *cotija* (Oaxacan cheese) and La Palma's own tangy tomatillo sauce. Get takeout or bring a small army to finish the meal at sunny sidewalk tables.

ST FRANCIS FOUNTAIN   DINER $
Map p302 (☑415-826-4210; https://stfrancis fountainsf.com; 2801 24th St; mains $8-13; ⊙8am-3pm; ☑; ☐12, 27, 33, 48) With more than 100 years under its belt, this wildly popular soda fountain is the Mission's oldest ice-cream parlor and diner. The milkshakes and American breakfasts are classically

delicious, but Mexican dishes and inventive vegetarian/vegan options, such as the beloved 'nebulous potato thing', also abound. The candy counter is full of vintage treats and trading cards.

TACOLICIOUS
MEXICAN $

Map p302 (☑415-649-6077; http://tacolicious. com; 741 Valencia St; tacos $5.50; ⊙11:30am-midnight; ⏃; ☐14, 22, 33, 49, Ⓑ16th St Mission, ⓂJ) Never mind the name: once you've sampled the *carnitas* (slow-roasted pork) tacos and passion-fruit-habañero margaritas, you'll be in no position to debate authenticity or grammar – or say anything besides *'uno mas, por favor'* ('another, please'). Choose four tacos for $20, including seasonal vegetarian options. No reservations, but while you wait you can work through the 100-tequila menu at the bar.

CRAFTSMAN & WOLVES
BAKERY $

Map p302 (☑415-913-7713; http://craftsman-wolves.com; 746 Valencia St; pastries $3-16; ⊙6am-5pm Mon-Fri, from 8am Sat & Sun; ☐14, 22, 33, 49, Ⓑ16th St Mission, ⓂJ) Breakfast routines are made to be broken by the infamous Rebel Within: a sausage-spiked Asiago-cheese muffin with a silken soft-boiled egg baked inside. SF's surest pick-me-up is a Bellwether latte with *matcha* (green tea) cookies; stone yuzu coconut cakes and concoctions of sesame praline, passion fruit and vanilla creme are ideal for celebrating unbirthdays and imaginary holidays.

MISSION CHEESE
CHEESE $

Map p302 (☑415-553-8667; www.mission cheese.net; 736 Valencia St; cheese flights $14; ⊙11am-9pm Tue-Thu & Sun, to 10pm Fri & Sat; ⏃; ☐14, 22, 33, 49, Ⓙ, Ⓑ16th St Mission) ⊘ Smile and say 'wine' at this cheese bar serving sublime pairings with expert advice and zero pretension. The all-domestic cheese menu ranges from triple creamy to extra stinky, raw cow's milk to sheep's milk, and California wines reign supreme. When in dairy doubt, try 'mongers choice' surprise cheese platters with pickles, nuts and dried fruit.

HUMPHRY SLOCOMBE
ICE CREAM $

Map p302 (☑415-550-6971; www.humphry slocombe.com; 2790 Harrison St; ice creams $4-7; ⊙1-11pm Mon-Fri, from noon Sat & Sun; ☐12, 14, 49, Ⓑ24th St Mission) Indie-rock organic ice cream that may permanently spoil you for Top 40 flavors. Once 'Elvis: The Fat Years' (banana and peanut butter) and 'Hibiscus Beet Sorbet' have rocked your taste buds, cookie dough seems basic. Ordinary sundaes can't compare to 'Secret Breakfast' (bourbon and cornflakes) and 'Blue Bottle Vietnamese Coffee' drizzled with hot fudge, California olive oil and sea salt.

BI-RITE CREAMERY
ICE CREAM $

Map p302 (☑415-626-5600; www.biritecream ery.com; 3692 18th St; ice creams $3.50-9; ⊙11am-10pm; ☐33, Ⓑ16th St Mission, ⓂJ) ⊘ On a sunny day the line snakes around the block for San Francisco's most iconic ice-cream shop. Big sellers include organic salted-caramel ice cream with housemade hot fudge and Sonoma honey-lavender ice cream in organic waffle cones. But if you're willing to settle for balsamic-strawberry soft serve, you can skip the line to the take-out window (hours vary).

LA TAQUERIA
MEXICAN $

Map p302 (☑415-285-7117; 2889 Mission St; items $3-11; ⊙11am-8:45pm Mon-Sat, to 7:45pm Sun; ☐12, 14, 48, 49, Ⓑ24th St Mission) SF's definitive burrito has no saffron rice, spinach tortilla or mango salsa – just perfectly grilled meats, slow-cooked beans and tomatillo or mesquite salsa wrapped in a flour tortilla. They're purists at James Beard Award–winning La Taqueria. You'll pay extra to go without beans because they add more meat – but spicy pickles and *crema* (sour cream) bring burrito bliss.

TARTINE
BAKERY $

Map p302 (☑415-487-2600; www.tartinebakery. com; 600 Guerrero St; pastries $4-6, sandwiches $10-14; ⊙8am-7pm Mon, from 7:30am Tue-Fri, 8am-8pm Sat & Sun; ⏃; ☐14, 22, 33, 49, ⓂJ, Ⓑ16th St Mission) Riches beyond your wildest dreams: butter-golden *pains au chocolat*, cappuccinos with ferns drawn in dense foam and croque monsieurs turbo-loaded with ham, two kinds of cheese and béchamel. Don't be dismayed by the inevitable line out the door – it moves fast – but be aware that lolling in Dolores Park is the only possible post-Tartine activity.

★AL'S PLACE
CALIFORNIAN $$

Map p302 (☑415-416-6136; www.alsplacesf.com; 1499 Valencia St; share plates $15-21; ⊙5:30-10pm Wed-Sun; ⏃; ☐12, 14, 49, ⓂJ, Ⓑ24th St Mission) ⊘ The Golden State dazzles on Al's plates, featuring homegrown heirloom ingredients, pristine Pacific seafood and grass-fed meat. Painstaking preparation

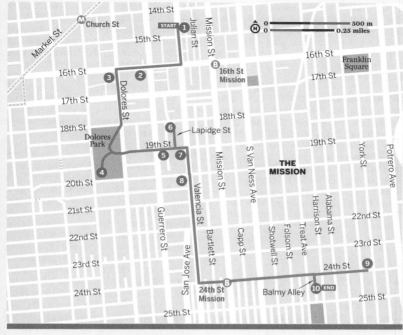

Neighborhood Walk
Colorful Mission Characters

START FOUR BARREL
END BALMY ALLEY
LENGTH 2.8 MILES; THREE HOURS

Begin by fueling up with house roast in the parklet at ❶ **Four Barrel Coffee** (p158) and buzz right past boutiques to ❷ **Creativity Explored** (p149), where the window showcases works by artists with developmental disabilities. Ahead is the city's first building: adobe ❸ **Mission Dolores** (p147), built by some 5000 conscripted Ohlone and Miwok laborers. You can glimpse the Miwok memorial hut through the mission fence on Chula Lane.

Climb to the upper southwestern corner of ❹ **Dolores Park** (p146) for panoramic views. Then walk down 19th St past Daniel Doherty's impressionist-inspired 2009 mural ❺ **Dejeuner Dolores**, showing Dolores Park's regular cast of characters, including frolicking pugs and handlebar-mustachioed men in matching Speedos. Swing left on Lapidge St to spot Georgia O'Keeffe and

goddesses galore in the ❻ **Women's Building** (p146) murals.

Back on Valencia St, you'll see the Chris Ware mural and storefront art installation of ❼ **826 Valencia** (p146), where you can duck inside for pirate supplies. Down the street, pause to pay your respects to bygone celebrities at ❽ **Dog Eared Books** (p162) – the front window features hand-drawn obituary cartoons of luminaries from Liz Taylor to Susan Sontag. Window-shop down Valencia then hang a left onto 24th St, San Francisco's Latino Cultural District. Here you'll pass mural-covered bodegas, taquerias and *panaderias* all the way to ❾ **24th & York Mini Park** (p145), where Aztec serpent-god Quetzalcoatl rears his mighty mosaic head from the rubberized playground yard.

Double back along 24th St, cross over and swing down to ❿ **Balmy Alley** (p145), where you may recognize beatified activist Archbishop Romero and surrealist painter Frida Kahlo among the colorful characters illuminating garage doors.

yields sun-drenched flavors and exquisite textures: crispy-skin cod with frothy preserved-lime dip, and grilled peach melting into velvety foie gras. Dishes are half the size but thrice the flavor of mains elsewhere – get two or three and you'll be California dreaming.

★TARTINE MANUFACTORY   CALIFORNIAN $$

Map p302 (☑415-757-0007; www.tartinemanufactory.com; 595 Alabama St; mains $16-38; ⊗8am-10pm; ☑; ☐12, 22, 27, 33) What began as a baking powerhouse has evolved into a veritable smorgasbord of delicious, collaborative, artisanal everything, set within an expansive yet deeply Instagram-worthy space appointed in light wood and exposed concrete. Need your morning caffeine fix? The Manufactory has its own coffee brand. Looking for a grab-and-go pastry? A sit-down breakfast? A lazy weekend brunch? Done, done and done.

DELFINA   ITALIAN $$

Map p302 (☑415-552-4055; http://delfinasf.com; 3611 18th St; mains $14-32; ⊗5-10:30pm Mon-Thu, to 11pm Fri & Sat, to 10pm Sun; ☐14, 22, 33, 49, MJ, B16th St Mission) Twenty years ago Delfina opened its doors on what was then a sketchy corner of the Mission. It served simple Italian cuisine prepared with fresh California ingredients, including a basic and deeply satisfying bowl of spaghetti that still packs the place today. Its winning concept has launched many similar restaurants and its location has become the city's hottest dining corridor.

PRAIRIE   ITALIAN $$

Map p302 (☑415-483-1112; http://prairiesf.com; 3431 19th St; mains $10-29; ⊗5:30-10pm Sun & Tue-Thu, to 11pm Fri & Sat; ☐14, 22, 33, 49, B16th St Mission) This is not your *nonni*'s Italian, and actually she might take issue with whether it's Italian at all. Many of the ingredients more commonly appear on Asian menus: a *guanciale*-wrapped mochi (rice wrapped in cured pork) appetizer or pork spareribs with a Calabrian-style XO (a spicy Chinese seafood sauce). Instead of gnocchi, there's Korean-style rice cakes with pioppini mushrooms, stinging nettles, sherry and pine nuts.

FARMHOUSE KITCHEN
THAI CUISINE   THAI $$

Map p302 (☑415-814-2920; www.farmhousethai.com; 710 Florida St; share plates $10-24; ⊗11am-2pm & 5-10pm Mon-Thu, to 10:30pm Fri, noon-10:30pm Sat, to 10pm Sun; ☑; ☐22, 27) California farm-to-table gets Thai street smarts in this warehouse restaurant showcasing organic local ingredients and regional Thai street-food inspirations. Skewered Sonoma BBQ chicken marinated in fresh turmeric packs a savory punch, but spicy eggplant with blue rice teaches your taste buds Thai kickboxing. Pricey for lunch, but worth it – embrace the decadence with local wines and croissant-bread pudding.

NAMU GAJI   KOREAN $$

Map p302 (☑415-431-6268; www.namusf.com; 499 Dolores St; share plates $10-21; ⊗5:30-10pm Tue, 11:30am-3pm & 5:30-10pm Wed-Fri, 10:30am-4pm & 5-10pm Sat & Sun; ☐14, 22, 33, 49, MJ, B16th St Mission) ⊘ SF's unfair culinary advantages – organic local ingredients, Pacific Rim roots and street-skater, try-anything attitude – are showcased in Namu's Korean-inspired soul food. Bold flavors abound in ultra-savory shiitake-mushroom dumplings, meltingly tender lamb meatballs and Namu's version of bibimbap: Wagyu beef, organic vegetables, kimchi, spicy *gochujang* (Korean chili sauce) and an egg atop *koshihikari* rice, served sizzling in a stone pot.

PIZZERIA DELFINA   PIZZA $$

Map p302 (☑415-437-6800; www.pizzeriadelfina.com; 3621 18th St; pizzas $14-19; ⊗5-10pm Tue, 11:30am-10pm Mon, Wed & Thu, to 11pm Fri, noon-11pm Sat, to 10pm Sun; ☐14, 22, 33, 49, MJ, B16th St Mission) ⊘ One bite explains why SF is obsessed with pizza lately: Delfina's thin crust heroically supports the weight of fennel sausage and fresh mozzarella without drooping or cracking. On sauce-free white pizzas, chefs freestyle with California ingredients such as broccoli rabe, maitake mushrooms and artisan cheese. No reservations; sign the chalkboard and wait with a glass of wine at next-door Delfina.

EL TECHO   LATIN AMERICAN $$

Map p302 (Lolinda Rooftop; ☑415-550-6970; http://eltechosf.com; 2516 Mission St; small plates $8-13; ⊗4-10pm Mon-Thu, to 11pm Fri, 11am-11pm Sat, to 10pm Sun; ☐14, 33, 49, B24th St Mission) Savor Latin street food six floors above Mission St, with views over cinema marquees, palm trees and bodegas all the way downtown. Sunny brunches call for eggs Benedict with jalapeño cornbread, a Chilcano (pisco, lime, ginger, passion fruit and bitters) and sunblock; foggy days require empanadas, La Avenida (rum, lemon and vermouth) and a windbreaker.

⭐CALIFORNIOS
LATIN AMERICAN $$$

Map p302 (✆415-757-0994; www.californiossf.com; 3115 22nd St; 16-course tasting menu $197; ◷5:30-8:30pm Tue-Thu, to 9pm Fri & Sat; ☐12, 14, 49, ⓑ24th St Mission) Parades – from Carnaval to Día de los Muertos – are a Mission specialty, and the parade of Latin-inspired flavors nightly at Californios does justice to the neighborhood's roots and unbridled creativity. Chef Val Cantu collaborates with local farms and artisan producers to reinvent staples with the seasons: imagine sourdough tortillas, foie-gras tamales, Dungeness crab ceviche and wild-strawberry flan. Reserve ahead.

COMMONWEALTH
CALIFORNIAN $$$

Map p302 (✆415-355-1500; www.commonwealthsf.com; 2224 Mission St; small plates $15-22; ◷5:30-10pm Sun-Thu, to 11pm Fri & Sat; ✐; ☐14, 22, 33, 49, ⓑ16th St Mission) Wildly imaginative farm-to-table dining in a converted cinderblock Mission dive. Chef Jason Fox serves adventurous compositions like *uni* (sea urchin) and bone-marrow cream with nasturtium flowers, and lamb with beets and seaweed on a redwood plank. Dishes are dainty but pack wallops of earthy flavor. Savor the six-course tasting menu ($95; $160 with wine pairings); a portion benefits local charities.

FOREIGN CINEMA
CALIFORNIAN $$$

Map p302 (✆415-648-7600; www.foreigncinema.com; 2534 Mission St; mains $28-36; ◷5:30-10pm Sun-Wed, to 11pm Thu-Sat, brunch 11am-2:30pm Sat & Sun; ☐12, 14, 33, 48, 49, ⓑ24th St Mission) Chef Gayle Pirie's acclaimed California classics such as grilled Monterey calamari and crisp sesame fried chicken are the star attractions here – but subtitled films by Luis Buñuel and François Truffaut screening in the courtyard are mighty handy when conversation lags with first dates or in-laws. Get the red-carpet treatment with valet parking ($15) and a well-stocked oyster bar.

LAZY BEAR
AMERICAN $$$

Map p302 (✆415-874-9921; www.lazybearsf.com; 3416 19th St; tasting menu $185-205; den snacks $9-19; ◷6-11pm Tue-Sat; ☐14, 22, 33, 49, ⓑ16th St Mission) Dinner at Lazy Bear actually requires quite a bit of (worthwhile) effort. Tickets for the supper club must be purchased in advance and tend to sell out. Guests are given assigned seats at communal tables. Before each course there's an announcement about the dish, which might be something playful like dry-aged squab (baby pigeon), blueberries, chanterelle mushrooms and sumac flowers.

LOCANDA
ITALIAN $$$

Map p302 (✆415-863-6800; www.locandasf.com; 557 Valencia St; mains $19-36; ◷5:30-10pm Wed & Thu, to 11pm Fri & Sat, brunch 10:30-2pm Sat & Sun; ☐14, 22, 33, 49, ⓑ16th St Mission) Friends, Romans, San Franciscans – join the crowd for Roman fried artichokes, pizza *bianca*, prosciutto, blood orange and beet salads, and scrumptious tripe melting into rich tomato-mint sauce. Pasta dishes are less adventurous than the small plates and mains created with market-fresh organic ingredients, like the whole fish of the day (served head on) and roast meats worthy of imperial feasts.

DRINKING & NIGHTLIFE

The Mission sets cocktail and coffee trends, while barflies hit Potrero Flats dives and toasts are raised in Dogpatch wine bars.

⭐TRICK DOG
BAR

Map p302 (✆415-471-2999; www.trickdogbar.com; 3010 20th St; ◷3pm-2am; ☐12, 14, 49) Drink adventurously with ingenious cocktails inspired by local obsessions: San Francisco muralists, Chinese diners or conspiracy theories. Every six months, Trick Dog adopts a new theme and the menu changes – proof you can teach an old dog new tricks and improve on classics like the Manhattan. Arrive early for bar stools or hit the mood-lit loft for high-concept bar bites.

⭐ZEITGEIST
BAR

Map p302 (✆415-255-7505; www.zeitgeistsf.com; 199 Valencia St; ◷9am-2am; ☐14, 22, 49, ⓑ16th St Mission) You've got two seconds flat to order from tough-gal barkeeps used to putting macho bikers in their place – but with 48 beers on draft, you're spoiled for choice. Epic afternoons unfold in the beer garden, with folks hanging out and smoking at long tables. SF's longest happy hour lasts 9am to 6pm weekdays. Cash only; no photos (read: no evidence).

WORTH A DETOUR

POTRERO FLATS CREATIVE UPSTARTS

San Francisco's historic Design District has rediscovered its edge with the arrival of avant-garde galleries, showing art that easily upstages beige sofas. Between SoMa and Potrero Hill is a flat expanse dotted with warehouse design-trade showrooms long overlooked, unless you were in the business of selecting window treatments. But ever since the **California College of the Arts** (Wattis Institute; Map p305; ✐Wattis Institute 415-355-9670; www.wattis.org; 360 Kansas St; ⊘during school sessions noon-6pm Tue-Sat; ☐10, 19, 22, 33) FREE creatively repurposed the neighborhood's old bus depot for its campus, the emerging Potrero Flats district (also called 'SoMissPo,' for SoMa, Mission and Potrero) is becoming an eye-catcher. Stop at CCA's campus to discover fresh provocations in student-curated **PLAySPACE** and the **Wattis Institute for Contemporary Arts.**

Head under the highway overpass to discover **SOMArts** (Map p302; ✐415-863-1414; www.somarts.org; 934 Brannan St; ⊘gallery noon-7pm Tue-Fri, to 5pm Sat; ☐8, 9, 10, 19, 27, 47), a nonprofit community hub for creative thinking that hosts shows featuring edible murals, global street dance-offs and new meanings for old words supplied by the pop-up Bureau of Linguistical Reality. Just down the street, the **San Francisco Center for the Book** (Map p305; ✐415-906-6417; www.sfcb.org; 375 Rhode Island St; gallery free; ⊘gallery 10am-5:30pm; ☐8, 10, 19, 22, 33) features shows of handmade pop-up books and matchbook-sized zines, plus workshops for making your own.

The creative pull of Potrero Flats is irresistible now that several of San Francisco's leading galleries have moved to the neighborhood. The **Catharine Clark Gallery** (Map p302; ✐415-399-1439; www.cclarkgallery.com; 248 Utah St; ⊘10:30am-5:30pm Tue-Fri, 11am-6pm Sat; ☐9, 10, 19, 22, 33) FREE instigates art revolutions with Masami Teraoka's monumental paintings of geisha superheroines fending off wayward priests, while the **Hosfelt Gallery** (Map p302; ✐415-495-5454; http://hosfeltgallery.com; 260 Utah St; ⊘10am-5:30pm Tue, Wed & Fri & Sat, 11am-7pm Thu; ☐9, 10, 19, 22, 27, 33) FREE mesmerizes visitors with Emil Lukas' drawings made by thousands of fly larvae dragging ink across paper. Meanwhile, collage artists at the **Jack Fischer Gallery** (Map p302; ✐415-522-1178; www.jackfischergallery.com; 311 Potrero Ave; ⊘11am-5:30pm Tue-Sat; ☐8, 9, 22, 27, 33) FREE bring intriguing interior worlds to life inside a warehouse space off Hwy 101. Friendly art debates continue around the corner at **Thee Parkside** (Map p305; ✐415-252-1330; www.theeparkside.com; 1600 17th St; ⊘11am-2am Mon-Sat, to 8pm Sun; ☐10, 19, 22), where bikers and art students converge for cheap drinks, parking-lot BBQ and vintage photo booth photo-ops. But once alt-rock and punk bands start playing at Bottom of the Hill (p159), artistic differences are set aside and mosh-pit mayhem reigns supreme.

★**UNGRAFTED**   WINE BAR
Map p305 (✐415-814-2129; www.ungraftedsf.com; 2419 3rd St; ⊘5-10pm Mon-Sat, to 9pm Sun; ☐22, 48, Ⓜ️T) At this industrial-chic, champagne-focused Dogpatch wine bar, you can't launch a cork without hitting a sommelier. The married owners are both sommeliers and every server in the place is, too. Your bubbly arrives in vintage champage buckets and the still wines are popular by the half-bottle, especially for commitment-phobes.

★**JOLENE'S**   LESBIAN
Map p302 (✐415-913-7948; http://jolenessf.com; 2700 16th St; ⊘4pm-2am Thu-Fri, from 11am Sat & Sun; ☐12, 22, 55, Ⓑ16th Mission St) For those who identify as ladies and also like others who identify as ladies, there's a shiny new bar. A huge neon sign announces 'you are safe here', while custom-made boob wallpaper similarly encourages abandon. Lip-loosening cocktails include the Purple Vesper (tanqueray, vodka, Cocchi Americano and blue pea flower), and rosemary fries and popcorn chicken are served until late.

★**BON VOYAGE**   COCKTAIL BAR
Map p302 (http://bonvoyagebar.com; 584 Valencia St; cocktails $9-15; ⊘bar 2pm-2am Mon-Fri, from noon Sat & Sun; kitchen from 5pm Mon-Fri, from noon Sat & Sun; ☐14, 22, 33, 49, Ⓑ16th St Mission) So, imagine a 1950s traveler who sets out to experience Southeast Asia and Africa, picking up art and curios along the

way. Now think about this traveler repatriating to Palm Springs in the 1970s and throwing massive parties involving a giant disco ball, Chinese food and innovative, exotic cocktails.

★ **EL RIO** CLUB

Map p302 (☑415-282-3325; www.elriosf.com; 3158 Mission St; cover free-$10; ⊙1pm-2am Mon-Sat, to midnight Sun; ☐12, 14, 27, 49, Ⓑ24th St Mission) Work it all out on the dance floor with SF's most down and funky crowd – the full rainbow spectrum of colorful characters is here to party. Highlights include Salsa Sunday, free oysters from 5:30pm Friday, drag-star DJs, backyard bands and ping-pong. Expect knockout margaritas and shameless flirting on a patio that's seen it all since 1978. Cash only on weekends.

20 SPOT WINE BAR

Map p302 (☑415-624-3140; www.20spot.com; 3565 20th St; ⊙5pm-11pm Mon-Thu, to 12:30am Fri & Sat; ☐14, 22, 33, Ⓑ16th St Mission) Find your California mellow at this neighborhood wine lounge in an 1885 Victorian building. After decades as Force of Habit punk-record shop – note the vintage sign – this corner joint has earned the right to unwind with a glass of Berkeley's Donkey and Goat sparkling wine and not get any guff. Caution: oysters with pickled persimmon could become a habit.

DALVA & HIDEOUT LOUNGE

Map p302 (☑415-252-7740; http://dalvasf.com; 3121 16th St; ⊙4pm-2am, Hideout from 7pm; ☐14, 22, 33, 49, Ⓑ24th St Mission) SF's best bars are distinguished not just by their drinks but by the conversations they inspire – by both measures Dalva is top-shelf. Over ice-cold mugs of Pliny the Elder or curious seasonal brews, patrons discuss indie flicks they just caught at the Roxie (p159). Meanwhile, in the backroom Hideout, Dolores Park gossip spills over Dirty Pigeons (mezcal, lime, grapefruit, gentian bitters).

%ABV COCKTAIL BAR

Map p302 (☑415-400-4748; www.overproofsf.com; 3174 16th St; ⊙2pm-2am; ☐14, 22, Ⓑ16th St Mission, ⓂJ) As kindred spirits will deduce from the name (the abbreviation for 'percent alcohol by volume'), this bar is backed by cocktail crafters who know their Rittenhouse rye from their Japanese malt whiskey. Top-notch hooch is served promptly and without pretension, including excellent Cali wine and beer, and original historically inspired cocktails like the Sutro Swizzle (Armagnac, grapefruit shrub, maraschino liqueur).

ELIXIR BAR

Map p302 (☑415-522-1633; www.elixirsf.com; 3200 16th St; ⊙3pm-2am Mon-Fri, from noon Sat & Sun; ☐14, 22, 33, 49, Ⓑ16th St Mission, ⓂJ) 🍷 Do the planet a favor and have another drink at SF's first certified green bar, in an actual 1858 Wild West saloon. Elixir blends farm-fresh seasonal mixers with local small-batch, organic, biodynamic spirits – Meyer lemon and rye sours and Mission Pimm's Cup with pisco and cucumber vodka get everyone air-guitar rocking to the killer jukebox. 'Drink-for-a-cause' Wednesdays support local charities.

RITUAL COFFEE ROASTERS CAFE

Map p302 (☑415-641-1011; www.ritualroasters.com; 1026 Valencia St; ⊙6am-8pm Mon-Fri, from 7am Sat & Sun; ☐14, 49, Ⓑ24th St Mission) Cults wish they inspired the same devotion as Ritual, where regulars solemnly queue for house-roasted cappuccino with ferns drawn in foam and specialty drip coffees with highly distinctive flavor profiles – descriptions comparing roasts to grapefruit peel or hazelnut aren't exaggerating. Electrical outlets are limited to encourage conversation, so you can eavesdrop on dates and political-protest plans.

OBISPO COCKTAIL BAR

Map p302 (☑415-529-2099; www.obisposf.com; 3266 24th St; ⊙6pm-2am Mon-Sat; ☐12, 14, 48, 49, Ⓑ16th Street Mission) This is no tiki bar. The setting is austere and designed to keep patrons focused on the origin and quality of the small-batch rums that the owner personally selected from around the Caribbean. The cocktails are balanced and potent, pairing exceedingly well with plates of oxtail stew, jerk chicken and Cuban sandwiches. Servers translate the Spanish menu with a smile.

Meanwhile, there are plans to adorn the walls with reproductions of folk-art by Bill Traylor, an artist born into slavery in Alabama. The art is part of a collaboration with SF's Museum of the African Diaspora (p83), which has partnered with the bar, along with Calle 24 (p147). Some proceeds will go toward these organizations, perhaps countering arguments that bars like Obispo are contributing to the gentrification of the Mission.

THE MISSION, DOGPATCH & POTRERO HILL DRINKING & NIGHTLIFE

NAEBLYS / SHUTTERSTOCK ©

1. Mission Dolores (p147)
San Francisco's oldest building (1776).

2. Dog Eared Books (p162)
An iconic Mission bookstore.

3. Community Thrift (p160)
Find yourself a bargain outfit at this Mission nonprofit.

4. Dolores Park (p146)
Relax and take in spectacular views of downtown San Francisco.

WILD SIDE WEST
LESBIAN

(☑415-647-3099; www.wildsidewest.com; 424 Cortland Ave; ⊙2pm-2am; 📑24) Lesbian-owned since 1962, Wild Side West has kept its clientele busy making herstory in the beer garden and making out on the pool table (Janis Joplin started it). The sculpture garden began in the 1970s, when killjoy neighbors chucked junk over the fence to protest women enjoying themselves – but cast-offs upcycled into art became the pride of the Wild Side.

PHONE BOOTH
BAR

Map p302 (☑415-648-4683; 1398 S Van Ness Ave; ⊙2pm-2am; 📑14, 49, 🅱24th St Mission) Classic SF dive celebrating defunct technology, with naked Barbie chandeliers and year-round Christmas lights. Art-school students mingle with sundry techies (oh, hi, Mark Zuckerberg) over pool tables and make out in dark corners. Cheap beer, Jameson and Bloody Marys flow freely, and the jukebox is perpetually on fire.

DOC'S CLOCK
BAR

Map p302 (☑415-824-3627; www.docsclock.com; 2577 Mission St; ⊙5pm-2am Mon-Thu, 4pm-2am Fri & Sat, 3pm-2am Sun; 📱; 📑12, 14, 49, 🅱24th St Mission) 🍸 Tickle in your throat? Time to see the Doc – head directly to the Prescriptions Counter at this gruffly lovable green-certified dive for local craft brews and spirits, free shuffleboard, Barbie Mutilation Nights, tricky pinball and easy conversation. Dog-friendly happy hours run 5pm to 9pm daily, with a percentage of proceeds supporting city dog rescues. Cash only.

LATIN AMERICAN CLUB
BAR

Map p302 (☑415-647-2732; 3286 22nd St; ⊙5pm-2am Mon-Fri, from noon Sat & Sun; 📑12, 14, 49, 🅱24th St Mission) Margaritas served in beer glasses go the distance here – just don't stand up too fast. Ninja *piñatas* and *papel picado* (cut-paper banners) add a festive atmosphere, and rosy lighting and generous pours enable shameless flirting. Cash only.

HOMESTEAD
BAR

Map p302 (☑415-282-4663; www.homesteadsf.com; 2301 Folsom St; ⊙2pm-2am; 📱; 📑12, 14, 22, 33, 49, 🅱16th St Mission) Your friendly Victorian corner dive c 1893, complete with carved-wood bar, pressed-tin ceiling, salty roast peanuts in the shell and Mission characters and their sweet dogs. SF's creative

contingent packs the place to celebrate art openings, grants and writing assignments with cheap draft beer – and when Iggy Pop or David Bowie hit the jukebox, stand back.

FOUR BARREL COFFEE
CAFE

Map p302 (☑415-896-4289; www.fourbarrelcoffee.com; 375 Valencia St; ⊙7am-8pm; 📱; 📑14, 22, 🅱16th St Mission) Surprise: the hippest cafe in town is also the friendliest, with upbeat baristas and no outlets or wi-fi to hinder conversation. Drip roasts are complex and powerful; the fruity espresso is an acquired taste. The front-bar, Slow Pour, offers cold coffee in a can and caffeinating crowds mingle in the sunny parklet with bike parking and patio seating.

☆ ENTERTAINMENT

The Mission's replete with art-house theaters, cocktail lounges and dive bars, while Potrero Hill features one of the city's legendary punk venues.

★ALAMO DRAFTHOUSE CINEMA
CINEMA

Map p302 (☑415-549-5959; https://drafthouse.com/sf; 2550 Mission St; tickets $6-20; 📑14, 🅱24th St Mission) The landmark 1932 New Mission cinema, now restored to its original Timothy Pfleuger–designed art deco glory, has a new mission: to upgrade dinner-and-a-movie dates. Staff deliver microbrews and tasty fare to plush banquette seats, so you don't miss a moment of premieres, cult revivals (especially Music Mondays) or SF favorites, from *Mrs Doubtfire* to *Dirty Harry* – often with filmmaker Q&As.

★ODC THEATER
DANCE

Map p302 (Oberlin Dance Collective; ☑box office 415-863-9834, classes 415-549-8519; www.odctheater.org; 3153 17th St; drop-in classes from $15, shows $20-50; 📑12, 14, 22, 33, 49, 🅱16th St Mission) For 45 years ODC has been redefining dance with risky, raw performances and the sheer joy of movement. ODC's season runs from September to December, but its stage presents year-round shows featuring local and international artists.

★BRAVA THEATER
THEATER

Map p302 (☑415-641-7657; www.brava.org; 2781 24th St; 📑12, 27, 33, 48) Brava's been producing women-run theater for 30-plus years, hosting acts from comedian Sandra Bernhard to V-day monologist Eve Ensler, and it's the nation's first company with a commitment to producing original works by women of color and LGBTIQ+ playwrights. Brava honors the Mission's Mexican heritage with music and dance celebrations, plus hand-painted show posters modeled after Mexican cinema billboards.

LOST CHURCH LIVE MUSIC
Map p302 (www.thelostchurch.com; 65 Capp St; cover $10-20, cash only; ⊙7:30-10:30pm Wed-Sat; 🚇14, 22, 33, 🄱16th Mission St) Enter the unmarked door on a quiet street and proceed upstairs to an intimate theater that has the distinct air of a vampire's parlor – albeit one with very good taste. Flowing drapes frame a small stage in front of folding chairs, and the room's acoustics are excellent, making an ideal space to experience emerging talents in theater, music and comedy.

BRICK & MORTAR LIVE MUSIC
Map p302 (📞415-678-5099; http://brickand mortarmusic.com; 1710 Mission St; cover $10-20; 🚇14, 49, 🄱16th St Mission) Some bands are too outlandish for regular radio – to hear them, you need San Francisco's Brick & Mortar. The bill here has featured national acts from brass-band showcases to the US air-guitar championships, plus homegrown SF upstarts like post-punk Magic Bullet, ironic 'indie-rock avalanche' the Yellow Dress and psychedelically groovy Loco Tranquilo.

CHAPEL LIVE MUSIC
Map p302 (📞415-551-5157; www.thechapelsf. com; 777 Valencia St; cover $15-40; ⊙bar 7pm-2am; 🚇14, 33, 🄼J, 🄱16th St Mission) Musical prayers are answered in a 1914 California arts-and-crafts landmark with heavenly acoustics. The 40ft roof is regularly raised by shows by New Orleans brass bands, folkYEAH! Americana groups, legendary rockers like Peter Murphy and hip-hop icons such as Prince Paul. Many shows are all ages, except when comedians like W Kamau Bell test edgy material.

If you get the munchies, head next door to Curio, Chapel's new, mortuary-inspired sister bar. They specialize in craft cocktails and shellfish towers.

ROXIE CINEMA CINEMA
Map p302 (📞415-863-1087; www.roxie.com; 3117 16th St; regular screening/matinee $12-13/10; 🚇14, 22, 33, 49, 🄱16th St Mission) This vintage 1909 cinema is a neighborhood nonprofit

BOTTOM OF THE HILL

Quite literally at the bottom of Potrero Hill, **Bottom of the Hill** (Map p305; 📞415-621-4455; www.bottomofthehill. com; 1233 17th St; $5-20; ⊙shows generally 9pm Tue-Sat; 🚇10, 19, 22) is always top of the list for alt-rocking out with punk legends the Avengers, Pansy Division and Nerf Herder, and newcomers worth checking out for their names alone (Summer Salt, the Regrettes, Sorority Noise). The smokers' patio is covered in handbills and ruled by a cat that enjoys music more than people – totally punk rock. There's Anchor Steam on tap at the cash-only bar; check the website for lineups.

with an international reputation for distributing documentaries and showing controversial films banned elsewhere. Tickets to film-festival premieres, rare revivals and raucous Oscars telecasts sell out – buy them online – but if the main show's packed, discover riveting documentaries in teensy next-door Little Roxy instead. No ads, plus personal introductions to every film.

MARSH THEATER
Map p302 (📞415-641-0235; www.themarsh. org; 1062 Valencia St; tickets $15-55; ⊙box office 10am-5pm Mon-Fri; 🚇12, 14, 48, 49, 🄱24th St Mission) Choose your seat wisely: you may spend the evening on the edge of it. One-acts and monologues here involve the audience in the creative process, from comedian W Kamau Bell's riffs to live tapings of National Public Radio's *Philosophy Talk*. Sliding-scale pricing allows everyone to participate and a few reserved seats are sometimes available (tickets $55).

REVOLUTION CAFE LIVE PERFORMANCE
Map p302 (📞415-642-0474; www.revolutioncafe sf.com; 3248 22nd St; ⊙9am-midnight Sun-Thu, to 1:30am Fri & Sat; 📶; 🚇12, 14, 49, 🄱24th St Mission) Musicians, you're among friends: classically trained musicians and jazz artists jam here daily. Hot weekend days call for iced coffee and live Latin jazz, and weeknights are redeemed with Belgian brews and rollicking chamber music. Arrive by 7pm to snag a table, or hang on the sidewalk with free wi-fi. Bring cash for drinks and musicians' tip jars.

THE MISSION, DOGPATCH & POTRERO HILL SHOPPING

MAKE-OUT ROOM
LIVE PERFORMANCE

Map p302 (www.makeoutroom.com; 3225 22nd St; cover free-$10; ⊙6pm-2am; 🚌12, 14, 49, **B**24th St Mission) Velvet curtains and round booths invite you to get comfortable under the disco ball for an evening of utterly unpredictable entertainment, ranging from Toychestra performances on kids' instruments to dancehall and *cumbia* DJ mash-ups, and painfully funny readings at Writers with Drinks. Booze is a bargain (happy hour 6pm to 8pm weeknights; drinks $5); cash only, with an on-site ATM.

AMNESIA
LIVE MUSIC

Map p302 (www.facebook.com/amnesiaSF; 853 Valencia St; cover free-$10; ⊙5pm-2am; 🚌14, 33, 49, **B**16th St Mission) Forget standard playlists – this closet-sized boho dive will make you lose your mind for Monday bluegrass jams, Tuesday Troubled Comedy sessions, Wednesday gaucho jazz, random readings and breakout dance parties. Shows are cheap and often sliding scale, the crowd is pumped and the beer flows freely. Check Facebook or go with the flow; $5 craft beer from 4pm to 7pm.

VERDI CLUB
LIVE PERFORMANCE

Map p302 (✆415-861-9199; www.verdiclub.net; 2424 Mariposa St; cover free-$25; 🚌22, 27, 33) Throwing swanky soirees since 1916, the Verdi Club hosts bawdy storytelling nights, swing-dancing lessons, drag-star comedy shows, the odd *lucha libre* (freestyle) wrestling night and regular rock concerts performed entirely by elementary-school kids. Check the website for events and bring cash for the velvet-swagged bar.

SHOPPING

SF's best boutique shopping is along Valencia from 14th to 26th St. Dogpatch has design boutiques around 22nd and 3rd Sts and Potrero Flats has upstart galleries wedged between design showrooms.

★RECCHIUTI AT THELAB
CHOCOLATE

Map p305 (✆415-489-2881; www.recchiuti.com; 801 22nd St; ⊙noon-7pm Mon-Fri, 11am-6pm Sat, noon-5pm Sun; 🚌22, 48, **M**T) Star chocolatier Michael Recchiuti sells confections at the Ferry Building (p78) but invents them in Dogpatch – taste his latest concoctions here

first. Go for dark-chocolate cocoa in winter, brownie sundaes in summer, or whatever oddity is on today's menu – recent standouts include chocolate-covered candied orange peels, burnt caramel truffles and gourmet s'mores kits (serious props on the handmade vanilla bean marshmallows).

★COMMUNITY THRIFT
CLOTHING

Map p302 (✆415-861-4910; www.communitythriftsf.org; 623 Valencia St; ⊙10am-6:30pm; 🚌14, 22, 33, 49, **B**16th St Mission) 🌿 When local collectors and retailers have too much of a good thing, they donate it to nonprofit Community Thrift, where proceeds go to 200-plus local charities – all the more reason to gloat over your $5 totem-pole teacup, $10 vintage windbreaker and $14 disco-era glitter romper. Donate your cast-offs (until 5pm daily) and show some love to the Community.

★BAGGU
FASHION & ACCESSORIES

Map p302 (https://baggu.com; 911 Valencia St; ⊙noon-7pm Mon-Fri, from 11am Sat & Sun; 🚌12, 14, 33, 49, **M**J) Plastic bags are banned in San Francisco, which is a perfect excuse to stock up on SF designer Baggu's reusable Ripstop nylon totes in bright colors and quirky prints: sharks, alpacas and, ay, Chihuahuas. They're durable, lightweight and crushable – totes fabulous. Striped canvas backpacks are destined for hauling Adobe Books (p162), and little leather circle purses hold Mission Litquake (p36) essentials.

★MISSION COMICS & ART
COMICS, ART

Map p302 (✆415-695-1545; www.missioncomics andart.com; 2250 Mission St; ⊙noon-8pm Mon, Tue & Thu-Sat, from 11am Wed, noon-6pm Sun; 🚌12, 14, 33, 49, **B**16th St Mission) Heads will roll, fists will fly and furious vengeance will be wreaked inside this mild-mannered shop stocking big-name and indie comics. Staff picks range from marquee (*Walking Dead, Star Wars*) to niche (*Snotgirl, Head Lopper*), and artists headlining signings and gallery shows here have included *Supergirl* writer Mariko Tamaki, *Ancestor* surrealist artist Matt Sheean and *New Yorker* constructivist cartoonist Roman Muradov.

★TIGERLILY PERFUMERY
PERFUME

Map p302 (✆415-896-4665; www.tigerlilysf.com; 973 Valencia St; ⊙noon-6:30pm Mon-Fri, to 7pm Sat, noon-5pm Sun; 🚌14, 33, 49, **B**24th St Mission) If you want to bottle San Francisco and take it home with you, you've come to the right place. Tigerlily stocks an intoxicating variety of local perfumers' creations, which will transport you from beach days to Barbary Coast nights. Options range from Yosh Han's California-sunbeam scent, appropriately called U4EAHH!, to Ikiryo's kinky, leather-bound Bad Omen. Check for in-person perfume events.

★ BI-RITE
FOOD & DRINKS

Map p302 (☎415-241-9760; www.biritemarket. com; 3639 18th St; ☺8am-9pm; ⊛; ☐14, 22, 33, 49, Ⓑ16th St Mission, ⓂJ) ✐ Diamond counters can't compare to the foodie dazzle of Bi-Rite's sublime wall of local artisan chocolates, treasure boxes of organic fruit and California wine and cheese selections expertly curated by upbeat, knowledgeable staff. Step up to the altar-like deli counter to provision five-star Dolores Park picnics. An institution since 1940, Bi-Rite champions good food for all through its nonprofit 18 Reasons (p163).

★ NEEDLES & PENS
ARTS & CRAFTS

Map p302 (☎415-872-9189; www.needles-pens. com; 1173 Valencia St; ☺noon-7pm; ☐14, 33, 49, Ⓑ24th St Mission) This scrappy zine shop/how-to source/art gallery/publisher delivers inspiration to create your own artworks, zines and repurposed fashion statements. Nab limited-edition printings of Xara Thustra's manifesto *Friendship Between Artists Is an Equation of Love and Survival* and H Finn Cunningham's *Mental Health Cookbook* – plus alphabet buttons to pin your own credo onto a handmade messenger bag.

GRAVEL & GOLD
HOMEWARES

Map p302 (☎415-552-0112; www.gravelandgold. com; 3266 21st St; ☺noon-7pm Mon-Sat, to 5pm Sun; ☐12, 14, 49, Ⓑ24th St Mission) ✐ Get back to the land and in touch with California's roots without leaving sight of a Mission sidewalk. Gravel & Gold celebrates California's hippie homesteader movement with hand-printed smock-dresses, signature boob-print totes and wiggly stoner-striped throw pillows. It's homestead California-style with hand-thrown stoneware mugs, Risograph posters and rare books on '70s beach-shack architecture – plus DIY maker workshops (see website).

HARVEST OFF MISSION
CANNABIS

(☎415-814-3272; www.harvestshop.com/harvest-off-mission-menu; 33 29th St; ☺10am-9pm; ☐14, 49, ⓂJ, Ⓑ24th St Mission) This tidy Bernal Heights dispensary is tops for its 'farm-to-feeling' edibles, which include things like animal cookies, Black Ice and Pineapple Love Bombs. Also, it may or may not be a co-incidence that the incomparable Mitchell's Ice Cream (p149) is right down the block.

WORKSHOP RESIDENCE
DESIGN

Map p305 (☎415-285-2050; http://workshop residence.com; 797 22nd St; ☺noon-6pm Tue-Fri, from 10am Sat; ☐22, 48, ⓂT) Cottage industry is alive at Workshop Residence, where artists and designers collaborate with Bay Area fabricators to produce limited-edition designs – Ann Hamilton's welcome mats quote the children's book *Heidi*, Bruno Fazzolari's scents are inspired by drying oil paintings, and Lauren DiCioccio's nylon bags are embroidered with the slogan 'Thank you – have a nice day.' Check website for upcoming artist talks.

HEATH CERAMICS & NEWSSTAND
CERAMICS

Map p302 (☎415-361-5552; www.heathceramics. com; 2900 18th St; ☺8am-6pm Sun-Wed, to 7pm Thu-Sat; ☐12, 22, 27, 33) No local artisan SF restaurant decor is complete without earthy Heath stoneware, including the hand-glazed tiles found at this Mission studio-showroom. New Heath models are sold here alongside a design-mag newsstand, artisan pop-ups and jewelry trunk shows. Factory tours are available weekends at 11:30am; working tours are held the first and third Fridays of each month at 11:30am.

POCO DOLCE
CHOCOLATE

Map p305 (☎415-817-1551; http://pocodolce. com; 2421 3rd St; ☺11am-6pm Tue-Fri, noon-5pm Sat; ☐22, 48, ⓂT) ✐ People who swear they're not into dessert can't get enough Poco Dolce, San Francisco's award-winning, sustainably sourced chocolates with a touch of sea salt. Popcorn-toffee chocolates upgrade movie nights, and Aztec chili-chocolate tiles are ideal with Dogpatch wine tastings – but Legion of Honor (p194) art-inspired bars with silky California olive oil are a reason to leave your heart in San Francisco.

BETABRAND
CLOTHING

Map p302 (☎855-694-8766, 415-692-7433; www. betabrand.com; 780 Valencia St; ☺11am-7pm Mon-Fri, to 8pm Sat, noon-6pm Sun; ☐14, 22, 33, 49, Ⓑ16th St Mission) Crowdsource fashion choices at Betabrand, where experimental designs are put to an online vote and

LOCAL KNOWLEDGE

THE COMMUNITY-SUPPORTED BOOKSTORE SCENE

San Francisco may be the global hub for all things digital, but an analog revolution is afoot in the Mission. The district has rallied around the once-struggling **Adobe Books** (Map p302; ☑415-864-3936; www.adobebooks.com; 3130 24th St; ◷noon-8pm Mon-Fri, from 11am Sat & Sun; ☐12, 14, 48, 49, Ⓑ24th St Mission), now reinvented as a member-supported collective hosting raucous readings and Backroom Gallery art openings with a track record of launching Whitney Biennial stars. Down 24th St from Adobe, **Alley Cat Books** (Map p302; ☑415-824-1761; www.alleycatbookshop.com; 3036 24th St; ◷10am-9pm Mon-Sat, to 8pm Sun; ☐12, 14, 48, 49, Ⓑ24th St Mission) is part bookstore, part community center, with books in front, local art shows and art books in the back. On Valencia St, Alley Cat's sibling bookstore **Dog Eared Books** (Map p302; ☑415-282-1901; www.dogearedbooks.com; 900 Valencia St; ◷10am-10pm; ☐12, 14, 33, 49) supports new releases and small presses with author readings, and commemorates bygone cultural figures in hand-drawn obituaries.

winners produced in limited editions. Recent approved designs include an age-defier blouse, Timberland Gladiator sandals and trouser-cut 'dress pant yoga pants'. Some styles have been clunkers – including the 'chillmono,' a kimono-style down puffer jacket – but at these prices you can afford to take fashion risks.

NOOWORKS
CLOTHING

Map p302 (☑415-829-7623; www.nooworks. com; 395 Valencia St; ◷11am-7pm Tue-Sat, to 5pm Sun & Mon; ☐14, 22, 33, 49, Ⓑ16th St Mission) Get a streetwise Mission edge with Nooworks' locally designed, US-made fashions, most under $100. Nooworks' open-mouth shirts are ideal for Pancho-Villa-burrito-and-Roxie-documentary dates and 'Muscle Beach' maxi dresses are Dolores Park-ready with psychedelic rainbows and Schwarzenegger-esque flexing bodybuilders. Kids are good to go to any Mission gallery opening in soft leggings and tees in feather-, forest- and desert-inspired graphic prints.

VOYAGER
FASHION & ACCESSORIES

Map p302 (☑415-779-2712; www.thevoyager shop.com; 365 Valencia St; ◷11am-7pm; ☐14, 22, 33, 49, Ⓑ16th St Mission) Post-apocalyptic art-school surf shack is the vibe inside this curated storefront, featuring the work of sundry indie makers on plywood planks. Items for sale range from cultish denim shirts and sculptural ninja pants to surf wear and art books in the geodesic submarine gallery. Monthly pop-ups showcase statement jewelry, minimalist dresses and artistically inclined office supplies by SF makers.

MISSION SKATEBOARDS
FASHION & ACCESSORIES

Map p302 (☑415-647-7888; 3045 24th St; ◷noon-6pm Mon-Fri, from 11am Sat & Sun; ☑; ☐12, 14, 48, 49, Ⓑ24th St Mission) Street cred comes easy with locally designed Mission decks, custom tees to kick-flip over and cult skate shoes at this shop owned by SF street-skate legend Scot Thompson. Cool deal: kids who show report cards with GPAs over 3.0 get discounts. This shop is handy to Potrero del Sol/La Raza Skatepark (p46) and, for newbies too cool for kneepads, SF General (p272).

BLACK & BLUE TATTOO
BODY ART

Map p302 (☑415-626-0770; www.blackand bluetattoo.com; 381 Guerrero St; ◷noon-7pm; ☐14, 22, 33, 49, Ⓑ16th St Mission) This women-owned tattoo parlor gets it in ink with designs ranging from honeycomb-pattern bicep graphics to shoulder-to-shoulder Golden Gate Bridge spans. Check out artists' work at the shop or online, then book a consultation. Once you've talked over the design, you can book your tattoo – you'll need to show up sober, well fed, fragrance free and clear headed for your transformation.

PAXTON GATE
GIFTS & SOUVENIRS

Map p302 (☑415-824-1872; www.paxtongate. com; 824 Valencia St; ◷11am-7pm Sun-Wed, to 8pm Thu-Sat; ☐12, 14, 33, 49, Ⓑ16th St Mission) Salvador Dalí probably would've shopped here for all his taxidermy and gardening needs. Get a surrealist home makeover with animal-skull puppets, terrariums sprouting from lab beakers and mounted heads of African game. The kids' shop down the street (at 766 Valencia) maximizes playtime with volcano-making kits, shadow puppets and rocket-ship dollhouses. Check DIY taxidermy workshop dates online.

RAINBOW GROCERY
FOOD & DRINKS

Map p302 (415-863-0620; www.rainbow.coop; 1745 Folsom St; 9am-9pm; 9, 12, 33, 47) This legendary cooperative attracts crowds to buy eco/organic/fair-trade products in bulk, sample the bounty of local cheeses and flirt in the artisan-chocolate aisle. To answer your questions about where to find what in the Byzantine bulk section, ask a fellow shopper – staff can be elusive. Small though well-priced wine and craft-beer selections; no meat products.

MISSION CANNABIS CLUB
CANNABIS

Map p302 (415-970-9333; www.missioncannabisclub.com; 2441 Mission St; 10am-10pm Mon-Sat, 11am-8pm Sun; 12, 14, 49, 24th St Mission) A pot dispensary with a great reputation for customer service and a wide range of products, from flowers to edibles, vapes to tropical rubs. The trippy local art is also a selling point and there are plans to add an upstairs lounge featuring a coffee bar, ping-pong tables, arcade games and an area for live entertainment.

SAN FRANCYCLE
FASHION & ACCESSORIES

Map p302 (SFC; 415-374-7550; www.wearesfc.com; 976 Valencia St; 11am-6:30pm; 14, 33, 49, 24th St Mission) Keep those muscles warm and show local cyclist pride as you whip through downtown streets wearing San Francycle's California-bear-on-a-bicycle tee and SF bike-district hoodie (Mission is represented by fixies, Castro by exercise bikes). Designer-owner and cyclist Tommy Pham prints his designs here in SF, so your souvenir tee has neighborhood street cred that earns bike-messenger nods, if not right of way.

MEL RICE CERAMICA
CERAMICS

Map p302 (415-685-6665; www.melriceceramica.com; 853 1/2 Valencia St; noon-6pm Sat & Sun; 14, 33, 49, MJ) Barn doors on the front of Amnesia bar magically open to reveal the ultimate Mission hipster china cupboard. Mel Rice stocks these shelves with her handmade Mission housewares in earthy colors and organic shapes: generous indigo-glazed wine cups, pot-bellied cookie jars with cork stoppers and emphatically undecided 'f*** yes/f*** no' coffee mugs.

AGGREGATE SUPPLY
HOMEWARES

Map p302 (415-474-3190; www.aggregatesupplysf.com; 806 Valencia St; 11am-7pm Mon-Sat, noon-6pm Sun; 14, 33, 49, 16th St Mission) Wild West modern is the look at Aggregate Supply, purveyors of California-cool fashion and home decor. Local designers and indie makers get pride of place; souvenirs don't get more authentically local than the pins, towels, posters, jams and candles created around the Bay Area.

🏃 SPORTS & ACTIVITIES

★ URBAN PUTT
MINIGOLF

Map p302 (415-341-1080; www.urbanputt.com; 1096 S Van Ness Ave; adult/child $12/8; 4pm-midnight Mon-Thu, to 1am Fri, 11am-1am Sat, to midnight Sun; 14, 24th St Mission) Leave it to the town that brought you Burning Man and the Exploratorium to turn innocent mini-golf games into total trips. Urban Putt's course looks like a Tim Burton hallucination, from tricky windmill Transamerica Pyramid hole 5 to Día de los Muertos–themed hole 9. Enjoy big beers with wee snacks, including mini corndogs and tiny chicken-and-waffle stacks on sticks.

★ 18 REASONS
COOKING

Map p302 (415-568-2710; https://18reasons.org; 3674 18th St; classes & dining events $12-125; ; 22, 33, MJ) Go gourmet at this Bi-Rite–affiliated community food nonprofit (p150), offering deliciously educational events: wine tastings, knife-skill and cheese-making workshops, and chef-led classes. Mingle with fellow foodies at family-friendly $12 community suppers and multicourse winemaker dinners ($95 to $125). The website lists bargain guest-chef pop-ups and low-cost classes with cookbook authors. Spots fill quickly for hands-on cooking classes – book early.

DANCE MISSION
DANCING

Map p302 (415-826-4441; www.dancemission.com; 3316 24th St; ; 12, 14, 48, 49, 24th St Mission) Step out and find your niche at this nonprofit Mission dance hub, featuring contact improv, dance jams and classes in styles from Afro-Caribbean to vogue – there's a class here for every interest, age and skill level. Check the website for dance showcases in the 140-seat theater, plus

WORTH A DETOUR

BUMPIN' AROUND BERNAL HEIGHTS

For a quick getaway from the Mission's urban grit, veer off Mission St south of 30th St onto colorful **Cortland Ave**, lined with quirky Victorian storefront boutiques and laid-back local hangouts. Weekends start just over the hill at Alemany Farmers Market (p26), where California's first farmers market has been held on Saturdays since 1943; it's also the site of Sunday-morning flea markets that unearth hidden treasures from Victorian attics. Urban hikers summit **Bernal Heights Park** (https://sfrecpark.org/destination/bernal-heights-park/; ⊗5am-midnight; 🐾; 🚌67) and go flying down the **Winfield St double hillside slides** – adults and kids alike – to get good and hungry for crispy rice-ball salad at **Mae Krua** (✆415-574-7334; 331 Cortland Ave; mains $7-13; ⊗10am-5:45pm Wed-Mon; 🚌24). For more adult entertainment, find prime patio seating at **Virgil's Sea Room** (Map p302; ✆415-829-2233; www.virgilssf.com; 3152 Mission St; ⊗4pm-2am Mon-Fri, from 2pm Sat & Sun; 🚌12, 14, 27, 49, Ⓑ24th St Mission) for cocktails and Drag Queen Bingo, hit **Holy Water** (http://holywatersf.com; 309 Cortland Ave; ⊗4pm-2am Mon-Sat, from 2pm Sun; 🐾; 🚌14, 24, 49) for happy-hour ablutions and/or head to landmark lesbian bar Wild Side West (p158) to chill in the junk-sculpture beer garden. Nothing tops such a sunny Bernal Heights afternoon – except maybe **Ichi Sushi** (✆415-525-4750; www.ichisushi.com; 3369 Mission St; sushi $5-8, mains $11-16; ⊗5:30-9:30pm Sun-Thu, to 10:30pm Fri & Sat; 🚌14, 24, 49, Ⓑ24th St Mission, ⓂJ) 🍜 *omakase* (chef's selection) and epic backyard dance parties at El Rio (p155).

events and guest-artist workshops ranging from beginner *taiko* drumming to dancing in stilts.

ANCHOR BREWING COMPANY   BREWERY

Map p305 (✆415-863-8350; www.anchorbrewing. com; cnr 1705 Mariposa & De Haro Sts; tours adult/ child $25/free; ⊗tours 1:30pm & 4pm daily plus 11am Fri-Sun; 🚌10, 19, 22) Beer-lovers, here's your best-ever excuse for daytime drinking: the Anchor Brewing Company shares its steam-brewing secrets on tours with extensive tastings. The 45-minute tour covers Anchor's landmark 1937 building, shiny-copper equipment and 2017 extension, followed by a 45-minute tasting featuring several half-pints of Anchor brews (sorry, kids: no beer for under-21s). Reserve via website.

MISSION CULTURAL CENTER FOR LATINO ARTS   ART

Map p302 (✆415-821-1155; www.missioncultural center.org; 2868 Mission St; ⊗5-10pm Mon, from 10am Tue-Sat, 10am-5:30pm Sun; 🚼; 🚌14, 49, Ⓑ24th St Mission) Join a class in tango, take up the conga, get crafty with your kids or silkscreen a protest poster at the printmaking studio at the Mission's Latinx arts hub. Teachers are friendly and participants range from *niños* (kids) to *abuelos* (grandparents). Check the online calendar for upcoming gallery openings, and don't miss November's Día de los Muertos altar displays.

MISSION BOWLING CLUB   BOWLING

Map p302 (✆415-863-2695; www.missionbowling club.com; 3176 17th St; ⊗3-11pm Mon-Wed, to midnight Thu & Fri, 11am-midnight Sat, to 11pm Sun; 🚌12, 22, 33, 49, Ⓑ16th St Mission) Don't mock until you try bowling Mission style: six lanes in a mood-lit warehouse, where the bar pours smoky mezcal sours and Sonoma Saison ales, and $1 off happy-hour orders of draft beer and seasonal menu items goes to local nonprofits. Book online or bide your time for walk-in lanes at the bar. Under-21s are only allowed at weekends 11am-7pm.

The Castro

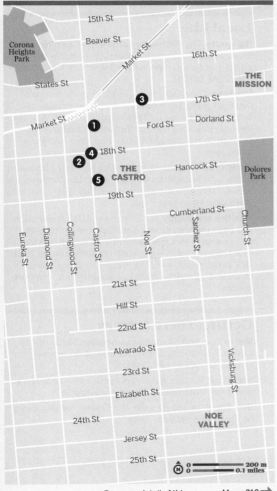

Neighborhood Top Five

1 **Castro Theatre** (p173) Catching a movie premiere, sing-along musical or drag show and hearing the Mighty Wurlitzer's pipes roar before showtime.

2 **GLBT History Museum** (p167) Time-traveling through 50 years in the Castro at America's first gay museum.

3 **Frances** (p171) Feasting on Melissa Perello's renegade rustic cuisine.

4 **Rainbow Honor Walk** (p167) Seeing how far we've come along Castro sidewalks honoring LGBTIQ+ pioneers.

5 **Human Rights Campaign Action Center** (p167) Admiring the mural and messages of civil rights leader Harvey Milk in his former camera store.

For more detail of this area see Map p312 ➡

Lonely Planet's Top Tip

Historic streetcars that look like toy trains run to Castro from Fisherman's Wharf, covering the Market St through downtown. Trouble is, they sometimes get stuck in traffic and you can wait what feels like forever. Check arrival times at www.nextmuni.com, which uses GPS tracking; use the 'live map' to determine streetcars' exact locations. If the F-Market service is far away or running slow, take underground-metro K, L or M trains, which move (much) faster beneath Market St – same ticket, same price.

Best Places to Eat

➡ Frances (p171)
➡ Kantine (p170)
➡ Mauerpark (p170)
➡ Gai Chicken Rice (p170)
➡ Beit Rima (p170)

For reviews, see p170.

Best Places to Drink

➡ 440 Castro (p172)
➡ Twin Peaks Tavern (p172)
➡ Last Rites (p172)
➡ Beaux (p172)

For reviews, see p171.

🔒 Best Shopping

➡ Apothecarium (p174)
➡ Cliff's Variety (p175)
➡ Omnivore (p174)
➡ Local Take (p174)
➡ Stag & Manor (p174)

For reviews, see p174. ➡

Explore The Castro

The Castro's main crossroads is at the intersection of 18th and Castro Sts, linked by rainbow crosswalks. Mornings are quiet, but the Castro kicks into gear in afternoons and evenings, especially weekends, when crowds come to people-watch, shop and drink. At night, semiclad partiers and buttoned-up moviegoers mingle on the Castro's wide sidewalks.

The best dining is off the main drag, clustered around 16th St. Castro-area shops line Market St between Church and Castro Sts, and Castro St itself, from Market to 19th Sts, with a few scattered along 18th St. Castro St is surrounded by residential streets, good for strolling, with many pretty Victorian buildings.

Local Life

Hangouts The Wednesday-afternoon Castro Farmers Market (March through November) provides the best glimpse of locals, especially from sidewalk tables at Cafe Flore (p173).

Drinking The Castro is packed with bars, but most don't get going till evening – except on Sunday afternoons, in a local tradition dating from WWII. For listings, pick up a copy of *BARtab* magazine – supplement to the local LGBTIQ+ *Bay Area Reporter* newspaper.

What (not) to wear Everyone flaunts their physique in the exhibitionist Castro, but once the afternoon fog blows, carry a jacket or shiver – locals spot tourists by their shorts and tank tops.

Healthy and happy San Francisco AIDS Foundation has been pioneering safe-sex initiatives since 1982 and now provides free and low-cost health services at Strut (p39), offering private consultations on PrEP HIV prophylaxis, screenings and substance abuse treatment as well as walk-in counseling and support groups.

Getting There & Away

Metro K, L and M trains run beneath Market St to Castro Station. J trains travel from downtown along Church to 18th St and beyond.

Streetcar Vintage streetcars operate on the F-Market line, from Fisherman's Wharf to Castro St.

Bus Buses 24 and 33 serve the Castro, but there may be long waits between runs.

◉ SIGHTS

Major sights are scattered along Castro between Market and 19th Sts, plus a few that make conquering nearby hills worth your while.

HUMAN RIGHTS CAMPAIGN
ACTION CENTER   HISTORIC SITE

Map p312 (☎415-431-2200; http://shop.hrc.org/san-francisco-hrc-store; 575 Castro St; ☺10am-8pm Mon-Sat, to 7pm Sun; ⓜCastro St) Harvey Milk's former camera storefront was featured in the Academy Award–winning movie *Milk,* and now it's home to the civil rights advocacy group championing for marriage equality and transgender identity rights. A rainbow mural quotes Milk: 'If a bullet should enter my brain, let that bullet destroy every closet door.' Activists scan the bulletin board and sign petitions, while shoppers score stylish HRC designer tees, with proceeds supporting LGBTIQ+ civil-rights initiatives.

GLBT HISTORY MUSEUM   MUSEUM

Map p312 (☎415-621-1107; www.glbthistory.org/museum; 4127 18th St; $5, 1st Wed of month free; ☺11am-6pm Mon-Sat, noon-5pm Sun, closed Tue fall-spring; ⓜCastro St) America's first gay-history museum showcases a century of San Francisco LGBTIQ+ ephemera – Harvey Milk's campaign literature, matchbooks from long-gone bathhouses, photographs of early marches – alongside insightful installations highlighting queer culture milestones and struggles for acceptance throughout history. Multimedia stories put civil rights efforts into personal perspective, and provide community introductions for queer folk and allies alike. The shop sells reproductions of '80s pink triangle tees,'70s pride pins, and Harvey Milk fridge magnets citing his words: 'You gotta give 'em hope.' Indeed.

RANDALL JUNIOR MUSEUM   MUSEUM

Map p312 (☎415-554-9600; www.randallmuseum.org; 199 Museum Way; ☺10am-5pm Tue-Sat; P ♿; ☒24, 37, ⓜF, K, L, M) FREE While adults are asleep downhill, eight-year-olds are making scientific discoveries atop Corona Heights Park. After Josephine Randall became a pioneering Stanford zoologist in 1910, she turned a jail into a kids' science and arts center as San Francisco's first Rec & Parks Superintendent. Today the kids' museum named after her features state-of-

RAINBOW HONOR WALK

You're always in excellent company in the Castro, where sidewalk plaques honor LGBTIQ+ heroes. The **Rainbow Honor Walk** (Map p312; http://rainbowhonorwalk.org; Castro St & Market St; ⓜCastro St) runs along Market St from Noe St to Castro St and down Castro St from Market St to 20th St. Portraits are etched into the bronze plaques, and many are familiar faces: civil rights activist James Baldwin, artist Keith Haring, author Virginia Woolf, disco diva Sylvester. Honorees are suitably bathed in glory every night, when they're illuminated by rainbow LEDs.

Each also has a brief bio, so you can get better acquainted with the likes of astronaut Sally Ride, trans Zuni leader We'Wha, and Iranian singer Fereydoun Farrokhzad. Some people leave offerings like flowers or notes by the plaques of their favorite icons – check the website to see who's featured where.

THE CASTRO SIGHTS

the-art science and tech labs, woodworking and ceramics studios. Highlights include a habitat for 100 stray and wounded animals, plus Lionel trains chugging along the Golden Gate Model Railroad.

CORONA HEIGHTS PARK   PARK

Map p312 (Museum Hill; btwn 16th St & Roosevelt Way; ☒37, ⓜCastro St) Scramble up the red rocks of 520ft-high Corona Heights for jaw-dropping, 180-degree views at the summit. Face east as the sun sets, and watch the city unfurl below in a carpet of light. Take tiny Beaver St uphill to the steps through the bushes, then head right up the trail, past tennis courts and rock climbers. For an easier hike, enter via Roosevelt Way.

BARBIE-DOLL WINDOW   ART

Map p312 (4099 19th St; ☒24, ⓜCastro) No first-time loop through the Castro would be complete without a peek at this window display featuring trans Barbies and Billy Doll, a gay alternative to Ken who's more than just a little anatomically correct. Dolls are dressed – well, some of them – in outrageous costumes and arranged in protest lines, complete with signs. One says it best: 'It's Castro, Bitch.'

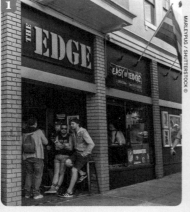

1. Edge (p173)
One of the Castro's favorite gay bars.

2. Human Rights Campaign Action Center (p167)
Harvey Milk's former camera storefront is now home to a civil rights advocacy group.

3. Twin Peaks Tavern (p172)
The world's first gay bar with windows open to the street.

4. Castro Theatre (p173)
Catch a musical, movie or drag show at this classic Castro venue.

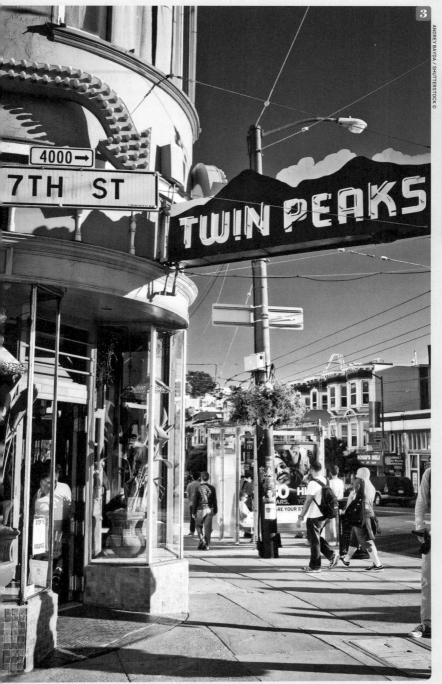

HARVEY MILK & JANE WARNER PLAZAS
SQUARE

Map p312 (cnr Market & Castro Sts; MCastro St) Somewhere over the rainbow is Harvey Milk Plaza, where a huge rainbow flag flaps. Rainbow-lit escalators lead toward Castro Muni station and a display honoring Milk's legacy of gay civic pride and political clout. Across Castro at the F-train terminus is Jane Warner Plaza, named for the pioneering lesbian officer who patrolled the Castro for 20 years. Rainbow-themed seating and bizarre public art make a great backdrop for people-watching – including glimpses of Castro nudists, legally obliged to cover up with strategically placed socks.

✕ EATING

There are many quick, convenient spots for a bite on Castro St, but tastier options and better values are along Market St to Church St. The very best places are off the main drag, including a cluster of bistros and bargain eats around 16th and 17th Sts.

★KANTINE
SCANDINAVIAN $

Map p312 (☑415-735-7123; http://kantinesf. com; 1906 Market St; dishes $10-19; ⏰7:30am-3pm Tue-Fri, from 9am Sat & Sun; ☑⛹; ☒22, MF, J, K, L, M) ✎ Brunch is served with a side of *hygge* (cozy happiness) at Kantine. Take your pick of five to seven seasonal Scandinavian-inspired dishes – velvety bay-shrimp-egg salad, lemony pickled herring – or hearty *smørrebrød* (open-faced sandwich) on nutty, toothsome, just-baked sprouted rye. Chef-owner Nichole Achettola turns local, sustainable, organic ingredients into decadent, curative, clean fare that honors Castro's Scandinavian heritage and Kantine's location in an ex-laundromat (love the laundry-bagged lights).

★GAI CHICKEN RICE
HAINAN $

Map p312 (☑415-535-0451; www.gaiandrice.com; 3463 16th St; dishes $11-13; ⏰11:30am-8:30pm; ☑⛹; ☒22, MF, J, K, L, M) Who's got the solution to cold snaps and tentative tummies? This Gai. The tender Hainan-style poached chicken here is free-range and antibiotic-free, accompanied by jasmine or brown rice cooked in chicken broth, with sweet-and-sour cucumbers and your choice of gingery Hainan, tangy Vietnamese, Thai soy or housemade *habanero* sauces. Soulful soup gets you back on your feet; sweetened Vietnamese coffee gets you Castro-club-hopping.

★MAUERPARK
GERMAN, BAKERY $

Map p312 (☑415-525-4429; http://mauerpark sf.com; 500 Church St; platters $12-13; ⏰7am-5pm Tue & Wed, to 9pm Thu & Fri, 8am-9pm Sat, 8am-5pm Sun; ⛹; ☒22, 33, MJ, K, L, M) Break *brot* (bread) with friends, and share platters piled with wurst, salami and cheese. Raised by German immigrants in the Bay Area, Salome Buelow serves sustaining, unfussy, soulful fare: thick yogurt and nutty Emmantaler cheese accompany *müsli*, while pretzel bread and wheat beer make *leberwurst* (liverwurst) sing. Mauerpark is named after Berlin's demilitarized zone – this *brot* builds bridges, not walls.

BEIT RIMA
PALESTINIAN $

Map p312 (☑415-710-2397; 138 Church St; small plates $8-12; ☑⛹; ☒22, MJ, K, L, M, N) Bond over mezze inspired by chef-owner Samir Mogannam's mom, plus stints at the Bay's top Mediterranean restaurants. Hummus tahina traditionalists and root-vegetable radicals kiss and make up over Samir's classic version, with just enough lemon to make you pucker up – *kibbe*-style spiced beef optional. Palestinian lager pairs with garlicky *ful* (fava spread), juicy, smokey *shish taouk* (grilled chicken) and nutty, tangy *muhamarra* (almond/pepper spread) .

THOROUGHBREAD
BAKERY $

Map p312 (☑415-558-0690; http://thorough breadandpastry.com; 248 Church St; pastries $3-6; ⏰7am-6pm Tue-Sat, from 8am Sun; ☑⛹; ☒22, 33, MJ, K, L, M, N) Pastries come with pedigree at Thoroughbread – they're creations of Michelin-starred Michel Suas, founder of the San Francisco Baking Institute. If you're unsure what to order, check the racks behind the counter – baking continues all day. Tantalizing aromas and upbeat bakers make this a beloved neighborhood hangout, where people put down phones and chat on the back patio.

THAI HOUSE EXPRESS
THAI $

Map p312 (☑415-864-5000; www.thaihousesf. com; 599 Castro St; dinner mains $10-17; ⏰noon-10pm; ☒24, MCastro St) Bright, fresh flavors and comforting Thai classics make Thai House a foggy-day staple, and attention is also paid to tasty $10 lunchtime rice plates – a rare value on high-rent, high-turnover Castro St. All-day service is handy when you're late or jetlagged, though it gets loud at peak times. Next time you come, the staff welcomes you back.

DINOSAURS   SANDWICHES $

Map p312 (☎415-503-1421; 2275 Market St, lower level; sandwiches $8-9; ⏰10am-10pm; 🚗♿🐕; Ⓜ Castro St) Monster *banh mi* (Vietnamese sandwiches) stomp hunger with your choice of beef, lemongrass chicken, portobello, or pork with pâté on crusty French bread. For a smashing lunch, ask friendly counter folk for all the fixings – jalapeños, mayo, and pickled vegetables, cilantro and Sriracha hot sauce optional – and Vietnamese iced coffee with sweetened condensed milk, and grab a sunny sidewalk seat.

SUPER DUPER BURGER   BURGERS $

Map p312 (www.superdupersf.com; 2304 Market St; burgers $5.75-8.25; ⏰11am-11pm; ♿; 🚌24, Ⓜ F, K, L, M) 🌱 Upgrade from drive-thru dinners at Super Duper, serving made-to-order burgers with top-quality, humanely raised beef, non-GMO fries, and dreamy milkshakes made with organic cream from Sonoma. This local chain has locations across SF, but this sunny glassed-in corner location is good for people-watching – and the Castro has a particular appreciation of beefcake.

STARBELLY   CALIFORNIAN, PIZZA $$

Map p312 (☎415-252-7500; https://starbellysf.com; 3583 16th St; dishes $8-25; ⏰11:30am-3:30pm & 5-11pm Mon-Thu, to midnight Fri, 10am-3:30pm & 5pm-midnight Sat, to 11pm Sun; 🚗♿; Ⓜ Castro St) 🌱 All the laid-back charm and sun-drenched flavors you'd expect from California, at totally chill prices. The Castro farmer's market is right across the street, and you can taste it in Starbelly's sustainably sourced, market-fresh salads, seasonal dumplings, and thin-crusted pizzas with cave-aged gruyere and wild local mushrooms. Salumi is house-cured and Prather Ranch burgers are the Castro's best.

LOVEJOY'S TEA ROOM   BRITISH $$

(☎415-648-5895; www.lovejoystearoom.com; 1351 Church St; tea service $18-30, pub fare $11-19; ⏰11am-6pm Wed-Sun, last seating 4:30pm; ♿; 🚌24, Ⓜ J) All the chintz you'd expect from an English tearoom, only with a San Francisco crowd: curators talk interactive art over Darjeeling, scones and clotted cream, while dual dads treat daughters and dolls to 'wee tea' of mini-sandwiches, petits fours and hot chocolate. For savory lunches, go with pub fare – especially fluffy sausage rolls and crocks of sausage pies. Make reservations.

POESIA   ITALIAN $$

Map p312 (☎415-252-9325; http://poesiasf.com; 4072 18th St; mains $23-34; ⏰5-10:30pm Mon-Sat, to 10pm Sun; Ⓜ F, K, L, M) Get cozy at this bay-window *osteria* with a sunny disposition, feel-good handmade pastas, excellent DOC Italian wines by the glass, and banquettes that invite lingering. Arrive before 6:30pm for half-off happy hour negronis and Aperol spritz, plus bargain crostini. Fun fact: this is where Oprah ate when she visited the Castro.

ANCHOR OYSTER BAR   SEAFOOD $$

Map p312 (☎415-531-3990; www.anchoroyster bar.com; 579 Castro St; mains $18-28; ⏰11:30am-10pm Mon-Sat, 4-9:30pm Sun; 🚌24, 33, Ⓜ F, K, L, M) Since 1977, Anchor has been Castro's port of call for sustainably sourced local oysters, Dungeness crab, seafood salads, and San Francisco *cioppino* (seafood stew). The nautical-themed room seats 24 at stainless-steel tables; for faster service, sit at the marble-top bar. They don't take reservations – get on the list, then chill with a glass of wine on the outdoor bench until called.

★ FRANCES   CALIFORNIAN $$$

Map p312 (☎415-621-3870; www.frances-sf.com; 3870 17th St; mains $26-34; ⏰5-10pm Sun & Tue-Thu, to 10:30pm Fri & Sat; 🚌24, 33, Ⓜ F, K, L, M) 🌱 Rebel chef-owner Melissa Perello earned a Michelin star for fine dining, then ditched downtown to start this market-inspired neighborhood bistro. Daily menus showcase rustic flavors and luxurious textures with impeccable technique – handmade ricotta *malfatti* pasta with buttery squash and crunchy pepitas, juicy pork chops with blood orange and earthy Japanese sweet potatoes – plus cult wine served by the ounce, directly from Wine Country.

🍷⚓ DRINKING & NIGHTLIFE

Castro bars open earlier than in other neighborhoods; on weekends most open at noon. An abundance of cafes offer excellent coffee and unbeatable people-watching.

★ LAST RITES
TIKI BAR

Map p312 (www.lastritesbar.com; 718 14th St; ⊙6pm-2am; ☃; ☐22, ⓜF, J, K, L, M) An airplane crashed on a desert island, and out of the wreckage came this killer Castro tiki bar. Enter through the airplane door to discover a long-lost jungle world, where tattoo artists and software engineers clink flaming rum drinks over steamer-trunk tables. A giant skull glowers from fern-covered walls, daring you to finish that second Zombie Killer. Brace for impact.

★ TWIN PEAKS TAVERN
GAY

Map p312 (⌨415-864-9470; www.twinpeaks tavern.com; 401 Castro St; ⊙noon-2am Mon-Fri, from 8am Sat & Sun; ⓜCastro St) The vintage rainbow neon sign points the way to a local landmark – Twin Peaks was the world's first gay bar with windows open to the street. If you're not here for the Castro's best people-watching, cozy up to the Victorian carved-wood bar for cocktails and conviviality, or grab a back booth to discuss movies at the Castro over wine by the glass.

VERVE COFFEE ROASTERS
CAFE

Map p312 (⌨415-780-0867; www.vervecoffee. com; 2101 Market St; ⊙6am-8pm; ☐22, ⓜF, J, K, L, M) Cults wish they had the devoted following of this Santa Cruz roaster, justifiably worshipped for small-batch, single-origin roasts prepared with pride. Chipper baristas will ask if you want your milk microfoamed for denser consistency – say yes and tip in cash. Tasty breakfast biscuits and a sunny corner spot encourage people-watching – don't let the silent stressy laptop crowd kill your vibe.

EUREKA
LOUNGE

Map p312 (⌨415-431-6000; www.eurekarestau rant.com; 4063 18th St; ⊙5:30-9:30pm Sun, to 10:30pm Mon-Thu, to 11:30pm Fri & Sat; ☐24, 33, ⓜF, K, L, M) Most Castro bars only serve eye candy with well drinks – but Eureka! You've found a class-act lounge that pairs Southern cooking with craft cocktails. Head upstairs and settle into white-leather communal booths or bar stools before 7pm to score HOMO Cosmos with Hanson Organic Mandarin vodka or Dark-n-Stormy with Kraken spiced rum for $7 – but splurge for fried chicken.

SWIRL
WINE BAR

Map p312 (⌨415-864-2262; www.swirloncastro. com; 572 Castro St; ⊙1:30-8pm Mon-Thu, 1:30-

9pm Fri, noon-9pm Sat, noon-8pm Sun; ☐24, 33, ⓖF, ⓜK, L, M) Come as you are – pinstripes or leather, gay, straight or whatever – to toast freedom with sublime bubbly after GLBT History Museum (p167) visits, or find liquid courage for sing-alongs at the Castro Theatre in flights of bold reds. This wine shop with a bar in the back has universal appeal, with reliably delicious wine at fair prices in neighborly company.

BEAUX
GAY & LESBIAN

Map p312 (www.beauxsf.com; 2344 Market St; cover free-$5; ⊙4pm-2am Mon-Fri, noon-2am Sat & Sun; ☐24, 33, ⓜF, K, L, M) The candy store of Castro clubs, Beaux serves every gay flavor. Highlights include Club Papi Wednesdays, '90s–'00s Throwback Thursdays, go-go Manimal Fridays, and Nitty Gritty dirty disco Saturdays (find the mezzanine for best views over the floor). On Big Top Sundays, *Rupaul's Drag Race* stars emcee. Weekends are rainbow-spectrum and straight-but-questioning; arrive before 10pm to beat lines and cover.

440 CASTRO
GAY

Map p312 (⌨415-621-8732; www.the440.com; 440 Castro St; ⊙noon-2am; ☐24, 33, ⓜF, K, L, M) The most happening bar on the street, 440 draws bearded, gym-fit 30- and 40-something dudes – especially on furry Sundays and weekend nights, when go-go boys twirl – and an odd mix of Peter Pans for Monday's underwear night. If you think the monthly Battle of the Bulge contest has something to do with WWII, this is not your bar, honey.

BLACKBIRD
GAY

Map p312 (⌨415-503-0630; www.blackbirdbar. com; 2124 Market St; ⊙3pm-2am Mon-Fri, from 2pm Sat & Sun; ☐33, 37, ⓜF, J, K, L, M) Mysterious tinctures and housemade bitters make creative cocktails with magnetic powers, drawing Castro regulars and straight-friendly after-work crowds to this cozy neighborhood den next to the Church St Muni stop. Mix it up while you wait for your turn at billiards or the photo booth. Happy hours run 5pm to 8pm weekdays; weekends get ear-splittingly loud.

MIDNIGHT SUN
GAY

Map p312 (⌨415-861-4186; www.midnightsunsf. com; 4067 18th St; ⊙2pm-2am Mon-Fri, from 1pm Sat & Sun; ☐24, 33, ⓜF, K, L, M) 'Servicing the Castro for over 40 years' is no small claim to fame – and Midnight Sun lives up to its motto daily with a steady flow of good vibes and strong drinks (two for one until 9pm every day). Bare some hair at wildly popular Bear Happy Hour Fridays and get dolled up for Mister Sister Mondays, hosted by drag star Honey Mahogany.

HITOPS
SPORTS BAR

Map p312 (📞415-551-2500; www.hitopsbar.com; 2247 Market St; ⏰11:30am-midnight Mon-Wed, to 2am Thu & Fri, 10am-2am Sat & Sun; 🚌22, 33, Ⓜ️F, J, K, L, M) At Castro's first gay sports bar, you can wear rainbows and team colors (as long as they're either blue and yellow, or orange and black). Giant-screen TVs and supersized snacks set the scene for instant bonding – and Thursday Gym Class amps up locker-room antics with whiskey shots and go-go boys. For friendly competition, hit the shuffleboard table and Tuesday trivia nights.

EDGE
GAY

Map p312 (www.edgesf.com; 4149 18th St; ⏰1pm-2am Mon-Fri, noon-2am Sat & Sun; 🚌24, 33, Ⓜ️F, K, L, M) When you're feeling kinda ratty and you're looking for a daddy, it's the Edge. Drag divas and leather daddies bond over show-tune sing-alongs Musical Sundays, Mondays and Wednesdays – but it takes a PhD in MTV to prevail at cut-throat Tuesday pop-music trivia nights. Thursday Monster drag shows and daily two-for-one drink specials do not disappoint.

THE CAFE
GAY & LESBIAN

Map p312 (📞415-523-0133; www.cafesf.com; 2369 Market St; cover free-$6; ⏰6pm-2am Mon-Fri, from 3pm Sat & Sun; Ⓜ️Castro St) With a Harvey Milk mural and rainbow light-up dance floor, The Cafe is the obvious place to throw your own coming-out party. Most nights the crowd seems recently graduated, and parties range from Latinx Picante Thursdays to lesbian Sugar Saturdays; check the calendar. Kick-ass sound and trippy light shows pack the dance floor; cruise the open-air patio between sets. Cash only.

MIX
GAY

Map p312 (📞415-431-8616; www.mixbarsf.com; 4086 18th St; ⏰7am-2am Mon-Fri, from 6am Sat & Sun; Ⓜ️Castro St) The last Castro bar to open at 6am, Mix lives up to its name with a full rainbow of colorful neighborhood characters – acclaimed lesbian playwrights, AIDS LifeCycle champs, and off-duty drag queens alike. The front bar is snug and sociable, but the open-roofed smokers patio is where the action is. Drink specials run $2–5 and good vibes are free.

CAFE FLORE
CAFE

Map p312 (📞415-621-8579; http://flore415.com; 2298 Market St; ⏰5-10pm Mon & Wed, 9am-10pm Thu & Fri, to 11pm Sat, to 8pm Sun; 🐾; 🚌24, 33, Ⓜ️F, K, L, M) Watch the entire gay world go by on the sun-drenched patio at the Flore, the Castro's hub since 1973. Weekdays regulars hold court over Purple Arnold Palmers and Ritual coffee outdoors, especially during Wednesday Castro farmers markets. Share cocktail carafes and make friends instantly; food's just average. Wi-fi weekdays only, and no electrical outlets; occasional DJs and drag karaoke.

BADLANDS
GAY

Map p312 (📞415-626-9320; www.sfbadlands.com; 4121 18th St; ⏰2pm-2am; 🚌24, 33, Ⓜ️F, K, L, M) The Castro's long-standing dance bar gets packed with gay college boys, their wide-eyed straight girlfriends, and sundry chicken hawks. A tame scene by SF standards, it's an easy point of entry for freshly out gays, with Top 40 music videos, standard vodka cocktails, and two-for-one drinks until 9pm. Expect lines at weekends.

⭐ ENTERTAINMENT

★CASTRO THEATRE
CINEMA

Map p312 (📞415-621-6120; www.castrotheatre.com; 429 Castro St; adult $13, child, senior & matinee $10; Ⓜ️Castro St) Every night at the Castro, crowds roar as the mighty organ rises – and no, that's not a euphemism. Showtime at this 1922 art deco movie palace is heralded with Wurlitzer organ show tunes, culminating in sing-alongs to the Judy Garland anthem 'San Francisco.' Architect Timothy Pflueger's OTT Spanish-Moorish-Asian style inspired the *Wizard of Oz* sets, but earthquake-shy San Franciscans avoid sitting under his pointy metal chandelier.

★SWEDISH AMERICAN HALL & CAFE DU NORD
LIVE MUSIC

Map p312 (📞415-375-3370; www.swedishamericanhall.com; 2170 Market St; shows $12-35; ⏰shows start 6:30-8pm; Ⓜ️Church St) The Castro was once known as Little Scandinavia

LOCAL KNOWLEDGE

SEWARD STREET SLIDES

Race ya! The twin concrete **Seward Slides** (Map p312; Seward St, cnr Douglass St; ⊙daylight hours; 👪; 🚌33, Ⓜ F, K, L, M) snake down a steep hill – it's an urban luge, built in 1973. Cardboard is necessary for descents, and there's usually a stack by the slides – but BYO waxed paper for faster speeds. Bring kids: a park sign reads, 'No adults unless accompanied by children.' Neighbors don't love noise, but sometimes it can't be helped ... wheeee!

after the sailors who docked here – and the secret to their community spirit was the speakeasy running in the basement of their meeting hall since 1907. Today the updated Cafe du Nord speakeasy is an atmospheric singer-songwriter hotspot, while shipshape Swedish American Hall hosts the bigger Noise Pop and folkYEAH! concert series.

MINT KARAOKE

Map p312 (📱415-626-4726; www.themint.net; 1942 Market St; ⊙3pm-2am Mon-Fri, from 2pm Sat & Sun; 🚌22, Ⓜ F, J, K, L, M) Big voices at this mixed straight-gay karaoke bar could rattle pennies in the US mint uphill. If you can't decide what to sing from the 30,000-plus playlist, know this: George Michael never fails, and the two-drink minimum practically guarantees applause. Reserve seating online, bring a posse, and tip the DJ if you want to sing any time soon.

SHOPPING

Most of the shops lining Castro St sell clothing, souvenirs and sex toys. For gifts, vintage and pot, head to Market St between Castro and Dolores St.

⭐APOTHECARIUM CANNABIS

Map p302 (📱415-500-2620; https://apothecarium.com; 2029 Market St; ⊙9am-9pm; 🚌22, 37, Ⓜ F, J, K, L, M) What's that alluring frosted-glass emporium – the lovechild of an Apple Store and Victorian lingerie boutique? Just as you suspected: it's America's best-designed marijuana dispensary, according to *Architectural Digest*. For the full effect, consult staff about edibles for your desired

state, from mellow to giddy – and then you can *really* appreciate the local art from designer couches. It's 18+ only; ID required.

⭐STAG & MANOR HOMEWARES, DESIGN

Map p312 (📱415-997-8241; https://stagandmanor.com; 2327 Market St; ⊙noon-7pm Tue-Thu & Sat, to 5pm Fri & Sun; 🚌24, 33, Ⓜ F, J, K, L, M) Dashingly handsome decor from indie design boutique Stag & Manor lets you take the Castro home. Macrame wall hangings give your pad California creds, brass-ball lanterns wink welcome at your guests, and minimalist fair-trade throw pillows hint to dates that you're thoughtful, laid-back, and well-traveled. Well-priced, globally minded, and neighbor-owned – friendly Castro owner Seth Morrison is here to solve design dilemmas.

⭐CHARLIE'S CORNER BOOKS

(📱415-641-1104; https://charliescorner.com; 4102 24th St; ⊙9:30am-6pm Mon-Fri, 10am-5pm Sat & Sun; 👪; 🚌24, 48, Ⓜ J) For Castro kids, the biggest neighborhood attraction is over the hill at Charlie's Corner, a storybook world where kids are invited to read, draw and sing along. This bookstore is a magical forest, where kids gather around a tree and sit on toadstools for story hours four times daily in English, Spanish and French – sometimes with live music and art projects.

⭐LOCAL TAKE GIFTS & SOUVENIRS

Map p312 (📱415-556-5300; http://localtakesf.com; 3979b 17th St; ⊙11am-7pm; 🚌24, 33, Ⓜ F, K, L, M) 🍃 Take in the local scenery at Local Take, a gallery of original SF souvenirs made and designed by locals. Bring home your very own Castro landmark – like a Castro Theatre marquee print, Sutro Tower tote, F Castro streetcar T-shirt or belt buckle featuring vintage Muni maps – and support SF's creative economy. Check online for events with local makers.

⭐OMNIVORE BOOKS

(📱415-282-4712; www.omnivorebooks.com; 3885a Cesar Chavez St; ⊙11am-6pm Mon-Sat, noon-5pm Sun; Ⓜ J) Salivate over signed cookbooks by chef-legend Alice Waters and signed first editions of Berkeley chef Samin Nosrat's *Salt Fat Acid Heat,* and stay for standing-room-only in-store events with star chefs and food luminaries like Michael Pollan. Satisfy insatiable appetites with specialty titles covering ancient Filipino diets, Lebanese preservation methods, and

DIY moonshine. Don't miss vintage cookbooks and ephemera like antique absinthe labels.

★CLIFF'S VARIETY   HOMEWARES
Map p312 (www.cliffsvariety.com; 479 Castro St; ☺10am-8pm Mon-Sat, to 6pm Sun; ⓂCastro St) None of the hardware maestros at Cliff's will raise an eyebrow if you express a dire need for a jar of rubber nuns, some silver body paint, and a case of cocktail toothpicks – though they might angle for an invitation. A community institution since 1936, Cliff's stocks drag supplies galore in the annex and celebrates the seasons with gay-gasp-worthy window displays.

DOG EARED BOOKS   BOOKS
Map p312 (www.dogearedbooks.com; 489 Castro St; ☺10am-10pm; ⓂF, K, L, M) For vacation reading that matches the Castro scenery, head into Dog Eared for a wide selection of San Francisco literature, LGBTIQ+ memoirs and novels censored elsewhere. Readings here are magnets for local characters, and the bulletin board at the back of the store will give you the lowdown on local activism and literary events.

SUI GENERIS   FASHION & ACCESSORIES
Map p312 (☎415-437-2231; www.suigeneris consignment.com; 2265 Market St; ☺11am-7pm Mon-Sat, to 5pm Sun; ⓂCastro St) Emerge with confidence into this men's designer resale boutique, sure that nobody but you will be working your look. The well-curated collection of contemporary resale and vintage clothing skews runway, best for skinny dudes with fat wallets – but because it's mostly secondhand, prices are way lower than normal retail, and occasionally even negotiable. Women's boutique is on Union St.

GIDDY   CHOCOLATE
Map p312 (☎415-857-4198; www.giddycandy. com; 2299 Market St; ☺11:30am-9pm Sun-Thu, to 10pm Fri & Sat; ⌖; ⌂F, ⓂK, L, M) All the candy you dreamed about as a kid is here, with a twist: candy-cane malt balls, cookies-and-cream caramels, extra-sour chewy skulls, and an entire rainbow of gummy bears. Friendly staff will help you put adorable care packages together, so that everyone gets Giddy together. Show the people back home some California Love – Compartés' dark-chocolate-covered-pretzel candy bar.

UNIONMADE   CLOTHING
Map p312 (☎415-861-3373; www.unionmade goods.com; 493 Sanchez St; ☺11am-7pm Mon-Sat, noon-6pm Sun; ⌂24, 33, ⓂF, J) Upgrade California casual to definitely dateworthy with Unionmade's gender-fluid modern classics. This is one-stop-shopping for your West Coast look: SF-made Golden Bear longshoremen's coats, Pendleton plaid shirts, vintage Levi's, Devaux tweed cashmere turtlenecks, handmade Alden workboots. Not cheap and not entirely unionmade, despite the name – but good quality and great sales.

CASTRO FARMERS MARKET   MARKET
Map p312 (www.pcfma.com; Noe St, cnr Market St; ☺4-8pm Wed Mar-Dec; ⓂCastro St) Find local and organic produce and artisan foods at moderate prices, plus charmingly offbeat folk music March through December.

KENNETH WINGARD   HOMEWARES
Map p312 (☎415-431-6900; www.kennethwing ard.com; 2319 Market St; ☺noon-8pm Mon-Fri, 11am-7pm Sat & Sun; ⓂCastro St) Give the gift of sass with cheeky accessories for him and home from Kenneth Wingard, San Francisco designer to the stars. He works for Oprah and Martha, but he hasn't lost his sense of humor – Kenneth's your go-to for *Tequila Mockingbird* cocktail cookbooks, 'So Rachet' tees, *This Annoying Life* coloring books for scribbling outside the lines, and motel keychains with inspirational mottos like 'Make today your bitch.'

The Haight & Hayes Valley

Neighborhood Top Five

① **Haight St** (p178) Bringing back the Summer of Love: wearing flowers, making a manifesto, singing folk songs on the corner of Haight and Ashbury Sts.

② **SFJAZZ** (p186) Toasting jazz giants between sets in front of Sandow Birk's tiled music-history mural.

③ **Alamo Square Park** (p179) Admiring Victorian mansions that have hosted earthquake refugees and hippie communes, speakeasies and satanic rites.

④ **Haight Street Art Center** (p180) Finding inspiration at poster-art shows, glimpsing works in progress

and spotting the hidden WPA mural.

⑤ **Bound Together Anarchist Book Collective** (p187) Checking out the *Anarchists of the Americas* mural and perusing prison lit.

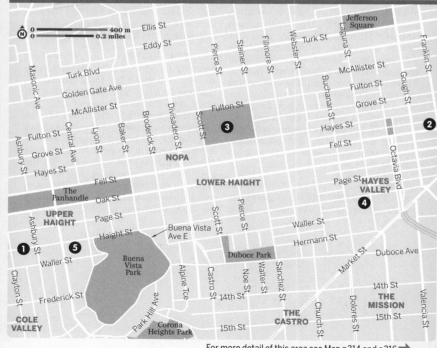

For more detail of this area see Map p314 and p316 ➡

Explore The Haight & Hayes Valley

Pick up picnic fixings for lunch amid Victorian architecture atop Alamo Square Park (p179) – or, in case of fog, brunch in NoPa and shop hip Divisadero boutiques. Go highbrow with Hayes Valley boutiques and fine dining, or skate to the Lower Haight to see rock-legendary shows at Haight Street Art Center (p180) and Family Affair (p180) and discuss them over Rosamunde (p183) sausages and Toronado (p185) beer. Overcome powerful bar-stool inertia for world-class SFJAZZ (p186) shows or epic mosh-pit action at the Independent (p186).

Local Life

Cheap eats with fancy drinks Go high/low with Rosamunde sausages (p183) and Toronado (p185) Belgian ales, oyster po' boy sliders and rare bourbon at Alembic (p185), DragonEats (p183) duck *banh mi* and agricole-rum drinks at Smuggler's Cove (p184).

Hangouts Aspiring flower children gather at Coffee to the People (p186), skaters hit up Haight Street Art Center (p180) shows, and hipsters grab bites in NoPa before shows at the Independent (p186).

Musical stylings Go acoustic on the corner of Haight and Ashbury Sts, improvise at SFJAZZ (p186) workshops, belt it out at the Mint (p174), sing along at Martuni's (p185) or rock out at free concerts at Amoeba Music (p186).

Getting There & Away

Bus Market St buses 6 and 7 run up Haight St to Golden Gate Park. The 22 links Lower Haight to the Mission and Japantown/Marina. Bus 24 runs along Divisadero, connecting NoPa and the Haight to the Castro and Pacific Heights. Bus 37 connects the Haight and the Castro, bus 43 goes from the Upper Haight to the Marina, and bus 33 runs through the Upper Haight between the Richmond District and the Mission. Buses 21 and 5 connect Hayes Valley with downtown and Golden Gate Park.

Streetcar The N line offers a shortcut from downtown and the Lower Haight to the Upper Haight, and onward to Ocean Beach.

BART Civic Center BART station is four blocks east of Hayes Valley.

 Best Places to Eat

➡ Rich Table (p183)
➡ Indian Paradox (p181)
➡ The Mill (p181)
➡ Brenda's Meat & Three (p183)
➡ RT Rotisserie (p181)

For reviews, see p181.➡

 Best Places to Drink

➡ Smuggler's Cove (p184)
➡ Toronado (p185)
➡ Madrone Art Bar (p184)
➡ Aub Zam Zam (p184)
➡ Noc Noc (p184)

For reviews, see p184.➡

Best Shopping

➡ Amoeba Music (p186)
➡ Bound Together Anarchist Book Collective (p187)
➡ Paloma (p187)
➡ Isotope (p188)
➡ Rare Device (p187)
➡ MAC (p187)

For reviews, see p186.➡

THE HAIGHT & HAYES VALLEY

Photo credit: MICHAEL URMANN / SHUTTERSTOCK ©

TOP SIGHT
HAIGHT STREET

Was it the fall of 1966 or the winter of '67? As the saying goes, if you can remember the Summer of Love, you probably weren't there. The fog was laced with pot, sandalwood incense and burning draft cards, and the corner of Haight and Ashbury Sts became the turning point for nonconformists dubbed 'hippies.'

Hippie tie-dyes and ideals have never entirely gone out of fashion in the Haight – hence the prized vintage rock tees on the wall at Wasteland (p188) and organic-farming manuals in their umpteenth printing at Bound Together Anarchist Book Collective (p187). To see where rock-star residents lived and loved freely, take a self-guided Flashback Walking Tour (p182) – and if you want to join a commune for a night, request a stay at the Red Victorian (p236).

Flashbacks are a given in the Haight, where the fog is fragrant downwind of Haight St's legal marijuana dispensaries. You'll notice the clock on the northeast corner of Haight and Ashbury reads 4:20 – a term coined in the Bay Area circa 1971, now recognized globally as a reference to International Bong Hit time. Recently, a local clockmaker took it upon himself to get the vintage clock running again. Within days, stoned pranksters reset it to 4:20.

Since the '60s, bad trips and unfortunate itches have been mercifully treated gratis at the **Haight-Ashbury Free Clinic** (HealthRIGHT 360; ☎415-746-1950; www.healthright360.org; 558 Clayton St; ☺by appointment 8:45am-noon & 1-5pm; ☑6, 7, 33, 37, 43, ⓂN). From the same era, Haight St has separated into two camps, divided by the Divisadero St strip of indie boutiques, trendy bars and restaurants now called **NoPa** (North of the Panhandle). The **Upper Haight** specializes in potent coffee, radical literature and retail therapy for rebels, while the **Lower Haight** has better beer selections and fantastic rock art openings at Haight Street Art Center (p180) and Family Affair (p180).

DON'T MISS

➡ 4:20 clock at Haight and Ashbury Sts

➡ Rock posters and a trippy 1937 fresco at Haight Street Art Center

➡ *Anarchists of the Americas* mural at Bound Together Anarchist Book Collective

PRACTICALITIES

➡ Map p314, B4

➡ btwn Central & Stanyan Sts

➡ ☑7, 22, 33, 43, ⓂN

TOP SIGHT
ALAMO SQUARE PARK

San Franciscans seldom miss an opportunity to show off, as you can see from the outrageous Victorian homes ringing Alamo Square Park.

The pastel, cookie-cutter Painted Ladies (pictured) of famed Postcard Row on Alamo Sq's eastern side pale in comparison with the colorful buildings along the northern side of the park and along parallel McAllister St and Golden Gate Ave. Here you'll spot true Barbary Coast baroque: Queen Anne mansions bedecked with fish-scale shingles, swagged stucco garlands, gingerbread trim dripping from peaked roofs – and carved theater masks. Local legend has it that masks were originally carved above certain doors so that San Franciscans would know when they were about to enter a bordello.

On the park's northwestern corner, the olive-green, gilded Stick-style Italianate Victorian capped by an ornamental watchtower was built by candy mogul William Westerfeld in 1889, and survived subsequent tenancies by czarist Russian bootleggers, Fillmore jazz musicians and hippie communes. Filmed rituals held in the tower by Church of Satan founder Anton LaVey involved candle fire hazards and a grumpy lion, coaxed up four flights of stairs.

DON'T MISS

➡ East-facing views of the downtown skyline

➡ Westerfeld House

➡ Postcard Row's pastel Painted Ladies

➡ Queen Anne mansions ornamented with theater masks

PRACTICALITIES

➡ Map p314, F2

➡ www.sfparksalliance.org/our-parks/parks/alamo-square

➡ cnr Hayes & Steiner Sts

➡ ☉ sunrise-sunset

➡ 👪 👹

➡ 🚌 5, 21, 22, 24

⊙ SIGHTS

Weekends are a major scene in the Upper Haight, with hippies reminiscing about glory days trailed by teenage relations pretending not to know them, suburban punks wearing too much aftershave and Harajuku hipsters loading suitcases full of vintage fashion for resale in Tokyo. Also in the mix are Green Party candidates, cafe regulars who greet one another by name and street musicians who play a mean banjo.

Wedged between the Lower Haight and Civic Center is little Hayes Valley, which packs in many of the city's best restaurants, design boutiques and two major but low-key landmarks: the Zen Center and SFJAZZ.

HAIGHT STREET   STREET
See p178.

ALAMO SQUARE PARK   PARK
See p179.

★**HAIGHT STREET**
ART CENTER   ARTS CENTER
Map p316 (☑415-363-6150; https://haight streetart.org; 215 Haight St; ⊙noon-6pm Wed-Sun; ☐6, 7, 22, **MF**) **FREE** Jeremy Fish's bronze bunny-skull sculpture hints at the weird wonders inside this nonprofit dedicated to works on paper and San Francisco's signature art form: screen-printed posters. Glimpse rock-concert posters currently in progress at the on-site screen-printing studio, plus jaw-dropping gallery shows – recently featuring Ralph Steadman's original illustrations for Hunter S Thompson's *Fear and Loathing in Las Vegas*. Gracing the stairwell is a hidden SF treasure: Ruben Kaddish's 1937 WPA fresco *Dissertation on Alchemy,* surely the trippiest mural ever commissioned by the US government.

★**FAMILY AFFAIR**   GALLERY
Map p314 (☑415-757-0670; www.facebook.com/familyaffairhq; 683 Haight St; ⊙noon-7pm Wed-Sat; ☐6, 7, 22, 24) **FREE** Can you see sound? The answer is always yes at this music-inspired art gallery, named for the anthem by SF soul supergroup Sly and the Family Stone. Recent shows include video art illustrating DJ J Dilla's sonic collages, lost album art by Bay Area hip-hop legends, and photographs of Prince taken before he was famous by his Bay Area producer.

ST JOHN COLTRANE CHURCH   CHURCH
Map p314 (☑415-673-7144; www.coltrane church.org; 2097 Turk Blvd, at St Cyprian's Center; ⊙services noon Sun; ☐5, 21, 38) When the bass thumbs out the opening notes to 'A Love Supreme,' you'll know the Sunday liturgy has begun at San Francisco's legendary Church of St John Coltrane. For 50 years, this African Orthodox church has honored the revelatory music and social justice activism of legendary jazz saxophonist John Coltrane in foot-stomping, singalong musical Sunday services. Sanctuary icons show the canonized musician in his glory, fire leaping from his saxophone.

ZEN CENTER   HISTORIC BUILDING
Map p316 (☑415-863-3136; http://sfzc.org; 300 Page St; ⊙9:30am-12:30pm & 1:30-4pm Mon-Fri, 8:30am-noon Sat; bookstore 1:30-5:30pm & 6:30-7:30pm Mon-Thu, 1:30-5:30pm Fri, 11am-1pm Sat; ☐6, 7, 21, 22) With its sunny courtyard and generous cased windows, this uplifting 1922 building is an interfaith landmark. Since 1969, it's been home to the largest Buddhist community outside Asia. Before she built Hearst Castle, Julia Morgan (California's first licensed woman architect) designed this Italianate brick structure to house the Emanu-El Sisterhood, a residence for low-income Jewish working women – note the ironwork Stars of David on the 1st-floor loggia.

HAIGHT & ASHBURY   LANDMARK
Map p314 (☐6, 7, 33, 37, 43) This legendary intersection was the epicenter of the psychedelic '60s, and 'Hashbury' remains a counterculture magnet. On average Saturdays here, you can sign Green Party petitions, commission a poem and hear Hare Krishna on keyboards and Bob Dylan on banjo.

GRATEFUL DEAD HOUSE   NOTABLE BUILDING
Map p314 (710 Ashbury St; ☐6, 7, 33, 37, 43) Like surviving members of the Grateful Dead, this purple Victorian sports a touch of gray – but during the Summer of Love, this was where Jerry Garcia and bandmates blew minds, amps and brain cells. After they were busted for drugs in 1967, the Dead held a press conference here arguing for decriminalization. They claimed if everyone who smoked marijuana were arrested, San Francisco would be empty. Point taken, eventually – in 2016, California legalized adult recreational marijuana use in private (read: not the sidewalk, dude).

HAYES VALLEY'S SHIPPING-CONTAINER SCENE

After the 1989 earthquake damaged freeway ramps around Fell and Octavia Sts, urban blight struck the neighborhood – until San Franciscan voters nixed the overpass and reinvented Octavia Blvd as a walkable, palm-tree-lined community hub. The social center is **Patricia's Green** (Map p316; http://proxysf.net; cnr Octavia Blvd & Fell St; ☐5, 21), featuring a playground, picnic tables and Burning Man–inspired sculpture installations flanked by shipping containers. These upcycled containers are part of SF's PROXY (http://proxysf.net) project, which hosts food trucks, pop-up galleries and shipping-container shops. Spring through fall, free Friday-night 'bike-in' movies are shown on the big outdoor screen at PROXY's creatively repurposed parking lot. On sunny days, graze your way across Patricia's Green to PROXY gourmet attractions **Biergarten** (Map p316; http://biergartensf.com; 424 Octavia St; ⊙3-9pm Mon-Sat, 1-7pm Sun; 🖭🖭; ☐5, 21, 47, 49) and Ritual Coffee (p185).

BUENA VISTA PARK
PARK
Map p314 (http://sfrecpark.org; Haight St, btwn Central Ave & Baker St; ⊙sunrise-sunset; 🖭; ☐6, 7, 37, 43) True to its name, this hilltop park offers splendid vistas over the city to Golden Gate Bridge and the Bay. Founded in 1867, this is one of the oldest city parks – and it's ringed by stately, century-old California oaks. Brave trails weaving uphill through the park, then take Buena Vista Ave West downhill to spot Victorian mansions that survived the 1906 earthquake and fire. Note that after-hours boozing or cruising here is risky, due to minor criminal activity.

 EATING

Hayes Valley is a hot spot for dinner and a show – reserve ahead for memorable meals and tickets to SFJAZZ, Opera or Symphony. Haight St is a cheap-eats destination worth the detour, and NoPa is gourmet all day with brunch options galore.

★RT ROTISSERIE
CALIFORNIAN $
Map p316 (www.rtrotisserie.com; 101 Oak St; dishes $9-14; ⊙11am-9pm; 🖭🖭; ☐5, 6, 7, 21, 47, 49, Ⓜ Van Ness) 🖉 An all-star menu makes ordering mains easy – you'll find bliss with entire chickens hot off the spit, succulent lamb and pickled onions, or surprisingly decadent roast cauliflower with earthy beet-tahini sauce – but do you choose porcini-powdered fries or signature salad with that? A counter staffer calls it: 'Look, I don't normally go for salads, but this one's next-level.' So true. No reservations.

★THE MILL
BAKERY $
Map p314 (☎415-345-1953; www.themillsf.com; 736 Divisadero St; toast $4-7; ⊙7am-9pm; 🖉🖭; ☐5, 21, 24, 38) Baked with organic wholegrain stone-ground on-site, hearty Josey Baker Bread sustains Haight skaters and start-uppers alike. You might think SF hipsters are gullible for queuing for pricey toast, until you taste the truth: slathered in housemade hazelnut spread or California-grown almond butter, it's a proper meal. Housemade granola with Sonoma yogurt starts SF days right, and hearty seasonal sandwiches fuel Alamo Sq hikes.

★INDIAN PARADOX
INDIAN $
Map p314 (☎415-593-5386; http://indianparadoxsf.com; 258 Divisadero St; share plates $6-15; ⊙5-10pm Tue-Thu, to 11pm Fri, 11am-2pm & 5-10pm Sat, 11am-2pm Sun; 🖉; ☐6, 7, 24, Ⓜ N) Hit the high-low sweet spot between the Upper and Lower Haight at this cozy storefront serving zesty Indian street food with inspired wine pairings. Coconut chutney melting into fluffy *adai* (lentil pancakes) deserves bubbles; paper cones of *bhei-puri* (puffed-rice crackers) with spicy mango and mint chutney require refreshing rosé; and masala-laced Sonoma lamb kebabs will have you waxing rhapsodic over deep-red Aglianico.

SOUVLA
GREEK $
Map p316 (☎415-400-5458; www.souvlasf.com; 517 Hayes St; sandwiches & salads $12-15; ⊙11am-10pm; ☐5, 21, 47, 49, Ⓜ Van Ness) Ancient Greek philosophers didn't think too hard about lunch, and neither should you at Souvla. Get in line and make no-fail choices: pita or salad, wine or not. Instead of go-to gyros, get signature spit-fired lamb atop kale with yogurt dressing, or tangy chicken salad with

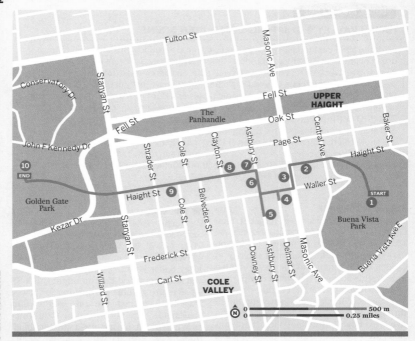

🏃 Neighborhood Walk
Haight Flashback

START BUENA VISTA PARK
END GOLDEN GATE PARK
LENGTH 1.3 MILES; ONE HOUR

Start in ① **Buena Vista Park** (p181), with panoramic city views that moved San Franciscans to tears after the 1906 earthquake.

Heading west up Haight St, you may recognize Emma Goldman in the *Anarchists of the Americas* mural at ② **Bound Together Anarchist Book Collective** (p186) – if not, staff can recommend biographical comics by way of introduction.

Neighborhood old-timers claim the Symbionese Liberation Army used ③ **1235 Masonic Ave** as a safe house for kidnapped-heiress-turned-revolutionary-bank-robber Patty Hearst. To live here now, you'd have to rob a bank – a one-bedroom apartment recently sold for $1.5 million.

Turn right onto Waller St and left uphill past ④ **32 Delmar St,** site of the Sid Vicious overdose that broke up the Sex Pistols in 1978.

A block over, pay your respects to Jerry Garcia, Bob Weir and Pigpen at the ⑤ **Grateful Dead House** (p180). Down the block, ⑥ **635 Ashbury St** is one of many known SF addresses for Janis Joplin, who had a hard time hanging onto leases in the 1960s.

At the corner of Haight and Ashbury, the ⑦ **clock** overhead always reads 4:20, better known in 'Hashbury' as International Bong-Hit Time. For trips that became bummers, ⑧ **Haight-Ashbury Free Clinic** (p178) offered free recovery treatment. This legendary 'rock clinic' still provides care to all.

Cross Haight and Cole Sts, and across the street from the apartment where Charles Manson once lived, you'll spot a Summer of Love relic: Joana Zegri's 1967 ⑨ **Evolution Rainbow mural**. Follow your bliss to the drum circle at ⑩ **Hippie Hill in Golden Gate Park**, where free spirits have gathered since the '60s to flail to the beat.

pickled onion and *mizithra* cheese. Go early/late for skylit communal seating, or head to Patricia's Green (p181) with takeout.

DRAGONEATS
VIETNAMESE $

Map p316 (☎415-795-1469; http://dragoneats.com; 520 Gough St; sandwiches & bowls $6-7; ⊗11am-6pm Mon-Sat, to 5pm Sun; 🖋; 🚇5, 21, 47, 49, Ⓜ Civic Center) Velvety roast-duck *banh mi* (Vietnamese sandwich) gives opera stars something to sing about at this sunny Vietnamese deli, right around the corner from San Francisco's opera house and symphony hall. Hungry divas order theirs with a shrimp-roll side, while tenors in tight corsets opt for five-spice-chicken 'fresh bowls' with vegetables and brown rice. For picnics in Golden Gate Park, visit their Haight location (1671 Haight St).

LITTLE CHIHUAHUA
MEXICAN $

Map p314 (☎415-255-8225; www.thelittlechihuahua.com; 292 Divisadero St; tacos $5-5.75, burritos $9.50-13.50; ⊗11am-11pm Mon-Fri, from 10pm Sat & Sun; 🖋🚸; 🚇6, 7, 21, 24) 🖋 Who says sustainable, organic food has to be expensive or French? Grass-fed meats and organic veggies and beans are packed into organic tortillas, all washed down with $5 draft craft beer. Burritos are a two-meal deal, especially the decadent *al pastor* (grilled pork with pineapple salsa and jack cheese) and garlic shrimp (sustainably sourced). Kids' menu available.

ROSAMUNDE SAUSAGE GRILL
FAST FOOD $

Map p314 (☎415-437-6851; http://rosamundesausagegrill.com; 545 Haight St; sausages $8-9; ⊗11:30am-10pm Mon-Wed, to 11pm Thu-Sat, to 9pm Sun; 🖋; 🚇6, 7, 22, Ⓜ N) 🖋 Impress a dinner date on the cheap: load up Coleman Farms pork brats, wild-boar sausages, or fig-brandy free-range duck links with complimentary roasted peppers, grilled onions, whole-grain mustard and mango chutney, and enjoy with seasonal draft brews at Toronado (p185) next door. Plant-based sausage options show vegetarian dates how thoughtful you are.

ESCAPE FROM NEW YORK PIZZA
PIZZA $

Map p314 (☎415-668-5577; www.escapefromnewyorkpizza.com; 1737 Haight St; slices $5-6.50; ⊗10am-midnight Sun-Thu, to 2am Fri & Sat; 🖋🚸; 🚇6, 7, 33, 43, Ⓜ N) The Haight's obligatory mid-bender stop for a hot slice. Pesto with roasted garlic and potato will send you blissfully off to carbo-loaded sleep, but the

sun-dried tomato with goat's cheese, artichoke hearts and spinach will recharge you to go another round. Art donated by fans includes signed rocker head-shots (hello Elvis Costello and Metallica), plus cartoons by *The Simpsons*' Matt Groening.

★ RICH TABLE
CALIFORNIAN $$

Map p316 (☎415-355-9085; http://richtablesf.com; 199 Gough St; mains $17-37; ⊗5:30-10pm Sun-Thu, to 10:30pm Fri & Sat; 🚇5, 6, 7, 21, 47, 49, Ⓜ Van Ness) 🖋 Impossible cravings begin at Rich Table, where mind-bending dishes like porcini doughnuts, sardine chips, and *burrata* (mozzarella and cream) funnel cake blow up Instagram feeds nightly. Married co-chefs and owners Sarah and Evan Rich riff on seasonal San Francisco cuisine with the soul of SFJAZZ stars and the ingenuity of Silicon Valley regulars.

★ BRENDA'S MEAT & THREE
SOUTHERN US $$

Map p314 (☎415-926-8657; http://brendasmeatandthree.com; 919 Divisadero St; mains $9-20; ⊗8am-10pm Wed-Mon; 🚇5, 21, 24, 38) The name means one meaty main course plus three sides – though only superheroes finish ham steak with Creole red-eye gravy and exemplary grits, let alone cream biscuits and eggs. Chef Brenda Buenviaje's portions are defiantly Southern, which explains brunch lines of marathoners and partiers who forgot to eat last night. Arrive early, share sweet-potato pancakes, and pray for crawfish specials.

LITTLE GEM
CALIFORNIAN $$

Map p316 (www.littlegem.restaurant; 400 Grove St; dishes $13-28; ⊗11am-9pm Sun-Thu, to 10pm Fri & Sat; 🖋; 🚇5, 21, 49) 🖋 Sunny flavors, healthful ingredients, and easygoing elegance make Little Gem a San Francisco treasure. Chef David Cruz combines fine-dining tradecraft honed at French Laundry with a Californian devotion to cross-cultural, locally sourced, nourishing fare: he gives equal, heartfelt attention to every julienned vegetable in Korean bibimbap, and slathers sustainable Wagyu beef brisket with BBQ sauce that tastes like a Napa summer's day.

RAGAZZA
PIZZA $$

Map p314 (☎415-255-1133; www.ragazzasf.com; 311 Divisadero St; pizzas $15-19; ⊗5-10pm; 🚸; 🚇6, 7, 21, 24) 'Girl' is what the name means – as in, 'Oooh, *girl*, did you try the wild-nettle pizza?!' Artisan *salumi* is the star of many

Ragazza pizzas, from the Amatriciana with pecorino, pancetta and egg to the Moto with Calabrian chili and sausage – best with SF's own Fort Point beer or carafes of rustic Montepulciano reds. Arrive early to avoid waits.

PETIT CRENN
CALIFORNIAN, FRENCH $$$

Map p316 (☎415-864-1744; www.petitcrenn.com; 609 Hayes St; dinner tasting menu $95, brunch mains $15-24; ⏰5-9:30pm Tue-Thu, 11am-2pm & 5-9:30pm Sat, 11am-2pm & 5-9pm Sun; 🚌5, 21) Leave gimmicky waterfront bistros behind and find higher ground here, with rustic French seafood and easy social graces. Triple-Michelin-starred chef Dominique Crenn offers a Brittany-inspired tasting menu nightly – items change seasonally, but include standout canapés (puffy *gougères* – cheese choux pastries – will haunt your dreams) and inspired coastal dishes like truffled steelhead and pistachio-oiled sea urchin. Reservations and prepayment required; meal price includes service.

CALA
MEXICAN, CALIFORNIAN $$$

Map p316 (☎415-660-7701; www.calarestaurant. com; 149 Fell St; share plates $14-36; ⏰5-10pm Sun-Wed, to 11pm Thu-Sat, taco bar 11am-2pm Mon-Fri; 🚌6, 7, 21, 47, 49, MVan Ness) Like discovering a long-lost twin, Cala's California roots cuisine is a revelation. San Francisco's Mexican-*ranchera* origins are deeply honored here: silky bone-marrow salsa and fragrant heritage-corn tortillas grace a sweet potato slow-cooked in ashes with sea salt. For even wilder flavors, pair mezcal margaritas with NorCal foragers' surf-and-turf: bottarga pasta with trumpet mushrooms and chickweed. Original and unforgettable, capped with silken coconut flan.

ZUNI CAFE
AMERICAN $$$

Map p316 (☎415-552-2522; www.zunicafe.com; 1658 Market St; mains $15-33; ⏰11:30am-11pm Tue-Thu, to midnight Fri & Sat, 11am-11pm Sun; 🚌6, 7, 47, 49, MVan Ness) 🍴 Gimmickry is for amateurs – Zuni has been turning basic menu staples into gourmet go-tos since 1979. Reservations and fat wallets are key for oyster-and-martini lunches, but the see-and-be-seen seating is a kick and the local, sustainably sourced signatures beyond reproach: Caesar salad with house-cured anchovies, brick-oven-roasted free-range chicken with Tuscan bread salad, and mesquite-grilled, grass-fed-beef burgers on focaccia (shoestring fries $9 extra).

🍷 DRINKING & NIGHTLIFE

Hayes Valley has high-rolling wine bars and sneaky rum punches, while Haight St is a beer bonanza.

★SMUGGLER'S COVE
BAR

(☎415-869-1900; www.smugglerscovesf.com; 650 Gough St; ⏰5pm-1:15am; 🚌5, 21, 47, 49, MCivic Center, BCivic Center) Yo-ho-ho and a bottle of rum...wait, make that a Dead Reckoning (Nicaraguan rum, port, pineapple, bitters), unless you'll split the flaming Scorpion Bowl? Pirates are bedeviled by choice at this Barbary Coast–shipwreck tiki bar, hidden behind tinted-glass doors. With 550 rums and 70-plus cocktails gleaned from rum-running around the world – and $2 off 5pm to 6pm daily – you won't be dry-docked long.

★AUB ZAM ZAM
BAR

Map p314 (☎415-861-2545; 1633 Haight St; ⏰3pm-2am Mon-Fri, 1pm-2am Sat & Sun; 🚌6, 7, 22, 33, 43, MN) Persian arches, *One Thousand and One Nights* murals, 1930s jazz on the jukebox and top-shelf cocktails at low-shelf prices have brought Bohemian bliss to Haight St since 1941. Legendary founder Bruno used to throw people out for ordering vodka martinis, but he was a softie in the end, bequeathing his beloved bar to regulars who'd become friends. Phones down, please; cash only.

★MADRONE ART BAR
BAR

Map p314 (☎415-241-0202; www.madroneartbar. com; 500 Divisadero St; cover free-$5; ⏰4pm-2am Tue-Sat, 3pm-1:30am Sun; 🚌5, 6, 7, 21, 24) Drinking becomes an art form at this Victorian parlor crammed with graffiti installations and absinthe fountains. Motown Mondays feature the Ike Turner drink special – Hennessy served with a slap – but nothing beats the monthly Prince/Michael Jackson throwdown dance party. Performers redefine genres: punk-grass (bluegrass and punk), blunt-funk (reggae and soul) and church, no chaser (Sunday-morning jazz organ). Cash only.

★NOC NOC
BAR

Map p314 (☎415-861-5811; www.nocnoc. com; 557 Haight St; ⏰5pm-2am Mon-Thu, from 3:30pm Fri, from 3pm Sat & Sun; 🚌6, 7, 22, 24, MN) Who's there? Steampunk blacksmiths, anarchist hackers, trance DJs practicing for Burning Man, and other San Francisco characters straight out of an R Crumb comic, that's who. Happy hour lasts until 7pm daily with $4 local drafts (no PBR here), and hot sake is $1 after 10pm – but mixing black-and-tans with potent house sake will Noc-knock you off your junkyard-art stool.

★ TORONADO   PUB

Map p314 (☑ 415-863-2276; www.toronado.com; 547 Haight St; ⊙11:30am-2am; ☐6, 7, 22, Ⓜ N) Glory hallelujah, beer-lovers: your prayers are answered. Genuflect before the chalkboard altar that lists 40-plus beers on tap and hundreds more bottled, including sensational seasonal microbrews. Bring cash and score sausages from Rosamunde (p183) to accompany ale made by Trappist monks. It sometimes gets too loud to hear your date talk, but you'll hear angels sing.

EMPORIUM   ARCADE, BAR

Map p314 (https://emporiumsf.com; 616 Divisadero St; ⊙4pm-2am Mon-Fri, 2pm-2am Sat & Sun; ☐5, 21, 24) Game on, gamers – this former movie palace is an adult playground with full bar, video games, billiards, air hockey and themed pinball. Beat Dirty Harry at his own game, or curse in Klingon over *Star Trek: The Next Generation* game. Check website for weekend DJ lineups and open hours – Emporium gets booked for tech industry events. Bring ID; 21+ only.

RIDDLER   WINE BAR

Map p316 (☑ 415-589-7002; www.theriddlersf.com; 528 Laguna St; ⊙4-10pm Tue-Thu, to 11pm Fri, 11am-11pm Sat, 11am-9pm Sun; ☐5, 6, 7, 21) Riddle me this: how can you ever thank the women in your life? As the Riddler's all-women sommelier-chef-investor team points out, champagne makes a fine start. Bubbles begin at $14 and include Veuve Clicquot, the brand named after the woman who invented riddling, the process that gives champagne its unclouded sparkle. But after one Chambong, you won't remember any of this. Cheers!

RITUAL COFFEE   CAFE

Map p316 (www.ritualroasters.com; PROXY, 432b Octavia St; ⊙7am-7pm; ☃; ☐5, 21, 47, 49) The Hayes Valley shipping-container outpost of the Mission roastery offers creamy single-origin espresso and powerful pour-overs to rival those at Blue Bottle around the corner – but beware, those are fighting words among SF's hardcore coffee loyalists.

BLUE BOTTLE COFFEE KIOSK   CAFE

Map p316 (www.bluebottlecoffee.net; 315 Linden St; ⊙6:30am-6pm Mon-Fri, 7am-6:30pm Sat &

BEST PLACES TO LET YOUR FREAK FLAG FLY

Haight St (p178) Sing songs, join cults, sign petitions, spout poetry, be alive.

Noc Noc (p184) Postapocalyptic party time is now.

Independent (p186) Head-bang with Japanese rockers and groove with reggae legends.

Distractions (p188) Get steampunked for parties, Burning Man, and the odd Wednesday.

Aub Zam Zam (p184) Find boho bliss in a 1940s Persian jazz bar.

Sun; ❤❄; ☐5, 21, 47, 49, Ⓜ Van Ness) Don't mock SF's coffee geekery until you've tried the elixir from this back-alley kiosk. The Bay Area's Blue Bottle built its reputation on microroasted organic coffee – especially Blue Bottle–invented, off-the-menu Gibraltar, the barista-favorite drink with foam and espresso poured together into the eponymous short glass. Expect a (short) wait and seats outside on creatively repurposed traffic curbs.

ALEMBIC   BAR

Map p314 (☑ 415-666-0822; www.alembicbar.com; 1725 Haight St; ⊙4pm-midnight Tue & Wed, to 2am Thu & Fri, 11am-2am Sat, 11am-midnight Sun; ☐6, 7, 33, 37, 43, Ⓜ N) The Victorian tin ceilings are hammered, and you could be too unless you sip these potent concoctions slowly – all crafted from 250 specialty spirits. Classics include the newfangled old fashioned with brown-butter bourbon, but the seasonal menu features limited-edition wonders like summer's Swizzle Me This (gin, run, black pepper, strawberry, Angostura bitters) and winter's Warm Core (citrus, pickled pineapple, Brugal 188 rum float).

MARTUNI'S   GAY & LESBIAN

Map p316 (☑ 415-241-0205; 4 Valencia St; ⊙4pm-2am; ☐6, 7, Ⓜ Van Ness) Slip behind the velvet curtains into the city's top piano bar, where the rainbow spectrum of regulars seems to have memorized the words to every show tune. Comedy nights are a blast and singalongs a given – especially after a couple of top-notch pepper-cucumber, lemon-drop or chocolate martinis under $10. Straight-friendly, especially if you sing from the heart.

THE HAIGHT & HAYES VALLEY DRINKING & NIGHTLIFE

COFFEE TO THE PEOPLE CAFE

Map p314 (☎415-626-2435; 1206 Masonic Ave; ⊙6am-6:30pm Mon-Fri, 7am-7pm Sat & Sun; 🛜🍴; 🚌6, 7, 33, 37, 43) ✐ The people united will never be decaffeinated at this radical coffee house. Choose a bumper-sticker-covered table to match your politics (peace is perennially popular), admire hippie macramé on the walls and browse consciousness-raising books. Hemp-milk cappuccinos and turmeric lattes are acquired tastes, but beware the quadruple-shot Freak Out, which has enough fair-trade espresso to revive the Sandinista movement.

ENTERTAINMENT

Not a night goes by in the Haight without a live jazz performance or a decent live show at the Independent. Bookish folks will appreciate the literary events over in Hayes Valley.

★**SFJAZZ CENTER** JAZZ

Map p316 (☎866-920-5299; www.sfjazz.org; 201 Franklin St; tickets $25-120; 🍴; 🚌5, 6, 7, 21, 47, 49, Ⓜ Van Ness) ✐ Jazz legends and singular talents from Argentina to Yemen are showcased at North America's newest, largest jazz center. Hear fresh takes on classic jazz albums and poets riffing with jazz combos in the downstairs Joe Henderson Lab, and witness extraordinary main-stage collaborations by legendary Afro-Cuban All Stars, raucous all-women mariachis Flor de Toluache, and Balkan barnstormers Goran Bregović and his Wedding and Funeral Orchestra.

★**BOOKSMITH** LIVE PERFORMANCE

Map p314 (☎415-863-8688; www.booksmith.com; 1644 Haight St; events free-$25; ⊙10am-10pm Mon-Sat, to 8pm Sun; 🍴; 🚌6, 7, 43, Ⓜ N) Throw a stone in SF and you'll probably hit a writer (ouch) or reader (ouch again) headed to/from Booksmith. Literary figures organize Booksmith book signings, raucous poetry readings, extra-short fiction improv, and politician-postcard-writing marathons. Head to sister shop-salon-bar the Bindery (1727 Haight St) for boozy book swaps, comedy nights, and silent reading parties hosted by Daniel Handler (aka Lemony Snicket).

★**INDEPENDENT** LIVE MUSIC

Map p314 (☎415-771-1421; www.theindependentsf.com; 628 Divisadero St; tickets $12-45; ⊙box office 11am-6pm Mon-Fri, show nights to 9:30pm; 🚌5, 6, 7, 21, 24) Bragging rights are earned with breakthrough shows at the small but mighty Independent, featuring indie dreamers (Magnetic Fields, Death Cab for Cutie), music legends (George Clinton, Meat Puppets), alt-pop (the Killers, T-Pain) and international bands (Tokyo Chaotic). Ventilation is poor in this max-capacity-800, age 21+ venue, but the sound is stellar, drinks reasonable and bathrooms improbably clean.

CLUB DELUXE JAZZ

Map p314 (☎415-555-1555; www.clubdeluxe.co; 1511 Haight St; cover free-$10; ⊙4pm-2am Mon-Fri, 2pm-2am Sat & Sun; 🚌6, 7, 33, 37, 43) Blame it on the bossa nova or the ginned-up Deluxe Spa Collins – you'll be swinging before the night is through. Nightly jazz combos bring the zoot suits and lindy-hoppers to the dance floor. Expect mood lighting, cats who wear hats well and dames who can swill $7 happy-hour highballs (4pm to 7pm weekdays, 2pm to 5pm weekends) without losing their matte-red lipstick.

SHOPPING

Discover local designers in Hayes Valley, only-in-SF scores on Divisadero and the Lower Haight, and vintage, vinyl, music and anarchy in the Upper Haight.

★**AMOEBA MUSIC** MUSIC

Map p314 (☎415-831-1200; www.amoeba.com; 1855 Haight St; ⊙11am-8pm; 🚌6, 7, 33, 43, Ⓜ N) ✐ Enticements are hardly necessary to lure the masses to the West Coast's most eclectic collection of new and used music and video, but Amoeba offers listening stations, free zines with uncannily accurate staff reviews, and a free concert series that recently starred Billy Bragg, Karl Denson's Tiny Universe, Violent Femmes, and Mike Doughty – plus a foundation that's saved one million acres of rainforest.

★**BOUND TOGETHER ANARCHIST BOOK COLLECTIVE** BOOKS

Map p314 (☎415-431-8355; http://boundtogetherbooks.wordpress.com; 1369 Haight St; ⊙11:30am-7:30pm; 🚌6, 7, 33, 37, 43) Since 1976 this volunteer-run, nonprofit anarchist bookstore has kept free thinkers supplied with organic-permaculture manuals, prison literature, and radical comics, all while coordinating the annual spring Anarchist Book Fair and expanding the *Anarchists of the*

Americas storefront mural – makes us tools of the state look like slackers. Hours are impressively regular, but call ahead to be sure.

⭐**AMOUR VERT**   FASHION & ACCESSORIES
Map p316 (☑415-800-8576; https://amourvert. com; 437 Hayes St; ⊗11am-7pm Sun-Thu, to 8pm Fri & Sat; ☐5, 21, 47, 49, Ⓜ Van Ness) 🖊 Looking smart comes easily with effortless wardrobe essentials that casually blend style, comfort, and sustainability. Wear your heart on your sleeve with feel-good fabrics ingeniously engineered from renewable sources, including Italian flax linen, beechwood modal, eucalyptus-tree Tencel and organic cotton. Find soft, flattering pieces at down-to-earth prices, designed in San Francisco and made locally to last a lifetime.

⭐**TANTRUM**   TOYS
Map p314 (☑415-504-6980; www.shoptantrum. com; 858 Cole St; ⊗10am-7pm; 👶; ☐6, 7, 33, 37, 43, Ⓜ N) Overbooked kids and overworked adults deserve a time-out for Tantrum, delightfully stocked with musical otters, wooden ducks on wheels, and a mechanical seal kids can ride for a quarter. Mid-century-modern circus is the design aesthetic in new and vintage items, including a tiny big-top tent with a cast of toy mice, and animal masks to start your own circus.

⭐**RARE DEVICE**   GIFTS & SOUVENIRS
Map p314 (☑415-863-3969; www.raredevice. net; 600 Divisadero St; ⊗noon-8pm Mon-Fri, 11am-7pm Sat, to 6pm Sun; ☐5, 6, 7, 21, 24) Sly San Francisco wit is the rare device that makes this well-curated selection of gifts for all ages so irresistible. Block kits help kids build their own Victorians; rainbow-

handled mugs help friends feel Pride every day; lipstick in a berry-stained hue, dubbed Divisadero, is dinner-date-worthy; and 826 Valencia's Adventure Calendar finds time for play in start-up schedules.

⭐**PALOMA**   FASHION & ACCESSORIES
Map p316 (☑415-342-2625; https://instagram. com/palomahayesvalley; 112 Gough St; ⊗noon-7pm Tue-Sat; ☐5, 6, 7, 21, 47, 49, Ⓜ Van Ness) Like ransacking a poet's attic, this SF maker collective yields evocative, imaginative handmade finds. You might discover hand-patched indigo scarves, caps made from camp blankets, wallets made from footballs, and real buffalo nickels adorning handbags made on-site by artisan Laureano Faedi. His love of history shows in SF motorcycle-gang coasters and tees advertising long-lost amusement park Playland at the Beach.

⭐**MAC**   FASHION & ACCESSORIES
Map p316 (☑415-863-3011; http://macmodern appealingclothing.com; 387 Grove St; ⊗11am-7pm Mon-Sat, noon-6pm Sun; ☐5, 21, 47, 49) 'Modern Appealing Clothing' is what this store promises – and it delivers for men and women alike, with streamlined chic from Engineered Garments, graphic Minä Perhonen shifts, and lines made exclusively for MAC by Bay Area designers. Fashion-forward-thinking staff are on your side, finding perfect fits and scores from the 40%-to-75%-off sales rack – including that luxe Dries Van Noten suit Jay-Z rocked.

⭐**NANCY BOY**   COSMETICS
Map p316 (☑415-552-3636; www.nancyboy.com; 347 Hayes St; ⊗11am-7pm Mon-Sat, to 6pm Sun; ☐5, 21, 47, 49) All you closet pomaders and

---

HOMELESS KIDS IN THE HAIGHT

Ever since the '60s, America's youth have headed to the Haight as a place to fit in, no questions asked. But in 2010, San Francisco's controversial Sit/Lie Ordinance made 7am to 11pm sidewalk loitering punishable by $50 to $100 fines. Critics note that the law has been primarily enforced in the Haight, ticketing homeless teens – but with 1145 shelter beds to accommodate 6400 to 13,000 homeless people citywide, many street kids have no place else to go.

Many homeless San Franciscans have jobs, but struggle to afford rent in the city on minimum wage. So in 2018, San Francisco voters passed a measure requiring San Francisco companies with more than $50 million in revenue to pay a 0.5% tax on profits, shouldering their share of responsibility for displacing low-income residents. These funds will double the city's budget to provide transitional housing and services for homeless families and individuals in need. While you're in town, volunteering or donations to homeless service nonprofits are thoughtful gestures to repay San Francisco hospitality, and ensure everyone has a chance to feel at home here.

after-sun balmers: wear those potions with pride, without feeling like the dupe of some cosmetics conglomerate. Clever Nancy Boy knows you'd rather pay for the product than for advertising campaigns featuring the starlet du jour, and delivers locally made wares with effective plant oils that are tested on boyfriends, never animals.

★ISOTOPE
COMICS

Map p316 (📞415-621-6543; www.isotopecomics. com; 326 Fell St; ⊙11am-7pm Tue-Fri, to 6pm Sat & Sun; 🖢; 🚍5, 21, 47, 49) Toilet seats signed by famous cartoonists over the front counter show just how seriously Isotope takes comics. Newbies tentatively flip through superhero serials, while superfans eye the latest limited-edition graphic novels and head upstairs to lounge with local cartoonists – some of whom teach classes here. Don't miss signings and epic over-21 launch parties.

RELIQUARY
FASHION & ACCESSORIES

Map p316 (📞415-431-4000; www.reliquarysf.com; 544 Hayes St; ⊙11am-7pm Mon-Sat, noon-6pm Sun; 🚍5, 21, 47, 49) Enter the well-traveled wardrobe of Leah Bershad, a former Gap designer whose folksy jet-set aesthetic is SF's antidote to khaki-and-fleece global domination. Hand-crafted and vintage items – peasant blouses, hand-knitted ponchos, silver jewelry banged together by Humboldt hippies – share the spotlight with cult-brand finds like Black Crane overalls, Rachel Comey mules and DS Durga's enticing unisex scents (Cowboy Grass, mmm).

COVE
GIFTS & SOUVENIRS

Map p314 (📞415-863-8199; www.covertcove. com; 206 Fillmore St; ⊙noon-7pm; 🚍6, 7, 22, MN) Sand-cast cocktail rings, succulents dripping from sea-urchin shells, scented candles in the shape of a doll's hand: such unique gifts lead grateful recipients to believe you've spent weeks combing San Francisco's curiosity shops. Owner Jean regularly stocks rare finds at reasonable prices and will wrap them for you, too. Call ahead; hours can be erratic.

GREEN ARCADE
BOOKS

Map p316 (📞415-431-6800; www.thegreenar cade.com; 1680 Market St; ⊙noon-8pm Mon-Sat, to 7pm Sun; 🚍6, 7, 47, 49, MVan Ness) Everything you always wanted to know about mushroom foraging, worm composting and running for office on an environmental platform – plus poetry and autographed books by SF authors. This bookstore emphasizes visionary possibility over eco-apocalypse doom, so you'll leave with a rosier outlook on making the world a greener place. Check website for author events.

WASTELAND
VINTAGE, CLOTHING

Map p314 (📞415-863-3150; www.shopwaste land.com; 1660 Haight St; ⊙11am-8pm Mon-Sat, to 7pm Sun; 🚍6, 7, 33, 37, 43, MN) 🍃 Take center stage in this converted-cinema vintage superstore in barely worn designer rompers, vintage concert tees and a steady supply of go-go boots. Hip occasionally verges on hideous with sequined sweaters and '80s power suits, but, at reasonable (not bargain) prices, anyone can afford fashion risks. If you've got excess baggage, Wasteland buys clothes noon to 6pm daily.

SPARC
CANNABIS

Map p314 (📞415-805-1085; https://sparcsf.org; 473 Haight St; ⊙10am-10pm; 🚍6, 7, 22, MN) The reception area looks more like a doctor's office than a Haight hippie den, because Sparc has been a medical marijuana pioneer since 1998 – and to be sure you're not ingesting toxic chemicals, they grow house-label cannabis biodynamically and source pesticide-free Farm Direct bud. To make SF hosts happy, the Coppola 'Growers Series' sampler comes in a wine-bottle-shaped gift box.

LOVED TO DEATH
GIFTS & SOUVENIRS

Map p314 (📞415-551-1036; www.lovedtodeath. net; 1681 Haight St; ⊙noon-7pm Wed-Mon; 🚍6, 7, 33, 37, 43, MN) Stuffed deer exchange glassy stares with skeletons over rusty dental tools: the signs are ominous, and for sale. Head upstairs for Goth gifts, including Victorian hair lockets and portable last-rites kits. Not for the faint of heart, vegans or shutterbugs – no photos allowed, though you might recognize staff from the Science Channel's *Oddities: San Francisco* reality show.

DISTRACTIONS
FASHION & ACCESSORIES

Map p314 (📞415-252-8751; 1552 Haight St; ⊙11am-7pm Sun-Fri, to 8pm Sat; 🚍6, 7, 33, 37, 43) Strap on goggles and hang onto your top hat: with steampunk styling from Distractions you're gonna party like it's 1899. This gold-rush mad-inventor look is SF's go-to alt-party style, from historically correct Edwardian-ball ensembles to post-apocalyptic Burning Man getups. So hang a compass from your lace corset and rock that creepy whaler's mask – you're among friends here.

Golden Gate Park & the Avenues

THE RICHMOND | THE SUNSET

Neighborhood Top Five

1 **Golden Gate Park**
(p191) Doing what comes naturally: skipping, lolling or Lindy-Hopping through America's most outlandish stretch of urban wilderness, and racing bison toward the Pacific Ocean.

2 **de Young Museum**
(p191) Following Andy Goldsworthy's sidewalk fault

lines to discover ground-breaking global art from Oceania to South Africa, Afghanistan to Alaska.

3 **California Academy of Sciences** (p192) Enjoying sunsets on the wildflower-topped roof and wild nights at kids-only Academy sleepovers and 21-plus NightLife events.

4 **Coastal Trail** (p200)
Glimpsing seals, sunsets and shipwrecks along San Francisco's wild waterfront walk.

5 **Ocean Beach** (p195)
Numbing your toes in the Pacific and expanding your horizons to Asia over bonfires in artist-designed firepits.

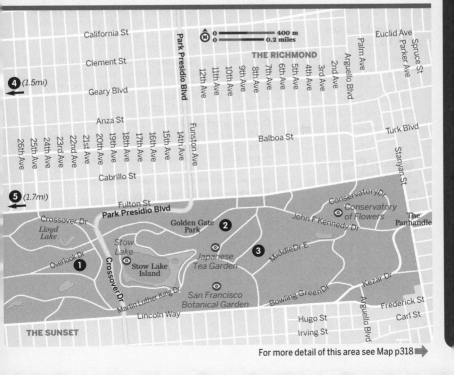

For more detail of this area see Map p318

Lonely Planet's Top Tip

Hear that echo across Golden Gate Park? It's probably a concert – and quite possibly a free one. Opera divas, indie acts, bluegrass greats and hip-hop heavies take turns rocking SF gratis, from the often wintry days of June through golden October afternoons. Most concerts are held in Sharon Meadow or Polo Fields at weekends; for upcoming events, consult the park calendar at www.golden-gate-park.com.

Best Places for Urban Wildlife

➡ Golden Gate Park (p191)
➡ Fort Funston (p195)
➡ Ocean Beach (p195)
➡ California Academy of Sciences (p192)

Best Places to Eat

➡ Pearl 6101 (p196)
➡ King of Noodles (p197)
➡ Spruce (p196)
➡ Arsicault Bakery (p196)
➡ Hook Fish Co (p197)

For reviews, see p195. ➡

Best Places to Drink

➡ Tommy's Mexican Restaurant (p198)
➡ Beach Chalet (p198)
➡ Woods Outbound (p197)
➡ Grand Hot Pot Lounge (p198)
➡ Violet's Tavern (p197)

For reviews, see p197. ➡

Explore Golden Gate Park & the Avenues

Golden Gate Park is a sprawling and wonderful place – your time here and in the surrounding neighborhood should largely be based on your interests. Are you mad to see the carnivorous plants gobbling insects at the Conservatory of Flowers (p193)? Keen to spot the blue butterflies in the rainforest dome at the California Academy of Sciences (p192)? Perhaps you'd prefer globe-trotting from Oceanic masks to James Turrell light installations among the art exhibits of the de Young Museum. You'll want to allot at least a couple of hours to sip green tea in the Japanese Tea Garden (p192), to take respite in the redwood grove at San Francisco Botanical Garden (p192), and to summit Strawberry Hill, which rewards with views past Stow Lake to the Pacific. When you've had your fill of the park, hop the N streetcar all the way to Ocean Beach (p195). Stroll the 4-mile stretch of sand to the Richmond for decadent dumplings at Dragon Beaux (p195) and hurricanes at Trad'r Sam (p198), or stay put in the Sunset District for surf-shopping at Mollusk (p200) and a poke burrito at Hook Fish Co (p197).

Local Life

Foggy days Stay warm with Trouble Coffee (p198), matinees at Balboa Theatre (p199), noir-movie fedoras at Paul's Hat Works (p199), and sultry rainforest strolls inside the California Academy of Sciences (p192) and the Conservatory of Flowers (p193).

Goose bumps, guaranteed Get delicious chills with bare feet on Ocean Beach (p195), eerily lifelike masks at the de Young Museum, cliff's-edge views along the Coastal Trail (p200) and steep concrete slides at the Children's Playground (p193).

Out-there art outposts Outlandishness is an SF way of life; take in the scene with Park Life (p199) art openings, original '60s pop art at Legion of Honor (p194) and surf photography at Mollusk (p200).

Getting There & Away

Bus Buses 1, 31 and 38 run from downtown through the Richmond, while 7 and 6 head from downtown to the Sunset. Buses 5 and 21 skirt the northern edge of Golden Gate Park, while north–south buses 28, 29 and 44 cut across the park. Bus 2 covers Clement St, 33 connects to the Haight and Castro, and 18 spans the Great Hwy.

Streetcar The N line runs from downtown through the Sunset to Ocean Beach.

TOP SIGHT
GOLDEN GATE PARK

When San Franciscans refer to 'the park,' there's only one that gets the definite article: Golden Gate Park. Everything they hold dear is here: free spirits, free music, redwoods, Frisbee, protests, fine art, bonsai and bison.

de Young Museum

The oxidized-copper building may keep a low profile, but there's no denying the park's all-star attraction: the **de Young Museum** (pictured; Map p318; ☏415-750-3600; http://deyoung.famsf.org; 50 Hagiwara Tea Garden Dr; adult/child $15/free, 1st Tue of month free; ☺9:30am-5:15pm Tue-Sun; ☐5, 7, 44, Ⓜ N). The cross-cultural collection featuring African masks and Turkish kilims alongside California crafts and avant-garde American art has been broadening artistic horizons for a century, and its acclaimed building by Swiss architects Herzog & de Meuron (of Tate Modern fame) is suitably daring.

The 144ft sci-fi observation **tower** is one futuristic feature that seems incongruous with the park setting – but access to the 360-degree tower viewing room is free, and Ruth Asawa's mesmerizing filigreed pods make elevator waits worthwhile.

Upstairs, don't miss 19th-century **Oceanic collection** ceremonial oars and stunning Afghani rugs from the 11,000-plus **textile collection**. **Blockbuster basement shows** range from psychedelic hand-sewn hippie fashions to Ed Ruscha paintings of Route 66 gas stations – but rotating **main-floor installations** are just as riveting and diverse, from early Inuit carvings to documentary prison photography.

Access to the **garden cafe** is free, as is entry to the **Osher Sculpture Garden** and its subterranean masterpiece: James Turrell's **Skyspace**.

DON'T MISS

➡ de Young Museum
➡ California Academy of Sciences
➡ San Francisco Botanical Garden
➡ Japanese Tea Garden
➡ Conservatory of Flowers

PRACTICALITIES

➡ Map p318, E4
➡ https://goldengate park.com
➡ btwn Stanyan St & Great Hwy
➡ admission free
➡ Ⓟ ♿
➡ ☐5, 7, 18, 21, 28, 29, 33, 44, Ⓜ N

TOURIST INFORMATION

To plan a picnic, concert or protest in the park and get detailed maps, check in at **McLaren Lodge** (Map p318; ☎415-831-2700; www. golden-gate-park.com; 501 Stanyan St, cnr Fell St; ☺8am-5pm Mon-Fri; ☐5, 7, 21, 33) at the eastern entrance, under the splendid cypress that's the city's official tree.

Though a local newspaper once cautioned that Golden Gate Park's scenic benches led to 'excess hugging,' San Franciscans have flocked to the park since its inception. On a sunny day in 1886, almost a fifth of the city's entire population made the trip to the park – canoodling shamelessly, no doubt.

TOP TIPS

➡ John F Kennedy Dr is closed to motor vehicles east of Crossover Dr (around 8th Ave) all day Sunday and Saturday mornings to accommodate runners, skateboarders, unicyclists and meandering dreamers.

➡ Don't attempt to visit everything in this huge park in a single day; it's more rewarding and relaxing to take in a few sights at a leisurely pace.

California Academy of Sciences

Leave it to San Francisco to dedicate a glorious four-story monument entirely to freaks of nature: the **California Academy of Sciences** (Map p318; ☎415-379-8000; www.calacademy.org; 55 Music Concourse Dr; adult/student/child $35.95/30.95/25.95; ☺9:30am-5pm Mon-Sat, from 11am Sun; ▣🚼; ☐5, 6, 7, 21, 31, 33, 44, Ⓜ N) 🍃. The Academy's tradition of weird science dates from 1853, with thousands of live animals and 100 research scientists now under a 2.5-acre wildflower-covered roof. Butterflies alight on visitors in the glass **Osher Rainforest Dome**, penguins paddle the tank in the **African Hall**, and Claude the albino alligator stalks the **mezzanine swamp**. Glimpse infinity in the **Morrison Planetarium** and ride the elevator to the blooming Living Roof for park panoramas, before checking out the Giants of Land and Sea exhibit, where you can brave an earthquake simulation, virtually climb a redwood and get lost in a fog room.

Children will enjoy the basement **Steinhart Aquarium**, where they can duck inside a glass bubble to enter an **Eel Garden**, find Dorys in the tropical fish tanks and pet starfish in the hands-on **Discovery Tidepool**. And while they might not technically sleep during Academy Sleepovers, kids just might jump-start promising careers as scientists (ages five to 17, plus adult chaperones; $119 per person including snack and breakfast; events 6pm to 8am; book ahead).

Meanwhile, adult night owls party on at the Academy's after-hours events. At the over-21 NightLife, nature-themed cocktails are served and strange mating rituals observed (ID required; $15 entry; 6pm to 10pm Thursday).

San Francisco Botanical Garden

Sniff your way around the world inside the 55-acre **San Francisco Botanical Garden** (Strybing Arboretum; Map p318; ☎415-661-1316; www.sfbg.org; 1199 9th Ave; adult/child $9/2, before 9am daily & 2nd Tue of month free; ☺7:30am-5pm, extended hours in summer & spring, last entry 1hr before closing, bookstore 10am-4pm; ☐6, 7, 44, Ⓜ N) 🍃, from South African savanna grasses to Japanese magnolias. Don't miss the California native-plant meadow, redwood grove and **Ancient Plant Garden**, with plants dating back to California's dinosaur days. **Free tours** take place daily; for details, stop by the bookstore inside the entrance.

Japanese Tea Garden

Since 1894 this 5-acre **garden** (Map p318; ☎415-752-1171; www.japaneseteagardensf.com; 75 Hagiwara Tea Garden Dr; adult/child $8/2, before 10am Mon, Wed & Fri free; ☺9am-6pm Mar-Oct, to 4:45pm Nov-Feb; ▣; ☐5, 7, 44, Ⓜ N) has blushed pink with cherry blossoms in spring, turned flaming red with maple leaves in fall and induced visitors to lose all track of time in its meditative **Zen Garden**. The century-old **bonsai grove** was cultivated by the Hagiwara family, who returned from WWII Japanese American internment camps to discover that many of their prized miniature evergreens had been sold – and spent decades recovering the precious trees.

Stop by the **Tea House** for traditional green tea and fortune cookies – first introduced to the US right here, over 120 years ago.

Conservatory of Flowers

Flower power is alive and well at SF's **Conservatory of Flowers** (Map p318; ☑415-831-2090; www.conservatoryofflowers.org; 100 John F Kennedy Dr; adult/student/child $9/6/3, 1st Tue of month free; ☺10am-6pm Tue-Sun; ☐5, 7, 21, 33, Ⓜ N). Inside this gloriously restored 1878 Victorian greenhouse, orchids command center stage like opera divas, lilies float contemplatively in ponds and gluttonous carnivorous plants gulp down insects.

Outside you'll find the **Dahlia Garden** (Map p318; ☺sunrise-sunset; ☝) 🎕 FREE and its spiky, in-your-face neon blooms cultivated by the city's many hardcore dahlia devotees. The flowers burst onto the scene each June and reach peak punk-rock glory in August or September.

Shakespeare Garden

Sonnets dot the flower beds in this romantic gated **garden** (Garden of Shakespeare's Flowers; Map p318; Martin Luther King Jr Dr, cnr Middle Dr E; ☺sunrise-sunset; ☐7, 44, Ⓜ N) 🎕 FREE , home since 1928 to more than 200 flowering plants mentioned in Shakespeare's writings. With all the poetry and perfume, this is an ideal secluded spot for a smooch – and a favorite setting for weddings.

Stow Lake

A park within the park, **Stow Lake** (Map p318; www.sfrecpark.org; ☺5am-midnight; ☐7, 44, Ⓜ N) is the place to come for waterfall views, picnics in the **Taiwanese pagoda** and bird-watching on a picturesque island called **Strawberry Hill**. Pedal boats and rowboats are available daily in good weather at the 1946 boathouse (p201). Ghost-hunters come at night seeking the **White Lady** – legend has it she has haunted Stow Lake for a century, searching these shores for her lost child.

Buffalo Paddock

Since 1899, this **paddock** (Map p318; ☺sunrise-sunset; ☐5, 21) FREE has been Golden Gate Park's home where the buffalo roam – though technically, they're bison. SF's mellow, well-fed herd rarely moves – but when their tails point upwards, you may be about to witness bison bucking.

National AIDS Memorial Grove

This tranquil, 10-acre **memorial grove** (Map p318; ☑415-765-0446; www.aidsmemorial.org; Bowling Green Dr; ☺sunrise-sunset; ☐44, 71, Ⓜ N) FREE graced with poetic paving-stone tributes was founded in 1991 to commemorate millions of lives lost to the AIDS epidemic and to strengthen national resolve for compassionate care and a lasting cure. Volunteer work days (8:30am to 12:30pm) are held the third Saturday of each month, March to October.

Children's Playground

Kids have had the run of the park's southeastern end since 1887. Highlights of this historic **children's playground** (Koret Children's Quarter; Map p318; ☑415-831-2700; carousel per ride adult/child $2/1; ☺sunrise-sunset, carousel 10am-4:15pm; ☝; ☐7, 33, Ⓜ N) include 1970s concrete slides, a climbing wall and a vintage 1912 carousel.

◉ SIGHTS

With its fine museums and expansive gardens, Golden Gate Park is the epicenter of the neighborhood's sightseeing. But avid explorers of the outer Avenues will stumble on things like a hidden mosaicked stairway, an art nouveau columbarium or the ruins of a 19th-century waterfront bathing complex, named for populist millionaire Adolph Sutro, who built a public railway in the 1890s to transport Downtown tenement-dwellers to breezy Ocean Beach. South of Golden Gate Park are candy-colored Sunset District homes, and surf hangouts pop up around Judah and 45th.

◉ The Richmond

GOLDEN GATE PARK   PARK
See p191.

LANDS END   PARK
Map p318 (☑(415) 426-5240; www.nps.gov; 680 Point Lobos Ave; ☺24hr; 🚌38) Looking out from Lands End feels like surveying the edge of the world. Nestled on the point of land between Golden Gate Park and the Presidio, the park's hiking trails cross the rugged landscape with alternating ocean vistas and views of the Golden Gate Bridge. The Lands End visitor center and cafe are located at Point Lobos Ave and Merrie Way, overlooking the Sutro Bath ruins.

INTERNET ARCHIVE   ARCHIVES
Map p318 (☑415-561-6767; www.archive.org; 300 Funston Ave; ☺events only; 🚌2, 38) FREE Follow trails of deleted White House tweets, lost Grateful Dead tapes and defunct Nintendo gamer magazines to this 1923 Greek Revival landmark. In a former Christian Science church, the nonprofit Internet Archive hosts more than 30 petabytes (that's 300 million gigabytes) of bygone media, and counting. The archive is run by 100-plus dedicated volunteer archivists, depicted in ceramic sculptures by artist Nuala Creed.

CLIFF HOUSE   LANDMARK
Map p318 (☑415-386-3330; www.cliffhouse.com; 1090 Point Lobos Ave; ☺9am-10:30pm Mon-Thu, to 11:30pm Fri & Sat, 8:30am-9:30pm Sun; 🚌5, 18, 31, 38) FREE Populist millionaire Adolph Sutro imagined the Cliff House as a work-ing man's paradise in 1863, but Sutro's dream has been rebuilt three times. The latest reworking, a $19-million 2004 facelift, turned the Cliff House into a largely generic, if panoramic, complex housing two restaurants, two bars, two lounges and a gift shop. The key attractions remain: sea lions barking on **Seal Rocks** and the **Camera Obscura**, a vintage 1946 attraction projecting sea views onto a parabolic screen.

LEGION OF HONOR   MUSEUM
Map p318 (☑415-750-3600; http://legionof honor.famsf.org; 100 34th Ave; adult/child $15/ free, discount with Muni ticket $2, 1st Tue of month free; ☺9:30am-5:15pm Tue-Sun; 🚌1, 2, 18, 38) A museum as eccentric and illuminating as San Francisco itself, the Legion showcases a wildly eclectic collection ranging from Monet water lilies to John Cage soundscapes, ancient Iraqi ivories to R Crumb comics. Upstairs are blockbuster shows of old masters and Impressionists, but don't miss selections from the Legion's Achenbach Foundation of Graphic Arts collection of 90,000 works on paper, ranging from Rembrandt to Ed Ruscha. Ticket price includes free same-day entry to the de Young Museum (p191).

SUTRO BATHS   PARK
Map p318 (www.nps.gov/goga/historyculture/ sutro-baths.htm; 680 Point Lobos Ave; ☺sunrise-sunset, visitor center 9am-5pm; 🅿; 🚌5, 31, 38) 🖋FREE It's hard to imagine from these ruins, but Victorian dandies and working stiffs once converged here for bracing baths in woolen rental swimsuits. Millionaire Adolph Sutro built hot and cold indoor pools to accommodate 10,000 unwashed souls in 1896, but the masses apparently preferred dirt – despite added attractions including trapezes and Egyptian mummies, the baths went bust in 1952. At low tide, follow the steep path past the now-ruined baths and through the sea-cave tunnel to find sublime Pacific panoramas.

LINCOLN PARK   PARK
Map p318 (www.sfrecpark.org; Clement St; ☺sunrise-sunset; 🚌1, 18, 38) America's legendary coast-to-coast Lincoln Hwy officially ends at 100-acre Lincoln Park, which served as San Francisco's cemetery until 1909. The city's best urban hike leads through Lincoln Park around Lands End, following a partially paved coastline trail with glorious Golden Gate views and low-tide sightings of coastal shipwrecks. Pick up the trailhead

north of the Legion of Honor, or head up the tiled **Lincoln Park Steps** near 32nd Ave. Book in advance for scenic **Lincoln Park Golf Course**.

◉ The Sunset

OCEAN BEACH
BEACH

Map p318 (☎415-561-4323; www.parksconservancy.org; Great Hwy; ☺sunrise-sunset; P; ⬜5, 18, 31, MN) The sun sets over the Pacific just beyond the fog at this blustery beach. Most days are too chilly for bikini-clad clambakes but fine for hardy beachcombers and hardcore surfers braving riptides (casual swimmers, beware). Ocean Beach allows bonfires in 16 artist-designed firepits until 9:30pm; no alcohol permitted. Stick to paths in the fragile southern dunes, where skittish snowy plover shorebirds shelter in winter.

FORT FUNSTON
PARK

(☎415-561-4700; www.parksconservancy.org; Fort Funston Rd; ☺sunrise-sunset; P; ML) ⊘ Grassy dunes up to 200ft high at Fort Funston give an idea of what the Sunset District looked like until the 20th century. A defunct military installation, Fort Funston still has 146-ton WWII guns aimed seaward and abandoned Nike missile silos near the parking lot. Nuclear missiles were never launched from the fort; today hang gliders launch and land here. Butterflies and shorebirds also flock to the surrounding park, which is now part of the Golden Gate National Recreation Area.

WINDMILLS
LANDMARK

Map p318 (Dutch & Murphy Windmills; www.golden-gate-park.com/windmills.html; ☺sunrise-sunset; ⬜5, 18, 21, MN) Surfers aiming for Ocean Beach keep in sight these twin landmarks on Golden Gate Park's extreme western edge. The 1902 Dutch windmill at the northwestern end is closed due to structural concerns, but photographers swarm its magnificent Queen Wilhelmina Tulip Garden February to April. At the park's southwestern end, the restored 95ft-tall 1908 Murphy Windmill has resumed its original irrigation function. The windmills are off the Great Hwy near John F Kennedy and Martin Luther King Jr Drs.

SAN FRANCISCO ZOO
ZOO

(☎415-753-7080; www.sfzoo.org; 1 Zoo Rd; adult/child 4-14yr/0-3yr $22/16/free; ☺10am-

WORTH A DETOUR

THE COLUMBARIUM

Art nouveau stained-glass windows and a dome skylight illuminate more than 8000 niches honoring dearly departed San Franciscans and their beloved pets. San Francisco's **Columbarium** (Map p318; ☎415-771-0717; www.neptune-society.com/columbarium; 1 Loraine Ct; ☺9am-5pm Mon-Fri, 10am-3pm Sat & Sun; ⬜5, 31, 33, 38) FREE revived the ancient Roman custom of sheltering cremated remains in 1898, when burial grounds crowded the Richmond District. The Columbarium was neglected from 1934 until its 1979 restoration by the Neptune Society, a cremation advocacy group. Today visitors admire the neoclassical architecture and pay their respects to pioneering gay city supervisor Harvey Milk.

4pm, last entry 3pm; P ♿; ⬜18, 23, ML) Crafty kids find ways to persuade parents to brave traffic and chilly fog to reach SF Zoo – but everyone ends up enjoying the well-kept habitats, including the Lemur Forest and the Savanna (featuring giraffes, zebras and ostriches). Other star attractions include Bear Country, the Gorilla Preserve, the barnyard-style petting zoo, the Dentzel carousel (rides $4) and the miniature steam train (rides $6). Interactive storybook features are activated with a keepsake Zoo Key ($5); strollers and wheelchairs available.

✕ EATING

Dining options line the Avenues, from bargain hole-in-the-wall hot spots to California-cuisine destinations.

✕ The Richmond

DRAGON BEAUX
DIM SUM $

Map p318 (☎415-333-8899; www.dragonbeaux.com; 5700 Geary Blvd; dumplings $5-9; ☺11am-2:30pm & 5:30-9:45pm Mon-Fri, 10am-3pm & 5:30-9:45pm Sat & Sun; ⬜2, 38) Hong Kong meets Vegas at SF's most glamorous, decadent Cantonese restaurant. Say yes to cartloads of succulent roast meats – hello, duck and pork belly – and creative dumplings, especially XO dumplings with plump, brandy-laced shrimp in spinach wrappers. Expect premium teas, sharp service and impeccable Cantonese standards, including Chinese doughnuts, *har gow* (shrimp dumplings) and Chinese broccoli in oyster sauce.

ORSON'S BELLY   TURKISH, CAFE $

Map p318 (☏415-340-3967; www.orsonsbelly. com; 1737 Balboa St; mains $8-15; ☺8:30am-9pm Tue-Fri, 9am-7pm Sat, 9am-5pm Sun; ☎☝; ☐5, 18, 31, 38) The fastest way to a San Franciscan's heart is through Orson's Belly, where Coastal Trail–blazers devour Turkish breakfasts of feta, organic eggs and freshly baked pita, and Balboa (p199) movie-goers debate cafe-namesake Orson Welles' best film over *amaro* (herbal liqueur) and Turkish tapas. Laze days away over wine and Turkish coffee, served with Turkish delight on owl-shaped platters.

HALU   JAPANESE $

Map p318 (☏415-221-9165; 312 8th Ave; yakitori $5-15; ramen $12-15; ☺5-10pm Tue-Thu, to 11pm Fri & Sat; ☐1, 2, 38, 44) Nibbling creative yakitori (skewers) at this snug six-table joint plastered with Beatles memorabilia is like dining aboard the Yellow Submarine. Twin owners Erika and Sayaka took over the place from their dad, a former drummer with John Lennon's Plastic Ono Band, and though they rock ramen, sticks – from scallops to yuzu chicken thighs and trumpet mushrooms – are still the specialty.

★PEARL 6101   MEDITERRANEAN $$

Map p318 (☏415-592-9777; www.pearl6101.com; 6101 California St; mains $19-28; ☺8am-2pm Tue-

---

BAKERY HITS THE BIGTIME

Armando Lacayo left his job in finance because he, like his Parisian grandparents before him, was obsessed with making croissants. After perfecting his technique, Lacayo opened the modest **Arsicault Bakery** (Map p318; ☏415-750-9460; 397 Arguello Blvd; pastries $3-7; ☺7am-2:30pm Mon-Fri, to 3:30pm Sat & Sun; ☐1, 2, 33, 38, 44) in the Inner Richmond in 2015. Within a year, Bon Appétit magazine had declared it the best new bakery in America and the golden, flaky, buttery croissants regularly sell out. Now there is talk of a new location near Civic Center, expected to open in 2019.

Fri, 10am-2pm Sat & Sun, 5-10pm Tue-Sun; ☐1, 2, 29, 38) Stop by this little neighborhood gem for coffee and wood-fired bagels on your way to the Presidio, or return in the evening for unmissable martinis. Start with some hamachi crudo (raw fish) and Miyagi oysters, continue with handmade spaghetti or pork chops, and if your party is large enough, splurge on the massive shared plate of tomahawk rib-eye chop.

CASSAVA   CALIFORNIAN $$

Map p318 (☏415-640-8990; www.cassavasf. com; 3519 Balboa St; mains breakfast & lunch $7-18, dinner $15-30; ☺8:30am-2:30pm & 5:30-9pm Mon & Wed-Fri, 10am-2:15pm & 5:30-9pm Sat, 10am-2:30pm & 5:30-7:45pm Sun; ☝; ☐5, 18, 31, 38) Early risers and park joggers are rewarded with SF-roasted Ritual coffee and Cassava's housemade, multilingual breakfasts – choose from a Japanese breakfast, slow-braised pork-rib hash, or baked burrata and a poached egg with veggies and toast. Book ahead for brunch before a Balboa Theatre (p199) matinee, and return to debrief over four-course dinners ($48) with beverage pairing ($34).

★WAKO   JAPANESE $$$

Map p318 (☏415-682-4875; www.sushiwakosf. com; 211 Clement St; 9-course menu $135; ☺5:30-10pm Tue-Sat; ☐1, 2, 33, 38, 44) Chef-owner Tomoharu Nakamura's driftwood-paneled bistro is as quirkily San Franciscan as the bonsai grove at the nearby Japanese Tea Garden (p192). Each *omakase* (chef's choice) dish is a miniature marvel of Japanese seafood with a California accent – Santa Cruz abalone *nigiri* (sushi), seared tuna belly with California caviar, crab *mushimono* (steamed crab) with yuzu grown by a neighbor. *Domo arigato* (thanks very much), dude.

★SPRUCE   CALIFORNIAN $$$

(☏415-931-5100; www.sprucesf.com; 3640 Sacramento St; mains $19-44; ☺11:30am-2pm & 5-10pm Mon-Thu, 11:30am-2pm & 5-11pm Fri, 10am-2pm & 5-11pm Sat, 10am-2pm & 5-9pm Sun; ☐1, 2, 33, 43) ☝ VIP all the way: Baccarat crystal chandeliers, tawny leather chairs, rotating art collections and 2500 wines. Ladies who lunch dispense with polite conversation, tearing into grass-fed burgers on house-baked English muffins loaded with pickled onions and heirloom tomatoes grown on the restaurant's own organic farm. Want fries with that? Oh, yes, you do: Spruce's are cooked in duck fat.

✗ The Sunset

★ HOOK FISH CO   SEAFOOD $
Map p318 (www.hookfishco.com; 4542 Irving St; mains $13-16; ⊙11:30am-9pm Mon-Fri, from 9am Sat & Sun; ☐18, Ⓜ N) There's a reason you packed that puffy coat: to visit this delightful fish joint out in the windy abyss also known as the Outer Sunset. Order over a small wooden counter from a short menu of locally sourced seafood, including a poke burrito, trout salad and an array of fish-of-the-day tacos, grilled or fried (choose grilled) on warm corn tortillas.

KING OF NOODLES   NOODLES $
Map p318 (☑415-566-8318; 1639 Irving St; dim sum $6-9.50, noodles $8-11; ⊙11:30am-3:30pm & 5-9:30pm Mon, Tue & Thu; ☐7, 28, 29, Ⓜ N) It's no surprise that Anthony Bourdain dropped by this casual dim sum and noodle establishment, where the menu features oddities like marinated pork elbow, black fungus with fresh cucumber and crispy lotus roots (these are amazing, BTW). But it's the delicious hand-pulled noodles in flavorful soups that draw people back, along with the outstanding onion pancakes and the classic Shanghai dumplings.

MANNA   KOREAN $
Map p318 (☑415-665-5969; www.mannasanfran cisco.com; 845 Irving St; mains $11-15; ⊙11am-9:30pm Tue-Sun; ☐6, 7, 43, 44, Ⓜ N) As Korean grandmothers and other Sunset District dwellers will tell you, nothing cures fog chills like home-style Korean cooking. Manna's *kalbi* (barbecue short ribs) and *dol-sot bibimbap* (rice, vegetables, steak and egg in a sizzling stone pot) are surefire toe-warmers, especially with addictive *gojujang* (sweetly spicy Korean chili sauce). Weekday lunch specials; parties of four maximum; expect waits.

MASALA DOSA   INDIAN $
Map p318 (☑415-566-6976; www.masaladosasf. com; 1375 9th Ave; mains $11-17; ⊙11am-11pm; ☑; ☐6, 7, 33, 43, 44, Ⓜ N) Warm up on Golden Gate Park's south side with South Indian fare in a low-lit storefront bistro. The house specialty is paper dosa, a massive crispy lentil-flour pancake served with *sambar* (spicy stew) and chutney – but onion-and-pea *uthappam* (pancake) is heartier and equally gluten free. Standout mains include chicken Madras rich with coconut milk and fragrant tilapia masala.

NOPALITO   MEXICAN $$
Map p318 (☑415-233-9966; www.nopalitosf. com; 1224 9th Ave; mains $13-21; ⊙11:30am-10pm; ☑; ☐6, 7, 43, 44, Ⓜ N) Head south of Golden Gate Park's border for upscale, sustainably sourced Cal-Mex, including succulent grass-fed beef empanadas, melt-in-your-mouth carnitas (beer-braised pork) with handmade organic-corn tortillas, and cinnamon-laced Mexican hot chocolate. Reservations aren't accepted – at sunny weekends when every park-goer craves margaritas and ceviche, show up well in advance to join the paper wait list.

OUTERLANDS   CALIFORNIAN $$
Map p318 (☑415-661-6140; www.outerlandssf. com; 4001 Judah St; sandwiches & small plates $8-14, mains $15-28; ⊙9am-3pm & 5-10pm; ☑; ☐18, Ⓜ N) When windy Ocean Beach leaves you feeling shipwrecked, drift into this chic beach bistro for organic Californian comfort food. Brunch demands Dutch pancakes baked in a cast iron pan, while lunch calls for pork belly sandwiches and citrusy beach cocktails. Dinner means creative regional fare like Washington manilla clams and California Holstein coulotte steak. Reserve.

🍷 DRINKING & NIGHTLIFE

Authentic Irish pubs, throwback tiki cocktail bars, cult coffee shacks, tequila schools – the Avenues spoil drinkers for choice.

★ VIOLET'S TAVERN   COCKTAIL BAR
Map p318 (☑415-682-4861; www.violets-sf.com; 2301 Clement St; ⊙bar 5-10:30pm Mon, to 11pm Tue-Thu, to midnight Fri, 11am-midnight Sat, 11am-10pm Sun; ☐1, 2, 29, 38) Here's another neighborhood cocktail bar that doubles as a delectable brunch and dinner spot, but the drinks are really where it's at. Case in point, the Siberian Tea Service, a warm concoction of Japanese whiskey, plum wine, oolong tea and hibiscus. Or how about the Violet Skies, with mezcal, strawberry brandy and some crème de violette?

★ WOODS OUTBOUND   CRAFT BEER
Map p318 (☑415-571-8025; www.woodsbeer. com/outbound; 4045 Judah St; ⊙4-10pm Mon-Wed, to midnight Thu, 3pm-midnight Fri, noon-midnight Sat, noon-10pm Sun; ☐18, Ⓜ N) On a

chilly evening, squeeze into this narrow, cozy craft-beer bar and give some inventive brews a try. The brewmasters are known for throwing unusual ingredients into their 20-gallon brewing system – yerba maté or yams, for instance – and the Morpho herbal ale is an unusual organic favorite.

★ANDYTOWN COFFEE   COFFEE
Map p318 (☑415-753-9775; www.andytownsf. com; 3655 Lawton St; ☉7am-5pm; ☎; 🚌18, Ⓜ️N) Since 2014, Andytown Coffee has spread like afternoon fog, unstoppable thanks to its yummy drip coffee, Irish-inspired soda bread and one-of-a-kind 'snowy plover', a delightful concoction of Pellegrino, ice, two shots of espresso and a scoop of whipped cream. In the last few years, outlets have opened on the increasingly hip **Taraval St** (☑415-571-8052; 3629 Taraval St; ☉7am-5pm; ☎; 🚌18, Ⓜ️L), and downtown near the Salesforce Transit Center.

TOYOSE   BAR
Map p318 (☑415-731-0232; www.toyose.org; 3814 Noriega St; ☉6pm-1am; 🚌7, 18, Ⓜ️N) Hidden in a converted garage in the Outer Sunset, this little Korean late-night spot has adorable environs in which to throw back pitchers of Hite beer or sweet soju cocktails (delivered in large bottles, to pour out and then sip from shot glasses). The food isn't spectacular, but the decent seafood pancakes will ward off an otherwise inevitable hangover.

SIP TEA ROOM   TEAHOUSE
Map p318 (☑415-683-5592; www.siptearoom. com; 721 Lincoln Way; ☉11am-5pm Wed & Fri-Sun, last seating 4:30pm, to 8pm Thu; 🚌6, 7, 43, 44, Ⓜ️N) After zipping around Golden Gate Park and touring a museum or two, relaxing with traditional English afternoon tea ($29 per person) is just the thing. This cozy little tea shop offers everything from Darjeeling to Lapsang Souchong, Ceylon to China Congou, and your pot comes with an array of sandwiches, scones and clotted cream, piled onto a three-tier serving stand.

GRAND HOT POT LOUNGE   KARAOKE
Map p318 (☑415-387-8989; www.hotpotsf.com; 3565 Geary Blvd; ☉11am-10pm; 🚌5, 31, 33, 38) For a night of exoticism, gluttony, intoxication and utter abandon, look no further than Grand Hot Pot Lounge, the Inner Richmond's gift to spicy-food enthusiasts and aspiring *American Idol* contestants everywhere. If you've got a crew and you

want to sing your hearts out, reserve a small karaoke and hot-pot room in advance.

TROUBLE COFFEE CO   CAFE
Map p318 (4033 Judah St; ☉7am-7pm; 🚌18, Ⓜ️N) Coconuts are unlikely near blustery Ocean Beach, but here comes Trouble with the 'Build Your Own Damn House' breakfast special: coffee, thick-cut cinnamon-laced toast and an entire young coconut. Join surfers sipping house roasts on driftwood perches outside, or toss back espresso at the reclaimed-wood counter. Featured on National Public Radio, but not Instagram – sorry, no indoor photos or laptops.

TRAD'R SAM   BAR
Map p318 (☑415-221-0773; 6150 Geary Blvd; ☉11am-2am; 🚌1, 5, 29, 31, 38) Island getaways at this vintage tiki dive will make you forget that Ocean Beach chill. Sailor-strength hot buttered rum will leave you three sheets to the wind, and five-rum Zombies will have you wondering what happened to your brain. Kitsch-lovers order the Hurricane and the Scorpion Bowl, which come with multiple straws: drink these solo and they'll blow you away.

TOMMY'S MEXICAN RESTAURANT   BAR
Map p318 (☑415-387-4747; www.tommys tequila.com; 5929 Geary Blvd; ☉noon-11pm Wed-Mon; 🚌1, 29, 31, 38) Welcome to SF's temple of tequila since 1965. Tommy's serves enchiladas as a cover for day drinking until 7pm, when margarita pitchers with *blanco, reposado* or *añejo* tequila rule. Cuervo Gold is displayed 'for educational purposes only' – it doesn't meet Tommy's strict criteria of unadulterated 100% agave, preferably aged in small barrels. Luckily for connoisseurs, 400 tasty tequilas do.

BEACH CHALET   BREWERY, BAR
Map p318 (☑415-386-8439; www.beachchalet. com; 1000 Great Hwy; ☉9am-10pm Mon-Thu, to midnight Fri, 8am-midnight Sat, 8am-11pm Sun; 🚌5, 18, 31) Microbrews with views: watch Pacific sunsets through pint glasses of the Beach Chalet's Riptide Red ale from the comfort of the formal upstairs dining room. Downstairs, splendid 1930s Works Project Administration (WPA) frescoes celebrate the building of Golden Gate Park. In the backyard, Park Chalet, the casual bar-restaurant, hosts raucous Taco Tuesdays, lazy Sunday brunch, and live music at weekends.

⭐ ENTERTAINMENT

★ NOISE
LIVE MUSIC

Map p318 (☑415-702-6006; www.sanfrancisco
noise.com; 3427 Balboa St; ⊘noon-7pm Mon &
Wed-Fri, to 5pm Tue, 10am-7pm Sat & Sun; ◻5,
18, 31, 38) The more San Francisco changes,
the more this incredible indie record store,
art gallery and performance space stays the
same. Vinyl enthusiasts will want to hang
here for days browsing the vast collection,
which is first organized by genre, then carefully alphabetized, and then described and
rated on handwritten sticky notes by the
store-owner's mom, Sara (who knows her
stuff).

PLOUGH & STARS
LIVE MUSIC

Map p318 (☑415-751-1122; www.theploughand
stars.com; 116 Clement St; ⊘3pm-2am Mon &
Tue, from 2pm Wed-Sun, shows 9pm; ◻1, 2, 33,
38, 44) Bands who sell out shows from Ire-
land to Appalachia and headline SF's Hardly Strictly Bluegrass festival (p35) jam here
on weeknights, taking breaks to clink pint
glasses of Guinness at long union-hall tables. Mondays compensate for no live music
with an all-day happy hour, plus free pool
and blarney from regulars; expect modest
cover charges ($6 to $10) for barnstorming
weekend shows.

NECK OF THE WOODS
LIVE MUSIC

Map p318 (☑415-387-6343; www.neckofthe
woodssf.com; 406 Clement St; ⊘6pm-2am; ◻1,
2, 33, 38, 44) A vast yet cozy venue with all
the right moves, including Monday salsa
dance classes, Russian karaoke (no lan-
guage skills required) and indie rock acts
regularly pounding the upstairs stage.
Downstairs the lounge serves $5 happy-
hour well drinks and beer, and hosts whol-
ly unpredictable open-mike nights.

BALBOA THEATRE
CINEMA

Map p318 (☑415-221-8184; www.balboamovies.
com; 3630 Balboa St; adult/child $12.50/10, mat-
inees $10; ◻5, 18, 31, 38) First stop Cannes;
next stop Balboa and 37th, where film-fest
favorites split the bill with Bogart noir
classics, family-friendly Saturday-morning
matinees and B-movie marathons with
in-person director commentary. This 1926
movie palace is run by the nonprofit San
Francisco Neighborhood Theater Foundation, which keeps tickets affordable and
programming exciting.

🛍 SHOPPING

**Find offbeat boutiques and kids' treats
on Clement St (around 5th) in the
Richmond, and on Irving St (around
9th) and Judah St (around 45th) in the
Sunset.**

★ PARK LIFE
GIFTS & SOUVENIRS

Map p318 (☑415-386-7275; www.parklifestore.
com; 220 Clement St; ⊘10am-7pm Mon-Sat, to
6pm Sun; ◻1, 2, 33, 38, 44) The Swiss Army
knife of hip SF emporiums, Park Life is design store, indie publisher and art gallery
rolled into one. Browse among presents too
clever to give away, including toy soldiers
in yoga poses, Park Life catalogs of Shaun
O'Dell paintings of natural disorder, sinister Todd Hido photos of shaggy cats on shag
rugs, and a Picasso bong.

★ PAUL'S HAT WORKS
HATS

Map p318 (☑415-221-5332; www.hatworksby
paul.com; 6128 Geary Blvd; ⊘10am-3pm Wed-Fri,
noon-4pm select Sat; ◻1, 38) Psst...keep this
SF style secret under your hat: there is no
Paul. Started in 1918 by a Peruvian hatmaker named Napoleon, Paul's has been
maintained by three generations of 'master
hatters' handcrafting noir-novel fedoras
on-site. Head downtown in Paul's jazz-
standard porkpie, social-climb Nob Hill in
Paul's stovepipe top hat or storm Trad'r Sam
down the block in Paul's classic panama.

★ JADE CHOCOLATES
FOOD

Map p318 (☑415-350-3878; www.jadechoco
lates.com; 4207 Geary Blvd; ⊘11am-7pm Tue-Sat;
◻2, 31, 38, 44) SF-born chocolatier Mindy
Fong hits the sweet spot between East and
West with only-in-SF treats like passion-
fruit caramels, Thai-curry hot chocolate
and the legendary peanut Buddha with
mango jam. Fusion flavors originally inspired by Fong's pregnancy cravings have
won national acclaim, but Jade keeps its SF
edge with experimental chocolates featuring ingredients like miso and curry powder.

GREEN APPLE BOOKS
BOOKS

Map p318 (☑415-387-2272; www.greenapple
books.com; 506 Clement St; ⊘10am-10:30pm;
◻2, 38, 44) Stagger out of this literary opium den while you still can, laden with re-
maindered art books, used cookbooks and
just-released novels signed by local authors.
If two floors of bookish bliss aren't enough,
check out more new titles, in-store readings

WHERE TO GEAR UP FOR OCEAN BEACH

Mollusk (Map p318; ☑415-564-6300; www.mollusksurfshop.com; 4500 Irving St; ☉10am-6:30pm Mon-Sat, to 6pm Sun; ☐18, Ⓜ N) The geodesic-dome tugboat marks the spot where ocean meets art in this surf gallery. Legendary shapers (surfboard makers) create limited-edition boards for Mollusk, and signature T-shirts and hoodies win nods of recognition on Ocean Beach. Kooks (newbies) get vicarious thrills from coffee-table books on California surf culture, Thomas Campbell ocean collages and other works by SF surfer-artists.

Aqua Surf Shop (Map p318; ☑415-242-9283; www.aquasurfshop.com; 3847 Judah St; rental per day bodyboard/wetsuit $10/15, surfboard $25-35; ☉10am-5:30pm Sun-Tue, to 7pm Wed-Sat; ☐18, Ⓜ N) Earn Sunset street cred the hardcore way, with Aqua's rental surf gear plus referrals for surf instructors (see website). Ocean Beach riptides are challenging, so Aqua only offers rentals when conditions are safe. For instant cool without getting wet, join Aqua pop-up events and Monday sunset yoga ($10).

On the Run (Map p318; ☑415-682-2042; www.ontherunshoes.com; 1310 9th Ave; ☉10am-7pm Mon-Fri, to 6pm Sat, 11am-6pm Sun; ☐6, 7, 43, 44, Ⓜ N) If your morning jog leaves your feet or shins hurting, get your gait checked here before you hit Ocean Beach or Golden Gate Park trails. The pros will recommend the right orthopedic inserts or shoes to relieve the pressure for free – and if you choose to buy inserts here, they'll mold them to fit while you wait.

and events at Green Apple Books on the Park (1231 9th Ave).

FOGGY NOTION
GIFTS & SOUVENIRS

Map p318 (☑415-683-5654; www.foggy-notion.com; 124 Clement St; ☉11am-7pm Mon-Fri, from 10am Sat, 10am-6pm Sun; ☐1, 2, 38, 49) 🏵 You can't take Golden Gate Park home with you – the city would seem naked without it – but Foggy Notion specializes in sense memories of SF's urban wilderness. The all-natural, all-artisan gift selection includes Juniper Ridge's hiking-trail scents, Golden Gate Park honey, SF artist Julia Canright's hand-printed canvas backpacks, and one of the largest candle selections in the city.

SAN FRANPSYCHO
GIFTS & SOUVENIRS

Map p318 (☑415-213-5442; http://sanfranpsycho.com; 1248 9th Ave; ☉10am-9pm Thu-Sat, to 8pm Sun-Wed; ☐6, 7, 43, 44, Ⓜ N) Blow minds with souvenirs that get visitors mistaken for locals. Go from downtown protests in tees featuring the Golden Gate Bridge and the city's unofficial slogan, 'Build bridges, not walls,' to beach bonfires with a six-pack of the store's signature IPA and a comfy Mexican blanket. Complete Cali-casual looks with enamel pins and matching hoodies for you and your dog.

LAST STRAW
GIFTS & SOUVENIRS

Map p318 (☑415-566-4692; 4540 Irving St; ☉noon-6pm Tue-Sat; ☐7, 18, Ⓜ N) Gifts come from the heart inside this front-parlor gift shop, packed with outer-avenues necessities: flax clothing, indigo beach totes and fisherman's scarves crocheted on a nearby houseboat. Open jewelry chests to find hidden treasures under $50, including Amano's Sonoma-made chiseled-silver señorita hoops. Owner Marge accepts cash, checks, credit cards and – proof that SF idealism lives on – IOUs.

SPORTS & ACTIVITIES

★ COASTAL TRAIL
HIKING

Map p318 (www.californiacoastaltrail.info; ☉sunrise-sunset; ☐1, 18, 38) Hit your stride on this 10.5-mile stretch, starting at Fort Funston, crossing 4 miles of sandy Ocean Beach and wrapping around the Presidio to the Golden Gate Bridge. Casual strollers can pick up the restored trail near Sutro Baths and head around the Lands End bluffs for end-of-the-world views and glimpses of shipwrecks at low tide.

SAN FRANCISCO DISC GOLF
SPORTS

Map p318 (www.sfdiscgolf.org; 900 John F Kennedy Dr; ☉sunrise-sunset; ☐5, 28, 29, 31, 38) **FREE** Wander the tranquil fairy-tale woods of outer Golden Gate Park and you'll find fierce Frisbee golf games in progress at a permanent 18-hole disc-golf course. Rent tournament discs at Golden Gate Park Bike & Skate and register online to mingle with disc-tossing singles on Sunday (8:30am to 10am; $5) or join Tuesday doubles tournaments (5pm; $5).

LAWN BOWLING CLUB BOWLING

Map p318 (✐415-487-8787; www.sflbc.org; Bowling Green Dr; ◷11am-4pm Tue-Sun, weather permitting; ☒5, 7, 21, 33, Ⓜ️N) Pins seem ungainly and bowling shirts unthinkable once you've joined sweater-clad enthusiasts on America's first public lawn-bowling green. Free lessons are available from volunteers on Wednesday at noon and occasional afternoons in spring and summer. Flat-soled shoes are mandatory, but otherwise bowlers dress for comfort and the weather – though all-white clothing has been customary at club social events since 1901.

GOLDEN GATE MUNICIPAL
GOLF COURSE GOLF

Map p318 (✐415-751-8987; www.goldengatepark golf.com; 970 47th Ave; adult/child Mon-Thu $22/8, Fri-Sun $26/10; ◷7am-5pm; 🚻; ☒5, 18, 31) With sunlight filtering through majestic Monterey cypress trees, even the rough is glorious at this challenging nine-hole, par-27 public course sculpted from park sand dunes in 1951. Equipment rental (adult/child $15/8) and practice range available; kids welcome. Book ahead online, especially before 9am weekdays, weekends and after school.

SAN FRANCYCLO CYCLING

Map p318 (✐415-831-8031; www.sanfrancyclo. com; 746 Arguello Blvd; rental bike per hour incl helmet $10-40; ◷11am-7pm Wed-Fri, 10am-5pm Sat & Sun; 🚻; ☒5, 21, 31, 33, 38) Glide around Golden Gate Park and zip across the bridge on sleek new bikes, including hybrid options. The storefront for pickup/drop-off is just north of Golden Gate Park. Seats and bikes for children are available.

GOLDEN GATE JOAD ARCHERY

Map p318 (www.goldengatejoad.com; Golden Gate Park Archery Range, cnr Fulton St & 47th Ave; 30min lesson incl archery gear rental $30; ◷classes morning Sat; 🚻; ☒5, 18, 31) Blockbusters like *The Avengers*, *The Hunger Games* and *Brave* have revived San Francisco's Victorian-era archery craze, and you can take aim Saturday mornings in Golden Gate Park with SF's nonprofit Junior Olympic Archery Division (JOAD). Patient, certified coaches offer traditional bow archery classes for adults and kids aged eight and

up (with guardian consent). Book online; beginner classes fill quickly.

GOLDEN GATE
PARK BIKE & SKATE CYCLING

Map p318 (✐415-668-1117; www.goldengatepark bikeandskate.com; 3038 Fulton St; skates per hour $5-6, per day $20-24, bikes per hour $3-5, per day $15-25, tandem bikes per hour/day $15/75, discs per hour/day $6/25; ◷10am-6pm Mon-Fri, to 7pm Sat & Sun; 🚻; ☒5, 21, 31, 44) Besides bikes and skates (four-wheeled and inline), this rental shop just outside Golden Gate Park rents disc putters and drivers for the park's free Frisbee golf course. Bargain rates; helmets, locks and maps included with rentals. Call ahead to confirm it's open if the weather looks iffy.

SAN FRANCISCO
MODEL YACHT CLUB BOATING

Map p318 (www.sfmyc.org; Spreckels Lake; ◷sunrise-sunset; ☒5, 18, 31) America's Cup races can't compare to these exciting remote-controlled miniature regattas. Kids cheer for scale-model yachts built and operated by local collectors on weekend afternoons, plus occasional weekdays in fine weather. Spreckels Lake is also a refuge for turtles, who snooze on the shore, unfazed by nautical events. When members are around, check out the vintage boats in the clubhouse.

STOW LAKE BOATHOUSE BOATING

Map p318 (✐415-386-2531; http://stowlakeboat house.com; 50 Stow Lake Dr; boats per hour $22.50-38.50; ◷10am-5pm; ☒5, 7, 29, 44) ✐ Push off from the dock of this vintage 1946 boathouse in a pedal-powered or rowing boat to glide across Stow Lake (p193), and return for a quick bite, a glass of wine or some organic Three Twins ice cream at the renovated boathouse cafe (open 11am to 5pm).

GOLDEN GATE PARK
HORSESHOE PITS OUTDOORS

Map p318 (https://goldengatepark.com/horse shoe-pits.html; ◷sunrise-sunset; 🚻; ☒5, 7, 21, 33) Hidden on a hillside at Golden Gate Park's eastern end, an equine giant is permanently poised for triumph. Since 1926, the concrete Horseshoe Thrower has witnessed epic horseshoe-pitching showdowns – after a massive neighborhood restoration effort, he now smiles upon courts which ring with the sound of iron striking posts most weekends. For upcoming tournaments and local horseshoe vendors, see www. sfhorseshoepitching.com.

Day Trips from San Francisco

Berkeley & Oakland p203

The legendary counterculture hubs of 'Bezerkely' and 'Oaktown' keep busy reinventing music, art, history and politics – but dinnertime is sacred in this culinary hub.

Muir Woods to Stinson Beach p210

Some of the world's tallest trees reach skyward in primordial forests near windblown beaches, just across the Golden Gate Bridge.

Sausalito & Tiburon p213

Picturesque bayside towns, perfect for strolling, are a fast ferry-ride away in Marin County. Meet for sunset drinks and seafood by the water.

Napa Valley p218

Sun-washed valleys and cool coastal fog have turned Napa into an iconic wine-growing region – but redwood groves, organic farms and natural hot springs keep things diverse.

Sonoma Valley p222

With its 19th-century California mission town, farm-to-table kitchens and pastoral wineries that welcome picnicking, Sonoma retains its folksy ways.

Berkeley & Oakland

Explore

Berkeley and Oakland are what most San Franciscans think of as the East Bay, though the area includes numerous other suburbs that swoop up from the bayside flats into exclusive enclaves in the hills. Many residents of the 'West Bay' would like to think they needn't ever cross the Bay Bridge or take a Bay Area Rapid Transit (BART) train through an underwater tunnel. But a wealth of museums and historical sites, a world-famous university, excellent restaurants and bars, a creative arts scene, offbeat shopping, woodsy parks and better weather are just some of the attractions that lure travelers from San Francisco over to the sunny side of the Bay.

The Best...

Sight Tilden Regional Park

Place to Eat Chez Panisse (p207)

Entertainment Fox Theater (p209)

Top Tip

You can cross between the East and West Bay via the **Bay Bridge Path** (www.baybridge info.org/path; ⊙hours vary), which spans the Bay Bridge between Oakland and Yerba Buena Island (2.2 miles total).

Getting There & Away

BART (Bay Area Rapid Transit; www.bart.gov) Trains run approximately every 10 or so minutes from around 5am to 12:30am on weekdays, with more limited service from 6am on Saturday and from 8am on Sunday and holidays.

Bus Regional company AC Transit (p268) operates a number of buses from San Francisco's Transbay Temporary Terminal to the East Bay (one-way fare $5.50).

Car Approach the East Bay from San Francisco by taking the Bay Bridge. Driving back westbound to San Francisco, the bridge toll is $5 to $7, depending on the time and day of the week.

Ferry Offering splendid views, the San Francisco Bay Ferry (p267) is the most enjoyable way of traveling between San Francisco and the East Bay, though also the slowest and most expensive.

Need to Know

Area Code ⊘510

Location Berkeley is 11 miles northeast of San Francisco; Oakland is about 8 miles west.

Visit Berkeley (⊘510-549-7040; www.visitberkeley.com; 2030 Addison St; ⊙9am-1pm & 2-5pm Mon-Fri; Ⓑ Downtown Berkeley)

Visit Oakland (⊘510-839-9000; www.visitoakland.com; 481 Water St; ⊙9am-5pm Mon-Fri, 10am-5pm Sat & Sun)

⊙ SIGHTS

★TILDEN REGIONAL PARK   PARK

(⊘510-544-2747; www.ebparks.org/parks/tilden/; ⊙5am-10pm; Ⓟ🚻🐕; 🚌AC Transit 67) 🎫 FREE
This 2079-acre park, up in the hills east of town, is Berkeley's best. It has nearly 40 miles of hiking and multiuse trails of varying difficulty, from paved paths to hilly scrambles, including part of the magnificent Bay Area Ridge Trail. There's also a miniature steam train ($3), a children's farm and environmental education center, a wonderfully wild-looking botanical garden and an 18-hole golf course. Lake Anza is good for picnics and from spring through fall you can swim ($3.50).

★OAKLAND MUSEUM OF CALIFORNIA   MUSEUM

(OMCA; ⊘510-318-8400; www.museumca.org; 1000 Oak St; adult/child $16/7, 1st Sun each month free; ⊙11am-5pm Wed & Thu, to 9pm Fri, 10am-6pm Sat & Sun; Ⓟ🛜♿; Ⓑ Lake Merritt) Every museum has an educational mission, and this one is dedicated to California. You'll find rotating exhibitions on artistic and scientific themes, and permanent galleries dedicated to the state's diverse ecology and history, as well as California art, from traditional landscapes to re-imagined cartography. Start your weekend here on a Friday night (after 5pm), when DJs, food trucks and free art workshops for kids make it a fun hangout.

★CHABOT SPACE & SCIENCE CENTER   MUSEUM

(⊘510-336-7300; www.chabotspace.org; 10000 Skyline Blvd; adult/child $18/14; ⊙10am-5pm

Berkeley & Oakland

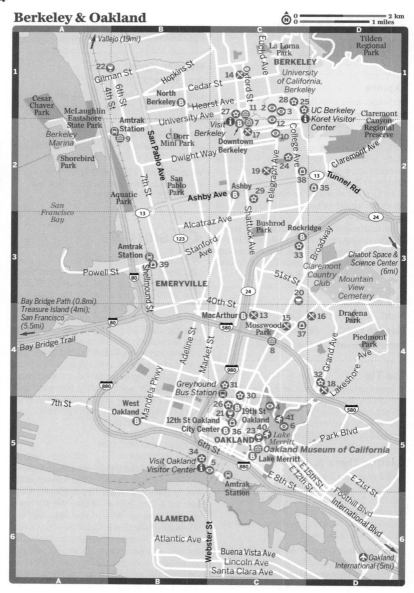

Wed-Sun; ⓟ 🚻; 🚌AC Transit 339) 🖋 Stargazers will go gaga over this kid-oriented science and technology center in the Oakland Hills with loads of exhibits on subjects such as space travel and eclipses, as well as cool planetarium shows. When the weather's good, check out the free Friday and Saturday evening viewings (7:30pm to 10:30pm) using a 20in refractor telescope.

Admission is just $5 on the first Friday evening of each month (6pm to 10pm), when the museum organizes hands-on activities, science demonstrations, movies and night hikes.

Berkeley & Oakland

CROWN MEMORIAL STATE BEACH BEACH
(☏510-544-3175; www.ebparks.org/parks/crown
_beach; 8th St & Otis Dr, Alameda; per car $5;
☺5am-10pm; P⛵♿) Along the western
shore of Alameda Island, Robert W Crown
Memorial State Park sees flocks of East
Bay locals on a sunny day. The sandy beach
stretches 2.5 miles along the San Francisco
Bay, and windsurfers love riding the gusts
from across the bay. There are picnic spots
and grilling stations throughout the park.

**MUSEUM OF ART &
DIGITAL ENTERTAINMENT** MUSEUM
(MADE; ☏510-457-0211; www.themade.org;
3400 Broadway Ave; $10; ☺noon-midnight Fri,
10am-10pm Sat, noon-6pm Sun; 🚌AC Transit 51A)
If you love video games, the MADE is the
heaven you go to when you die and are all
out of extra lives. It's a museum of sorts, but
more a sort of time-travel arcade filled with
video game consoles ranging from Playsta-
tion 4s to Neo Geos to Atari 2600s. There
are 5300 playable games inside, and you
can lose a day playing them all in happy,
pew-pew-pew, bleeping bliss. Only open on
weekends.

**UNIVERSITY OF
CALIFORNIA, BERKELEY** UNIVERSITY
(☏510-642-6000; www.berkeley.edu; ☺hours
vary; P☂; 🚇Downtown Berkeley) 'Cal' is one
of the country's top universities, California's
oldest university (1866), and home to 40,000
diverse, politically conscious students. Next
to **California Memorial Stadium** (☏510-642-
2730; www.californiamemorialstadium.com), the
Koret Visitor Center (☏510-642-5215; http://
visit.berkeley.edu; 2227 Piedmont Ave; ☺8:30am-
4:30pm Mon-Fri, 9am-1pm Sat & Sun; 🚌AC Transit

36) has information and maps, and leads free campus walking tours (reservations required). Cal's landmark is the 1914 **Campanile** (Sather Tower; http://campanile.berkeley.edu; adult/child $4/3; ☺10am-3:45pm Mon-Fri, 10am-4:45pm Sat, to 1:30pm & 3-4:45pm Sun; 🚼), with elevator rides ($4) to the top and carillon concerts. The **Bancroft Library** (📞510-642-3781; www.lib.berkeley.edu/libraries/bancroft-library; University Dr; ☺archives 10am-4pm or 5pm Mon-Fri; 🚻) FREE displays the small gold nugget that started the California gold rush in 1848.

UC BERKELEY ART MUSEUM MUSEUM
(BAMPFA; 📞510-642-0808; www.bampfa.berkeley.edu; 2155 Center St; adult/child $13/free; ☺11am-7pm Sun, Wed & Thu, to 9pm Fri & Sat; 🚻; ⓑDowntown Berkeley) With a stainless-steel exterior wrapping around a 1930s printing plant, this museum holds multiple galleries showcasing a limited number of artworks, from ancient Chinese to cutting-edge contemporary. The complex also houses a bookstore, cafe and the much-loved **Pacific Film Archive** (PFA; adult/child from $13/9; ☺hours vary; 🚼).

JACK LONDON SQUARE SQUARE
(📞510-645-9292; www.jacklondonsquare.com; Broadway & Embarcadero; ☺24hr, shop, restaurant & bar hours vary; ℗; 🚌Broadway Shuttle) The area where writer and adventurer Jack London once raised hell now bears his name. The pretty waterfront location is worth a stroll, especially when the Sunday **farmers market** (📞415-291-3276; www.cuesa.org; ☺10am-3pm Sun; 🚼 🚻) 🍴 takes over, or get off your feet and kayak around the harbor. Contemporary redevelopment has added a cinema complex, condo development and popular restaurants and bars.

A replica of Jack London's Yukon **cabin** stands at the eastern end of the square. Oddly, people throw coins inside as if it's a fountain.

TAKARA SAKE MUSEUM
(📞510-540-8250; www.takarasake.com; 708 Addison St; tasting fee $5-15; ☺noon-6pm, last tasting 5:30pm; 🚌AC Transit 51B, 80) Stop in to see the traditional wooden tools used for making sake and a short video of the brewing process. Tours of the factory aren't offered, but you can view elements of modern production and bottling through a window. Sake flights are poured in a spacious tasting room constructed with reclaimed wood and floor tiles fashioned from recycled

glass, all set beneath 'Song of the Sky,' a kinetic sculpture by Susumu Shingu.

MAGNES COLLECTION
OF JEWISH ART AND LIFE MUSEUM
(📞510-643-2526; www.magnes.berkeley.edu; 2121 Allston Way; ☺11am-4pm Tue-Fri; ⓑDowntown Berkeley) FREE This museum boasts a fine collection – almost 15,000 pieces – of art and cultural artifacts sourced from across the Jewish diaspora, particularly Jewish communities in the American West. Note that the museum is open during the academic year, and closed outside of fall and spring semester.

TELEGRAPH AVENUE STREET
(☺shop & restaurant hours vary; ℗; 🚌AC Transit 6) Telegraph Ave has traditionally been the throbbing heart of studentville in Berkeley, the sidewalks crowded with undergrads, postdocs and youthful shoppers squeezing their way past throngs of vendors, buskers and panhandlers. Street stalls hawk everything from crystals to bumper stickers to self-published tracts. Several cafes and budget eateries cater to students.

LAKE MERRITT LAKE
(📞510-238-7275; www.lakemerritt.org; ☺7:30am-sunset; ℗ 🚼; ⓑLake Merritt) 🚶 FREE An urban respite, Lake Merritt is a popular place to stroll or go running (a 3.5-mile paved path circles the lake), with bonsai and botanical gardens, a children's amusement park, bird sanctuary, green spaces, a **boathouse** (📞510-238-2196; www.oaklandnet.com; 568 Bellevue Ave; boat rentals per hour $15-25; ☺daily Mar-Oct, Sat & Sun Nov-Feb; 🚼; 🚌AC Transit 12) and **gondola rides** (📞510-663-6603; www.gondolaservizio.com; 1520 Lakeside Dr; 30/50min cruise $60/85). The two main commercial streets skirting Lake Merritt are Grand Ave, running along the north shore, and Lakeshore Ave on the eastern edge of the lake.

CHILDREN'S FAIRYLAND AMUSEMENT PARK
(📞510-452-2259; www.fairyland.org; 699 Bellevue Ave; $10, child under 1yr free; ☺10am-4pm Mon-Fri, to 5pm Sat & Sun Jun-Aug, off-season hours vary; ℗ 🚼; 🚌AC Transit 12) This 10-acre kiddie attraction dates from 1950, and we're not sure if it's been overhauled since. We mean that as a compliment! Children's Fairyland, with its little Aesop and Grimm Bros themed attractions, has all of the nostalgia feels. There's a raw authenticity to the faded Peter Rabbit gardens and Alice in Wonderland labyrinth,

a stark contrast to most hyper-frenetic contemporary kids' play parks. Located on the northern side of Lake Merritt.

 EATING & DRINKING

★**TAQUERIA EL PAISA@.COM** MEXICAN $

(☎510-534-2180; www.facebook.com/pg/elpaisa77; 4610 International Blvd; tacos $2.50; ⊗9am-9pm; 🚌AC Transit 1, 901) Yes that is the name of this place, and no, we don't know how to say it out loud (a lot of locals just call it 'El Paisa'). Honestly, we would call this taco joint whatever it wants to be named, because the tacos are good beyond all superlative: simple, fresh, garnished with cilantro, onions, nopales (cactus); hands down delicious.

★**FENTONS** ICE CREAM $

(☎510-658-7000; www.fentonscreamery.com; 4226 Piedmont Ave; mains $8-13; ⊗11am-11pm Mon-Thu, 9am-midnight Fri & Sat, 9am-11pm Sun; 🚼; 🚌AC Transit 12, C) If you have children, or love ice cream, you owe it to yourself to stop by this institution. The range of ice cream flavors is encyclopedic in range, stretching from banana nut to green tea, and the scoops are more than generous. Plenty of sundae options, plus burgers and grilled sandwiches for those not indulging their sweet tooth.

OAKLAND–GRAND LAKE FARMERS MARKET MARKET $

(☎415-472-6100; www.agriculturalinstitute.org; Lake Park Ave, at Grand Ave; ⊗9am-2pm Sat; 🍴🚼; 🚌AC Transit 12) 🌿 A rival to San Francisco's Ferry Plaza Farmers Market, this bountiful weekly market hauls in bushels of fresh fruit, vegetables, seafood, ranched meats, artisanal cheese and baked goods from as far away as Marin County and the Central Valley. The northern side of the market is cheek-to-jowl with food trucks and hot-food vendors – don't skip the dim-sum tent.

BEAUTY'S BAGEL SHOP JEWISH $

(☎510-788-6098; www.beautysbagelshop.com; 3838 Telegraph Ave; mains $6-11; ⊗8am-3pm Tue-Fri, 7am-3pm Sat & Sun; 🚇MacArthur) Few breakfasts can match the sheer perfection of a good bagel loaded with cream cheese, salmon, tomatoes and capers, and the version at Beauty's is, well, a beauty. All of its bagels are excellent, as are other Jewish soul-food specialties like a chopped liver and Swiss cheese sandwich, matzo-ball soup, and egg salad.

★**ROYAL RANGOON** BURMESE $$

(☎510-647-9744; www.royalrangoon.com; 2826 Telegraph Ave; mains $10-20; ⊗11:30am-2:30pm & 5-9:30pm; 🍴; 🚌AC Transit 18, 800) Excellent Burmese fare includes some of the Bay Area's more authentic takes on *mohinga* (fish noodle soup), *ohn no kauk swe* (coconut-curry chicken soup), fried tofu and pork and mango curry, among many other goodies. The setting is elegant, but the price point is appealingly modest.

GREAT CHINA RESTAURANT CHINESE $$

(☎510-843-7996; www.greatchinaberkeley.com; 2190 Bancroft Way; mains $13-21; ⊗11:30am-2:30pm Wed-Mon, 5:30-9pm Mon, Wed & Thu, to 9:30pm Fri, 5-9:30pm Sat & Sun; 🚇Downtown Berkeley) Berkeley does not lack for good Chinese food, but this enormous, upscale restaurant elevates the genre with Northern Chinese specialties like duck-bone soup, cumin-braised lamb, steamed fish with ginger and scallions, and thrice-cooked pork belly. Come with friends and order as much as you can – your taste buds will thank you.

★**CHEZ PANISSE** CALIFORNIAN $$$

(☎cafe 510-548-5049, restaurant 510-548-5525; www.chezpanisse.com; 1517 Shattuck Ave; cafe dinner mains $21-35, restaurant prix-fixe dinner $75-125; ⊗cafe 11:30am-2:45pm & 5-10:30pm Mon-Thu, 11:30am-3pm & 5-11pm Fri & Sat, restaurant seatings 5:30pm & 8pm Mon-Sat; 🍴; 🚌AC Transit 7) 🌿 Foodies come to worship here at the church of Alice Waters, inventor of California cuisine. Panisse is located in a lovely arts-and-crafts house in Berkeley's 'Gourmet Ghetto,' and you can choose to pull out all the stops with a prix-fixe meal downstairs or go less expensive and a tad less formal in the upstairs cafe. Reservations accepted one month ahead.

COMMIS CALIFORNIAN $$$

(☎510-653-3902; www.commisrestaurant.com; 3859 Piedmont Ave; 8-course dinner $175, with wine & beer pairings $260; ⊗5:30-9:30pm Wed-Sat, 5-9pm Sun; 🚌AC Transit 51A) The East Bay's only Michelin-starred restaurant, the signless and discreet dining room counts a minimalist decor and some coveted counter real estate where patrons can watch a two-Michelin-star award-winning team piece together creative and innovative dishes – maybe Monterey Bay abalone, soy-milk custard with chanterelles or a perfectly ripe peach topped with oats, beeswax creme and marigolds. Reservations essential.

WORTH A DETOUR

SIGHTS OF SILICON VALLEY

Touted as the largest computer-history exhibition in the world, the **Computer History Museum** (650-810-1010; www.computerhistory.org; 1401 N Shoreline Blvd, Mountain View; adult $17.50, student & senior $13.50; 10am-5pm Wed-Sun; P) has rotating exhibits drawn from its 100,000-item collection. Artifacts include Cray-1 supercomputers, a Babbage difference engine (a Victorian-era automatic computing engine) and the first Google server.

At the impressive **Apple Park Visitor Center** (408-974-5050; www.apple.com/retail/appleparkvisitorcenter; 10600 N Tantau Ave, Cupertino; 9am-7pm Mon-Fri, 10am-7pm Sat, 11am-6pm Sun; P), hardcore fans can play with all the latest Apple products, take short classes led by staff, explore the new space-age Apple Park via iPad and commiserate that yes, Steve Jobs has left the building.

There are no official tours of Google's corporate headquarters, **Googleplex** (650-214-3308; www.google.com/about/company/facts/locations; 1600 Amphitheatre Pkwy, Mountain View; store 10am-6:30pm Mon-Fri; P), but visitors can stroll the campus and gawk at the public art on the leafy grounds. Check out the toothy T rex festooned in pink flamingos, and discover the lawn sculptures of Android operating systems (a cupcake! A doughnut! A robot!) a short drive away at 1981 Landings Dr, where the **Google company store** sells logo-branded merchandise.

Facebook Headquarters (1 Hacker Way, Menlo Park) doesn't allow visitors but that doesn't stop throngs of fans stopping to get a selfie at the thumbs-up sign.

The **Intel Museum** (408-765-5050; www.intel.com/museum; 2200 Mission College Blvd, Santa Clara; 9am-6pm Mon-Fri, 10am-5pm Sat; P) FREE has displays on the birth and growth of the computer industry with special emphasis, not surprisingly, on microchips and Intel's involvement. Call ahead to check opening hours.

In San Jose, be wowed by exhibits on robotics, biotechnology and virtual reality at the **Tech Museum of Innovation** (The Tech; 408-294-8324; www.thetech.org; 201 S Market St; adult/child $25/20, incl IMAX movie $31/24; 10am-5pm;), then snap a selfie inside the Tesla electric-car showroom and interactive design studio at **Santana Row** (408-551-4611; www.santanarow.com; 377 Santana Row; 10am-9pm Mon-Sat, 11am-7pm Sun) shopping mall.

⭐ **BLUE BOTTLE COFFEE COMPANY** CAFE

(510-653-3394; www.bluebottlecoffee.com; 4270 Broadway; 6am-6:30pm Mon-Fri, 6:30am-6pm Sat & Sun; AC Transit 51A) 🍴 This Blue Bottle cafe is inside the beautiful WC Morse Building, a 1920s truck showroom. Communal tables, lofty ceilings and minimalist decor invite sipping a Gibraltar – similar to a cortado (espresso with a dash of milk), but made with more milk – or a cold-brew iced coffee.

⭐ **CAFE VAN KLEEF** BAR

(510-763-7711; www.facebook.com/cafevankleef; 1621 Telegraph Ave; 4pm-2am Mon, from noon Tue-Fri, from 6pm Sat, from 7pm Sun; B19th St Oakland) Order a greyhound and take a gander at the profusion of antique musical instruments, fake taxidermy heads, sprawling formal chandeliers and bizarro ephemera clinging to every surface possible. Quirky even *before* you get lit, it features live blues, jazz and the occasional rock band on weekends.

FIELDWORK BREWING COMPANY BREWERY

(510-898-1203; www.fieldworkbrewing.com; 1160 6th St; 11am-10pm Sun-Thu, to 11pm Fri & Sat; AC Transit 12) At this industrial brewery taproom you can sit down on the outdoor patio with a tasting flight of IPAs or a glass of rich Mexican hot-chocolate stout. It's dog-friendly, and there are racks for hanging up your bicycle inside the front door. There's a short menu of Mexican-Californian food too.

RUBY ROOM BAR

(510-444-7224; www.facebook.com/darkest.bar.ever; 132 14th St; 4pm-2am; AC Transit 14) This dive lives up to the promise of its website – if it's not the darkest bar ever, it's in the running. What lighting does exist is red and moody, which gives the spot an atmosphere straddling sexy and dangerous. Drinks are strong, and DJs spin on some nights, making for some very low-lit dance parties.

⭐ ENTERTAINMENT

★FOX THEATER
THEATER

(☎510-302-2250; www.thefoxoakland.com; 1807 Telegraph Ave; tickets from $35; ☺hours vary; Ⓑ19th St Oakland) A phoenix arisen from the urban ashes, this restored 1928 art deco stunner adds dazzle and neon lights to Telegraph Ave, where it's a cornerstone of the happening Uptown theater and nightlife district. Once a movie house, it's now a popular concert venue for edgy and independent Californian, national and international music acts. Buy tickets early, since many shows sell out.

YOSHI'S
JAZZ

(☎510-238-9200; www.yoshis.com; 510 Embarcadero W; ☺hours vary; 🚌Broadway Shuttle) Yoshi's has a solid jazz calendar, with talent from around the world passing through on a near-nightly basis. It's also a Japanese restaurant, so if you enjoy a sushi dinner before the show, you'll be rewarded with reserved cabaret-style seating. Otherwise, resign yourself to limited high-top tables squeezed along the back walls of this intimate club.

PARAMOUNT THEATRE
THEATER, CINEMA

(☎510-465-6400; www.paramounttheatre.com; 2025 Broadway; ☺hours vary; Ⓑ19th St Oakland) This massive 1931 art deco masterpiece shows classic films a few times each month and is also home to the Oakland Symphony and Oakland Ballet. It periodically books big-name concerts and screens classic flicks.

Guided tours ($5) are given at 10am on the first and third Saturdays of the month (no reservations).

GREEK THEATRE
LIVE PERFORMANCE

(☎510-871-9225; www.thegreekberkeley.com; 2001 Gayley Rd; ⒷDowntown Berkeley) This outdoor, Greek-style amphitheater has been around since 1903, and is the oldest venue of its type in the country. Excellent sight lines, tons of history, and a great lineup of talent makes for a brilliant concert venue.

BERKELEY PLAYHOUSE
THEATER

(☎510-845-8542; https://tickets.berkeleyplayhouse.org; 2640 College Ave; tickets $20-45; 📶) This lively little theater runs plenty of musicals, including a fair number of shows (*Pippin, The Wizard of Oz,* and *The Little Mermaid,* for example) that are family friendly. On that note, the Playhouse also runs a few youth productions every year. Shows are performed at the Julia Morgan Theater.

FREIGHT & SALVAGE COFFEEHOUSE
LIVE MUSIC

(☎510-644-2020; www.thefreight.org; 2020 Addison St; tickets $5-45; ☺shows daily; 📶; ⒷDowntown Berkeley) This legendary club has almost 50 years of history and is conveniently located in the downtown arts district. It features great traditional folk, country, bluegrass and world music, and welcomes all ages, with half-price tickets for patrons under 21.

LA PEÑA CULTURAL CENTER
WORLD MUSIC

(☎510-849-2568; www.lapena.org; 3105 Shattuck Ave; ☺hours vary; ⒷAshby) This warmhearted community center presents dynamic dance classes and musical and visual arts events with a social justice bent. Look for a vibrant mural outside and the on-site Mexican cafe, perfect for grabbing drinks and a preshow bite.

STARLINE SOCIAL CLUB
LIVE PERFORMANCE

(☎510-593-2109; www.starlinesocialclub.com; 2236 Martin Luther King Way; ☺4pm-2am; 🚌AC Transit 18) A local favorite for live music, art shows, dance parties, comedy sets, readings and other events, the Starline has a vintage feel, which makes sense, as this three-story Victorian building used to be a saloon. A dining area serves Cali-style bar food (buffalo wings *and* chicory salad), and there are regular DJs, jazz on Tuesdays and karaoke on Sundays.

GRAND LAKE THEATRE
CINEMA

(☎510-452-3556; www.renaissancerialto.com; 3200 Grand Ave; tickets $11; ☺hours vary; 📶; 🚌AC Transit 12) Once a vaudeville theater and silent-movie house, this 1926 beauty near Lake Merritt lures you in with its huge corner marquee (which sometimes displays left-leaning political messages) and keeps you coming with a fun balcony and a Wurlitzer organ playing on weekends.

THE ALLEY
LIVE MUSIC

(☎510-444-8505; www.thealleyoakland.com; 3325 Grand Ave; ☺5pm-2am Tue-Sat, from 6pm Sun & Mon; 🚌AC Transit 12) There's live music every night of the week at this ramshackle locals' favorite, which feels like a roadside juke joint plopped onto Grand Ave. The tunes are basically good-time piano and guitar stuff, and make for a nice backdrop to getting pleasantly sloshed.

THE RIC
LIVE PERFORMANCE

(Rockridge Improvement Club; ☎510-597-1940; www.facebook.com/thericbar; 5515 College Ave;

⊘9am-1am Mon-Thu, to 2am Fri-Sun; ⒷRock-ridge) The RIC straddles that line between a bar and a performance space; the beers are good and the bartenders are friendly, but for us, the big draw is a fantastically unique slate of shows, from drag shows to cabaret to Magic Mike nights to random art classes (why not?). Attracts a 30- to 40-something crowd still looking to party.

 SHOPPING

★**DARK CARNIVAL** BOOKS
(☑510-654-7323; www.darkcarnival.com; 3086 Claremont Ave; ⊘10:30am-7pm Mon-Sat, noon-6pm Sun; ⊒AC Transit 51B, 605, 851) Rumor has it this is the oldest science-fiction, fantasy and horror bookstore in the country. Whether true or not, those who love this sort of genre of literature will enter this explosion of books and experience a spontaneous combustion of happiness. We gotta stress: it's all controlled chaos, but half the joy is losing yourself in the stacks.

★**ZENTNER COLLECTION** ANTIQUES
(☑510-653-5181; www.zentnercollection.com; 5757 Horton St, Emeryville; ⊘11am-5pm Wed-Sat; ⊒AC Transit 36, C, F) The Zenter has been called the Bay Area's 'other Asian art museum,' and while that designation is tongue in cheek, it's not entirely inaccurate either. You'll see what we mean if you peruse this vast collection of Asian antiquities, ranging from scroll paintings to full suits of samurai armor to mind-boggling galleries of gorgeous furniture.

★**OAKLANDISH** GIFTS & SOUVENIRS
(☑510-251-9500; www.oaklandish.com; 1444 Broadway; ⊘11am-7pm Mon-Fri, 10am-7pm Sat, to 6pm Sun) Urban fashions for anyone who 'hella' loves Oaktown are sold downtown at this signature shop. T-shirts, hats and stickers make a statement with original graphics depicting the Port of Oakland cranes, BART lines and other East Bay icons.

STRANDED MUSIC
(☑510-808-5505; www.strandedrecords.com; 14 Glen Ave; ⊘noon-7pm; ⊒AC Transit C) Stranded is the kind of cool record store you wished you had worked at when you were younger (or maybe now). It only carries vinyl, and offers a thoughtfully curated selection and showcasing of labels you may not know, but should:

Pinkflag, Kranky, Black Truffle and others. Plenty of cool books and band merch too.

WALDEN POND BOOKS BOOKS
(☑510-832-4438; www.waldenpondbooks.com; 3316 Grand Ave; ⊘10am-9pm Sun-Thu, to 10pm Fri & Sat) This excellent independent bookstore is a community fixture with a well curated selection of literature and nonfiction that reflects Oakland's lefty political leanings.

AFIKOMEN JUDAICA GIFTS & SOUVENIRS
(☑510-655-1977; www.afikomen.com; 3042 Claremont Ave; ⊘11am-6pm Mon-Wed, to 8pm Thu, 10am-2pm Fri, 11am-5pm Sun; ⊒AC Transit 51B) This store boasts one of the most voluminous collections of Jewish gifts, souvenirs and general *tchotckes* (trinkets) anywhere. Need something religious, like a *shofar* (ram's horn)? They got you. Home decor inspired by the Jewish diaspora? Check. Kosher craft beer? Oh yeah.

SWEET DREAMS TOYS
(☑toy store 510-548-8697; http://stores.sweetdreamscandyandtoys.com; 2921 College Ave; ⊘10am-6pm Mon-Sat, 11am-5:30pm Sun; ⊒AC Transit 80) If you've got kids and don't take them to Sweet Dreams, they may never forgive you. This independent toy store has a great range of well-curated goodness, from costumes to stuffed animals to board games.

Muir Woods to Stinson Beach

························

Explore

Walking through an awe-inspiring stand of the world's tallest trees is an experience to be had only in Northern California and a small part of southern Oregon. The old-growth redwoods at Muir Woods, just 12 miles north of the Golden Gate Bridge, make up the closest redwood stand to San Francisco; more grandiose redwood forests are found further north in Mendocino and Humboldt counties. The trees were initially eyed by loggers, and Redwood Creek, as the area was known, seemed ideal for a dam. Those plans were halted when congressman and naturalist William Kent bought a section of Redwood Creek and, in 1907, donated 295

BEST MARIN COUNTY HIKES

Hiking is a main draw of Marin County with its bay and Pacific coastline, the magnificent lakes and forests of Mt Tamalpais and the surrounding foothills. You can't go wrong taking a walk anywhere in the county, but these are our favorite outdoor jaunts:

Alamere Falls (www.nps.gov/pore/planyourvisit/alamere_falls.htm) This 8.4-mile round-trip hike leads to a 40ft cascade that tumbles to the beach. Busy and steep in parts but worth it.

Cataract Falls & Alpine Lake A 3.3-mile out-and-back hike leading upriver past a series of falls from Alpine Lake, a large wooded reservoir.

Angel Island (p217) Walk the relatively flat island perimeter (5.5 miles) to the 788ft peak of Mt Livermore or to a few uncrowded beaches.

Dipsea Trail (www.dipsea.org) An ambitious 7-mile trail that runs from Mill Valley to Stinson Beach over Mt Tam through serene forests to Pacific Ocean vistas.

Point Bonita Lighthouse (p213) It's only 1 mile round-trip but this hike will give you a long-spanning view of the Golden Gate Bridge and San Francisco out to the Pacific.

acres to the federal government. President Theodore Roosevelt made the site a national monument in 1908, the name honoring John Muir, naturalist and founder of environmental organization the Sierra Club.

The Best...
Sight Cathedral Grove

Hike Dipsea Trail

Place to Eat The Siren Canteen (p212)

Top Tip
To beat the crowds, come early in the day, before sunset or midweek; otherwise the parking lots fill up. Consider riding the seasonal shuttle bus to Muir Woods.

Getting There & Away
Car Drive north on Hwy 101, exit at Hwy 1 and continue north along Hwy 1/Shoreline Hwy to the Panoramic Hwy (a right-hand fork). Follow that for about 1 mile to Four Corners, where you turn left onto Muir Woods Rd (there are plenty of signs).

Shuttle During busy periods (most weekends and during summer), you'll be required to take a shuttle to/from Sausalito. The Muir Woods Shuttle leaves from Sausalito, where the ferries from San Francisco arrive.

Ferry & Bus West Marin Stagecoach route 61 runs a few daily minibuses ($2) from Marin City (one hour), with more frequent weekend and holiday services connecting with Sausalito ferries (75 minutes).

Need to Know
Area Code ☎415

Location 12 miles northwest of SF

 SIGHTS

★MUIR WOODS
NATIONAL MONUMENT   FOREST
(☎415-561-2850; www.nps.gov/muwo; 1 Muir Woods Rd, Mill Valley; adult/child $15/free; ⊗8am-8pm mid-Mar–mid-Sep, to 7pm mid-Sep–early Oct, to 6pm Feb–mid-Mar & early Oct–early Nov, to 5pm early Nov-Jan; P) ✐ Wander among an ancient stand of the world's tallest trees in 550-acre Muir Woods. The shortest option, the 1-mile Main Trail Loop, is a gentle walk alongside Redwood Creek to the 1000-year-old trees at **Cathedral Grove**; it returns via Bohemian Grove, where the tallest tree in the park stands 258ft high. It's a good 2-mile hike up to the top of the aptly named Cardiac Hill to reach the **Dipsea Trail**.

STINSON BEACH   BEACH
(☎415-868-0942; www.nps.gov/goga/stbe.htm; off Hwy 1; ⊗from 9am daily, closing time varies seasonally; P) Stinson Beach (3 miles long) is a popular surf spot, with swimming advised from late May to mid-September only. For updated weather and surf conditions call ☎415-868-1922.

MUIR BEACH   BEACH
(www.nps.gov/goga/planyourvisit/muirbeach.htm; off Pacific Way; P) ✐ The turnoff from

HIKING & BIKING MT TAM

Standing guard over Marin County, majestic Mt Tamalpais (Mt Tam) holds more than 200 miles of hiking and biking trails, lakes, streams, waterfalls and an impressive array of wildlife – from plentiful newts and hawks to rare foxes and mountain lions. Wind your way through meadows, oaks and madrone trees to breathtaking vistas over the San Francisco Bay, Pacific Ocean, towns, cities and forested hills rolling into the distance. This serene 2572ft mountain is still a bit of a secret and is the pride, love and *raison d'être* for many Marin County residents.

One of the best hikes on the mountain is the **Steep Ravine Trail**. From **Pantoll Station** (☑415-388-2070; www.parks.ca.gov; 801 Panoramic Hwy; ⊘hours vary; 🛜), it follows a wooded creek on to the coast (about 2.1 miles each way). For a longer hike, veer right (northwest) after 1.5 miles onto the Dipsea Trail (p211), which meanders through trees for 1 mile before ending at Stinson Beach (p211). Grab some lunch, then walk north through town and follow signs for the **Matt Davis Trail**, which leads 2.7 miles back to Pantoll Station, making a good loop. Other top picks include the woodsy and watery 6-mile round-trip Cataract Falls & Alpine Lake (p211) hike and a 2.5 mile ramble with the best views of the Bay Area at the **East Peak**.

Cyclists must stay on the fire roads (and off the single-track trails) and keep to speeds under 15mph. The most popular ride is the **Old Railroad Grade** from Mill Valley to Mt Tam's East Peak. Alternatively, from just west of Pantoll Station, cyclists can take either the **Deer Park Fire Road** – which runs close to the Dipsea Trail (p211) through giant redwoods to the main entrance of Muir Woods (p211) – or the aptly named **Coast View Trail**, which joins Hwy 1 north of **Muir Beach Overlook** (www.nps. gov/goga/planyourvisit/muirbeach.htm; Shoreline Hwy; 🅿). Both options require a return to Mill Valley via Frank Valley/Muir Woods Rd, which climbs steadily (800ft) to Panoramic Hwy, then becomes Sequoia Valley Rd as it drops toward Mill Valley.

Hwy 1 is next to the coast's longest row of mailboxes at Mile 5.7, just before Pelican Inn. Aside from the beach, there are wetlands, creeks, lagoons and sand dunes providing a habitat for birds, California red-legged frogs and coho salmon. In winter you might spot monarch butterflies roosting in Monterey pines, and migratory whales offshore.

✕ EATING & DRINKING

★ THE SIREN CANTEEN AMERICAN $

(☑415-868-1777; www.thesirencanteen.com; 3201 Hwy 1, Stinson Beach; mains around $10; ⊘11am-7pm Fri-Sat & Mon, to 6pm Sun; 🚼) This beach-chic canteen with bench seating sits just under the lifeguard tower. Order quality, fresh tacos, nachos, fish and chips, crepes and burgers to eat here or take out to your towel near the surf.

PARKSIDE CAFE $$

(☑415-868-1272; www.parksidecafe.com; 43 Arenal Ave, Stinson Beach; restaurant mains $16-30, snack bar $4-9; ⊘7:30am-9pm, coffee bar from 6am; 🍴🚼) Famous for its hearty breakfasts and lunches, this cozy eatery next to the beach serves wood-fired pizzas and excellent coastal cuisine such as Tomales Bay oysters and king salmon at dinner, when reservations are recommended.

Very popular with families, beachgoers, hikers and cyclists, Parkside's outdoor snack bar serves burgers, sandwiches, smoothies, baked goods and ice cream. Expect a queue.

SAND DOLLAR AMERICAN $$

(☑415-868-0434; www.stinsonbeachrestaurant. com; 3458 Hwy 1, Stinson Beach; mains $14-28; ⊘11:30am-9pm Fri-Mon, 3-9pm Tue-Thu) Stinson Beach's oldest establishment isn't on the beach but there's a great outdoor patio, local vibe, live jazz every night of the week and live bluegrass during the day on weekends. The food is good enough and includes tacos, burgers, salads and local oysters.

PELICAN INN PUB FOOD $$$

(☑415-383-6000; www.pelicaninn.com; 10 Pacific Way, Muir Beach; dinner mains $18-36; ⊘8-11am Sat & Sun, 11:30am-3pm & 5:30-9pm daily; 🚼) The oh-so-English Pelican Inn lures in visitors almost as much as the beach itself. Hikers, cyclists and families come for pub lunches inside its dark, timbered restaurant and cozy bar, perfect for a pint, and bangers and mash. Enjoy the lawn in sunshine or warm up beside the open fire when it's colder.

Sausalito & Tiburon

Explore

Perfectly arranged on a secure little harbor on the bay, Sausalito is undeniably lovely. Named for the tiny willows that once populated the banks of its creeks, it's famous for its colorful houseboats bobbing in the bay. Much of the well-heeled downtown has uninterrupted views of San Francisco and Angel Island; and, due to the ridgeline at its back, fog generally skips it. It's the first town you encounter after crossing the Golden Gate Bridge from San Francisco, so daytime crowds turn up in droves and make parking difficult. Ferrying over from San Francisco makes for a more relaxing excursion.

Opposite Sausalito, at the end of a small peninsula, Tiburon is blessed with gorgeous views. The name comes from its original Spanish title, Punta de Tiburon (Shark Point). Take the ferry from San Francisco, browse the shops on Main St, grab a bite to eat and you've seen downtown Tiburon.

The Best...

Sight Sausalito Houseboats (p215)

Place to Eat Avatar's (p217)

Activity Sea Trek (p218)

Top Tip

Walking or cycling across the Golden Gate Bridge (p58) to Sausalito is a fun way to avoid traffic, enjoy some great ocean views and

---

MARIN HEADLANDS

The headland cliffs and hillsides rise majestically at the north end of the Golden Gate Bridge, their rugged beauty all the more striking given the fact that they're only a few miles from San Francisco's urban core. A few forts and bunkers are left over from a century of US military occupation – which is, ironically, the reason the headlands are today protected parklands, free of development. It's no mystery why this is one of the Bay Area's most popular hiking and cycling destinations: as the trails wind through the headlands, they afford stunning views of the sea, the Golden Gate Bridge and San Francisco and lead to isolated beaches and secluded picnic spots.

This historical **Point Bonita Lighthouse** (🖉415-331-1540; www.nps.gov/goga/pobo.htm; ☺12:30-3:30pm Sat-Mon; Ⓟ) **FREE** is a breathtaking half-mile walk from Field Rd parking area. From the tip of Point Bonita, you can see the Golden Gate Bridge and the San Francisco skyline. Harbor seals haul out seasonally on nearby rocks. It's worth coming out here even when the lighthouse is closed (but note the whole area closes in bad weather).

For those who opt for an exhilarating bicycle ride across the Golden Gate Bridge, there's also a good 12-mile dirt loop. The **Coastal Trail** (www.nps.gov/goga/planyour visit/coastal-trail.htm) heads west from the fork of Conzelman and McCullough Rds, bumping and winding down to Bunker Rd where it meets **Bobcat Trail**, which joins **Marincello Trail** and descends steeply into the **Tennessee Valley** (www.nps.gov/ goga/planyourvisit/tennessee_valley.htm; ⛟) parking area. The **Old Springs Trail** and the **Miwok Trail** take you back to Bunker Rd a bit more gently than the Bobcat Trail, though any attempt to avoid at least a couple of hefty climbs is futile.

If you're driving to the headlands, take the Alexander Ave exit just after crossing north over the Golden Gate Bridge and dip left under the freeway. Conzelman Rd, to the right, takes you up along the bluffs; you can also take Bunker Rd, which leads to the headlands through a one-way tunnel. Arrive before 2pm on weekends to avoid traffic and parking congestion, or cycle over the bridge instead.

On Saturdays, Sundays and holidays, **Muni** (www.sfmta.com; fare $2.75) bus 76X runs every 60 to 90 minutes from San Francisco's Financial District to the **Marin Headlands Visitor Center** (www.nps.gov/goga/marin-headlands.htm; Bunker Rd, Fort Barry; ☺9:30am-4:30pm), **Rodeo Beach** (www.parksconservancy.org/visit/park-sites/rodeo-beach.html; off Bunker Rd; Ⓟ ⛟) and several other stops. Buses are equipped with bicycle racks.

Marin County

bask in that refreshing Marin County air. You can also simply hop on a ferry back to SF. The trip is about 4 miles from the south end of the bridge and takes less than an hour. Check the bridge website (www.goldengatebridge.org/bikesbridge/bikes.php) for updates.

Getting There & Away

Car Drive Hwy 101 north across the Golden Gate Bridge. For Sausalito, take the Alexander Ave exit; for Tiburon, exit at Tiburon Blvd/E Blithedale Ave/Hwy 131.

Ferry Golden Gate Ferry (p74) sails from San Francisco's Ferry Building to Sausal-ito ($12.50, 25 to 30 minutes) and Tibu-ron ($12.50, 30 minutes). **Blue & Gold Fleet** (☑415-705-8200; www.blueandgoldfleet.com) sails to Sausalito from Fisherman's Wharf ($12.50, 30 to 55 minutes) and to Tiburon from Pier 41 or 39 ($12.50, 30 to 50 minutes).

Bus From downtown San Francisco **Golden Gate Transit** (☑415-455-2000, 511; www.goldengatetransit.org) bus 30 runs hourly to Sausalito ($6.50, 40 to 55 minutes). Commuter bus 8 runs direct between San Francisco and Tiburon ($6.50, 60 to 80 minutes) once or twice on weekdays. On weekends and holidays, **West Marin Stagecoach**

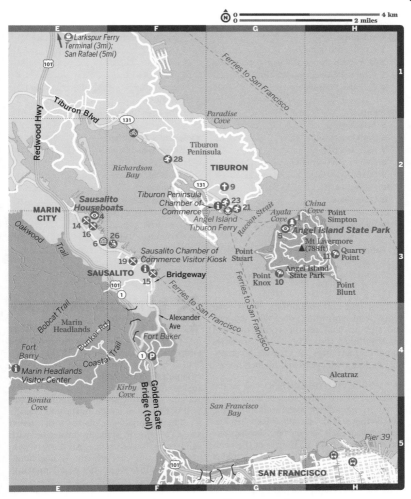

(📞415-226-0825; www.marintransit.org/stage.html) route 61 ($2) extends to Sausalito.

Need to Know

Area Code 📞415

Location Sausalito is 5 miles north of San Francisco; Tiburon is 12 miles northeast.

Sausalito Chamber of Commerce Visitor Kiosk (📞415-331-1093; www.sausalito.org; foot of El Portal St; ⏰10am-4pm)

Tiburon Peninsula Chamber of Commerce (📞415-435-5633; www.tiburonchamber.org; 96b Main St; ⏰hours vary)

◉ SIGHTS

★**SAUSALITO HOUSEBOATS**   ARCHITECTURE

(Richardson Bay) Bohemia still thrives along the shoreline of Richardson Bay, where free spirits inhabit hundreds of quirky homes that bob in the waves among the seabirds and seals. Structures range from psychedelic mural-splashed castles to dilapidated salt-sprayed shacks and immaculate three-story floating mansions. You can poke around the houseboat docks located off Bridgeway Blvd between Gate 5 and Gate 6½ Rds.

Marin County

It's a tight-knit community, where residents tend sprawling dockside gardens and stop to chat on the creaky wooden boardwalks as they wheel their groceries home. Etiquette tips for visitors: no smoking, no pets, no bicycles and no loud noise.

BAY MODEL VISITOR CENTER MUSEUM
(☑415-332-3871; www.spn.usace.army.mil/mis sions/recreation/baymodelvisitorcenter.aspx; 2100 Bridgeway Blvd, Sausalito; ◷9am-4pm Tue-Fri, 10am-5pm Sat & Sun summer, 9am-4pm Tue-Sat rest of year; Ⓟ⚿) FREE One of the coolest things in town, fascinating to both kids and adults, is the Army Corps of Engineers' solar-powered visitor center. Housed in one of the old (and cold!) Marinship warehouses, it's a 1.5-acre hydraulic model of San Francisco Bay and the delta region.

OLD ST HILARY'S CHURCH
(☑415-435-1853; http://landmarkssociety.com/ landmarks/st-hilarys; 201 Esperanza St, Tiburon; ◷1-4pm Sun Apr-Oct) This fine 19th-century example of Carpenter Gothic architectural style can be seen from almost anywhere in Tiburon. Hiking trails lead from above it onto Old St Hilary's Open Space Reserve where there are tons of wildflowers in spring (many endemic to the area) and incredible views of the bay year-round.

✕ EATING & DRINKING

★AVATAR'S INDIAN $$
(☑415-332-8083; www.enjoyavatars.com; 2656 Bridgeway Blvd, Sausalito; mains $13-19; ◷11am-3pm & 5-9:30pm Mon-Sat; ✈) Boasting a cuisine of 'ethnic confusions,' the Indian-fusion dishes here incorporate Mexican, Italian and Caribbean ingredients and will bowl you over with flavor and creativity. Think Punjabi enchiladas with curried sweet potato or spinach fettuccine with mild-curry tomato sauce. All diets (vegan, gluten-free etc) are graciously accommodated. It sounds weird, but it's all amazing.

FISH SEAFOOD $$
(☑415-331-3474; www.331fish.com; 350 Harbor Dr, Sausalito; mains $17-36; ◷11:30am-8:30pm) ∅ Chow down on seafood sandwiches, BBQ oysters or a Dungeness-crab roll at redwood picnic tables facing Richardson Bay. A local leader in promoting fresh and sustainably caught fish, this place has wonderful wild salmon in season and refuses to serve the farmed stuff. It's *really* pricey, but so worth it. Cash only. Expect a queue.

BARREL HOUSE TAVERN CALIFORNIAN $$
(☑415-729-9593; www.barrelhousetavern.com; 660 Bridgeway Blvd, Sausalito; shared dishes $4-18, mains $16-36; ◷11:30am-9pm Mon-Fri, 11am-9pm

Sat & Sun) You can practically dangle your legs out over the water on the sunny back deck, which has spectacular bay views. It's a short dash from the ferry terminal, and the California wine, craft beer and cocktail lists complement a raw bar, hot flatbreads and charcuterie and cheese platters.

COPITA TEQUILERIA Y COMIDA   MEXICAN **$$**
(✆415-331-7400; www.copitarestaurant.com; 739 Bridgeway Blvd, Sausalito; mains $12-19; ⊙11:30am-9:30pm Sun-Thu, to 10:30pm Fri & Sat) Upscale fresh Mexican with a Mediterranean twist is served in bright, modern, lively surrounds. The ceviches and slow-cooked meats are especially yummy. You could also turn up for a tasting flight of tequilas or mezcals ($22 to $42) or one of Copita's outrageous margaritas. Everything is gluten-free.

SUSHI RAN   JAPANESE **$$$**
(✆415-332-3620; www.sushiran.com; 107 Caledonia St, Sausalito; shared dishes $5-38; ⊙11:45am-2:45pm Mon-Fri, 5-10pm Sun-Thu, 5-11pm Fri & Sat) Many Marin residents claim this place is the best sushi spot around and it's hard to argue. If you didn't reserve ahead, the wine and sake bar next door eases the pain of the long wait for a table.

ACTIVITIES

SEA TREK   KAYAKING
(✆415-332-8494; www.seatrek.com; 2100 Bridgeway, Sausalito; kayak or SUP rental per hour from $25, tours from $75; ⊙9am-5pm Mon-Fri & 8:30am-5pm Sat & Sun Apr-Oct, 9am-4pm daily Nov-Mar)

ANGEL ISLAND

One of the most under-visited destinations in San Francisco Bay, **Angel Island State Park** (✆415-435-5390; www.parks.ca.gov/AngelIsland; ♿) `FREE` has beaches, hiking and biking trails with some of the best views in the region. On a sunny day, you can picnic in a protected cove looking out at the seemingly close yet distant urban grid.

Beaches
Quarry Beach is the island's best stretch of sand, a long white protected stretch backed by beautiful hills and fronted with a view of the East Bay. Adventurous folks can try and find, then navigate, the unmaintained trail that leads to beautiful – but often rough and windy – **Perles Beach**, which looks out to Alcatraz Island, the Golden Gate Bridge and San Francisco. If you just want a quick dip, the beach at **Ayala Cove** is a bit small and mucky but works in a pinch. There's a nice picnic area behind it and the views through the cove to Tiburon look like the Mediterranean.

Biking
Angel Island's 6-mile **Perimeter Trail** is perfect for biking; it gives a 360-degree view of the bay and is easy enough for kids. Most non-paved trails on the island are off-limits to bikes so you don't need a mountain bike. Bicycle rentals on the island with the **Angel Island Company** (✆415-435-3392; www.angelisland.com; tram tour adult/child $16.50/10.50, bike rental incl helmet per hour/day $15/60, ebikes $25/90; ⊙varies seasonally) are convenient but pricey. If you don't have your own bike it can be cheaper to rent one on the mainland and bring it over on the ferry.

Hiking
You'll find maps at the visitor center and on panels in Ayala Cove and along the Perimeter Rd. Many of the trails link up so you can mix and match. Top trails include **North Ridge & Sunset Trail,** a 4.8-mile loop trail that leads around the upper part of the island for views over the entire bay; **Mt Livermore** (788ft), which gets you to the top of the island with a 4.6-mile round-trip hike from the ferry dock; and **Perimeter Trail,** which is under 6 miles long and follows the paved road all the way around the island.

Getting There & Away
All ferry tickets are sold on a first-come, first-served basis. From San Francisco's Pier 41, take a Blue & Gold Fleet (p214) ferry (one way adult/child $9.75/5.50). From Tiburon, take the **Angel Island Tiburon Ferry** (✆415-435-2131; http://angelislandferry.com; 21 Main St; round-trip adult/child/bicycle $15/13/1).

On a sunny day, Richardson Bay is irresistible. Kayaks and stand up paddleboard (SUP) sets can be rented here. No experience is necessary; lessons and group outings are also available. Guided kayaking excursions include full-moon and starlight tours and an adventurous crossing to Angel Island. May through October is the best time to paddle.

BAY CRUISES   CRUISE

(☑415-435-2131; http://angelislandferry.com; 21 Main St, Tiburon; 90-minute cruise adult/child $30/15; ⊗usually 6:30-8pm Fri & Sat mid-May–mid-Oct) The Angel Island Tiburon Ferry (p217) runs San Francisco Bay sunset cruises on weekend evenings in summer and fall. Reserve ahead and bring your own picnic dinner to enjoy outside on the deck.

TIBURON BIKE PATH   CYCLING

This paved trail runs for 2.6 miles, mostly along outrageously scenic Richardson's Bay with views of Mt Tamalpais and the Golden Gate Bridge. It runs from downtown Tiburon to Blackie's Pasture where there's a big parking lot and a statue of Blackie, the swaybacked horse who lived in the field here for 28 years.

Bring your own bike or rent one at **Demosport** (☑415-435-5111; www.demosport.com; 1690 Tiburon Blvd, Tiburon; bicycle rentals 2/24hr $30/50; ⊗10am-6pm Fri-Sun, usually Mar-Nov).

Napa Valley

Explore

Napa Valley is exactly what you expect when you think of Wine Country: hillside chateau wineries, bold cabernets, vast expanses of perfectly ordered grape vines, grassy slopes speckled by the tungsten sun, restaurant dinners that go on for hours, and some of the finest and most luxurious small-scale boutique hotels anywhere in California.

Beyond the typical, Napa has some great hiking in the hillsides, exhilarating mud baths up north in the more working-class town of Calistoga, and plenty of small shops, wineries and classy bistros in the tony village settings of St Helena and Yountville.

Most journeys here start and end in the city of Napa proper. In the town center there are tasting rooms, live jazz and plenty of fine-dining options, plus the option to party late into the night at down-home pubs and eateries that draw a young local crowd.

The Best...

Sight di Rosa

Place to Eat Oxbow Public Market (p221)

Place to Drink Hess Collection

Top Tip

Most vineyard wine-tasting rooms open daily 10am or 11am to 4pm or 5pm, but call ahead for appointments, especially in Napa. Fees for wine tasting range from $10 to $50, and you must be 21 to taste.

Getting There & Away

Car From San Francisco, take Hwy 101 north over the Golden Gate Bridge, then Hwy 37 east to Hwy 121 north; continue to the junction of Hwy 12/121 and take that east. Plan 70 minutes in light traffic, two hours during the weekday commute.

Ferry Baylink Ferry (☑877-643-3779; www.sanfranciscobayferry.com) Downtown ferry from San Francisco to Vallejo (adult/child $14.60/7.30, 60 minutes); connect with Napa Valley Vine bus 29 (weekdays) or bus 11 (daily).

Train & Bus Amtrak (☑800-872-7245; www.amtrak.com) trains travel to Martinez (south of Vallejo), with connecting buses to Napa (45 minutes). From San Francisco, **BART Trains** (☑415-989-2278; www.bart.gov) connecting to Richmond station can deliver you to Amtrak. BART also runs from San Francisco to El Cerrito del Norte ($4.45, 30 minutes). **Napa Valley Vine** (☑707-251-2800, 800-696-6443; www.ridethevine.com; Napa) bus 29 runs weekdays from that same BART stop to Calistoga, via Napa ($5.50); on Saturdays take **SolTrans** (☑707-648-4666; www.soltransride.com) from BART to Vallejo ($5, 30 minutes), then connect with Napa Valley Vine bus 11 to Napa and Calistoga ($1.60); on Sundays, there's no connecting bus service from BART.

Need to Know

Area Code ☑707

Location 50 miles northeast of San Francisco

Napa Valley Welcome Center (☑707-251-5895, 855-847-6272; www.visitnapavalley.com; 600 Main St; ⊗9am-5pm; ⊕)

WORTH A DETOUR

POINT REYES

Windswept Point Reyes peninsula is a rough-hewn beauty that has always lured marine mammals and migratory birds; it's also home to scores of shipwrecks. **Point Reyes National Seashore** (📞415-654-5100; www.nps.gov/pore; P 🚻) 🅿 FREE protects 110 sq miles of pristine ocean beaches and coastal wilderness and has excellent hiking and camping opportunities. The point's edge-of-the-world **lighthouse** (📞415-669-1534; www.nps.gov/pore; end of Sir Francis Drake Blvd; ⏰10am-4:30pm Fri-Mon, lens room 2:30-4pm Fri-Mon; P) FREE offers the best whale-watching along the coast. Be sure to bring warm clothing, as even the sunniest days can quickly turn cold and foggy.

Before setting out for a hike or a paddle, stop through Point Reyes Station, the hub of western Marin County. Dominated by dairies and ranches, the region was invaded by artists in the 1960s. Today Main St is a diverting blend of art galleries, tourist shops, restaurants and cafes. The town has a rowdy saloon and the occasional smell of cattle on the afternoon breeze.

You can get to Point Reyes by car a few different ways. The curviest is along Hwy 1, through Stinson Beach and Olema. More direct is to exit Hwy 101 in San Rafael and follow Sir Francis Drake Blvd all the way to the tip of Point Reyes. By either route, it's less than 1½ hours to Olema from San Francisco barring weekend and rush-hour traffic jams. Just north of Olema, where Hwy 1 and Sir Francis Drake Blvd come together, is Bear Valley Rd; turn left to reach **Bear Valley Visitor Center** (📞415-464-5100; www.nps.gov/pore; 1 Bear Valley Rd, Point Reyes Station; ⏰10am-5pm Mon-Fri, 9am-5pm Sat & Sun). If you're heading to the outermost reaches of Point Reyes, follow Sir Francis Drake Blvd north toward Point Reyes Station, turning left and heading out onto the peninsula.

West Marin Stagecoach (p214) route 68 from San Rafael stops several times daily at the Bear Valley Visitor Center ($2, 70 minutes) before continuing to the town of Point Reyes Station.

🅾 SIGHTS

⭐DI ROSA ARTS CENTER
(📞707-226-5991; www.dirosaart.org; 5200 Hwy 121, Napa; admission incl tour $18; ⏰10am-4pm Wed-Sun; P) West of downtown, scrap-metal sculptures dot Carneros vineyards at the 217-acre di Rosa Art and Nature Preserve, a stunning collection of Northern California art, displayed indoors in galleries and outdoors in gardens by a giant lake. Reservations recommended for tours.

⭐HESS COLLECTION WINERY, GALLERY
(📞707-255-1144; www.hesscollection.com; 4411 Redwood Rd, Napa; museum & tours free, tasting $25-35; ⏰10am-5pm, last tasting 5pm) 🅿 Art-lovers: don't miss Hess Collection, whose galleries display mixed-media and large-canvas works, including pieces by Francis Bacon and Robert Motherwell. In the elegant stone-walled tasting room, find well-known cabernet sauvignon and chardonnay, but also try the Viognier. There's garden service in the warmer months, which is lovely, as Hess overlooks the valley. Make reservations and be prepared to drive a winding road. Bottles are $30 to $100.

⭐FROG'S LEAP WINERY
(📞707-963-4704; www.frogsleap.com; 8815 Conn Creek Rd, Rutherford; tasting incl tour $25-35; ⏰10am-4pm by appointment only; P 🚻🐾) 🅿 Meandering paths wind through magical gardens and fruit-bearing orchards surrounding an 1884 barn and farmstead with cats and chickens. The vibe is casual and down-to-earth, with a major emphasis on *fun*. Sauvignon blanc is its best-known wine but the merlot merits attention. There's also a dry, restrained cabernet, atypical of Napa.

⭐ROBERT SINSKEY VINEYARDS WINERY
(📞707-944-9090; www.robertsinskey.com; 6320 Silverado Trail, Napa; bar tasting $40, seated food & wine pairings $70-175; ⏰10am-4:30pm; P) 🅿 The fabulous hillside tasting room, constructed of stone, redwood and teak, resembles a small cathedral – fitting, given the sacred status here bestowed upon food and wine. It specializes in bright-acid organic pinot noir, plus exceptional aromatic white varietals, dry rosé and Bordeaux varietals such as merlot and cab franc, all crafted for the dinner table. Small bites accompany bar tastings, and seated food and wine experiences are curated by chef Maria Sinskey

Wine Country

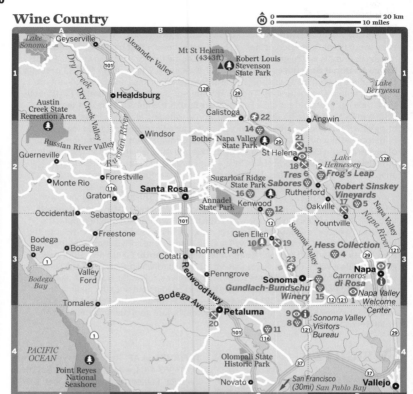

herself. Reserve ahead for sit-down tastings and culinary tours.

★ **TRES SABORES** WINERY
(☎707-967-8027; www.tressabores.com; 1620 Sth Whitehall Lane, St Helena; tour & tasting $40; ◷10:30am-3pm, by appointment; 🖼) 🏷 At the valley's westernmost edge, where sloping vineyards meet wooded hillsides, Tres Sabores is a portal to old Napa – no fancy tasting room, no snobbery, just great wine in a spectacular setting. Bucking the cabernet custom, Tres Sabores crafts elegantly structured, Burgundian-style zinfandel and spritely sauvignon blanc, which the *New York Times* dubbed a top 10 of its kind in California. Reservations are essential.

SCHRAMSBERG WINERY
(☎800-877-3623, 707-942-4558; www.schrams berg.com; 1400 Schramsberg Rd, Calistoga; tour & tasting $70, tour & sparkling-wine tasting $95, reserve wine & cheese pairing $125; ◷by appoint-

ment at 9:30am, 10am, 11:30am, noon, 1:30pm, & 2:30pm) Napa's second-oldest winery, Schramsberg makes some of California's best brut sparkling wines, and in 1972 was the first domestic wine served at the White House. Blanc de blancs is the signature. The appointment-only tasting and tour (book well ahead) is expensive, but you'll sample all the *tête de cuvées* (best of each vintage), not just the low-end wines. Tours include a walk through the caves; bring a sweater. Bottles cost $24 to $150.

LONG MEADOW RANCH FARM
(☎707-963-4555; www.longmeadowranch.com; 738 Main St, St Helena; tasting $10-25, chef's table $170; ◷11am-6pm) 🏷 Long Meadow stands out for olive-oil tastings ($10), plus good estate-grown cabernet, sauvignon blanc, chardonnay and pinot noir, served inside an 1874 farmhouse surrounded by lovely gardens. It also has a whiskey flight for $30; sells housemade products such as pre-

Wine Country

serves, BBQ sauce and Bloody Mary mix; and hosts chef's tables (four- to five-course food-and-wine experiences) at lunch and dinner daily. Reservations for chef's table required. Bottles $20 to $50.

CIA AT COPIA   CENTER
(Culinary Institute of America; ☑707-967-2500; www.ciaatcopia.com; 500 1st St; ☺10:30am-9pm) The former food museum beside Napa's famous Oxbow Public Market has been revived as a center of all things edible by the prestigious Culinary Institute of America. In its new life as Copia, the 80,000-sq-ft campus offers wine tastings, interactive cooking demos, an innovative restaurant, a massive fork statue (composed of many thousands of smaller forks) and more food-related features.

✖ EATING

★ OXBOW PUBLIC MARKET   MARKET **$**
(☑707-226-6529; www.oxbowpublicmarket.com; 610 & 644 1st St, Napa; items from $3; ☺7:30am-9:30pm; ⚟🅿) 🍴 Graze at this gourmet market and plug into the Northern California food scene. Standouts: **Hog Island Oyster Co**; comfort cooking at celeb-chef Todd Humphries' **Kitchen Door**; great Cal-Mexican tacos at **C Casa & Taco Lounge**; the India pale ales (IPAs) and sour beers

at **Fieldwork Brewing Company**; espresso from **Ritual Coffee**; and **Three Twins** certified-organic ice cream.

BOUCHON BAKERY   BAKERY **$**
(☑707-944-2253; www.bouchonbakery.com; 6528 Washington St, Yountville; items from $3; ☺7am-7pm Mon-Fri, 6:30am-7pm Sat-Sun; 🅿) Bouchon makes as-good-as-in-Paris French pastries and strong coffee. There's always a line and rarely a seat: get it to go.

FARMSTEAD   MODERN AMERICAN **$$**
(☑707-963-4555; www.longmeadowranch.com; 738 Main St, St Helena; mains $19-33; ☺11:30am-9:30pm Mon-Thu, to 10pm Fri & Sat, 11am-9:30pm Sun; 🅿) 🍴 An enormous open-truss barn with leather booths and rocking-chair porch, Farmstead draws an all-ages crowd and farms many of its own ingredients – including grass-fed beef and lamb – for an earthy menu highlighting wood-fired cooking.

★ FRENCH LAUNDRY   CALIFORNIAN **$$$**
(☑707-944-2380; www.thomaskeller.com/tfl; 6640 Washington St, Yountville; prix-fixe dinner from $325; ☺seatings 11am-12:30pm Fri-Sun, 5-9pm daily) The pinnacle of California dining, Thomas Keller's three-Michelin-star rated French Laundry is epic, a high-wattage culinary experience on par with the world's best. Book one month ahead on the online app Tock, where tickets are

WINE COUNTRY WITHOUT A CAR

Beyond the Label (☎707-363-4023; www.btlnv.com; per couple from $995; �︎11am-4pm) Personalized tours, including lunch at home with a vintner, guided by a knowledgeable Napa native.

Napa Valley Vine Trail (☎707-252-3547; www.vinetrail.org) This multiuse trail in Napa Valley connects vineyards, wineries, downtown Napa and Yountville via 12.5 miles of walking and cycling paths. The trail is just a piece of an ambitious 47-mile stretch that will eventually connect the Vallejo Ferry Terminal to Calistoga.

Active Wine Adventures (☎707-927-1058; www.activewineadventures.com; per person $125) This innovative tour company in Napa Valley pairs wine and food with scenic hikes, local art, literary adventures and, most recently, microbreweries.

Napa Valley Wine Train (☎707-253-2111, 800-427-4124; www.winetrain.com; 1275 McKinstry St; ticket incl dining from $146) A cushy, if touristy, way to see Wine Country, the Wine Train offers three-hour daily trips in vintage Pullman dining cars, from Napa to St Helena and back, with optional winery tours. It also offers six-hour journeys visiting multiple wineries with Napa Valley cuisine served between visits.

Platypus Wine Tours (☎707-253-2723; www.platypustours.com; join-in tour per person $110) Billed as the anti-wine-snob tour, Platypus specializes in backroad vineyards, historic wineries and family-owned operations. There's a daily 'join-in' tour that shuttles guests to four wineries and provides a picnic lunch, and private tours with a dedicated driver and vehicle.

released in groupings. This is the meal you can brag about the rest of your life.

★ RESTAURANT AT MEADOWOOD
CALIFORNIAN $$$

(☎707-967-1205; www.meadowood.com; 900 Meadowood Lane, St Helena; 12-course menu $275; �︎5:30-9:30pm Tue-Sat) If you couldn't score reservations at French Laundry, fear not: Meadowood – the valley's only other three-Michelin-star restaurant – has a slightly more sensibly priced menu, elegantly unfussy dining room and lavish haute cuisine that's not too esoteric.

CICCIO
ITALIAN $$$

(☎707-945-1000; www.ciccionapavalley.com; 6770 Washington St, Yountville; mains $25-32; �︎5-9pm Wed-Sun) The small, frequently changing menu at this family-owned Italian place is dependent on the season and likely to include just a couple of veggies, pastas, meat options and four to six wood-fired pizzas. But wow! You cannot go wrong, especially if you're lucky enough to show up when whole sea bass and garlicky pea tendrils are available.

LOVINA
CALIFORNIAN $$$

(☎707-942-6500; www.lovinacalistoga.com; 1107 Cedar St, Calistoga; mains lunch $12-18, dinner $20-36; �︎5:30pm-late Thu, 11:30am-3pm & 5:30pm-late Fri & Sat, 9:30am-3pm Sun) A sparsely decorated cottage surrounded by a white picket fence, Lovina is especially good for lunch. The menu changes frequently, featuring unique takes from around the world with special nods to Eastern flavors, plus a few tried and true California favorites like savory cioppino (fish stew). Thursdays have no corkage, so bring your own bottle.

🏃 ACTIVITIES

★ INDIAN SPRINGS SPA
SPA

(☎844-378-3635; www.indianspringscalistoga.com; 1712 Lincoln Ave, Calistoga; mud bath & massage $240; �︎by appointment 9am-7pm) California's longest continually operating spa, and original Calistoga resort, has concrete mud tubs and mines its own ash. Treatments include use of the huge, hot-spring-fed pool.

Sonoma Valley

Explore

Delightfully laid-back, unapologetic and fun-loving, the Sonoma Valley, or Valley of the Moon as it's sometimes called, is bordered to the east by the Mayacamas and to the west by the Sonoma Mountain Range. Here in the fertile valley wine makers ply their craft, foodies flock to amazing restaurants, and there are plenty of adventures to be had in the 13,000 acres of parkland.

Easily accessed from San Francisco, most journeys in the area start in the town of Sonoma itself, with its gorgeous town square, fun tasting rooms and excellent eateries.

Heading up valley, you pass through the tiny village of Glen Ellen, which has a handful of small eateries and access to the valley's best natural area at Jack London State Park and then on to the gorgeous wineries and roadside attractions of the Kenwood area.

The Best...
Sight Sonoma Plaza
Place to Eat Cafe La Haye (p225)
Place to Drink Gundlach-Bundschu Winery

Top Tip
If you're not up for driving, hit downtown Sonoma's tasting rooms around shady Sonoma Plaza, where it's legal to drink wine on the grass from 11am until dark.

Getting There & Away
Car From San Francisco, take Hwy 101 north over the Golden Gate Bridge, then Hwy 37 east to Hwy 121 north; continue to the junction of Hwy 12/121 and take it north. Sonoma Valley is a 90-minute drive from San Francisco.

Bus Golden Gate Transit (p268) has routes from San Francisco to Petaluma (adult/youth $11.75/5.75) and Santa Rosa (adult/youth $13/6.50); board at 1st and Mission Sts. Connects with Sonoma County Transit buses.

Train & Bus Amtrak trains travel to Martinez (south of Vallejo), with connecting buses to Santa Rosa (1¼ hours). From San Francisco, BART Trains connecting to Richmond station can deliver you to Amtrak.

Need to Know
Area Code ☑707
Location 45 miles north–northeast of San Francisco.
Sonoma Valley Visitors Bureau (☑707-996-1090; www.sonomavalley.com; 23,570 Hwy 121, Sonoma; ⊙10am-4pm)

⦿ SIGHTS

★**SONOMA PLAZA** SQUARE
(www.sonomaplaza.com; btwn Napa, Spain & 1st Sts) This is the largest plaza in California, and the veritable center for politics, love and community in the Sonoma Valley. Smack in the center of the plaza, the Mission Revival–style city hall, built 1906–08, has identical facades on four sides, reportedly because plaza businesses all demanded City Hall face their direction. The weekly farmers market (5:30pm to 8pm Tuesdays, April to October) showcases Sonoma's incredible produce.

★**GUNDLACH-BUNDSCHU WINERY** WINERY
(☑707-938-5277; www.gunbun.com; 2000 Denmark St, Sonoma; tasting $20-30, incl tour $30-60; ⊙11am-5:30pm Sun-Fri, to 7pm Sat Apr-Oct, to 4:30pm Nov-Mar; ℗) ⌀ California's oldest family-run winery looks like a castle but has a down-to-earth vibe. Founded in 1858 by a Bavarian immigrant, its signatures are gewürztraminer and pinot noir, but 'Gun-Bun' was the first American winery to produce 100% merlot. Down a winding lane, it's a terrific bike-to winery with picnicking, hiking, a lake and frequent concerts, including a two-day folk-music festival in June. Tour the 1800-barrel cave by reservation only. Bottles are $20 to $50.

ST FRANCIS WINERY & VINEYARDS WINERY
(☑707-538-9463; www.stfranciswinery.com; 100 Pythian Rd at Hwy 12, Santa Rosa; tasting $15, wine & cheese pairing $25, wine & food pairing $68; ⊙10am-5pm) The vineyards are scenic and all, but the real reason to visit St Francis is the much-lauded food-pairing experience. The mouthwatering, multicourse affair is hosted by amiable and informative wine experts and includes things such as braised Kurobuta pork with Okinawan sweet potatoes paired with cab franc, and American Wagyu strip loin and chanterelles paired with an old-vine zin. Seatings at 11am, 1pm and 3pm, Thursday to Monday. Spots fill fast; book well in advance.

BENZIGER WINERY
(☑707-935-3000, 888-490-2739; www.benziger. com; 1883 London Ranch Rd, Glen Ellen; tasting $20-50, tours $25-50; ⊙11am-5pm Mon-Fri, 10am-5pm Sat & Sun; ℗ ⌀ If you're new to wine, make Benziger your first stop for Sonoma's best crash course in winemaking. The worthwhile tour (reserve ahead)

WORTH A DETOUR

SOUTH OF SAN FRANCISCO: HIGHWAY 1 HIGHLIGHTS

Pacifica The lazy beach town of Pacifica, just 15 miles from downtown San Francisco, signals the end of the city's urban sprawl and the start of wild Pacific coastline. Immediately south of Pacifica is the Devil's Slide, a gorgeous coastal cliff area with a good **hiking trail** (☑650-355-8289; http://parks.smcgov.org/devils-slide-trail; Hwy 1; ☺8am-8pm Apr-Aug, closes earlier Sep-Mar).

Half Moon Bay (☑650-726-8819; www.parks.ca.gov/HalfMoonBaySB; off Hwy 1; per car $10; ☺8am-sunset; P) Home to a long coastline, mild weather and Mavericks – one of the biggest and scariest surf breaks on the planet – Half Moon Bay is prime real estate. Its long stretches of beach still attract rambling weekenders and die-hard surfers.

Pescadero (☑650-726-8819; www.parks.ca.gov; off Hwy 1; per car $8; ☺8am-sunset; P) A foggy speck of coastal crossroads between Half Moon Bay and Santa Cruz, 160-year-old Pescadero is a close-knit rural town of sugar-lending neighbors and community pancake breakfasts.

Año Nuevo State Park (☑park office 650-879-2025, recorded info 650-879-0227, tour reservations 800-444-4445; www.parks.ca.gov/anonuevo; 1 New Years Creek Rd; per car $10, 2½hr tour per person $7; ☺8:30am-sunset Apr-Nov, tours only Dec 15–Mar 31; P) Año Nuevo State Natural Reserve is home base for one of the world's largest mainland breeding colonies of northern elephant seals. More raucous than a full-moon beach rave, thousands of boisterous elephant seals party down year-round on the dunes of Año Nuevo Point.

includes an open-air tram ride (weather permitting) through biodynamic vineyards and a five-wine tasting. Great picnicking, excellent for families. The large-production wine is OK (head for the reserves); the tour's the thing. Bottles are $20 to $80.

SCRIBE
WINERY

(☑707-939-1858; www.scribewinery.com; 2100 Denmark St, Sonoma; tasting $35, food pairing $65; ☺11:30am-4pm Thu-Mon, by appointment only) With Scribe, a new generation has found its place in Wine Country. Bantering groups of bespectacled, high-waisted-jeans-wearing millennials frequent this hip winery designed to resemble a French château, and at outdoor picnic tables they hold forth on the terroir-driven rosé of pinot, the skin-fermented chardonnay and the bold cab. The food pairing both hits and misses, with delectable charred asparagus and fantastically citrusy salad, but a lackluster main of rock-cod tacos drowning in avocado crema.

KELLER ESTATE
WINERY

(☑707-765 2117; www.kellerestate.com; 5875 Lakeville Hwy, Petaluma; tour & tasting $25-40; ☺tour/tastings at 11:30am, 1pm, 2:30pm Fri-Mon) This 42-acre estate sits in the newly dubbed 'Petaluma Gap,' where pinot noir and chardonnay grapes are tormented by wind and fog, urging them to produce elegant and

complex wines. Keller also pours a brut and a pinot gris. Bottles are $30 to $54.

KUNDE
WINERY

(☑707-833-5501; www.kunde.com; 9825 Hwy 12, Kenwood; tasting $15-50, cave tours free; ☺10:30am-5pm; P) This family-owned winery on a historic ranch has vineyards that are more than a century old. It offers mountaintop tastings with impressive valley views and seasonal guided hikes (advance reservations recommended), though you can also just stop for a tasting and a tour. Elegant, 100% estate-grown wines include crisp chardonnay and unfussy red blends, all made sustainably. Bottles $17 to $100.

CLINE CELLARS
WINERY

(☑707-940-4030; www.clinecellars.com; 24737 Arnold Dr, Hwy 121, Sonoma; tasting free-$10; ☺tasting room 10am-6pm, museum to 4pm) Balmy days are for pondside picnics and rainy ones for fireside tastings of old-vine zinfandel and Mourvèdre inside an 1850s farmhouse. Stroll out back to the **California Mission Museum**, housing 1930s miniature replicas of California's original 21 Spanish Colonial missions.

CORNERSTONE SONOMA
GARDENS

(☑707-933-3010; www.cornerstonesonoma.com; 23570 Arnold Dr; ☺10am-5pm, gardens to 4pm; P) **FREE** This roadside Wine Country marketplace showcases 25 walk-through (in some cases edible) gardens, along with a bunch of innovative and adorable shops, wine-tasting parlors and on-site Sonoma Valley Visitors Bureau (p223). There's a good, if pricey, cafe, and an outdoor 'test kitchen.' Look for the enormous orange Adirondack chair at road's edge.

JACK LONDON STATE HISTORIC PARK   PARK

(☑707-938-5216; www.jacklondonpark.com; 2400 London Ranch Rd, Glen Ellen; per car $10, cottage $3; ⊘9:30am-5pm; P ⊞) ✎ Napa has Robert Louis Stevenson, but Sonoma has Jack London. This 1400-acre park frames that author's last years; don't miss the excellent on-site **museum**. Miles of **hiking trails** (some open to mountain bikes) weave through oak-dotted woodlands, between 600ft and 2300ft elevations; an easy 2-mile loop meanders to **London Lake**, great for picnicking. On select summer evenings, the park transforms into a theater for 'Broadway Under the Stars.' Be alert for poison oak.

✖ EATING & DRINKING

SUNFLOWER CAFFÉ & WINE BAR   CAFE $

(☑707-996-6645; www.sonomasunflower.com; 421 1st St W; dishes $8-15; ⊘7am-4pm; ☜) The big back garden at this local hangout is a great spot for breakfast, a no-fuss lunch or afternoon wine.

PETALUMA CREAMERY   MARKET, CAFE $

(☑707-762-9038; www.springhillcheese.com; 711 Western Ave; items $3-7; ⊘7am-6pm Mon-Fri, 9am-6pm Sat & Sun; ☑ ⊞) Taste organic Sonoma and Marin cheeses, buy a scoop of lavender ice cream, or order a tri-tip barbecue sandwich or fresh spinach salad at this small market inside the historic 1913 Petaluma Creamery.

★ CAFE LA HAYE   CALIFORNIAN $$

(☑707-935-5994; www.cafelahaye.com; 140 E Napa St; mains $19-25; ⊘5:30-9pm Tue-Sat) ✎ One of Sonoma's top tables for earthy New American cooking, La Haye only uses produce sourced from within 60 miles. Its dining room gets packed cheek-by-jowl and

service can border on perfunctory, but the clean simplicity and flavor-packed cooking make it many foodies' first choice. Reserve well ahead.

FIG CAFE & WINEBAR   FRENCH, CALIFORNIAN $$

(☑707-938-2130; www.thefigcafe.com; 13690 Arnold Dr, Glen Ellen; mains $21-24, 3-course dinner $36; ⊘dinner from 5pm) The Fig's earthy California-Provençal comfort food includes flash-fried calamari with spicy lemon aioli, fig and arugula salad and *steak frites*. Good wine prices and friendly service give reason to return. No reservations; complimentary corkage.

GLEN ELLEN STAR   CALIFORNIAN, ITALIAN $$$

(☑707-343-1384; www.glenellenstar.com; 13648 Arnold Dr, Glen Ellen; pizzas $15-20, mains $24-50; ⊘5:30-9pm Sun-Thu, to 9:30pm Fri & Sat; ☑) ✎ Helmed by chef Ari Weiswasser, who once worked at Thomas Keller's French Laundry (p222), this petite Glen Ellen bistro shines a light on the best of Sonoma farms and ranches. Local, organic and seasonal ingredients star in dishes such as spring-lamb ragù, whole roasted fish with broccoli Di Cicco or golden beets with harissa crumble. Reservations recommended.

🏃 ACTIVITIES

WILLOW STREAM SPA AT SONOMA MISSION INN   SPA

(☑877-289-7354; www.fairmont.com/sonoma; 100 Boyes Blvd; ⊘9am-6pm) Few Wine Country spas compare with glitzy Sonoma Mission Inn. Purchasing a treatment or paying $89 (make reservations) allows use of three outdoor and two indoor mineral pools, gym, sauna and herbal steam room at the Romanesque bathhouse. No under 18s.

RAMEKINS SONOMA VALLEY CULINARY SCHOOL   COOKING

(☑707-933-0450; www.ramekins.com; 450 W Spain St; ⊞) Offers excellent demonstrations and hands-on classes for home chefs, covering things such as hors d'oeuvres and cheese-and-wine pairings. The school also hosts culinary tours of local farms and dinners with vintners and chefs.

Sleeping

San Francisco hotel rates are among the world's highest. Plan ahead – well ahead – and grab bargains when you see them. If you have the choice, San Francisco's boutique properties beat chains for a sense of place – but take what you can get at a price you can afford.

When to Book

Travelers often only consider the cost of an airline ticket when choosing the dates of their trip, but you should confirm the availability of good hotel rates before booking flights. 'Citywide sellouts' happen several times a year when there's a big convention or event in town. Check the **SF Convention & Visitors Bureau convention calendar** (www.sanfrancisco.travel/article/hotel-availability), which shows the availability 'opportunity' for meeting planners. Look for times that list 'high opportunity' – this means many rooms are available in convention hotels and, by extension, smaller hotels. But if the calendar lists a specific convention, choose other dates or pay a premium – sometimes double or triple base rates.

Room Rates & Fees

San Francisco is in a boom cycle – this is the epicenter of tech and the whole world wants to be here. But there simply aren't enough beds. Between 2012 and 2019, rates at many downtown hotels jumped more than 100%. Day-to-day rates fluctuate wildly. Brace yourself. The best prices for a basic double room can be found from April to October, excluding citywide sellouts, when hotels charge 'compression rates' – a handy term when negotiating with hotels.

To get the best prices at chains, where rates change daily, call the hotel during business hours and speak with in-house reservations, rather than toll-free central reservations, for up-to-date information about inventories and specials. Some hotels have internet-only deals but, when booking online, know that 'best rate' does not necessarily mean lowest available rate. When in doubt, call the hotel directly. Online booking engines (eg Priceline) offer lower rates but have many restrictions and may be nonrefundable.

Although hostels and budget hotels are cheapest, rooms are never truly cheap in SF: expect to pay $100 for a private hostel room, $200 at a budget motel and over $300 at midrange hotels. Note the hefty 15% room tax on top of quoted rates. Most hotels offer free wi-fi (only luxury hotels charge, claiming it's for secured lines). Prices run higher June to August and plummet from November to April. Ask about weekly rates. At weekends and on holidays, rates for business and luxury hotels decrease, but they increase for tourist hotels; on weekdays the opposite is true.

Apartment Rentals

Short-term rentals are an attractive alternative for families and longer-term visitors, but options are limited in San Francisco – even though home-sharing site Airbnb was founded here. City law restricts SF home rentals to 90 days per year while spare bedrooms may be rented more frequently. Local taxes also apply, which can make the cost of short-term rentals comparable to a motel or B&B. But to stay in neighborhoods outside the downtown tourist fray like the Mission, Castro, Haight and Avenues, apartment rentals are often your only option besides B&Bs. Check Airbnb and VRBO for available options. Book well in advance.

Lonely Planet's Top Choices

Hotel Drisco (p229) Stately boutique hotel overlooking the Marina.

Argonaut Hotel (p229) Nautical-themed hotel at Fisherman's Wharf.

Hotel Vitale (p232) Contemporary downtowner with knockout waterfront vistas.

Inn at the Presidio (p229) National-park lodge in historic building surrounded by nature.

Hotel Bohème (p234) Artsy, affordable boutique charmer in the heart of North Beach.

Best By Budget: $

HI San Francisco Fisherman's Wharf (p229) Waterfront hostel with million-dollar views.

San Remo Hotel (p234) Spartan furnishings, shared bathrooms, great rates.

Yotel (p230) Smart downtown digs with shared workspace.

Best By Budget: $$

Inn at the Presidio (p229) Small luxury inn surrounded by national-park land.

Hotel Carlton (p231) Jet-set vibe with good-value rooms.

Marker (p231) Snazzy design, useful amenities and a central location..

Hotel Zeppelin (p230) Psychedelic SF style in the heart of downtown.

Best By Budget: $$$

Loews Regency (p232) Five-star service and knockout views.

Palace Hotel (p233) Stately classical hotel that is also a century-old landmark.

Hotel Zetta (p233) Tech-centric downtowner filled with art.

Argonaut Hotel (p229) Bay views in a converted Fisherman's Wharf warehouse.

Best Family-Friendly

Hotel Zephyr (p229) Games everywhere and a vast outdoor courtyard.

Hotel del Sol (p229) Colorful theme rooms, plus a heated outdoor pool.

Argonaut Hotel (p229) The Wharf's best hotel, with a giant lobby to explore.

Americania Hotel (p232) Better-than-average motel with pool.

Best Views

Loews Regency (p232) Bridge-to-bridge views from an SF skyscraper.

Hotel Drisco (p229) Billion-dollar bay views atop a mansion-lined ridge.

Fairmont San Francisco (p234) Hilltop vistas plus SF's grandest lobby.

Mark Hopkins Intercontinental (p235) Nob Hill's stately charmer.

Best for Victorian Splendor

Chateau Tivoli (p236) Legendary boarding house where Mark Twain and sundry opera divas caroused and crashed.

Queen Anne Hotel (p235) An 1890 mansion and former girls' boarding school that sets the scene for novels and cozy hideaways.

Parsonage (p236) Period-perfect Italianate mansion with airy, glamorous rooms.

NEED TO KNOW

Price Ranges
The following price ranges refer to a double room with bathroom in high season (June to August); you can sometimes do better, except when there's a convention. Unless otherwise stated, breakfast is not included in the price.

$ less than $150

$$ $150–$350

$$$ more than $350

Parking
Hotel parking costs $40 to $60 per night extra – very few offer a *free* self-service lot. Hotels without parking often have valet parking or an agreement with a nearby garage; call ahead.

Reconfirming
If you're arriving after 4pm, guarantee with a credit card or your reservation may be cancelled.

Tipping
Tipping housekeepers in US hotels is standard practice; leave $2 to $5 on your pillow each morning and be guaranteed excellent housekeeping.

SLEEPING

Where to Stay

Neighborhood	For	Against
The Marina, Fisherman's Wharf & the Piers	Near the northern waterfront; good for kids; lots of restaurants and nightlife at the Marina.	Fisherman's Wharf is all tourists; street parking at the Marina and Wharf is a nightmare.
Downtown, Civic Center & SoMa	Biggest selection of hotels; walkable to many sights, restaurants, shopping and theaters; near all public transportation. Parts of SoMa are close to major downtown sights; great nightlife.	Downtown is quiet at night; Civic Center feels rough – the worst area extends three blocks in all directions from Eddy and Jones Sts. SoMa: few restaurants, gritty streets at night.
North Beach & Chinatown	Culturally colorful; great strolling; lots of cafes, bars and restaurants; terrific sense of place; access by cable car.	Street noise; limited choice and transportation options.
Nob Hill & Russian Hill	Stately, classic hotels atop Nob Hill; great restaurants and shopping in Russian Hill.	The Hills are steep, hard on the out-of-shape; slightly removed from major sights.
Japantown, Fillmore & Pacific Heights	Distinctive hotels, great shopping and restaurant choices in Pacific Heights and Japantown; iconic entertainment in the Fillmore.	Sleeping options limited; sights thin on the ground in the Fillmore and Pacific Heights; Pacific Heights hills are steep.
The Mission, Dogpatch & Potrero	The Mission's flat terrain makes walking easier; good for biking; easy access to BART.	Limited choice; distance from sights; gritty street scene on main thoroughfares.
The Castro	Great nightlife, especially for LGBTIQ+ travelers; lots of cafes and restaurant choices; easy access to Market St transit.	Distance from major tourist sights; few sleeping choices.
The Haight & Hayes Valley	Lots of bars and restaurants; Hayes Valley near cultural sights; the Haight near Golden Gate Park.	Gritty street scene at night on major thoroughfares; limited public transportation in the Haight.
Golden Gate Park & the Avenues	Quiet nights; good for outdoor recreation.	Very far from major sights; foggy and cold; restaurants and bars limited to main strips; limited public transportation.

🛏 The Marina, Fisherman's Wharf & the Piers

⭐ HI SAN FRANCISCO FISHERMAN'S WHARF
HOSTEL $

Map p292 (📞415-771-7277; www.hiusa.org; Fort Mason, Bldg 240; dm $40-64, r $116-160; 🅿 @ 🛜; 🚍28, 30, 47, 49) Trading downtown convenience for a glorious park-like setting with million-dollar waterfront views, this hostel occupies a former army-hospital building, with bargain-priced private rooms and dorms (some co-ed) with four to 22 beds (avoid bunks one and two – they're by doorways). All bathrooms are shared. There's a huge kitchen and a cafe overlooking the bay. Limited free parking.

⭐ INN AT THE PRESIDIO
HOTEL $$

Map p291 (📞415-800-7356; www.presidiolodging.com; 42 Moraga Ave; r $310-495; 🅿 🐾 @ 🛜🐕; 🚍43, PresidiGo Shuttle) 🍃 Built in 1903 as bachelor quarters for army officers, this three-story, redbrick building in the Presidio was transformed in 2012 into a smart national-park lodge, styled with leather, linen and wood. Oversized rooms are plush, including feather beds with Egyptian-cotton sheets. Suites have gas fireplaces. Nature surrounds you, with hiking trailheads out back, but taxis downtown cost $25 to $30.

HOTEL ZEPHYR
DESIGN HOTEL $$

Map p289 (📞415-617-6565, 844-617-6555; www.hotelzephyrsf.com; 250 Beach St; r $250-500; 🅿 🐾 @ 🛜; 🚍8, 39, 47, 🚋Powell-Mason, Ⓜ E, F) 🍃 Completely revamped in 2015, this vintage 1960s hotel surrounds a vast courtyard with fire pits and lounge chairs, modern art from nautical junk, and games like table tennis in a tube – reminders you're here to play, not work. Rooms are fresh and spiffy, with up-to-date amenities, including smart TVs that link with your devices. Best rooms face the water.

HOTEL DEL SOL
MOTEL $$

Map p292 (📞415-921-5520; www.jdvhotels.com; 3100 Webster St; d $259-359; 🅿 🐾 @ 🛜🐕🐕; 🚍22, 28, 30, 43) 🍃 The kid-friendly Marina District Hotel del Sol is a riot of color, with tropical-themed decor. This quiet, revamped 1950s motor lodge with a palm-lined central courtyard is one of the few San Francisco hotels with a heated outdoor pool. Family suites have trundle beds and board games. Parking costs $30 a night.

COVENTRY MOTOR INN
MOTEL $$

Map p292 (📞415-567-1200; www.coventrymotorinn.com; 1901 Lombard St; r $158-228; 🅿 🐾 🐾 🛜; 🚍22, 28, 30, 43) Of the many motels lining Lombard St, the generic Coventry has the highest quality-to-value ratio, with spacious, well-maintained (if plain) rooms and extras like air-con (good for quiet sleeps) and covered parking. Parents: there's plenty of floor space to unpack kids' toys, but no pool.

MARINA MOTEL
MOTEL $$

Map p292 (📞415-921-9406; www.marinamotel.com; 2576 Lombard St; r $189-269; 🅿 🐾🐕; 🚍28, 30, 41, 43, 45) Established in 1939 to accommodate visitors arriving via the new Golden Gate Bridge, the Marina has an inviting Spanish-Mediterranean look, with a quiet bougainvillea-lined courtyard. Rooms are homey, simple and well maintained; some have full kitchens (extra $10 to $20). Rooms on Lombard St are loud; request one in back. Free parking.

⭐ ARGONAUT HOTEL
BOUTIQUE HOTEL $$$

Map p289 (📞415-345-5519, 415-563-0800; www.argonauthotel.com; 495 Jefferson St; r from $389; 🅿 🐾 🛜🐕; 🚍19, 47, 49, 🚋Powell-Hyde) 🍃 Fisherman's Wharf's top hotel was built as a cannery in 1908 and has century-old wooden beams and exposed-brick walls. Rooms sport an over-the-top nautical theme, with porthole-shaped mirrors and plush, deep-blue carpets. Though all rooms have the amenities of an upper-end hotel – ultra-comfy beds, iPod docks – some are tiny with limited sunlight. Parking starts at $65.

HOTEL DRISCO
BOUTIQUE HOTEL $$$

Map p292 (📞415-346-2880, 800-634-7277; www.hoteldrisco.com; 2901 Pacific Ave; r $377-1099; @ 🛜; 🚍3, 24, 45) One of the few hotels in Pacific Heights, this stately 1903 apartment-hotel tucked between mansions stands high on the ridgeline. It's notable for its architecture, attentive service and newly revamped rooms with elegant decor and heated bathroom floors. The high-on-a-hill location is convenient only to the Marina; anywhere else requires a bus or taxi. Still, for a real boutique hotel, it's tops.

LODGE AT THE PRESIDIO
BOUTIQUE HOTEL $$$

Map p291 (📞415-561-1234; www.presidiolodging.com/lodge-at-the-presidio; 105 Montgomery St; r $275-450; 🛜🐕; 🚍43, PresidiGo shuttle) During the Spanish-American war, officers living within these former barracks did not sleep on the custom-made pillow-top mattresses that today's guests enjoy. But this modern, 42-room redbrick stay does preserve the military past via the original art and historic photographs. Aim for a room with a view of the Golden Gate Bridge and San Francisco Bay.

HOTEL ZOE BOUTIQUE HOTEL $$$
Map p289 (415-561-1100; www.hotelzoesf. com; 425 North Point St; r $309-800; ❄☎❄; ❑47, ❑Powell-Mason, ⓜF) Drawing inspiration from luxury yachts for its $16 million redesign, this little sister to the Argonaut Hotel (p229) was reborn in 2017 to parent Noble House Hotels. The location's tops if Alcatraz, Fisherman's Wharf and Pier 39 are on your must-do list, and the cozy fireplace, plush modern furnishings and earthy tones make Zoe a relaxing retreat from the action.

🛏 Downtown, Civic Center & SoMa

⭐**HI SAN FRANCISCO CITY CENTER** HOSTEL $
Map p296 (415-474-5721; www.sfhostels.org; 685 Ellis St; dm $33-70, r $90-165; @☎; ❑19, 38, 47, 49) ✏ The seven-story, 1920s Atherton Hotel was remodeled in 2001 into a much-better-than-average hostel, with private baths in all rooms, including dorms. And it scores bonus points for eco-friendliness: the place is powered mainly by solar panels and shower heads change color based on the length of a shower.

⭐**YOTEL SAN FRANCISCO** HOTEL $
Map p296 (415-829-0000; www.yotel.com/en/ hotels/yotel-san-francisco; 1095 Market St; d $149-209; ❄☎; ❑6, 7, 9, 21, ⒷCivic Center, ⓜCivic Center) Newly situated within the long-standing Grant building, this chic downtown hotel is a West Coast first for parent company Yotel, a chain of compact, technology-forward luxury stays. Design choices conserve time and space at every turn, from the self-check-in kiosks to the adjustable 'smartbeds' (which morph into couches) to the playful 'sky cabins,' cozy lofted sleeping quarters with extra-long mattresses and large flat-screens.

USA HOSTELS HOSTEL $
Map p296 (877-483-2950, 415-440-5600; www. usahostels.com; 711 Post St; dm $43-73, r $145-194; ☎; ❑2, 3, 27, 38) This 1909 hotel was cleverly converted into a sharp-looking hostel with a college-dorm vibe and international students chilling out in the lounge. Private rooms have fridge, microwave and TV.

Dorms have built-in 'privacy pod' screens, reading lights and electrical outlets, and lockers contain outlets to charge electronics. Common areas include a big kitchen, laundry, yoga room and games space.

FITZGERALD HOTEL HOTEL $
Map p296 (415-775-8100; www.fitzgeraldhotel. com; 620 Post St; r $119-200; ☎; ❑2, 3, 27, 38) Upgrade from hostel to hotel at the cheerful Fitzgerald, whimsically decorated with mismatched furniture liquidated from fancier hotels. The old-fashioned building (built in 1910) needs upgrades (note the creepy elevator) and rooms are tiny and have occasional scuff marks and torn curtains – but bathrooms are clean, and most rooms have fridges and microwaves.

HI SAN FRANCISCO DOWNTOWN HOSTEL $
Map p294 (415-788-5604; www.sfhostels.com; 312 Mason St; dm $46-60, r $139-164; @☎; ⓜPowell, ⒷPowell) You've come to the right place – a block from Union Sq, this well-managed hostel looks fresh, clean and colorful, with contemporary furnishings. Dorms have four beds; private rooms sport low-slung platform beds (beware sharp corners) and some even have down pillows (by request). Extras include free continental breakfast, quiet area, social lounge, clean kitchen, laundry facility and full activities calendar.

⭐**AXIOM** BOUTIQUE HOTEL $$
Map p294 (415-392-9466; www.axiomhotel. com; 28 Cyril Magnin St; d $189-342; @☎❄; ❑Powell-Mason, Powell-Hyde, ⒷPowell, ⓜPowell) Of all the downtown SF hotels aiming for high-tech appeal, this one gets it right. The lobby is razzle-dazzle LED, marble and riveted steel, but the game room looks like a start-up HQ, with arcade games and foosball tables. Guest rooms have low-slung, gray-flannel couches, king platform beds, dedicated routers for high-speed wireless streaming to Apple/Google/Samsung devices, and Bluetooth-enabled everything.

HOTEL ZEPPELIN BOUTIQUE HOTEL $$
Map p296 (415-563-0303; www.viceroyhotels andresorts.com; 545 Post St; d from $169; ❄☎; ❑2, 3, 38, ❑Powell-Mason, Powell-Hyde) A block west of Union Sq and a half-century back in time, this trippy boutique stay is replete with throw-back details. A Gothic fireplace and mod furnishings anchor the rock-n-roll-inspired lobby, while a giant peace sign constructed of license plates livens up the basement game parlor.

MARKER
BOUTIQUE HOTEL **$$**

Map p296 (📞844-736-2753, 415-292-0100; http://themarkersanfrancisco.com; 501 Geary St; r from $209; ❄@🛜🏊; 🚌38, 🚃Powell-Hyde, Powell-Mason) 🏅 Snazzy Marker gets details right, with guest-room decor in bold colors – lipstick-red lacquer, navy-blue velvet and shiny purple silk – and thoughtful amenities like high-thread-count sheets, ergonomic workspaces, digital-library access, multiple electrical outlets and ample space in drawers, closets and bathroom vanities. Extras include a small gym, an evening wine reception and bragging rights to stylish downtown digs.

HOTEL CARLTON
DESIGN HOTEL **$$**

Map p296 (📞415-673-0242, 800-922-7586; www.hotelcarltonsf.com; 1075 Sutter St; r from $269; @🛜🏊; 🚌2, 3, 19, 38, 47, 49) 🏅 World travelers feel right at home at the Carlton amid Moroccan tea tables, Indian bedspreads, West African wax-print throw pillows and carbon-offsetting LEED-certified initiatives (note the rooftop solar panels). It's not the most convenient location – 10 minutes from Union Sq – but offers good value for colorful, spotlessly clean rooms. The quietest rooms are those with the suffix -08 to -19.

PHOENIX HOTEL
MOTEL **$$**

Map p296 (📞415-776-1380, 800-248-9466; www.phoenixsf.com; 601 Eddy St; r $134-224; 🅿🛜❄🏊; 🚌19, 31, 47, 49) This rocker crash pad lures revelers to a 1950s motor lodge with mod paint jobs and hipster amenities (hello, Pendleton blankets). There's a courtyard pool and a happening lounge – but Tenderloin bar crawls and Great American Music Hall shows beckon. Free parking and admission to Kabuki Springs & Spa (p142). Bring earplugs; no smoking.

HOTEL TRITON
BOUTIQUE HOTEL **$$**

Map p294 (📞415-394-0500; www.hoteltriton.com; 342 Grant Ave; r $269-389; ❄@🛜🏊; 🚇Montgomery, 🚋Montgomery) 🏅 Forget boring business hotels: Triton's lobby thumps with club music and pops with comic-book color. Upstairs, recently redesigned rooms are bright and cozy, sporting shag-worthy beds with Frette linens and eco-friendly amenities (including organic snacks). Note that baths have limited space to primp.

HOTEL UNION SQUARE
HOTEL **$$**

Map p294 (📞415-397-3000, bookings 415-969-2301; www.hotelunionsquare.com; 114 Powell St; r $196-299; ❄@🛜🏊; 🚇Powell, 🚋Powell) Cleverly stylish Hotel Union Square adds soft touches like tufted headboards and down comforters to complement the original brick walls. The main drawbacks are lack of sunlight and very small rooms, but designers compensated with concealed lighting, mirrored walls and plush fabrics.

WESTIN ST FRANCIS HOTEL
HOTEL **$$**

Map p294 (📞415-397-7000; www.westinstfrancis.com; 335 Powell St; r from $199; ❄@🛜🏊; 🚇Powell, 🚋Powell, 🚃Powell-Mason, Powell-Hyde) This is one of SF's most storied hotels – Gerald Ford was shot right outside, and Reagan was kept awake by Union Sq protests. Tower rooms offer stellar views but generic architecture, while the landmark 1904 building has old-fashioned charm, with high ceilings, crown moldings, gleaming marble and brass. Westin beds set the industry standard for comfort, but service can be lax.

PROPER HOTEL
DESIGN HOTEL **$$**

Map p296 (📞415-735-7777; www.properhotel.com/hotels/san-francisco; 1100 Market St; d from $275; ❄🛜; 🚌6, 7, 9, 21, 🚇Civic Center, 🚋Civic Center) Ensconced in a historic flatiron building, this design-forward hotel feels a little bit like *Alice in Wonderland*, only Alice is all grown up and has gotten really into secessionist art and cubism. Contrasting bright colors, busy patterns and reupholstered vintage furnishings give the place an undeniable pizzazz, and the rooms feature ultra-comfortable beds with Italian linens and hypoallergenic pillows.

GOOD HOTEL
MOTEL **$$**

Map p298 (📞415-621-7001; www.thegoodhotel.com; 112 7th St; r $199-279; @🛜❄; 🚇Civic Center, 🚋Civic Center) 🏅 A revamped motel full of green ideas: reclaimed-wood headboards, repurposed-bottle light fixtures and soft fleece bedspreads made from recycled soda bottles. It's youthful and upbeat, like a smartly decorated college dorm. The Good Hotel is in a bad neighborhood, with street scenes and noise; book in back. Parking costs $35. There's a pool across the street at the Americania Hotel (p232).

HOTEL ABRI
HOTEL **$$**

Map p294 (📞415-392-8800; www.hotelabrisf.com; 127 Ellis St; r $245-359; ❄@🛜🏊; 🚇Powell, 🚋Powell) Inside a remodeled early-20th-century building, the Abri has an updated deco sensibility, with jazz-age black-and-tan motifs, sleek wood-paneled headboards for pillow-top beds, and flat-screen TVs hung above workstations for multitasking. Few bathrooms have tubs, but rainfall shower-heads compensate. The hotel's popularity has meant wear-and-tear on the once-fresh furnishings, but rooms remain comfy, and staff friendly and accommodating.

CARRIAGE INN
MOTEL **$$**

Map p298 (☑415-552-8600, 800-444-5817; www.carriageinnsf.com; 140 7th St; r $229-349; ❋@❡☎; MCivic Center, BCivic Center) A kooky motor lodge in an ersatz Victorian offers bigger-than-average rooms named for San Francisco icons, swathed in colorful fabrics and festooned with poignant por-traits and old-timey typewriters. The Car-riage Inn offers good bang for your buck, but it's on a sometimes-sketchy street – keep your earplugs and street smarts ready. Self-parking costs $35. The pool is across the street at the Americania Hotel.

AMERICANIA HOTEL
MOTEL **$$**

Map p298 (☑415-626-0200, bookings 800-444-5816; www.americaniahotel.com; 121 7th St; r $229-399; @❡☎; MCivic Center, BCivic Center) Retro rooms at this revamped mid-century mo-tor lodge face a central courtyard and look sharp, with black-and-teal-checkerboard car-peting, studded white-vinyl headboards, Op Art linens and '60s swivel chairs. Kids love the small outdoor heated pool, while par-ents love the fitness center and microbrews at the downstairs restaurant and lounge – but might not be so thrilled about the gritty neighborhood and paid parking ($45).

HOTEL VIA
HOTEL **$$**

Map p298 (☑415-200-4977; www.hotelviasf.com; 138 King St; d from $229; ❋❡; MN, T) The clear choice for traveling baseball fans, Hotel VIA right across from AT&T Park sports a fabu-lous guests-only rooftop bar with giant heat lamps, fire pits and swanky cabanas (not to mention views for days). The 159 rooms are spacious with contemporary furnishings, while provided tablets allow guests to order car service, request privacy and control the lights from anywhere in the hotel.

HOTEL DIVA
BOUTIQUE HOTEL **$$**

Map p294 (☑415-885-0200; www.hoteldiva. com; 440 Geary St; r $279-350; ❋@❡☎; ▢38, ▢Powell-Hyde, Powell-Mason) Industrial-chic Diva has a stainless-steel and black-granite dominatrix aesthetic that appeals to techies and club kids alike. Beds are comfy, with good sheets, feather pillows and down com-forters adding much needed softness to the hard-edged design. Best for a party, but if you're here on business, escape your room to take calls in your lounge.

HOTEL DES ARTS
HOTEL **$$**

Map p294 (☑415-956-3232; www.sfhoteldesarts. com; 447 Bush St; r $189-239, with shared bath $179-219; ❡; MMontgomery, BMontgomery) Wel-come, art freaks: who needs red carpet when your room is painted with jaw-dropping mu-rals by underground Bay Area artists? Service is weak, linens are thin, and some bathrooms have separate hot and cold taps – but you're basically sleeping inside a painting in the heart of downtown SF, right near Geary St galleries and SFMOMA. Bring earplugs.

GALLERIA PARK
BOUTIQUE HOTEL **$$$**

Map p294 (☑415-781-3060; www.galleriapark. com; 191 Sutter St; r $325-369; ❋@❡☎; MMont-gomery, BMontgomery) ✿ Exuberant staff greet your arrival at this certified-green, recently renovated boutique, a 1911 hotel re-styled with contemporary art and handsome furnishings. Some rooms (and beds) run small, but they include Frette linens, down pillows, high-end bath amenities, free even-ing martinis and – most importantly – good service. Rooms on Sutter St are noisier, but get more light; interior rooms are quietest.

HOTEL VITALE
BOUTIQUE HOTEL **$$$**

Map p298 (☑888-890-8688, 415-278-3700; www.hotelvitale.com; 8 Mission St; r $385-675; ❋@❡☎; MEmbarcadero, BEmbarcadero) When your love interest or executive re-cruiter books you into the waterfront Vitale, you know it's serious. The office-tower ex-terior disguises a snazzy hotel with sleek, up-to-the-minute luxuries. Beds are dressed with silky-soft 450-thread-count sheets, and there's an excellent on-site spa with two rooftop hot tubs. Rooms facing the bay of-fer spectacular Bay Bridge views, and Ferry Building dining awaits across the street.

LOEWS REGENCY
HOTEL **$$$**

Map p301 (☑415-276-9888, 877-672-1575; www. loewshotels.com/regency-san-francisco; 222 San-some St; r from $600; ❋@❡☎; ▢California, MMontgomery, BMontgomery) On the top 11 floors of SF's third-tallest building, Loews offers sweeping bird's-eye views from every room. There's nothing earth-shattering about the classic decor, but the details are sumptuous and, oh, those vistas – you're eye level with the Transamerica Pyramid. Splash out on a 'Golden Gate Suite' (from $1999), with floor-to-ceiling windows overlooking the Golden Gate Bridge from your bathtub.

PALACE HOTEL
HOTEL $$$

Map p294 (☑415-512-1111; www.rycollection. com; 2 New Montgomery St; r from $300; ✳@⚡☒☒; Ⓜ Montgomery, Ⓑ Montgomery) The 1906 landmark Palace remains a monument to turn-of-the-century grandeur, with 100-year-old Austrian-crystal chandeliers and Maxfield Parrish paintings. Cushy (if staid) accommodations cater to expense-account travelers, but prices drop at weekends. Even if you're not staying here, visit the opulent Garden Court to sip tea beneath a translucent glass ceiling. There's also a spa; kids love the big pool.

HARBOR COURT HOTEL
BOUTIQUE HOTEL $$$

Map p298 (☑415-882-1300, bookings 855-212-6775; www.harborcourthotel.com; 165 Steuart St; r $299-599; ✳@⚡☒; Ⓜ Embarcadero, Ⓑ Embarcadero) This repurposed 1928 YMCA hotel right off the waterfront has tiny rooms, all of which were redesigned in attractive textures and colors as part of a $14 million renovation completed in 2018. Book a bay-view room and drift off watching the Bay Bridge lights at night. Downstairs, guests gather fireside at the bayfront common area, and there's a new coffee shop in the lobby.

HOTEL ZETTA
HOTEL $$$

Map p294 (☑415-543-8555, bookings 888-720-7004; www.hotelzetta.com; 55 5th St; r from $324; ✳@⚡☒; Ⓑ Powell St, Ⓜ Powell St) ⚡ Opened in 2013, this savvy eco-conscious downtowner by the Viceroy group caters to overworked techies ready to play – above the art-filled lobby there's a mezzanine-level 'play room' with billiards, shuffleboard and two-story-high Plinko wall. Upstairs, bigger-than-average rooms beckon with padded black-leather headboards and low-slung platform beds. Web-enabled flat-screen TVs link with your devices, because we invented that stuff here, mmmkay?

INN AT UNION SQUARE
BOUTIQUE HOTEL $$$

Map p294 (☑800-288-4346, 415-397-3510; www.unionsquare.com; 440 Post St; r $259-359; ✳@⚡; ⬛ Powell-Hyde, Powell-Mason, Ⓜ Powell, Ⓑ Powell) ⚡ Get comfortable without giving up personalized service at this understated boutique charmer, best for travelers who want a central location without compromising on quiet or details like Carrara-marble bathrooms. The hotel was fully renovated in 2017, and is ideal for days of shopping and nights at the theater. Valet parking costs $53 per car, more for an SUV.

SIR FRANCIS DRAKE HOTEL
HOTEL $$$

Map p294 (☑800-795-7129, 415-392-7755; www. sirfrancisdrake.com; 450 Powell St; r $269-449; ✳@⚡; ⚡ Powell-Mason, Powell-Hyde, Ⓜ Powell, Ⓑ Powell) ⚡ The city's most famous doormen, clad like cartoon Beefeaters, greet you at this 1920s tower. The Spanish-Moorish lobby is magnificent, but the smallish, neutral-toned guest rooms targeted to conventioneers are less glamorous than you'd expect from such a grand entrance. Still, rooms do have business-class amenities and proper beds. Book 16th-to 20th-floor rooms for expansive views.

TAJ CAMPTON PLACE
HOTEL $$$

Map p294 (☑415-955-5521; www.tajhotels.com; 340 Stockton St; r from $425; ✳@⚡; ⬛30, 45, Ⓜ Montgomery) Impeccable service sets the Campton Place apart – this is the place to put your fur-clad rich aunt when she wants discretion above all. Details are lavish, if beige. The cheapest rooms are tiny; pay to upgrade or be imprisoned in a jewelry box. It's in a prime Union Sq location for shopping and dining, including at the formal California-Indian restaurant on-site.

🛏 North Beach & Chinatown

PACIFIC TRADEWINDS HOSTEL
HOSTEL $

Map p308 (☑415-433-7970; www.san-francisco-hostel.com; 680 Sacramento St; dm $35-45 plus $20 refundable security deposit; ⏱ front desk 8am-midnight; ⚡@⚡; ⬛1, Ⓑ Montgomery, ⬛ California) San Francisco's smartest all-dorm hostel has a blue-and-white nautical theme, a fully equipped kitchen (free coffee, tea, and peanut butter and jelly sandwiches), spotless glass-brick showers, a laundry (free sock wash – so smart), luggage storage and no lockout time. Bunks are bolted to the wall, so there's no bed-shaking when bunkmates roll. No elevator means hauling bags up three flights – but it's worth it. Great service; fun staff.

SAN REMO HOTEL
HOTEL $

Map p308 (☑415-776-8688, 800-352-7366; www. sanremohotel.com; 2237 Mason St; r with shared bath $99-159; @⚡☒; ⬛30, 47, ⬛ Powell-Mason, Ⓜ T) One of the city's best-value stays, the San Remo was built in 1906, right after the Great Earthquake. More than a century later, this upstanding North Beach boarding house still offers sunny, cheerful Italian *nonna* (grandma)–styled rooms with eclectic turn-of-the-century furnishings and shared bathrooms. Snug rooms facing the interior corridor are bargains; family suites accommodate up to five. No elevator.

★HOTEL BOHÈME
BOUTIQUE HOTEL **$$**

Map p308 (☑415-433-9111; www.hotelboheme.com; 444 Columbus Ave; r $195–295; ◉@🛜; 🚇10, 12, 30, 41, 45, Ⓜ T) Eclectic, historic and unabashedly romantic, this quintessential North Beach boutique hotel has jazz-era color schemes, wrought-iron beds, paper-umbrella lamps, Beat poetry and artwork on the walls. The vintage rooms are smallish, some face noisy Columbus Ave (quieter rooms are in back) and bathrooms are teensy, but novels beg to be written here – especially after bar crawls. No elevator or parking lot.

WASHINGTON SQUARE INN
B&B **$$**

Map p308 (☑415-981-4220, 800-388-0220; www.wsisf.com; 1660 Stockton St; r $199-289; @🛜; 🚇30, 41, 45, 🚋Powell-Mason, Ⓜ T) On sunny Washington Sq, this restored 1910 inn offers European style, complete with wine-and-cheese receptions and continental breakfasts in bed. The rooms are traditionally styled, with brocade curtains, antique tables and tapestry pillows. The least-expensive rooms don't leave much space for North Beach shopping, and one has a bathroom across the hall – but this is a stellar location. No elevator.

★ORCHARD GARDEN HOTEL
BOUTIQUE HOTEL **$$$**

Map p308 (☑415-393-9917, 844-332-5240; www.theorchardgardenhotel.com; 466 Bush St; r $278-332; 🅿◉❄@🛜; 🚇2, 3, 30, 45, Ⓑ Montgomery) 🍃 San Francisco's original LEED-certified, all-green-practices hotel uses sustainably grown wood, chemical-free cleaning products and recycled fabrics in its soothingly quiet rooms. Don't think you'll be trading comfort for conscience: rooms have unexpectedly luxe touches, like high-end down pillows, Egyptian-cotton sheets and organic bath products. Toast sunsets with a cocktail on the rooftop terrace. Book directly for deals, free breakfast and parking.

🛏 Nob Hill & Russian Hill

HOTEL MAYFLOWER
HISTORIC HOTEL **$**

Map p306 (☑415-673-7010; www.sfmayflowerhotel.com; 975 Bush St; d $130-190; 🅿◉❄🛜; 🚇2, 3, 27) Location, comfort and character at half the cost of places down the block. Built in 1926, Hotel Mayflower has a Span-

ish Mission–style cloister lobby and vintage cage elevator straight out of a Hitchcock movie. Guest rooms are snug and simple but ship-shape, with sepia-toned San Francisco murals and wrought iron bed frames. Rates include muffin breakfasts; parking is a bargain at $20.

★WHITE SWAN INN
BOUTIQUE HOTEL **$$**

Map p306 (☑415-775-1755; www.whiteswaninnsf.com; 845 Bush St; r $237-305; 🅿@🛜; 🚇2, 3, 27) Imagine a Nob Hill socialite had a fling with English gentry: there you have romantic White Swan. Each room has its own eccentric English character – cabbage-rose wallpaper, terrier portraits, mod lamps, fireplaces – without sacrificing Californian creature comforts: soaking tubs, pillow-top beds, gourmet pizza delivery. Don't miss high tea in Christian Lacroix wingback lounge chairs, or fireside yoga in the library (yes, really).

★FAIRMONT SAN FRANCISCO
HOTEL **$$**

Map p306 (☑415-772-5000, 800-257-7544; www.fairmont.com; 950 Mason St; r from $259; 🅿❄@🛜; 🚋California, Powell-Mason, Powell-Hyde) Heads of state choose the Fairmont for its grand hotel swagger – magnificent marble lobby, opulent mosaic penthouse suite, bacchanalian brunches – plus San Francisco eccentricity, including tiki Tonga Room and deco circus-mural Cirque bar. Guest rooms offer business-class comfort, but comparatively less character and luxury than public spaces. For historic appeal, reserve in the original 1906 building; for jaw-dropping views, go for the tower.

PETITE AUBERGE
BOUTIQUE HOTEL **$$**

Map p306 (☑415-928-6000; www.petiteaubergesf.com; 863 Bush St; r $219-264; 🛜; 🚇2, 3, 27) Gracing the slope of Nob Hill is this unexpected French country inn – all sunshine yellow and floral prints, with vintage books flanking cozy gas fireplaces. This is one of downtown SF's most charming boutique stays, though some darker rooms overlook an alley where rubbish is collected (request a quiet room). Breakfast and afternoon wine are served fireside in the salon.

GOLDEN GATE HOTEL
HOTEL **$$**

Map p306 (☑415-392-3702, 800-835-1118; www.goldengatehotel.com; 775 Bush St; r $225-245, with shared bath $145; @🛜; 🚇2, 3, 🚋Powell-Hyde, Powell-Mason) Like an old-fashioned *pension*, the Golden Gate has kindly owners and simple rooms with eclectic furniture, in a 1913 Edwardian hotel perched above the downtown fray. Rooms are snug, clean and comfortable, and most have private bathrooms – some with antique clawfoot bathtubs. Enormous croissants, homemade cookies, and a resident cat provide TLC after long days of sightseeing.

MARK HOPKINS INTERCONTINENTAL
HOTEL $$$

Map p306 (☎888-424-6835, 415-392-3434; www.intercontinentalmarkhopkins.com; 999 California St; r from $300; ⓟ❄@🛜🐾; 🚋California) Moods lift and everyone glows under the crystal lobby chandeliers of this 1926 San Francisco landmark. Mark Hopkins' gilded-age style is clearly continental, and a bit formal for California – but this 19-story tower is beloved for end-of-the-world views by locals and celebrities (including Michelle Obama). Rooms are business-class beige, with Frette linens on plush beds – but service can be inattentive.

🛏 Japantown, Fillmore & Pacific Heights

⭐HOTEL KABUKI
HOTEL $$

Map p310 (☎800-533-4567, 415-922-3200; www.jdvhotels.com; 1625 Post St; r $160-570; ⓟ@🛜🐾; 🚌2, 3, 38) Welcome to the Steve Jobs of SF hotels – minimalist and austere outside, but inside sneaky psychedelic touches make you wonder who's been microdosing magic mushrooms. Japanese mid-century modern meets '60s SF in cleverly updated decor: Noguchi tables flank *shibori* tie-dyed bedheads and slate-gray walls feature trippy Jonathan Adler prints. Book directly to score free passes to Kabuki Springs & Spa (p142).

⭐THE KIMPTON BUCHANAN
BOUTIQUE HOTEL $$

Map p310 (☎415-921-4000, bookings 855-454-4644; www.thebuchananhotel.com; 1800 Sutter St; r$218-294; 🐾ⓟ) Roll out of bed and find shopping, spas and shabu-shabu dining at your doorstep. Mid-century modern luxe city-view rooms offer views of Japantown's Peace Pagoda from the considerable comfort of your king bed and spa king corner rooms have Japanese soaking tubs. Cheeky style – like the whiskey-crate-paneled lounge – and thoughtful amenities, including PUBLIC bicycles at your disposal.

QUEEN ANNE HOTEL
B&B $$

Map p310 (☎800-227-3970, 415-441-2828; www. queenanne.com; 1590 Sutter St; r $134-429; @🛜; 🚋2, 3) Call the 1890 pink Victorian mansion of your San Francisco dreams home for the night. This exemplary Queen Anne was once a girls' boarding school and the decor is downright princessy: carved wood beds, antique vanities and tasseled curtains to throw open so you can lord it over neighboring millionaires. Rooms are comfy, though the wallpaper is too close for comfort in some. Don't miss afternoon sherry.

🛏 The Mission, Dogpatch & Potrero Hill

INN SAN FRANCISCO
B&B $$

Map p302 (☎800-359-0913, 415-641-0188; www.innsf.com; 943 S Van Ness Ave; r $175-400, with shared bath $155-215, cottages $370-495; ⓟ♿@🛜🐾; 🚌14, 49) An elegant 1872 Italianate-Victorian mansion has become a stately Mission District inn, impeccably maintained and packed with antiques. All rooms have fresh-cut flowers and sumptuous mattresses with feather beds; some have Jacuzzis. The freestanding garden cottage sleeps four adults and two children. Outside there's an English garden and a redwood hot tub open 24 hours – a rarity in SF.

🛏 The Castro

BECK'S MOTOR LODGE
MOTEL $$

Map p312 (☎415-621-8212; www.becksmotorlodge.com; 2222 Market St; d $169-299; ⓟ❄🐾; Ⓜ Castro St) Back when it opened in 1958, Beck's rooms cost $5 a night – but after recent upgrades, this mid-century motel is good as new, clean, sharp, even a tad upscale. Though not LGBTIQ-specific, its central Castro location makes it the gay go-to. During summer and major events like Pride or Folsom St Fair, rooms book out months ahead. Free parking.

INN ON CASTRO
B&B $$

Map p312 (☎415-861-0321; www.innoncastro. com; 321 Castro St; d $165-250, with shared bath $135-155, self-catering apt $205-225; 🛜; Ⓜ Castro St) A portal to the Castro's disco heyday, this Edwardian townhouse is decked out with '70s-mod furnishings, trippy artwork and a jungle's worth of exotic plants. Rooms are spotless and retro cool, with eye-opening colors and pop art pillows. Exceptional breakfasts – the owner is a chef. Several nearby, great-value apartments are also available for rent. No elevator; parking available nearby.

★ PARKER GUEST HOUSE   B&B $$$

Map p312 (☑415-621-3222, 888-520-7275; www.
parkerguesthouse.com; 520 Church St; d $249-
289, with shared bath $209-249; P @ 🛜; 🚇33,
M J) 🗲 Make your gay getaway in grand
style at this Edwardian estate, covering
two sunny yellow mansions linked by secret
gardens. Guest rooms hit the swanky mod-
ern sweet spot: stately, inviting beds piled
with down duvets and gleaming retro-tiled
bathrooms. Unwind over wine in the sun-
room, linger over continental breakfasts, or
get cozy with sherry by the library fireplace.

🛌 The Haight & Hayes Valley

HAYES VALLEY INN   HOTEL $

Map p316 (☑800-930-7999, 415-431-9131; www.
hayesvalleyinn.com; 417 Gough St; d with shared
bath $109-189; @ 🛜🐾; 🚇21, M Van Ness) Like
a European *pension,* this amazingly rea-
sonable find has simple, small rooms with
shared bathrooms, a napping doggie in the
parlor, and welcoming staff. Turret rooms
have bay windows and accommodate three
guests. Drawbacks: street noise and too
few bathrooms. Bonuses: world-class din-
ing and entertainment at your doorstep. No
elevator.

RED VICTORIAN   COMMUNE $

Map p314 (https://redvic.com; 1665 Haight St; r
with shared bath $94-107; 🛜; 🚇6, 7, 33, 43, M N)
For the complete Haight experience, stay in
a historic commune. This rambling 1904
Victorian houses a dozen quasi-resident ide-
alists plus guests who share six bathrooms,
kitchen, and ground-floor makerspace
hosting events ranging from homebrew
tastings to 'Digital Tools for Menstrual
Health' lectures – guests can attend and/or
host. Of the six snug, tidy guest rooms, bay-
windowed Golden Gate's the sunniest – but
here people bring their own sunshine.

METRO HOTEL   HOTEL $

Map p314 (☑415-861-5364; www.metrohotelsf.
com; 319 Divisadero St; d $107-121, q $153-168;
@ 🛜; 🚇6, 7, 24) Trendy Divisadero St is lined
with boutiques and restaurants, and Metro
Hotel has a prime position – some rooms
overlook the patio of top-notch Ragazza
pizzeria (p183). Rooms are cheap and clean,
if bland – ask for the SF mural room. One
room sleeps six ($182), and the studio dou-
ble has a kitchenette. Handy to the Haight,
with 24-hour reception but no elevator.

★ CHATEAU TIVOLI   B&B $$

Map p314 (☑800-228-1647, 415-776-5462; www.
chateautivoli.com; 1057 Steiner St; d $205-215,
with shared bath $160-185, q $220-325; 🛜; 🚇5,
22) The source of neighborhood gossip since
1892, this gilded and turreted mansion
graciously hosted Isadora Duncan, Mark
Twain and (rumor has it) the ghost of a Victorian opera diva – and now you too can be
Chateau Tivoli's guest. Nine antique-filled
rooms and suites set the scene for romance;
most have claw-foot bathtubs, though two
share a bathroom. No elevator or TVs.

★ PARSONAGE   B&B $$

Map p316 (☑415-863-3699; www.theparsonage.
com; 198 Haight St; r $240-280; @ 🛜; 🚇6, 71,
M F) With rooms named for San Francisco's
grand dames, this 23-room 1883 Italianate
Victorian retains gorgeous original de-
tails, including rose-brass chandeliers and
Carrara-marble fireplaces. Spaciousrooms
offer antique beds with cushy SF-made
McRoskey mattresses; some rooms have
wood-burning fireplaces. Take breakfast in
the formal dining room, and brandy and
chocolates before bed. Two-night minimum.

SLEEP OVER SAUCE   B&B $$

Map p316 (☑415-621-0896; www.sleepsf.com; 135
Gough St; d $150-195, ste $245-295; @ 🛜; 🚇21, 47,
49, M Van Ness) At this eight-room inn above a
tempting Hayes Valley bar, you're down the
block from great restaurants and world-class
entertainment at SFJAZZ, SF Opera, Symphony and Ballet. Simple rooms have dark-
wood furniture; guests share a living room
with fireplace. Bathrooms are sparkling
clean with Egyptian-cotton towels, but not
all are en suite. No elevator or front desk –
check in at the restaurant downstairs.

🛌 Golden Gate Park & the Avenues

SEAL ROCK INN   MOTEL $$

Map p318 (☑415-752-8000, 888-732-5762; www.
sealrockinn.com; 545 Point Lobos Ave; s $160-
207, d $170-217; P 🛜; 🚇38) Far from down-
town, this vintage 1950s ocean-side motel
has big rooms, where Hunter S Thompson
holed up in to write in the '70s. Today it's
a mellow, family-friendly getaway with
beach, park and coastal hike access; ask
if the pool has reopened. All rooms have
refrigerators and microwaves; some have
kitchenettes. Reserve for 3rd-floor rooms
with views and gas fireplaces.

Understand San Francisco

San Francisco Today

Congratulations: you're right on time for SF's latest tech boom, art show, green initiative, civil rights movement and (fair warning) marriage proposal. SF has its ups and downs, but, as anyone who's clung on to the side of a cable car will tell you, this town gives you one hell of a ride.

Best on Film & TV

Milk (2008) Sean Penn won an Oscar for his portrayal of America's first openly gay elected official.

Tales of the City (1993) Laura Linney opens her mind and unravels a mystery in SF's swinging '70s.

Chan Is Missing (1982) When Chan disappears, two cabbies realize they don't know Chan, Chinatown or themselves.

Harold and Maude (1971) The Conservatory of Flowers and Sutro Baths make metaphorically apt backdrops for this May–December romance.

Best in Print

Howl and Other Poems (Allen Ginsberg; 1956) Mind-altering, law-changing words defined a generation of 'angel-headed hipsters.'

Slouching Towards Bethlehem (Joan Didion; 1968) Scorching truth burns through San Francisco fog during the Summer of Love.

Time and Materials (Robert Hass; 2007) Every Pulitzer Prize–winning syllable is as essential as a rivet in the Golden Gate Bridge.

On the Road (Jack Kerouac; 1957) Banged out in a San Francisco attic, Kerouac's travelogue set postwar America free.

Green City, USA

According to the North American Green Cities Index, San Francisco is the greenest of them all. Practices that are standard-setting elsewhere were pioneered here, including LEED-certified green hotels, organic cocktail bars, sustainable dining from tacos to tasting menus, and dozens of car-parking spaces that have been converted into public green oases. San Francisco mandates citywide composting and has banned plastic bags as part of its initiative to become a zero-waste city by 2030. San Franciscans also support more environmental nonprofits than other US cities.

Welcome to Boomtown

The Bay Area currently leads the nation in job creation: mobile apps and social media are booming SF industries, with restaurants, bars, clubs and performance spaces flourishing as the tech money flows in. San Franciscans also rank above the national average in charitable giving. The economic upturn does have downsides, however, and longtime San Franciscans struggle to keep pace with rising house and food prices. Private buses whisking SF-based tech workers to Silicon Valley jobs have come to symbolize a growing income divide, as service workers commute long distances into SF via floundering public transit. Your patience with service workers while you're in town will help ease the burden of increasingly long commutes to low-wage jobs.

Sanctuary City

San Francisco was the first city worldwide to declare itself a 'Sanctuary City.' In the 1980s, Central American refugees escaping civil war settled in San Francisco but were unable to obtain official refugee status. To ensure these new San Franciscans were afforded some protection under the law, a 1989 'City of Refuge' ordinance prohibited SF police from detaining people based on immigration status alone. The city strengthened its Sanctuary status in 2013, with an ordinance prohibiting police cooperation with federal immigration agents – a rule that provoked criticism from Donald Trump.

On January 25, 2017, Trump issued an executive order threatening Sanctuary Cities with withdrawal of federal funds – including a projected loss to San Francisco of $1.3 billion in funding for roads, homeless shelters and other safety-net programs. San Francisco promptly filed a lawsuit against the order – and California passed a 2017 law declaring all of California a 'Sanctuary State.' Meanwhile, Sanctuary City pride has hit San Francisco streets at City Hall rallies and on T-shirts bearing the city's new motto: 'Build bridges, not walls.'

Marijuana Legalization

California voters passed a law legalizing marijuana for recreational and medical use starting in 2018, but it was a long time coming. Legalization activists first got organized in San Francisco in 1964. But the movement didn't get much press until San Francisco's Summer of Love in 1967, when police raided a crash pad on 710 Ashbury St – home to the Grateful Dead rock band. Eleven members of the household were arrested for possession of marijuana.

The raid backfired. The Grateful Dead quickly posted bail and held a press conference. Rather than protesting their innocence, they demanded the decriminalization of marijuana claiming that the dangers of pot were exaggerated. And besides, if everyone who used pot in San Francisco were arrested, the city would be empty.

The case made headlines, and with rock-star backing, the legalization movement took off. California put decriminalization to a vote in 1972, but it didn't pass. The issue became urgent during the AIDS crisis, when caregivers found that terminal patients' pain and wasting could be alleviated by medical marijuana use. In 1996, California's Compassionate Care Act made California the first US state allowing patients access to marijuana by prescription.

Today California's legalization of pot for recreational and medical use enables the state to tax, license and monitor an industry that's been (ahem) budding for decades. For your own safety, avoid street dealers, who may adulterate their pot. Reputable, trailblazing, licensed cannabis dispensaries are available citywide, and many deliver through reliable, fast, tamper-proof delivery services such as HelloMD (www.hellomd.com).

You must be aged 18 or over with ID to buy pot, and you're expected to consume it responsibly in private spaces. Stay safe and, as the Grateful Dead would say: 'if you get confused, just let the music play.'

population per sq mile

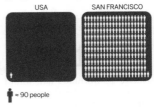

USA   SAN FRANCISCO

👤 ≈ 90 people

politics
(% of population)

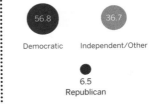

56.8
Democratic

36.7
Independent/Other

6.5
Republican

if San Francisco were 100 people

40 would be Caucasian
36 would be Asian
15 would be Latinx
5 would be African American
4 would be other/multiracial

History

Native Californians had found gold in California long before 1849 – but it hardly seemed worth mentioning, as long as there were oysters for lunch and venison for dinner. Once word circulated, San Francisco was transformed almost overnight from bucolic trading backwater to gold-rush metropolis. Over 170 years of booms, busts, history-making high jinks and lowdown dirty dealings later, SF remains the wildest city in the west.

Cowboys on a Mission

When Spanish cowboys brought 340 horses, 302 head of cattle and 160 mules to settle Misión San Francisco de Asís (Mission San Francisco) in 1776, there was a slight hitch: the area had already been settled by Native Americans for over 14,300 years. There was plenty of shellfish and wild foods to go around, so the arrival of Captain Juan Bautista de Anza, Father Francisco Palou and their livestock initially met with no apparent resistance – until the Spaniards began to demand more than dinner.

The new arrivals expected the local Ohlone to build them a mission and to take over its management within 10 years. In exchange, the Ohlone were allowed one meager meal a day, if any, and a place in God's kingdom – which came much sooner than expected for many. Smallpox and other introduced diseases reduced the Ohlone population by almost three-quarters during the 50 years of Spanish rule in California.

As the name suggests, Mission Dolores ('mission of the sorrows') settlement never really prospered. Spain wasn't especially sorry to hand over the troublesome settlement to the newly independent nation of Mexico, but Mexico soon made this colony a profitable venture with a bustling hide and tallow trade at Yerba Buena Cove, where the Financial District now stands. Much of the land was owned by a woman: Juana Briones, rancher, dairy farmer, trader, midwife, mother of 11 children, and *fundadora* (founder) of San Francisco.

Meanwhile, US–Mexico relations steadily deteriorated, and things were made worse by rumors that Mexico was entertaining a British buyout offer for California. The Mexican–American War broke out in 1846

TIMELINE	June 1776	1835	1846
	Captain Juan Bautista de Anza and Father Francisco Palou arrive in SF with cattle and settlers. With Ohlone conscripts, they build the Misión San Francisco de Asís (now Mission Dolores).	President Andrew Jackson's emissary makes an offer of $500,000 to buy Northern California. Mexico testily refuses and tries to sell California to Britain.	The Mexican–American War breaks out and drags on for two years, with much posturing but little actual bloodshed in California.

and dragged on for two years before ending with the Treaty of Guadalupe Hidalgo. This treaty formally ceded California and the present-day southwestern states to the USA – a loss that was initially reckoned by missionizing Church fathers in souls, but within months could be counted in ingots.

Gold! Gold! Gold!

In 1848 Sam Brannan, the San Francisco real-estate speculator and tabloid founder, published rumors of a find 120 miles away near Sutter's Mill, where sawmill employees had found gold flakes in the water. Hoping to scoop other newspapers and maybe sell swampland to rubes back East, Brannan published golden gossip as solid fact.

When San Franciscans proved skeptical, Brannan traveled to Sutter's Fort and convinced fellow Mormons to entrust him with a vial of gold for the church, swearing to keep their secret. Brannan kept his word for about a day. Upon his return to San Francisco, he ran through Portsmouth Sq, brandishing the vial and shouting, 'Gold! Gold! Gold on the American River!'

But Brannan's plan backfired. Within weeks San Francisco's population shrank to 200, as every able-bodied individual headed to the hills to pan for gold. Brannan's newspaper folded; there was no one around to read, write or print it. Good thing Brannan had a backup plan: he'd bought every available shovel, pick and pan, and he opened a general store near Sutter's Fort. Within its first 70 days, Brannan & Co sold $36,000 in equipment – almost a million bucks in today's terms. Brannan bought land from Juana Briones, and became San Francisco's largest landowner.

Other newspapers around the world hastily published stories of 'gold mountains' near San Francisco. Boatloads of prospectors arrived from Australia, China, South America and Europe. They weren't all miners – many were refugees, seeking safety from civil war in their home countries. Meanwhile, another 40,000 American prospectors trudged overland, seeking fortunes and freedom from slavery and strife in the lead-up to the American Civil War.

Lawless, Loose & Lowdown

By 1850, the year California was fast-tracked for admission as the 31st state in the Union, San Francisco's population had skyrocketed from 800 a year earlier to an estimated 25,000. But for all the new money in town, it wasn't exactly easy living.

Most of the early prospectors (called '49ers,' after their arrival date) were men under the age of 40, and to keep them entertained – and fleece the gullible – some 500 saloons, 20 theaters and numerous venues of ill repute opened within five years. A buck might procure

Top Five Sites for Native History

Mission Dolores (The Mission)

Alcatraz

The Presidio

Rincon Center Murals (Financial District)

San Francisco Historical Society (Downtown)

HISTORY GOLD! GOLD! GOLD!

1848	1850	1851	1860
Gold is discovered near present-day Placerville. San Francisco's newspaper publisher Sam Brannan spills the secret, and the gold rush is on.	With hopes of solid-gold tax revenues, the US hastily dubs California the 31st state.	Gold discovery in Australia leads to cheering in the streets of Melbourne – and panic in the streets of San Francisco as the price for California gold plummets.	Defying her abusive husband, SF entrepreneur Juana Briones wins a landmark US Supreme Court case, establishing women's property rights in the US.

whiskey, opium or the company of women frolicking on swings over the bar on San Francisco's 'Barbary Coast.'

Wise prospectors arrived early and got out quick. As gold became harder to find, backstabbing became more common, sometimes literally. Successful Peruvians and Chileans were harassed and denied renewals of their mining claims, and most left California by 1855. Native Californian laborers who had helped the 49ers strike it rich were also denied the right to hold claims. Despite San Francisco's well-earned reputation for freewheeling lawlessness, crime was swiftly and conveniently blamed on Australian newcomers. Along with Australians, Chinese – the most populous group in California by 1860 – were on the receiving end of misplaced resentment.

The View from Gold Mountain

Within a year of the 1849 gold rush, Chinatown was already established in San Francisco – better known in Cantonese as Gam Saan ('Gold Mountain'). At first Chinatown wasn't exclusively Chinese at all, but a bachelor community of Mexican, American, European, African American and Chinese miners who bunked, prospected and caroused side by side. But when gold prices came crashing down with the discovery of gold in Australia, miners turned their irrational resentment onto resident Australians and Chinese. Australian lodging houses were burned to the ground, anti-Chinese riots broke out, and Chinese land claims were voided. In 1870, San Francisco officially restricted housing and employment for anyone born in China.

The 1882 US Chinese Exclusion Act prevented new immigration from China, barred Chinese from citizenship until 1943 and spurred the passage of 100 parallel ordinances limiting rights for Japanese San Franciscans. Not coincidentally, anti-Chinese laws served the needs of local magnates looking for cheap labor to build the first cross-country railroad. With little other choice of legitimate employment, an estimated 12,000 Chinese laborers did the dangerous work of dynamiting rail tunnels through the Sierra Nevada.

After the 1906 earthquake and fire, city officials planned to oust Chinese residents altogether and develop the prime property of Chinatown, but the Chinese consulate and rifle-toting Chinatown merchants persuaded the city otherwise. They rebuilt while Chinatown was still smoldering, using clinker bricks – and developed a new architectural style.

Today Chinatown is a major tourism boon to the city, yet many residents scrape by on less than $10,000 a year – not exactly a Gold Mountain. Upwardly mobile residents tend to leave Chinatown, new arrivals move in, and the cycle begins anew.

William Hammond Hall briefly quit his job building Golden Gate Park in 1886 over proposals to convert the park into a racetrack lined with cookie-cutter housing. When a casino and carnival were established for the 1893 Midwinter's Fair, Hammond Hall fought to get the park returned to its intended purpose.

1861–65	May 1869	1882	April 18, 1906
While the US Civil War divides North from South out East, SF perversely profits in the West, as industry diverted from factories burdened by the war effort heads to San Francisco.	The Golden Spike completes the first transcontinental railroad. The news travels via San Franciscan David Brooks' invention: the telegraph.	The US Chinese Exclusion Act suspends new immigration from China; these racially targeted laws remain until 1943.	A massive earthquake levels entire blocks of SF in 47 seconds, setting off fires that rage for three days. Survivors start rebuilding while the town is still smoldering.

Keeping the West Wild

Naturalist John Muir came through San Francisco in 1868, but he soon left, with a shudder, for greener pastures in Yosemite. But with the backing of fellow nature enthusiasts in San Francisco, he founded a trailblazing environmentalist organization called the Sierra Club. The miles of Californian wilderness that Muir and his organization successfully lobbied to protect includes one of San Francisco's most popular escapes: Muir Woods.

San Franciscans determined to preserve the city's natural splendors also pushed to establish the city's first park in 1867, when squatters were paid to vacate the area now known as Buena Vista Park. With a mandate from San Francisco voters to transform sand dunes into a vast city park, tenacious engineer William Hammond Hall saw the development of Golden Gate Park through to completion from 1870 to 1887 – despite developers' best attempts to scuttle park plans in favor of casinos, amusement parks, resorts, racetracks and an igloo village.

Populist millionaire Adolph Sutro decided that every working stiff should be able to escape downtown tenements for the sand dunes and sunsets of Ocean Beach, accessible for a nickel on his public railway. By way of thanks, he was elected mayor in 1894 – the first of many city officials to succeed with a green platform.

Built in 1907, soon after the earthquake, the Great American Music Hall shows the unabashed flamboyance of post-earthquake San Francisco. Carved gilt decor recalls the city's gold-rush heyday, and scantily clad frescoed figures hint at other possible backstage entertainments – this music hall once did double duty as a bordello.

Double Disaster

On April 18, 1906, a quake estimated at a terrifying 7.8 to 8.3 on today's Richter scale struck the city. In 47 seconds, San Franciscans discovered just how many corners had been cut on government contracts. Unreinforced buildings collapsed, including City Hall. The sole functioning downtown water source was a fountain donated to the city by opera prodigy Lotta Crabtree. Assembly lines were formed to haul buckets of water from Lotta's Fountain, but the water couldn't reach the crest of steep hills fast enough. Chinatown burned for days and, even further uphill, Nob Hill mansions were reduced to ashes.

Survivors fled to Potrero Hill and Buena Vista Park, and for three days they watched their city and its dreams of grandeur go up in smoke. The Mission was saved by one functioning fire hydrant at the top of Dolores Park – and grateful residents still paint it gold every year.

Second Acts

Yet San Francisco had learned one thing through 50 years of booms and busts: how to stage a comeback. All but one of the city's 20 historic

1910	1913	1915	1927
Angel Island opens as the West Coast immigration station. Over 30 years, 175,000 arrivals from Asia are subjected to months or years of interrogation and prison-like conditions.	California's Alien Land Law prohibits property ownership by Asians, including Japanese, Koreans and Indians. Lawyer Juichi Soyeda immediately files suit; he wins in 1952, 23 years after his death.	Post-quake San Francisco hosts the Panama–Pacific International Exposition. The city cements its reputation as a showplace for new technology, outlandish ideas and the arts.	After a year of tinkering, 21-year-old Philo Farnsworth transmits the first successful TV broadcast of...a straight line.

theaters were completely destroyed by the earthquake and fire, but theater tents were soon set up amid the rubble. Surviving entertainers began marathon performances to lift the city's spirits. Soprano Luisa Tetrazzini ditched New York's Metropolitan Opera to return to San Francisco and sang on Market St to an audience of 250,000 – virtually every surviving San Franciscan.

San Franciscans rose to the occasion and rebuilt their city at an astounding rate of 15 buildings a day. In a show of popular priorities, San Francisco's theaters were rebuilt long before City Hall's grandiose Civic Center was completed. Most of the Barbary Coast had gone up in flames, so the theater scene and most red-light entertainments decamped to the Tenderloin, where they remain.

The Left Coast

San Francisco's port thrived in 1934, but when local longshoremen protested dangerous working conditions, shipping tycoons sought dockworkers elsewhere – only to discover that San Francisco's longshoremen had coordinated their strike with 35,000 workers all along the West Coast. After 83 days, police and the National Guard broke the strike, killing two strikers and hospitalizing 85 protestors. Public sympathy forced concessions from shipping magnates. Coit Tower frescoes completed in 1934 capture the pro-worker sentiment that swept the city – known henceforth as America's 'Left Coast.'

When WWII brought a shipbuilding boom to town, it created opportunities for African Americans and for women to take key roles in San Francisco's workforce. In their downtime, they founded new musical, literary, and artistic movements. After the war, their technical skills were instrumental in creating microprocessors, in a budding business zone south of the city that came to be known as Silicon Valley.

But with misplaced anxiety about possible attacks from the Pacific, Japanese San Franciscans and Japantown became convenient targets for public animosity. Two months after the attack on Pearl Harbor in Hawaii, President Franklin D Roosevelt signed Executive Order 9066, ordering the relocation of 120,000 Japanese Americans to internment camps. The San Francisco–based Japanese American Citizens League (JACL) immediately challenged the grounds for internment and lobbied tirelessly for more than 40 years to overturn the executive order, gain symbolic reparations for internees, and restore the community's standing with a formal letter of apology signed by President George HW Bush in 1988. By setting key legal precedents from the 1940s onward, JACL paved the way for the 1964 Civil Rights Act.

On November 20, 1969, 79 Native American activists defied Coast Guard blockades to symbolically reclaim Alcatraz as native land. Hundreds of supporters joined the protest, until FBI raids ousted the protestors on June 11, 1971. Public support for the protesters strengthened self-rule for Native territories, signed into law by Richard Nixon.

1934	1937	February 1942	1957
A West Coast longshoremen's strike ends with strikers and sympathizers shot by police. A citywide strike follows; longshoremen win historic concessions.	After four years of dangerous labor in treacherous riptides, the Golden Gate Bridge is complete.	Executive Order 9066 mandates internment of 120,000 Japanese Americans. The Japanese American Citizens League immediately files civil rights claims.	City Lights wins a landmark ruling against book banning over the publication of Allen Ginsberg's Howl, and free speech and free spirits enjoy a reprieve from McCarthyism.

Beats, Free Speech, Free Spirits

Members of the armed services dismissed from service for homosexuality and other 'subversive' behavior during WWII were discharged onto the streets of San Francisco, as if that would teach them a lesson. Instead, the new arrivals found themselves at home in the low-rent, laissez-faire neighborhoods of North Beach and the Haight. So when the rest of the country took a sharp right turn with McCarthyism in the 1950s, rebels and romantics headed for San Francisco – including Jack Kerouac. By the time his cross-country chronicle *On the Road* was published in 1957, the motley crowd of writers, artists, dreamers and unclassifiable characters Kerouac called 'the mad ones' had found their way to like-minded San Francisco.

San Francisco didn't always take kindly to the nonconformists derisively referred to in the press as 'beatniks,' and police and poets were increasingly at odds on the streets of North Beach. Officers tried to fine 'beatnik chicks' for wearing sandals, only to be mercilessly taunted in verse by self-described African American Jewish voodoo anarchist and legendary street-corner Beat poet Bob Kaufman. Poet Lawrence Ferlinghetti and bookstore manager Shigeyoshi Murao of City Lights were arrested for 'willfully and lewdly' printing Allen Ginsberg's magnificent, incendiary epic poem *Howl*. But artistic freedom prevailed in 1957, when City Lights won its landmark ruling against book banning.

The kindred Beat spirits Ginsberg described in *Howl* experimented with art, radical politics, marijuana and one another, defying 1950s social-climbing conventions and Senator Joe McCarthy's alarmist call to weed out 'communists in our midst.' When McCarthy's House Un-American Activities Committee (HUAC) convened in San Francisco in 1960 to expose alleged communists, UC Berkeley students organized a disruptive sing-along sit-in at City Hall. After police turned fire hoses on the protesters, thousands of San Franciscans rallied, and HUAC split town, never to return. It was official: the '60s had begun.

Flower Power

San Francisco was a testing ground for freedom of expression in the 1960s, as comedian Lenny Bruce uttered the f-word on stage and burlesque dancer Carol Doda bared it all for titillated audiences in North Beach clubs. But neither jokes nor striptease would pop the last button of confining 1950s social norms – no, that was a job for the CIA. In a major lapse in screening judgment, the CIA hired local writer Ken Kesey to test psychoactive drugs intended to create the ultimate soldier. Instead, they inspired Kesey to write the novel *One Flew Over the Cuckoo's Nest,* drive psychedelic busloads of Merry Pranksters across

Top Five Beat Scenes

City Lights Books
(North Beach)

Beat Museum
(North Beach)

Vesuvio
(North Beach)

Li Po (Chinatown)

Bob Kaufman Alley
(North Beach)

1959	January 1966	August 1966	October 1966
Mayor George Christopher authorizes measures against gay citizens. Openly gay WWII veteran José Sarria runs for public office – in drag.	The Trips Festival is organized by techno-futurist Stewart Brand and features Ken Kesey, the Grateful Dead and Native American activists, plus Bill Graham handling promotion.	Transgender patrons protest police harassment at Compton's Cafeteria in the Tenderloin; the uprising kicks off the US transgender rights movement.	In Oakland, Huey Newton and Bobby Seale found the Black Panther Party for Self-Defense, demanding 'Land, Bread, Housing, Education, Clothing, Justice and Peace.'

the country, and introduce San Francisco to LSD and the Grateful Dead at the legendary Acid Tests. San Francisco's 1966 Trips Festival led co-organizer and veteran CIA tester Stewart Brand to a revelation: vast computing machines should shrink to fit into the human hand...a wild hallucination, obviously.

After the Civil Rights movement anything seemed possible, and for a while it seemed that the freaky force of free thinking would stop the unpopular Vietnam War. At the January 14, 1967, Human Be-In in Golden Gate Park, trip-master Timothy Leary urged a crowd of 20,000 to dream a new American dream and 'turn on, tune in, drop out.' Free music rang out in the streets, free food was provided by community activists the Diggers, free LSD was circulated by Owsley Stanley, free crash pads were all over the Haight and free love transpired on some very dubious free mattresses. For the duration of the Summer of Love it seemed possible to make love, not war.

But a chill soon settled over San Francisco. Civil rights hero Martin Luther King Jr was assassinated on April 8, 1968, followed by the fatal shooting of Robert Kennedy on June 5 after he'd won California's presidential primary. Radicals worldwide called for revolution, and separatist groups like Oakland's Black Panther Party for Self-Defense took up arms.

How to Revive the Summer of Love

Give a free Haight St concert

·······

Commune with nature at Hippie Hill in Golden Gate Park

·······

Take the Haight Flashback walking tour

·······

Volunteer or show kindness to strangers

Meanwhile, recreational drug-taking was turning into a thankless career for many, a distinct itch in the nether regions was making the rounds of Haight squats, and still more busloads of teenage runaways were arriving in the ill-equipped, wigged-out Haight. Haight Ashbury Free Clinic helped with the rehabbing and the itching, but disillusionment seemed incurable when Hells Angels beat protestors in Berkeley and turned on the crowd at a free Rolling Stones concert at Altamont.

Many idealists headed 'back to the land' in the bucolic North Bay, jump-starting California's organic farming movement with Stewart Brand's *Whole Earth Catalog* as their DIY resource. But a dark streak emerged among those who remained, including young Charles Manson, the Symbionese Liberation Army (better known post-1974 as Patty Hearst's kidnappers) and an evangelical egomaniac named Jim Jones, who would oblige 900 followers to commit mass suicide in 1978.

By the time Be-In LSD supplier Stanley was released from a three-year jail term in 1970, the party seemed to be over. But in the Castro, it was just getting started.

Pride

By the 1970s, San Francisco's gay community was fed up with police raids, done with hetero Haight communes, and ready for music with an actual beat. In 1959, after an opponent accused then-mayor George

January 1967	1969	November 1969	April 1977
The Summer of Love begins with the Human Be-In, with draft cards used as rolling papers, free Grateful Dead gigs and Allen Ginsberg naked, as usual.	A computer link is established between Stanford Research Institute and UCLA via ARPANET, and an unsolicited group message is sent: email and spam are born.	Native American activists reclaim the abandoned island of Alcatraz as reparation for broken treaties. The occupation lasts 19 months, until FBI agents forcibly oust the activists.	The Apple II is introduced in SF at the first West Coast Computer Faire and stuns the crowd with its computing speed (1MHz).

Christopher of allowing San Francisco to become 'the national head-quarters of the organized homosexuals,' Christopher authorized crackdowns on gay bars and started a blacklist of gay citizens.

Never one to be harassed or upstaged, WWII veteran and drag star José Sarria became the first openly gay man to run for public office, in 1962, on a platform to end police harassment of gay San Franciscans. He won 5600 votes. Undaunted, he declared himself Absolute Empress of San Francisco, the widow and true heir of Emperor Norton. When local media echoed the Empress' criticism of the continuing raids, police crackdowns stopped.

By the mid-1970s, the rainbow flag was flying high over gay businesses and homes in the out-and-proud Castro, and the sexual revolution was in full swing at gay clubs and bathhouses on Polk St and in SoMa. The Castro was triumphant when Castro camera-store owner Harvey Milk was elected the city's Supervisor, becoming the nation's first openly gay elected official – but as Milk himself eerily predicted, his time in office would be cut short by an act of extremist violence.

Dan White, a washed-up politician hyped on Hostess Twinkies, fatally shot Milk and then-mayor George Moscone at City Hall in 1978. The charge was reduced to manslaughter due to the infamous 'Twinkie Defense' faulting the ultra-sweet junk food, sparking an outpouring of public outrage dubbed the 'White Riot.' White was deeply disturbed, and committed suicide a year after his 1984 release.

By then San Francisco had another problem. A strange illness began to appear at local hospitals, and it seemed to be hitting the gay community especially hard. The first cases of AIDS reported in San Francisco were mistakenly referred to as GRID (Gay-Related Immune Deficiency), and a social stigma became attached to the virus. But San Francisco health providers and gay activists rallied to establish global standards for care and prevention, with vital early HIV/AIDS health initiatives funded not through federal agencies but with tireless local efforts – the Empress herself organized trailblazing fundraisers. Caregivers noticed that marijuana eased pain and symptoms for some people living with HIV/AIDS, and backed the legalization of marijuana for medical use in California in 1996.

Civil rights organizations, religious institutions and LGBTIQ+ organizations increasingly popped the question: why couldn't same-sex couples get married too? Early backing came from the Japanese American Citizens League, which publicly endorsed marriage for same-sex couples as a civil right in 1994. Just 45 days after taking office in 2004, San Francisco mayor Gavin Newsom authorized same-sex weddings in San Francisco.

The first couple to be married were Phyllis Lyon and Del Martin, a San Francisco couple who had spent 52 years together. California courts

---

How to Celebrate Gay Pride

Come out and join the Pride Parade

Meet fabulous, fearless pioneers at the GLBT Museum

Peruse petitions at Human Rights Campaign

Binge-watch at the LGBTQ Film Festival

Get inspired at City Hall to run for office like Harvey Milk did

HISTORY PRIDE

1977	November 1978	1981	1989
Harvey Milk becomes the first openly gay man elected to US public office. Milk sponsors a gay-rights bill and trend-setting 'pooper-scooper' ordinance before his murder in 1978.	After moving his People's Temple from SF to Guyana, Jim Jones orders the murders of a congressman and four journalists and the mass suicide of 900 followers.	The first cases of AIDS are identified in an epidemic that would claim 30 million lives. Early intervention in SF institutes key prevention measures and sets global treatment standards.	Hundreds of sea lions haul out on the yacht slips near Pier 39. State law and wildlife officials grant them squatters' rights, and the beach bums become San Francisco mascots.

ultimately voided their and 4036 other San Francisco same-sex marriage contracts, but Lyon and Martin weren't dissuaded: they married again on June 18, 2008, with Mayor Newsom personally officiating. Martin passed away two months later at age 83, her wife by her side.

California courts struck down laws prohibiting same-sex marriage as unconstitutional in 2010. Upon appeal, the US Supreme Court upheld California's state ruling in July 2015, effectively legalizing same-sex marriage nationwide.

New Technologies, New Prospects

Industry dwindled steadily in San Francisco after WWII, as Oakland's port took over container-ship traffic and San Francisco's Presidio military base was deactivated. But onetime military contractors found work in a stretch of scrappy firms south of San Francisco nicknamed 'Silicon Valley.' When a company called Hewlett-Packard, based in a South Bay garage, introduced the 9100A 'computing genie' in 1968, a generation of unconventional thinkers and tinkerers took note.

Ads breathlessly gushed that Hewlett-Packard's 'light' (40lb) machine could 'take on roots of a fifth-degree polynomial, Bessel functions, elliptic integrals and regression analysis' – all for the low price of $4900 (about $29,000 today). Consumers didn't know what to do with such a computer, until its potential was explained in simple terms by Trips Festival co-organizer and techno-futurist Stewart Brand. In a 1969 issue of his DIY-promoting *Whole Earth Catalog,* Brand reasoned that the technology governments used to run countries could empower ordinary people. He called it 'personal computing.'

That same year, University of California, Los Angeles (UCLA) professor Len Kleinrock sent the first rudimentary email from his computer to another at Stanford. The message he typed was 'L,' then 'O,' then 'G' – at which point the computer crashed.

The next wave of California techies was determined to create a personal computer that could compute and communicate without crashing. When 21-year-old Steve Jobs and Steve Wozniak introduced the Apple II at San Francisco's West Coast Computer Faire in 1977, techies were awed by the memory (4KB of RAM!) and the microprocessor speed (1MHz!). The Mac II originally retailed for the equivalent today of $4300 (or, for 48KB of RAM, more than twice that amount) – a staggering investment for what seemed like a glorified calculator/typewriter. Even if machines could talk to one another, pundits reasoned, what would they talk about?

A trillion web pages and a few million mobile apps later, it turns out machines have plenty to communicate. By the mid-1990s, the dot-com

Top Five for Weird Technology

Exploratorium (Fisherman's Wharf)

San Francisco Museum of Modern Art (SoMa)

Audium (Pacific Heights)

The Interval (Fort Mason)

Internet Archive (Richmond)

October 17, 1989	March 2000	2003	February 2004
The Loma Prieta earthquake hits 6.9 on the Richter scale; a freeway in SF and a Bay Bridge section collapse in 15 seconds, killing 41.	After the NASDAQ index peaks at double its value a year earlier, the dot-com bubble pops. Share prices drop dramatically, and the 'dot-bomb' closes businesses across SF within a month.	Republican Arnold Schwarzenegger is elected governor of California. Schwarzenegger breaks party ranks on environmental issues and wins 2007 re-election.	Defying a Californian ban, SF mayor Gavin Newsom licenses 4037 same-sex marriages. Courts declare the marriages void.

industry boomed in SoMa warehouses as start-up ventures rushed to put news, politics, fashion and, yes, sex online. But when venture-capital funding dried up, multimillion-dollar sites shriveled into oblivion.

The paper fortunes of the dot-com boom disappeared on one nasty NASDAQ-plummeting day, March 10, 2000, leaving San Francisco service-sector employees and 26-year-old vice-presidents alike without any immediate job prospects. City dot-com revenues vanished; a 1999 FBI probe revealed that a windfall ended up in the pockets of real-estate developers. But today San Francisco is again booming with start-ups aiming to succeed just like San Francisco–based Twitter, Pinterest, Instagram, Airbnb, Yelp, Uber and Lyft – and, just south of the city, Facebook, LinkedIn, Apple, Google, eBay, YouTube, Netflix, Adobe and hundreds more top tech companies.

Redesigning Humankind

Inside shiny new glass towers at SoMa's Mission Bay, start-ups are busy updating another old technology: the human body. Human augmentation, cancer-fighting nanobots and AI doctors may sound like science-fiction in other cities, but they're well-established fields here.

Biotech was pioneered over beer in San Francisco in 1976. Since Genetech's founders clinked glasses, their company has gained global recognition for cloning human insulin and introducing the hepatitis B vaccine. San Francisco's biotech industry got another boost in 2004, when California voters approved a $3-billion bond measure for stem-cell research. By 2008, California had become the nation's biggest funder of stem-cell research and genetic medicine.

With so many global health crises demanding funding and the attention of researchers, many cures still seem like impossible dreams, and not every Bay Area medical start-up makes good on its life-saving promises. In 2018 blood-testing start-up Theranos was shut down for making false claims and its founders were indicted for fraud. But hope is ever present: in 2017, the University of California, San Francisco successfully applied stem-cell research to produce the first known case of full HIV remission. And if history is any indication, the impossible is almost certain to happen in San Francisco.

2010	2014	2017	2018
After SF couples file suit, courts declare laws prohibiting same-sex marriage unconstitutional. In 2015, the US Supreme Court upholds the ruling, making it legal nationwide.	The San Francisco Giants win their third World Series title in five years; 'Fear the Beard' and 'Rally Thong' become SF cheers.	When Trump's executive order threatens Sanctuary Cities, San Francisco stands by its ground and slaps the federal government with a lawsuit.	California legalizes marijuana for private medical and recreational use by adults age 18 and over with ID.

Literary San Francisco

San Francisco has more writers than any other US city and hoards three times the national average of library books. Anachronistic though it may seem in the capital of new technology, San Franciscans still buy more books per capita than residents of other US cities. But the truth of San Francisco is even stranger than its fiction: where else could poetry fight the law and win? Yet that's exactly what happened in City Lights Books' 1957 landmark anti-censorship ruling in *People v Ferlinghetti*. The city remains a magnet for free thinkers and voracious readers, with its landmark Litquake festival, member-supported bookshops lining 24th St, authors mentoring kids at 826 Valencia, and literary events ranging from raucous booze-fueled book swaps to silent reading groups at Booksmith Bindery.

Poetry

San Franciscans swoon for a few well-chosen words. When the city has you waxing poetic, hit an open mike in the Mission. Key titles:

Howl and Other Poems (Allen Ginsberg; 1956) Each line of Ginsberg's epic title poem is an ecstatic improvised mantra, chronicling the waking dreams of the Beat generation and taking a stand against postwar conformity. Publisher Lawrence Ferlinghetti was taken to court for 'willfully and lewdly' publishing *Howl* – resulting in a landmark free-speech triumph.

A Coney Island of the Mind (Lawrence Ferlinghetti; 1958) This slim collection by San Francisco's Beat poet laureate is an indispensable doorstop for the imagination, letting fresh air and ideas circulate.

Native Tongue (Alejandro Murguía; 2012) The Mission's own San Francisco poet laureate is a master interpreter of San Franciscan behavior, rhythmic performance poet, and charismatic cofounder of Mission Cultural Center for Latino Arts.

Best for Readings

City Lights Books
(North Beach)

Booksmith
(The Haight)

San Francisco
Main Library
(Civic Center)

Adobe Books
(The Mission)

Green Apple
Books
(The Avenues)

Fiction

Many San Franciscans seem like characters in a novel – and after a few days here, you'll swear you've seen Armistead Maupin's corn-fed Castro newbies, Dashiell Hammett's dangerous redheads and Amy Tan's American-born daughters explaining slang to their moms. Key titles:

Tales of the City (Armistead Maupin) The 1976 *San Francisco Chronicle* serial follows classic San Francisco characters: pot-growing landladies of mystery, ever-hopeful Castro club-goers and wide-eyed Midwestern arrivals. See also the miniseries version, which broke PBS ratings records.

The Joy Luck Club (Amy Tan; 1989) The stories of four Chinese-born women and their American-born daughters are woven into a textured tale of immigration and aspiration in San Francisco's Chinatown. Director Wayne Wang's film version is charming, but the novel is more richly nuanced.

The Maltese Falcon (Dashiell Hammett; 1930) In this classic noir novel, private eye Sam Spade risks his reputation on a case involving an elusive redhead, a gold statuette, the Holy Roman Empire and an unholy cast of thugs. Humphrey Bogart made his career as Sam Spade in the movie version.

Nonfiction & Memoir

People-watching rivals reading as a preferred SF pastime, and the result is stranger-than-fiction nonfiction – hence Tom Wolfe's trip-happy tales and Joan Didion's core-shaking takedowns. Key titles:

Slouching Towards Bethlehem (Joan Didion; 1968) Like hot sun through San Francisco summer fog, Didion's 1968 essays burn through the hippie haze to reveal glassy-eyed teenagers adrift in the Summer of Love.

On the Road (Jack Kerouac; 1957) The book Kerouac banged out on one long scroll of paper in a San Francisco attic over a couple of sleepless months of 1951 shook America awake.

The Electric Kool-Aid Acid Test (Tom Wolfe; 1968) His groovy slang may seem dated, but Wolfe had extraordinary presence of mind to capture SF in the '60s with Ken Kesey, the Merry Pranksters, the Grateful Dead and the Hells Angels.

Graphic Novels

Ambrose Bierce and Mark Twain set the standard for sardonic wit, but recently Bay Area graphic novelists like Robert Crumb and Daniel Clowes have added a twist to tradition. Key titles:

Meanwhile in San Francisco (Wendy MacNaughton; 2014) The San Franciscan illustrator captures the city's stories as they unfold on street corners and public spaces, with a pen attuned to the city's ironies and poetry.

Ghost World (Daniel Clowes; 1997) The Oakland-based graphic novelist's sleeper hit follows recent high-school grads Enid and Rebecca as they make plans, make do, grow up and grow apart.

American Born Chinese (Gene Luen Yang & Lark Pien; 2008) Chinese Monkey King fables are intricately interwoven with teenage tales of assimilation – no wonder this won the Eisner Award for best graphic novel, plus the Harvey comic-art award for SF cartoonist Lark Pien.

Zines

The local zine scene has been the underground mother lode of riveting reading since the '70s brought punk, DIY spirit and V Vale's groundbreaking *RE/Search* to San Francisco. The SF Public Library has been collecting local zines since 1966 – check out historic examples in the Little Maga/Zine Collection on the 6th floor of the SF Main Library (p86). For zines you can take with you for eye-opening airplane reading, check out the wide-ranging selection at Needles & Pens (p161).

The most successful local zine is *McSweeney's,* founded by Dave Eggers, who achieved first-person fame with *A Heartbreaking Work of Staggering Genius* (2000) and generously used the proceeds to launch 826 Valencia (p146), a nonprofit writing program for teens. Besides zines written by kids, McSweeney's also publishes an excellent map of literary San Francisco, so you can walk the talk.

Spoken Word

San Francisco's literary tradition doesn't just hang out on bookshelves. Beat authors like Jack Kerouac and Bob Kauffman freed generations of open-mike monologuists from the tyranny of tales with morals and punctuation. Allen Ginsberg's ecstatic readings of *Howl* are commemorated at the Beat Museum (p111), and continue to inspire slam poets at Litquake (p36) and at regular, raucous open mikes in the Mission, Tenderloin, and North Beach.

Best for Comics & Graphic Novels

Mission Art & Comics (The Mission)

Isotope (Hayes Valley)

Kinokuniya Books & Stationery (Japantown)

Cartoon Art Museum (Fisherman's Wharf)

Bound Together Anarchist Book Collective (The Haight)

Best for Zines

Needles & Pens (The Mission)

826 Valencia (The Mission)

Adobe Books (The Mission)

Bound Together Anarchist Book Collective (The Haight)

The Magazine (Tenderloin)

Visual Arts

Art explodes from frames and jumps off the pedestal in San Francisco, where murals, street performances and impromptu sidewalk altars flow from alleyways right into galleries. Velvet ropes would only get in the way of SF's enveloping installations and interactive new-media art – often provocative, sometimes overwhelming, but never standoffish.

Media & Methods

San Francisco has some unfair artistic advantages: it's a photogenic city with a colorful past, with 150-year-old photography and painting traditions to prove it. Homegrown traditions of '50s Beat collage, '60s psychedelia, '70s punk, '80s graffiti, '90s skater graphics and 2000s new-media art keep San Francisco's art scene vibrant.

Photography

Pioneering 19th-century photographer Pirkle Jones saw expressive potential in California landscape photography – but SF native Ansel Adams' photos of Northern California's sublime wilds and his accounts of photography in Yosemite in the 1940s drew generations of camera-clutching visitors to San Francisco. Adams founded Group f/64 with pioneering street photographer Imogen Cunningham and still-life master Edward Weston, who kept a studio in SF and made frequent visits from his permanent base in nearby Carmel.

Adams and Cunningham taught at the San Francisco Art Institute alongside the definitive documentarian of the Great Depression, Dorothea Lange. Among her many poignant photographs are portraits of Californian migrant farm laborers and Japanese Americans forced to leave their San Francisco homes for WWII internment camps. Many of Lange's internment photographs conflicted with official propaganda and were impounded by the Army, not to be shown for 50 years.

After the censorship of her photographs, Lange cofounded the groundbreaking art-photography magazine *Aperture* with Adams and fellow photographers in San Francisco. Today her legacy of cultural critique continues with the colorful Californian suburban dystopias of Larry Sultan and Todd Hido. *Aperture* still publishes, and SF Camerawork continues the proud San Franciscan tradition of boundary-pushing photography shows and publications. Photography fans should book SFMOMA tickets even before air travel – this world-class collection continues to redefine photography past, present and future with landmark shows.

Best for Photography

....

SFMOMA
(Downtown)

....

SF Camerawork
(Civic Center)

....

de Young Museum
(Golden Gate Park)

....

Fraenkel Gallery
at 49 Geary
(Union Square)

....

Chinese Historical Society of America
(Chinatown)

....

Casemore Kirkeby
(Dogpatch)

Social Commentary

The 1930s social-realist movement brought Mexican muralist Diego Rivera and vivid surrealist painter Frida Kahlo to San Francisco, where Rivera was invited to paint a cautionary fresco of California on the San Francisco Stock Exchange Lunch Club and Kahlo painted some of her first portrait commissions. In over a decade spent working on projects in the city and hosting open-studio salons in North Beach, the modern-art power couple inspired bold new approaches to public art in San Francisco. Starting in the 1970s, their larger-than-life figures and leftist leanings have been reprised in works by Mission *muralistas,* as seen on the Women's Building and along Balmy Alley.

The Depression-era Work Projects Administration (WPA) sponsored several SF muralists to create original works for the Rincon Annex Post Office, Coit Tower, Aquatic Park Bathhouse and Beach Chalet. When the murals at Rincon Post Office and Coit Tower turned out to be more radical than the government-sponsored arts program had anticipated, censors demanded changes before the murals could be unveiled. But the artworks outlasted the censors and today are celebrated national landmarks.

Offsetting high-minded revolutionary art is gutsy, irreverent SF satire. Tony Labatt's 1970s video of disco balls dangling from his nether regions sums up SF's disco-era narcissism, while Lynn Hershman Leeson's performances as alter ego Roberta Breitmore chronicled 1970s encounters with feminism, self-help movements and diet fads. San Francisco provocateur Enrique Chagoya invents archaeological artifacts from a parallel universe in which Mexico colonized America – he borrows a page from Philip K Dick's alternative-reality novel *The Man in the High Castle,* and turns it into a fascinating Mayan codex.

VISUAL ARTS MEDIA & METHODS

Abstract Thinking

Local art schools attracted major abstract expressionists during SF's vibrant postwar period, when Clyfford Still, David Park and Elmer Bischoff taught at the San Francisco Art Institute. Still and Park founded the misleadingly named Bay Area Figurative Art movement, an elemental style often associated with San Francisco painter Richard Diebenkorn's fractured, color-blocked landscapes. Diebenkorn influenced San Francisco Pop artist Wayne Thiebaud, who tilted Sunset District street grids into giddy abstract cityscapes.

PUBLIC SCULPTURE

San Francisco owes its sculpture tradition to a nude sculptor's model: 'Big Alma' Spreckels. Her 'sugar daddy' Adolph Spreckels left her sugar-plantation fortunes, which she generously donated to build the Legion of Honor and its Rodin sculpture court. The next benefactor was the WPA, whose government-funded Aquatic Park Bathhouse commissions included the totemic seal by Beniamino Bufano and a sleek green-slate nautical frieze by trailblazing African American artist Sargent Johnson.

But the sculptor who made the biggest impact on the San Francisco landscape in terms of sheer scale is Richard Serra, whose contributions range from the lobby sculpture maze at SFMOMA to the University of California San Francisco's Mission Bay campus. Serra's massive, rusted-metal minimalist shapes have been favorably compared to ship's prows – and, less generously, to Soviet factory seconds.

Public sculptures have been favorite San Franciscan subjects of debate since 1894, when vigilante art critics pulled down the Washington Square Park statue of dentist Henry D Cogswell over a public drinking fountain he'd donated. Claes Oldenburg and Coosje van Bruggen's 2002 *Cupid's Span* represents the city's reputation for romance with a giant bow and arrow sunk into the Embarcadero. But the city wasn't smitten: a recent poll ranks it among SF's most despised public artworks. Tony Bennett's musical anthem 'I Left My Heart in San Francisco' inspired the SF General Hospital's Hearts in San Francisco fundraising project, but the cartoon hearts are regularly graffitied, denounced as eyesores and marked by territorial canine critics.

High Concept, High Craft

San Francisco's peculiar dedication to craft and personal vision can get obsessive. Consider *The Rose,* the legendary painting Beat artist Jay DeFeo began in the 1950s and worked on for eight years, layering it with 2000lb of paint – until a hole had to be cut in the wall of her apartment to forklift it out. Sculptor Ruth Asawa started weaving not with wool but with metal in the 1950s, following a childhood behind barbed wire in Japanese American internment camps. Her legacy includes de Young Museum sculptures that look like jellyfish within onion domes within mushrooms, and Union Sq's beloved bronze San Francisco fountain, incorporating figures by more than 200 San Franciscans. SF's latest obsessive is San Francisco–raised new-media artist Matthew Barney, who made his definitive debut at SFMOMA with *Cremaster Cycle* videos involving vats of Vaseline.

Posters & Street Smarts

Posters are a quintessential San Francisco art form, from 1960s psychedelic Fillmore posters by Stanley Mouse, advertising bands, to political protest posters still wheatpasted onto walls across the city. In Mission storefronts you might spot silk-screened posters by the late artist Susan O'Malley, who collected advice from San Franciscans on the street for her 'Advice from My 80-year-old Self' poster series. To see the art form in action, head to Haight Street Art Center, where you can catch gallery poster shows and glimpse artists silk-screening new posters in the working studio.

With Balmy Alley murals and renegade poster art as inspiration, SF skateboard decks and Clarion Alley garage doors were transformed in the 1990s with boldly outlined, oddly poignant graphics, dubbed 'Mission School' for their storytelling *muralista* sensibilities and graffiti-tag urgency. The Mission School's professor emeritus was the late Margaret Kilgallen, whose closely observed character studies blended hand-painted street signage, comic-book pathos and a miniaturist's attention to detail.

Clare Rojas expanded on these principles with urban folk-art wall paintings, featuring looming, clueless California grizzly bears and tiny, fierce girls in hoodies. Street-art star Barry McGee paints piles of found bottles with freckled, feckless characters, and still shows at the Luggage Store Gallery. Some Mission School art is critiqued as the faux-naive work of stoned MFAs – but when its earnestness delivers, it hits you where it counts.

New Media

For 40 years, the Bay Area has been the global hub for technical breakthroughs – and local artists have been using technology creatively to pioneer new-media art. Since the '80s, Silicon Valley artist Jim Campbell has been building motherboards to misbehave. On the top of Saleforce Tower, his nine-story, 11,000 LED installation **Day for Night** (Salesforce Tower; Map p298; 415 Mission St; ☉dusk-dawn) projects scenes of dancers and passersby interacting on city streets, 52 stories below. But artist Leo Villereal's Bay Lights (p79) installation is even bigger: each night, 25,000 LEDs illuminate the entire western span of the Bay Bridge in mesmerizing, ever-changing patterns.

San Francisco Music

Only an extremely eclectic DJ can cover all of SF's varied musical tastes. Symphonies, bluegrass tunes, Latin music, electronica and both Chinese and Italian opera have lifted San Franciscan spirits through earthquakes and fires, booms and busts. Music trends that started around the Bay never really went away: '50s free-form jazz and folk; '60s psychedelic rock; '70s disco bathhouse anthems; '80s new wave; '90s West Coast rap and Berkeley's pop-punk revival; and 2000s EDM. Today DJ mash-ups put SF's entire back catalog to work.

Classical Music & Opera

Changes in the SF Giants lineup would be less surprising than the Symphony's shakeup in 2018, when Finnish innovator Esa-Pekka Salonen was lured away from LA's Disney Symphony Hall and his own compositions to replace Michael Tilson Thomas as musical director of the San Francisco Symphony. Since 1995, the Symphony has won more Grammys than the Beatles – 18 and counting. And you can see why: nightly programs enthrall audiences with an unpredictable mix of full-throttle classics, collaborations with the likes of Metallica and the Kronos Quartet, and genuinely odd experimental music.

The San Francisco Opera is the US's second-largest opera company after New York's Metropolitan Opera, but it's second to none with risk-taking. You'd never guess that San Francisco's opera roots go back to the 19th century, from avant-garde original productions like *Harvey Milk* and *The (R)evolution of Steve Jobs* to the Chinese courtesan epic *Dream of the Red Chamber*.

Rock

Lately, San Francisco's rock of choice is preceded by the prefix alt- or indie- at music extravaganzas like Outside Lands, Noise Pop and Napa's Bottle Rock (www.bottlerocknapavalley.com). SF acts like Rogue Wave, Peggy Honeywell and Joanna Newsom add acoustic roots stylings even when they're not playing Berkeley's twangy Freight & Salvage Coffeehouse or Golden Gate Park's Hardly Strictly Bluegrass festival. Vintage SF sounds become new again with local bands playing any given night at Public Works, Brick & Mortar, Bottom of the Hill, the Independent or Hotel Utah.

But San Francisco rock isn't all California sunshine and acoustic twang. Metalheads need no introduction to SF's mighty Metallica, the triumphant survivors of a genre nearly smothered in the '80s by its own hair. Black Rebel Motorcycle Club and Deerhoof throw Mission grit into their walls of sound.

Before you arrived, you may have had the impression San Francisco's rock scene had OD'd long ago. Fair enough. SF has the ignominious distinction of being a world capital of rocker drug overdoses. In the Haight, you can pass places where Janis Joplin nearly met her maker; 32 Delmar St, where Sid Vicious went on the heroin bender that finally broke up the Sex Pistols; and the Grateful Dead flophouse, where the

Best for Classical & Opera

San Francisco Symphony (Civic Center)

San Francisco Opera (Civic Center)

Stern Grove Festival (Golden Gate Park)

Zellerbach Hall (Berkeley)

SoundBox (Hayes Valley)

Classical music is accessible and often free in San Francisco – a local tradition started when opera divas performed gratis to raise SF's spirits after the 1906 earthquake and fire. For listings of free concerts around town, see www.sfcv.org.

At the Fillmore Auditorium (p139)

band was drug-raided – and held a press conference calling for the legalization of marijuana. Grateful Dead guitarist Jerry Garcia eluded the bust and survived for decades, until his death in rehab in 1995.

But baby boomers keep the sound of San Francisco in the '60s alive, and much of it stands the tests of time and sobriety. After Joan Baez and Bob Dylan had their Northern California fling, folk turned into folk rock, and Jimi Hendrix turned the American anthem into a jam suitable for an acid trip. When Janis Joplin and Big Brother & the Holding Company applied their rough musical stylings to 'Me and Bobby McGee,' it was like taking a necessary pass of sandpaper to the sometimes clunky, wooden verses of traditional folk songs. Jefferson Airplane held court at the Fillmore, turning Lewis Carroll's opium-inspired children's classic into the psychedelic anthem 'White Rabbit,' with singer Grace Slick's piercing wail.

The '60s were quite a trip, but the '70s rocked around the Bay. Crosby, Stills, Nash & Young splintered, but Neil Young keeps his earnest, bluesy whine going from his ranch south of San Francisco. Since the 1970s, California-born, longtime Sonoma resident Tom Waits has been singing poetry in an after-hours honky-tonk voice with a permanent catch in the throat. SF's own Steve Miller Band turned out stoner hits like 'The Joker,' Van Morrison lived in Marin and regularly played SF clubs in the '70s, and the Doobie Brothers have played bluesy stoner rock around the Bay since the 1970s. But SF's most iconic '70s rocker is Mission-born Carlos Santana, who combined a guitar moan and a Latin backbeat in 'Black Magic Woman,' 'Evil Ways' and 'Oye Como Va.' Santana made a crossover comeback with 1999's Grammy-winning *Supernatural* and 2005's *All That I Am,* featuring fellow San Franciscan Kirk Hammett of Metallica.

The ultimate SF rock anthem is an '80s power ballad by San Francisco supergroup Journey: 'Lights.' Giants fans also warm up for games

Best for Rock & Punk

Fillmore Auditorium (Japantown)

Warfield (Union Square)

Bottom of the Hill (Potrero Hill)

Great American Music Hall (Tenderloin)

Slim's (SoMa)

Hardly Strictly Bluegrass (October; Golden Gate Park)

by air-guitar-rocking to Journey's 'Don't Stop Believing,' the unofficial theme song of the Giants' World Series championships.

Funk & Hip-Hop

If there's anything San Francisco loves more than an anthem, it's an anthem with a funky groove. The '60s were embodied by freaky-funky, racially integrated San Francisco supergroup Sly and the Family Stone, whose number-one hits are funk manifestos: 'Everyday People,' 'Stand' and 'Thank You (Falettinme Be Mice Elf Agin).' The '70s sexual revolution is summed up in the disco anthem 'You Make Me Feel (Mighty Real)' by Sylvester – the Cockettes drag diva who was tragically lost to the HIV/AIDS epidemic, yet still brings SF crowds to the dance floor.

San Francisco's '70s funk was reverb from across the bay in Oakland, where Tower of Power worked a groove with taut horn arrangements. Meanwhile in Marin, a startlingly talented young musician was recording his first album: the record was *Controversy,* and his name was Prince. All this trippy funk worked its way into the DNA of the Bay Area hip-hop scene, spawning the jazz-inflected Charlie Hunter, freeform Broun Fellinis and the infectious wokka-wokka baseline of rapper Lyrics Born. Oakland's MC Hammer was an '80s crossover hip-hop hit maker best known for inflicting harem pants on the world, though his influence is heard in E-40's bouncing hyphy sound.

Political commentary and pop hooks became East Bay hip-hop signatures with Michael Franti and Spearhead, Blackalicious and the Coup. But the Bay Area is still best known as the home of the world's most talented and notorious rapper: Tupac Shakur, killed in 1996 by an assailant out to settle an East Coast–West Coast gangsta rap rivalry. Lately San Francisco rappers are less pugnacious and more tech savvy, as you hear in SF MC San Quinn's tech-name-checking 'San Francisco Anthem.'

Punk

London may have been more political and Los Angeles more hardcore, but San Francisco's take on punk was way weirder. Dead Kennedys frontman Jello Biafra ran for mayor in 1979 with a platform written on

Best for Funk & Hiphop

Mezzanine (SoMa)

Outside Lands (August; Golden Gate Park)

Independent (Haight/NoPa)

Boom Boom Room (Japantown)

Warfield (Union Square)

SAN FRANCISCO MUSIC FUNK & HIP-HOP

SF ECLECTIC HITS PLAYLIST

➡ 'Take Five' by the Dave Brubeck Quartet (1959)

➡ 'I Left My Heart in San Francisco' by Tony Bennet (1962)

➡ 'Everyday People' by Sly and the Family Stone (1968)

➡ 'Evil Ways' by Santana (1969)

➡ 'Ripple' by the Grateful Dead (1970)

➡ 'Me and Bobby McGee' by Janis Joplin (1971)

➡ 'Lights' by Journey (1978)

➡ 'The American in Me' by The Avengers (1979)

➡ 'Welcome to Paradise' by Green Day (1992)

➡ 'Make You Feel That Way' by Blackalicious (2002)

➡ 'California' by Rogue Wave (2005)

➡ 'Stay Human (All the Freaky People)' by Michael Franti & Spearhead (2007)

➡ 'San Francisco Anthem' by San Quinn (2008)

➡ 'Sing Sang Saing' by Peggy Honeywell (2009)

➡ 'Grace Cathedral Hill' by The Decembrists (2014)

➡ 'Restless Year' by Ezra Furman (2015)

Search & Destroy was San Francisco's shoddily photocopied and totally riveting chronicle of the '70s punk scene as it happened from 1977 to 1979, starting with an initial run financed with $100 from Allen Ginsberg and Lawrence Ferlinghetti, and morphing into V Vale's seminal zine RE/Search in the 1980s.

the back of a bar napkin: ban cars, set official rates for bribery and force businessmen to dress as clowns. He received 6000 votes, and his political endorsement is still highly prized. But for oddity, even Jello can't top the Residents, whose identities remain unknown after 60 records and three decades of performances wearing giant eyeballs over their heads.

Today, punk's not dead in the Bay Area. The Avengers played with the Sex Pistols the night they broke up in San Francisco and, by all accounts, lead singer Penelope Houston upstaged Johnny Rotten for freakish intensity. Unlike the Pistols, the Avengers are still going strong. In the '90s, ska-inflected Rancid and pop-punk Green Day brought punk staggering out of Berkeley's 924 Gilman into the mass-media spotlight. Hardcore punks sneered at Green Day's chart-topping hits, but the group earned street cred (and Grammys) in 2004 with the dark social critique of *American Idiot* – at least until that album became a Broadway musical.

Landmark clubs like Bottom of the Hill and Slim's keep SF punk alive and pogoing. Following the early success of *Punk in Drublic*, SF-based NOFX recorded an impressively degenerate show at Slim's called *I Hear They've Gotten Worse Live!* Punk continues to evolve in San Francisco, with queercore Pansy Division, glam-punk songwriter Ezra Furman and the brass-ballsiness of Latin ska-punk La Plebe.

Jazz

Ever since house bands pounded out ragtime hits to distract Barbary Coast audiences from barroom brawls, San Francisco has echoed with jazz. SFJAZZ Center is the nation's biggest jazz center and a magnet for global talents as artists-in-residence. But jazz will find you all around town, from the Mission's stalwart Revolution Cafe and the Tenderloin's Black Cat, to the Fillmore's Sheba Piano Lounge and the Haight's swinging Club Deluxe.

Best for Jazz

....

SFJAZZ
(Hayes Valley)

....

Black Cat
(Tenderloin)

....

Revolution Cafe
(The Mission)

....

Yerba Buena
Center for the
Arts (SoMa)

....

The Chapel
(The Mission)

SF played it cool in the 1950s with West Coast jazz innovated by the legendary Dave Brubeck Quartet, whose *Time Out* is among the best-selling jazz albums of all time. Bebop had disciples among the Beats, and the SF scene is memorably chronicled in Jack Kerouac's *On the Road*. Billie Holiday and Miles Davis recorded here at the Black Cat, and today John Coltrane is revered as a saint at the African Orthodox Church of St John Coltrane.

During the '60s, the SF jazz scene exploded into a kaleidoscope of styles. Trumpeter Don Cherry blew minds with Ornette Coleman's avant-garde ensemble, while Dixieland band Turk Murphy kept roots jazz relevant.

Today, jazz takes many unexpected turns in SF and pops up where you least expect to find it. At newer venues like SFJAZZ and the Chapel, tempos shift from Latin jazz to klezmer, acid jazz to Afrofunk. So where are the jazz traditionalists? Playing the Hardly Strictly Bluegrass festival and sharing the stage at Symphony Hall. But you can't miss SF jazz at Christmas: San Franciscan Vince Guaraldi wrote the jazzy score for *A Charlie Brown Christmas,* the beloved antidote to standard Christmas carols.

San Francisco Architecture

Superman wouldn't be so impressive in San Francisco, where most buildings are low enough for even a middling superhero to leap in a single bound. The Transamerica Pyramid, Salesforce Tower and Ferry Building clock tower are helpful pointers to orient newcomers, and Coit Tower adds emphatic punctuation to the skyline – but SF's low-profile buildings are its highlights, from Mission adobe and Haight Victorians to wildflower-covered roofs in Golden Gate Park. Lining SF streets are Western storefronts, their squared-off rooflines as iconic as a cowboy's hat.

The Mission & Early SF

Not much is left of San Francisco's original Ohlone-style architecture, beyond the grass memorial hut you'll see in the graveyard of Mission Dolores and the wall of the original Presidio (military post) – both built in adobe with conscripted Ohlone labor. When the gold rush began, buildings were slapped together from ready-made sawn-timber components, sometimes shipped from the East Coast or Australia – an early precursor to postwar prefab.

In SF's Barbary Coast days, City Hall wasn't much to look at, at least from the outside: it was housed in the burlesque Jenny Lind Theater at Portsmouth Sq. Most waterfront buildings from SF's hot-headed Wild West days were lost to arson, including San Francisco's long-lost waterfront neighborhoods of Sydneytown, Manilatown and Chiletown, named for early gold-rush arrivals. Eventually, the builders of Jackson Sq got wise and switched to brick.

But masonry was no match for the 1906 earthquake and fire. The waterfront was almost completely leveled, with the mysterious exception of the Italianate 1866 AP Hotaling's Warehouse – which at the time housed SF's largest whiskey stash. The snappiest comeback in SF history is now commemorated in a bronze plaque on the building: 'If, as they say, God spanked the town/For being over-frisky/Why did He burn His churches down/And spare Hotaling's whiskey?'

Uphill toward North Beach, you'll spot a few other original 1860s to 1880s Italianate brick storefronts wisely built on bedrock. Elevated false facades are capped with jutting cornices, straight rooflines and graceful arches over tall windows.

Victoriana

To make room for new arrivals with the gold, silver, railroad, lumber and shipping booms, San Francisco had to expand fast. Wooden Victorian row houses cropped up almost overnight, with a similar underlying floor plan, but with eye-catching color and embellishments. Legend has it that inhabitants stumbling home after Barbary Coast nights needed these pointers to recognize their homes. Some of these 'Painted Ladies' proved surprisingly sturdy: several upstanding Victorian row houses remain in Pacific Heights, the Haight and the Mission.

Best for Early Architecture

Mission Dolores
(The Mission)

Presidio

Cottage Row
(Japantown)

Jackson Square
(Downtown)

Waverly Place
(Chinatown)

Octagon House
(Cow Hollow)

Some Victorian mansions are now B&Bs, so you too can live large in swanky San Francisco digs of yore: look for places in the Haight, Pacific Heights, the Mission and Castro.

The Victorian era was a time of colonial conquest and the culmination of the European Age of Discovery, and the Victorians liked to imagine themselves as the true successors of great early civilizations. San Franciscans incorporated designs from ancient Rome, Egypt and the Italian Renaissance into grand mansions around Alamo Sq, giving fresh-out-of-the-box San Francisco a hodge-podge instant culture. Look closely, and you'll notice theater masks decorating some of these mansion facades. According to local legends, these theatrical symbols distinguished neighborhood bordellos.

Best for Victorians

....

Alamo Square (The Haight)

....

Haas-Lilienthal House (Pacific Heights)

....

Conservatory of Flowers (Golden Gate Park)

....

Palace Hotel (Downtown)

....

The Mission

Pacific Polyglot Architecture

A trip across town or even down the block will bring you face to facade with San Francisco's Spanish and Mexican heritage, Asian ancestry and California arts-and-crafts roots. Italianate-and-box San Francisco dance halls like the 1907 Great American Music Hall, while Chinatown merchants designed their own streamlined, pagoda-topped Chinatown deco to attract tourists to Grant St.

San Francisco's cinemas and theaters dispense with all geographical logic in favor of pure fantasy, starting with the scalloped Moorish arches of Thomas Patterson Ross' 1913 Exotic Revivalist Alcazar Theater (at 650 Geary St). Chinoiserie- and Mayan-inspired deco elements grace Timothy Pflueger's Bay Area movie palaces: 1922 Castro Theatre, Oakland's 1931 Paramount Theater, and the 1932 cinema on Mission St – now the Alamo Drafthouse Cinema.

Mission & Meso-American

Never mind that Mexico and Spain actually fought over California, and missionaries and Mayans had obvious religious and cultural differences: San Francisco's flights of architectural fancy paved over historical differences with cement, tile and stucco. Meso-American influences are obvious in the stone-carved Aztec motifs on Sansome St banks, not to mention the 1929 Mayan deco gilt reliefs that add jaw-dropping grandeur to architect Timothy Pflueger's 450 Sutter St – surely the world's most mystical dental-office building.

San Francisco's 1915 to 1935 Mission Revival paid tribute to California's Hispanic heritage, influenced by the 1915 Panama–Pacific International Exposition held in San Francisco. Spanish baroque fads flourished with the 1918 construction of a new churrigueresque (Mexican-style Spanish baroque) Mission Dolores basilica, replacing the earlier brick Gothic cathedral damaged in the 1906 earthquake.

The look proved popular for secular buildings, including Pflueger's Mexican baroque Castro Theatre marquee. Pflueger also invited the great Mexican muralist Diego Rivera to San Francisco to create the 1931 *Allegory of California* fresco for San Francisco's Stock Exchange Lunch Club – sparking a mural trend that continues in Mission streets today.

Chinatown Deco

Chinatown was originally hastily constructed by non-Chinese landlords from brick, which promptly collapsed into rubble in the 1906 earthquake. Fire swept the neighborhood, warping bricks into seemingly useless clinker bricks. But, facing City Hall plans for forced relocation, Chinatown residents ingeniously repurposed clinker bricks and rebuilt their neighborhood.

Clinker brickwork became a California arts-and-crafts signature, championed by Chinatown YWCA architect Julia Morgan. The first licensed female architect in California and the chief architect of over-the-top Spanish-Gothic-Greek-Persian Hearst Castle, Morgan showed tasteful restraint and finesse, combining cultural traditions in her designs for the pagoda-topped brick Chinatown YWCA (now the Chinese Historical Society of America) and the graceful Italianate Emanu-El Sisterhood Residence (now home to San Francisco Zen Center).

To attract business to the devastated neighborhood, Chinatown mounted a redevelopment initiative. A forward-thinking group of Chinatown merchants led by Look Tin Eli consulted with a cross section of architects and rudimentary focus groups to create a signature Chinatown art-deco architectural style in the 1920s and '30s. Using this approach, they reinvented brothel-lined Dupont St as tourist-friendly, pagoda-topped Grant Ave, with dragon lanterns and crowd-pleasing modern chinoiserie buildings including the Pacific Telephone Exchange.

California Arts & Crafts

California arts-and-crafts style combines Mission influences with English arts-and-crafts architecture, as seen in Bay Area Craftsman cottages and earthy ecclesiastical structures like San Francisco's Swedenborgian Church.

Berkeley-based architect Bernard Maybeck reinvented England's arts-and-crafts movement with the down-to-earth California bungalow, a small, simple single-story design derived from summer homes favored by British officers serving in India. Though Maybeck's Greco-Roman 1915 Palace of Fine Arts was intended as a temporary structure, the beloved but crumbling plaster ruin was recast in concrete in the 1960s – and it continues to serve as San Franciscans' favorite wedding-photo backdrop.

Modern Skyline

Once steel-frame buildings stood the test of the 1906 earthquake, San Francisco began to think big with its buildings. The city aspired to rival the capitols of Europe and commissioned architect Daniel Burnham to build a grand City Hall in the neoclassical Parisian beaux arts, or 'city beautiful,' style. But City Hall was reduced to a mere shell by the 1906 earthquake, and it wasn't until 1924 that Pflueger built San Francisco's first real skyscraper: the Gothic deco, 26-story 1924 Pacific Telephone Building at 140 New Montgomery St. The telecom megalith is now the headquarters of Yelp and home to Mourad restaurant.

Flatirons

Chicago and New York started a trend raising skylines to new heights, and San Francisco borrowed their flatiron skyscraper style to maximize prime real estate along Market St. The street cuts a diagonal across San Francisco's tidy east–west grid, leaving both flanks of four attractive, triangular flatiron buildings exposed to view.

Among the head shops and triple-X-rated dives around 1020 Market St at Taylor, you'll find the lacy white flatiron featured as broody Brad Pitt's apartment in the film *Interview with a Vampire*. On a less seedy block above the Powell St cable-car turnaround is the stone-cold silver fox known as the James Flood Building, a flinty character that has seen it all: fire, earthquakes and the Gap's attempts to revive bell-bottoms at its ground-floor flagship store. The Flood's opulent cousin is the 1908 Phelan Building at 760 Market St, while that charming slip of a building at 540 Market St is the 1913 Flatiron Building.

SAN FRANCISCO ARCHITECTURE MODERN SKYLINE

Top Low-Profile SF Landmarks

California Academy of Sciences (Golden Gate Park)

de Young Museum (Golden Gate Park)

Swedenborgian Church (Pacific Heights)

Chinese Historical Society of America (Chinatown)

Frank Lloyd Wright Building – VC Morris Store (Union Square)

Streamlined SF

San Francisco became a forward-thinking port city in the 1930s, introducing the ocean-liner look of the 1939 Streamline Moderne Aquatic Park Bathhouse and SF's signature art deco Golden Gate Bridge. But, except for the exclamation point of Coit Tower, most new SF buildings kept a low, sleek profile. Until the '60s, San Francisco was called 'the white city' because of its vast, low swaths of white stucco.

Skyscrapers

SF's skyline scarcely changed until the early 1960s, when seismic retrofitting and innovations made upward mobility possible in this shaky city. The 1959 Crown Zellerbach Building at 1 Bush St became a prototype for downtown buildings: a minimalist, tinted-glass rectangle with open-plan offices. The Financial District morphed into a Manhattanized forest of glass boxes, with one pointed exception: the Transamerica Pyramid. High-rises are now springing up in SoMa around the 61-story Salesforce Tower, with slots for 'urban village' shops, condos, restaurants and cafes. This latest attempt at instant culture is consistent with the city's original Victorian vision – only bigger and blander.

Proponents of SoMa's Mission Bay development say it's a forward-thinking green scheme, with mixed-use space and high-density housing. Critics argue that such costly real estate only attracts tech millionaires and high-priced retailers. A 2014 proposal to allow further development was quashed by voters, still waiting for Mission Bay to make good on its community promises.

Prefab

Amid Victorian prefab row houses in San Francisco neighborhoods, you might also spot some newcomers that seem to have popped right out of the box. Around Patricia's Green in Hayes Valley, shipping containers have been repurposed into stores, cafes and a beer garden. San Francisco's *Dwell* magazine championed architect-designed, eco-prefab homes innovated in the Bay Area, and you can spot some early adopters in Diamond Heights and Bernal Heights. The exteriors can seem starkly minimal, but their interior spaces make the most of air and light.

Adaptive Reuse

Instead of starting from scratch, avant-garde architects are repurposing San Francisco's eclectic architecture to meet the needs of a modern city. Daniel Libeskind's design for the 2008 Contemporary Jewish Museum turned a historic power station into the Hebrew word for life, with a blue-steel pavilion as an emphatic accent.

Once the Embarcadero freeway collapsed in the 1989 earthquake, the sun shone on the Embarcadero at last – and the potential of the waterfront and its Ferry Building was revealed. San Francisco's neglected, partly rotten Piers 15 and 17 sheds have been retrofitted and connected with Fujiko Nakaya's Fog Bridge to form a stunning, solar-powered new home for the Exploratorium. SFMOMA's new addition envelops the original Mario Botta–designed brick box with undulating white sails constantly poised for launch.

But raising the roof on standards for adaptive reuse is the 2008 LEED–certified green building for the California Academy of Sciences. Pritzker Prize–winning architect Renzo Piano incorporated the previous building's neoclassical colonnaded facade, gutted the interior to make way for a basement aquarium and four-story rainforest, and capped it all with a domed 'living roof' of California wildflowers perforated with skylights to allow air to circulate.

Survival Guide

Transportation

ARRIVING IN SAN FRANCISCO

The Bay Area has three international airports: San Francisco (SFO), Oakland (OAK) and San Jose (SJC). Direct flights from Los Angeles take an hour; Chicago, four hours; Atlanta, five hours; New York, six hours. Factor in additional transit time – and cost – to reach San Francisco proper from Oakland or San Jose, and note that what you save in airfare you may wind up spending on ground transportation. However, if schedule is most important, note that SFO has more weather-related delays than OAK.

If you've unlimited time, consider taking the train instead of driving or flying, to avoid traffic hassles and excess carbon emissions.

Flights, cars and tours can be booked online at lonely planet.com/bookings.

San Francisco International Airport

One of America's busiest, **San Francisco International Airport** (www.flysfo. com; S McDonnell Rd) is 14 miles south of downtown off Hwy 101 and accessible by BART.

BART

Direct 30-minute ride to/from downtown San Francisco. The SFO BART station is connected to the International Terminal; buy tickets from machines inside stations.

Bus

SamTrans (☑800-660-4287; www.samtrans.com) Express bus 398 takes 30 to 45 minutes to reach Transbay Transit Center, in the South of Market (SoMa) area.

Airport Express (☑800-327-2024; www.airportexpressinc. com) Runs a scheduled shuttle every hour from 5:30am to 12:30am between San Francisco Airport and Sonoma ($38) and Marin ($30) counties.

Shuttle Bus

Airport shuttles (one way $19 to $25 plus tip) depart from *upper-level* ticketing areas (not lower-level baggage claim); anticipate 45 minutes to most SF locations. For service to the airport, call at least four hours before departure to reserve pick-ups from any San Francisco location. Companies include **Super-Shuttle** (☑800-258-3826; www.supershuttle.com), **Quake City** (☑415-255-4899; www. quakecityshuttle.com; $19-25) and **American Airporter Shuttle** (☑415-202-0733; www.americanairporter.com).

Taxi

Taxis to downtown San Francisco cost $50 to $65 plus tip and depart from the lower-level baggage-claim area of SFO.

Ride-share

Ride-share services such as Lyft and Uber serve SFO. Fares range from $35 to $60 off-peak for a direct-to-destination ride, depending on traffic and SF destination. Ride-shares meet curbside at the upstairs Departures level.

Car

The drive between the airport and the city can take as little as 25 minutes with no traffic, but give yourself an hour during the morning and evening rush hours. If you're headed to the airport via Hwy 101, take the San Francisco International Airport exit. Don't be misled by the Airport Rd exit, which leads to parking lots and warehouses.

Oakland International Airport

Travelers arriving at **Oakland International Airport** (OAK; ☑510-563-3300; www.oakland airport.com; 1 Airport Dr; ☎; ⒷOakland International Airport), 15 miles east of downtown, have a longer trip to reach San Francisco – but OAK has fewer weather-related flight delays than SFO.

BART

The cheapest way to reach San Francisco from the Oakland Airport. BART people-mover shuttles run every 10 to 20 minutes from Terminal 1 to the Coliseum station, where you connect with BART trains to downtown SF ($10.95, 35 minutes). Service operates 5am to midnight Monday to Friday, 6am to midnight Saturday, and 8am to midnight Sunday.

Shuttle Bus

Airport Express (☏800-327-2024; www.airportexpressinc.com) Runs a scheduled shuttle every two hours (from 5:30am to 9:30pm) between Oakland Airport and Sonoma ($38) and Marin ($30) counties.

SuperShuttle (☏800-258-3826; www.supershuttle.com) Offers shared van rides from OAK to downtown SF for $75 for up to three people (reservation required).

Taxi

Taxis leave curbside from OAK and average $35 to $55 to Oakland, $70 to $90 to SF.

Ride-share

Ride-share services such as Lyft and Uber serve OAK. Fares range from $40 to $80 off-peak for a direct-to-destination ride to SF, depending on traffic and destination.

Norman Y Mineta San Jose International Airport

Fifty miles south of downtown San Francisco, **Mineta San Jose International Airport** (☏408-392-3600; www.flysanjose.com; 1701 Airport Blvd) is the least convenient of SF's airports, but by car it's a straight shot to the city via Hwy 101; expect heavy traffic during peak times. The free **VTA** (Valley Transit Authority; ☏408-321-2300; www.vta.org) Airport Flyer (bus 10; runs 5am to 11:30pm) makes a continuous run every 15 to 30 minutes between the Santa Clara Caltrain station (Railroad Ave and Franklin St) and the airport terminals. From Santa Clara station, Caltrain (one way $10.50, 1½ hours) runs northbound trains to the SF terminus at 4th and King Sts from 5am to 10:30pm weekdays, 7am to 10:30pm Saturday and 8am to 9pm Sunday.

Bus

From the **Temporary Transbay Terminal** (Map p298; cnr Howard & Main Sts; ☐5, 38, 41, 71), you can catch the following buses:

AC Transit (☏510-891-4777; www.actransit.org; single ride East Bay/trans-Bay $2.35/5.50) Buses to the East Bay.

Greyhound (☏800-231-2222; www.greyhound.com) Buses leave daily for Los Angeles ($21 to $33, eight to 12 hours), Truckee ($32 to $40, 5½ hours) near Lake Tahoe and other major destinations.

Megabus (☏877-462-6342; https://us.megabus.com) Low-cost bus service to San Francisco from Los Angeles, Sacramento and Anaheim.

SamTrans (☏800-660-4287; www.samtrans.com) Southbound buses to Palo Alto and the Pacific coast.

Car & Motorcycle

Driving in San Francisco is a nightmare of traffic and stress, except in the middle of the night. If you arrive by car or motorcycle, plan to park your car until it's time to leave, and take public transit, ride-shares, bicycles or taxis to get around.

Train

Easy on the eyes and light on carbon emissions, train travel is a good way to visit the Bay Area and beyond.

Caltrain (www.caltrain.com; cnr 4th & King Sts) connects San Francisco with Silicon Valley hubs and San Jose.

Amtrak (☏800-872-7245; www.amtrak.com) serves San Francisco via stations in Oakland and Emeryville (near Oakland), with free shuttle-bus connections to

---

CLIMATE CHANGE & TRAVEL

Every form of transport that relies on carbon-based fuel generates CO_2, the main cause of human-induced climate change. Modern travel is dependent on airplanes, which might use less fuel per mile per person than most cars but travel much greater distances. The altitude at which aircraft emit gases (including CO_2) and particles also contributes to their climate change impact. Many websites offer 'carbon calculators' that allow people to estimate the carbon emissions generated by their journey and, for those who wish to do so, to offset the impact of the greenhouse gases emitted with contributions to portfolios of climate-friendly initiatives throughout the world. Lonely Planet offsets the carbon footprint of all staff and author travel.

BIKING AROUND THE BAY AREA

Within SF Muni has racks that can accommodate two bikes (only) on the front of most buses.

Marin County Bikes are allowed on the Golden Gate Bridge, so riding north to Marin County is no problem. You can transport bicycles on Golden Gate Transit buses, which usually have free racks (three bikes only; first come, first served). Ferries also allow bikes on board.

Wine Country To transport your bike to Wine Country, take Golden Gate Transit or the Vallejo Ferry. Within Sonoma Valley, take Arnold Dr instead of busy Hwy 12; through Napa Valley, take the Silverado Trail instead of busy Hwy 29. The most spectacular ride in Wine Country is sun-dappled, tree-lined West Dry Creek Rd, in Sonoma's Dry Creek Valley.

East Bay Cyclists can't use the Bay Bridge. Bikes are allowed on uncrowded BART trains, but during rush hours special limits apply: between 6:30am and 9am and from 4pm to 6:30pm, passengers with bikes can't board the first three cars. (Folded bikes are allowed in all cars at all times.) During commuting hours, you can also carry your bike across the Bay via the **Caltrans Bay Bridge Bicycle Commuter Shuttle** (Map p298; ☑510-286-6945; www.dot.ca.gov/dist4/shuttle.htm; cnr Main & Bryant Sts; tickets $1; ◷6:40-8:10am & 3:50-6:15pm Mon-Fri), which operates from the northwestern corner of Main and Bryant Sts in San Francisco, and from MacArthur BART station in Oakland (on 40th St, between Market St and the BART entrance); shuttles fill up – arrive early.

San Francisco's Ferry Building and Caltrain station, and Oakland's Jack London Sq. Amtrak offers rail passes good for 15 days of travel in California within a 330-day period (from $459).

Most Amtrak departures from Oakland are short hops to Sacramento, but several daily departures are long-haul trains, with coach service, sleepers and private rooms. The **Coast Starlight** (www.amtrak.com) makes its spectacular 35-hour run from Los Angeles to Seattle via Emeryville/Oakland.

California Zephyr (www.amtrak.com) runs from Chicago, through the Rockies and snow-capped Sierra Nevada, to Oakland (51 hours). It's almost always late, but what a ride. Chicago–Oakland fares cost from $174.

GETTING AROUND

BART

The fastest link between downtown and the Mission District also offers transit

to SF airport (SFO; $9.65), Oakland ($4) and Berkeley ($4.60). Four of the system's five lines pass through SF before terminating at Daly City or SFO. Within SF, one-way fares start at $2.50.

Tickets

Buy tickets at BART stations: you need a ticket to enter – and exit – the system. If your ticket still has value after you exit turnstiles, it's returned to you, with the remaining balance for later use. If your ticket's value is less than needed to exit, use an Addfare machine to pay the appropriate amount. The reloadable Clipper card (p268) can be used for BART for fare discounts.

Transfers

At San Francisco BART stations, a 50¢ transfer discount is available for Muni buses and streetcars; look for transfer machines before you pass through the turnstiles.

Bicycle

Contact the **San Francisco Bicycle Coalition** (☑415-431-2453; www.sfbike.org) for maps, information and laws regarding bicyclists. Bicycles can be taken on BART, but not aboard crowded trains, and never in the first car, nor in the first three cars during weekday rush hours; folded bikes are allowed in all cars at all times. On Amtrak, bikes can be checked as baggage for $5.

Bike Sharing

Ford GoBikes (☑855-480-2453; www.fordgobike.com; single ride/day pass $2/10) are available within SF for single trips, day use or with monthly access passes. Blue racks for Ford GoBike are located downtown, and at major intersections – but bikes come without helmets, and biking downtown without proper protection can be dangerous. Bring your own helmet and plan bike routes before you hit the road.

Boat

With the reinvention of the Ferry Building (p78) as a gourmet dining destination, commuters and tourists alike are dining before taking the scenic ferry across the bay.

Alcatraz

Alcatraz Cruises (Map p290; ☏415-981-7625; www.alcatrazcruises.com; Pier 33; tours day adult/child/family $38.35/23.50/115.70, night adult/child $45.50/27.05; ⓜE, F) has ferries departing Pier 33 for Alcatraz every half-hour from 8:45am to 3:50pm and at 5:55pm and 6:30pm for night tours. Reservations essential.

East Bay

San Francisco Bay Ferry (☏415-705-8291; http://sanfranciscobayferry.com) operates from both Pier 41 and the Ferry Building to Oakland/Alameda. During baseball season, a Giants ferry service runs directly from the landing at AT&T Park's Seals Plaza entrance to Oakland and Alameda. Fares cost $7.

Marin County

Golden Gate Transit Ferries (Map p301; ☏415-455-2000; www.goldengateferry.org; ⓧ6am-9:30pm Mon-Fri, 10am-6pm Sat & Sun) runs regular ferry services from the Ferry Building to Larkspur (one way $12) and Sausalito (one way $12.50). Transfers are available to Muni bus services and bicycles are permitted.

Blue & Gold Fleet (Map p289; ☏415-705-8200; www.blueandgoldfleet.com; Pier 41; adult/child 60min ferry tour $33/22, 30min high-speed boat ride $30/21; ⓧ9am-6:30pm, varies seasonally; ⓫; ⓠ47, ⓜE, F) operates ferries to Tiburon or Sausalito (one way $12.50) from Pier 41.

Napa Valley

Get to Napa car free (weekdays only) via the **Vallejo Ferry** (Map p301; ☏707-643-3779, 877-643-3779; http://sanfranciscobayferry.com; one way $14.60), with departures from the Ferry Building

docks about every hour from 6:30am to 7pm weekdays and roughly every 90 minutes from 10am to 9pm on weekends; bikes are permitted. Note, however, that the connecting bus from the Vallejo Ferry Terminal – Napa Valley Vine bus 29 to downtown Napa, Yountville, St Helena or Calistoga – operates only on weekdays. Fares are $14.60.

Bus, Streetcar & Cable Car

Schedules

For route planning and schedules, consult http://transit.511.org. For real-time departures, see www.nextmuni.com, which syncs with GPS on buses and streetcars to provide best estimates on arrival times. This is the system tied to digital displays posted inside bus shelters. It's accurate for most lines, but not always for the F-line vintage streetcars or cable cars. Nighttime and weekend service is less frequent than on weekdays. Owl service (half-hourly from 1am to 5am) operates only on a few principal lines; for schedules, see http://allnighter.511.org.

System Maps

A detailed *Muni Street & Transit Map* (www.sfmta.com) is available free online.

Tickets

The standard cash fare for buses or streetcars is $2.75, and each ticket is good for

120 minutes of travel on Muni buses or streetcars. Buy tickets on buses and streetcars from drivers (exact change required) or at underground Muni stations (where machines give change). With a reloadable Clipper card, discounted fare is $2.50. Cable-car tickets cost $7 per ride, and can be bought at cable-car-turnaround kiosks or on-board from the conductor. Hang onto your ticket even if you're not planning to use it again: if you're caught without one by the transit police, you're subject to a $100 fine (repeat offenders may be fined up to $500).

Transfers

At the start of your Muni journey, free transfer tickets are available for additional Muni trips within 90 minutes (not including cable cars or BART). After 8:30pm, buses issue a Late Night Transfer good for travel until 5:30am the following morning.

Discounts & Passes

MUNI PASSPORT

A **Muni Passport** (1/3/7 days $23/34/45) allows unlimited travel on all Muni transportation, including cable cars. It's sold at the Muni kiosk at the Powell St cable-car turnaround on Market St; SF's Visitor Information Center; the TIX Bay Area kiosk at Union Sq; and shops around town – see www.sfmta.com for exact locations. One-day (but not multiday) passports are

---

HOW TO FIND MUNI STOPS

Muni stops are indicated by a street sign and/or a yellow-painted stripe on the nearest lamppost, with route numbers stamped on the yellow stripe; if there is no street sign or lamppost, look on the pavement for a yellow bar with a route number painted on it. Ignore yellow circles and Xs on the pavement, or bars that do not also have route numbers; these other markings tell electric-trolley drivers when to engage or disengage the throttle; they do not indicate bus stops.

TRANSPORTATION BUS, STREETCAR & CABLE CAR

available from cable-car conductors.

CLIPPER CARD

Downtown Muni/BART stations have machines that issue the **Clipper card** (www. clippercard.com), a reloadable transit card that costs $3 with a $2 minimum that can be used on Muni, BART, AC Transit, Caltrain, SamTrans and Golden Gate Transit (but not cable cars). Clipper cards automatically deduct fares and apply transfers – only one Muni fare is deducted per 90-minute period. A Clipper Card will save you 50 cents per ride on Muni, so it's worth the investment if you're planning to take more than six Muni rides.

MUNI MONTHLY PASS

The **Muni Monthly Pass** (adult/child $78/39) offers unlimited Muni travel for the calendar month, including cable cars. Fast Passes are available at the Muni kiosk at the Powell St cable-car turnaround, and from many businesses around town; for exact locations, see www. sfmta.com.

Bus

Muni buses display their route number and final destination on the front and side. If the number is followed by the letter A, B, X or R, then it's a limited-stop or express service.

KEY ROUTES

22 Fillmore From Dogpatch (Potrero Hill), through the Mission on 16th St, along Fillmore St past Japantown to Pacific Heights and the Marina.

33 Stanyan From San Francisco General Hospital, through the Mission, the Castro and the Haight, past Golden Gate Park to Clement St.

38 Geary From the Salesforce Transit Center, along Market to Geary Blvd, north of Golden Gate Park through the Richmond district to Ocean Beach.

7 Haight From the Salesforce Transit Center, along Market and Haight Sts, along the southeastern side of Golden Gate Park through the Sunset District and to the Great Hwy at the beach.

Streetcar

Muni Metro streetcars run 5am to midnight on weekdays, with limited schedules at weekends. The K, L, M, N and T lines operate 24 hours, but above-ground Owl buses replace streetcars between 12:30am and 5:30am. The F-Market line runs vintage streetcars above ground along Market St to the Embarcadero, where they turn north to Fisherman's Wharf; the E-Embarcadero runs the same cars along the waterfront. The T line heads south along the Embarcadero through SoMa and Mission Bay, then down 3rd St. Other streetcars run underground below Market St to downtown.

KEY ROUTES

F Fisherman's Wharf and Embarcadero to the Castro.

J Downtown to the Mission, the Castro and Noe Valley.

K, L, M Downtown to the Castro and the western neighborhoods.

N Caltrain and SBC Ballpark to the Haight, Golden Gate Park and Ocean Beach.

T The Embarcadero to Caltrain and Bayview.

Cable Car

In this age of seat belts and airbags, a rickety cable-car ride is an anachronistic thrill. There are seats for about 30 passengers, who are often outnumbered by passengers clinging to creaking leather straps.

KEY ROUTES

California Street Runs east–west along California St, from the downtown terminus at Market and Davis Sts through Chinatown and Nob Hill to Van Ness Ave. It's the least-traveled route, with the shortest queues.

Powell-Mason Runs from the Powell St cable-car turnaround past Union Sq, turns west along Jackson St, and then descends

---

BUSES AROUND THE BAY

Three public bus systems connect San Francisco to the rest of the Bay Area. Most buses leave from clearly marked bus stops; for transit maps and schedules, see the bus-system websites.

AC Transit (☎510-891-4777; www.actransit.org; single ride East Bay/trans-Bay $2.35/5.50) East Bay bus services from the Transbay Transit Center. For public-transport connections from BART in the East Bay, get an AC Transit transfer ticket before leaving the BART station for 50¢ off your connecting fare, both to and from BART.

Golden Gate Transit (☎511, outside Bay Area 415-455-2000; http://goldengatetransit.org) Connects San Francisco to Marin ($6.50 to $8.50) and Sonoma ($12.75 to $13) counties; check schedules online, as service is erratic.

SamTrans (☎800-660-4287; www.samtrans.com) Connects San Francisco and the South Bay, including bus services to/from SF airport (SFO). Buses pick up/drop at from the Transbay Transit Center and other marked bus stops within the city.

north down Mason St, Columbus Ave and Taylor St toward Fisherman's Wharf. On the return trip it takes Washington St instead of Jackson St.

Powell-Hyde The most picturesque route follows the same tracks as the Powell-Mason line until Jackson St, where it turns down Hyde St to terminate at Aquatic Park; coming back it takes Washington St.

Car & Motorcycle

If you can, avoid driving in San Francisco: heavy traffic is a given, street parking is harder to find than true love, and meter readers are ruthless.

Traffic

San Francisco streets mostly follow a grid bisected by Market St, with signs pointing toward tourist zones such as North Beach, Fisherman's Wharf and Chinatown. Try to avoid driving during rush hours: 7:30am to 9:30am and 3:30pm to 6:30pm Monday to Friday. Before heading to any bridge, airport or other traffic choke-point, call 511 for a traffic update.

Parking

For real-time details on how to find parking in the city, and also how to pay your parking meter by telephone or smartphone (so you don't have to return to the car if your meter expires), see SF Park (http://sfpark.org). Parking is tricky and often costly, especially downtown – ask your hotel about parking, and inquire about validation at restaurants and entertainment venues.

GARAGES

Downtown parking garages charge from $5 to $8 per hour and $30 to $55 per day, depending on how long you park and whether you require in-and-out privileges. The most convenient down-

town parking lots are at the Embarcadero Center; at 5th and Mission Sts; under Union Sq; and at Sutter and Stockton Sts. For more public parking garages, see www.sfmta.com; for a map of garages and rates, see http://sfpark.org.

PARKING RESTRICTIONS

Parking restrictions are indicated by the following color-coded sidewalk curbs:

Blue Disabled parking only; placard required.

Green Ten-minute parking zone from 9am to 6pm.

Red No parking or stopping.

White For picking up or dropping off passengers only; note posted times.

Yellow Loading zone during posted times.

TOWING VIOLATIONS

Desperate motorists often resort to double-parking or parking in red zones or on sidewalks, but parking authorities are quick to tow cars. If this should happen to you, you'll have to retrieve your car at **Autoreturn** (☑415-865-8200; www.autoreturn.com; 450 7th St; ⊗24hr; ☒27, 42). Besides at least $200.75 in fines for parking violations, you'll also have to fork out a towing and storage fee ($229 for the first four hours, $50.75 for the rest of the first day, $60.75 for every additional day, plus a $32.50 transfer fee if your car is moved to a long-term lot). Cars are usually stored at 450 7th St, corner of Harrison St.

Rental

Typically, a small rental car might cost $55 to $75 a day or $175 to $300 a week, plus 8.75% sales tax and various licensing fees and tourism taxes that add another $10 to $30 beyond the tax. Unless your credit card, travel insurance or personal car insurance covers car-rental insurance, you'll need to add $10 to $20 per day for

a loss/damage waiver. Most rates include unlimited mileage; with cheap rates, there's often a per-mile charge above a certain mileage.

Booking ahead usually ensures the best rates. Airport rates are generally lower than city rates, but they carry a hefty facility charge of about $20 per day. As part of SF's citywide green initiative, rentals of hybrid cars and low-emissions vehicles from agencies at SF airport (SFO) are available at a discount.

GoCar (www.gocartours.com; per hr $56) rents mini-cars with audio GPS instructions to major attractions in multiple languages. To rent a motorcycle, contact **Dubbelju** (☑415-495-2774, 866-495-2774; www.dubbelju.com; 274 Shotwell St; per day from $99; ⊗9am-6pm Mon-Sat).

Major car-rental agencies include the following:

Alamo Rent-a-Car (☑888-826-6893, 415-693-0191; www.alamo.com; 750 Bush St; ⊗7am-4pm; ☒Powell-Mason, Powell-Hyde, ☒2, 3, 30, 45)

Avis (☑800-352-7900, 415-929-2555; www.avis.com; 675 Post St; ⊗6am-6pm Mon-Fri, to 6:30pm Sat & Sun; ☒2, 3, 27, 38)

Budget (☑415-674-1917, 800-527-7000; www.budget.com; 675 Post St; ⊗6am-6pm Mon-Fri, to 6:30pm Sat & Sun; ☒2, 3, 27, 38)

Dollar (☑866-434-2226; www.dollar.com; 364 O'Farrell St; ⊗7am-6pm; ☒38, ☒Powell)

Hertz (☑800-654-3131, 415-771-2200; www.hertz.com; 325 Mason St; ⊗6am-6pm; ☒38, ☒Powell)

Thrifty (☑800-367-2277, 415-788-8111; www.thrifty.com; 350 O'Farrell St; ⊗7am-6pm; ☒38, ☒Powell)

Car Share

Car sharing is a convenient alternative to rentals, and spares you pick-up/drop-off and parking hassles: reserve a car online for an hour or two, or all day, and you can usually pick up/drop off your car within blocks of where you're staying.

Zipcar (☎866-494-7227; www.zipcar.com) rents various car types by the hour, for flat rates starting at $11 per hour, including gas and insurance, or per day for $79; a $25 application fee and $50 prepaid usage are required. The maximum damage-loss insurance coverage, which brings the deductible to $0, is strongly recommended. Drivers without a US driver's license should follow instructions on the website. Once approved, cars can be reserved online or by phone, provided you have your member card in pocket. Check the website for pick-up/drop-off locations. Other current Zipcard holders may also drive the car; if you want to share the driving with someone, both of you should sign up.

Ride-share

Ride-share services Lyft and Uber were founded in SF, and they're widely used – which means you may have to wait or pay a premium during peak use times, such as weekend nights or right after conferences or events. Fares within SF range from $7 to $20 off-peak for a direct-to-destination ride, depending on traffic and SF destination.

Roadside Assistance

Members of **American Automobile Association** (AAA; ☎800-222-4357, 415-773-1900; https://calstate.aaa.com; 160 Sutter St; ⊙9am-6pm Mon-Fri; Ⓑ Montgomery, Ⓜ Montgomery) can call the 800 number any time for emergency road service and towing. AAA also provides travel insurance and free road maps of the region. A green alternative is **Better World Auto Club** (www.betterworldclub.com).

Taxi

Taxi fares start at $3.50 at flag flag and run about $3 per mile. Add 15% to the fare as a tip ($1 minimum). For quickest service in San Francisco, download the Flywheel app for smartphones, which dispatches the nearest taxi.

Lyft and Uber are available in San Francisco, but licensed taxis have greater access, specifically to dedicated downtown bus and taxi lanes, notably along Market St. Taxis also don't charge surge pricing at peak times.

Green Cab (☎415-626-4733; www.greencabsf.com) Fuel-efficient hybrids; worker-owned collective.

Homobiles (☎415-574-5023; www.homobiles.org; donations appreciated) Get home safely with secure, reliable, donation-based transport by and for the LGBTIQ+ community: drivers provide 24/7 taxi service – text for fastest service.

Luxor (☎415-282-4141; www.luxorcab.com)

Yellow Cab (☎415-333-3333; www.yellowcabsf.com)

Train

From the depot at 4th and King Sts in San Francisco, **Caltrain** (www.caltrain.com; cnr 4th & King Sts) heads south to Millbrae (connecting to BART and San Francisco airport; 30 minutes), Palo Alto (one hour) and San Jose (1½ hours). This is primarily a commuter line, with frequent departures during weekday rush hours and less frequent service outside rush hours and at weekends.

Directory A–Z

Accessible Travel

All Bay Area transit companies offer wheelchair-accessible service and travel discounts for travelers with disabilities. Major car-rental companies can usually supply hand-controlled vehicles with one or two days' notice. For people with visual impairment, major intersections emit a chirping signal to indicate when it is safe to cross the street.

San Francisco Bay Area Regional Transit Guide (https://511.org/transit/accessibility/overview) Covers accessibility for people with disabilities.

Muni's Street & Transit (www.sfmta.com/accessibility) Details wheelchair-friendly bus routes and streetcar stops.

Independent Living Resource Center of San Francisco (📞415-543-6222, TTY 415-543-6698; www.ilrcsf.org; ⏰9am-4:30pm Mon-Thu, to 4pm Fri) Provides information about wheelchair accessibility on Bay Area public transit and in hotels and other local facilities.

Environmental Traveling Companions (Map p292; 📞415-474-7662; www.etctrips.org) Leads excellent outdoor trips in California – white-water rafting, kayaking and cross-country skiing – for kids with disabilities.

Download Lonely Planet's free Accessible Travel guides from http://lptravel.to/AccessibleTravel.

Customs Regulations

Each person over 21 years old is allowed to bring 1L of liquor and 200 cigarettes duty-free into the USA. Non-US citizens are allowed to bring $100 worth of duty-free gifts. If you're carrying over $10,000 in US and foreign cash, traveler's checks or money orders, you must declare the excess amount – undeclared sums in excess of $10,000 may be subject to confiscation.

Dangers & Annoyances

Keep your city smarts and wits about you, especially at night in the Tenderloin, South of Market (SoMa), the Upper Haight and the Mission. If you're alone in these areas at night, consider ride-share or a taxi instead of waiting for a bus.

➡ Avoid using your smartphone unnecessarily on the street – phone-snatching does happen.

➡ The Bayview–Hunters Point neighborhood (south of Potrero Hill, along the water) isn't suitable for wandering tourists, due to policing and crime issues.

➡ After dark, Mission Dolores Park, Buena Vista Park and the entry to Golden Gate Park at Haight and Stanyan Sts are used for drug deals and casual sex hookups. If you're there at night, you may get propositioned.

Discount Cards

Some green-minded venues, such as the de Young Museum, the California Academy of Sciences and the Legion of Honor, also offer discounts to ticket-bearing Muni riders.

City Pass (www.citypass.com; adult/child $94/74) Covers three days of cable cars and Muni, plus entry to four attractions, including the California Academy of Sciences, Blue & Gold Fleet Bay Cruise, the Aquarium of the Bay and either the Exploratorium or SFMOMA.

Go Card (www.smartdestinations.com; adult/child one day $74/54, two days $109/89, three days $139/124) Provides access to the city's major attractions, including the California Academy of Sciences, the de Young Museum, the Aquarium of the Bay, SFMOMA, USS Pampanito, the Beat Museum and Exploratorium, plus discounts on packaged tours and waterfront restaurants and cafes.

Electricity

Electric current in the USA is 110 to 115 volts, 60Hz AC. Outlets may be suited for flat two-prong or three-prong plugs. If your appliance is made for another electrical system, get a transformer or adapter at Walgreens.

Type A
120V/60Hz

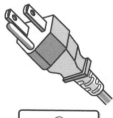

Type B
120V/60Hz

Emergency

Emergency	☑911
Non-emergency	☑311
San Francisco city/ area code	☑415
US country code	☑1

Internet Access

SF has free wi-fi hot spots citywide including in some parks and public spaces. Connect for free at most cafes and hotel lobbies. See **Free Wifi Near Me** (https:// wifispc.com/articles/free-wi-fi-near-me.html) and **San Francisco WiFi** (http://sf gov.org/sfc/sanfrancisco wifi) wi-fi hot spots.

Legal Matters

San Francisco police usually have more urgent business than fining you for picking a protected orange California poppy on public land (up to $500), littering ($250 and up), loitering on sidewalks against the Sit/Lie law ($50 to $500), jaywalking (ie crossing streets outside a pedestrian crosswalk; $75 to $250) or failing to clean up after your puppy (up to $320, plus shaming glares from fellow dog owners).

Drinking alcoholic beverages outdoors is not officially allowed, though beer and wine are often permissible at street fairs and other outdoor events. Marijuana consumption is legal for private use by adults aged 18 and over with ID – emphasis on private. Many San Franciscans prefer not to have smoke blown in their direction, cigarette or otherwise. In recent years the police have also cracked down on park squatters and illegal camping.

If you are arrested for any reason, it's your right to remain silent, but never walk away from an officer until given permission or you could be charged with resisting arrest. Anyone arrested gets the right to make one phone call. If you want to call your consulate, the police will give you the number on request. In accordance with San Francisco's Sanctuary City Laws, San Francisco police do not share your visa status with federal immigration authorities.

LGBTIQ+ Travelers

Information for LGBTIQ+ travelers can be found on p38.

Medical Services

Before traveling, contact your health-insurance provider to learn what medical care they will cover outside your hometown (or home country). Overseas visitors should acquire travel insurance that covers medical situations in the US, where nonemergency care for un-insured patients can be very expensive.

For nonemergency appointments at hospitals, you'll need proof of insurance, or credit card or cash. Even with insurance, you'll most likely have to pay up front for nonemergency care and then wrangle afterward with your insurance company to get reimbursed. San Francisco has excellent medical facilities, plus alternative medical practices and herbal apothecaries.

University of California San Francisco Medical Center (☑415-476-1000; www.ucsf health.org; 505 Parnassus Ave; ⊙24hr; 🚍6, 7, 43, Ⓜ N) ER at leading university hospital.

San Francisco General Hospital (Zuckerberg San Francisco General Hospital and Trauma Center; ☑emergency 415-206-8111, main hospital 415-206-

8000; https://zuckerberg
sanfranciscogeneral.org; 1001
Potrero Ave; ⊙24hr; ⊡9, 10,
33, 48) Best ER for serious
trauma.

Health Insurance

Make sure your health-
insurance policy covers travel to California. If it does not,
consider a travel-insurance
policy that covers emergency medical services.

Recommended Vaccinations

No specific vaccinations are
required for travel to the US,
though it is always sensible
to ensure that your routine
vaccinations are up to date.

Money

ATMs are widely available;
credit cards are accepted
at most hotels, stores and
restaurants. Many farmers-
market stalls and food trucks
and some bars are cash only.
Keep small bills for cafes,
bars and hotel service, where
cash tips are appreciated.

ATMs

Most banks have 24-hour
ATMs, except in areas where
street crime is a problem
(such as near the BART stop
at 16th and Mission Sts).
You can withdraw cash from
an ATM using a credit card
(service charge applies);
check with your bank about
fees and immediately applied
interest.

Changing Money

Though there are exchange
bureaus at airports, the best
rates are generally in town.
You can change money
downtown at **Currency
Exchange International**
(⊡415-974-6600; www.san
franciscocurrencyexchange.
com; 865 Market St, Westfield
Centre, Level 1; ⊙10am-
8:30pm Mon-Sat, 11am-7pm
Sun; ⓂPowell, ⒷPowell) and
Bank of America (⊡415-

837-1394; www.bankamerica.
com; 1 Powell St, downstairs;
⊙9am-5pm Mon-Fri, 10am-
2pm Sat; ⓂPowell, ⒷPowell).

Traveler's Checks

In the US, traveler's checks
in US dollars are virtually
as good as cash; you don't
necessarily have to go to a
bank to cash them, as some
establishments – particularly
hotels – will accept them like
cash. Fair warning, though:
more SF venues accept
Apple Pay than traveler's
checks.

Tipping

Tipping is *essential*, as most
workers in service-industry
jobs make only the minimum
wage and rely almost entirely
on tips for their income.
However, if service is truly
terrible, tip less than 15% –
or else reduce the following
standard amounts:

Bartenders $1 to $2 per drink,
or 15% of the bill. Note: good
tippers get stronger drinks.

Bellhops and airport skycaps
$2 per bag, plus $5 to $10
extra for special service.

Concierges Nothing for simple
information (like directions); $2
to $20 for securing restaurant
reservations or concert tickets,
or for providing exceptional
service.

Housekeeping staff $2 to $5
daily, left on the pillow each
day; more if you're messy.

Parking valets $2; extra for
special service.

Restaurant servers 15% to
20% of the pretax bill.

Taxis and ride-shares 10% to
15% of the metered fare.

Opening Hours

Typical opening hours in San
Francisco:

Banks 9am–4:30pm or 5pm
Monday to Friday, plus occasionally 9am–noon Saturday

Offices 8:30am–5:30pm
Monday to Friday

Restaurants Breakfast 8am–
10am; lunch 11:30am–2:30pm;
dinner 5:30pm, with last service 9pm–9:30pm weekdays or
10pm weekends; Saturday and
Sunday brunch 10am–2:30pm

MEDIA

San Francisco has plenty of print information sources:
San Francisco Chronicle (www.sfgate.com) City's
main daily newspaper.

SF Weekly (www.sfweekly.com) Free weekly with local
gossip and entertainment.

San Francisco Examiner (www.sfexaminer.com) Free
daily with news, events, opinions and culture.

For local listening in San Francisco and online via
podcasts and/or streaming audio, check out these
stations:

KQED (8.5 FM; www.kqed.org) National Public Radio
(NPR) and Public Broadcasting (PBS) affiliate offering
podcasts and streaming audio.

KALW (91.7 FM; www.kalw.org) Local NPR affiliate:
news, talk, music, original programming.

KPOO (89.5 FM; www.kpoo.com) Community nonprofit radio with jazz, R&B, blues and reggae.

KPFA (94.1 FM; www.kpfa.org) Alternative news and
music.

Shops 10am–6pm or 7pm Monday to Saturday, though hours may run 11am–8pm Saturday and 11am–6pm Sunday

Post

US Postal service remains reliable, though hours are limited, especially on weekends. Check www.usps.com for post-office locations throughout San Francisco.

Public Holidays

Most shops remain open on public holidays (with the exception of Independence Day, Thanksgiving, Christmas Day and New Year's Day), but banks, schools and offices are usually closed. Holidays that may affect business hours and transit schedules include the following:

New Year's Day January 1

Martin Luther King Jr Day Third Monday in January

Presidents' Day Third Monday in February

Easter Sunday (and Good Friday and Easter Monday) in March or April

Memorial Day Last Monday in May

Independence Day July 4

Labor Day First Monday in September

Columbus Day Second Monday in October

Veterans Day November 11

Thanksgiving Fourth Thursday in November

Christmas Day December 25

Smoking

Smoking is prohibited almost everywhere. Some hotels have smoking rooms, but most are entirely nonsmoking. Bars with outdoor patios allow smoking in these areas; otherwise, you must go outside to the sidewalk and stay away from the doorways of

open businesses. Smoking marijuana in private is legal for adults 18 and over, but only in designated smoking areas – and watch out for smoke alarms.

Taxes & Refunds

SF's 8.75% sales tax is added to virtually everything, including meals, shopping and car rentals; the hotel-room tax is 14%, plus 1% to 1.5% tourism district assessment. Groceries are about the only items not taxed. Unlike the value-added tax (VAT) in the EU, sales tax is not refundable.

In response to city laws mandating health-care benefits for restaurant workers, some restaurants pass those costs on to diners by tacking an additional 3% to 5% 'Healthy SF' charge onto the bill – it's usually mentioned in the menu's fine print.

Telephone

The US country code is 1. San Francisco's city/area code is 415. When calling local numbers in San Francisco you must dial the area code; thus, all local numbers begin with 1-415.

To place an international call, dial 011 + country code + city code + number (make sure to drop the 0 that precedes foreign city codes or your call won't go through). When calling Canada, there's no need to dial the international access code (011). When dialing from a landline, you must precede any area code by 1 for direct dialing, 0 for collect calls and operator assistance (both expensive); from cell phones, dial only the area code and number.

Area Codes in the Bay Area

East Bay ☑510

Marin County ☑415

Peninsula ☑650

San Francisco ☑415

San Jose ☑408

Santa Cruz ☑831

Wine Country ☑707

Toll-free numbers start with 800, 855, 866, 877 or 888; phone numbers beginning with 900 usually incur high fees.

Cell Phones

Most US cell (mobile) phones operate on CDMA or GSM 850/1900, not the European standard GSM 900/1800 – check compatibility with your phone-service provider. North American travelers can use their cell phones in San Francisco and the Bay Area, but should check with their carriers about roaming and data-use charges.

Operator Services

International operator ☑00

Local directory ☑411

Long-distance directory information ☑1 + area code + 555-1212

Operator ☑0

Toll-free number information ☑800-555-1212

Time

San Francisco is on Pacific Standard Time (PST), three hours behind the East Coast's Eastern Standard Time (EST) and eight hours behind Greenwich Mean Time (GMT/UTC). March through October is daylight-saving time in the US.

Toilets

Many toilets in public or shared spaces in San Francisco are designated for use by all genders, denoted by a triangle. All-gender toilets usually have stalls instead of open urinals.

Citywide Self-cleaning, coin-operated outdoor kiosk commodes cost 25¢ or require a free token to enter; there are 28 citywide, mostly in North Beach, Fisherman's Wharf, the Financial District and the Tenderloin. Toilet paper isn't always available, and there's a 20-minute time limit. Public library branches and some city parks also have restrooms.

Downtown Most hotel lobbies have restrooms. Clean toilets and baby-changing tables can be found at Westfield San Francisco Centre and Macy's.

Civic Center San Francisco Main Library has restrooms.

Haight-Ashbury & Mission District Woefully lacking in public toilets; you may have to buy coffee, beer or food to gain access to locked customer-only bathrooms.

Tourist Information

SF Visitor Information Center (www.sanfrancisco.travel/ visitor-information-center) Muni Passports, activities deals, culture and event calendars.

Visas

Canadians

Canadian citizens currently only need proof of identity and citizenship to enter the US – but check the US Department of State for updates, as requirements may change.

Visa Waiver Program

USA Visa Waiver Program (VWP) allows nationals from 38 countries to enter the US without a visa, provided they are carrying a machine-readable e-passport (with an embedded chip). For the updated list of countries included in the program and current requirements, see the **US Customs & Border Protection** (https://www.cbp.gov/travel/internation al-visitors) website.

Citizens of VWP countries need to register with the **US Department of Homeland Security** (https://esta.cbp. dhs.gov/esta) three days before their visit. There is a $14 fee for registration application.

Visas Required

You must obtain a visa from a US embassy or consulate in your home country if any of the following apply to you:

➡ You do not currently hold a passport from a VWP country.

➡ You are from a VWP country but don't have a machine-readable passport, aka an e-passport.

➡ You plan to stay longer than 90 days.

➡ You intend to work or study in the US.

Work Visas

Foreign visitors are not legally allowed to work in the USA without the appropriate working visa. The most common, the H visa, can be difficult to obtain. It usually requires a sponsoring organization, such as the company you will be working for in the US. The company will need to demonstrate why you, rather than a US citizen, are most qualified for the job.

The type of work visa you need depends on your work:

H visa For temporary workers.

L visa For employees in intra-company transfers.

O visa For workers with extraordinary abilities.

P visa For athletes and entertainers.

Q visa For international cultural-exchange visitors.

Volunteering

Volunteer opportunities abound at Bay Area non-profits, depending on your skill set, time availability and flexibility.

VolunteerMatch (www.volun teermatch.org) Matches your interests, talents and availability with a local nonprofit where you could donate your time, even if only for a few hours.

Craigslist (http://sfbay. craigslist.org/vol) Lists opportunities to support the Bay Area community, from nonprofit fashion-show fundraisers to teaching English to new arrivals.

Women & Nonbinary Travelers

SF is excellent for solo women and nonbinary travelers: you can eat, stay, dine and go out alone without anyone making presumptions about your availability, interests, sexual orientation or gender identification. That said, women and nonbinary travelers should apply their street smarts here as in any other US city. US crime rates are higher than the global average, and crime disproportionately affects women and nonbinary people in the US – even in historically progressive San Francisco.

The Women's Building (p146) has a Community Resource Room offering information on health care, domestic violence, childcare, harassment, legal issues, employment and housing.

Behind the Scenes

SEND US YOUR FEEDBACK

We love to hear from travelers – your comments keep us on our toes and help make our books better. Our well-traveled team reads every word on what you loved or loathed about this book. Although we cannot reply individually to your submissions, we always guarantee that your feedback goes straight to the appropriate authors, in time for the next edition. Each person who sends us information is thanked in the next edition – the most useful submissions are rewarded with a selection of digital PDF chapters.

Visit **lonelyplanet.com/contact** to submit your updates and suggestions or to ask for help. Our award-winning website also features inspirational travel stories, news and discussions.

Note: We may edit, reproduce and incorporate your comments in Lonely Planet products such as guidebooks, websites and digital products, so let us know if you don't want your comments reproduced or your name acknowledged. For a copy of our privacy policy visit lonelyplanet.com/privacy.

WRITER THANKS

Ashley Harrell

Thanks to my editor Sarah Stocking and to my co-author Alison Bing for all their sound advice and enthusiasm for the project. Thanks to Andy Wright, David Roth, Amy Benziger, Kara Levy, Lauren Smiley, Laurie Prill, Paul Stockamore, Osa Peligrosa, Freda Moon, Lois Beckett, Margie Benziger and Peter Benziger for the friendship, shared meals and ideas. Most of all thanks to my amazing boyfriend Steven Sparapani. I love you the absolute most.

ACKNOWLEDGEMENTS

Cover photograph: Cable car, Matteo Colombo/ AWL Images ©
Illustration on pp56–7 by Michael Weldon.

THIS BOOK

This 12th edition of Lonely Planet's *San Francisco* guidebook was curated by Ashley Harrell, and re-searched and written by Ashley, Alison Bing, Greg Benchwick, Celeste Brash and Adam Karlin. The previous edition was written by Ashley, Sara Benson, Alison and John A Vlahides. This guidebook was produced by the following:

Destination Editor
Sarah Stocking
Senior Product Editors
Martine Power,
Victoria Smith
Regional Senior Cartographer Alison Lyall
Product Editors
Kathryn Rowan, Ross Taylor
Book Designer
Fergal Condon
Assisting Book Designer
Gwen Cotter

Assisting Editors
Janice Bird, Kate Daly,
Gabrielle Innes, Lou
McGregor, Alison Morris,
Rosie Nicholson, Lauren
O'Connell, Monique Perrin,
Tamara Sheward,
Monica Woods
Cartographer
Valentina Kremenchutskaya
Cover Researcher
Meri Blazevski
Thanks to Hannah Cartmel

Index

see also separate subindexes for:

✕ **EATING P281**

🍷 **DRINKING & NIGHTLIFE P283**

☆ **ENTERTAINMENT P283**

🔒 **SHOPPING P284**

🏃 **SPORTS & ACTIVITIES P285**

🛏 **SLEEPING P285**

🛍 **SHOPPING**

🏃 SPORTS & ACTIVITIES

🛏 SLEEPING

San Francisco Maps

Sights

- Beach
- Bird Sanctuary
- Buddhist
- Castle/Palace
- Christian
- Confucian
- Hindu
- Islamic
- Jain
- Jewish
- Monument
- Museum/Gallery/Historic Building
- Ruin
- Shinto
- Sikh
- Taoist
- Winery/Vineyard
- Zoo/Wildlife Sanctuary
- Other Sight

Activities, Courses & Tours

- Bodysurfing
- Diving
- Canoeing/Kayaking
- Course/Tour
- Sento Hot Baths/Onsen
- Skiing
- Snorkelling
- Surfing
- Swimming/Pool
- Walking
- Windsurfing
- Other Activity

Sleeping

- Sleeping
- Camping
- Hut/Shelter

Eating

- Eating

Drinking & Nightlife

- Drinking & Nightlife
- Cafe

Entertainment

- Entertainment

Shopping

- Shopping

Information

- Bank
- Embassy/Consulate
- Hospital/Medical
- Internet
- Police
- Post Office
- Telephone
- Toilet
- Tourist Information
- Other Information

Geographic

- Beach
- Gate
- Hut/Shelter
- Lighthouse
- Lookout
- Mountain/Volcano
- Oasis
- Park
- Pass
- Picnic Area
- Waterfall

Population

- Capital (National)
- Capital (State/Province)
- City/Large Town
- Town/Village

Transport

- Airport
- Border crossing
- Bus
- Cable car/Funicular
- Cycling
- Ferry
- Metro station
- Monorail
- Parking
- Petrol station
- Subway station
- Taxi
- Train station/Railway
- Tram
- Underground station
- Other Transport

Routes

- Tollway
- Freeway
- Primary
- Secondary
- Tertiary
- Lane
- Unsealed road
- Road under construction
- Plaza/Mall
- Steps
- Tunnel
- Pedestrian overpass
- Walking Tour
- Walking Tour detour
- Path/Walking Trail

Boundaries

- International
- State/Province
- Disputed
- Regional/Suburb
- Marine Park
- Cliff
- Wall

Hydrography

- River, Creek
- Intermittent River
- Canal
- Water
- Dry/Salt/Intermittent Lake
- Reef

Areas

- Airport/Runway
- Beach/Desert
- Cemetery (Christian)
- Cemetery (Other)
- Glacier
- Mudflat
- Park/Forest
- Sight (Building)
- Sportsground
- Swamp/Mangrove

Note: Not all symbols displayed above appear on the maps in this book

MAP INDEX

Treasure Island

San Francisco Bay

Alcatraz

Golden Gate National Recreation Area

Bonita Cove

Kirby Cove

Golden Gate

PACIFIC OCEAN

PRESIDIO

Presidio National Park

Mountain Lake Park

Lincoln Park

Fort Miley

THE RICHMOND

Golden Gate Park

Spreckels Lake

Stow Lake

Lily Pond

San Francisco Botanical Garden & Strybing Arboretum

Laguna Honda

THE SUNSET

Sunset Reservoir

Marina Green

Fort Mason

THE MARINA

PACIFIC HEIGHTS

FISHERMAN'S WHARF

RUSSIAN HILL

NOB HILL

NORTH BEACH

CHINATOWN

FINANCIAL DISTRICT (FID)

UNION SQUARE

THE TENDERLOIN

CIVIC CENTER

SOUTH OF MARKET (SOMA)

MISSION BAY

POTRERO HILL

JAPANTOWN

WESTERN ADDITION

HAYES VALLEY

LOWER HAIGHT

The Panhandle

UPPER HAIGHT

COLE VALLEY

THE CASTRO

NOE VALLEY

THE MISSION

Bernal Heights Park

Twin Peaks

McCovey Cove

1 2 3 4 5 6 7 8 9 10 11 12 13 14 15 16 17

N

0 2 km
0 1 miles

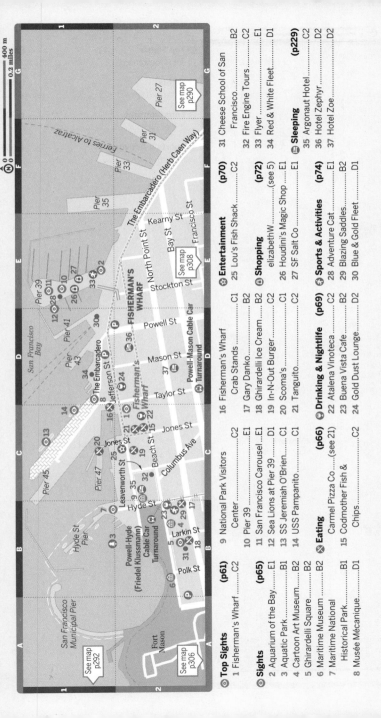

◎ **Top Sights** (p61)
1 Fisherman's Wharf C2

◎ **Sights** (p65)
2 Aquarium of the Bay......E1
3 Aquatic Park..................B1
4 Cartoon Art Museum.....B2
5 Ghirardelli Square..........B2
6 Maritime Museum............B2
7 Maritime National
  Historical Park..............B1
8 Musée Mécanique.........D1
9 National Park Visitors
  Center C2
10 Pier 39 ....E1
11 San Francisco Carousel...E1
12 Sea Lions at Pier 39.......D1
13 SS Jeremiah O'Brien.....C1
14 USS Pampanito............C1

✕ **Eating** (p66)
  Carmel Pizza Co ....(see 21)
15 Codmother Fish &
  Chips..........................C2
16 Fisherman's Wharf
  Crab Stands C1
17 Gary Danko...................B2
18 Ghirardelli Ice Cream......B2
19 In-N-Out Burger.............C2
20 Scoma's.......................C1
21 Tanguito.......................C2

◑ **Drinking & Nightlife** (p66)
  Atalena Vinoteca ....(see 21)
22 Atalena Vinoteca..........C2
23 Buena Vista Cafe..........B2
24 Gold Dust Lounge.........D2

✿ **Entertainment** (p70)
25 Lou's Fish Shack C2

🛍 **Shopping** (p72)
  elizabethW ....(see 5)
26 Houdini's Magic Shop E1
27 SF Salt Co...................E1

◉ **Sports & Activities** (p74)
28 Adventure Cat...............E1
29 Blazing Saddles............B2
30 Blue & Gold Fleet..........D2
31 Cheese School of San
  Francisco...................B2
32 Fire Engine Tours...........C2
33 Flyer............................E1
34 Red & White Fleet.........D1

◑ **Sleeping** (p229)
35 Argonaut Hotel...............C2
36 Hotel Zephyr.................D2
37 Hotel Zoe.....................D2

400 m
0.2 miles

Ferries to Alcatraz

The Embarcadero (Herb Caen Way)

San Francisco Bay

Fisherman's Wharf

FISHERMAN'S WHARF

Powell-Mason Cable Car
Turnaround

Powell-Hyde
(Friedel Klussmann)
Cable Car
Turnaround

San Francisco Municipal Pier

Hyde St Pier

Fort Mason

See map p292
See map p306
See map p290
See map p308

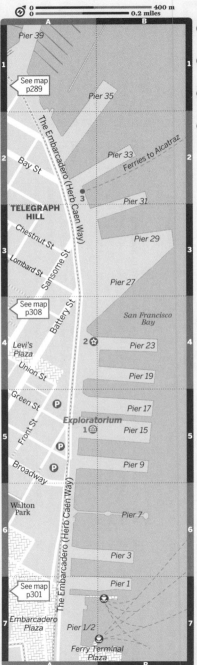

◎ **Top Sights** **(p64)**

◎ **Sights** **(p64)**

✪ **Entertainment** **(p70)**

✪ **Sports & Activities** **(p55)**

THE PRESIDIO

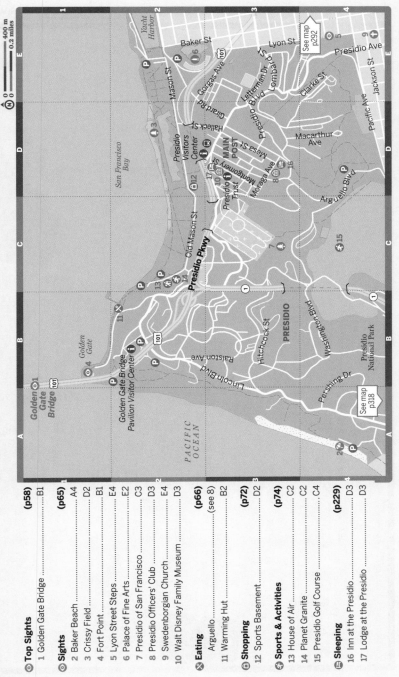

© Top Sights (p58)
1 Golden Gate Bridge B1

◎ Sights (p65)
2 Baker Beach A4
3 Crissy Field D2
4 Fort Point B1
5 Lyon Street Steps E4
6 Palace of Fine Arts E2
7 Presidio of San Francisco C3
8 Presidio Officers' Club D3
9 Swedenborgian Church E4
10 Walt Disney Family Museum D3

✕ Eating (p66)
Arguello .... (see 8)
11 Warming Hut B2

🛍 Shopping (p72)
12 Sports Basement D2

⊕ Sports & Activities (p74)
13 House of Air C2
14 Planet Granite C2
15 Presidio Golf Course C4

⊟ Sleeping (p229)
16 Inn at the Presidio D3
17 Lodge at the Presidio D3

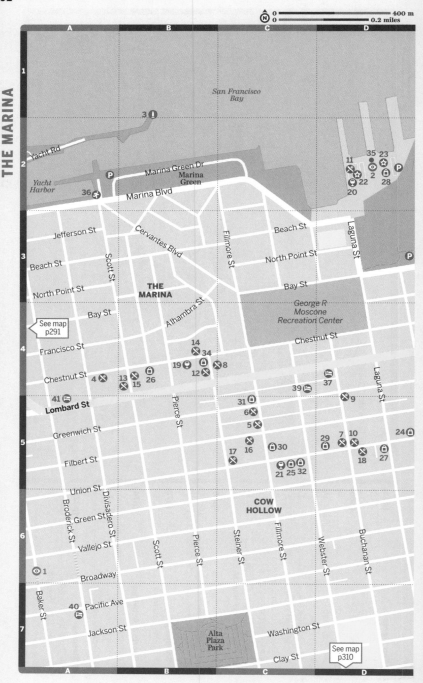

THE MARINA

San Francisco Bay

Yacht Rd

Yacht Harbor

Jefferson St

Cervantes Blvd

Marina Green Dr
Marina Green

Marina Blvd

Beach St

North Point St

Bay St

THE MARINA

Scott St

Alhambra St

Fillmore St

Laguna St

George R Moscone Recreation Center

Chestnut St

See map p291

Francisco St

Chestnut St

Bay St

North Point St

Lombard St

Pierce St

Greenwich St

Filbert St

Union St

Green St

Vallejo St

Broadway

Broderick St

Divisadero St

Scott St

Pierce St

Steiner St

Fillmore St

Webster St

Buchanan St

Laguna St

COW HOLLOW

Baker St

Pacific Ave

Jackson St

Alta Plaza Park

Washington St

Clay St

See map p310

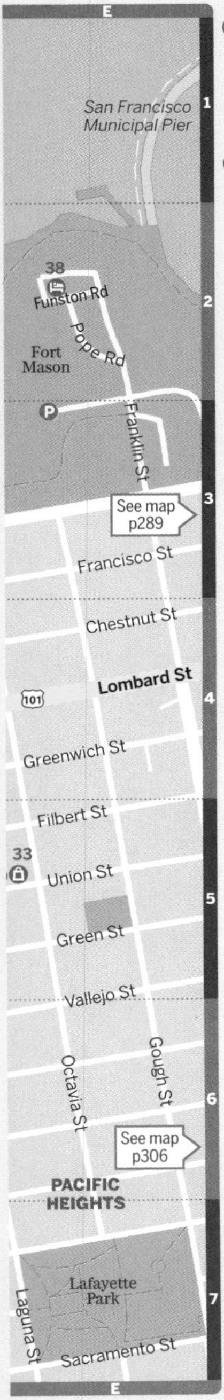

THE MARINA

San Francisco
Municipal Pier

38
Funston Rd

Fort
Mason

Pope Rd

Franklin St

See map
p289

Francisco St

Chestnut St

Lombard St

101

Greenwich St

Filbert St

33

Union St

Green St

Vallejo St

Octavia St

Gough St

See map
p306

PACIFIC
HEIGHTS

Laguna St

Lafayette
Park

Sacramento St

UNION SQUARE

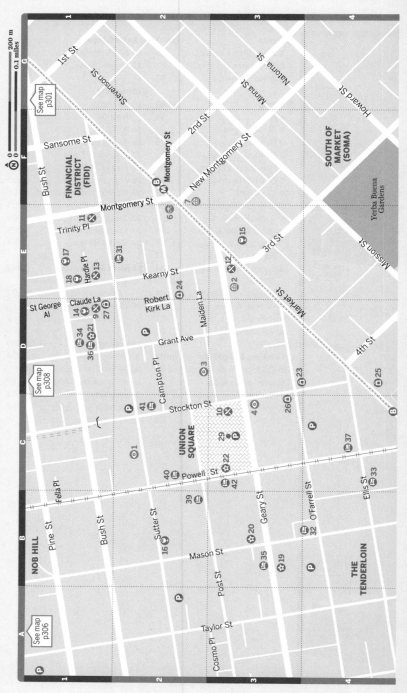

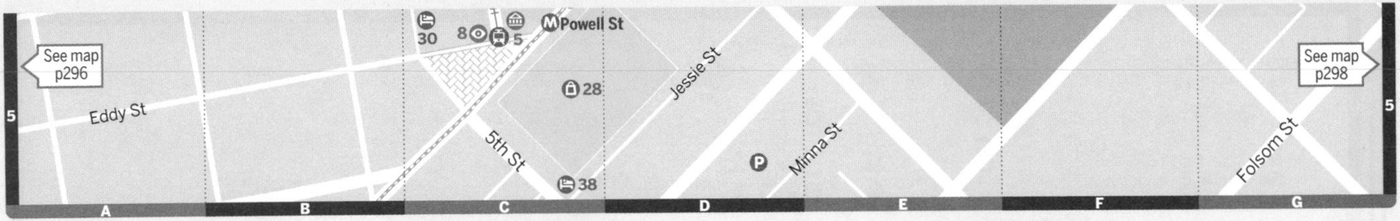

See map p296
Eddy St
30
8
5
Powell St
28
5th St
38
Jessie St
Minna St
Folsom St
See map p298
A
B
C
D
E
F
G
5
5

Sights (p82)

1 450 Sutter St C2
2 49 Geary E3
3 Frank Lloyd Wright Building D2
4 I Magnin Building C3
5 James Flood Building C5
6 One Montgomery Terrace E2
7 Palace Hotel F2
8 Powell St Cable Car Turnaround C5

Eating (p89)

9 Cafe Claude D1
10 Emporio Rulli C3
11 Golden West E1
12 Hakkasan E3
13 Sushirrito E1

Drinking & Nightlife (p93)

Gaspar Brasserie & Cognac Room .... (see 31)
14 Irish Bank D1
15 Local Edition E3
16 Pacific Cocktail Haven B2
17 Pagan Idol E1
18 Rickhouse E1

Entertainment (p97)

19 American Conservatory Theater B3
20 August Hall B3
21 Bar Fluxus D1
22 TIX Bay Area C3

Shopping (p102)

23 Barneys D3
24 Britex Fabrics E2
Isaia .... (see 3)
25 Levi's Flagship Store D4
26 Macy's C3
27 Margaret O'Leary D1
28 Westfield San Francisco Centre C5

Sports & Activities (p104)

29 Emperor Norton's Fantastic Time Machine C3

Sleeping (p230)

30 Axiom C5
31 Galleria Park E2
32 HI San Francisco Downtown B4
33 Hotel Abri C4
34 Hotel des Arts D1
35 Hotel Diva B3
36 Hotel Triton D1
37 Hotel Union Square C4
38 Hotel Zetta C5
39 Inn at Union Square B2
Palace Hotel .... (see 7)
40 Sir Francis Drake Hotel C2
41 Taj Campton Place C2
42 Westin St Francis Hotel C3

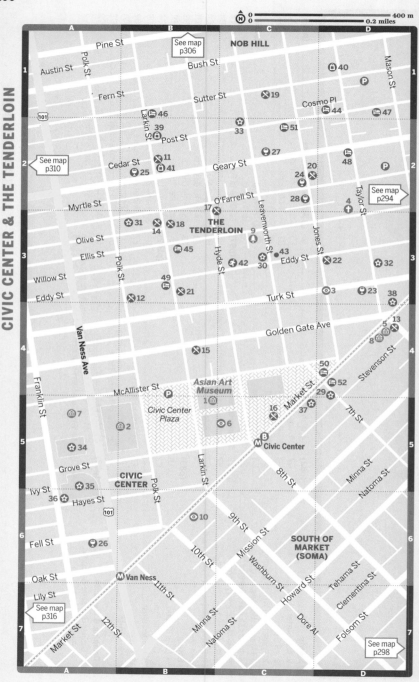

CIVIC CENTER & THE TENDERLOIN

0 400 m
0 0.2 miles

NOB HILL

THE TENDERLOIN

CIVIC CENTER

SOUTH OF MARKET (SOMA)

Asian Art Museum

Civic Center Plaza

See map p306
See map p310
See map p294
See map p298
See map p316

CIVIC CENTER & THE TENDERLOIN

Key on p300

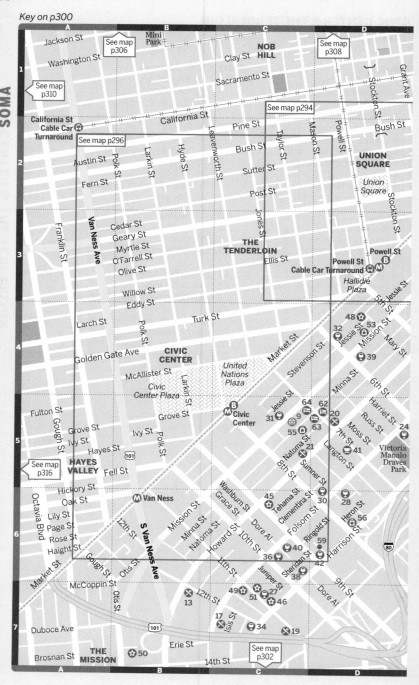

SOMA

See map p306
See map p308
See map p310
See map p294
See map p296
See map p316
See map p302

Jackson St
Washington St
Mini Park
Clay St
NOB HILL
Sacramento St

California St
Cable Car Turnaround
California St
Pine St
Bush St
Taylor St
Mason St
Powell St
Stockton St
Grant Ave
Bush St

Austin St
Polk St
Larkin St
Hyde St
Leavenworth St
Sutter St
UNION SQUARE
Fern St
Post St
Union Square
Jones St
Stockton St

Cedar St
Geary St
Myrtle St
O'Farrell St
Olive St
THE TENDERLOIN
Ellis St
Powell St
Cable Car Turnaround
Powell St
Hallidie Plaza

Franklin St
Willow St
Eddy St
5th St
Jessie St

Larch St
Polk St
Turk St
48
32
Jessie St
53
Mission St
May St

CIVIC CENTER
Golden Gate Ave
Market St
Stevenson St
39
Minna St
6th St

McAllister St
United Nations Plaza
Civic Center Plaza
Larkin St
Harriet St
Russ St
24

Fulton St
Gough St
Grove St
Grove St
Civic Center
Jessie St
31
64
9
62
20
Moss St
7th St
Russ St
Victoria Manalo Draves Park

Ivy St
Hayes St
Polk St
55
63
Natoma St
41

HAYES VALLEY
Fell St
21
Sumner St
Langton St

Hickory St
Oak St
Van Ness
Washburn St
Grace St
Mission St
Minna St
Dore Al
45
Tehama St
Clementina St
Folsom St
30
28
56
Heron St

Octavia Blvd
Lily St
Page St
Rose St
Haight St
12th St
S Van Ness Ave
Natoma St
Howard St
10th St
Ringold St
59
42
I-80

Market St
Gough St
Otis St
McCoppin St
36
40
Sheridan St
38
Harrison St
9th St
Dore Al

Duboce Ave
Otis St
12th St
49
51
27
46
13
Juniper St

THE MISSION
Brosnan St
50
Erie St
14th St
17
34
19

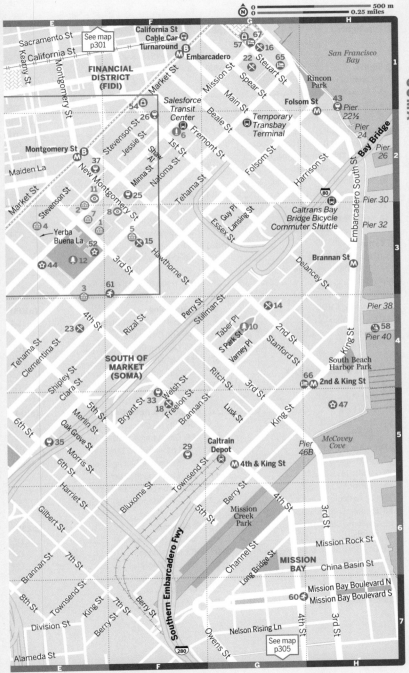

SOMA

SOMA *Map on p298*

THE MISSION

See map p305
See map p298
See map p314
See map p312

Key on p304

400 m
0.2 miles

Vermont St
San Bruno Ave
James Lick Fwy
Potrero Ave

San Bruno Ave
17th St
Utah St
Division St

11

8
4
9

66

Franklin Square

16th St
17th St
Mariposa St
18th St
19th St

21
12
51

Treat Ave

46

59

36

45

Shotwell St

Chan
Kaajal
Park

89
63

18th St
19th St

Erie St
14th St
15th St

84

S Van Ness Ave
Capp St

60
17

B 16th St
Mission

17th St

Mission St

57

San Carlos St

18
79
26
32

Julian St

93
53

87
44
82

5

75

34
58

Duboce Ave
Clinton Park
Brosnan St
15th St

27

28
13

72

68
83
2

43
65
39

Dearborn St

Linda St

55

40
37

74

Guerrero St

6

Dorland St

15
19
35

Dolores St

10

31
73

Market St

70

Chula La

7

THE
CASTRO

Landers St
Church St

Dorland St
18th St
Hancock St
19th St

Sharon St

Church St

N

McKinley Square

101

22nd St

San Francisco General Hospital

San Bruno Ave

Utah St

25th St

Potrero del Sol Park

91

Potrero Ave

Hampshire St

York St

56

1

33

Bryant St

23rd St

Bryant St

24

Florida St

Alabama St

92

Harrison St

69 23

80

3

Treat Ave

Lucky St

Garfield Square

Treat Ave

Folsom St

Folsom St

Shotwell St

22nd St

Shotwell St

THE MISSION

67

Calle 24 Latino Cultural District

S Van Ness Ave

York St

Bryant St

Florida St

Alabama St

Harrison St

Shotwell St

Cesar Chavez St

Precita Park

Precita Ave

Harvest Off Mission (0.2mi);
Holy Water (0.7mi);
Ichi Sushi (0.3mi);
Mae Krua (0.7mi);
Wild Side West (0.8mi)

Bernal Heights Park (0.3mi)

20th St

95

41

78

16 94

Capp St

49

48

30

25

90

Mission St

24th St Mission

25th St

Valencia St

20

54

22

29

64

61

Bartlett St

88

52

42

Mission St

San Jose Ave

14

Mitchell's Ice Cream (0.2mi)

71

38

86

85

77

81

76

Liberty St

21st St

50

Hill St

62

47

23rd St

Guerrero St

Ames St

Fair Oaks St

Fair Oaks St

Quane St

Dolores St

Jersey St

Clipper St

26th St

NOE VALLEY

Chattanooga St

Church St

Vicksburg St

Sanchez St

Cesar Chavez St

27th St

Cumberland St

21st St

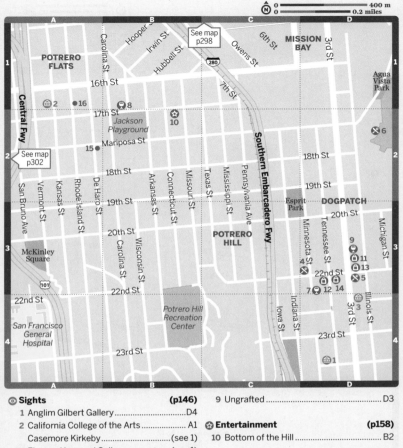

200 m
0.1 miles

See map p289

Chestnut St

Chestnut St

Polk St

Lombard St

8

3

Greenwich St

7

Filbert St

2

RUSSIAN HILL

See map p292

16

19

Union St

22 23

Macondray La

9

Russell St

25

6 12

18

Green St

Taylor St

Eastman Pl

Larkin St

Vallejo St

Hyde St

Leavenworth St

Glover St

Jones St

Florence St

Broadway Tunnel

Van Ness Ave

Broadway

Morrell St

Lynch St

Bernard St

36

15

Pacific Ave

20

39

Jackson St

17

Mini Park

24

Priest St

35 37

38

Washington St

NOB HILL

13

28 26

Pleasant St

29

Clay St

14

34

Sacramento St

4

California St Cable Car Turnaround

21

California St

27 10

Franklin St

30

Pine St

See map p310

Polk St

Austin St

Larkin St

Hyde St

Bush St

Leavenworth St

Jones St

See map p296

41

101

RUSSIAN & NOB HILLS

NORTH BEACH & CHINATOWN

See map p289

Basically Free Bike Rentals (130yd)

Powell-Mason Cable Car Turnaround

72

55

56

64

66

Francisco St

Water St

Mason St

Jansen St

Taylor St

Valparaiso St

Filbert St

Columbus Ave

North Beach Playground

Powell St

Union St

Green St

Pfeiffer St

Chestnut St

Lombard St

Stockton St

Grant Ave

Kearny St

Montgomery St

12

Pioneer Park/ Telegraph Hill

Greenwich St

Coit Tower

1

NORTH BEACH

11

31 30

Filbert St

73

20

33 37 39
52

54 32

26

22

57

Genoa Pl

Varennes St

Kearny St

Sonoma St

69

38

35 45

23 29

Broadway

50 43 14

2 36

25

8

13 53

51

40

49

59

46

Jasper Pl

Telegraph Hill Blvd

Greenwich St

58

RUSSIAN HILL

Ina Coolbrith Park

Vallejo St

See map p306

Broadway Tunnel

Bernard St

Pacific Ave

28

9

61

CHINATOWN

42

41

Jones St

Taylor St

Mason St

Jackson St

Washington St

Stockton St

Grant Ave

Kearny St

62

17

27 4

18

44

21

19

47

7

65

67

16

5

68

NOB HILL

Priest St

Clay St

6

Sacramento St

Joice St

34 60

63

15

71

Huntington Park

California St

Quincy St

St Mary's Square

48

See map p296

Pine St

See map p294

Bush St

70

10

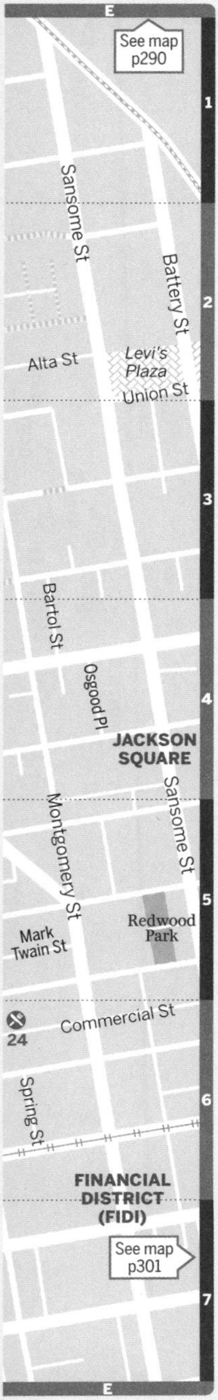
E
See map p290
1
2
3
4
5
6
7
Sansome St
Battery St
Alta St
Levi's Plaza
Union St
Bartol St
Osgood Pl
JACKSON SQUARE
Sansome St
Montgomery St
Mark Twain St
Redwood Park
Commercial St
24
Spring St
FINANCIAL DISTRICT (FIDI)
See map p301
E

Top Sights **(p110)**

1 Coit Tower D2

Sights **(p111)**

2 Beat Museum D4
3 Bob Kaufman Alley C2
4 Chinatown Alleyways C5
5 Chinese Culture Center D5
6 Chinese Historical Society of America C6
7 Chinese Telephone Exchange D5
8 City Lights Books D4
9 Columbus Tower D5
10 Dragon's Gate D7
11 Filbert Street Steps D2
12 Francisco Street Steps C1
13 Jack Kerouac Alley D4
14 Mule Gallery D4
15 Old St Mary's Cathedral & Square D6
16 Portsmouth Square D5
17 Ross Alley C5
18 Spofford Alley C5
19 Tin How Temple D6
20 Washington Square C3
21 Waverly Place D5

Eating **(p113)**

22 Cafe Jacqueline C3
23 China Live C4
24 City View E6
25 E' Tutto Qua D4
26 Golden Boy C3
27 Good Mong Kok C5
28 House of Nanking D5
29 Lai Hong Lounge C4
30 Liguria Bakery C2
31 Mama's C2
32 Mara's Italian Pastry C3
33 Mario's Bohemian Cigar Store Cafe C3
34 Mister Jiu's D6
35 Molinari C4
36 Naked Lunch D4
37 Park Tavern C3
38 Ristorante Ideale C4
39 Tony's Coal-Fired Pizza & Slice House C3
40 Tosca Cafe D4
41 Trestle D5
42 Z & Y D5

Drinking & Nightlife **(p119)**

43 15 Romolo D4
44 Buddha Lounge D5
Cafe Zoetrope .... (see 9)
45 Caffe Trieste C4
46 Comstock Saloon D4
Devil's Acre .... (see 25)
47 Li Po D5
48 PlenTea D7
49 Réveille D4
50 Saloon D4
51 Specs D4
52 Tony Nik's C3
53 Vesuvio D4

Entertainment **(p122)**

54 Beach Blanket Babylon C3
55 Bimbo's 365 Club A1
56 Cobb's Comedy Club A2

Shopping **(p122)**

57 101 Music C3
58 Al's Attire D3
59 Artist & Craftsman Supply D4
60 Chinatown Kite Shop D6
61 Eden & Eden D5
62 Golden Gate Fortune Cookies C5
63 Kim + Ono D6
64 Real Old Paper A2
65 Red Blossom Tea Company D5
66 San Francisco Rock Posters & Collectibles B2

Sports & Activities **(p121)**

67 Chinatown Alleyway Tours D5
68 Chinatown Heritage Walking Tours D5
Drag Me Along Tours .... (see 16)

Sleeping **(p233)**

69 Hotel Bohème C3
70 Orchard Garden Hotel D7
71 Pacific Tradewinds Hostel D6
72 San Remo Hotel A1
73 Washington Square Inn C3

JAPANTOWN & PACIFIC HEIGHTS

See map p306

See map p292

JAPANTOWN & PACIFIC HEIGHTS

See map p296

⊙ Sights (p136)
1 Cottage Row	D4
2 Haas-Lilienthal House	F1
3 Japan Center	E4
4 Peace Pagoda	E4

⊗ Eating (p136)
5 b. patisserie	A3
6 Benkyodo	E4
7 Marufuku Ramen	D4
8 Nijiya Supermarket	D4
9 Noosh	C3
10 Out the Door	C3
11 Pizzeria Delfina	C3
12 Sasa	E4
13 State Bird Provisions	D5
14 The Progress	D5
15 Wise Sons Bagel & Bakery	D5

⊙ Drinking & Nightlife (p139)
16 Boba Guys	C3
17 Elite Cafe	C3
18 Scopo Divino	A3
19 Social Study	D5

⊙ Entertainment (p139)
20 AMC Kabuki 8	D4
21 Audium	C3
22 Boom Boom Room	C3
23 Fillmore Auditorium	E4
24 New People Cinema	D4
25 Sheba Piano Lounge	D5

⊙ Shopping (p140)
26 Bite Lip Lab	C2
27 Crossroads Trading	C3
28 Ichiban Kan	E4
29 Jonathan Adler	D4
30 Katsura Garden	D4
31 Kinokuniya Books	D4
Kohshi	(see 8)
32 Margaret O'Leary	C2
New People	(see 24)
33 Paper Tree	D5
34 Sanko Kitchen Essentials	D5
35 Soko Hardware	E4

⊙ Sports & Activities (p142)
36 Japanese Arts & Cooking Workshops at JCCNC	D4
37 Japantown Cultural & Historical Walking Tour	E4
38 Kabuki Springs & Spa	D5
39 Playland Japan	D4

⊙ Sleeping (p235)
40 Hotel Kabuki	E4
41 Queen Anne Hotel	F3
42 The Kimpton Buchanan	E4

THE CASTRO

See map p314

THE HAIGHT

See map p316

See map p302

See map p318

THE CASTRO

Church St

Duboce Ave

Noe St

Duboce Park

LOWER HAIGHT

Castro St

Divisadero St

Alpine Tce

Buena Vista Park

Buena Vista Ave E

UPPER HAIGHT

Central Ave

COLE VALLEY

WESTERN ADDITION

NOPA

University of San Francisco

Golden Gate Park

400 m
0.2 miles

Webster St

Ivy St

Webster St

Fillmore St

Haight St

Oak St

Page St

Steiner St

Fillmore St

Pierce St

Alamo Square Park

Scott St

Fulton St

McAllister St

Golden Gate Ave

Steiner St

Grove St

Hayes St

Fell St

Divisadero St

Broderick St

Golden Gate Ave

Fulton St

Grove St

Hayes St

Fell St

Oak St

Page St

Baker St

Lyon St

Turk Blvd

Baker St

Lyon St

McAllister St

Central Ave

Masonic Ave

Masonic Ave

Ashbury St

Clayton St

Haight St

Waller St

Haight Street

Ashbury St

Clayton St

Hayes St

Grove St

Cole St

Page St

Oak St

Fell St

The Panhandle

Shrader St

Parker Ave

Waller St

Waller St

Haight St

Scott St

THE HAIGHT

HAYES VALLEY

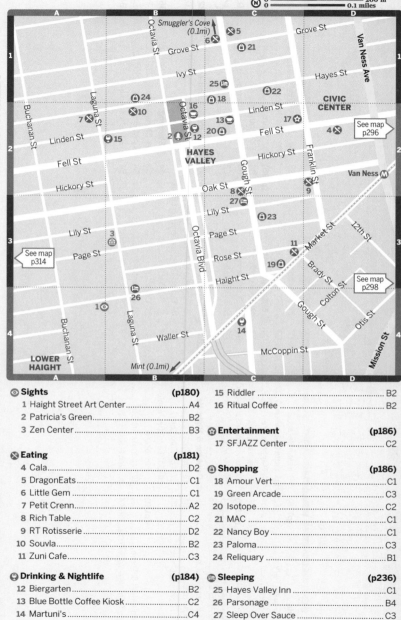

GOLDEN GATE PARK & THE AVENUES *Map on p318*

HAYES VALLEY

GOLDEN GATE PARK & THE AVENUES

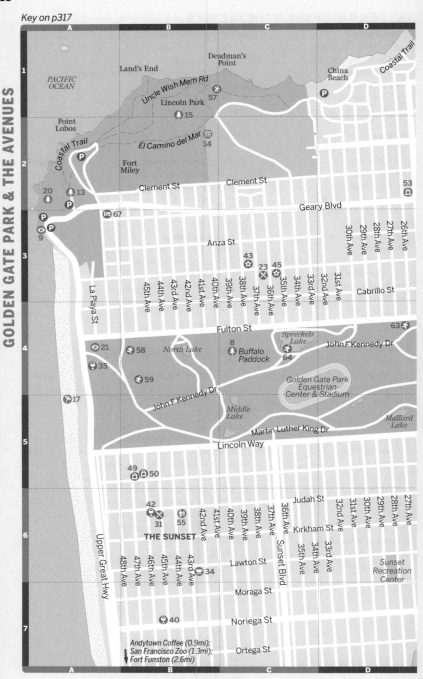

PACIFIC
OCEAN

Land's End

Deadman's
Point

China
Beach

Coastal Trail

Uncle Wish Mem Rd

57

Lincoln Park

15

Point
Lobos

Coastal Trail

El Camino del Mar

14

Fort
Miley

Clement St

Clement St

20

13

Geary Blvd

67

9

Anza St

43

23

45

45th Ave
44th Ave
43rd Ave
42nd Ave
41st Ave
39th Ave
38th Ave
37th Ave
36th Ave
35th Ave
34th Ave
33rd Ave
32nd Ave
31st Ave

30th Ave
29th Ave
28th Ave
27th Ave
26th Ave

53

Cabrillo St

La Playa St

Fulton St

Spreckels
Lake

63

21

58

North Lake

8

Buffalo
Paddock

64

John F Kennedy Dr

35

John F Kennedy Dr

59

Golden Gate Park
Equestrian
Center & Stadium

Mallard
Lake

17

Middle
Lake

Martin Luther King Dr

Lincoln Way

49

50

42

31

55

THE SUNSET

48th Ave
47th Ave
46th Ave
45th Ave
44th Ave
43rd Ave
42nd Ave
41st Ave
40th Ave
39th Ave
38th Ave
37th Ave
36th Ave
35th Ave
34th Ave
33rd Ave

32nd Ave
31st Ave
30th Ave
29th Ave
28th Ave
27th Ave

Judah St

Kirkham St

Sunset Blvd

Lawton St

34

Sunset
Recreation
Center

Upper Great Hwy

Moraga St

40

Noriega St

Ortega St

Andytown Coffee (0.9mi);
San Francisco Zoo (1.3mi);
Fort Funston (2.6mi)

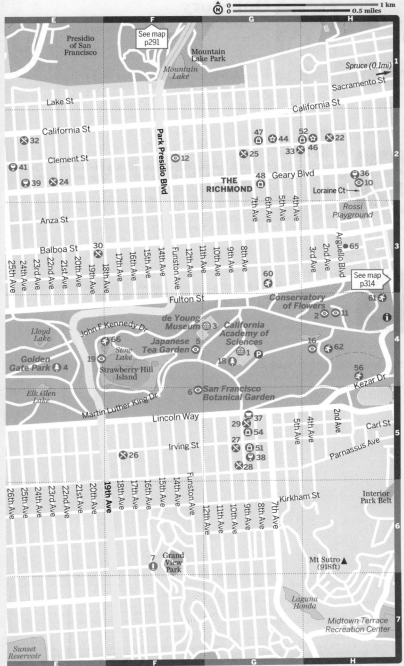

Our Story

A beat-up old car, a few dollars in the pocket and a sense of adventure. In 1972 that's all Tony and Maureen Wheeler needed for the trip of a lifetime – across Europe and Asia overland to Australia. It took several months, and at the end – broke but inspired – they sat at their kitchen table writing and stapling together their first travel guide, *Across Asia on the Cheap*. Within a week they'd sold 1500 copies. Lonely Planet was born.

Today, Lonely Planet has offices in Franklin, London, Melbourne, Oakland, Dublin, Beijing and Delhi, with more than 600 staff and writers. We share Tony's belief that 'a great guidebook should do three things: inform, educate and amuse'.

Our Writers

Ashley Harrell

Downtown, Civic Center & SoMa; Golden Gate Park & the Avenues; The Marina, Fisherman's Wharf & the Piers; The Mission, Dogpatch & Potrero Hill After a brief stint selling day spa coupons door-to-door in South Florida, Ashley decided she'd rather be a writer. She went to journalism grad school, convinced a newspaper to hire her, and starting covering wildlife, crime and tourism, sometimes all in the same story. Fueling her zest for storytelling and the unknown, she traveled widely and moved often, from a tiny NYC apartment to a vast California ranch to a jungle cabin in Costa Rica, where she started writing for Lonely Planet.

Alison Bing

Japantown, Fillmore & Pacific Heights; Nob Hill & Russian Hill; North Beach & Chinatown; The Castro; The Haight & Hayes Valley Over 10 guidebooks and 20 years in San Francisco, author Alison has spent more time on Alcatraz than some inmates, become an aficionado of drag and burritos, and willfully ignored Muni signs warning that safety requires avoiding unnecessary conversation.

Contributing writers: Greg Benchwick (Napa & Sonoma Valleys), Celeste Brash (Marin County) and Adam Karlin (Berkeley & Oakland) contributed to the Day Trips from San Francisco chapter.

Published by Lonely Planet Global Limited
CRN 554153
12th edition – December 2019
ISBN 978 1 78701 410 7
© Lonely Planet 2019   Photographs © as indicated 2019
10 9 8 7 6 5 4 3 2 1
Printed in Singapore

Although the authors and Lonely Planet have taken all reasonable care in preparing this book, we make no warranty about the accuracy or completeness of its content and, to the maximum extent permitted, disclaim all liability arising from its use.